Odoo 14 Development Cookbook

Fourth Edition

Rapidly build, customize, and manage secure and efficient business apps using Odoo's latest features

Parth Gajjar

Alexandre Fayolle

Holger Brunn

Daniel Reis

BIRMINGHAM—MUMBAI

Odoo 14 Development Cookbook
Fourth Edition

Copyright © 2020 Packt Publishing

All rights reserved. No part of this book may be reproduced, stored in a retrieval system, or transmitted in any form or by any means, without the prior written permission of the publisher, except in the case of brief quotations embedded in critical articles or reviews.

Every effort has been made in the preparation of this book to ensure the accuracy of the information presented. However, the information contained in this book is sold without warranty, either express or implied. Neither the authors, nor Packt Publishing or its dealers and distributors, will be held liable for any damages caused or alleged to have been caused directly or indirectly by this book.

Packt Publishing has endeavored to provide trademark information about all of the companies and products mentioned in this book by the appropriate use of capitals. However, Packt Publishing cannot guarantee the accuracy of this information.

Group Product Manager: Aaron Lazar

Associate Publishing Product Manager: Shweta Bairoliya

Senior Editor: Rohit Singh

Content Development Editor: Dwayne Fernandes, Tiksha Lad

Technical Editor: Pradeep Sahu

Copy Editor: Safis Editing

Project Coordinator: Deeksha Thakkar

Proofreader: Safis Editing

Indexer: Pratik Shirodkar

Production Designer: Prashant Ghare

First published: April 2016

Second edition: January 2018

Third edition: April 2019

Fourth edition: December 2020

Production reference: 2150221

Published by Packt Publishing Ltd.

Livery Place

35 Livery Street

Birmingham

B3 2PB, UK.

ISBN 978-1-80020-031-9

www.packt.com

I dedicate this book to my parents with love and gratitude. Thank you for giving me the freedom and support to follow my ambitions throughout my childhood.

– Parth Gajjar

Packt.com

Subscribe to our online digital library for full access to over 7,000 books and videos, as well as industry leading tools to help you plan your personal development and advance your career. For more information, please visit our website.

Why subscribe?

- Spend less time learning and more time coding with practical eBooks and videos from over 4,000 industry professionals
- Improve your learning with Skill Plans built especially for you
- Get a free eBook or video every month
- Fully searchable for easy access to vital information
- Copy and paste, print, and bookmark content

Did you know that Packt offers eBook versions of every book published, with PDF and ePub files available? You can upgrade to the eBook version at packt.com and, as a print book customer, you are entitled to a discount on the eBook copy. Get in touch with us at customercare@packtpub.com for more details.

At www.packt.com, you can also read a collection of free technical articles, sign up for a range of free newsletters, and receive exclusive discounts and offers on Packt books and eBooks.

Contributors

About the authors

Parth Gajjar is an Odoo expert with a deep understanding of the Odoo framework. He started his career at Odoo and spent 7 years in the R&D department at Odoo India. During his time at Odoo, he worked on several key features, including a marketing automation app, mobile application, report engine, domain builder, and more. He also worked as a code reviewer and helped manage the code quality of the new features. Later, he started his own venture named Droggol and now provides various development services related to Odoo. He loves working on Odoo and solving real-world business problems with different technologies. He often gives technical training to Odoo developers.

> *I would like to thank my parents and family members for all of the support they have given throughout the writing of this book.*

Alexandre Fayolle started working with Linux and free software in the mid-1990s and quickly became interested in the Python programming language. In 2012, he joined Camptocamp to share his expertise on Python, PostgreSQL, and Linux with the team implementing Odoo. He currently manages projects for Camptocamp and is strongly involved in the Odoo Community Association. In his spare time, he likes to play jazz on the vibraphone.

Holger Brunn has been a fervent open source advocate since he came into contact with the open source market sometime in the nineties.

He has programmed for ERP and similar systems in different positions since 2001. For the last 10 years, he has dedicated his time to TinyERP, which became OpenERP and evolved into Odoo. Currently, he works at Therp BV in the Netherlands as a developer and is an active member of the Odoo Community Association.

Daniel Reis has had a long career in the IT industry, largely as a consultant implementing business applications in a variety of sectors, and today works for Securitas, a multinational security services provider.

He has been working with Odoo (formerly OpenERP) since 2010, is an active contributor to the Odoo Community Association projects, is currently a member of the board of the Odoo Community Association, and collaborates with ThinkOpen Solutions, a leading Portuguese Odoo integrator.

About the reviewer

Kishan Gajjar is a lead developer at Droggol and has been working on Odoo for the last 4 years. Previously, he worked at the Indian branch of Odoo for 3 years in the R&D department. During his time at Odoo, he mostly worked on the website builder, themes, and the backend JavaScript framework. Later, he established Droggol as one of the co-founders. He has expertise in website and theme development and loves creating beautiful and eye-catching websites in Odoo. Aside from development, he loves playing video games.

To begin with, I would like to thank my parents for allowing me to follow my ambitions throughout my childhood, and also my brother, who encourages me in his own particular way. He has been my inspiration and motivation.

Packt is searching for authors like you

If you're interested in becoming an author for Packt, please visit `authors.packtpub.com` and apply today. We have worked with thousands of developers and tech professionals, just like you, to help them share their insight with the global tech community. You can make a general application, apply for a specific hot topic that we are recruiting an author for, or submit your own idea.

Table of Contents

Preface

1
Installing the Odoo Development Environment

Understanding the Odoo ecosystem	**30**
Odoo editions	30
Git repositories	31
Runbot	31
Odoo app store	32
Odoo Community Association	33
Official Odoo help forum	33
Odoo's eLearning platform	33
Easy installation of Odoo from source	**34**
Getting ready	34
How to do it...	35
How it works...	36
Managing Odoo server databases	**40**
Getting ready	40
How to do it...	40
How it works...	48
There's more...	49
Storing the instance configuration in a file	**50**
How to do it...	50
How it works...	51
Activating Odoo developer tools	**54**
How to do it...	54
How it works...	56
Updating the add-on modules list	**56**
Getting ready	56
How to do it...	57
How it works...	58

2
Managing Odoo Server Instances

Configuring the add-ons path	**60**
Getting ready	60
How to do it...	60
How it works...	61
There's more...	61
Standardizing your instance directory layout	**62**
How to do it...	63

How it works...	65	How it works...	75
There's more...	66	There's more...	75
Installing and upgrading local add-on modules	**67**	**Applying changes to add-ons**	**75**
Getting ready	67	Getting ready	75
How to do it...	67	How to do it...	76
How it works...	71	How it works...	76
There's more...	73	See also	77
Installing add-on modules from GitHub	**74**	**Applying and trying proposed pull requests**	**77**
Getting ready	74	Getting ready	77
How to do it...	74	How to do it...	77
		How it works...	78
		There's more...	78

3
Creating Odoo Add-On Modules

Technical requirements	**82**	Getting ready	89
What is an Odoo add-on module?	**82**	How to do it...	89
Creating and installing a new add-on module	**83**	How it works...	91
Getting ready	83	**Adding models**	**92**
How to do it...	**84**	Getting ready	92
How it works...	85	How to do it...	93
Completing the add-on module manifest	**86**	How it works...	94
		Adding menu items and views	**95**
Getting ready	86	Getting ready	95
How to do it...	86	How to do it...	95
How it works...	87	How it works...	99
There's more...	88	**Adding access security**	**101**
Organizing the add-on module file structure	**89**	Getting ready	101
		How to do it...	101
		How it works...	103
		See also	103

Using the scaffold command to create
a module   103

Getting ready   103
How to do it...   104
How it works...   105

4
Application Models

Technical requirements	108
Defining the model representation and order	**108**
Getting ready	108
How to do it...	109
How it works...	110
There's more...	111
Adding data fields to a model	**112**
Getting ready	112
How to do it...	112
How it works...	114
There's more...	117
Using a float field with configurable precision	**119**
Getting ready	119
How to do it...	119
How it works...	120
Adding a monetary field to a model	**120**
Getting ready	120
How to do it...	120
How it works...	121
Adding relational fields to a model	**122**
Getting ready	122
How to do it...	123
How it works...	124
There's more...	125

Adding a hierarchy to a model	**127**
Getting ready	127
How to do it...	127
How it works...	128
There's more...	129
Adding constraint validations to a model	**129**
Getting ready	130
How to do it...	130
How it works...	131
There's more...	132
Adding computed fields to a model	**132**
Getting ready	133
How to do it...	133
How it works...	135
There's more...	136
Exposing related fields stored in other models	**137**
Getting ready	137
How to do it...	137
How it works...	138
There's more...	138
Adding dynamic relations using reference fields	**138**
Getting ready	139
How to do it...	139
How it works...	139

Adding features to a model using inheritance	140	Using delegation inheritance to copy features to another model	144
Getting ready	140	Getting ready	144
How to do it…	141	How to do it…	145
How it works…	141	How it works…	145
		There's more…	146
Copy model definition using inheritance	142	Using abstract models for reusable model features	147
Getting ready	142	Getting ready	147
How to do it…	142	How to do it…	147
How it works…	143	How it works…	148
There's more…	144	There's more…	149

5
Basic Server-Side Development

Technical requirements	152	How it works…	162
Defining model methods and using API decorators	152	There's more…	163
Getting ready	152	Updating values of recordset records	164
How to do it…	153	Getting ready	164
How it works…	154	How to do it…	164
Reporting errors to the user	156	How it works…	165
Getting ready	156	There's more…	165
How to do it…	156	Searching for records	166
How it works…	157	Getting ready	167
There's more…	157	How to do it…	167
Obtaining an empty recordset for a different model	158	How it works…	167
		There's more…	169
Getting ready	159	Combining recordsets	169
How to do it…	159	Getting ready	169
How it works…	159	How to do it…	169
See also	160	How it works…	170
Creating new records	160	Filtering recordsets	171
Getting ready	160	Getting ready	171
How to do it…	161	How to do it…	171

How it works...	172	There's more...	178
There's more...	172	**Extending write() and create()**	**179**
Traversing recordset relations	**172**	Getting ready	179
Getting ready	173	How to do it...	180
How to do it...	173	How it works...	181
How it works...	173	There's more...	181
There's more...	174	**Customizing how records are searched**	**182**
See also	174	Getting ready	183
Sorting recordsets	**174**	How to do it...	183
Getting ready	174	How it works...	184
How to do it...	175	There's more...	185
How it works...	175	See also	185
There's more...	175	**Fetching data in groups using read_group()**	**186**
Extending the business logic defined in a model	**176**	Getting ready	186
Getting ready	176	How to do it...	187
How to do it...	177	How it works...	187
How it works...	177		

6
Managing Module Data

Technical requirements	**190**	**Using the noupdate and forcecreate flags**	**198**
Using external IDs and namespaces	**190**	How to do it...	198
How to do it...	190	How it works...	198
How it works...	191	There's more...	199
There's more...	192	See also	199
See also	193	**Loading data using CSV files**	**200**
Loading data using XML files	**193**	How to do it...	200
How to do it...	194	How it works...	200
How it works...	195	There's more...	201
There's more...	197		

Add-on updates and data migration	**202**	Getting ready	205
		How to do it...	205
How to do it...	202	How it works...	206
How it works...	203	**Invoking functions from XML files**	**206**
There's more...	204		
See also	205	How to do it...	206
Deleting records from XML files	**205**	How it works...	207
		There's more...	207

7
Debugging Modules

The auto-reload and --dev options	**210**	How to do it...	216
		How it works...	217
Getting ready	210	There's more...	218
How to do it...	210	**Using the Python debugger to trace method execution**	**218**
How it works...	210		
Producing server logs to help debug methods	**211**	Getting ready	218
		How to do it...	218
Getting ready	212	How it works...	221
How to do it...	212	There's more...	223
How it works...	213	See also	223
There's more...	214	**Understanding the debug mode options**	**223**
Using the Odoo shell to interactively call methods	**215**		
		How to do it...	224
Getting ready	216	How it works...	224

8
Advanced Server-Side Development Techniques

Technical requirements	**230**	How to do it...	231
Changing the user that performs an action	**230**	How it works...	232
		There's more...	233
		See also	233
Getting ready	230		

Calling a method with a modified context	233	Getting ready	249
		How to do it...	249
Getting ready	234	How it works...	250
How to do it...	234	See also	250
How it works...	235	Defining onchange with the compute method	250
There's more...	235		
See also	236		
Executing raw SQL queries	236	Getting ready	250
		How to do it...	251
Getting ready	236	How it works...	251
How to do it...	236	There's more...	251
How it works...	237		
There's more...	238	See also	252
See also	239	Defining a model based on a SQL view	252
Writing a wizard to guide the user	239	Getting ready	252
		How to do it...	253
Getting ready	239	How it works...	254
How to do it...	240	There's more...	254
How it works...	241		
There's more...	242	See also	255
		Adding custom settings options	255
See also	245	Getting ready	255
Defining onchange methods	245	How to do it...	255
Getting ready	246	How it works...	258
How to do it...	246	There's more...	258
How it works...	247		
There's more...	247	Implementing init hooks	259
		Getting ready	259
Calling onchange methods on the server side	248	How to do it...	260
		How it works...	260

9
Backend Views

Technical requirements	262	How to do it...	263
Adding a menu item and window actions	263	How it works...	264
		There's more...	266
Getting ready	263	See also	267

Having an action open a specific view	**267**	See also	291
How to do it...	267	**Adding a search filter side panel**	**291**
How it works...	269	Getting ready	291
There's more...	270	How to do it...	291
Adding content and widgets to a form view	**270**	How it works...	292
		There's more...	293
How to do it...	271	**Changing existing views – view inheritance**	**293**
How it works...	272		
There's more...	275	How to do it...	293
See also	276	How it works...	294
Adding buttons to forms	**276**	There's more...	296
How to do it...	276	**Defining document-style forms**	**298**
How it works...	276	How to do it...	298
There's more...	277	How it works...	299
Passing parameters to forms and actions – context	**277**	See also	300
		Dynamic form elements using attrs	**300**
Getting ready	277		
How to do it...	278	How to do it...	301
How it works...	278	How it works...	301
There's more...	279	There's more...	301
See also	280	**Defining embedded views**	**301**
Defining filters on record lists – domain	**281**	How to do it...	302
		How it works...	302
How to do it...	281	There's more...	302
How it works...	282	**Displaying attachments on the side of the form view**	**303**
There's more...	283		
See also	285	How to do it...	304
Defining list views	**285**	How it works...	304
How to do it...	285	There's more...	305
How it works...	286	**Defining kanban views**	**305**
There's more...	287	How to do it...	305
Defining search views	**287**	How it works...	307
How to do it...	288	There's more...	308
How it works...	289	**See also**	**308**
There's more...	290		

Showing kanban cards in columns according to their state	308	How it works...	314
		Defining the dashboard view	315
Getting ready	308	Getting ready	315
How to do it...	309	How to do it...	315
How it works...	309	How it works...	316
There's more...	310	There's more....	317
Defining calendar views	310	Defining the gantt view	317
How to do it...	310	Getting ready	317
How it works...	311	How to do it...	317
There's more...	311	How it works...	318
		There's more...	318
Defining graph view and pivot view	311	Defining the activity view	319
Getting ready	311	Getting ready	319
How to do it...	312	How to do it...	319
How it works...	312	How it works...	320
There's more...	313	Defining the map view	320
Defining the cohort view	313	Getting ready	320
Getting ready	314	How to do it...	321
How to do it...	314	How it works...	321

10
Security Access

Technical requirements	324	How to do it...	330
Creating security groups and assigning them to users	324	How it works...	330
		There's more...	332
Getting ready	324	See also	332
How to do it...	324	Limiting access to fields in models	333
How it works...	326		
There's more...	328	Getting ready	333
See also	329	How to do it...	333
Adding security access to models	329	How it works...	333
		There's more...	334
Getting ready	329	See also	335

Limiting record access using record rules — 335
Getting ready — 335
How to do it... — 335
How it works... — 336
There's more... — 338

Using security groups to activate features — 339
Getting ready — 339
How to do it... — 339
How it works... — 343
There's more... — 344

Accessing recordsets as a superuser — 345
How to do it... — 345
How it works... — 346
There's more... — 347

Hiding view elements and menus based on groups — 347
Getting ready — 347
How to do it... — 347
How it works... — 348
See also — 348

11
Internationalization

Installing a language and configuring user preferences — 350
How to do it... — 350
How it works... — 352
There's more... — 352

Configuring language-related settings — 353
Getting ready — 353
How to do it... — 354
How it works... — 354
There's more... — 355

Translating texts through the web client user interface — 355
Getting ready — 355
How to do it... — 355
How it works... — 357
There's more... — 358

Exporting translation strings to a file — 358
Getting ready — 358

How to do it... — 359
How it works... — 360
There's more... — 361

Using gettext tools to make translations easier — 362
How to do it... — 362
How it works... — 363
There's more... — 364

Importing translation files into Odoo — 364
Getting ready — 364
How to do it... — 364
How it works... — 365

Changing the custom language URL code for a website — 365
Getting ready — 366
How to do it... — 366
How it works... — 367

12
Automation, Workflows, Emails, and Printing

Technical requirements	370
Managing dynamic record stages	**370**
Getting ready	370
How to do it...	371
How it works...	373
There's more...	374
See more	375
Managing kanban stages	**375**
Getting started	375
How to do it...	375
How it works...	377
There's more...	378
See more	378
Adding a quick create form to a kanban card	**378**
Getting started	378
How to do it...	379
How it works...	380
Creating interactive kanban cards	**380**
Getting started	380
How to do it...	380
How it works...	383
Adding a progress bar in kanban views	**384**
Getting started	384
How to do it...	384
How it works...	385
Creating server actions	**386**
Getting ready	386
How to do it...	386
How it works...	388
There's more...	389
Using Python code server actions	**390**
Getting ready	390
How to do it...	390
How it works...	392
There's more...	392
See more	392
Using automated actions on time conditions	**393**
Getting ready	393
How to do it...	393
How it works...	395
There's more...	396
See more	396
Using automated actions on event conditions	**397**
Getting ready	397
How to do it...	397
How it works...	399
There's more...	400
Creating QWeb-based PDF reports	**400**
Getting ready	401
How to do it...	401
How it works...	403
There's more...	404
Managing activities from a kanban card	**405**
Getting started	405
How to do it...	405
How it works...	406

There's more…	407	See also	409
See also	407	**Enabling the archive option for records**	**410**
Adding a stat button to a form view	**407**	Getting started	410
Getting started	407	How to do it…	410
How to do it…	408	How it works…	411
How it works…	409	There's more…	411

13
Web Server Development

Technical requirements	**414**	to your handlers	**422**
Making a path accessible from the network	**414**	How to do it…	422
		How it works…	423
Getting ready	414	There's more…	423
How to do it…	414	See also	424
How it works…	416	**Modifying an existing handler**	**424**
There's more…	418	Getting ready	424
See also	419	How to do it…	424
Restricting access to web-accessible paths	**419**	How it works…	425
		There's more…	426
Getting ready	419	See also	427
How to do it…	419	**Serving static resources**	**427**
How it works…	421	Getting ready	427
There's more…	421	How to do it…	427
Consuming parameters passed		How it works…	428

14
CMS Website Development

Managing static assets	**430**	There's more…	433
What are asset bundles and different assets in Odoo?	430	**Adding CSS and JavaScript for a website**	**435**
Custom assets	432	Getting ready	435
How to do it…	432	How to do it…	435
How it works…	433		

How it works...	437	How to do it...	465
There's more...	439	How it works...	465
		There's more...	466

Creating or modifying templates – QWeb — 439

Getting ready	439	**Managing sitemaps for the website**	**466**
How to do it...	439	Getting ready...	467
How it works...	441	How to do it...	467
There's more...	447	How it works...	468
See also	448	There's more...	468

Managing dynamic routes — 448

Getting a visitor's country information — 468

Getting ready	448	Getting ready	469
How to do it...	449	How to do it...	469
How it works...	451	How it works...	470
There's more...	451		

Offering static snippets to the user — 452

Tracking a marketing campaign — 471

Getting ready	452	Getting ready	471
How to do it...	452	How to do it...	471
How it works...	454	How it works...	472
There's more...	455		

Offering dynamic snippets to the user — 455

Managing multiple websites — 473

Getting ready	455	Getting ready	473
How to do it...	455	How to do it...	474
How it works...	458	How it works...	475
There's more...	459		

Getting input from website users — 460

Redirecting old URLs — 476

Getting ready	460	Getting ready	476
How to do it...	461	How to do it...	476
How it works...	463	How it works...	477
There's more...	464		

Managing SEO options — 464

Publish management for website-related records — 478

Getting ready	464	Getting ready	478
		How to do it...	478
		How it works...	479
		There's more...	480

15
Web Client Development

Technical requirements	483	Getting ready	495
Creating custom widgets	483	How to do it…	496
Getting ready	483	How it works…	503
How to do it…	483	There's more…	506
How it works…	487	**Debugging your client-side code**	**507**
There's more…	488	Getting ready	507
Using client-side QWeb templates	**489**	How to do it…	507
Getting ready	489	How it works…	508
How to do it…	489	There's more…	509
How it works…	490	**Improving onboarding with tours**	**510**
There's more…	491	Getting ready	510
See also	492	How to do it…	510
Making RPC calls to the server	**492**	How it works…	512
Getting ready	492	**Mobile app JavaScript**	**513**
How to do it…	492	Getting ready	513
How it works…	494	How to do it…	513
There's more…	494	How it works…	515
See also	495	There's more…	515
Creating a new view	**495**		

16
The Odoo Web Library (OWL)

Technical requirements	518	Getting ready	521
Creating an OWL component	518	How to do it…	521
Getting ready	518	How it works…	523
How to do it…	518	There's more…	523
How it works…	520	**Making OWL components reactive**	**523**
There's more…	521	Getting ready	524
Managing user actions in an OWL component	**521**	How to do it…	524

How it works...	526	There's more...	529
Understanding the OWL component life cycle	**526**	**Adding an OWL field to the form view**	**529**
Getting ready	526	Getting ready	529
How to do it...	527	How to do it...	530
How it works...	528	How it works...	534

17

In-App Purchasing with Odoo

Technical requirements	538	Getting ready	551
IAP concepts	538	How to do it...	552
How it works...	538	How it works...	554
The IAP service flow	539	There's more...	556
There's more...	540	See also	557
Registering an IAP service in Odoo	**541**	**Creating an IAP client module**	**557**
		Getting ready	557
Getting ready	541	How to do it...	558
How to do it...	541	How it works...	561
How it works...	544	There's more...	562
Creating an IAP service module	**545**	**Displaying offers when an account lacks credits**	**563**
Getting ready	545	Getting ready	563
How to do it...	546	How to do it...	563
How it works...	550	How it works...	566
Authorizing and charging IAP credits	**551**	There's more...	566

18

Automated Test Cases

Technical requirements	568	There's more...	571
Adding Python test cases	**569**	**Running tagged Python test cases**	**571**
Getting ready	569		
How to do it...	569	Getting ready	571
How it works...	570	How to do it...	572

How it works...	572	from the UI	583
There's more...	573	How to do it...	583
Setting up Headless Chrome for client-side test cases	**574**	How it works...	586
		Debugging client-side test cases	**586**
How to do it...	574	Getting ready	586
How it works...	575	How to do it...	586
Adding client-side QUnit test cases	**575**	How it works...	587
		Generating videos/screenshots for failed test cases	**588**
Getting ready	575		
How to do it...	575	How to do it...	588
How it works...	577	How it works...	589
There's more...	579	**Populating random data for testing**	**589**
Adding tour test cases	**579**		
Getting ready	579	Getting ready	589
How to do it...	580	How to do it...	590
How it works...	582	How it works...	590
Running client-side test cases		There's more...	592

19
Managing, Deploying, and Testing with Odoo.sh

Technical requirements	**594**	**Adding and installing custom modules**	**601**
Exploring some basic concepts of Odoo.sh	**594**		
		Getting ready	601
What is Odoo.sh?	594	How to do it...	602
Why was Odoo.sh introduced?	595	How it works...	603
When should you use Odoo.sh?	595	There's more...	604
What are the features of Odoo.sh?	596	**Managing branches**	**604**
Creating an Odoo.sh account	**597**	Getting ready	605
Getting ready	597	How to do it...	605
How to do it...	598	How it works...	609
How it works...	600	**Accessing debugging options**	**610**
There's more...	601	How to do it...	610
		There's more...	616

Getting a backup of your instance — 616
How to do it... — 616
How it works... — 617

Checking the status of your builds — 617
How to do it... — 617
How it works... — 618
There's more... — 618

All Odoo.sh options — 619
Getting ready — 619
How to do it... — 619
There's more... — 624

20
Remote Procedure Calls in Odoo

Technical requirements — 626
Logging in to/connecting Odoo with XML-RPC — 626
Getting ready — 627
How to do it... — 627
How it works... — 628
There's more... — 628

Searching/reading records through XML-RPC — 629
Getting ready — 629
How to do it... — 629
How it works... — 631
There's more... — 632

Creating/updating/deleting records through XML-RPC — 633
Getting ready — 633
How to do it... — 634
How it works... — 636
There's more... — 636

Calling methods through XML-RPC — 637
Getting ready — 637
How to do it... — 638
How it works... — 639
There's more... — 640

Logging in to/connecting Odoo with JSON-RPC — 640
Getting ready — 640
How to do it... — 640
How it works... — 642
There's more... — 642

Fetching/searching records through JSON-RPC — 643
Getting ready — 643
How to do it... — 644
How it works... — 645
There's more... — 646

Creating/updating/deleting records through JSON-RPC — 647
Getting ready — 647
How to do it... — 647
How it works... — 649
There's more... — 649

Calling methods through JSON-RPC — 650
Getting ready — 650
How to do it... — 650
How it works... — 652

The OCA odoorpc library — 652

Getting ready	653	See also	656
How to do it...	653	**Generating API keys**	**656**
How it works...	654	How to do it...	656
There's more...	655	How it works...	658

21
Performance Optimization

The prefetching pattern for recordsets	**660**	How it works...	669
		There's more...	671
How to do it...	660	See also	671
How it works...	661	**Creating or writing multiple records**	**671**
There's more...	662		
The in-memory cache – ormcache	**662**	How to do it...	671
		How it works...	672
How to do it...	663	There's more...	673
How it works...	665	**Accessing records through database queries**	**674**
There's more...	665		
Generating differently sized images	**666**	How to do it...	674
		How it works...	675
How to do it...	666	There's more...	676
How it works...	667	**Profiling Python code**	**677**
There's more...	668	How to do it...	677
Accessing grouped data	**668**	How it works...	678
How to do it...	668	There's more...	678

22
Point of Sale

Technical requirements	**682**	There's more...	685
Adding custom JavaScript/SCSS files	**682**	**Adding an action button on the keyboard**	**685**
Getting ready	682	Getting ready	685
How to do it...	683	How to do it...	685
How it works...	684	How it works...	687

There's more…	688	How it works…	695
Making RPC calls	**689**	**Modifying existing business logic**	**695**
Getting ready	689		
How to do it…	689	Getting ready	695
How it works…	691	How to do it…	696
There's more…	692	How it works…	697
Modifying the Point of Sale screen UI	**693**	**Modifying customer receipts**	**698**
		Getting ready	698
Getting ready	693	How to do it…	698
How to do it…	693	How it works…	700

23
Managing Emails in Odoo

Technical requirements	**702**	There's more…	711
Configuring incoming and outgoing email servers	**702**	**Sending emails using the Jinja template**	**711**
Getting ready	702	Getting ready	711
How to do it…	703	How to do it…	712
How it works…	705	How it works…	714
There's more…	706	There's more…	716
Managing chatter on documents	**707**	**Sending emails using the QWeb template**	**716**
Getting ready	707	Getting ready	716
How to do it…	707	How to do it…	716
How it works…	708	How it works…	718
There's more…	709	There's more…	720
Managing activities on documents	**709**	**Managing the email alias**	**721**
Getting ready	709	Getting ready	721
How to do it…	709	How to do it…	722
How it works…	710	How it works…	723
		There's more…	725

Logging user changes in a chatter	725	Sending periodic digest emails	727
Getting ready	725	Getting ready	727
How to do it...	725	How to do it...	727
How it works...	726	How it works...	729

24
Managing the IoT Box

Technical requirements	732	Taking input from devices	746
Flashing the IoT Box image for Raspberry Pi	732	Getting ready	747
		How to do it...	747
Getting ready	732	How it works...	748
How to do it...	732	There's more...	749
How it works...	733	Accessing the IoT Box through SSH	749
There's more...	734		
Connecting the IoT Box with a network	735	Getting ready	749
		How it works...	750
Getting ready	735	How to do it...	750
How to do it...	735	There's more...	751
How it works...	737	Configuring a point of sale	752
Adding the IoT Box to Odoo	738	Getting ready	752
Getting ready	738	How to do it...	752
How to do it...	738	How it works...	753
How it works...	741	There's more...	754
There's more...	743	Sending PDF reports directly to a printer	755
Loading drivers and listing connected devices	743	Getting ready	755
		How to do it...	755
Getting ready	744	How it works...	756
How to do it...	744		
How it works...	746		

Other Books You May Enjoy

Index

Preface

Odoo 14 Development Cookbook, Fourth Edition, is a complete resource that provides various development scenarios to help you build complex business applications with the Odoo framework. Whether you want to customize existing modules, create new ones, or customize the website or backend web client (JS), this book covers every aspect of Odoo development.

With its latest release, the powerful Odoo framework released a wide variety of features for rapid application development. This updated Odoo development cookbook will help you explore the new features in Odoo 14 and learn how to use them to develop Odoo applications from scratch. You'll learn about the new website concepts in Odoo 14 and get a glimpse of Odoo's new web client framework, **OWL** (short for **Odoo Web Library**).

Once you've completed the installation, you'll begin to explore the Odoo framework with real-world examples. You'll then create a new Odoo module from the ground up and progress to advanced framework concepts. You'll also learn how to modify existing applications, including **Point of Sale** (**PoS**). This book isn't just limited to backend development; you'll discover advanced JavaScript recipes for creating new views and widgets. As you progress, you'll learn website development and become a quality Odoo developer by studying performance optimization, debugging, and automated testing. Finally, you'll delve into advanced concepts such as multi-website, **In-App Purchasing** (**IAP**), Odoo.sh, IoT Box, and deployment.

You will build beautiful websites with Odoo CMS using dynamic building blocks; get to grips with advanced concepts, such as caching, prefetching, and debugging; modify backend JavaScript components and POS with the new OWL framework; connect and access any object in Odoo via **Remote Procedure Calls** (**RPC**); manage, deploy, and test an Odoo instance with Odoo.sh; configure IoT Box to add and upgrade POS hardware, and find out how to implement IAP services.

By the end of the book, you'll have all the knowledge you need to build impressive Odoo applications and you'll become well versed in development best practices that will come handy when working with the Odoo framework.

Who this book is for

This book is suitable for both newcomers and experienced Odoo developers who want to develop a highly efficient business application with the Odoo framework. Basic knowledge of Python and JavaScript is necessary to get the most out of the book.

What this book covers

Chapter 1, *Installing the Odoo Development Environment*, explains how to create a development environment for Odoo, start Odoo, create a configuration file, and activate Odoo's developer tools.

Chapter 2, *Managing Odoo Server Instances*, provides useful tips for working with add-ons installed from GitHub and organizing the source code of your instance.

Chapter 3, *Creating Odoo Add-On Modules*, explains the structure of an Odoo add-on module and gives a step-by-step guide for creating a simple module from scratch.

Chapter 4, *Application Models*, focuses on the Odoo model structure, and explains all types of fields with their attributes. It also covers techniques to extend existing database structures via extended modules.

Chapter 5, *Basic Server-Side Development*, explains various framework methods to perform CRUD operations in Odoo. This chapter also includes different ways to inherit and extend existing methods.

Chapter 6, *Managing Module Data*, shows how to ship data along with the code of your module. It also explains how to write a migration script when a data model provided by an add-on is modified in a new release.

Chapter 7, *Debugging Modules*, proposes some strategies for server-side debugging and an introduction to the Python debugger. It also covers techniques to run Odoo in developer mode.

Chapter 8, *Advanced Server-Side Development Techniques*, covers more advanced topics of the ORM framework. It is useful for developing wizards, SQL views, installation hooks, on-change methods, and more. This chapter also explains how to execute raw SQL queries in the database.

Chapter 9, Backend Views, explains how to write business views for your data models and how to call server-side methods from these views. It covers the usual views (list view, form view, and search view), as well as some complex views (kanban, graph, calendar, pivot, and so on).

Chapter 10, Security Access, explains how to control who has access to what in your Odoo instance by creating security groups, writing access control lists to define what operations are available to each group on a given model, and, if necessary, by writing record-level rules.

Chapter 11, Internationalization, shows how language translation works in Odoo. It shows how to install multiple languages and how to import/export translated terms.

Chapter 12, Automation, Workflows, Emails, and Printing, illustrates the different tools available in Odoo to implement business processes for your records. It also shows how server actions and automated rules can be used to support business rules. This also covers the QWeb report to generate dynamic PDF documents.

Chapter 13, Web Server Development, covers the core of the Odoo web server. It shows how to create custom URL routes to serve data on a given URL, and also shows how to control access to these URLs.

Chapter 14, CMS Website Development, shows how to manage a website with Odoo. It also shows how to create and modify beautiful web pages and QWeb templates. This chapter also includes how to create dynamic building blocks with options. It includes some dedicated recipes for managing SEO, user forms, UTM tracking, sitemaps, and fetching visitor location information. This chapter also highlights the latest concept of a multi-website in Odoo.

Chapter 15, Web Client Development, dives into the JavaScript part of Odoo. It covers how to create a new field widget and make RPC calls to the server. This also includes how to create a brand-new view from scratch. You will also learn how to create onboarding tours.

Chapter 16, The Odoo Web Library (OWL), gives introductions to the new client-side framework called OWL. It covers the life cycle of the OWL component. It also covers recipes to create a field widget from scratch.

Chapter 17, In-App Purchasing with Odoo, covers everything related to the latest concept of IAP in Odoo. In this chapter, you will learn how to create client and service modules for IAP. You will also learn how to create an IAP account and draw IAP credits from the end user.

Chapter 18, Automated Test Cases, includes how to write and execute automated test cases. This includes both server-side and client-side test cases. This chapter also covers tour test cases and setting up headless Chrome to get videos for failed test cases.

Chapter 19, Managing, Deploying, and Testing with Odoo.sh, explains how to manage, deploy, and test Odoo instances with the PaaS platform, Odoo.sh. It covers how you can manage different types of instances, such as production, staging, and development. This chapter also covers various configuration options for Odoo.sh.

Chapter 20, Remote Procedure Calls in Odoo, covers different ways to connect Odoo instances from external applications. This chapter teaches you how to connect to and access the data from an Odoo instance through XML-RPC, JSON-RPC, and the odoorpc library.

Chapter 21, Performance Optimization, explains the different concepts and patterns used to gain performance improvements in Odoo. This chapter includes the concept of prefetching, ORM-cache, and profiling the code to detect performance issues.

Chapter 22, Point of Sale, covers customization in a PoS application. This includes customization of the user interface, adding a new action button, modifying business flow, and extending customer recipes.

Chapter 23, Managing Emails in Odoo, explains how to manage email and chatter in Odoo. It starts by configuring mail servers and then moves to the mailing API of the Odoo framework. This chapter also covers the Jinja2 and QWeb mail templates, chatters on the form view, field logs, and activities.

Chapter 24, Managing IoT Box, gives you the highlights of the latest hardware of IoT Box. This chapter covers how to configure, access, and debug IoT Box. It also includes a recipe to integrate IoT Box with your custom add-ons.

To get the most out of this book

This book includes the installation steps for Odoo, so the only thing you require is Ubuntu 18.04 or any other Linux-based OS. On other OSes, you can use it via a virtual machine. If you are using Windows, you can also install Ubuntu as a subsystem:

Software/hardware covered in the book	OS requirements
Odoo v14	Ubuntu recommended (or any version of Linux)

This book is intended for developers who have basic knowledge of the Python programming language, as the Odoo backend runs on Python. In Odoo, data files are created with XML, so basic knowledge of XML is required.

This book also covers the backend JavaScript framework, PoS applications, and the website builder, which requires basic knowledge of JavaScript, jQuery, and Bootstrap 4. The Community Edition of Odoo is open source and freely available, but a few features, including IoT, cohort, and the dashboard, are available only in the Enterprise Edition, so to follow along with that recipe, you will need the Enterprise Edition.

To follow *Chapter 24*, *Managing IoT Box*, you will require the Raspberry Pi 3 Model B+, which is available at `https://www.raspberrypi.org/products/raspberry-pi-3-model-b-plus/`.

If you are using the digital version of this book, we advise you to type the code yourself or access the code via the GitHub repository (link available in the next section). Doing so will help you avoid any potential errors related to the copying and pasting of code.

Download the example code files

You can download the example code files for this book from GitHub at `https://github.com/PacktPublishing/Odoo-14-Development-Cookbook-Fourth-Edition`. If there's an update to the code, it will be updated on the existing GitHub repository.

We also have other code bundles from our rich catalog of books and videos available at `https://github.com/PacktPublishing/`. Check them out!

Download the color images

We also provide a PDF file that has color images of the screenshots/diagrams used in this book. You can download it here:

`https://static.packt-cdn.com/downloads/9781800200319_ColorImages.pdf`

Conventions used

There are a number of text conventions used throughout this book.

`Code in text`: Indicates code words in text, database table names, folder names, filenames, file extensions, pathnames, dummy URLs, user input, and Twitter handles. Here is an example: "Given that `book` is a browse record, we can simply recycle the first example's function by passing `book.id` as a `book_id` parameter to give out the same content."

A block of code is set as follows:

```
@http.route('/my_library/books/json', type='json',
auth='none')
def books_json(self):
    records = request.env['library.book'].sudo().search([])
    return records.read(['name'])
```

Any command-line input or output is written as follows:

```
$ ./odoo-bin -d mydb --i18n-export=mail.po --modules=mail
$ mv mail.po ./addons/mail/i18n/mail.pot
```

Bold: Indicates a new term, an important word, or words that you see on screen. For example, words in menus or dialog boxes appear in the text like this. Here is an example: "Another important usage is providing demonstration data, which is loaded when the database is created with the **Load demonstration data** checkbox checked."

> Tips or important notes
> Appear like this.

Get in touch

Feedback from our readers is always welcome.

General feedback: If you have questions about any aspect of this book, mention the book title in the subject of your message and email us at `customercare@packtpub.com`.

Errata: Although we have taken every care to ensure the accuracy of our content, mistakes do happen. If you have found a mistake in this book, we would be grateful if you would report this to us. Please visit www.packtpub.com/support/errata, selecting your book, clicking on the Errata Submission Form link, and entering the details.

Piracy: If you come across any illegal copies of our works in any form on the internet, we would be grateful if you would provide us with the location address or website name. Please contact us at `copyright@packt.com` with a link to the material.

If you are interested in becoming an author: If there is a topic that you have expertise in, and you are interested in either writing or contributing to a book, please visit `authors.packtpub.com`.

Reviews

Please leave a review. Once you have read and used this book, why not leave a review on the site that you purchased it from? Potential readers can then see and use your unbiased opinion to make purchase decisions, we at Packt can understand what you think about our products, and our authors can see your feedback on their book. Thank you!

For more information about Packt, please visit `packt.com`.

1
Installing the Odoo Development Environment

There are several ways to set up an Odoo development environment. This chapter proposes one of them; you will certainly find a number of other tutorials on the web explaining other approaches. Keep in mind that this chapter is about a development environment that has different requirements from a production environment.

If you are new to Odoo development, you must know about certain aspects of the Odoo ecosystem. The first recipe will give you a brief introduction to the Odoo ecosystem, and then we will move on to the installation of Odoo for development.

In this chapter, we will cover the following recipes:

- Understanding the Odoo ecosystem
- Easy installation of Odoo from source
- Managing Odoo server databases
- Storing the instance configuration in a file

- Activating Odoo developer tools
- Updating the add-on modules list

Understanding the Odoo ecosystem

Odoo provides the developer with out-of-the-box modularity. Its powerful framework helps the developer to build projects very quickly. There are various characters in the Odoo ecosystem that you should be familiar with before embarking on your journey of becoming a successful Odoo developer.

Odoo editions

Odoo comes with two different editions. The first one is the **Community Edition**, which is open source, and the second one is the **Enterprise Edition**, which has licensing fees. Unlike other software vendors, Odoo Enterprise Edition is just a pack of extra applications that adds extra features or new apps to the Community Edition. Basically, the Enterprise Edition runs on top of the Community Edition. The Community Edition comes under the **Lesser General Public License v3.0 (LGPLv3)** license and comes with all of the basic **Enterprise Resource Planning (ERP)** applications, such as sales, **Customer Relationship Management (CRM)**, invoicing, purchases, and website builder. Alternatively, the Enterprise Edition comes with the Odoo Enterprise Edition License, which is a proprietary license. Odoo Enterprise Edition has a number of advanced features, such as full accounting, studio, **Voice over Internet Protocol (VoIP)**, mobile responsive design, e-sign, marketing automation, delivery and banking integrations, IoT, and more. The Enterprise Edition also provides you with unlimited *bugfix support*. The following diagram shows that the Enterprise Edition depends on the Community Edition, which is why you need the latter in order to use the former:

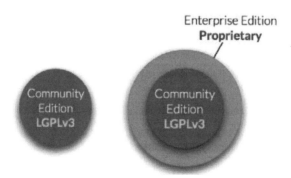

Figure 1.1 – Differences between the Community and Enterprise Editions

You can see a full comparison of both editions here: `https://www.odoo.com/page/editions`.

> **Note**
> Odoo has the largest number of community developers, which is why you will find a large number of third-party apps (modules) on the app store. Some of the free apps use an **Affero General Public License version 3 (AGPLv3)**. You cannot use the proprietary license on your app if your application has dependencies on such apps. Apps with an Odoo proprietary license can be developed only on modules that have LGPL or other proprietary licenses.

Git repositories

The entire code base of Odoo is hosted on GitHub. You can post bugs/issues for stable versions here. You can also propose a new feature by submitting **Pull Requests (PR)**. There are several repositories in Odoo. See the following table for more information:

Repositories	Purpose
`https://github.com/odoo/odoo`	This is the Community Edition of Odoo. It's available publicly.
`https://github.com/odoo/enterprise`	This is the Enterprise Edition of Odoo. It's available to official Odoo partners only.
`https://github.com/odoo-dev/odoo`	This is an ongoing development repository. It's available publicly.

Table 1.1

Every year, Odoo releases one major (**Long-Term Support (LTS)**) version and a few minor versions. Minor versions are mostly used in Odoo's online SaaS service, meaning that Odoo SaaS users get early access to these features. Major version branches have names such as 14.0, 13.0, and 12.0, while minor version branches have names such as saas-14.1, and saas-14.2 on GitHub. These minor versions are mostly used for Odoo's SaaS platform. The `master` branch is under development and is unstable, so it is advisable not to use this for production since it might break down your database.

Runbot

Runbot is Odoo's automated testing environment. Whenever there is a new commit in Odoo's GitHub branch, Runbot pulls those latest changes and creates the builds for the last four commits. Here, you can test all stable and in-development branches. You can even play with the Enterprise Edition and its development branches.

Every build has a different background color, which indicates the status of the test cases. A green background color means that all of the test cases run successfully and you can test that branch, while a red background color means that some test cases have failed on this branch and some features might be broken on that build. You can view the logs for all test cases, which show exactly what happens during installation. Every build has two databases. The `all` database has all of the modules installed on it, while the `base` database only has base Odoo modules installed. Every build is installed with basic demo data, and therefore you can test it quickly without extra configurations.

> **Note**
>
> You can access Runbot from the following URL: `http://runbot.odoo.com/runbot`.

The following credentials can be used to access any Runbot build:

- **Login ID**: admin **Password**: admin
- **Login ID**: demo **Password**: demo
- **Login ID**: portal **Password**: portal

> **Note**
>
> This is a public testing environment, so sometimes it is possible that other users are using/testing the same branch that you are testing.

Odoo app store

Odoo launched the app store a few years back, and this was an instant hit. Right now, there are over 22,000+ different apps hosted there. In the app store, you will find lots of free and paid applications for different versions. This includes specific solutions for different business verticals, such as education, food industries, and medicine. It also includes apps that extend or add new features to existing Odoo applications. The app store also provides numerous beautiful themes for the Odoo website builder. In *Chapter 3, Creating Odoo Add-On Modules*, we will look at how you can set pricing and currency for your custom module.

You can access the Odoo app store via the following URL: `https://www.odoo.com/apps`.

You can access the Odoo themes via the following URL: `https://www.odoo.com/apps/themes`.

> **Note**
> Odoo has open sourced several themes with versions 13 and 14. Note that these were paid themes in previous versions. This means that, in Odoo versions 13 and 14, you can download and use those beautiful themes at no extra cost.

Odoo Community Association

Odoo Community Association (OCA) is a non-profit organization that develops/manages community-based Odoo modules. All OCA modules are open source and maintained by Odoo community members. Under the OCA's GitHub account, you will find multiple repositories for different Odoo applications. Apart from Odoo modules, it also contains various tools, a migration library, accounting localizations, and so on.

Here is the URL for OCA's official GitHub account: `https://github.com/OCA`.

Official Odoo help forum

Odoo has a very powerful framework, and tons of things can be achieved just by using/activating options or by following specific patterns. Consequently, if you run into some technical issues or if you are not sure about some complex cases, then you can post your query on Odoo's official help forum. Lots of developers are active on this forum, including some official Odoo employees.

You can search your questions or post your new questions at the following URL: `https://help.odoo.com.help.odoo.com`.

Odoo's eLearning platform

Recently, Odoo has launched a new eLearning platform. This platform has lots of videos that explain how to use different Odoo applications. At the time of writing this book, this platform does not have technical videos, just functional ones.

Here is the URL for Odoo's eLearning platform: `https://www.odoo.com/slides`.

Easy installation of Odoo from source

It is highly recommended to use the **Linux Ubuntu** operating system for the installation of Odoo, since this is the operating system that Odoo uses for all its tests, debugging, and installations of Odoo Enterprise, in addition to the fact that most developers of Odoo also use GNU/Linux distributions, and is much more likely to get support from the Odoo community for OS-level issues that occur in **GNU/Linux** than **Windows** or **macOS**.

It is also recommended to develop Odoo add-on modules using the same environment (the same distribution and the same version) as the one that will be used in production. This will avoid nasty surprises, such as discovering on the day of deployment that a library has a different version than expected, with a slightly different and incompatible behavior. If your workstation is using a different OS, a good approach is to set up a **Virtual Machine (VM)** on your workstation and install a GNU/Linux distribution in the VM.

> **Note**
> Ubuntu is available as an app in **Microsoft Store** so you can use that too, if you do not want to switch to Ubuntu OS.

For this book, we will be using Ubuntu Server 18.04 LTS, but you can use any another Debian GNU/Linux OS. Whatever Linux distribution you choose, you should have some notion of how to use it from the command line, and having knowledge of system administration will certainly not do any harm.

Getting ready

We are assuming that you have Ubuntu 18.04 up and running and that you have an account with root access or that `sudo` has been configured. In the following sections, we will install Odoo's dependencies and download Odoo's source code from GitHub.

> **Note**
> Some of the configurations require a system login username, so we will use `$(whoami)` whenever a login username is required in a command line. This is a shell command that will substitute your login in the command you are typing.

Some operations will definitely be easier if you have a GitHub account. If you don't have one already, go to `https://github.com` and create one.

How to do it...

To install Odoo from source, perform the following steps:

1. Run the following commands to install the main dependencies:

   ```
   $ sudo apt-get update
   $ sudo apt install git python3-pip build-essential wget python3-dev python3-venv python3-wheel libxslt-dev libzip-dev libldap2-dev libsasl2-dev python3-setuptools libpng12-0 libjpeg-dev gdebi -y
   ```

2. Download and install `wkhtmltopdf`:

   ```
   $ wget https://github.com/wkhtmltopdf/wkhtmltopdf/releases/download/0.12.5/wkhtmltox_0.12.5-1.trusty_amd64.deb
   $ sudo dpkg -i wkhtmltox_0.12.5-1.trusty_amd64.deb
   ```

   If you find errors in a previous command, force install the dependencies with the following command:

   ```
   $ sudo apt-get install -f
   ```

3. Now, install the PostgreSQL database:

   ```
   $ sudo apt install postgresql -y
   ```

4. Configure PostgreSQL:

   ```
   $ sudo -u postgres createuser --superuser $(whoami)
   ```

5. Configure `git`:

   ```
   $ git config --global user.name "Your Name"
   $ git config --global user.email youremail@example.com
   ```

6. Clone the Odoo code base:

   ```
   $ mkdir ~/odoo-dev
   $ cd ~/odoo-dev
   $ git clone -b 14.0 --single-branch --depth 1 https://github.com/odoo/odoo.git
   ```

7. Create an `odoo-14.0` virtual environment and activate it:

   ```
   $ python3 -m venv ~/venv-odoo-14.0
   $ source ~/venv-odoo-14.0/bin/activate
   ```

8. Install the Python dependencies of Odoo in `venv`:

   ```
   $ cd ~/odoo-dev/odoo/
   $ pip3 install -r requirements.txt
   ```

9. Create and start your first Odoo instances:

   ```
   $ createdb odoo-test
   $ python3 odoo-bin -d odoo-test -i base --addons-path=addons --db-filter=odoo-test$
   ```

10. Point your browser to `http://localhost:8069` and authenticate it by using the **admin** account and using `admin` as the password.

> **Note**
>
> If you need RTL support, please install `node` and `rtlcss` via the following command:
>
> ```
> sudo apt-get install nodejs npm -y
> sudo npm install -g rtlcss
> ```

How it works...

In *step 1*, we installed several core dependencies. These dependencies include various tools, such as `git`, `pip3`, `wget`, Python setup tools, and more. These core tools will help us install other Odoo dependencies using simple commands.

In *step 2*, we downloaded and installed the `wkhtmltopdf` package, which is used in Odoo to print PDF documents such as sale orders, invoices, and other reports. Odoo 14.0 needs version 0.12.5 of `wkhtmltopdf`, and that exact version might be not included in the current Linux distributions. Fortunately for us, the maintainers of `wkhtmltopdf` provide pre-built packages for various distributions at `http://wkhtmltopdf.org/downloads.html` and we have downloaded and installed it from that URL.

PostgreSQL configuration

In *step 3*, we installed the PostgreSQL database.

In *step 4*, we created a new database user with the login name of your system. `$(whoami)` is used to fetch your login name, and the `-s` option is used to give super user rights. Let's see why we need these configurations.

Odoo uses the `psycopg2` Python library to connect with a PostgreSQL database. To access a PostgreSQL database with the `psycopg2` library, Odoo uses the following values by default:

- By default, `psycopg2` tries to connect to a database with the same username as the current user on local connections, which enables password-less authentication (this is good for the development environment).
- The local connection uses Unix domain sockets.
- The database server listens on port `5432`.

That's it! Your PostgreSQL database is now ready to be connected with Odoo.

As this is a development server, we have given `--superuser` rights to the user. It is OK to give the PostgreSQL user more rights as this will be your development instance. For a production instance, you can use the `--createdb` command line instead of `--superuser` to restrict rights. The `-superuser` rights in a production server will give additional leverage to an attacker exploiting a vulnerability in some part of the deployed code.

If you want to use a database user with a different login, you will need to provide a password for the user. This is done by passing the `--pwprompt` flag on the command line when creating the user, in which case the command will prompt you for the password.

If the user has already been created and you want to set a password (or modify a forgotten password), you can use the following command:

```
$ psql -c "alter role $(whoami) with password 'newpassword'"
```

If this command fails with an error message saying that the database does not exist, it is because you did not create a database named after your login name in *step 4* of this recipe. That's fine; just add the `--dbname` option with an existing database name, such as `--dbname template1`.

Git configuration

For the development environment, we are using Odoo sourced from GitHub. With `git`, you can easily switch between different Odoo versions. Also, you can fetch the latest changes with the `git pull` command.

In *step 5*, we configured your `git` user.

In *step 6*, we downloaded the source code from Odoo's official GitHub repository. We have used the `git clone` command to download Odoo's source code. We have used a single branch as we only want a branch for the 14.0 version. Also, we have used `--depth 1` to avoid downloading the full commit history of the branch. These options will download the source code very quickly, but if you want, you can omit those options.

Odoo developers also propose nightly builds, which are available as tarballs and distribution packages. The main advantage of using `git clone` is that you will be able to update your repository when new bug fixes are committed in the source tree. You will also be able to easily test any proposed fixes and track regressions so that you can make your bug reports more precise and helpful for developers.

> **Note**
> If you have access to the enterprise edition source code, you can download that too in a separate folder under the `~/odoo-dev` directory.

Virtual environments

Python **virtual environments**, or `venv` for short, are isolated Python workspaces. These are very useful to Python developers because they allow different workspaces with different versions of various Python libraries to be installed, possibly on different Python interpreter versions.

You can create as many environments as you wish using the `python3 -m venv ~/newvenv` command. This will create a `newvenv` directory in the specified location, containing a `bin/` subdirectory and a `lib/python3.6` subdirectory.

In *step 7*, we created a new virtual environment in the `~/venv-odoo-14.0` directory. This will be our isolated Python environment for Odoo, and all of Odoo's Python dependencies will be installed in this environment.

To activate the virtual environment, we need to use the source command. With the `source ~/venv-odoo-14.0/bin/activate` command, we have activated the virtual environment.

Installing Python packages

Odoo's source code has a list of Python dependencies in `requirements.txt`. In *step 8*, we installed all those requirements via the `pip3 install` command.

That's it. Now you can run the Odoo instance.

Starting the instance

Now comes the moment you've been waiting for. To start our first instance, in *step 9*, we first created a new empty database, used the `odoo-bin` script, and then started the Odoo instance with the following command:

```
python3 odoo-bin -d odoo-test -i base --addons-path=addons --db-filter=odoo-test$
```

You can also omit `python3` by using `./` before `odoo-bin` as it is an executable Python script, as follows:

```
./odoo-bin -d odoo-test -i base --addons-path=addons --db-filter=odoo-test$
```

With `odoo-bin`, a script with the following command-line arguments are used:

- `-d database_name`: Use this database by default.
- `--db-filter=database_name$`: Only try to connect to databases that match the supplied regular expression. One Odoo installation can serve multiple instances that live in separate databases, and this argument limits the available databases. The trailing `$` is important as the regular expression is used in match mode. This enables you to avoid selecting names starting with the specified string.
- `--addons-path=directory1,directory2,...`: This is a comma-separated list of directories in which Odoo will look for add-ons. This list is scanned at instance creation time to populate the list of available add-on modules in the instance. If you want to use Odoo's Enterprise Edition, then add its directory with this option.
- `-i base`: This is used to install a base module. This is required when you have created a database via the command line.

If you are using a database user with a database login that is different from your Linux login, you need to pass the following additional arguments:

- `--db_host=localhost`: Use a TCP connection to the database server.
- `--db_user=database_username`: Use the specified database login.
- `--db_password=database_password`: This is the password for authenticating against the PostgreSQL server.

To get an overview of all available options, use the `--help` argument. We will see more of the `odoo-bin` script later in this chapter.

When Odoo is started on an empty database, it will first create the database structure that's needed to support its operations. It will also scan the add-ons path to find the available add-on modules and insert some into the initial records in the database. This includes the **admin** user with the default `admin` password, which you will use for authentication.

Pointing your web browser to `http://localhost:8069/` leads you to the login page of your newly created instance, as shown in the following screenshot:

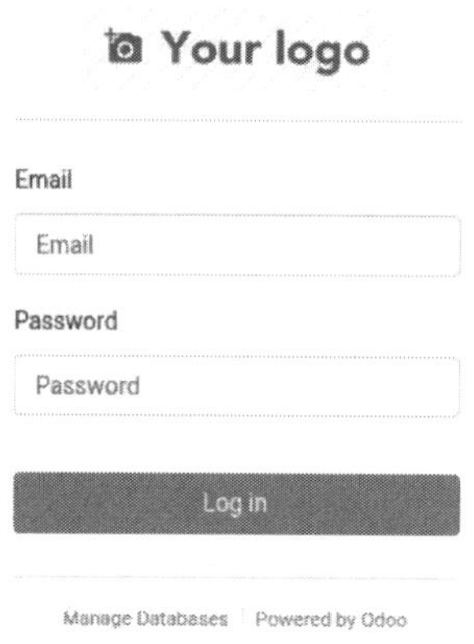

Figure 1.2 – Login screen of the Odoo instance

This is due to the fact that Odoo includes an HTTP server. By default, it listens on all local network interfaces on TCP port `8069`.

Managing Odoo server databases

When working with Odoo, all the data in your instance is stored in a PostgreSQL database. All the standard database management tools you are used to are available, but Odoo also proposes a web interface for some common operations.

Getting ready

We are assuming that your work environment is set up and that you have an instance running.

How to do it...

The Odoo database management interface provides tools to create, duplicate, remove, back up, and restore a database. There is also a way to change the master password, which is used to protect access to the database management interface.

Accessing the database management interface

To access the database, perform the following steps:

1. Go to the login screen of your instance (if you are authenticated, log out).
2. Click on the **Manage Databases** link. This will navigate to `http://localhost:8069/web/database/manager` (you can also point your browser directly to that URL):

Figure 1.3 – Database manager

Setting or changing the master password

If you've set up your instance with default values and haven't modified it yet, as we will explain in the following section, the database management screen will display a warning, telling you that the **master password** hasn't been set and will advise you to set one with a direct link:

Figure 1.4 – Master password warning

To set the master password, perform the following steps:

1. Click on the **Set Master Password** button. You will get a dialog box asking you to fill in the **New Master Password** field:

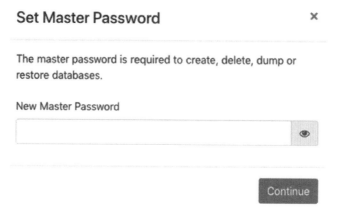

Figure 1.5 – Setting a new master password dialog

2. Type in a non-straightforward new password and click **Continue**.

If the master password is already set, click on the **Set Master Password** button at the bottom of the screen to change it. In the displayed dialog box, type the previous master password and the new one and then click on **Continue**.

> **Note**
> The master password is the server configuration file under the `admin_password` key. If the server was started without specifying a configuration file, a new one will be generated in `~/.odoorc`. Refer to the next recipe for more information about the configuration file.

Creating a new database

This dialog box can be used to create a new database instance that will be handled by the current Odoo server:

1. In the database management window, click on the **Create Database** button, which can be found at the bottom of the screen. This will bring up the following dialog:

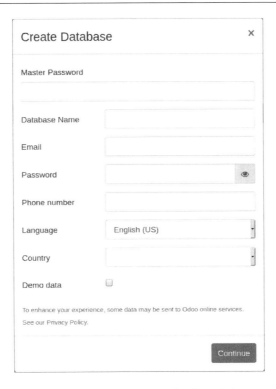

Figure 1.6 – Creating a new database dialog

2. Fill in the form, as follows:

- **Master Password**: This is the master password for this instance.
- **Database Name**: Input the name of the database you wish to create.
- **Email**: Add your email address here; this will be your username later.
- **Password**: Type in the password you want to set for the admin user of the new instance.
- **Phone Number**: Set the phone number (optional).
- **Language**: Select the language you wish to be installed by default in the new database in the drop-down list. Odoo will automatically load the translations for the selected language.
- **Country**: Select the country of the main company in the drop-down list. Selecting this will automatically configure a few things, including company currency.
- **Demo data**: Check this box to obtain demonstration data. This is useful for running interactive tests or setting up a demonstration for a customer, but it should not be checked for a database that is designed to contain production data.

> **Note**
>
> If you wish to use the database to run the automated tests of the modules (refer to *Chapter 7, Debugging Modules*), you need to have the demonstration data, as the vast majority of the automated tests in Odoo depend on these records in order to run successfully.

3. Click on the **Continue** button and wait for a while until the new database is initialized. You will then be redirected to the instance and connected as the administrator.

> **Troubleshooting**
>
> If you are redirected to a login screen, this is probably because the `--db-filter` option was passed to Odoo and the new database name didn't match the new database name. Note that the `odoo-bin start` command does this silently, making only the current database available. To work around this, simply restart Odoo without the `start` command, as shown in the *Easy installation of Odoo from source* recipe of this chapter. If you have a configuration file (refer to the *Storing the instance configuration in a file* recipe later in this chapter), and then check that the `db_filter` option is unset or set to a value matching the new database name.

Duplicating a database

Often, you will have an existing database, and you will want to experiment with it to try a procedure or run a test, but without modifying the existing data. The solution here is simple: duplicate the database and run the test on the copy. Repeat this as many times as required:

1. In the database management screen, click on the **Duplicate Database** link next to the name of the database you wish to clone:

Figure 1.7 – Duplicate Database dialog

2. Fill in the form as follows:

   - **Master Password**: This is the master password of the Odoo server.
   - **New Name**: The name you want to give to the copy.

3. Click on the **Continue** button.

4. You can then click on the name of the newly created database in the database management screen to access the login screen for that database.

Removing a database

When you have finished your tests, you will want to clean up the duplicated databases. To do this, perform the following steps:

1. In the database management screen, you will find the **Delete** button next to the name of the database. Clicking on it will bring up a dialog like the following screenshot:

Figure 1.8 – Delete Database dialog

2. Fill in the form and complete the **Master Password** field, which is the master password of the Odoo server.

3. Click on the **Delete** button.

> **Caution! Potential data loss!**
> If you selected the wrong database, and have no backup, there is no way to recover the lost data.

Backing up a database

To create a backup, perform the following steps:

1. In the database management screen, you will find the **Backup** button next to the database name. Clicking on it will bring up dialog like the following screenshot:

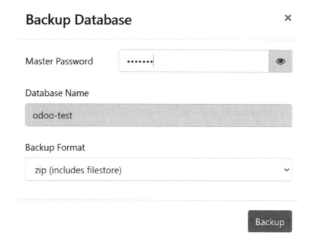

Figure 1.9 – Backup Database dialog

2. Fill in the form as follows:

- **Master Password**: This is the master password of the Odoo server.

- **Backup Format**: Always use zip for a production database, as this is the only real full backup format. Only use the `pg_dump` format for a development database when you don't really care about the file store.

3. Click on the **Backup** button. The backup file will then be downloaded to your browser.

Restoring a database backup

If you need to restore a backup, this is what you need to do:

1. In the database management screen, you will find a **Restore Database** button at the bottom of the screen. Clicking on it will bring up a dialog like the following screenshot:

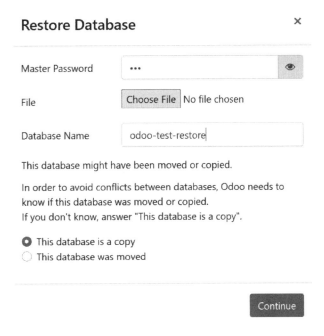

Figure 1.10 – Restore Database dialog

2. Fill in the form as follows:

- **Master Password**: This is the master password of the Odoo server.
- **File**: This is a previously downloaded Odoo backup.
- **Database Name**: Provide the name of the database in which the backup will be restored. The database must not exist on the server.
- **This database might have been moved or copied**: Choose **This database was moved** if the original database was on another server or if it has been deleted from the current server. Otherwise, choose **This database is a copy**, which is the safe default option.

3. Click on the **Continue** button.

> Note
> It isn't possible to restore a database on top of itself. If you try to do this, you will get an error message (**Database restore error: Database already exists**). You need to remove the database first.

How it works...

These features, apart from the **Change master password** screen, run PostgreSQL administration commands on the server and report back through the web interface.

The master password is a very important piece of information that only lives in the Odoo server configuration file and is never stored in the database. There used to be a default value of `admin`, but using this value is a security liability, which is well-known. In Odoo v9 and later, this is identified as an *unset* master password, and you are urged to change it when accessing the database administration interface. Even if it is stored in the configuration file under the `admin_passwd` entry, this is not the same as the password of the `admin` user; these are two independent passwords. The master password is set for an Odoo server process, which itself can handle multiple database instances, each of which has an independent `admin` user with their own password.

> **Security considerations**
>
> Remember that we are considering a development environment in this chapter. The Odoo database management interface is something that needs to be secured when you are working on a production server, as it gives access to a lot of sensitive information, especially if the server hosts Odoo instances for several different clients.

To create a new database, Odoo uses the PostgreSQL `createdb` utility and calls the internal Odoo function to initialize the new database in the same way as when you start Odoo on an empty database.

To duplicate a database, Odoo uses the `--template` option of `createdb`, passing the original database as an argument. This essentially duplicates the structure of the template database in the new database using internal and optimized PostgreSQL routines, which is much faster than creating a backup and restoring it (especially when using the web interface, which requires downloading the backup file and uploading it again).

Backup and restore operations use the `pg_dump` and `pg_restore` utilities, respectively. When using the `zip` format, the backup will also include a copy of the file store that contains a copy of the documents when you configure Odoo to not keep these in the database, which is the default option in 14.0. Unless you change it, these files reside in `~/.local/share/Odoo/filestore`.

If the backup gets large, downloading it may fail. This is either because the Odoo server itself is unable to handle the large file in memory or because the server is running behind a reverse proxy because there is a limit to the size of HTTP responses that were set in the proxy. Conversely, for the same reasons, you will likely experience issues with the database restore operation. When you start running into these issues, it is time to invest in a more robust external backup solution.

There's more...

Experienced Odoo developers generally don't use the database management interface and perform operations from the command line. To initialize a new database with demo data, for instance, the following single-line command can be used:

```
$ createdb testdb && odoo-bin -d testdb
```

The additional bonus of this command line is that you can request the installation of add-ons while you are using, for instance, `-i sale,purchase,stock`.

To duplicate a database, stop the server and run the following commands:

```
$ createdb -T dbname newdbname
$ cd ~/.local/share/Odoo/filestore  # adapt if you have changed the data_dir
$ cp -r dbname newdbname
$ cd -
```

Note that, in the context of development, the file store is often omitted.

> **Note**
> The use of `createdb -T` only works if there are no active sessions on the database, which means that you have to shut down your Odoo server before duplicating the database from the command line.

To remove an instance, run the following command:

```
$ dropdb dbname
$ rm -rf ~/.local/share/Odoo/filestore/dbname
```

To create a backup (assuming that the PostgreSQL server is running locally), use the following command:

```
$ pg_dump -Fc -f dbname.dump dbname
$ tar cjf dbname.tgz dbname.dump ~/.local/share/Odoo/filestore/dbname
```

To restore the backup, run the following command:

```
$ tar xf dbname.tgz
$ pg_restore -C -d dbname dbname.dump
```

> **Caution!**
> If your Odoo instance uses a different user to connect to the database, you need to pass `-U username` so that the correct user is the owner of the restored database.

Storing the instance configuration in a file

The `odoo-bin` script has dozens of options, and it is tedious to remember them all, as well as remembering to set them properly when starting the server. Fortunately, it is possible to store them all in a configuration file and to only specify by hand the ones you want to alter, for example, for development.

How to do it...

For this recipe, perform the following steps:

1. To generate a configuration file for your Odoo instance, run the following command:

   ```
   $ ./odoo-bin --save --config myodoo.cfg --stop-after-init
   ```

2. You can add additional options, and their values will be saved in the generated file. All the unset options will be saved with their default value set. To get a list of possible options, use the following command:

   ```
   $ ./odoo-bin --help | less
   ```

   This will provide you with some help about what the various options perform.

3. To convert from the command-line form to the configuration form, use the long option name, remove the leading dashes, and convert the dashes in the middle into underscores. `--without-demo` then becomes `without_demo`. This works for most options, but there are a few exceptions, which are listed in the following section.

4. Edit the `myodoo.cfg` file (use the table in the following section for some parameters you may want to change). Then, to start the server with the saved options, run the following command:

```
$ ./odoo-bin -c myodoo.cfg
```

> **Note**
> The `--config` option is commonly abbreviated as `-c`.

How it works...

At startup, Odoo loads its configuration in three passes. First, a set of default values for all options is initialized from the source code, then the configuration is parsed, and then any value that's defined in the file overrides the defaults. Finally, the command-line options are analyzed, and their values override the configuration that was obtained from the previous pass.

As we mentioned earlier, the names of the configuration variables can be found from the names of the command-line options by removing the leading dashes and converting the middle dashes into underscores. There are a few exceptions to this, notably the following:

Command line	Configuration file
`--db-filter`	`dbfilter`
`--no-http`	`http_enable = True/False`
`--database`	`db_name`
`--dev`	`dev_mode`
`--i18n-import`/`--i18n-export`	Unavailable

Table 1.2

Here is a list of options that are commonly set through the configuration file:

Option	Format	Usage
`without_demo`	Comma-separated list of module names	This prevents module demo data from being loaded. Give the value `all` to disable demo data for all modules, or `False` to enable demo data for all modules. To disable demo data for specific modules, provide module names, for example, `sale,purchase,crm`.
`addons_path`	Comma-separated list of paths	This is a list of directory names in which the server will look for add-ons.
`admin_passwd`	Text	This is the master password (take a look at the preceding recipe).
`data_dir`	Path to a directory	This is a directory in which the server will store session information, add-ons downloaded from the internet, and documents if you enable the file store.
`http_port` `longpolling_port`	Port number	These are the ports on which the Odoo server will listen. You will need to specify both to run multiple Odoo servers on the same host; `longpolling_port` is only used if `workers` is not 0. `http_port` defaults to `8069`, and `longpolling_port` defaults to `8072`.
`logfile`	Path to a file	The file in which Odoo will write its logs.
`log_level`	Log verbosity level	Specifies the level of logging. Accepted values (in increasing order of verbosity) include `critical`, `error`, `warn`, `info`, `debug`, `debug_rpc`, and `debug_rpc_answer`, `debug_sql`.
`workers`	Integer	The number of worker processes. Refer to *Chapter 3*, *Server Deployment*, for more information.
`proxy_mode`	True/False	Activate reverse proxy WSGI wrappers. Only enable this when running behind a trusted web proxy!

Table 1.3

Here is a list of configuration options related to the database:

Options	Format	Usage
db_host	Hostname	This is the name of the server running the PostgreSQL server. Use False to use local Unix domain sockets, and localhost to use TCP sockets locally.
db_user	Database user login	This is generally empty if db_host is False. This will be the name of the user used to connect to the database.
db_password	Database user password	This is generally empty if db_host is False and when db_user has the same name as the user running the server. Read the main page of pg_hba.conf for more information on this.
db_name	Database name	This is used to set the database name on which some commands operate by default. This does not limit the databases on which the server will act. Refer to the following dbfilter option for this.
db_sslmode	Database SSL mode	This is used to specify the database SSL connection mode.
dbfilter	A regular expression	The expression should match the name of the databases that are considered by the server. If you run the website, it should match a single database, so it will look like ^databasename$. More information on this can be found in *Chapter 3, Server Deployment*.
list_db	True/False	Set to **True** to disable the listing of databases. See *Chapter 3, Server Deployment*, for more information.

Table 1.4

The parsing of the configuration file by Odoo is now using the Python ConfigParser module. However, the implementation in Odoo 11.0 has changed, and it is no longer possible to use variable interpolation. So, if you are used to defining values for variables from the values of other variables using the %(section.variable)s notation, you will need to change your habits and revert to explicit values.

Some options are not used in config files, but they are widely used during development:

Options	Format	Usage
`-i` or `--init`	Comma-separated list of module names	It will install given modules by default while initializing the database.
`-u` or `--update`	Comma-separated list of module names	It will update given modules when you restart the server. It is mostly used when you modify source code or update the branch from git.
`--dev`	`all`, `reload`, `qweb`, `werkzeug`, and `xml`	This enables developer mode and the auto-reload feature.

Table 1.5

Activating Odoo developer tools

When using Odoo as a developer, you need to know how to activate **developer mode** in the web interface so that you can access the technical settings menu and developer information. Enabling debug mode will expose several advance configuration options and fields. These options and fields are hidden in Odoo for better usability because they are not used on a daily basis.

How to do it...

To activate developer mode in the web interface, perform the following steps:

1. Connect to your instance and authenticate as `admin`.
2. Go to the **Settings** menu.
3. Scroll to the bottom and locate the **Developer Tools** section:

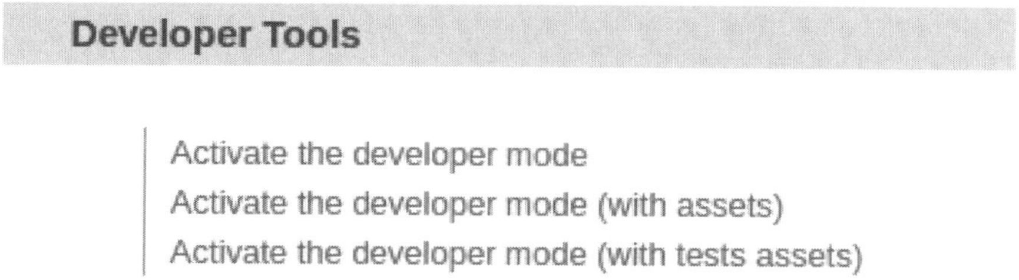

Developer Tools

Activate the developer mode
Activate the developer mode (with assets)
Activate the developer mode (with tests assets)

Figure 1.11 – Links to activate different developer modes

4. Click on the **Activate the developer mode** link.
5. Wait for the UI to reload.

> **Alternative way**
>
> It is also possible to activate the developer mode by editing the URL. Before the # sign, insert `?debug=1`.
>
> For example, if your current URL is `http://localhost:8069/web#menu_id=102&action=94` and you want to enable developer mode, then you need to change that URL to `http://localhost:8069/web?debug=1#menu_id=102&action=94`. Furthermore, if you want debug mode with assets, then change the URL to `http://localhost:8069/web?debug=assets#menu_id=102&action=94`.

To exit developer mode, you can perform any one of the following operations:

- Edit the URL and write `?debug=0` in the query string.
- Use **Deactivate the developer mode** from the same place in the **Settings** menu.
- Click on the bug icon in the top menu and click on the **Leave Developer Tools** option.

Lots of developers are using browser extensions to toggle debug mode. By using this, you can toggle debug mode quickly without accessing the settings menu. These extensions are available for Firefox and Chrome. Take a look at the following screenshot. It will help you to identify the plugin in the Chrome store:

Figure 1.12 – Browser extension for debug mode

> **Note**
>
> The behavior of debug mode has changed since Odoo v13. Since v13, the status of the debug mode is stored in session, implying that even if you have removed `?debug` from the URL, debug mode will still be active.

How it works...

In developer mode, two things happen:

- You get tooltips when hovering over a field in a form view or over a column in list view, providing technical information about the field (internal name, type, and so on)

- A drop-down menu with a bug icon is displayed next to the user's menu in the top-right corner, giving access to technical information about the model being displayed, the various related view definitions, the workflow, custom filter management, and so on.

There is a variant of developer mode – **Developer mode (with assets)**. This mode behaves like the normal developer mode, but additionally, the JavaScript and CSS code that's sent to the browser is not minified, which means that the web development tools of your browser are easy to use for debugging the JavaScript code (more on this in *Chapter 15, Web Client Development*).

> **Caution!**
> Test your add-ons both with and without developer mode, as the unminified versions of the JavaScript libraries can hide bugs that only bite you in the minified version.

Updating the add-on modules list

When you add a new module, Odoo is unaware of the new module. In order to list the module in Odoo, you will need to update module list. In this recipe, you will learn how to update the app list.

Getting ready

Start your instance and connect to it using the **Administrator** account. After doing this, activate developer mode (if you don't know how to activate developer mode, refer to *Chapter 1, Installing the Odoo Development Environment*).

How to do it...

To update the list of available add-on modules in your instance, you need to perform the following steps:

1. Open the **Apps** menu.
2. Click on **Update Apps List**:

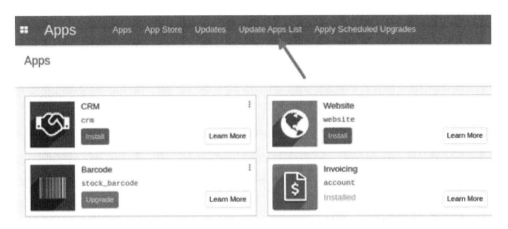

Figure 1.13 – Menu item to update the apps list

3. In the dialog, click on the **Update** button:

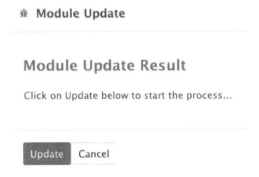

Figure 1.14 – Dialog to update the apps list

4. At the end of the update, you can click on the **Apps** entry to see the updated list of available add-on modules. You will need to remove the default filter on **Apps** in the search box to see all of them.

How it works...

When the **Update** button is clicked, Odoo will read the add-ons path configuration variable. For each directory in the list, it will look for immediate subdirectories containing an add-on manifest file, which is a file named __manifest__.py that's stored in the add-on module directory. Odoo reads the manifest, expecting to find a Python dictionary. Unless the manifest contains a key `installable` instance set to `False`, the add-on module metadata is recorded in the database. If the module was already present, the information is updated. If not, a new record is created. If a previously available add-on module is not found, the record is not deleted from the list.

> **Note**
> An updated apps list is only required if you added the new add-on path after initializing the database. If you add the new add-on path to the configuration file before initializing the database, then there will be no need to update the module list manually.

To summarize what we have learned so far, after installing, you can start the Odoo server by using the following command line (if you are using a virtual environment, then you need to activate it first):

```
python3 odoo-bin -d odoo-test -i base --addons-path=addons
 --db-filter=odoo-test
```

Once you run the module, you can access Odoo from `http://localhost:8069`.

You can also use a configuration file to run Odoo as follows:

```
./odoo-bin -c myodoo.cfg
```

Once you start the Odoo server, you can install/update modules from the **App** menu.

2
Managing Odoo Server Instances

In *Chapter 1, Installing the Odoo Development Environment*, we looked at how to set up an Odoo instance using only the standard core add-ons that are shipped with source. This chapter focuses on adding non-core or custom add-ons to an Odoo instance. In Odoo, you can load add-ons from multiple directories. In addition, it is recommended that you load your third-party add-ons or your own custom add-ons from separate folders to avoid conflicts with Odoo core modules. Even Odoo Enterprise Edition is a type of add-on directory, and you need to load this just like a normal add-ons directory.

In this chapter, we will cover the following recipes:

- Configuring the add-ons path
- Standardizing your instance directory layout
- Installing and upgrading local add-on modules
- Installing add-on modules from GitHub
- Applying changes to add-ons
- Applying and trying proposed pull requests

> **About the terminology**
>
> In this book, we will use the terms `add-on` or `module` or `app` or `add-on module` interchangeably. All of them refer to the Odoo app or Extension app that can be installed in Odoo from the user interface.

Configuring the add-ons path

With the help of the `addons_path` parameter, you can load your own add-on modules into Odoo. When Odoo initializes a new database, it will search for add-on modules within directories that have been provided in the `addons_path` configuration parameter. Odoo will search in these directories for the potential add-on module.

Directories listed in `addons_path` are expected to contain subdirectories, each of which is an add-on module. Following initialization of the database, you will be able to install modules that are given in these directories.

Getting ready

This recipe assumes that you have an instance ready with a configuration file generated, as described in the *Storing the instance configuration in a file* recipe in *Chapter 1, Installing the Odoo Development Environment*. Note that the source code of Odoo is available in `~/odoo-dev/odoo`, and the configuration file in `~/odoo-dev/myodoo.cfg`.

How to do it...

To add the `~/odoo-dev/local-addons` directory to `addons_path` of the instance, perform the following steps:

1. Edit the configuration file for your instance, that is, `~/odoo-dev/myodoo.cfg`.
2. Locate the line starting with `addons_path=`. By default, this should look like the following:

   ```
   addons_path = ~/odoo-dev/odoo/addons
   ```

3. Modify the line by appending a comma, followed by the name of the directory you want to add to `addons_path`, as shown in the following code:

   ```
   addons_path = ~/odoo-dev/odoo/addons,~/odoo-dev/local-addons
   ```

4. Restart your instance from the terminal:

   ```
   $ ~/odoo-dev/odoo/odoo-bin -c my-instance.cfg
   ```

How it works...

When Odoo is restarted, the configuration file is read. The value of the `addons_path` variable is expected to be a comma-separated list of directories. Relative paths are accepted, but they are relative to the current working directory and therefore should be avoided in the configuration file.

At this point, we have only listed the add-on directory in Odoo, but no add-on modules are present in `~/odoo-dev/local-addons`. And even if you add a new add-on module to this directory, Odoo does not show this module in the user interface. For this, you need to perform an extra operation, as explained in the next recipe, *Updating the add-on modules list*.

> **Note**
>
> The reason behind this is that when you initialize a new database, Odoo automatically lists your custom modules in available modules, but if you add new modules following database initialization, then you need to manually update the list of available modules, as shown in the *Updating the add-on modules list* recipe.

There's more...

When you call the `odoo-bin` script for the first time to initialize a new database, you can pass the `--addons-path` command-line argument with a comma-separated list of directories. This will initialize the list of available add-on modules with all of the add-ons found in the supplied add-ons path. When you do this, you have to explicitly include the base add-ons directory (`odoo/odoo/addons`), as well as the core add-ons directory (`odoo/addons`). A small difference with the preceding recipe is that the local add-ons must not be empty; they must contain at least one sub-directory, which has the minimal structure of an add-on module.

In *Chapter 3, Creating Odoo Add-On Modules*, we will look at how to write your own modules. In the meantime, here's a quick hack to produce something that will make Odoo happy:

```
$ mkdir -p ~/odoo-dev/local-addons/dummy
$ touch ~/odoo-dev/local-addons/dummy/__init__.py
$ echo '{"name": "dummy", "installable": False}' > \
~/odoo-dev/local-addons/dummy/__manifest__.py
```

You can use the `--save` option to save the path to the configuration file:

```
$ odoo/odoo-bin -d mydatabase \
--add-ons-path="odoo/odoo/addons,odoo/addons,~/odoo-dev/local-addons" \
--save -c ~/odoo-dev/my-instance.cfg --stop-after-init
```

In this case, using relative paths is OK, since they will be converted into absolute paths in the configuration file.

> **Note**
> Since Odoo only checks directories in the add-ons path for the presence of add-ons when the path is set from the command line, not when the path is loaded from a configuration file, the dummy module is no longer necessary. You may, therefore, remove it (or keep it until you're sure that you won't need to create a new configuration file).

Standardizing your instance directory layout

We recommend that your development and production environments all use a similar directory layout. This standardization will prove helpful when you have to perform maintenance operations, and it will also ease your day-to-day work.

This recipe creates a directory structure that groups files with similar life cycles or similar purposes in standardized subdirectories.

> **Note**
> This recipe is only useful if you want to manage similar folder structure development and production environments. If you do not want this, you can skip this recipe.
>
> Also, it is not compulsory to observe the same folder structure as in this recipe. Feel free to alter this structure to suit your needs.

How to do it...

To create the proposed instance layout, you need to perform the following steps:

1. Create one directory per instance:

    ```
    $ mkdir ~/odoo-dev/projectname
    $ cd ~/odoo-dev/projectname
    ```

2. Create a Python `virtualenv` object in a subdirectory called `env/`:

    ```
    $ python3 -m venv env
    ```

3. Create some subdirectories, as follows:

    ```
    $ mkdir src local bin filestore logs
    ```

    The functions of the subdirectories are as follows:

    - `src/`: This contains the clone of Odoo itself, as well as the various third-party add-on projects (we have added Odoo source code to the next step in this recipe).
    - `local/`: This is used to save your instance-specific add-ons.
    - `bin/`: This includes various helper executable shell scripts.
    - `filestore/`: This is used as a file store.
    - `logs/` (optional): This is used to store the server log files.

4. Clone Odoo and install the requirements (refer to *Chapter 1*, *Installing the Odoo Development Environment*, for details on this):

    ```
    $ git clone -b 14.0 --single-branch --depth 1 https://github.com/odoo/odoo.git src/odoo
    $ env/bin/pip3 install -r src/odoo/requirements.txt
    ```

5. Save the following shell script as `bin/odoo`:

   ```
   #!/bin/sh ROOT=$(dirname $0)/..
   PYTHON=$ROOT/env/bin/python3 ODOO=$ROOT/src/odoo/odoo-bin
   $PYTHON $ODOO -c $ROOT/projectname.cfg "$@" exit $?
   ```

6. Make the script executable:

   ```
   $ chmod +x bin/odoo
   ```

7. Create an empty dummy local module:

   ```
   $ mkdir -p local/dummy
   $ touch local/dummy/__init__.py
   $ echo '{"name": "dummy", "installable": False}' >\
   local/dummy/__manifest__.py
   ```

8. Generate a configuration file for your instance:

   ```
   $ bin/odoo --stop-after-init --save \
   --addons-path src/odoo/odoo/addons,src/odoo/addons,local \
   --data-dir filestore
   ```

9. Add a `.gitignore` file, which is used to tell GitHub to exclude given directories so that Git will ignore these directories when you commit the code, for example, `filestore/`, `env/`, `logs/`, and `src/`:

   ```
   # dotfiles, with exceptions:
   .*
   !.gitignore
   # python compiled files
   *.py[co]
   # emacs backup files
   *~
   # not tracked subdirectories
   /env/
   /src/
   /filestore/
   /logs/
   ```

10. Create a Git repository for this instance and add the files you've added to Git:

```
$ git init
$ git add .
$ git commit -m "initial version of projectname"
```

How it works...

We generate a clean directory structure with clearly labeled directories and dedicated roles. We are using different directories to store the following:

- The code maintained by other people (in `src/`)
- The local-specific code
- `filestore` of the instance

By having one `virtualenv` environment per project, we are sure that the project's dependencies will not interfere with the dependencies of other projects that may be running a different version of Odoo or will use different third-party add-on modules, which require different versions of Python dependencies. This comes at the cost of a little disk space.

In a similar way, by using separate clones of Odoo and third-party add-on modules for our different projects, we are able to let each of these evolve independently and only install updates on the instances that need them, hence reducing the risk of introducing regressions.

The `bin/odoo` script allows us to run the server without having to remember the various paths or activate the `virtualenv` environment. This also sets the configuration file for us. You can add additional scripts in there to help you in your day-to-day work. For instance, you can add a script to check out the different third-party projects that you need to run your instance.

Regarding the configuration file, we have only demonstrated the bare minimum options to set up here, but you can obviously set up more, such as the database name, the database filter, or the port on which the project listens. Refer to *Chapter 1, Installing the Odoo Development Environment*, for more information on this topic.

Finally, by managing all of this in a Git repository, it becomes quite easy to replicate the setup on a different computer and share the development among a team.

> **Speedup tip**
>
> To facilitate project creation, you can create a template repository containing the empty structure, and fork that repository for each new project. This will save you from retyping the `bin/odoo` script, the `.gitignore` file, and any other template file you need (continuous integration configuration, `README.md`, `ChangeLog`, and so on).

There's more...

The development of complex modules requires various configuration options, which leads to updating the configuration file whenever you want to try any configuration option. Updating the configuration file frequently can be a headache, and to avoid this, an alternative way is to pass all configuration options from the command line, as follows:

1. Activate `virtualenv` manually:

   ```
   $ source env/bin/activate
   ```

2. Go to the Odoo source directory:

   ```
   $ cd src/odoo
   ```

3. Run the server:

   ```
   ./odoo-bin --addons-path=addons,../../local -d test-14 -i account,sale,purchase --log-level=debug
   ```

In *step 3*, we passed a few configuration options directly from the command line. The first is `--add-ons-path`, which loads Odoo's core add-ons directory, `addons`, and your add-ons directory, `local`, in which you will put your own add-on modules. Option `-d` will use the `test-14` database or create a new database if it isn't present. The `-i` option will install the `account`, `sale`, and `purchase` modules. Next, we passed the `log-level` option and increased the log level to `debug` so that it will display more information in the log.

> **Note**
> By using the command line, you can quickly change the configuration options. You can also see live logs in the terminal. For all available options, refer to *Chapter 1, Installing the Odoo Development Environment*, or use the `--help` command to view a list of all options and the description of each option.

Installing and upgrading local add-on modules

The core functionality of Odoo comes from its add-on modules. You have a wealth of add-ons available as part of Odoo itself, as well as add-on modules that you can download from the app store or that have been written by yourself.

In this recipe, we will demonstrate how to install and upgrade add-on modules through the web interface and from the command line.

The main benefits of using the command line for these operations include being able to act on more than one add-on at a time and having a clear view of the server logs as the installation or update progresses, which is very useful when in development mode or when scripting the installation of an instance.

Getting ready

Make sure that you have a running Odoo instance with its database initialized and the add-ons path properly set. In this recipe, we will install/upgrade a few add-on modules.

How to do it...

There are two possible methods to install or update add-ons—you can use the web interface or the command line.

From the web interface

To install a new add-on module in your database using the web interface, perform the following steps:

1. Connect to the instance using the **Administrator** account and open the **Apps** menu:

Figure 2.1 – List of Odoo apps

2. Use the search box to locate the add-on you want to install. Here are a few instructions to help you with this task:

   - Activate the **Not Installed** filter.
   - If you're looking for a specific functionality add-on rather than a broad functionality add-on, remove the **Apps** filter.
   - Type a part of the module name in the search box and use this as a **Module** filter.
   - You may find that using the list view gives something more readable.

3. Click on the **Install** button under the module name in the card.

Note that some Odoo add-on modules have external Python dependencies. If Python dependencies are not installed in your system, then Odoo will abort the installation and it will show the following dialog:

Installing and upgrading local add-on modules   69

Figure 2.2 – Warning for external library dependency

To fix this, just install the relevant Python dependencies on your system.

To update a pre-installed module in your database, perform the following steps:

1. Connect to the instance using the **Administrator** account.
2. Open the **Apps** menu.
3. Click on **Apps**:

Figure 2.3 – Odoo apps list

4. Use the search box to locate the add-on you want to install. Here are a few tips:

- Activate the **Installed** filter.
- If you're looking for a specific functionality add-on rather than a broad functionality add-on, remove the **Apps** filter.
- Type a part of the add-on module name into the search box and then press *Enter* to use this as a **Module** filter. For example, type CRM and press *Enter* to search CRM apps.
- You may find that using the list view gives you something more readable.

5. Click on the three dots in the top right-corner of the card and click on the **Upgrade** option:

Figure 2.4 – Drop-down link for upgrading the module

Activate developer mode to see the technical name of the module. See *Chapter 1, Installing the Odoo Development Environment*, if you don't know how to activate developer mode:

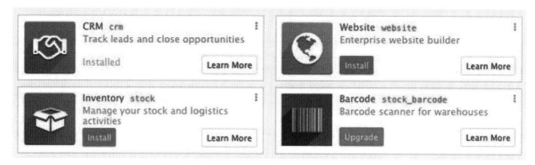

Figure 2.5 – Application's technical names

After activating developer mode, it will show the module's technical name in red. If you are using Odoo Community Edition, you will see some extra apps with the **Upgrade** button. Those apps are Odoo Enterprise Edition apps, and in order to install/use them, you need to purchase a license.

From the command line

To install new add-ons in your database, perform the following steps:

1. Find the names of the add-ons. This is the name of the directory containing the _manifest_.py file, without the leading path.
2. Stop the instance. If you are working on a production database, make a backup.

3. Run the following command:

    ```
    $ odoo/odoo-bin -c instance.cfg -d dbname -i addon1,addon2 \
    --stop-after-init
    ```

    You may omit -d dbname if this is set in your configuration file.

4. Restart the instance.

To update an already installed add-on module in your database, perform the following steps:

1. Find the name of the add-on module to update; this is the name of the directory containing the _manifest_.py file, without the leading path.
2. Stop the instance. If you are working on a production database, make a backup.
3. Run the following command:

    ```
    $ odoo/odoo-bin -c instance.cfg -d dbname -u addon1 \
    --stop-after-init
    ```

    You may omit -d dbname if this is set in your configuration file.

4. Restart the instance.

How it works...

The add-on module installation and update are two closely related processes, but there are some important differences, as highlighted in the following two sections.

Add-on installation

When you install an add-on, Odoo checks its list of available add-ons for an uninstalled add-on with the supplied name. It also checks for the dependencies of that add-on and, if there are any, it will recursively install them before installing the add-on.

The installation process of a single module consists of the following steps:

1. If there are any, run the add-on `preinit` hook.
2. Load the model definitions from the Python source code and update the database structure, if necessary (refer to *Chapter 4, Application Models*, for details).
3. Load the data files of the add-on and update the database contents, if necessary (refer to *Chapter 6, Managing Module Data*, for details).

4. Install the add-on demo data if demo data has been enabled in the instance.
5. If there are any, run the add-on `postinit` hook.
6. Run a validation of the view definitions of the add-on.
7. If demo data is enabled and a test is enabled, run the tests of the add-on (refer to *Chapter 18, Automated Test Cases*, for details).
8. Update the module state in the database.
9. Update the translations in the database from the add-on's translations (refer to *Chapter 11, Internationalization*, for details).

> **Note**
>
> The `preinit` and `postinit` hooks are defined in the `__manifest__.py` file using the `pre_init_hook` and `post_init_hook` keys, respectively. These hooks are used to invoke Python functions before and after the installation of an add-on module. To learn more about `init` hooks, refer to *Chapter 3, Creating Odoo Add-On Modules*.

Add-on update

When you update an add-on, Odoo checks in its list of available add-on modules for an installed add-on with the given name. It also checks for the reverse dependencies of that add-on (these are the add-ons that depend on the updated add-on). If any, it will recursively update them, too.

The update process of a single add-on module consists of the following steps:

1. Run the add-on module's pre-migration steps, if any (refer to *Chapter 6, Managing Module Data*, for details).
2. Load the model definitions from the Python source code and update the database structure if necessary (refer to *Chapter 4, Application Models*, for details).
3. Load the data files of the add-on and update the database's contents if necessary (refer to *Chapter 6, Managing Module Data*, for details).
4. Update the add-on's demo data if demo data is enabled in the instance.
5. If your module has any migration methods, run the add-on post-migration steps (refer to *Chapter 6, Managing Module Data*, for details).
6. Run a validation of the view definitions of the add-on.

7. If demo data is enabled and a test is enabled, run the tests of the add-on (refer to *Chapter 18, Automated Test Cases*, for details).

8. Update the module state in the database.

9. Update the translations in the database from the add-on's translations (refer to *Chapter 11, Internationalization*, for details).

> **Note**
> Note that updating an add-on module that is not installed does nothing at all. However, installing an add-on module that is already installed reinstalls the add-on, which can have some unintended effects with some data files that contain data that is supposed to be updated by the user and not updated during the normal module update process (refer to the *Using the noupdate and forcecreate flags* recipe in *Chapter 6, Managing Module Data*). There is no risk of error from the user interface, but this can happen from the command line.

There's more...

Be careful with dependency handling. Consider an instance where you want to have the sale, sale_stock, and sale_specific add-ons installed, with sale_specific depending on sale_stock, and sale_stock depending on sale. To install all three, you only need to install sale_specific, as it will recursively install the sale_stock and sale dependencies. To update all three, you need to update sale, as this will recursively update the reverse dependencies, sale_stock and sale_specific.

Another tricky part with managing dependencies is when you add a dependency to an add-on that already has a version installed. Let's understand this by continuing with the previous example. Imagine that you add a dependency on stock_dropshipping in sale_specific. Updating the sale_specific add-on will not automatically install the new dependency, and neither will requesting the installation of sale_specific. In this situation, you can get very nasty error messages because the Python code of the add-on is not successfully loaded, but the data of the add-on and the models' tables in the database are present. To resolve this, you need to stop the instance and manually install the new dependency.

Installing add-on modules from GitHub

GitHub is a great source of third-party add-ons. A lot of Odoo partners use GitHub to share the add-ons they maintain internally, and the **Odoo Community Association** (**OCA**) collectively maintains several hundred add-ons on GitHub. Before you start writing your own add-on, ensure that you check that nothing already exists that you can use as is or as a starting point.

This recipe will show you how to clone the partner-contact project of the OCA from GitHub and make the add-on modules it contains available in your instance.

Getting ready

Suppose you want to add new fields to the customers (partner) form. By default, the Odoo customers model doesn't have a gender field. If you want to add a gender field, you need to create a new module. Fortunately, someone on a mailing list tells you about the partner_contact_gender add-on module, which is maintained by the OCA as part of the partner-contact project.

The paths that are used in this recipe reflect the layout that was proposed in the *Standardizing your instance directory layout* recipe.

How to do it...

To install partner_contact_gender, perform the following steps:

1. Go to your project's directory:

   ```
   $ cd ~/odoo-dev/my-odoo/src
   ```

2. Clone the 14.0 branch of the partner-contact project in the src/ directory:

   ```
   $ git clone --branch 14.0 \
   https://github.com/OCA/partner-contact.git src/partner-contact
   ```

3. Change the add-ons path to include that directory and update the add-ons list of your instance (refer to the *Configuring the add-ons path* recipe and *Updating the add-on modules list* recipes in this chapter). The add-ons_path line of instance.cfg should look like this:

   ```
   addons_path = ~/odoo-dev/my-odoo/src/odoo/odoo/addons, \
   ~/odoo-dev/my-odoo/src/odoo/addons, \
   ```

```
~/odoo-dev/my-odoo/src/, \
~/odoo-dev/local-addons
```

4. Install the `partner_contact_gender` add-on (if you don't know how to install the module, take a look at the previous recipe, *Installing and upgrading local add-on modules*).

How it works...

All of the Odoo Community Association code repositories have their add-ons contained in separate subdirectories, which is coherent in accordance with what is expected by Odoo regarding the directories in the add-ons path. Consequently, just cloning the repository somewhere and adding that location in the add-ons path is enough.

There's more...

Some maintainers follow a different approach and have one add-on module per repository, living at the root of the repository. In that case, you need to create a new directory, which you will add to the add-ons path and clone all of the add-ons from the maintainer you need in this directory. Remember to update the add-on modules list each time you add a new repository clone.

Applying changes to add-ons

Most add-ons that are available on GitHub are subject to change and do not follow the rules that Odoo enforces for its stable release. They may receive bug fixes or enhancements, including issues or feature requests that you have submitted, and these changes may introduce database schema changes or updates in the data files and views. This recipe explains how to install the updated versions.

Getting ready

Suppose you reported an issue with `partner_contact_gender` and received a notification that the issue was solved in the last revision of the `14.0` branch of the `partner-contact` project. In this case, you will want to update your instance with this latest version.

How to do it...

To apply a source modification to your add-on from GitHub, you need to perform the following steps:

1. Stop the instance using that add-on.
2. Make a backup if it is a production instance (refer to the *Manage Odoo server databases* recipe in *Chapter 1, Installing the Odoo Development Environment*).
3. Go to the directory where `partner-contact` was cloned:

    ```
    $ cd ~/odoo-dev/my-odoo/src/partner-contact
    ```

4. Create a local tag for the project so that you can revert to that version in case things break:

    ```
    $ git checkout 14.0
    $ git tag 14.0-before-update-$(date --iso)
    ```

5. Get the latest version of the source code:

    ```
    $ git pull --ff-only
    ```

6. Update the `partner_address_street3` add-on in your databases (refer to the *Installing and upgrading local add-on modules* recipe).
7. Restart the instance.

How it works...

Usually, the developer of the add-on module occasionally releases the newest version of the add-on. This update typically contains bug fixes and new features. Here, we will get a new version of the add-on and update it in our instances.

If `git pull --ff-only` fails, you can revert to the previous version using the following command:

```
$ git reset --hard 14.0-before-update-$(date --iso)
```

Then, you can try `git pull` (without `--ff-only`), which will cause a merge, but this means that you have local changes on the add-on.

See also

If the update step breaks, refer to the *Updating Odoo from Source* recipe in *Chapter 1, Installing the Odoo Development Environment*, for recovery instructions. Remember to always test an update on a copy of a database production first.

Applying and trying proposed pull requests

In the GitHub world, a **Pull Request (PR)** is a request that's made by a developer so that the maintainers of a project can include some new developments. Such a PR may contain a bug fix or a new feature. These requests are reviewed and tested before being pulled into the main branch.

This recipe explains how to apply a PR to your Odoo project in order to test an improvement or a bug fix.

Getting ready

As in the previous recipe, suppose you reported an issue with `partner_address_street3` and received a notification that the issue was solved in a PR, which hasn't been merged in the `14.0` branch of the project. The developer asks you to validate the fix in PR #123. You need to update a test instance with this branch.

You should not try out such branches directly on a production database, so first create a test environment with a copy of the production database (refer to *Chapter 1, Installing the Odoo Development Environment*).

How to do it...

To apply and try out a GitHub PR for an add-on, you need to perform the following steps:

1. Stop the instance.
2. Go to the directory where `partner-contact` was cloned:

    ```
    $ cd ~/odoo-dev/my-odoo/src/partner-contact
    ```

3. Create a local tag for the project so that you can revert to that version in case things break:

    ```
    $ git checkout 14.0
    $ git tag 14.0-before-update-$(date --iso)
    ```

4. Pull the branch of the `pull` request. The easiest way to do this is by using the number of the PR, which should have been communicated to you by the developer. In our example, this is PR number `123`:

   ```
   $ git pull origin pull/123/head
   ```

5. Update the `partner_contact_gender1` add-on module in your database and restart the instance (refer to the *Installing and upgrading local add-on modules* recipe if you don't know how to update the module).

6. Test the update—try to reproduce your issue, or try out the feature you wanted.

If this doesn't work, comment on the PR page of GitHub, explaining what you did and what didn't work so that the developer can update the PR.

If it works, say so on the PR page too; this is an essential part of the PR validation process, and it will speed up merging in the main branch.

How it works...

We are using a GitHub feature that enables pull requests to be pulled by number using the `pull/nnnn/head` branch name, where nnnn is the number of the PR. The Git pull command will merge the remote branch in ours, applying the changes in our code base. After this, we update the add-on module, test it, and report back to the author of the change with regard to any failures or success.

There's more...

You can repeat *step 4* of this recipe for different pull requests in the same repository if you want to test them simultaneously. If you are really happy with the result, you can create a branch to keep a reference to the result of the applied changes:

```
$ git checkout -b 14.0-custom
```

Using a different branch will help you remember that you are not using the version from GitHub, but a custom one.

> **Note**
> The `git branch` command can be used to list all of the local branches you have in your repository.

From then on, if you need to apply the latest revision of the `14.0` branch from GitHub, you will need to pull it without using `--ff-only`:

```
$ git pull origin 14.0
```

3
Creating Odoo Add-On Modules

Now that we have a development environment and know how to manage Odoo server instances and databases, you can learn how to create Odoo add-on modules.

Our main goal in this chapter is to understand how an add-on module is structured and the typical incremental workflow to add components to it. The various components that are mentioned in the recipe names of this chapter will be covered extensively in subsequent chapters.

In this chapter, we will cover the following recipes:

- Creating and installing a new add-on module
- Completing the add-on module manifest
- Organizing the add-on module file structure
- Adding models
- Adding menu items and views
- Adding access security
- Using the scaffold command to create a module

Technical requirements

For this chapter, you are expected to have Odoo installed and you are also expected to have followed the recipes in *Chapter 1, Installing the Odoo Development Environment*. You are also expected to be comfortable in discovering and installing extra add-on modules, as described in *Chapter 2, Managing Odoo Server Instances*.

All the code used in this chapter can be downloaded from the following GitHub repository at `https://github.com/PacktPublishing/Odoo-14-Development-Cookbook-Fourth-Edition/tree/master/Chapter03`.

What is an Odoo add-on module?

Except for the framework code, all of the code bases of Odoo are packed in the form of modules. These modules can be installed or uninstalled at any time from the database. There are two main purposes for these modules. Either you can add new apps/business logic, or you can modify an existing application. Put simply, in Odoo, everything starts and ends with modules.

Odoo is being used by companies of all sizes; each company has a different business flow and requirements. To deal with this issue, Odoo splits the features of the application into different modules. These modules can be loaded in the database on demand. Basically, the user can enable/disable these features at any time. Consequently, the same software can be adjusted for different requirements. Check out the following screenshot of Odoo modules; the first module in the column is the main application and others are designed for adding extra features in that app. To get a modules list grouped by the application's category, go to the **Apps** menu, and apply grouping by category:

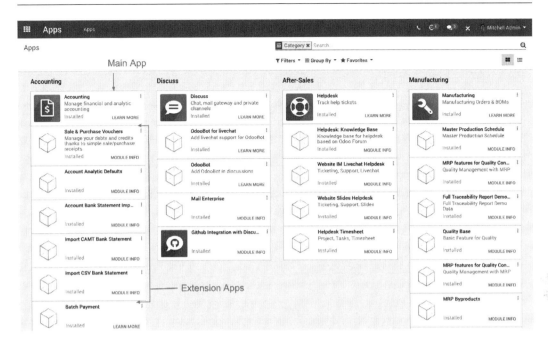

Figure 3.1 – Grouping apps by category

If you plan on developing the new application in Odoo, you should create boundaries for various features. This will be very helpful for dividing your application into different add-on modules. Now that you know the purpose of the add-on module in Odoo, we can start building our own add-on module.

Creating and installing a new add-on module

In this recipe, we will create a new module, make it available in our Odoo instance, and install it.

Getting ready

To begin, we will need an Odoo instance that's ready to use.

If you followed the *Easy installation of Odoo from source* recipe in *Chapter 1*, *Installing the Odoo Development Environment*, Odoo should be available at `~/odoo-dev/odoo`. For explanation purposes, we will assume this location for Odoo, although you can use any other location of your preference.

We will also need a location to add our own Odoo modules. For the purpose of this recipe, we will use a `local-addons` directory alongside the `odoo` directory, at `~/odoo-dev/local-addons`.

How to do it...

As an example, for this chapter, we will create a small add-on module for managing a list of the books for the library.

The following steps will create and install a new add-on module:

1. Change the working directory in which we will work and create the add-ons directory where our custom module will be placed:

   ```
   $ cd ~/odoo-dev
   $ mkdir local-addons
   ```

2. Choose a technical name for the new module and create a directory with that name for the module. For our example, we will use `my_library`:

   ```
   $ mkdir local-addons/my_library
   ```

   A module's *technical name* must be a valid Python identifier. It must begin with a letter, and only contain letters, numbers, and underscore characters. It is preferable that you only use lowercase letters in the module name.

3. Make the Python module importable by adding an `__init__.py` file:

   ```
   $ touch local-addons/my_library/__init__.py
   ```

4. Add a minimal module manifest for Odoo to detect it as an add-on module. Inside the `my_library` folder, create an `__manifest__.py` file with this line:

   ```
   {'name': 'My Library'}
   ```

5. Start your Odoo instance, including our module directory, in the add-ons path:

   ```
   $ odoo/odoo-bin --addons-path=odoo/addon/,local-addons/
   ```

   If the `--save` option is added to the Odoo command, the add-ons path will be saved in the configuration file. The next time you start the server, if no add-ons path option is provided, this will be used.

6. Make the new module available in your Odoo instance. Log in to Odoo using `admin`, enable **Developer Mode** in the **About** box, and in the **Apps** top menu, select **Update Apps List**. Now, Odoo should know about our Odoo module:

Figure 3.2 – Dialog to update the app list

7. Select the **Apps** menu at the top and, in the search bar in the top-right corner, delete the default Apps filter and search for `my_library`. Click on the **Install** button, and the installation will be concluded.

How it works...

An Odoo module is a directory that contains code files and other assets. The directory name that's used is the module's technical name. The `name` key in the module manifest is its title.

The `__manifest__.py` file is the module manifest. This contains a Python dictionary with module metadata including category, version, the modules it depends on, and a list of the data files that it will load. In this recipe, we used a minimal manifest file, but in real modules, we will need other important keys. These are discussed in the next recipe, *Completing the add-on module manifest*.

The module directory must be Python-importable, so it also needs to have an `__init__.py` file, even if it's empty. To load a module, the Odoo server will import it. This will cause the code in the `__init__.py` file to be executed, so it works as an entry point to run the module Python code. Due to this, it will usually contain import statements to load the module Python files and submodules.

Known modules can be installed directly from the command line using the `--init` or `-i` option. For example, if you want to install the `crm` and `website` app, you can use `-i crm,website`. This list is initially set when you create a new database from the modules found on the add-ons path provided at that time. It can be updated in an existing database with the **Update Module List** menu.

Completing the add-on module manifest

The manifest is an important piece for Odoo modules. It contains important metadata about the add-on module and declares the data files that should be loaded.

Getting ready

We should have a module to work with, already containing a `__manifest__.py` manifest file. You may want to follow the previous recipe to provide such a module to work with.

How to do it...

We will add a manifest file and an icon to our add-on module:

1. To create a manifest file with the most relevant keys, edit the module's `__manifest__.py` file so that it looks like this:

    ```python
    {
        'name': "My library",
        'summary': "Manage books easily",
        'description': """
        Manage Library
        ==============
        Description related to library.
        """,
        'author': "Your name",
        'website': "http://www.example.com",
        'category': 'Uncategorized',
        'version': '13.0.1',
        'depends': ['base'],
        'data': ['views/views.xml'],
        'demo': ['demo.xml'],
    }
    ```

2. To add an icon for the module, choose a PNG image to use and copy it to `static/description/icon.png`.

How it works...

The content in the manifest file is a regular Python dictionary, with keys and values. The example manifest we used contains the most relevant keys:

- name: This is the title for the module.
- summary: This is the subtitle with a one-line description.
- description: This is a long description written in plaintext or **ReStructuredText** (**RST**) format. It is usually surrounded by triple quotes and is used in Python to delimit multi-line texts. For an RST quick-start reference, visit http://docutils.sourceforge.net/docs/user/rst/quickstart.html.
- author: This is a string with the name of the authors. When there is more than one, it is common practice to use a comma to separate their names, but note that it should still be a string, not a Python list.
- website: This is a URL people should visit to learn more about the module or the authors.
- category: This is used to organize modules by areas of interest. The list of the standard category names available can be seen at https://github.com/odoo/odoo/blob/13.0/odoo/addons/base/data/ir_module_category_data.xml. However, it's also possible to define other new category names here.
- version: This is the module's version number. It can be used by the Odoo app store to detect newer versions for installed modules. If the version number does not begin with the Odoo target version (for example, 13.0), it will be automatically added. Nevertheless, it will be more informative if you explicitly state the Odoo target version, for example, by using 13.0.1.0.0 or 13.0.1.0, instead of 1.0.0 or 1.0.
- depends: This is a list with the technical names of the modules it directly depends on. If your module does not depend on any other add-on module, then you should at least add a base module. Don't forget to include any module defining XML IDs, views, or models that are referenced by this module. That will ensure that they all load in the correct order, avoiding hard-to-debug errors.
- data: This is a list of relative paths for the data files to load during module installation or upgrade. The paths are relative to the module root directory. Usually, these are XML and CSV files, but it's also possible to have YAML data files. These are discussed in depth in *Chapter 6, Managing Module Data*.

- `demo`: This is the list of relative paths to the files with demonstration data to load. These will only be loaded if the database was created with the Demo Data flag enabled.

The image that is used as the module icon is the PNG file at `static/description/icon.png`.

Odoo is expected to have significant changes between major versions, so modules that have been built for one major version are not likely to be compatible with the next version without conversion and migration work. For this reason, it's important to be sure about a module's Odoo target version before installing it.

There's more...

Instead of having the long description in the module manifest, it's possible to have a separate description file. Since version 8.0, it can be replaced by a `README` file, with either a `.txt`, `.rst`, or an `.md` (markdown) extension. Otherwise, include a `description/index.html` file in the module.

This HTML description will override the description that's defined in the manifest file.

There are a few more keys that are frequently used:

- `licence`: The default value is `LGPL-3`. This identifier is used for a license under the module that is made available. Other license possibilities include `AGPL-3`, `Odoo Proprietary License v1.0` (mostly used in paid apps), and `Other OSI Approved Licence`.

- `application`: If this is `True`, the module is listed as an application. Usually, this is used for the central module of a functional area.

- `auto_install`: If this is `True`, it indicates that this is a *glue* module, which is automatically installed when all of its dependencies are installed.

- `installable`: If this is `True` (the default value), it indicates that the module is available for installation.

- `external_dependencies`: Some Odoo modules internally use `Python/bin` libraries. If your modules are using such libraries, you need to put them here. This will stop users from installing the module if the listed modules are not installed on the host machine.

- `{pre_init, post_init, uninstall}_hook`: This is a Python function hook that's called during installation/uninstallation. For a more detailed example, refer to *Chapter 8, Advanced Server-Side Development Techniques*.

There are a number of special keys that are used for app store listing:

- `price`: This key is used to set the price for your add-on module. The value of this key should be an integer value. If a price is not set, this means your app is free.
- `currency`: This is the currency for the price. Possible values are USD and EUR. The default value for this key is EUR.
- `live_test_url`: If you want to provide a live test URL for your app, you can use this key to show the **Live Preview** button on the app store.
- `iap`: Set your IAP developer key if the module is used to provide an IAP service.
- `images`: This gives the path of images. This image will be used as a cover image in Odoo's app store.

Organizing the add-on module file structure

An add-on module contains code files and other assets, such as XML files and images. For most of these files, we are free to choose where to place them inside the module directory.

However, Odoo uses some conventions on the module structure, so it is advisable to follow them.

Getting ready

We are expected to have an add-on module directory with only the `__init__.py` and `__manifest__.py` files. In this recipe, we assume this is `local-addons/my_library`.

How to do it...

To create a basic skeleton for the add-on module, perform the following steps:

1. Create directories for the code files:

    ```
    $ cd local-addons/my_library
    $ mkdir models
    $ touch models/__init__.py
    $ mkdir controllers
    $ touch controllers/__init__.py
    $ mkdir views
    $ touch views/views.xml
    $ mkdir security
    ```

```
$ mkdir wizard
$ touch wizard/__init__.py
$ mkdir report
$ mkdir data
$ mkdir demo
$ mkdir i18n
```

2. Edit the module's top __init__.py file so that the code in the subdirectories is loaded:

```
from . import models
from . import controllers
from . import wizard
```

This should get us started with a structure containing the most frequently used directories, similar to this one:

```
my_library
├── __init__.py
├── __manifest__.py
├── controllers
|   └── __init__.py
├── data
├── demo
├── i18n
├── models
|   └── __init__.py
├── security
├── static
|   ├── description
|   └── src
|       ├── js
|       ├── scss
|       ├── css
|       └── xml
├── report
├── wizard
|   └── __init__.py
```

```
└── views
    └── __init__.py
```

How it works...

To provide some context, an Odoo add-on module can have three types of files:

- The **Python code** is loaded by the `__init__.py` files, where the `.py` files and code subdirectories are imported. Subdirectories containing Python code, in turn, need their own `__init__.py` file.

- **Data files** that are to be declared in the `data` and `demo` keys of the `__manifest__.py` module manifest in order to be loaded are usually XML and CSV files for the user interface, fixture data, and demonstration data. There may also be YAML files, which can include some procedural instructions that are run when the module is loaded, for instance, to generate or update records programmatically rather than statically in an XML file.

- **Web assets** such as JavaScript code and libraries, CSS, SASS, and QWeb/HTML templates. These files are used to build UI parts and manage user actions in those UI elements. These are declared through an XML file that's extending the master templates, which adds these assets to the web client or website pages.

The add-on files are to be organized into the following directories:

- `models/` contains the backend code files, thus creating the models and their business logic. One file per model is recommended with the same name as the model, for example, `library_book.py` for the `library.book` model. These are addressed in depth in *Chapter 4, Application Models*.

- `views/` contains the XML files for the user interface, with the actions, forms, lists, and so on. Like models, it is advised to have one file per model. Filenames for website templates are expected to end with the `_template` suffix. Backend views are explained in *Chapter 9, Backend Views*, and website views are addressed in *Chapter 14, CMS Website Development*.

- `data/` contains other data files with the module's initial data. Data files are explained in *Chapter 6, Managing Module Data*.

- `demo/` contains data files with demonstration data, which is useful for tests, training, or module evaluation.

- `i18n/` is where Odoo will look for the translation `.pot` and `.po` files. Refer to *Chapter 11, Internationalization*, for further details. These files don't need to be mentioned in the manifest file.

- `security/` contains the data files that define access control lists, which is usually a `ir.model.access.csv` file, and possibly an XML file to define access *groups and record rules* for row-level security. Take a look at *Chapter 10, Security Access*, for more details on this.

- `controllers/` contains the code files for the website controllers, and for modules providing that kind of feature. Web controllers are covered in *Chapter 13, Web Server Development*.

- `static/` is where all web assets are expected to be placed. Unlike other directories, this directory name is not just a convention. The files inside this directory are public and can be accessed without a user login. This directory mostly contains files such as JavaScript, style sheets, and images. They don't need to be mentioned in the module manifest but will have to be referred to in the web template. This is discussed in detail in *Chapter 14, CMS Website Development*.

- `wizard/` contains all of the files related to wizards. In Odoo, wizards are used to hold intermediate data. We learn more about wizards in *Chapter 8, Advanced Server-Side Development Techniques*.

- `report/`: Odoo provides a feature to generate PDF documents such as sales orders and invoices. This directory holds all the files related to PDF reports. We will learn more about PDF reports in *Chapter 12, Automation, Workflows, Emails, and Printing*.

When adding new files to a module, don't forget to declare them either in the `__manifest__.py` file (for data files) or `__init__.py` file (for code files), otherwise those files will be ignored and won't be loaded.

Adding models

Models define the data structures that will be used by our business applications. This recipe shows you how to add a basic model to a module.

In our example, we want to manage books for a library. To do this, we need to create a model to represent books. Each book will have a name and a list of authors.

Getting ready

We should have a module to work with. If you followed the first recipe in this chapter, *Creating and installing a new add-on module*, you will have an empty module called `my_library`. We will use that for our explanation.

How to do it...

To add a new `Model`, we need to add a Python file describing it and then to upgrade the add-on module (or install it, if this was not already done). The paths that are used are relative to our add-on module's location (for example, `~/odoo-dev/local-addons/my_library/`):

1. Add a Python file to the `models/library_book.py` module with the following code:

    ```python
    from odoo import models, fields
    class LibraryBook(models.Model):
        _name = 'library.book'
        name = fields.Char('Title', required=True)
        date_release = fields.Date('Release Date')
        author_ids = fields.Many2many(
            'res.partner',
            string='Authors'
        )
    ```

2. Add a Python initialization file with code files to be loaded by the `models/__init__.py` module with the following code:

    ```python
    from . import library_book
    ```

3. Edit the module's Python initialization file to have the `models/` directory loaded by the module:

    ```python
    from . import models
    ```

4. Upgrade the Odoo module either from the command line or from the **Apps** menu in the user interface. If you look closely at the server log while upgrading the module, you should see the following line:

    ```
    odoo.modules.registry: module my_library: creating or updating database table
    ```

After this, the new `library.book` model should be available in our Odoo instance. There are two ways to check whether our model has been added to the database.

First, you can check it in the Odoo user interface. Activate the developer tools and open the menu at **Settings | Technical | Database Structure | Models**. Search for the `library.book` model here.

The second way is to check the table entry in your PostgreSQL database. You can search for the `library_book` table in the database. In the following code example, we used `test-13.0` as our database. However, you can replace your database name in the following command:

```
$ psql test-13.0
test-13.0# \d library_book;
```

How it works...

Our first step was to create a Python file where our new module was created.

The Odoo framework has its own **Object Relational Mapping** (**ORM**) framework. This ORM framework provides abstraction over the PostgreSQL database. By inheriting the Odoo Python class `Model`, we can create our own model (table). When a new model is defined, it is also added to a central model registry. This makes it easier for other modules to make modifications to it later.

Models have a few generic attributes prefixed with an underscore. The most important one is _name, which provides a unique internal identifier that will be used throughout the Odoo instance. The ORM framework will generate the database table based on this attribute. In our recipe, we used _name = 'library.book'. Based on this attribute, the ORM framework will create a new table called `library_book`. Note that the ORM framework will create a table name by replacing . with _ in the value of the _name attribute.

The model fields are defined as class attributes. We began by defining the name field of the Char type. It is convenient for models to have this field because, by default, it is used as the record description when referenced by other models.

We also used an example of a relational field – author_ids. This defines a many-to-many relation between `Library Books` and their partners. A book can have many authors and each author can have written many books.

There's much more to say about models, and they will be covered in depth in *Chapter 4, Application Models*.

Next, we must make our module aware of this new Python file. This is done by the __init__.py files. Since we placed the code inside the models/ subdirectory, we need the previous __init__ file to import that directory, which should in turn contain another __init__ file, importing each of the code files there (just one, in our case).

Changes to Odoo models are activated by upgrading the module. The Odoo server will handle the translation of the `model` class into database structure changes.

Although no example is provided here, business logic can also be added to these Python files, either by adding new methods to the model's class, or by extending the existing methods, such as `create()` or `write()`. This is addressed in *Chapter 5, Basic Server-Side Development*.

Adding menu items and views

Once we have models for our data structure needs, we want a user interface so that our users can interact with them. This recipe builds on the `Library Book` model from the previous recipe and adds a menu item to display a user interface featuring list and form views.

Getting ready

The add-on module for implementing the `library.book` model, which was provided in the previous recipe, is needed. The paths that will be used are relative to our add-on module location (for example, `~/odoo-dev/local-addons/my_library/`).

How to do it...

To add a view, we will add an XML file with its definition to the module. Since it is a new model, we must also add a menu option for the user to be able to access it.

Be aware that the sequence of the following steps is relevant, since some of them use references to IDs that are defined in the preceding steps:

1. Create the XML file to add the data records describing the user interface, `views/library_book.xml`:

    ```xml
    <?xml version="1.0" encoding="utf-8"?>
    <odoo>
    <!-- Data records go here -->
    </odoo>
    ```

2. Add the new data file to the add-on module manifest, `__manifest__.py`, by adding it to `views/library_book.xml`:

    ```
    {
        'name': "My Library",
        'summary': "Manage books easily",
        'depends': ['base'],
    ```

```
        'data': ['views/library_book.xml'],
}
```

3. Add the action that opens the views in the `library_book.xml` file:

   ```xml
   <record id='library_book_action' model='ir.actions.act_window'>
       <field name="name">Library Books</field>
       <field name="res_model">library.book</field>
       <field name="view_mode">tree,form</field>
   </record>
   ```

4. Add the menu items to the `library_book.xml` file, making it visible to users:

   ```xml
   <menuitem name="My Library" id="library_base_menu" />
   <menuitem name="Books" id="library_book_menu" parent="library_base_menu" action="library_book_action"/>
   ```

5. Add a custom form view to the `library_book.xml` file:

   ```xml
   <record id="library_book_view_form" model="ir.ui.view">
       <field name="name">Library Book Form</field>
       <field name="model">library.book</field>
       <field name="arch" type="xml">
           <form>
               <group>
                   <group>
                       <field name="name"/>
                       <field name="author_ids" widget="many2many_tags"/>
                   </group>
                   <group>
                       <field name="date_release"/>
                   </group>
               </group>
           </form>
       </field>
   </record>
   ```

6. Add a custom tree (list) view to the `library_book.xml` file:

```xml
<record id="library_book_view_tree" model="ir.ui.view">
  <field name="name">Library Book List</field>
  <field name="model">library.book</field>
  <field name="arch" type="xml">
    <tree>
      <field name="name"/>
      <field name="date_release"/>
    </tree>
  </field>
</record>
```

7. Add custom `Search` options to the `library_book.xml` file:

```xml
<record id="library_book_view_search" model="ir.ui.view">
  <field name="name">Library Book Search</field>
  <field name="model">library.book</field>
  <field name="arch" type="xml">
    <search>
      <field name="name"/>
      <field name="author_ids"/>
      <filter string="No Authors"
              name="without_author"
              domain="[('author_ids','=',False)]"/>
    </search>
  </field>
</record>
```

When a new model is added in Odoo, the user doesn't have any access rights by default. We must define access rights for the new model in order to get access. In our example, we haven't defined any access rights, so the user doesn't have access to our new model. Without access, our menus and views are not visible either. Luckily, there is one shortcut! By switching to superuser mode, you can see menus for our app without having access rights.

Accessing Odoo as a superuser

By converting the `admin` user into a superuser type, you can bypass the access rights and therefore access menus and views without giving default access rights. To convert the `admin` user into a superuser, activate **Developer Mode**. After doing this, from the developer tool options, click on the **Become Superuser** option.

The following screenshot has been provided as reference:

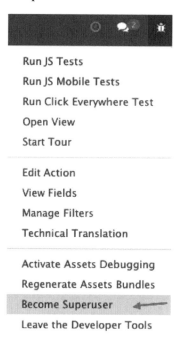

Figure 3.3 – Option to activate superuser mode

After becoming a superuser, your menu will have a striped background, as shown in the following screenshot:

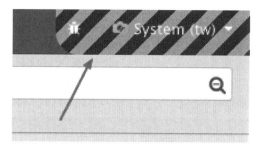

Figure 3.4 – Superuser mode activated

If you try and upgrade the module now, you should be able to see a new menu option (you might need to refresh your web browser). Clicking on the **Books** menu will open a list view for book models, as shown in the following screenshot:

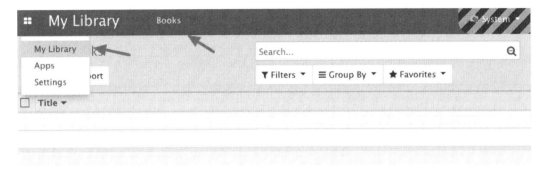

Figure 3.5 – Menu to access books

How it works...

At a low level, the user interface is defined by records stored in special models. The first two steps create an empty XML file to define the records to be loaded, and then add them to the module's list of data files to be installed.

Data files can be placed anywhere inside the module directory, but the convention is for the user interface to be defined inside a `views/` subdirectory. Usually, the name of these files is based on the name of the model. In our case, we are creating the user interface for the `library.book` model, so we created the `views/library_book.xml` file.

The next step is to define a window action to display the user interface in the main area of the web client. The action has a target model defined by `res_model`, and the `name` attribute is used to display the title to the user when the user opens the action. These are just the basic attributes. The window action supports additional attributes, giving much more control over how the views are rendered, such as what views are to be displayed, adding filters on the records that are available, or setting default values. These are discussed in detail in *Chapter 9, Backend Views*.

In general, data records are defined using a `<record>` tag, and we created a record for the `ir.actions.act_window` model in our example. This will create the window actions.

Similarly, menu items are stored in the `ir.ui.menu` model, and we can create these with the `<record>` tag. However, there is a shortcut tag called `<menuitem>` available in Odoo, so we used this in our example.

These are the menu item's main attributes:

- `name`: This is the menu item text to be displayed.
- `action`: This is the identifier of the action to be executed. We use the ID of the window action we created in the previous step.
- `sequence`: This is used to set the order in which the menu items of the same level are presented.
- `parent`: This is the identifier for the parent menu item. Our example menu item had no parent, meaning that it is to be displayed at the top of the menu.
- `web_icon`: This attribute is used to show the icon for the menu. This icon is only displayed in the Odoo Enterprise Edition.

At this point, we haven't defined any of the views in our module. However, if you upgrade your module at this stage, Odoo will automatically create them on the fly. Nevertheless, we will surely want to control how our views look, so, in the next two steps, a form and a tree view are created.

Both views are defined with a record on the `ir.ui.view` model. The attributes we used are as follows:

- `name`: This is a title identifying the view. In the source code of Odoo, you will find the XML ID repeated here, but if you want, you can add a more human readable title as a name.

    If the `name` field is omitted, Odoo will generate one using the model name and the type of view. This is perfectly fine for the standard view of a new model. It is recommended to have a more explicit name when you are extending a view, as this will make your life easier when you are looking for a specific view in the user interface of Odoo.

- `model`: This is the internal identifier of the target model, as defined in its `_name` attribute.
- `arch`: This is the view architecture, where its structure is actually defined. This is where different types of views differ from each other.

Form views are defined with a top `<form>` element, and its canvas is a two-column grid. Inside the form, `<group>` elements are used to vertically compose fields. Two groups result in two columns with fields, which are added using the `<field>` element. Fields use a default widget according to their data type, but a specific widget can be used with the help of the `widget` attribute.

Tree views are simpler; they are defined with a top `<tree>` element that contains `<field>` elements for the columns to be displayed.

Finally, we added a **Search** view to expand the search option in the box at the top-right. Inside the `<search>` top-level tag, we can have the `<field>` and `<filter>` elements. Field elements are additional fields that can be searched from the input given in the search view. Filter elements are predefined filter conditions that can be activated with a click. These subjects are discussed in detail in *Chapter 9*, *Backend Views*.

Adding access security

When adding a new data model, you need to define who can create, read, update, and delete records. When creating a totally new application, this can involve defining new user groups. Consequently, if a user doesn't have these access rights, then Odoo will not display your menus and views. In the previous recipe, we accessed our menu by converting an `admin` user into a superuser. After completing this recipe, you will be able to access menus and views for our `Library` module directly as an `admin` user.

This recipe builds on the `Library Book` model from the previous recipes and defines a new security group of users to control who can access or modify the records of the books.

Getting ready

The add-on module that implements the `library.book` model, which was provided in the previous recipe, is needed because, in this recipe, we will add the security rules for it. The paths that are used are relative to our add-on module location (for example, `~/odoo-dev/local-addons/my_library/`).

How to do it...

The security rules we want to add in this recipe are as follows:

- Everyone will be able to read library book records.
- A new group of users called **Librarians** will have the right to create, read, update, and delete book records.

To implement this, you need to perform the following steps:

1. Create a file called `security/groups.xml` with the following content:

   ```xml
   <?xml version="1.0" encoding="utf-8"?>
   <odoo>
     <record id="group_librarian" model="res.groups">
       <field name="name">Librarians</field>
       <field name="users" eval="[(4, ref('base.user_admin'))]"/>
     </record>
   </odoo>
   ```

2. Add a file called `security/ir.model.access.csv` with the following content:

   ```
   id,name,model_id:id,group_id:id,perm_read,perm_write,perm_create,perm_unlink
   acl_book,library.book default,model_library_book,,1,0,0,0
   acl_book_librarian,library.book_librarian,model_library_book,group_librarian,1,1,1,1
   ```

3. Add both files in the `data` entry of `__manifest__.py`:

   ```python
   # ...
   'data': [
       'security/groups.xml',
       'security/ir.model.access.csv',
       'views/library_book.xml'
   ],
   # ...
   ```

The newly defined security rules will be in place once you update the add-on in your instance.

How it works...

We are providing two new data files that we add to the add-on module's manifest so that installing or updating the module will load them in the database:

- The `security/groups.xml` file defines a new security group by creating a `res.groups` record. We also gave librarians' rights to the `admin` user by using its reference ID, `base.user_admin`, so that the admin user will have rights for the `library.book` model.
- The `ir.model.access.csv` file associates permissions on models with groups. The first line has an empty `group_id:id` column, which means that the rule applies to everyone. The last line gives all privileges to members of the group we just created.

The order of the files in the data section of the manifest is important. The file for creating the security groups must be loaded before the file listing the access rights, as the access right's definition depends on the existence of the groups. Since the views can be specific to a security group, we recommend putting the group's definition file in the list to be on the safer side.

See also

This book has a chapter dedicated to security. For more information on security, refer to *Chapter 10, Security Access*.

Using the scaffold command to create a module

When creating a new Odoo module, there is some boilerplate code that needs to be set up. To help quick-start new modules, Odoo provides the `scaffold` command.

This recipe shows you how to create a new module using the `scaffold` command, which will put in place a skeleton of the file for directories to use.

Getting ready

We will create the new add-on module in a custom module directory, so we need Odoo installed and a directory for our custom modules. We will assume that Odoo is installed at `~/odoo-dev/odoo` and that our custom modules will be placed in the `~/odoo-dev/local-addons` directory.

How to do it...

We will use the `scaffold` command to create boilerplate code. Perform the following steps to create new a module using the `scaffold` command:

1. Change the working directory to where we will want our module to be. This can be whatever directory you choose, but it needs to be within an add-on path to be useful. Following the directory choices that we used in the previous recipe, this should be as follows:

   ```
   $ cd ~/odoo-dev/local-addons
   ```

2. Choose a technical name for the new module, and use the `scaffold` command to create it. For our example, we will choose `my_module`:

   ```
   $ ~/odoo-dev/odoo/odoo-bin scaffold my_module
   ```

3. Edit the `__manifest__.py` default module manifest provided and change the relevant values. You will surely want to at least change the module title in the name key.

This is what the generated add-on module should look like:

```
$ tree my_module
my_module/
├── __init__.py
├── __manifest__.py
├── controllers
│   ├── __init__.py
│   └── controllers.py
├── demo
│   └── demo.xml
├── models
│   ├── __init__.py
│   └── models.py
├── security
│   └── ir.model.access.csv
└── views
    ├── templates.xml
    └── views.xml
```

```
5 directories, 10 files
```

You should now edit the various generated files and adapt them to the purpose of your new module.

How it works...

The `scaffold` command creates the skeleton for a new module based on a template.

By default, the new module is created in the current working directory, but we can provide a specific directory to create the module, passing it as an additional parameter.

Consider the following example:

```
$ ~/odoo-dev/odoo/odoo-bin scaffold my_module ~/odoo-dev/local-addons
```

A `default` template is used, but a `theme` template is also available for website theme authoring. To choose a specific template, the `-t` option can be used. We are also allowed to use a path for a directory with a template.

This means that we can use our own templates with the `scaffold` command. The built-in templates can be found in the `/odoo/cli/templates` Odoo subdirectory. To use our own template, we can use something like the following command:

```
$ ~/odoo-dev/odoo/odoo-bin scaffold -t path/to/template my_module
```

By default, Odoo has two templates in the `/odoo/cli/templates` directory. One is the `default` template, and the second is the `theme` template. However, you can create your own templates or use it with `-t`, as shown in the preceding command.

4
Application Models

The recipes in this chapter will make small additions to an existing add-on module. In the previous chapter, we registered our add-on module in the Odoo instance. In this chapter, we will dive deeply into the database side of the module. We will add a new model (database table), new fields, and constraints. We will also examine the use of inheritance in Odoo. We will be using the module we created in the recipes in *Chapter 3, Creating Odoo Add-On Modules*.

In this chapter, we will cover the following recipes:

- Defining the model representation and order
- Adding data fields to a model
- Using a float field with configurable precision
- Adding a monetary field to a model
- Adding relational fields to a model
- Adding a hierarchy to a model
- Adding constraint validations to a model
- Adding computed fields to a model

- Exposing related fields stored in other models
- Adding dynamic relations using reference fields
- Adding features to a model using inheritance
- Using abstract models for reusable model features
- Using delegation inheritance to copy features to another model

Technical requirements

To follow the examples in this chapter, you should have the module that we created in *Chapter 3, Creating Odoo Add-On Modules*, and the module must be ready to use.

All the code used in this chapter can be downloaded from the GitHub repository at https://github.com/PacktPublishing/Odoo-14-Development-Cookbook-Fourth-Edition/tree/master/Chapter04.

Defining the model representation and order

Models have structural attributes for defining their behavior. These are prefixed with an underscore. The most important attribute of the model is _name, as this defines the internal global identifier. Internally, Odoo uses this _name attribute to create a database table. For example, if you provide _name="library.book", then the Odoo ORM will create the library_book table in the database. And that's why the _name attribute must be unique across Odoo.

There are two other attributes that we can use on a model:

- _rac_name is used to set the field that's used as a representation or title for the records.
- The other one is _order, which is used to set the order in which the records are presented.

Getting ready

This recipe assumes that you have an instance ready with the my_library module, as described in *Chapter 3, Creating Odoo Add-On Modules*.

How to do it...

The my_library instance should already contain a Python file called models/library_book.py, which defines a basic model. We will edit it to add a new class-level attribute after _name:

1. To add a user-friendly title to the model, add the following code:

   ```
   _description = 'Library Book'
   ```

2. To sort the records first (from the newest to the oldest, and then by title), add the following code:

   ```
   _order = 'date_release desc, name'
   ```

3. To use the short_name field as the record representation, add the following code:

   ```
   _rec_name = 'short_name'
   short_name = fields.Char('Short Title', required=True)
   ```

4. Add the short_name field in the form view so that it can display the new field in the view:

   ```
   <field name="short_name"/>
   ```

   When we're done, our library_book.py file should appear as follows:

   ```
   from odoo import models, fields
   class LibraryBook(models.Model):
       _name = 'library.book'
       _description = 'Library Book'
       _order = 'date_release desc, name'
       _rec_name = 'short_name'
       name = fields.Char('Title', required=True)
       short_name = fields.Char('Short Title', required=True)
       date_release = fields.Date('Release Date')
       author_ids = fields.Many2many('res.partner', string='Authors')
   ```

   Your `<form>` view in the library_book.xml file will look as follows:

   ```
   <form>
       <group>
   ```

```xml
            <group>
                <field name="name"/>
                <field name="author_ids" widget="many2many_tags"/>
            </group>
            <group>
                <field name="short_name"/>
                <field name="date_release"/>
            </group>
        </group>
    </form>
```

We should then upgrade the module to activate these changes in Odoo. To update the module, you can open the **Apps** menu, search for the `my_library` module, and then update the module via a dropdown, as in the following screenshot:

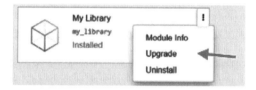

Figure 4.1 – Option to update the module

Alternatively, you can also use the `-u my_library` command in the command line.

How it works...

The first step adds a more user-friendly title to the model's definition. This is not mandatory, but can be used by some add-ons. For instance, it is used by the tracking feature in the `mail` add-on module for the notification text when a new record is created. For more details, refer to *Chapter 23, Managing Emails in Odoo*. If you don't use `_description` for your model, in that case, Odoo will show a warning in the logs.

By default, Odoo orders the records using the internal `id` value (autogenerated primary key). However, this can be changed so that we can use the fields of our choice by providing an `_order` attribute with a string containing a comma-separated list of field names. A field name can be followed by the `desc` keyword to sort it in descending order.

> **Important note**
> Only fields stored in the database can be used. Non-stored computed fields can't be used to sort records.

The syntax for the `_order` string is similar to `SQL ORDER BY` clauses, although it's stripped down. For instance, special clauses, such as `NULLS FIRST`, are not allowed.

Model records use a representation when they are referenced from other records. For example, a `user_id` field with the value `1` represents the **Administrator** user. When displayed in a form view, Odoo will display the username, rather than the database ID. In short, `_rec_name` is the display name of the record used by Odoo GUI to represent that record. By default, the `name` field is used. In fact, this is the default value for the `_rec_name` attribute, which is why it's convenient to have a `name` field in our models. In our example, the `library.book` model has a `name` field, so, by default, Odoo will use it as a display name. We want to change this behavior in *step 3*; we have used `short_name` as the `_rec_name`. After that, `library.book` model's display name is changed form `name` to `short_name` and Odoo GUI will use the value of `short_name` to represent the record.

> **Warning**
> If your model doesn't have a `name` field and you haven't specified `_rec_name` either in that case, your display name will be a combination of the model name and record ID, like this: (`library.book, 1`).

Since we have added a new field, `short_name`, to the model, the Odoo ORM will add a new column to the database table, but it won't display this field in the view. To do this, we need to add this field to the form view. In *step 4*, we added the `short_name` field to the form view.

There's more...

Record representation is available in a magic `display_name` computed field and has been automatically added to all models since version 8.0. Its values are generated using the `name_get()` model method, which was already in existence in the previous versions of Odoo.

The default implementation of `name_get()` uses the `_rec_name` attribute to find which field holds the data, which is used to generate the display name. If you want your own implementation for the display name, you can override the `name_get()` logic to generate a custom display name. The method must return a list of tuples with two elements: the ID of the record and the Unicode string representation for the record.

For example, to have the title and its release date in the representation, such as `Moby Dick (1851-10-18)`, we can define the following:

Take a look at the following example. This will add a release date in the record's name:

```
def name_get(self):
    result = []
    for record in self:
        rec_name = "%s (%s)" % (record.name, record.date_release)
        result.append((record.id, rec_name))
    return result
```

After adding the preceding code, your `display_name` record will be updated. Suppose you have a record with the name *Odoo Cookbook* and a release date of *19-04-2019*, then the preceding `name_get()` method will generate a name such as *Odoo Cookbook (19-04-2019)*.

Adding data fields to a model

Models are meant to store data, and this data is structured in fields. Here, you will learn about the several types of data that can be stored in fields, and how to add them to a model.

Getting ready

This recipe assumes that you have an instance ready with the `my_library` add-on module available, as described in *Chapter 3, Creating Odoo Add-On Modules*.

How to do it...

The `my_library` add-on module should already have `models/library_book.py`, defining a basic model. We will edit it to add new fields:

1. Use the minimal syntax to add fields to the `Library Books` model:

    ```
    from odoo import models, fields
    class LibraryBook(models.Model):
        # ...
        short_name = fields.Char('Short Title')
        notes = fields.Text('Internal Notes')
    ```

```python
        state = fields.Selection(
            [('draft', 'Not Available'),
             ('available', 'Available'),
             ('lost', 'Lost')],
            'State')
        description = fields.Html('Description')
        cover = fields.Binary('Book Cover')
        out_of_print = fields.Boolean('Out of Print?')
        date_release = fields.Date('Release Date')
        date_updated = fields.Datetime('Last Updated')
        pages = fields.Integer('Number of Pages')
        reader_rating = fields.Float(
            'Reader Average Rating',
            digits=(14, 4),  # Optional precision decimals,
        )
```

2. We have added new fields to the model. We still need to add these fields to the form view in order to reflect these changes in the user interface. Refer to the following code to add fields in the form view:

```xml
<form>
    <group>
        <group>
            <field name="name"/>
            <field name="author_ids" widget="many2many_tags"/>
            <field name="state"/>
            <field name="pages"/>
            <field name="notes"/>
        </group>
        <group>
            <field name="short_name"/>
            <field name="date_release"/>
            <field name="date_updated"/>
            <field name="cover" widget="image" class="oe_avatar"/>
            <field name="reader_rating"/>
        </group>
```

```
            </group>
            <group>
                <field name="description"/>
            </group>
        </form>
```

Upgrading the module will make these changes effective in the Odoo model.

Take a look at the following samples of different fields. Here, we have used different attributes on various types in the fields. This will give you a better idea of field declaration:

```
short_name = fields.Char('Short Title',translate=True,
index=True)
state = fields.Selection(
    [('draft', 'Not Available'),
        ('available', 'Available'),
        ('lost', 'Lost')],
    'State', default="draft")
description = fields.Html('Description', sanitize=True, strip_
style=False)
pages = fields.Integer('Number of Pages',
        groups='base.group_user',
        states={'lost': [('readonly', True)]},
        help='Total book page count', company_dependent=False)
```

How it works...

Fields are added to models by defining an attribute in their Python classes. The non-relational field types that are available are as follows:

- `Char` is used for string values.
- `Text` is used for multiline string values.
- `Selection` is used for selection lists. This has a list of values and description pairs. The value that is selected is what gets stored in the database, and it can be a string or an integer. The description is automatically translatable.

> **Important note**
> In fields of the Selection type, you can use integer keys, but you must be aware that Odoo interprets 0 as not having been set internally, and will not display the description if the stored value is zero. This can happen, so you will need to take this into account.

- Html is similar to the text field, but is expected to store rich text in an HTML format.
- Binary fields store binary files, such as images or documents.
- Boolean stores True/False values.
- Date stores date values. They are stored in the database as dates. The ORM handles them in the form of Python date objects. You can use fields.Date.today() to set the current date as a default value in the date field.
- Datetime is used for datetime values. They are stored in the database in a naive datetime, in UTC time. The ORM handles them in the form of Python datetime objects. You can use fields.Date.now() to set the current time as a default value in the datetime field.
- The Integer fields need no further explanation.
- The Float fields store numeric values. Their precision can optionally be defined with a total number of digits and decimal digit pairs.
- Monetary can store an amount in a certain currency. This will also be explained in the *Adding a monetary field* recipe in this chapter.

The *first step* of this recipe shows the minimal syntax to add to each field type. The field definitions can be expanded to add other optional attributes, as shown in *step 2*.

Here's an explanation for the field attributes that were used:

- string is the field's title, and is used in UI view labels. It is optional. If not set, a label will be derived from the field name by adding a title case and replacing the underscores with spaces.
- translate, when set to True, makes the field translatable. It can hold a different value, depending on the user interface language.
- default is the default value. It can also be a function that is used to calculate the default value; for example, default=_compute_default, where _compute_default is a method that was defined on the model before the field definition.

- `help` is an explanation text that's displayed in the UI tooltips.
- `groups` makes the field available only to some security groups. It is a string containing a comma-separated list of XML IDs for security groups. This is addressed in more detail in *Chapter 10, Security Access*.
- `states` allows the user interface to dynamically set the value for the `readonly`, `required`, and `invisible` attributes, depending on the value of the state field. Therefore, it requires a `state` field to exist and be used in the form view (even if it is invisible). The name of the `state` attribute is hardcoded in Odoo and cannot be changed.
- `copy` flags whether the field value is copied when the record is duplicated. By default, it is `True` for non-relational and `Many2one` fields, and `False` for `One2many` and computed fields.
- `index`, when set to `True`, creates a database index for the field, which sometimes allows for faster searches. It replaces the deprecated `select=1` attribute.
- The `readonly` flag makes the field read-only by default in the user interface.
- The `required` flag makes the field mandatory by default in the user interface.

  The various whitelists that are mentioned here are defined in `odoo/tools/mail.py`.

- The `company_dependent` flag makes the field store different values for each company. It replaces the deprecated `Property` field type.
- `group_operator` is an aggregate function used to display results in the group by mode. Possible values for this attribute include `count`, `count_distinct`, `array_agg`, `bool_and`, `bool_or`, `max`, `min`, `avg`, and `sum`. Integer, float, and monetary field types have the default value `sum` for this attribute.
- The `sanitize` flag is used by HTML fields and strips its content from potentially insecure tags. Using this performs a global cleanup of the input.

If you need finer control in HTML sanitization, there are a few more attributes that you can use, which only work if `sanitize` is enabled:

- `sanitize_tags=True`, to remove tags that are not part of a whitelist (this is the default)
- `sanitize_attributes=True`, to remove attributes of the tags that are not part of a whitelist
- `sanitize_style=True`, to remove style properties that are not part of a whitelist

- `strip_style=True`, to remove all style elements
- `strip_class=True`, to remove the class attributes

Finally, we updated the form view according to the newly added fields in the model. We placed `<field>` tags in an arbitrary manner here, but you can place them anywhere you want. Form views are explained in more detail in *Chapter 9, Backend Views*.

There's more...

The `Selection` field also accepts a function reference as its `selection` attribute instead of a list. This allows for dynamically generated lists of options. You can find an example relating to this in the *Adding dynamic relations using reference fields* recipe in this chapter, where a `selection` attribute is also used.

The `Date` and `Datetime` field objects expose a few utility methods that can be convenient.

For `Date`, we have the following:

- `fields.Date.to_date(string_value)` parses the string into a `date` object.
- `fields.Date.to_string(date_value)` converts the python `Date` object as a string.
- `fields.Date.today()` returns the current day in a string format. This is appropriate to use for default values.
- `fields.Date.context_today(record, timestamp)` returns the day of the `timestamp` (or the current day, if `timestamp` is omitted) in a string format, according to the time zone of the record's (or record set's) context.

For `Datetime`, we have the following:

- `fields.Datetime.to_datetime(string_value)` parses the string into a `datetime` object.
- `fields.Datetime.to_string(datetime_value)` converts the `datetime` object to a string.
- `fields.Datetime.now()` returns the current day and time in a string format. This is appropriate to use for default values.
- `fields.Datetime.context_timestamp(record, timestamp)` converts a `timestamp`-naive `datetime` object into a time zone-aware `datetime` object using the time zone in the context of `record`. This is not suitable for default values, but can be used for instances when you're sending data to an external system.

Other than the basic fields, we also have relational fields: Many2one, One2many, and Many2many. These are explained in the *Adding relational fields to a model* recipe in this chapter.

It's also possible to have fields with automatically computed values, defining the computation function with the compute field attribute. This is explained in the *Adding computed fields to a model* recipe.

A few fields are added by default in Odoo models, so we should not use these names for our fields. These are the id field, for the record's automatically generated identifier, and a few audit log fields, which are as follows:

- create_date is the record creation timestamp.
- create_uid is the user who created the record.
- write_date is the last recorded timestamp edit.
- write_uid is the user who last edited the record.

The automatic creation of these log fields can be disabled by setting the _log_access=False model attribute.

Another special column that can be added to a model is active. It must be a Boolean field, allowing users to mark records as inactive. It is used to enable the **archive/unarchive** feature on the records. Its definition is as follows:

```
active = fields.Boolean('Active', default=True)
```

By default, only records with active set to True are visible. To retrieve them, we need to use a domain filter with [('active', '=', False)]. Alternatively, if the 'active_test': False value is added to the environment's context, the ORM will not filter out inactive records.

In some cases, you may not be able to modify the context to get both the active and the inactive records. In this case, you can use the ['|', ('active', '=', True), ('active', '=', False)] domain.

> **Caution**
> [('active', 'in' (True, False))] does not work as you might expect. Odoo is explicitly looking for an ('active', '=', False) clause in the domain. It will default to restricting the search to active records only.

Using a float field with configurable precision

When using `float` fields, we may want to let the end user configure the decimal precision that is to be used. In this recipe, we will add a `Cost Price` field to the `Library Books` model, with the user-configurable decimal precision.

Getting ready

We will continue using the `my_library` add-on module from the previous recipe.

How to do it...

Perform the following steps to apply dynamic decimal precision to the model's `cost_price` field:

1. Activate **Developer Mode** from the link in the **Settings** menu (refer to the *Activating the Odoo developer tools* recipe in *Chapter 1, Installing the Odoo Development Environment*). This will enable the **Settings | Technical** menu.

2. Access the decimal precision configurations. To do this, open the **Settings** top menu and select **Technical | Database Structure | Decimal Accuracy**. We should see a list of the currently defined settings.

3. Add a new configuration, setting **Usage** to `Book Price`, and choosing the **Digits** precision:

Figure 4.2 – Creating new decimal precision

4. To add the `model` field using this decimal precision setting, edit the `models/library_book.py` file by adding the following code:

```
class LibraryBook(models.Model):
    cost_price = fields.Float(
        'Book Cost', digits='Book Price')
```

> **Tip**
> Whenever you add new fields in models, you will need to add them into views in order to access them from the user interface. In the previous example, we added the `cost_price` field. To see this in the form view, you need to add it with `<field name="cost_price"/>`.

How it works...

When you add a string value to the `digits` attribute of the field, Odoo looks up that string in the decimal accuracy model's **Usage** field and returns a tuple with 16-digit precision and the number of decimals that were defined in the configuration. Using the field definition, instead of having it hardcoded, allows the end user to configure it according to their needs.

> **Tip**
> If you are using a version older than v13, you require some extra work to use the `digits` attribute in float fields. In older versions, decimal precision was available in a separate module called `decimal_precision`. To enable custom decimal precision in your field, you have to use the `get_precision()` method of the `decimal_precision` module like this: `cost_price = fields.Float( 'Book Cost', digits=dp.get_precision('Book Price'))`.

Adding a monetary field to a model

Odoo has special support for **monetary** values related to a **currency**. Let's see how we can use this in a model.

Getting ready

We will continue to use the `my_library` add-on module from the previous recipe.

How to do it...

The monetary field needs a complementary currency field to store the currency for the amounts.

`my_library` already has `models/library_book.py`, which defines a basic model. We will edit this to add the required fields:

1. Add the field to store the currency that is to be used:

   ```
   class LibraryBook(models.Model):
       # ...
       currency_id = fields.Many2one(
           'res.currency', string='Currency')
   ```

2. Add the monetary field to store the amount:

   ```
   class LibraryBook(models.Model):
       # ...
       retail_price = fields.Monetary(
           'Retail Price',
           # optional: currency_field='currency_id',
       )
   ```

Now, upgrade the add-on module, and the new fields should be available in the model. They won't be visible in views until they are added to them, but we can confirm their addition by inspecting the `model` fields in **Settings | Technical | Database Structure | Models** in developer mode.

After adding them to the form view, it will appear as follows:

Figure 4.3 – Currency symbol in the monetary field

How it works...

Monetary fields are similar to float fields, but Odoo is able to represent them correctly in the user interface since it knows what their currency is through the second field.

This currency field is expected to be called `currency_id`, but we can use whatever field name we like as long as it is indicated using the optional `currency_field` parameter.

> **Tip**
> You can omit the `currency_field` attribute from the monetary field if you are storing your currency information in a field with the name `currency_id`.

This is very useful when you need to maintain the amounts in different currencies in the same record. For example, if we want to include the currency of the sale order and the currency of the company, you can configure the two fields as `fields.Many2one(res.currency)` and use the first one for the first amount and the other one for the second amount.

You might like to know that the decimal precision for the amount is taken from the currency definition (the `decimal_precision` field of the `res.currency` model).

Adding relational fields to a model

Relations between Odoo models are represented by relational fields. There are three different types of **relations**:

- **many-to-one**, commonly abbreviated as **m2o**
- **one-to-many**, commonly abbreviated as **o2m**
- **many-to-many**, commonly abbreviated as **m2m**

Looking at the `Library Books` example, we can see that each book can only have one publisher, so we can have a many-to-one relation between books and publishers.

Each publisher, however, can have many books. So, the previous many-to-one relation implies a one-to-many reverse relation.

Finally, there are cases in which we can have a many-to-many relation. In our example, each book can have several (many) authors. Also, inversely, each author may have written many books. Looking at it from either side, this is a many-to-many relation.

Getting ready

We will continue using the `my_library` add-on module from the previous recipe.

How to do it...

Odoo uses the partner model, `res.partner`, to represent people, organizations, and addresses. We should use it for authors and publishers. We will edit the `models/library_book.py` file to add these fields:

1. Add the many-to-one field for the book's publisher to `Library Books`:

   ```
   class LibraryBook(models.Model):
       # ...
       publisher_id = fields.Many2one(
           'res.partner', string='Publisher',
           # optional:
           ondelete='set null',
           context={},
           domain=[],
       )
   ```

2. To add the one-to-many field for a publisher's books, we need to extend the partner model. For simplicity, we will add that to the same Python file:

   ```
   class ResPartner(models.Model):
       _inherit = 'res.partner'
       published_book_ids = fields.One2many(
           'library.book', 'publisher_id',
           string='Published Books')
   ```

   The `_inherit` attribute we use here is for inheriting an existing model. This will be explained in the *Adding features to a model using inheritance* recipe later in this chapter.

3. We've already created the many-to-many relation between books and authors, but let's revisit it:

   ```
   class LibraryBook(models.Model):
       # ...
       author_ids = fields.Many2many(
           'res.partner', string='Authors')
   ```

4. The same relation, but from authors to books, should be added to the partner model:

```
class ResPartner(models.Model):
    # ...
    authored_book_ids = fields.Many2many(
        'library.book',
        string='Authored Books',
        # relation='library_book_res_partner_rel'  # optional
    )
```

Now, upgrade the add-on module, and the new fields should be available in the model. They won't be visible in the views until they are added to them, but we can confirm their addition by inspecting the `model` fields in **Settings | Technical | Database Structure | Models** in developer mode.

How it works...

Many-to-one fields add a column to the database table of the model, storing the database ID of the related record. At the database level, a foreign key constraint will also be created, ensuring that the stored IDs are a valid reference to a record in the related table. No database index is created for these relation fields, but this can be done by adding the `index=True` attribute.

We can see that there are four more attributes that we can use for many-to-one fields. The `ondelete` attribute determines what happens when the related record is deleted. For example, what happens to books when their publisher record is deleted? The default is `'set null'`, which sets an empty value on the field. It can also be `'restrict'`, which prevents the related record from being deleted, or `'cascade'`, which causes the linked record to also be deleted.

The last two (`context` and `domain`) are also valid for the other relational fields. These are mostly meaningful on the client-side, and, at the model level, they act as default values that will be used in the client-side views:

- `context` adds variables to the client context when clicking through the field to the related record's view. We can, for example, use it to set default values for new records that are created through that view.
- `domain` is a search filter that's used to limit the list of related records that are available.

Both context and domain are explained in more detail in *Chapter 9, Backend Views*.

One-to-many fields are the reverse of many-to-one relations, and although they are added to models just like other fields, they have no actual representation in the database. Instead, they are programmatic shortcuts, and they enable views to represent these lists of related records. That means that one-to-many fields need a many-to-one field in the reference model. In our example, we have added one-to-many field by inheriting a partner model. We will see model inheritance in detail in the *Adding features to a model using inheritance* recipe in this chapter. In our example, the one-to-many field `published_book_ids` has a reference to the `publisher_id` field of the `library.book` model.

Many-to-many relations don't add columns to the tables for the models, either. This type of relation is represented in the database using an intermediate relation table, with two columns to store the two related IDs. Adding a new relation between a book and an author creates a new record in the relation table with the ID of the book and the ID of the author.

Odoo automatically handles the creation of this relation table. The relation table name is, by default, built using the name of the two related models, alphabetically sorted, plus a `_rel` suffix. However, we can override this using the `relation` attribute.

A case to keep in mind is when the two table names are large enough for the automatically generated database identifiers to exceed the PostgreSQL limit of 63 characters. As a rule of thumb, if the names of the two related tables exceed 23 characters, you should use the `relation` attribute to set a shorter name. In the next section, we will go into more detail on this.

There's more...

The `Many2one` fields support an additional `auto_join` attribute. This is a flag that allows the ORM to use SQL joins on this field. Due to this, it bypasses the usual ORM control, such as user access control and record access rules. In specific cases, it can solve performance issues, but it is advised to avoid using it.

We have covered the shortest way to define the relational fields. Let's take a look at the attributes specific to this type of field.

The `One2many` field attributes are as follows:

- `comodel_name`: This is the target model identifier and is mandatory for all relational fields, but it can be defined position-wise, without the keyword.
- `inverse_name`: This only applies to `One2many` and is the field name in the target model for the inverse `Many2one` relation.

- **limit**: This applies to One2many and Many2many, and sets an optional limit in terms of the number of records to read that are used at the user interface level.

The Many2many field attributes are as follows:

- **comodel_name**: This is the same as it is for the One2many field.
- **relation**: This is the name to use for the table supporting the relation, overriding the automatically defined name.
- **column1**: This is the name for the Many2one field in the relational table linking to this model.
- **column2**: This is the name for the Many2one field in the relational table linking to comodel.

For Many2many relations, in most cases, the ORM will take care of the default values for these attributes. It is even capable of detecting inverse Many2many relations, detecting the already existing relation table, and appropriately inverting the column1 and column2 values.

However, there are two cases where we need to step in and provide our own values for these attributes:

- One is the case where we need more than one Many2many relations between the same two models. For this to be possible, we must provide ourselves with the relation table name for the second relation, which must be different from the first relation.
- The other case is when the database names of the related tables are long enough for the automatically generated relation name to exceed the 63-character PostgreSQL limit for database object names.

The relation table's automatic name is <model1>_<model2>_rel. However, this relation table also creates an index for its primary key with the following identifier:

```
<model1>_<model2>_rel_<model1>_id_<model2>_id_key
```

This primary key also needs to meet the 63-character limit. So, if the two table names combined exceed a total of 63 characters, you will probably have trouble meeting the limits and will need to manually set the relation attribute.

Adding a hierarchy to a model

Hierarchies are represented like a model having relations with the same model. Each record has a parent record in the same model, and many child records. This can be achieved by simply using many-to-one relations between the model and itself.

However, Odoo also provides improved support for this type of field by using the **nested set model** (https://en.wikipedia.org/wiki/Nested_set_model). When activated, queries using the `child_of` operator in their domain filters will run significantly faster.

Staying with the `Library Books` example, we will build a hierarchical category tree that can be used to categorize books.

Getting ready

We will continue using the `my_library` add-on module from the previous recipe.

How to do it...

We will add a new Python file, `models/library_book_categ.py`, for the category tree, as follows:

1. To load the new Python code file, add the following line to `models/__init__.py`:

    ```
    from . import library_book_categ
    ```

2. To create the `Book Category` model with the parent and child relations, create the `models/library_book_categ.py` file with the following code:

    ```python
    from odoo import models, fields, api
    class BookCategory(models.Model):
        _name = 'library.book.category'
        name = fields.Char('Category')
        parent_id = fields.Many2one(
            'library.book.category',
            string='Parent Category',
            ondelete='restrict',
            index=True)
        child_ids = fields.One2many(
    ```

```
                'library.book.category', 'parent_id',
                string='Child Categories')
```

3. To enable the special hierarchy support, also add the following code:

   ```
   _parent_store = True
   _parent_name = "parent_id" # optional if field is
   'parent_id'
   parent_path = fields.Char(index=True)
   ```

4. To add a check preventing looping relations, add the following line to the model:

   ```
   from odoo.exceptions import ValidationError
   ...
   @api.constraints('parent_id')
   def _check_hierarchy(self):
       if not self._check_recursion():
           raise models.ValidationError(
               'Error! You cannot create recursive
   categories.')
   ```

5. Now, we need to assign a category to a book. To do this, we will add a new many2one field to the `library.book` model:

   ```
   category_id = fields.Many2one('library.book.category')
   ```

Finally, a module upgrade will make these changes effective.

To display the `librart.book.category` model in the user interface, you will need to add menus, views, and security rules. For more details, refer to *Chapter 3, Creating Odoo Add-On Modules*. Alternatively, you can access all code at https://github.com/PacktPublishing/Odoo-13-Development-Cookbook-Fourth-Edition.

How it works...

Steps 1 and *2* create the new model with hierarchical relations. The Many2one relation adds a field to reference the parent record. For faster child record discovery, this field is indexed in the database using the `index=True` parameter. The `parent_id` field must have `ondelete` set to either `'cascade'` or `'restrict'`. At this point, we have all that is required to achieve a hierarchical structure, but there are a few more additions we can make to enhance it. The One2many relation does not add any additional fields to the database, but provides a shortcut to access all the records with this record as their parent.

In *step 3*, we activate the special support for the hierarchies. This is useful for high-read but low-write instructions, since it brings faster data browsing at the expense of costlier write operations. This is done by adding one helper field, `parent_path`, and setting the `model` attribute to `_parent_store=True`. When this attribute is enabled, the helper field will be used to store data in searches in the hierarchical tree. By default, it is assumed that the field for the record's parent is called `parent_id`, but a different name can also be used. In this case, the correct field name should be indicated using the additional model attribute, `_parent_name`. The default is as follows:

```
_parent_name = 'parent_id'
```

Step 4 is advised in order to prevent cyclic dependencies in the hierarchy, which means having a record in both the ascending and descending trees. This is dangerous for programs that navigate through the tree, since they can get into an infinite loop. `models.Model` provides a utility method for this (`_check_recursion`) that we have reused here.

Step 5 is to add the `category_id` field with the type `many2one` to the `libary.book` book, so that we can set a category on book records. This is just for the purpose of completing our example.

There's more...

The technique shown here should be used for *static* hierarchies, which are read and queried often but are updated less frequently. Book categories are a good example, since the library will not be continuously creating new categories; however, readers will often be restricting their searches to a category and its child categories. The reason for this lies in the implementation of the nested set model in the database, which requires an update of the `parent_path` column (and the related database indexes) for all records whenever a category is inserted, removed, or moved. This can be a very expensive operation, especially when multiple editions are being performed in parallel transactions.

If you are dealing with a very dynamic hierarchical structure, the standard `parent_id` and `child_ids` relations will often result in better performance by avoiding table-level locks.

Adding constraint validations to a model

Models can have validations preventing them from entering undesired conditions.

Odoo supports two different types of constraints:

- The ones checked at the database level
- The ones checked at the server level

Database-level constraints are limited to the constraints supported by PostgreSQL. The most commonly used ones are the UNIQUE constraints, but the CHECK and EXCLUDE constraints can also be used. If these are not enough for our needs, we can use Odoo server-level constraints written in Python code.

We will use the `Library Books` model that we created in *Chapter 3, Creating Odoo Add-On Modules,* and add a couple of constraints to it. We will add a database constraint that prevents duplicate book titles, and a Python model constraint that prevents release dates in the future.

Getting ready

We will continue using the `my_library` add-on module from the previous recipe. We expect it to contain at least the following:

```
from odoo import models, fields
class LibraryBook(models.Model):
    _name = 'library.book'
    name = fields.Char('Title', required=True)
    date_release = fields.Date('Release Date')
```

How to do it...

We will edit the `LibraryBook` class in the `models/library_book.py` Python file:

1. To create the database constraint, add a `model` attribute:

   ```
   class LibraryBook(models.Model):
       # ...
       _sql_constraints = [
           ('name_uniq', 'UNIQUE (name)',
            'Book title must be unique.'),
           ('positive_page', 'CHECK(pages>0)',
            'No of pages must be positive')
       ]
   ```

2. To create the Python code constraint, add a `model` method:

```python
from odoo import api, models, fields
from odoo.exceptions import ValidationError
class LibraryBook(models.Model):
    # ...
    @api.constrains('date_release')
    def _check_release_date(self):
        for record in self:
            if record.date_release and \
                    record.date_release > fields.Date.today():
                raise models.ValidationError(
                    'Release date must be in the past')
```

After these changes are made to the code file, an add-on module upgrade and a server restart are needed.

How it works...

The *first step* creates a database constraint on the model's table. It is enforced at the database level. The `_sql_constraints` model attribute accepts a list of constraints to create. Each constraint is defined by a three-element tuple. These are listed as follows:

- A suffix to use for the constraint identifier. In our example, we used `name_uniq`, and the resulting constraint name is `library_book_name_uniq`.
- The SQL to use in the PostgreSQL instruction to alter or create the database table.
- A message to report to the user when the constraint is violated.

In our example, we have used two SQL constraints. The first one is for a unique book name, and the second one is to check whether the book has a positive number of pages.

> **Warning**
> If you are adding SQL constraints to the existing model through model inheritance, make sure you don't have rows that violate the constraints. If you have such rows, then SQL constraints will not be added and an error will be generated in the log.

As we mentioned earlier, other database table constraints can also be used. Note that column constraints, such as `NOT NULL`, can't be added this way. For more information on PostgreSQL constraints in general and table constraints in particular, take a look at `http://www.postgresql.org/docs/current/static/ddl-constraints.html`.

In the *second step*, we added a method to perform Python code validation. It is decorated with `@api.constrains`, meaning that it should be executed to run checks when one of the fields in the argument list is changed. If the check fails, a `ValidationError` exception will be raised.

There's more...

Normally, if you need complex validation, you can use `@api.constrains`, but for some simple cases, you can use `_sql_constraints` with the `CHECK` option. Take a look at the following example:

```
_sql_constraints = [
    ( 'check_credit_debit',
     'CHECK(credit + debit>=0 AND credit * debit=0)',
     'Wrong credit or debit value in accounting entry!'
    )
]
```

In the preceding example, we have used the `CHECK` option, and we are checking multiple conditions in the same constraints with the `AND` operator.

Adding computed fields to a model

Sometimes, we need to have a field that has a value calculated or derived from other fields in the same record or in related records. A typical example is the total amount, which is calculated by multiplying a unit price by a quantity. In Odoo models, this can be achieved using computed fields.

To show you how computed fields work, we will add one to the `Library Books` model to calculate the days since the book's release date.

It is also possible to make computed fields editable and searchable. We will implement this to our example as well.

Getting ready

We will continue using the `my_library` add-on module from the previous recipe.

How to do it...

We will edit the `models/library_book.py` code file to add a new field and the methods supporting its logic:

1. Start by adding the new field to the `Library Books` model:

    ```python
    class LibraryBook(models.Model):
        # ...
        age_days = fields.Float(
            string='Days Since Release',
            compute='_compute_age',
            inverse='_inverse_age',
            search='_search_age',
            store=False,          # optional
            compute_sudo=True     # optional
        )
    ```

2. Next, add the method with the value computation logic:

    ```python
    # ...
    from odoo import api  # if not already imported
    # ...
    class LibraryBook(models.Model):
        # ...
        @api.depends('date_release')
        def _compute_age(self):
            today = fields.Date.today()
            for book in self:
                if book.date_release:
                    delta = today - book.date_release
                    book.age_days = delta.days
                else:
                    book.age_days = 0
    ```

3. To add the method and implement the logic to write on the computed field, use the following code:

```python
from datetime import timedelta
# ...
class LibraryBook(models.Model):
    # ...
    def _inverse_age(self):
        today = fields.Date.today()
        for book in self.filtered('date_release'):
            d = today - timedelta(days=book.age_days)
            book.date_release = d
```

4. To implement the logic that will allow you to search in the computed field, use the following code:

```python
from datetime import timedelta
class LibraryBook(models.Model):
    # ...
    def _search_age(self, operator, value):
        today = fields.Date.today()
        value_days = timedelta(days=value)
        value_date = today - value_days
        # convert the operator:
        # book with age > value have a date < value_date
        operator_map = {
            '>': '<', '>=': '<=',
            '<': '>', '<=': '>=',
        }
        new_op = operator_map.get(operator, operator)
        return [('date_release', new_op, value_date)]
```

An Odoo restart, followed by a module upgrade, is needed to correctly activate these new additions.

How it works...

The definition of a computed field is the same as that of a regular field, except that a `compute` attribute is added to specify the name of the method to use for its computation.

Their similarity can be deceptive, since computed fields are internally quite different from regular fields. Computed fields are dynamically calculated at runtime, and because of that, they are not stored in the database and so you cannot search or write on compute fields by default. You need to do some extra work in order to enable write and search support for compute fields. Let's see how to do it.

The computation function is dynamically calculated at runtime, but the ORM uses caching to avoid inefficiently recalculating it every time its value is accessed. So, it needs to know what other fields it depends on. It uses the `@depends` decorator to detect when its cached values should be invalidated and recalculated.

Ensure that the `compute` function always sets a value on the computed field. Otherwise, an error will be raised. This can happen when you have `if` conditions in your code that sometimes fail to set a value on the computed field. This can be tricky to debug.

Write support can be added by implementing the `inverse` function. This uses the value assigned to the computed field to update the origin fields. Of course, this only makes sense for simple calculations. Nevertheless, there are still cases where it can be useful. In our example, we make it possible to set the book release date by editing the **Days Since Release** computed field. The `inverse` attribute is optional; if you don't want to make the compute field editable, you can skip it.

It is also possible to make a non-stored computed field searchable by setting the search attribute to the method name (similar to `compute` and `inverse`). Like `inverse`, `search` is also optional; if you don't want to make the compute field searchable, you can skip it.

However, this method is not expected to implement the actual search. Instead, it receives the operator and value used to search on the field as parameters, and is expected to return a domain with the replacement search conditions to use. In our example, we translate a search of the **Days Since Release** field into an equivalent search condition on the **Release Date** field.

The optional `store=True` flag stores the field in the database. In this case, after being computed, the field values are stored in the database, and from there on, they are retrieved in the same way as regular fields, instead of being recomputed at runtime. Thanks to the `@api.depends` decorator, the ORM will know when these stored values need to be recomputed and updated. You can think of it as a persistent cache. It also has the advantage of making the field usable for search conditions, including sorting and grouping by operations. If you use `store=True` in your compute field, you no longer need to implement the `search` method because the field is stored in a database and you can search/sort based on the stored field.

The `compute_sudo=True` flag is to be used in cases in which the computations need to be done with elevated privileges. This might be the case when the computation needs to use data that may not be accessible to the end user.

> **Important note**
> The default value of `compute_sudo` is changed in Odoo v13. Prior to Odoo v13, the value of `compute_sudo` was `False`. But in v13, the default value of `compute_sudo` will be based on store attributes. If the value of the `store` attribute is `True`, then `compute_sudo` is `True` or it is `False`. However, you can always manually change it by explicitly putting `compute_sudo` in your field definition.

There's more...

Odoo v13 introduced a new caching mechanism for ORM. Earlier, the cache was based on the environment, but now in Odoo v13, we have one global cache. So, if you have a computed field that depends on context values, then you may get incorrect values on occasion. To fix this issue, you need to use the `@api.depends_context` decorator. Refer to the following example:

```
@api.depends('price')
@api.depends_context('company_id')
def _compute_value(self):
    company_id = self.env.context.get('company_id')
    ...
    # other computation
```

You can see in the preceding example that our computation is using `company_id` from the context. By using `company_id` in the `depends_context` decorator, we are ensuring that the field value will be recomputed based on the value of `company_id` in the context.

Exposing related fields stored in other models

When reading data from the server, Odoo clients can only get values for the fields that are available in the model and being queried. Client-side code, unlike server-side code, can't use dot notation to access data in the related tables.

However, these fields can be made available there by adding them as related fields. We will do this to make the publisher's city available in the `Library Books` model.

Getting ready

We will continue using the `my_library` add-on module from the previous recipe.

How to do it...

Edit the `models/library_book.py` file to add the new `related` field:

1. Ensure that we have a field for the book publisher:

    ```
    class LibraryBook(models.Model):
        # ...
        publisher_id = fields.Many2one(
            'res.partner', string='Publisher')
    ```

2. Now, add the related field for the publisher's city:

    ```
    # class LibraryBook(models.Model):
    #     ...
    publisher_city = fields.Char(
        'Publisher City',
        related='publisher_id.city',
        readonly=True)
    ```

Finally, we need to upgrade the add-on module for the new fields to be available in the model.

How it works...

Related fields are just like regular fields, but they have an additional attribute, `related`, with a string for the separated chain of fields to traverse.

In our case, we access the publisher-related record through `publisher_id`, and then read its `city` field. We can also have longer chains, such as `publisher_id.country_id.country_code`.

Note that in this recipe, we set the related field as `readonly`. If we don't do that, the field will be writable, and the user may change its value. This will have the effect of changing the value of the `city` field of the related publisher. While this can be a useful side effect, caution needs to be exercised. All the books that are published by the same publisher will have their `publisher_city` field updated, which may not be what the user expects.

There's more...

Related fields are, in fact, computed fields. They just provide a convenient shortcut syntax to read field values from related models. As a computed field, this means that the `store` attribute is also available. As a shortcut, they also have all the attributes from the referenced field, such as `name`, `translatable`, as required.

Additionally, they support a `related_sudo` flag similar to `compute_sudo`; when set to `True`, the field chain is traversed without checking the user access rights.

Using related fields in a `create()` method can affect performance, as the computation of these fields is delayed until the end of their creation. So, if you have a `One2many` relation, such as in `sale.order` and `sale.order.line` models, and you have a related field on the line model referring to a field on the order model, you should explicitly read the field on the order model during record creation, instead of using the related field shortcut, especially if there are a lot of lines.

Adding dynamic relations using reference fields

With relational fields, we need to decide the relation's target model (or co-model) beforehand. However, sometimes, we may need to leave that decision to the user and first choose the model we want and then the record we want to link to.

With Odoo, this can be achieved using reference fields.

Getting ready

We will continue using the `my_library` add-on module from the previous recipe.

How to do it...

Edit the `models/library_book.py` file to add the new related field:

1. First, we need to add a helper method to dynamically build a list of selectable target models:

    ```
    from odoo import models, fields, api
    class LibraryBook(models.Model):
        # ...
        @api.model
        def _referencable_models(self):
            models = self.env['ir.model'].search([
                ('field_id.name', '=', 'message_ids')])
            return [(x.model, x.name) for x in models]
    ```

2. Then, we need to add the reference field and use the previous function to provide a list of selectable models:

    ```
        ref_doc_id = fields.Reference(
            selection='_referencable_models',
            string='Reference Document')
    ```

Since we are changing the model's structure, a module upgrade is needed to activate these changes.

How it works...

Reference fields are similar to many-to-one fields, except that they allow the user to select the model to link to.

The target model is selectable from a list that's provided by the `selection` attribute. The `selection` attribute must be a list of two element tuples, where the first is the model's internal identifier, and the second is a text description for it.

Here's an example:

```
[('res.users', 'User'), ('res.partner', 'Partner')]
```

However, rather than providing a fixed list, we can use most common models. For simplicity, we are using all the models that have the messaging feature. Using the `_referencable_models` method, we provided a model list dynamically.

Our recipe started by providing a function to browse all the model records that can be referenced to dynamically build a list that will be provided to the `selection` attribute. Although both forms are allowed, we declared the function name inside quotes, instead of directly referencing the function without quotes. This is more flexible, and it allows for the referenced function to be defined only later in the code, for example, which is something that is not possible when using a direct reference.

The function needs the `@api.model` decorator because it operates on the model level, and not on the record set level.

While this feature looks nice, it comes with a significant execution overhead. Displaying the reference fields for a large number of records (for instance, in a list view) can create heavy database loads as each value has to be looked up in a separate query. It is also unable to take advantage of database referential integrity, unlike regular relation fields.

Adding features to a model using inheritance

One of the most important Odoo features is the ability of module add-ons to extend features that are defined in other module add-ons without having to edit the code of the original feature. This might be to add fields or methods, modify the existing fields, or extend the existing methods to perform additional logic.

According to the official documentation, Odoo provides three types of inheritance:

- Class inheritance (extension)
- Prototype inheritance
- Delegation inheritance

We will see each one of these in a separate recipe. In this recipe we will see **Class inheritance (extension)**. It is used to add new fields or methods to existing models.

We will extend the built-in partner model `res.partner` to add it to a computed field with the authored book count. This involves adding a field and a method to an existing model.

Getting ready

We will continue using the `my_library` add-on module from the previous recipe.

How to do it...

We will be extending the built-in partner model. If you remembered, we have already inherited the `res.parnter` model in the *Adding relational fields to a model* recipe in this chapter. To keep the explanation as simple as possible, we will reuse the `res.partner` model in the `models/library_book.py` code file:

1. First, we will ensure that the `authored_book_ids` inverse relation is in the partner model and add the computed field:

    ```
    class ResPartner(models.Model):
        _inherit = 'res.partner'
        _order = 'name'
        authored_book_ids = fields.Many2many(
            'library.book', string='Authored Books')
        count_books = fields.Integer( 'Number of Authored Books',
                compute='_compute_count_books' )
    ```

2. Next, add the method that's needed to compute the book count:

    ```
    # ...
    from odoo import api  # if not already imported
    # class ResPartner(models.Model):
        # ...
        @api.depends('authored_book_ids')
        def _compute_count_books(self):
            for r in self:
                r.count_books = len(r.authored_book_ids)
    ```

Finally, we need to upgrade the add-on module for the modifications to take effect.

How it works...

When a model class is defined with the `_inherit` attribute, it adds modifications to the inherited model, rather than replacing it.

This means that fields defined in the inheriting class are added or changed on the parent model. At the database layer, the ORM is adding fields to the same database table.

Fields are also incrementally modified. This means that if the field already exists in the superclass, only the attributes declared in the inherited class are modified; the other ones are kept as they are in the parent class.

Methods defined in the inheriting class replace methods in the parent class. If you don't invoke the parent method with the `super` call, in that case, the parent's version of the method will not be executed and we will lose the features. So, whenever you add a new logic by inheriting existing methods, you should include a statement with `super` to call its version in the parent class. This is discussed in more detail in *Chapter 5, Basic Server-Side Development*.

This recipe will add new fields to the existing model. If you also want to add these new fields to existing views (the user interface), refer to the *Changing existing views – view inheritance* recipe in *Chapter 9, Backend Views*.

Copy model definition using inheritance

We have seen class inheritance (extension) in the previous recipe. Now we will see **prototype inheritance**, which is used to copy the entire definition of the existing model. In this recipe, we will make a copy of the `library.book` model.

Getting ready

We will continue using the `my_library` add-on module from the previous recipe.

How to do it...

Prototype inheritance is executed by using the `_name` and `_inherit` class attributes at the same time. Perform the following steps to generate a copy of the `library.book` model:

1. Add new file called `library_book_copy.py` to the `/my_library/models/` directory.
2. Add the following content to the in `library_book_copy.py` file:

   ```
   from odoo import models, fields, api
   class LibraryBookCopy(models.Model):

       _name = "library.book.copy"
       _inherit = "library.book"
       _description = "Library Book's Copy"
   ```

3. Import a new file reference into the /my_library/models/__init__.py file. Following the changes, your __init__.py file will look like this:

```
from . import library_book
from . import library_book_categ
from . import library_book_copy
```

Finally, we need to upgrade the add-on module for the modifications to take effect. To check the new model's definition, go to the **Settings** | **Technical** | **Database Structure** | **Models** menu. You will see a new entry for the library.book.copy model here.

> **Tip**
>
> In order to see menus and views for the new model, you need to add the XML definition of views and menus. To learn more about views and menus, refer to the *Adding menu items and views* recipe in *Chapter 3, Creating Odoo Add-On Modules*.

How it works...

By using _name with the _inherit class attribute at the same time, you can copy the definition of the model. When you use both attributes in the model, Odoo will copy the model definition of _inherit and create a new model with the _name attribute.

In our example, Odoo will copy the definition of the library.book model and create a new model, library.book.copy. The new library.book.copy model has its own database table with its own data that is totally independent from the library.book parent model. Since it still inherits from the partner model, any subsequent modifications to it will also affect the new model.

Prototype inheritance copies all the properties of the parent class. It copies fields, attributes, and methods. If you want to modify them in the child class, you can simply do so by adding a new definition to the child class. For example, the library.book model has the _name_get method. If you want to use a different version of _name_get in the child, you need to redefine the method in the library.book.copy model.

> **Warning**
>
> Prototype inheritance does not work if you use the same model name in the _inherit and _name attributes. If you do use the same model name in the _inherit and _name attributes, it will just behave like a normal extension inheritance.

There's more...

In the official documentation, this is called prototype inheritance, but in practice, it is rarely used. The reason for this is that delegation inheritance usually answers to that need in a more efficient way, without the need to **duplicate data structures**. For more information on this, you can refer to the next recipe, *Using delegation inheritance to copy features to another model*.

Using delegation inheritance to copy features to another model

The third type of inheritance is **Delegation inheritance**. Instead of _inherit, it uses the _inherits class attribute. There are cases where, rather than modifying an existing model, we want to create a new model based on an existing one to use the features it already has. We can copy a model's definitions with prototype inheritance, but this will generate duplicate data structures. If you want to copy a model's definitions without duplicating data structures, then the answer lies in Odoo's delegation inheritance, which uses the _inherits model attribute (note the additional s).

Traditional inheritance is quite different from the concept in object-oriented programming. Delegation inheritance, in turn, is similar, in that a new model can be created to include the features from a parent model. It also supports polymorphic inheritance, where we inherit from two or more other models.

We have a library with books. It's about time our library also has members. For a library member, we need all the identification and address data that's found in the partner model, and we also want it to retain some information pertaining to membership: a start date, a termination date, and a card number.

Adding those fields to the partner model is not the best solution, since they will not be used for partners that are not members. It would be great to extend the partner model to a new model with some additional fields.

Getting ready

We will continue using the my_library add-on module from the previous recipe.

How to do it...

The new library member model should be in its own Python code file, but to keep the explanation as simple as possible, we will reuse the `models/library_book.py` file:

1. Add the new model, inheriting from `res.partner`:

```python
class LibraryMember(models.Model):
    _name = 'library.member'
    _inherits = {'res.partner': 'partner_id'}
    partner_id = fields.Many2one(
        'res.partner',
        ondelete='cascade')
```

2. Next, we will add the fields that are specific to library members:

```python
# class LibraryMember(models.Model):
#   ...
    date_start = fields.Date('Member Since')
    date_end = fields.Date('Termination Date')
    member_number = fields.Char()
    date_of_birth = fields.Date('Date of birth')
```

Now, we should upgrade the add-on module to activate the changes.

How it works...

The `_inherits` model attribute sets the parent models that we want to inherit from. In this case, we just have one—`res.partner`. Its value is a key-value dictionary, where the keys are the inherited models, and the values are the field names that were used to link to them. These are Many2one fields that we must also define in the model. In our example, `partner_id` is the field that will be used to link with the `Partner` parent model.

To better understand how this works, let's look at what happens at a database level when we create a new member:

- A new record is created in the `res_partner` table.
- A new record is created in the `library_member` table.
- The `partner_id` field of the `library_member` table is set to the ID of the `res_partner` record that is created for it.

The member record is automatically linked to a new partner record. It's just a many-to-one relation, but the delegation mechanism adds some magic so that the partner's fields are seen as if they belong to the member record, and a new partner record is also automatically created with the new member.

You may be interested in knowing that this automatically created partner record has nothing special about it. It's a regular partner, and if you browse the partner model, you will be able to find that record (without the additional member data, of course). All members are partners, but only some partners are also members.

So, what happens if you delete a partner record that is also a member? You decide by choosing the `ondelete` value for the relation field. For `partner_id`, we used `cascade`. This means that deleting the partner will also delete the corresponding member. We could have used the more conservative setting, `restrict`, to prohibit deleting the partner while it has a linked member. In this case, only deleting the member will work.

It's important to note that delegation inheritance only works for fields, and not for methods. So, if the partner model has a `do_something()` method, the members model will not automatically inherit it.

There's more...

There is a shortcut for this inheritance delegation. Instead of creating an `_inherits` dictionary, you can use the `delegate=True` attribute in the `Many2one` field definition. This will work exactly like the `_inherits` option. The main advantage is that this is simpler. In the given example, we have performed the same inheritance delegation as in the previous one, but in this case, instead of creating an `_inherits` dictionary, we have used the `delegate=True` option in the `partner_id` field:

```
class LibraryMember(models.Model):
    _name = 'library.member'
    partner_id = fields.Many2one('res.partner', ondelete='cascade', delegate=True)
    date_start = fields.Date('Member Since')
    date_end = fields.Date('Termination Date')
    member_number = fields.Char()
    date_of_birth = fields.Date('Date of birth')
```

A noteworthy case of delegation inheritance is the users model, `res.users`. It inherits from partners (`res.partner`). This means that some of the fields that you can see on the user are actually stored in the partner model (notably, the `name` field). When a new user is created, we also get a new, automatically created partner.

We should also mention that traditional inheritance with `_inherit` can also copy features into a new model, although in a less efficient way. This was discussed in the *Adding features to a model using inheritance* recipe.

Using abstract models for reusable model features

Sometimes, there is a particular feature that we want to be able to add to several different models. Repeating the same code in different files is a bad programming practice; it would be better to implement it once and reuse it.

Abstract models allow us to create a generic model that implements some features that can then be inherited by regular models in order to make that feature available.

As an example, we will implement a simple archive feature. It adds the `active` field to the model (if it doesn't exist already) and makes an archive method available to toggle the `active` flag. This works because `active` is a magic field. If present in a model by default, the records with `active=False` will be filtered out from the queries.

We will then add it to the `Library Books` model.

Getting ready

We will continue using the `my_library` add-on module from the previous recipe.

How to do it...

The archive feature certainly deserves its own add-on module, or at least its own Python code file. However, to keep the explanation as simple as possible, we will cram it into the `models/library_book.py` file:

1. Add the abstract model for the archive feature. It must be defined in the `Library Book` model, where it will be used:

   ```
   class BaseArchive(models.AbstractModel):
       _name = 'base.archive'
       active = fields.Boolean(default=True)
   ```

```
    def do_archive(self):
        for record in self:
            record.active = not record.active
```

2. Now, we will edit the `Library Book` model to inherit the archive model:

```
class LibraryBook(models.Model):
    _name = 'library.book'
    _inherit = ['base.archive']
    # ...
```

An upgrade of the add-on module is required in order for the changes to be activated.

How it works...

An abstract model is created by a class based on `models.AbstractModel`, instead of the usual `models.Model`. It has all the attributes and capabilities of regular models; the difference is that the ORM will not create an actual representation for it in the database. This means that it can't have any data stored in it. It only serves as a template for a reusable feature that is to be added to regular models.

Our archive abstract model is quite simple. It just adds the `active` field and a method to toggle the value of the `active` flag, which we expect to be used later, via a button on the user interface.

When a model class is defined with the `_inherit` attribute, it inherits the attribute methods of those classes, and the attribute methods that are defined in the current class add modifications to those inherited features.

The mechanism at play here is the same as that of a regular model extension (as per the *Adding features to a model using inheritance* recipe). You may have noticed that `_inherit` uses a list of model identifiers instead of a string with one model identifier. In fact, `_inherit` can have both forms. Using the list form allows us to inherit from multiple (usually `Abstract`) classes. In this case, we are inheriting just one, so a text string would be fine. A list was used instead, for illustration purposes.

There's more...

A noteworthy built-in abstract model is `mail.thread`, which is provided by the `mail (Discuss)` add-on module. On models, it enables the discussion features that power the message wall that's seen at the bottom of many forms.

Other than `AbstractModel`, a third model type is available: `models.TransientModel`. This has a database representation like `models.Model`, but the records that are created there are supposed to be temporary and regularly purged by a server-scheduled job. Other than that, transient models work just like regular models.

`models.TransientModel` is useful for more complex user interactions, known as **wizards**. The wizard is used to request inputs from the user. In *Chapter 8, Advanced Server-Side Development Techniques*, we explore how to use these for advanced user interaction.

5
Basic Server-Side Development

In *Chapter 4*, *Application Models*, we saw how to declare or extend business models in custom modules. The recipes in that chapter covered writing methods for computed fields, as well as methods to constrain the values of fields. This chapter focuses on the basics of server-side development in Odoo method definitions, recordset manipulation, and extending inherited methods. With this, you will be able to add/modify business logins in the Odoo module.

In this chapter, we will cover the following recipes:

- Defining model methods and using API decorators
- Reporting errors to the user
- Obtaining an empty recordset for a different model
- Creating new records
- Updating values of recordset records
- Searching for records
- Combining recordsets
- Filtering recordsets

- Traversing recordset relations
- Sorting recordsets
- Extending the business logic defined in a model
- Extending `write()` and `create()`
- Customizing how records are searched
- Fetching data in groups using `read_group()`

Technical requirements

The technical requirements for this chapter include Odoo's online platform.

All the code used in this chapter can be downloaded from the following GitHub repository at `https://github.com/PacktPublishing/Odoo-14-Development-Cookbook-Fourth-Edition/tree/master/Chapter05`.

Defining model methods and using API decorators

In Odoo models, a class is a mixture of field definitions and business logic methods. In *Chapter 4, Application Models*, we saw how to add fields to a model. Now we will see how to add methods and business logic to a model.

In this recipe, we will see how we can write a method that can be called by a button in the user interface, or by another piece of code in our application. This method will act on `LibraryBook` and perform the required actions to change the state of a selection of books.

Getting ready

This recipe assumes that you have an instance ready, with the `my_library` add-on module available, as described in *Chapter 3, Creating Odoo Add-On Modules*. You will need to add a `state` field to the `LibraryBook` model, which is defined as follows:

```
from odoo import models, fields, api
class LibraryBook(models.Model):
    # [...]
    state = fields.Selection([
        ('draft', 'Unavailable'),
```

```
        ('available', 'Available'),
        ('borrowed', 'Borrowed'),
        ('lost', 'Lost')],
    'State', default="draft")
```

Refer to the *Adding models* recipe in *Chapter 3, Creating Odoo Add-On Modules*, for more information.

How to do it...

To define a method on library books to change the state of a selection of books, you need to add the following code to the model definition:

1. Add a helper method to check whether a state transition is allowed:

    ```
    @api.model
    def is_allowed_transition(self, old_state, new_state):
        allowed = [('draft', 'available'),
                   ('available', 'borrowed'),
                   ('borrowed', 'available'),
                   ('available', 'lost'),
                   ('borrowed', 'lost'),
                   ('lost', 'available')]
        return (old_state, new_state) in allowed
    ```

2. Add a method to change the state of some books to a new state that is passed as an argument:

    ```
    def change_state(self, new_state):
        for book in self:
            if book.is_allowed_transition(book.state, new_state):
                book.state = new_state
            else:
                continue
    ```

3. Add a method to change the book state by calling the `change_state` method:

   ```
   def make_available(self):
       self.change_state('available')

   def make_borrowed(self):
       self.change_state('borrowed')

   def make_lost(self):
       self.change_state('lost')
   ```

4. Add a button and status bar in the `<form>` view. This will help us trigger these methods from the user interface:

   ```
   <form>
   ...
       <button name="make_available" string="Make Available" type="object"/>
       <button name="make_borrowed" string="Make Borrowed" type="object"/>
       <button name="make_lost" string="Make Lost" type="object"/>
       <field name="state" widget="statusbar"/>
   ...
   </form>
   ```

Update or install the module to make these changes available.

How it works...

The code in this recipe defines a few methods. They are normal Python methods that have `self` as their first argument, and can have additional arguments as well. Some methods are decorated with **decorators** from the `odoo.api` module.

> **Tip**
>
> The API decorators were initially introduced in Odoo 9.0 to support both old and new frameworks. As of Odoo 10.0, the old API is no longer supported, but some decorators, such as `@api.model`, are still being used.

When writing a new method, if you don't use any decorator, then the method is executed on a recordset. In such methods, self is a recordset that can refer to an arbitrary number of database records (this includes empty recordsets), and the code will often loop over the records in self to do something on each individual record.

The @api.model decorator is similar, but it's used on methods for which only the model is important, not the contents of the recordset, which is not acted upon by the method. The concept is similar to Python's @classmethod decorator.

In *step 1*, we created the is_allowed_transition() method. The purpose of this method is to verify whether a transition from one state to another is valid. The tuples in the allowed list are the available transitions. For example, we don't want to allow a transition from lost to borrow, which is why we haven't put ('lost, 'borrowed').

In *step 2*, we created the change_state() method. The purpose of this method is to change the status of the book. When this method is called, it changes the status of the book to the state given by the new_state parameter. It only changes the book status if the transition is allowed. We used a for loop here because self can contain multiple recordsets.

In *step 3*, we created the methods that change the state of the book by calling the change_state() method. In our case, this method will be triggered by the buttons that were added to the user interface.

In *step 4*, we added <button> in the <form> view. Upon clicking this button, the Odoo web client will invoke the Python function mentioned in the name attribute. Refer to the *Adding buttons to forms* recipe in *Chapter 9, Backend Views*, to learn how to call such a method from the user interface. We have also added the state field with the statusbar widget to display the status of the book in the <form> view.

When the user clicks on the button from the user interface, one of the methods from *step 3* will be called. Here, self will be the recordset that contains the record of the library.book model. After that, we call the change_state() method and pass the appropriate parameter based on the button that was clicked.

When change_state() is called, self is the same recordset of the library.book model. The body of the change_state() method loops over self to process each book in the recordset. Looping on self looks strange at first, but you will get used to this pattern very quickly.

Inside the loop, `change_state()` calls `is_allowed_transition()`. The call is made using the `book` local variable, but it can be made on any recordset for the `library.book` model, including, for example, `self`, since `is_allowed_transition()` is decorated with `@api.model`. If the transition is allowed, `change_state()` assigns the new state to the book by assigning a value to the attribute of the recordset. This is only valid on recordsets with a length of 1, which is guaranteed to be the case when iterating over `self`.

Reporting errors to the user

During method execution, it is sometimes necessary to abort processing because the action that's requested by the user isn't valid or an error condition has been met. This recipe shows you how to manage these cases by showing a helpful error message.

Getting ready

This recipe assumes that you have an instance ready, with the `my_library` add-on module available, as described in the previous recipe.

How to do it...

We will make a change to the `change_state` method from the previous recipe and display a helpful message when the user is trying to change the state that is not allowed by the `is_allowed_transition` method. Perform the following steps to get started:

1. Add the following import at the beginning of the Python file:

   ```
   from odoo.exceptions import UserError
   from odoo.tools.translate import _
   ```

2. Modify the `change_state` method and raise a `UserError` exception from the `else` part:

   ```
   def change_state(self, new_state):
       for book in self:
           if book.is_allowed_transition(book.state, new_state):
               book.state = new_state
           else:
               msg = _('Moving from %s to %s is not
   ```

```
        allowed') % (book.state, new_state)
                raise UserError(msg)
```

How it works...

When an exception is raised in Python, it propagates up the call stack until it is processed. In Odoo, the **RPC** (**remote procedure call**) layer that answers the calls made by the web client catches all exceptions and, depending on the exception class, triggers different possible behaviors on the web client.

Any exception not defined in `odoo.exceptions` will be handled as an internal server error (**HTTP status** `500`) with the stack trace. `UserError` will display an error message in the user interface. The code of the recipe raises `UserError` to ensure that the message is displayed in a user-friendly way. In all cases, the *current database transaction is rolled back*.

We are using a function with a strange name, `_()`, which is defined in `odoo.tools.translate`. This function is used to mark a string as translatable, and to retrieve the translated string at runtime, given the language of the end user that's found in the execution context. More information on this is available in *Chapter 11, Internationalization*.

> **Important note**
> When using the `_()` function, ensure that you pass only strings with the interpolation placeholder, not the whole interpolated string. For example, `_('Warning: could not find %s') % value` is correct, but `_('Warning: could not find %s' % value)` is incorrect because the first one will not find the string with the substituted value in the translation database.

There's more...

Sometimes, you are working on error-prone code, meaning that the operation you are performing may generate an error. Odoo will catch this error and display a traceback to the user. If you don't want to show a full error log to the user, you can cache the error and raise a custom exception with a meaningful message. In the example provided, we are generating `UserError` from the `try...cache` block so that instead of showing a full error log, Odoo will now show a warning with a meaningful message:

```
def post_to_webservice(self, data):
    try:
```

```
            req = requests.post('http://my-test-service.com',
data=data, timeout=10)
            content = req.json()
    except IOError:
            error_msg = _("Something went wrong during data
submission")
            raise UserError(error_msg)
    return content
```

There are a few more exception classes defined in `odoo.exceptions`, all deriving from the base legacy `except_orm` exception class. Most of them are only used internally, apart from the following:

- `ValidationError`: This exception is raised when a Python constraint on a field is not respected. In *Chapter 4*, *Application Models*, refer to the *Adding constraint validations to a model* recipe for more information.

- `AccessError`: This error is usually generated automatically when the user tries to access something that is not allowed. You can raise the error manually if you want to show the access error from your code.

- `RedirectWarning`: With this error, you can show a redirection button with the error message. You need to pass two parameters to this exception: the first parameter is the action ID, and the second parameter is the error message.

- `Warning`: In Odoo 8.0, `odoo.exceptions.Warning` played the same role as `UserError` in 9.0 and later. It is now deprecated because the name was deceptive (it is an error, not a warning) and it collided with the Python built-in `Warning` class. It is kept for backward compatibility only, and you should use `UserError` in your code.

Obtaining an empty recordset for a different model

When writing Odoo code, the methods of the current model are available through `self`. If you need to work on a different model, it is not possible to directly instantiate the class of that model; you need to get a recordset for that model to start working.

This recipe shows you how to get an empty recordset for any model that's registered in Odoo inside a model method.

Getting ready

This recipe will reuse the setup of the library example in the `my_library` add-on module.

We will write a small method in the `library.book` model and search for all `library.members`. To do this, we need to get an empty recordset for `library.members`. Make sure you have added the `library.members` model and access rights for that model.

How to do it...

To get a recordset for `library.members` in a method of `library.book`, you need to perform the following steps:

1. In the `LibraryBook` class, write a method called `get_all_library_members`:

   ```
   class LibraryBook(models.Model):
       # ...
       def log_all_library_members(self):
           # This is an empty recordset of model library.member
           library_member_model = self.env['library.member']
           all_members = library_member_model.search([])
           print("ALL MEMBERS:", all_members)
           return True
   ```

2. Add a button to the `<form>` view to invoke our method:

   ```
   <button name="log_all_library_members" string="Log Members" type="object"/>
   ```

Update the module to apply the changes. After that, you will see the **Log Members** button in the book's `<form>` view. Upon clicking that button, you will see the member's recordset in the server log.

How it works...

At startup, Odoo loads all the modules and combines the various classes that derive from `Model`, and also defines or extends the given model. These classes are stored in the Odoo **registry**, indexed by name. The `env` attribute of any recordset, available as `self.env`, is an instance of the `Environment` class defined in the `odoo.api` module.

The `Environment` class plays a central role in Odoo development:

- It provides shortcut access to the registry by emulating a Python dictionary. If you know the name of the model you're looking for, `self.env[model_name]` will get you an empty recordset for that model. Moreover, the recordset will share the environment of `self`.
- It has a `cr` attribute, which is a database cursor you may use to pass raw SQL queries. Refer to the *Executing raw SQL queries* recipe in *Chapter 8, Advanced Server-Side Development Techniques*, for more information on this.
- It has a `user` attribute, which is a reference to the current user performing the call. Take a look at *Chapter 8, Advanced Server-Side Development Techniques*, and the *Changing the user performing an action* recipe for more on this.
- It has a `context` attribute, which is a dictionary that contains the context of the call. This includes information about the language of the user, the time zone, the current selection of records, and much more. Refer to the *Calling a method with a modified context* recipe in *Chapter 8, Advanced Server-Side Development Techniques*, for more on this.

The call to `search()` is explained in the *Searching for records* recipe later.

See also

Sometimes, you want to use a modified version of the environment. One such example is that you want an environment with a different user and language. In *Chapter 8, Advanced Server-Side Development Techniques*, you will learn how to modify the environment at runtime.

Creating new records

A common requirement when writing business logic methods is the creation of new records. This recipe explains how to create records of the `library.book.category` model. For our example, we will add a method that will create dummy categories for the `library.book.category` model. To trigger this method, we will add a button to the `<form>` view.

Getting ready

You need to know the structure of the models for which you want to create a record, especially their names and types, as well as any constraints that exist on these fields (for example, whether some of them are mandatory).

For this recipe, we will reuse the `my_library` module from *Chapter 4, Application Models*. Take a look at the following example to quickly recall the `library.book.category` model:

```python
class BookCategory(models.Model):
    _name = 'library.book.category'

    name = fields.Char('Category')
    description = fields.Text('Description')
    parent_id = fields.Many2one(
        'library.book.category',
        string='Parent Category',
        ondelete='restrict',
        index=True
    )
    child_ids = fields.One2many(
        'library.book.category', 'parent_id',
        string='Child Categories')
```

Make sure you have added menus, views, and access rights for the `library.book.category` model.

How to do it...

To create a category with some child categories, you need to perform the following steps:

1. Create a method in the `library.book.category` model with the name `create_categories`:

   ```python
   def create_categories(self):
       ......
   ```

2. Inside the body of this method, prepare a dictionary of values for the fields of the first child category:

   ```python
   categ1 = {
       'name': 'Child category 1',
       'description': 'Description for child 1'
   }
   ```

3. Prepare a dictionary of values for the fields of the second category:

```
categ2 = {
    'name': 'Child category 2',
    'description': 'Description for child 2'
}
```

4. Prepare a dictionary of values for the fields of the parent category:

```
parent_category_val = {
    'name': 'Parent category',
    'email': 'Description for parent category',
    'child_ids': [
        (0, 0, categ1),
        (0, 0, categ2),
    ]
}
```

5. Call the `create()` method to create the new records:

```
record = self.env['library.book.category'].create(parent_category_val)
```

6. Add a button in the `<form>` view to trigger the `create_categories` method from the user interface:

```
<button name="create_categories" string="Create Categories" type="object"/>
```

How it works...

To create a new record for a model, we can call the `create(values)` method on any recordset related to the model. This method returns a new recordset with a length of 1 and contains the new record, with the field values specified in the `values` dictionary.

In the dictionary, the keys give the name of the fields, and the corresponding values correspond to the value of the field. Depending on the field type, you need to pass different Python types for the values:

- `Text` field values are given with Python strings.
- `Float` and `Integer` field values are given using Python floats or integers.
- `Boolean` field values are given preferably using Python Booleans or integers.

- `Date` field values are given with the Python `datetime.date` object.
- `Datetime` field values are given with the Python `datetime.datetime` object.
- `Binary` field values are passed as a Base64-encoded string. The `base64` module from the Python standard library provides methods such as `encodebytes(bytestring)` to encode a string in Base64.
- `Many2one` field values are given with an integer, which has to be the database ID of the related record.
- `One2many` and `Many2many` fields use a special syntax. The value is a list that contains tuples of three elements, as follows:

Tuple	Effect
(0, 0, dict_val)	Creates a new record that will be related to the main record.
(6, 0, id_list)	Creates a relation between the record being created and existing records, whose IDs are in the Python list called id_list. Caution: When used on a `One2many` field, this will remove the records from any previous relation.

Table 5.1

In this recipe, we create the dictionaries for two contacts in the company we want to create, and then we use these dictionaries in the `child_ids` entry of the dictionary for the company being created by using the `(0, 0, dict_val)` syntax we explained earlier.

When `create()` is called in *step 5*, three records are created:

- One for the parent book category, which is returned by `create`
- Two records for the child book category, which are available in `record.child_ids`

There's more...

If the model defined some **default values** for some fields, nothing special needs to be done. `create()` will take care of computing the default values for the fields that aren't present in the supplied dictionary.

The `create()` method also supports the creation of records in a batch. To create multiple records in a batch, you need to pass a list of multiple values to the `create()` method, as shown in the following example:

```
categ1 = {
    'name': 'Category 1',
    'description': 'Description for Category 1'
}
categ2 = {
    'name': 'Category 2',
    'description': 'Description for Category 2'
}
multiple_records = self.env['library.book.category'].
create([categ1, categ2])
```

Updating values of recordset records

Business logic often requires us to update records by changing the values of some of their fields. This recipe shows you how to modify the `date` field of the partner as we go.

Getting ready

This recipe will use the same simplified `library.book` definition of the *Creating new records* recipe. You may refer to this simplified definition to find out about the fields.

We have the `date_release` field in the `library.book` model. For illustration purposes, we will write in this field with the click of a button.

How to do it...

1. To update a book's `date_updated` field, you can write a new method called `change_update_date()`, which is defined as follows:

```
def change_release_date(self):
    self.ensure_one()
    self.date_release = fields.Date.today()
```

2. Then, you can add a button to the book's `<form>` view in xml, as follows:

   ```
   <button name="change_release_date" string="Update Date"
   type="object"/>
   ```

3. Restart the server and update the `my_library` module to see the changes. Upon clicking the **Update Date** button, `update_date` will be changed.

How it works...

The method starts by checking whether the book recordset that's passed as `self` contains exactly one record by calling `ensure_one()`. This method will raise an exception if this is not the case, and the processing will abort. This is necessary because we don't want to change the date of multiple records. If you want to update multiple values, you can remove `ensure_one()` and update the attribute using a loop on the recordset.

Finally, the method modifies the values of the attributes of the book record. It updates the `date_release` field with the current date. Just by modifying the field attributes of the recordset, you can perform write operations.

There's more...

There are three options available if you want to write new values to the fields of records:

- Option one is the one that was explained in this recipe. It works in all contexts by assigning values directly to the attribute representing the field of the record. It isn't possible to assign a value to all recordset elements in one go, so you need to iterate on the recordset, unless you are certain that you are only handling a single record.

- Option two is to use the `update()` method by passing dictionary mapping field names to the values you want to set. This also only works for recordsets with a length of 1. It can save some typing when you need to update the values of several fields at once on the same record. Here's *Step 2* of the recipe, rewritten to use this option:

  ```
  def change_update_date(self):
      self.ensure_one()
      self.update({
          'date_release': fields.Datetime.now(),
          'another_field': 'value'
          ...
      })
  ```

- Option three is to call the `write()` method, passing a dictionary that maps the field names to the values you want to set. This method works for recordsets of arbitrary size and will update all records with the specified values in one single database operation when the two previous options perform one database call per record and per field. However, it has some limitations: it does not work if the records are not yet present in the database (refer to the *Writing on change methods* recipe in *Chapter 8*, *Advanced Server-Side Development Techniques*, for more information on this). Also, it requires a special format when writing relational fields, similar to the one used by the `create()` method. Check the following table for the format that's used to generate different values for the relational fields:

Tuple	Effect
`(0, 0, dict_val)`	This creates a new record that will be related to the main record.
`(1, id, dict_val)`	This updates the related record with the specified ID with the values supplied.
`(2, id)`	This removes the record with the specified ID from the related records and deletes it from the database.
`(3, id)`	This removes the record with the specified ID from the related records. The record is not deleted from the database.
`(4, id)`	This adds an existing record with the supplied ID to the list of related records.
`(5, )`	This removes all the related records, equivalent to calling `(3, id)` for each related `id`.
`(6, 0, id_list)`	This creates a relation between the record being updated and the existing record, whose IDs are in the Python list called `id_list`.

Table 5.2

> **Important note**
> Operation types 1, 2, 3, and 5 cannot be used with the `create()` method.

Searching for records

Searching for records is also a common operation in business logic methods. This recipe shows you how to find the book by name and category.

Getting ready

This recipe will use the same `library.book` definition as the *Creating new records* recipe did previously. We will write the code in a method called `find_book(self)`.

How to do it...

To find the books, you need to perform the following steps:

1. Add the `find_book` method to the `library.book` model:

   ```
   def find_book(self):
       ...
   ```

2. Write the search domain for your criteria:

   ```
   domain = [
       '|',
           '&', ('name', 'ilike', 'Book Name'),
                ('category_id.name', 'ilike', 'Category Name'),
           '&', ('name', 'ilike', 'Book Name 2'),
                ('category_id.name', 'ilike', 'Category Name 2')
   ]
   ```

3. Call the `search()` method with the domain, which will return the recordset:

   ```
   books = self.search(domain)
   ```

The `books` variable will have a recordset of searched books. You can print or log that variable to see the result in the server log.

How it works...

Step 1 defines the method.

Step 2 creates a search domain in a local variable. Often, you'll see this creation inline in the call to search, but with complex domains, it is good practice to define it separately.

For a full explanation of the *search domain* syntax, refer to the *Defining filters on record lists – domain* recipe in *Chapter 9, Backend Views*.

Step 3 calls the `search()` method with the domain. The method returns a recordset that contains all the records that match the domain, which can then be processed further. In this recipe, we call the method with just the domain, but the following keyword arguments are also supported:

- `offset=N`: This is used to skip the first N records that match the query. This can be used along with `limit` to implement pagination or to reduce memory consumption when processing a very large number of records. It defaults to 0.

- `limit=N`: This indicates that, at most, N records should be returned. By default, there is no limit.

- `order=sort_specification`: This is used to force the order in the recordset returned. By default, the order is given by the `_order` attribute of the model class.

- `count=boolean`: If `True`, this returns the number of records instead of the recordset. It defaults to `False`.

> **Important note**
> We recommend using the `search_count(domain)` method rather than `search(domain, count=True)`, as the name of the method conveys the behavior in a much clearer way. Both will give the same result.

Sometimes, you need to search from another model so that searching for `self` will return a recordset of the current model. To search from another model, we need to get an empty recordset for the model. For example, let's say we want to search some contacts. To do that, we will need to use the `search()` method on the `res.partner` model. Refer to the following code. Here we get the empty recordset of `res.partner` to search the contacts:

```
def find_partner(self):
    PartnerObj = self.env['res.partner']
    domain = [
        '&', ('name', 'ilike', 'Parth Gajjar'),
            ('company_id.name', '=', 'Odoo')
    ]
    partner = PartnerObj.search(domain)
```

In the preceding code, you can omit the `'&'` from the domain, because when you do not specify the domain, then Odoo will take `'&'` as a default.

There's more...

We said previously that the `search()` method returned all the records matching the domain. This is not actually completely true. The security rules ensure that the user only gets those records to which they have `read` access rights. Additionally, if the model has a `boolean` field called **active** and no term of the search domain specifies a condition on that field, then an implicit condition is added by search to only return `active=True` records. So, if you expect a search to return something, but you only get empty recordsets, ensure that you check the value of the `active` field (if present) to check for **record rules**.

Refer to the *Calling a method with a different context* recipe in *Chapter 8, Advanced Server-Side Development Techniques*, for a way to not have the implicit `active=True` condition added. Take a look at the *Limiting record access using record rules* recipe in *Chapter 10, Security Access*, for more information about record-level access rules.

If, for some reason, you find yourself writing raw SQL queries to find record IDs, ensure that you use `self.env['record.model'].search([('id', 'in', tuple(ids))]).ids` after retrieving the IDs to ensure that security rules are applied. This is especially important in **multi-company** Odoo instances where the record rules are used to ensure proper discrimination between companies.

Combining recordsets

Sometimes, you will find that you have obtained recordsets that are not exactly what you need. This recipe shows various ways of combining them.

Getting ready

To use this recipe, you need to have two or more recordsets for the same model.

How to do it...

Perform the following steps to perform common operations on recordsets:

1. To merge two recordsets into one while preserving their order, use the following operation:

   ```
   result = recordset1 + recordset2
   ```

2. To merge two recordsets into one while ensuring that there are no duplicates in the result, use the following operation:

   ```
   result = recordset1 | recordset2
   ```

3. To find the records that are common to two recordsets, use the following operation:

```
result = recordset1 & recordset2
```

How it works...

The class for recordsets implements various Python operator redefinitions, which are used here. Here's a summary table of the most useful Python operators that can be used on recordsets:

Operator	Action performed
R1 + R2	This returns a new recordset containing the records from R1, followed by the records from R2. This can generate duplicate records in the recordset.
R1 - R2	This returns a new recordset consisting of the records from R1 that are not in R2. The order is preserved.
R1 & R2	This returns a new recordset with all the records that belong to both R1 and R2 (intersection of recordsets). The order is *not* preserved here, but there are no duplicates.
R1 | R2	This returns a new recordset with the records belonging to either R1 or R2 (union of recordsets). The order is *not* preserved, but there are no duplicates.
R1 == R2	True if both recordsets contain the same records.
R1 <= R2 R1 < R2	True if all records in R1 are a subset of R2. Both syntaxes are equivalent.
R1 >= R2	True if all records in R1 are a superset of R2. Both syntaxes are equivalent.
R1 != R2	True if R1 and R2 do not contain the same records.
R1 in R2	True if R1 (must be one record) is part of R2.
R1 not in R2	True if R1 (must be one record) is not part of R2.

Table 5.3

There are also in-place operators, +=, -=, &=, and |=, which modify the left-hand side operand instead of creating a new recordset. These are very useful when updating a record's One2many or Many2many fields. Refer to the *Updating values of recordset records* recipe for an example of this.

Filtering recordsets

In some cases, you already have a recordset, but only you need to operate on certain records. You can, of course, iterate on the recordset, checking for the condition on each iteration and acting depending on the result of the check. It can be easier, and in some cases, more efficient, to construct a new recordset containing only the interesting records and calling a single operation on that recordset.

This recipe shows you how to use the `filter()` method to extract a subset of recordsets based on a condition.

Getting ready

We will reuse the simplified `library.book` model that was shown in the *Creating new records* recipe. This recipe defines a method to extract books that have multiple authors from a supplied recordset.

How to do it...

To extract records that have multiple authors from a recordset, you need to perform the following steps:

1. Define the method to accept the original recordset:

   ```
   @api.model
   def books_with_multiple_authors(self, all_books):
   ```

2. Define an inner predicate function:

   ```
   def predicate(book):
       if len(book.author_ids) > 1:
           return True
       return False
   ```

3. Call `filter()`, as follows:

   ```
   return all_books.filter(predicate)
   ```

You can print or log the result of this method to see it in a server log. Refer to the example code of this recipe for more.

How it works...

The implementation of the `filter()` method creates an empty recordset. All the records for which the predicate function evaluates to `True` are added to this empty recordset. The new recordset is finally returned. The order of records in the original recordset is preserved.

The preceding recipe used a named internal function. For such simple predicates, you will often find an anonymous Lambda function being used:

```
@api.model
def books_with_multiple_authors(self, all_books):
    return all_books.filter(lambda b: len(b.author_ids) > 1)
```

Actually, you need to filter a recordset based on the fact that the value of a field is *truthy* in the Python sense (non-empty strings, non-zero numbers, non-empty containers, and so on). So, if you want to filter records that have a category set, you can pass the field name to filter like this: `all_books.filter('category_id')`.

There's more...

Keep in mind that `filter()` operates in memory. If you are trying to optimize the performance of a method on the critical path, you may want to use a search domain or even move to SQL, at the cost of readability.

Traversing recordset relations

When working with a recordset with a length of 1, various fields are available as record attributes. Relational attributes (`One2many`, `Many2one`, and `Many2many`) are also available with values that are recordsets, too. As an example, let's say we want to access the name of the category from the recordset of the `library.book` model. You can access the category name by traversing through the `Many2one` field's `category_id` as follows: `book.category_id.name`. However, when working with recordsets with more than one record, the attributes cannot be used.

This recipe shows you how to use the `mapped()` method to traverse recordset relations. We will write a method to retrieve the names of authors from the recordset of books, passed as an argument.

Getting ready

We will reuse the `library.book` model that was shown in the *Creating new records* recipe in this chapter.

How to do it...

To get the names of authors from the book recordset, you need to perform the following steps:

1. Define a method called `get_author_names()`:

   ```
   @api.model
   def get_author_names(self, books):
   ```

2. Call `mapped()` to get the email addresses of the contacts of the partner:

   ```
   return books.mapped('author_ids.name')
   ```

How it works...

Step 1 is just defining the method. In *step 2*, we call the `mapped(path)` method to traverse the fields of the recordset; `path` is a string that contains field names separated by dots. For each field in the path, `mapped()` produces a new recordset that contains all the records related by this field to all elements in the current recordset, and then the next element in the path applies to that new recordset. If the last field in the path is a relational field, `mapped()` will return a recordset; otherwise, a Python list is returned.

The `mapped()` method has two useful properties:

- If the path is a single scalar field name, then the returned list is in the same order as the processed recordset.
- If the path contains a relational field, then the order is not preserved, but duplicates are removed from the result.

> **Important information**
>
> This second property is very useful when you want to perform an operation on all the records that are pointed to by a `Many2many` field for all the records in `self`, but you need to ensure that the action is performed only once (even if two records of `self` share the same target record).

There's more...

When using `mapped()`, keep in mind that it operates in memory inside the Odoo server by repeatedly traversing relations and therefore making SQL queries, which may not be efficient. However, the code is terse and expressive. If you are trying to optimize a method on the critical path of the performance of your instance, you may want to rewrite the call to `mapped()` and express it as `search()` with the appropriate domain, or even move to SQL (at the cost of readability).

The `mapped()` method can also be called with a function as an argument. In this case, it returns a list containing the result of the function that's applied to each record of `self`, or the union of the recordsets that's returned by the function, if the function returns a recordset.

See also

- The *Searching for records* recipe in this chapter
- The *Executing raw SQL queries* recipe in *Chapter 8, Advanced Server-Side Development Techniques*

Sorting recordsets

When you fetch a recordset with the `search()` method, you can pass an optional argument order to get a recordset that's in a particular order. This is useful if you already have a recordset from a previous bit of code and you want to sort it. It may also be useful if you use a set operation to combine two recordsets, for example, which would cause the order to be lost.

This recipe shows you how to use the `sorted()` method to sort an existing recordset. We will sort books by release date.

Getting ready

We will reuse the `library.book` model that was shown in the *Creating new records* recipe in this chapter.

How to do it...

You need to perform the following steps to get the sorted recordset of books based on `release_date`:

1. Define a method called `sort_books_by_date()`:

   ```
   @api.model
   def sort_books_by_date(self, books):
   ```

2. Use the `sorted()` method, as in the given example, to sort book records based on the `release_date` field:

   ```
   return books.sorted(key='release_date')
   ```

How it works...

Step 1 is just defining the method. In *step 2*, we call the `sorted()` method in the recordset of books. Internally, the `sorted()` method will fetch the data of the field that's passed as the key argument. Then, by using Python's native `sorted` method, it returns a sorted recordset.

It also has one optional argument, `reverse=True`, which returns a recordset in reverse order. `reverse` is used as follows:

```
books.sorted(key='release_date', reverse=True)
```

There's more...

The `sorted()` method will sort the records in a recordset. Called without arguments, the `_order` attribute of the model will be used. Otherwise, a function can be passed to compute a comparison key in the same way as the Python built-in sorted (sequence, key) function.

> **Important note**
>
> When the default `_order` parameter of the model is used, the sorting is delegated to the database, and a new `SELECT` function is performed to get the order. Otherwise, the sorting is performed by Odoo. Depending on what is being manipulated, and depending on the size of the recordsets, there might be some important performance differences.

Extending the business logic defined in a model

It is a very common practice in Odoo to divide application features into different modules. By doing so, you can simply enable/disable features by installing/uninstalling the application. And when you add new features to the existing app, it then becomes necessary to customize the behavior of some methods that were defined in the original app. Sometimes, you also want to add new fields to an existing model. This is a very easy task in Odoo, and one of the most powerful features of the underlying framework.

In this recipe, we will see how you can extend the business logic of one method from the method in another module. We will also add new fields to an existing module from the new module.

Getting ready

For this recipe, we will continue to use the my_library module from the last recipe. Make sure that you have the library.book.category model in the my_library module.

For this recipe, we will create a new module called my_library_return, which depends on the my_library module. In this module, we will manage return dates for the borrowed book. We will also automatically calculate the return date based on the category.

In the *Adding features to a model using inheritance* recipe in *Chapter 4, Application Models*, we saw how to add a field to the existing model. In this module, extend the library.book model as follows:

```
class LibraryBook(models.Model):
    _inherit = 'library.book'

    date_return = fields.Date('Date to return')
```

Then, extend the library.book.category model, as follows:

```
class LibraryBookCategory(models.Model):
    _inherit = 'library.book.category'

    max_borrow_days = fields.Integer(
        'Maximum borrow days',
```

```
            help="For how many days book can be borrowed",
            default=10)
```

To add this field in views, you need to follow the *Changing existing views – view inheritance* recipe from *Chapter 9, Backend Views*. You can find a full example of the code at `https://github.com/PacktPublishing/Odoo-13-Development-Cookbook-Fourth-Edition`.

How to do it...

To extend the business logic in the `library.book` model, you need to perform the following steps:

1. From `my_library_return`, we want to set `date_return` in the books record when we change the book status to `Borrowed`. For this, we will override the `make_borrowed` method from the `my_module_return` module:

    ```python
    def make_borrowed(self):
        day_to_borrow = self.category_id.max_borrow_days or 10
        self.date_return = fields.Date.today() + timedelta(days=day_to_borrow)
        return super(LibraryBook, self).make_borrowed()
    ```

2. We also want to reset `date_return` when the book is returned and available to borrow, so we will override the `make_available` method to reset the date:

    ```python
    def make_available(self):
        self.date_return = False
        return super(LibraryBook, self).make_available()
    ```

How it works...

Steps 1 and *2* carry out the extension of the business logic. We define a model that extends `library.books` and redefines the `make_borrowed()` and `make_available()` methods. In the last line of both methods, the result that was implemented by the parent class is returned:

```python
return super(LibraryBook, self).make_borrowed()
```

In the case of Odoo models, the parent class is not what you'd expect by looking at the Python class definition. The framework has dynamically generated a class hierarchy for our recordset, and the parent class is the definition of the model from the modules that we depend on. So, the call to `super()` brings back the implementation of `library.book` from `my_module`. In this implementation, `make_borrowed()` changes the state of the book to `Borrowed`. So, calling `super()` will invoke the parent method and it will set the book state to `Borrowed`.

There's more...

In this recipe, we choose to extend the default implementation of the methods. In the `make_borrow()` and `make_available()` methods, we modified the returned result *before* the `super()` call. Note that, when you call `super()`, it will execute the default implementation. It is also possible to perform some actions *after* the `super()` call. Of course, we can also do both at the same time.

However, it is more difficult to change the behavior of the middle of a method. To do this, we will need to refactor the code so that we can extract an extension point to a separate method and override this new method in the extension module.

You may be tempted to completely rewrite a method. Always be very cautious when doing so. If you do not call the `super()` implementation of your method, you are breaking the extension mechanism and potentially breaking the add-ons that extend the method, meaning that the extension methods will never be called. Unless you are working in a controlled environment in which you know exactly which add-ons are installed and you've checked that you are not breaking them, avoid doing this. Also, if you have to, ensure that you document what you are doing in a very visible way.

What can you do before and after calling the original implementation of the method? There are lots of things, including (but not limited to) the following:

- Modifying the arguments that are passed to the original implementation (before)
- Modifying the context that is passed to the original implementation (before)
- Modifying the result that is returned by the original implementation (after)
- Calling another method (before and after)
- Creating records (before and after)
- Raising a `UserError` error to cancel the execution in forbidden cases (before and after)
- Splitting `self` into smaller recordsets, and calling the original implementation on each of the subsets in a different way (before)

Extending write() and create()

The *Extending the business logic defined in a model* recipe from this chapter showed us how to extend methods that are defined on a model class. If you think about it, methods that are defined on the parent class of the model are also part of the model. This means that all the base methods that are defined on `models.Model` (actually, on `models.BaseModel`, which is the parent class of `models.Model`) are also available and can be extended.

This recipe shows you how to extend `create()` and `write()` to control access to some fields of the records.

Getting ready

We will extend the library example from the `my_library` add-on module in *Chapter 3, Creating Odoo Add-On Modules*.

Add a `manager_remarks` field to the `library.book` model. We only want members of the `Library Managers` group to be able to write to that field:

```
from odoo import models, api, exceptions
class LibraryBook(models.Model):
    _name = 'library.book'
    manager_remarks = fields.Text('Manager Remarks')
```

Add the `manager_remarks` field to the `<form>` view of the `view/library_book.xml` file to access this field from the user interface:

```
<field name="manager_remarks"/>
```

Modify the `security/ir.model.access.csv` file to give write access to library users:

```
id,name,model_id:id,group_id:id,perm_read,perm_write,perm_create,perm_unlink
acl_book_user,library.book_default,model_library_book,base.group_user,1,1,0,0
acl_book_librarian,library.book_librarian,model_library_book,group_librarian,1,1,1,1
```

How to do it...

To prevent users who are not members of the librarian group from modifying the value of `manager_remarks`, you need to perform the following steps:

1. Extend the `create()` method, as follows:

```python
@api.model
def create(self, values):
    if not self.user_has_groups('my_library.acl_book_librarian'):
        if 'manager_remarks' in values:
            raise UserError(
                'You are not allowed to modify '
                'manager_remarks'
            )
    return super(LibraryBook, self).create(values)
```

2. Extend the `write()` method, as follows:

```python
def write(self, values):
    if not self.user_has_groups('my_library.acl_book_librarian'):
        if 'manager_remarks' in values:
            raise UserError(
                'You are not allowed to modify '
                'manager_remarks'
            )
    return super(LibraryBook, self).write(values)
```

Install the module to see the code in action. Now, only a manager type of user can modify the `manager_remarks` field. To test this implementation, you can log in as a demo user or revoke librarian access from the current user.

How it works...

Step 1 redefines the `create()` method. Before calling the base implementation of `create()`, our method uses the `user_has_groups()` method to check whether the user belongs to the `my_library.group_librarian` group (this is the XML ID of the group). If this is not the case and a value is passed for `manager_remarks`, a `UserError` exception is raised, preventing the creation of the record. This check is performed before the base implementation is called.

Step 2 does the same thing for the `write()` method. Prior to writing, we check the group and the presence of the field in the values to write and raise a `UserError` exception if there is a problem.

> **Important note**
> Having the field set to read-only in the web client does not prevent RPC calls from writing it. This is why we extend `create()` and `write()`.

In this recipe, you have seen how you can override the `create()` and `write()` methods. But note that this is not limited to the `create()` and `write()` methods. You can override any model method. For example, let's say you want to do something when the record is deleted. To do so, you need to override the `unlink()` method (the `unlink()` method will be called when the record is deleted). Here is the small code snippet to override the `unlink()` method:

```
def unlink(self):
    # your logic
    return super(LibraryBook, self).unlink()
```

> **Warning**
> When overriding a method in Odoo, never forgot to call the `super()` method, otherwise you will encounter an issue. This is because when you don't use the `super()` method, the code in the original method is never executed. If, in our previous code snippet, we didn't call `super(...).unlink()`, records would not be deleted.

There's more...

When extending `write()`, note that, before calling the `super()` implementation of `write()`, `self` is still unmodified. You can use this to compare the current values of the fields to the ones in the `values` dictionary.

In this recipe, we chose to raise an exception, but we could have also chosen to remove the offending field from the `values` dictionary and silently skipped updating that field in the record:

```python
def write(self, values):
    if not self.user_has_groups( 'my_library.group_librarian'):
        if 'manager_remarks' in values:
            del values['manager_remarks']
    return super(LibraryBook, self).write(values)
```

After calling `super().write()`, if you want to perform additional actions, you have to be wary of anything that can cause another call to `write()`, or you will create an infinite recursion loop. The workaround is to put a marker in the context that will be checked to break the recursion:

```python
class MyModel(models.Model):
    def write(self, values):
        sup = super(MyModel, self).write(values)
        if self.env.context.get('MyModelLoopBreaker'):
            return
        self = self.with_context(MyModelLoopBreaker=True)
        self.compute_things() # can cause calls to writes
        return sup
```

In the preceding example, we have added the `MyModelLoopBreaker` key before calling the `compute_things()` method. So, if the `write()` method is called again, it doesn't go in an infinite loop.

Customizing how records are searched

The *Defining the model representation and order* recipe in *Chapter 3*, *Creating Odoo Add-On Modules*, introduced the `name_get()` method, which is used to compute a representation of the record in various places, including in the widget that's used to display `Many2one` relations in the web client.

This recipe will show you how to search for a book in the `Many2one` widget by title, author, or ISBN by redefining `name_search`.

Getting ready

For this recipe, we will use the following model definition:

```python
class LibraryBook(models.Model):
    _name = 'library.book'
    name = fields.Char('Title')
    isbn = fields.Char('ISBN')
    author_ids = fields.Many2many('res.partner', 'Authors')

    def name_get(self):
        result = []
        for book in self:
            authors = book.author_ids.mapped('name')
            name = '%s (%s)' % (book.name, ', '.join(authors))
            result.append((book.id, name))
        return result
```

When using this model, a book in a Many2one widget is displayed as **Book Title** (**Author1, Author2**...). Users expect to be able to type in an author's name and find the list filtered according to this name, but this will not work since the default implementation of name_search only uses the attribute referred to by the _rec_name attribute of the model class, which, in our case, is 'name'. We also want to allow filtering by ISBN number.

How to do it...

You need to perform the following steps in order to execute this recipe:

1. To be able to search for library.book either by the book's title, one of the authors, or the ISBN number, you need to define the _name_search() method in the LibraryBook class, as follows:

```python
@api.model
def _name_search(self, name='', args=None,
operator='ilike',
                limit=100, name_get_uid=None):
    args = [] if args is None else args.copy()
    if not(name == '' and operator == 'ilike'):
        args += ['|', '|',
```

```
                    ('name', operator, name),
                    ('isbn', operator, name),
                    ('author_ids.name', operator, name)
                ]
            return super(LibraryBook, self)._name_search(
                name=name, args=args, operator=operator,
                limit=limit, name_get_uid=name_get_uid)
```

2. Add the `old_editions` Many2one field in the `library.book` model to test the `_name_search` implementation:

   ```
   old_edition = fields.Many2one('library.book', string='Old Edition')
   ```

3. Add the following field to the user interface:

   ```
   <field name="old_edition" />
   ```

4. Restart and update the module to reflect these changes.

You can invoke the `_name_search` method by searching in the `old_edition` Many2one field.

How it works...

The default implementation of `name_search()` actually only calls the `_name_search()` method, which does the real job. This `_name_search()` method has an additional argument, `name_get_uid`, which is used in some corner cases such as if you want to compute the results using `sudo()` or with a different user.

We pass most of the arguments that we receive unchanged to the `super()` implementation of the method:

- `name` is a string that contains the value the user has typed so far.
- `args` is either `None` or a search domain that's used as a prefilter for the possible records. (It can come from the domain parameter of the `Many2one` relation, for instance.)
- `operator` is a string containing the match operator. Generally, you will have `'ilike'` or `'='`.

- `limit` is the maximum number of rows to retrieve.
- `name_get_uid` can be used to specify a different user when calling `name_get()` to compute the strings to display in the widget.

Our implementation of the method does the following:

1. It generates a new empty list if `args` is `None`, and makes a copy of `args` otherwise. We make a copy to avoid our modifications to the list having side effects on the caller.
2. Then, we check that `name` is not an empty string or that `operator` is not `'ilike'`. This is to avoid generating a dumb domain, `[('name', ilike, '')]`, that doesn't filter anything. In this case, we jump straight to the `super()` call implementation.
3. If we have `name`, or if `operator` is not `'ilike'`, then we add some filtering criteria to `args`. In our case, we add clauses that will search for the supplied name in the title of the books, in their ISBNs, or in the authors' names.
4. Finally, we call the `super()` implementation with the modified domain in `args` and force `name` to be `''` and `operator` to be `ilike`. We do this to force the default implementation of `_name_search()` to not alter the domain it receives, and so the one we specified will be used.

There's more...

We mentioned in the introduction that this method is used in the `Many2one` widget. For completeness, it is also used in the following parts of Odoo:

- When using the `in` operator on the `One2many` and `Many2many` fields in the domain
- To search for records in the `many2many_tags` widget
- To search for records in the CSV file import

See also

The *Defining the model representation and order* recipe in *Chapter 3, Creating Odoo Add-On Modules*, demonstrates how to define the `name_get()` method, which is used to create a text representation of a record.

The *Defining filters on record lists – domain* recipe in *Chapter 9, Backend Views*, provides more information about search domain syntax.

Fetching data in groups using read_group()

In the previous recipes, we saw how we can search and fetch data from the database. But sometimes, you want results by aggregating records, such as *the average cost of last month's sales order*. Usually, we use `group by` and the `aggregate` function in SQL queries for such a result. Luckily, in Odoo, we have the `read_group()` method. In this recipe, you will learn how to use the `read_group()` method to get the aggregate result.

Getting ready

In this recipe, we will use the `my_library` add-on module from *Chapter 3*, *Creating Odoo Add-On Modules*.

Modify the `library.book` model, as shown in the following model definition:

```
class LibraryBook(models.Model):
    _name = 'library.book'

    name = fields.Char('Title', required=True)
    date_release = fields.Date('Release Date')
    pages = fields.Integer('Number of Pages')
    cost_price = fields.Float('Book Cost')
    category_id = fields.Many2one('library.book.category')
    author_ids = fields.Many2many('res.partner',
 string='Authors')
```

Add the `library.book.category` model. For simplicity, we will just add it to the same `library_book.py` file:

```
class BookCategory(models.Model):
    _name = 'library.book.category'

    name = fields.Char('Category')
    description = fields.Text('Description')
```

We will be using the `library.book` model and getting an average cost price per category.

How to do it...

To extract grouped results, we will add the `_get_average_cost` method to the `library.book` model, which will use the `read_group()` method to fetch the data in a group:

```python
@api.model
def _get_average_cost(self):
    grouped_result = self.read_group(
        [('cost_price', "!=", False)], # Domain
        ['category_id', 'cost_price:avg'], # Fields to access
        ['category_id'] # group_by
    )
    return grouped_result
```

To test this implementation, you need to add a button to the user interface that triggers this method. Then, you can print the result in the server log.

How it works...

The `read_group()` method internally uses the SQL `groupby` and `aggregate` functions to fetch the data. The most common arguments that are passed to the `read_group()` method are as follows:

- `domain`: This is used to filter records for grouping. For more information on the domain, refer to the *Searching views* recipe in *Chapter 9, Backend Views*.
- `fields`: This passes the names of fields you want to fetch with the grouped data. Possible values for this argument are as follows:

  `field name`: You can pass the field name into the `fields` argument, but if you are using this option, then you must pass this field name to the `groupby` parameter too, otherwise it will generate an error.

  `field_name:agg`: You can pass the field name with the `aggregate` function. For example, in `cost_price:avg`, `avg` is a SQL aggregate function. A list of PostgreSQL aggregate functions can be found at https://www.postgresql.org/docs/current/static/functions-aggregate.html.

  `name:agg(field_name)`: This is the same as the previous one, but, with this syntax, you can provide column aliases, such as `average_price:avg(cost_price)`.

- `groupby`: This argument accepts a list of field descriptions. Records will be grouped based on these fields. For the `date` and `datetime` column, you can pass `groupby_function` to apply date groupings based on different time durations, such as `date_release:month`. This will apply groupings based on months.

- `read_group()` also supports some optional arguments, as follows:

    `offset`: This indicates an optional number of records to skip.

    `limit`: This indicates an optional maximum number of records to return.

    `orderby`: If this option is passed, the result will be sorted based on the given fields.

    `lazy`: This accepts Boolean values and, by default, is `True`. If `True` is passed, the results are only grouped by the first `groupby` and the remaining `groupby` are put in the __context key. If `False`, all `groupby` function are done in one call.

> **Performance tip**
>
> `read_group()` is a lot faster than reading and processing values from a recordset. So, for KPIs or graphs, you should always use `read_group()`.

6
Managing Module Data

In this chapter, we'll look at how add-on modules can provide data at installation time. This is useful for us when providing default values, adding metadata, such as view descriptions, menus, or actions. Another important usage is providing demonstration data, which is loaded when the database is created with the **Load demonstration data** checkbox checked.

In this chapter, we will cover the following recipes:

- Using external IDs and namespaces
- Loading data using XML files
- Using the `noupdate` and `forcecreate` flags
- Loading data using CSV files
- Add-on updates and data migration
- Deleting records from XML files
- Invoking functions from XML files

Technical requirements

The technical requirements for this chapter include the online Odoo platform.

All the code that's used in this chapter can be downloaded from the following GitHub repository:

https://github.com/PacktPublishing/Odoo-13-Development-Cookbook-Fourth-Edition/tree/master/Chapter06

In order to avoid repeating a lot of code, we'll make use of the models that were defined in *Chapter 4, Application Models*. To follow these examples, make sure you grab the code for the my_library module from Chapter04/r6_hierarchy_model/my_library.

Using external IDs and namespaces

External IDs or XML IDs in Odoo are used to identify records. So far in this book, we have used XML IDs in areas such as views, menus, and actions. However, we haven't seen what an XML ID actually is. This recipe will give you a deeper understanding.

How to do it...

We will write in the already-existing records to demonstrate how to use cross-module references:

1. Update the manifest file of the my_library module by registering a data file like this:

   ```
   'data': [
       'data/data.xml',
   ],
   ```

2. Create a new book in the library.book model:

   ```xml
   <record id="book_cookbook" model="library.book">
       <field name="name"> Odoo 14 Development Cookbook </field>
   </record>
   ```

3. Change the name of the main company:

```xml
<record id="base.main_company" model="res.company">
    <field name="name">Packt publishing</field>
</record>
```

Install the module to apply the changes. After installation, a new record for the book *Odoo 14 Development Cookbook* will be created and the company will be renamed to `Packt publishing`.

How it works...

An XML ID is a string that refers to a record in the database. The IDs themselves are records of the `ir.model.data` model. This model contains the data such as the module name that declares the XML ID, the ID string, the referred model, and the referred ID.

Every time we use an XML ID on a `<record>` tag, Odoo checks whether the string is namespaced (that is, whether it contains exactly one dot), and, if not, it adds the current module name as a namespace. Then, it looks up whether there is already a record in `ir.model.data` with the specified name. If so, an UPDATE statement for the listed fields is executed; if not, a CREATE statement is executed. This is how you can provide partial data when a record already exists, as we did earlier.

In the first example of this recipe, the record has the ID `book_cookbook`. As it is not namespaced, the final external ID will have a module name like this: `my_library.book_cookbook`. Then Odoo will try to find a record for `my_library.book_cookbook`. As Odoo doesn't have a record for that external ID yet, it will generate the new record in the `library.book` model.

In the second example, we have used the external ID of the main company, which is `base.main_company`. As its namespace suggests, it is loaded from the `base` module. As the external ID is already present, instead of creating a record, Odoo will perform the `write` (UPDATE) operation so the company name will be changed to `Packt publishing`.

> **Important note**
>
> A widespread application for partial data, apart from changing records defined by other modules, is using a shortcut element to create a record in a convenient way and writing a `field` on that record, which is not supported by the shortcut element:
> ```xml
> <act_window id="my_action" name="My action" model="res.partner" />
> <record id="my_action" model="ir.actions.act_window">
>     <field name="auto_search" eval="False" />
> </record>
> ```

The `ref` function, as used in the *Loading data using XML files* recipe of this chapter, also adds the current module as a namespace if appropriate, but raises an error if the resulting XML ID does not exist already. This also applies to the `id` attribute if it is not namespaced already.

> **Tip**
>
> If you want to see the list of all external identifiers, start developer mode and open the menu to **Settings | Technical | Sequence & Identifiers | External Identifiers**.

There's more...

You will probably need to access records with an XML ID from your Python code sooner or later. Use the `self.env.ref()` function in these cases. This returns a browse record (recordset) of the referenced record. Note that here, you always have to pass the full XML ID. Here's an example of a full XML ID: `<module_name>.<record_id>`.

You can see the XML ID of any record from the user interface. For that, you need to activate developer mode in Odoo. Refer to *Chapter 1, Installing the Odoo Development Environment*, to activate developer mode in Odoo. After activating the developer mode, open the **Form View** of the record for which you want to find out the XML ID. You will see a bug icon in the top bar. From that menu, click on the **View Metadata** option. See the following screenshot for reference:

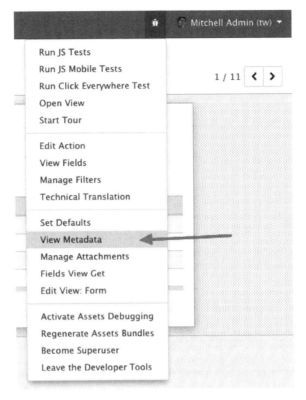

Figure 6.1 – Menu to open a record's metadata

See also

Consult the *Using the noupdate and forcecreate flags* recipe of this chapter to find out why the company's name is only changed during the installation of the module.

Loading data using XML files

In the previous recipe, we created the new book record with the external identifier book_cookbook. In this recipe, we will add a different type of data from the XML file. We'll add a book and an author as demonstration data. We'll also add a well-known publisher as normal data in our module.

How to do it...

Follow the given steps to create two data XML files and link them in your __manifest__.py file:

1. Add a file called `data/demo.xml` to your manifest, in the `demo` section:

    ```
    'demo': [
        'data/demo.xml',
    ],
    ```

2. Add the following content to this file:

    ```xml
    <odoo>
        <record id="author_pga" model="res.partner">
            <field name="name">Parth Gajjar</field>
        </record>
        <record id="author_af" model="res.partner">
            <field name="name">Alexandre Fayolle</field>
        </record>
        <record id="author_dr" model="res.partner">
            <field name="name">Daniel Reis</field>
        </record>
        <record id="author_hb" model="res.partner">
            <field name="name">Holger Brunn</field>
        </record>
        <record id="book_cookbook" model="library.book">
            <field name="name">Odoo Cookbook</field>
            <field name="short_name">cookbook</field>
            <field name="date_release">2016-03-01</field>
            <field name="author_ids"
                eval="[(6, 0, [ref('author_af'), ref('author_dr'),
                              ref('author_hb')])]"
            />
            <field name="publisher_id" ref="res_partner_packt" />
        </record>
    </odoo>
    ```

3. Add a file called `data/data.xml` to your manifest, in the `data` section:

```
'data': [
    'data/data.xml',
    ...
],
```

4. Add the following XML content to the `data/data.xml` file:

```xml
<odoo>
    <record id="res_partner_packt" model="res.partner">
        <field name="name">Packt Publishing</field>
        <field name="city">Birmingham</field>
        <field name="country_id" ref="base.uk" />
    </record>
</odoo>
```

When you update your module now, you'll see the publisher we created, and, if your database has demo data enabled, as pointed out in *Chapter 3, Creating Add-On Odoo Modules*, you'll also find this book and its authors.

How it works...

The data XML files uses the `<record>` tag to create a row in the database table. The `<record>` tag has two mandatory attributes, `id` and `model`. For the `id` attribute, consult the *Using external IDs and namespaces* recipe; the `model` attribute refers to a model's _name property. Then, we use the `<field>` element to fill the columns in the database, as defined by the model you named. The model also decides which fields it is mandatory to fill and also defines the default values. In this case, you don't need to give those fields a value explicitly.

There are two ways to register data XML files in a module manifest. One with the `data` key and the second is with the `demo` key. The XML files in the `data` key are loaded every time you install or update the module. While XML files with `demo` keys are loaded only if you enabled demo data for your database.

In *step 1*, we registered a `data` XML file in the manifest with the `demo` key. Because we are using the `demo` key, the XML file will be loaded only if you have enabled demo data for the database.

In *step 2*, the `<field>` element can contain a value as simple text in the case of scalar values. If you need to pass the content of a file (to set an image, for example), use the `file` attribute on the `<field>` element and pass the file's name relative to the add-ons path.

For setting up references, there are two possibilities. The simplest is using the `ref` attribute, which works for many2one fields and just contains the XML ID of the record to be referenced. For one2many and many2many fields, we need to use the `eval` attribute. This is a general-purpose attribute that can be used to evaluate Python code to use as the field's value; think of `strftime('%Y-01-01')` as an example to populate a `date` field. X2many fields expect to be populated by a list of three tuples, where the first value of the tuple determines the operation to be carried out. Within an `eval` attribute, we have access to a function called `ref`, which returns the database ID of an XML ID given as a string. This allows us to refer to a record without knowing its concrete ID, which is probably different in different databases, as shown here:

- `(2, id, False)`: This deletes the linked record with `id` from the database. The third element of the tuple is ignored.
- `(3, id, False)`: This detaches the record with `id`, from the one2many field. Note that this operation does not delete the record—it just leaves the existing record as it is. The last element of the tuple is also ignored.
- `(4, id, False)`: This adds a link to the existing record `id` and the last element of the tuple is ignored. This should be what you use most of the time, usually accompanied by the `ref` function to get the database ID of a record known by its XML ID.
- `(5, False, False)`: This cuts all links but keeps the linked records intact.
- `(6, False, [id, ...])`: This clears out currently referenced records to replace them with the ones mentioned in the list of IDs. The second element of the tuple is ignored.

Steps 3 and 4 are the same as the first two; they just use the `data` key instead of the `demo` key. This means the XML files will be loaded every time a module is installed or upgraded.

> **Important note**
> Note that order matters in data files and that records within data files can only refer to records defined in data files earlier in the list. This is why you should always check whether your module installs in an empty database, because during development, you often add records all over the place, which works because the records defined afterward are already in the database from an earlier update.
>
> Demo data is always loaded after the files from the `data` key, which is why the reference in this example works.

There's more...

While you can do basically anything with the `record` element, there are shortcut elements that make it more convenient for the developer to create certain kinds of records. These include menu items, templates, and act windows. Refer to *Chapter 9, Backend Views*, and *Chapter 14, CMS Website Development*, for information about these.

A `field` element can also contain the `function` element, which calls a function defined on a model to provide a field's value. Refer to the *Invoking functions from XML files* recipe for an application in which we simply call a function to directly write to the database, circumventing the loading mechanism.

The preceding list misses entries for 0 and 1 because they are not very useful when loading the data. They are entered, as follows, for the sake of completeness:

- `(0, False, {'key': value})`: This creates a new record of the referenced model, with its fields filled from the dictionary at position three. The second element of the tuple is ignored. As these records don't have an XML ID and are evaluated every time the module is updated, leading to double entries, it's better to avoid this. Instead, create the record in its own record element, and link it as explained in the *How it works* section of this recipe.

- `(1, id, {'key': value})`: This can be used to write on an existing linked record. For the same reasons that we mentioned earlier, you should avoid this syntax in your XML files.

These syntaxes are the same as the ones we explained in the *Creating new records* and *Updating values of records* recipes in *Chapter 5, Basic Server-Side Development*.

Using the noupdate and forcecreate flags

Most add-on modules have different types of data. Some data simply needs to exist for the module to work properly, other data shouldn't be changed by the user, and most data can be changed as the user wants and is only provided as a convenience. This recipe will detail how to address the different types. First, we'll write a field in an already-existing record, and then we'll create a record that is supposed to be recreated during a module update.

How to do it...

We can enforce different behaviors from Odoo when loading data by setting certain attributes on the enclosing `<odoo>` element or the `<record>` element itself:

1. Add a publisher that will be created at installation time, but not updated on subsequent updates. However, if the user deletes it, it will be recreated:

    ```xml
    <odoo noupdate="1">
        <record id="res_partner_packt" model="res.partner">
            <field name="name">Packt publishing</field>
            <field name="city">Birmingham</field>
            <field name="country_id" ref="base.uk"/>
        </record>
    </odoo>
    ```

2. Add a book category that is not changed during add-on updates and is not recreated if the user deletes it:

    ```xml
    <odoo noupdate="1">
        <record id="book_category_all" model="library.book.category"
                forcecreate="false">
            <field name="name">All books</field>
        </record>
    </odoo>
    ```

How it works...

The `<odoo>` element can have a `noupdate` attribute, which is propagated to the `ir.model.data` records that are created when reading the enclosed data records for the first time, thus ending up as a column in this table.

When Odoo installs an add-on (called `init` mode), all records are written, whether `noupdate` is `true` or `false`. When you update an add-on (called the `update` mode), the existing XML IDs are checked to see whether they have the `noupdate` flag set, and if so, elements that try to write to this XML ID are ignored. This is not the case if the record in question was deleted by the user, which is why you can force not recreating `noupdate` records in the `update` mode by setting the `forcecreate` flag on the record to `false`.

> **Important note**
> In legacy add-ons (prior to and including version 8.0), you'll often find an `<openerp>` element enclosing a `<data>` element, which contains `<record>` and other elements. This is still possible, but deprecated. Now, `<odoo>`, `<openerp>`, and `<data>` have exactly the same semantics; they are meant as a bracket to enclose XML data.

There's more...

If you want to load records even with the `noupdate` flag, you can run the Odoo server with the `--init=your_addon` or `-i your_addon` parameter. This will force Odoo to reload your records. This will also cause deleted records to be recreated. Note that this can cause double records and related installation errors if a module circumvents the XML ID mechanism, for example, by creating records in Python code called by the `<function>` tag.

With this code, you can circumvent any `noupdate` flag, but first, make sure that this is really what you want. Another option for solving the scenario presented here is to write a migration script, as outlined in the *Add-on updates and data migration* recipe.

See also

Odoo also uses XML IDs to keep track of which data is to be deleted after an add-on update. If a record has an XML ID from the module's namespace before the update, but the XML ID is not reinstated during the update, the record and its XML ID will be deleted from the database because they're considered obsolete. For a more in-depth discussion of this mechanism, refer to the *Add-on updates and data migration* recipe.

Loading data using CSV files

While you can do everything you need to with XML files, this format is not the most convenient when you need to provide larger amounts of data, especially given that many people are more comfortable preprocessing data in Calc or other spreadsheet software. Another advantage of the CSV format is that it is what you get when you use the standard export function. In this recipe, we'll take a look at importing table-like data.

How to do it...

Traditionally, **access-control lists** (**ACLs** – refer to *Chapter 10*, *Security Access*) are a type of data that is loaded through CSV files:

1. Add `security/ir.model.access.csv` to your data files:

    ```
    'data': [
        ...
        'security/ir.model.access.csv',
    ],
    ```

2. Add an ACL for our books in this file (we already have a few records from the *Adding access security* recipe from *Chapter 3*, *Creating Odoo Add-On Modules*):

    ```
    id,name,model_id:id,group_id:id,perm_read,perm_write,perm_create,perm_unlink
    acl_library_book_user,ACL for books,model_library_book,base.group_user,1,0,0,0
    ```

We now have an ACL that permits normal users to read book records, but does not allow them to edit, create, or delete them.

How it works...

You simply drop all your data files in your manifest's *data* list. Odoo will use the file extension to decide which type of file it is. A specialty of CSV files is that their filename must match the name of the model to be imported, in our case, `ir.model.access`. The first line needs to be a header with column names that match the model's field names exactly.

For scalar values, you can use a quoted (if necessary, because the string contains quotes or commas itself) or an unquoted string.

When writing `many2one` fields with a CSV file, Odoo first tries to interpret the column value as XML ID. If there's no dot, Odoo adds the current module name as a namespace and looks up the result in `ir.model.data`. If this fails, the model's `name_search` function is called with the column's value as a parameter, and the first result returned wins. If this also fails, the line is considered invalid and Odoo raises an error.

> **Important note**
> Note that data read from CSV files is always `noupdate=False`, and there's no convenient way around this. This means that subsequent updates of your add-on will always overwrite possible changes made by the user.
> If you need to load huge amounts of data and `noupdate` is a problem for you, load a CSV file from an `init` hook.

There's more...

Importing the `one2many` and `many2many` fields with CSV files is possible, but a bit tricky. In general, you're better off creating the records separately and setting up the relation with an XML file afterward, or working with a second CSV file that sets up the relationship.

If you really need to create related records within the same file, order your columns so that all scalar fields are to the left and the fields of the linked model are to the right, with a column header consisting of the linking field's name and the linked model's field, separated by a colon:

```
"id","name","model_id:id","perm_read","perm_read", "group_id:name"
"access_library_book_user","ACL for books","model_library_book",1,
"my group"
```

This will create a group called `my group`; you can write more fields in the group record by adding columns to the right. If you need to link multiple records, repeat the line and change the right-hand side columns as appropriate. Given that Odoo fills empty columns with the previous line's value, you don't need to copy all the data—you can simply add a line with empty values saved for the fields of the linked model you want to fill.

For x2m fields, just list the XML IDs of the records to be linked.

Add-on updates and data migration

The data model you choose when writing an add-on module might turn out to have some weaknesses, so you may need to adjust it during the life cycle of your add-on module. In order to allow that without a lot of hacks, Odoo supports versioning in add-on modules and running migrations if necessary.

How to do it...

We assume that in an earlier version of our module, the `date_release` field was a character field, where people wrote whatever they saw fit as the date. We now realize that we need this field for comparisons and aggregations, which is why we want to change its type to `Date`.

Odoo does a great job at type conversions, but, in this case, we're on our own, which is why we need to provide instructions as to how to transform a database with the previous version of our module installed on a database where the current version can run. Let's try this with the following steps:

1. Bump the version in your `__manifest__.py` file:

    ```
    'version': '13.0.1.0.1',
    ```

2. Provide the pre-migration code in `migrations/13.0.1.0.1/pre-migrate.py`:

    ```
    def migrate(cr, version):
        cr.execute('ALTER TABLE library_book RENAME COLUMN date_release
                                                        TO date_release_char')
    ```

3. Provide the post-migration code in `migrations/13.0.1.0.1/post-migrate.py`:

    ```
    from odoo import fields
    from datetime import date

    def migrate(cr, version):
        cr.execute('SELECT id, date_release_char FROM library_book')
        for record_id, old_date in cr.fetchall():
            # check if the field happens to be set in Odoo's
    ```

```
                internal
        # format
        new_date = None
        try:
            new_date = fields.Date.to_date(old_date)
        except ValueError:
            if len(old_date) == 4 and old_date.isdigit():
                # probably a year
                new_date = date(int(old_date), 1, 1)
        if new_date:
            cr.execute('UPDATE library_book SET date_
    release=%s',
                       (new_date,))
```

Without this code, Odoo would have renamed the old `date_release` column to `date_release_moved` and created a new one, because there's no automatic conversion from character fields to date fields. From the point of view of the user, the data in `date_release` will simply be gone.

How it works...

The first crucial point is that you increase the version number of your add-on, as migrations run only between different versions. During every update, Odoo writes the version number from the manifest at the time of the update into the `ir_module_module` table. The version number is prefixed with Odoo's major and minor versions if the version number has three or fewer components. In the preceding example, we explicitly named Odoo's major and minor version, which is good practice, but a value of `1.0.1` would have had the same effect, because, internally, Odoo prefixes short version numbers for add-ons with its own major and minor version number. Generally, using the long notation is a good idea because you can see at a glance which version of Odoo an add-on is meant for.

The two migration files are just code files that don't need to be registered anywhere. When updating an add-on, Odoo compares the add-on's version, as noted in `ir_module_module`, with the version in the add-on's manifest. If the manifest's version is higher (after adding Odoo's major and minor version), this add-on's `migrations` folder will be searched to see whether it contains folders with the version(s) in-between, up to and including the version that is currently updated.

Then, within the folders found, Odoo searches for Python files whose names start with `pre-`, loads them, and expects them to define a function called `migrate`, which has two parameters. This function is called with a database cursor as the first argument and the currently-installed version as the second argument. This happens before Odoo even looks at the rest of the code the add-on defines, so you can assume that nothing changes in your database layout compared to the previous version.

After all the `pre-migrate` functions run successfully, Odoo loads the models and the data declared in the add-on, which can cause changes in the database layout. Given that we renamed `date_release` in `pre-migrate.py`, Odoo will just create a new column with that name, but with the correct data type.

After that, with the same search algorithm, the `post-migrate` files will be searched and executed if found. In our case, we need to look at every value to see whether we can make something usable out of it; otherwise, we keep the data as `NULL`. Don't write scripts that iterate over a whole table if not absolutely necessary; in this case, we would have written a very big, unreadable SQL switch.

> **Important tip**
>
> If you simply want to rename a column, you don't need a migration script. In this case, you can set the `oldname` parameter of the field in question to the field's original column name; Odoo then takes care of the renaming itself.

There's more...

In both the pre- and post-migration steps, you only have access to a cursor, which is not very convenient if you're used to Odoo environments. It can lead to unexpected results to use models at this stage, because in the pre-migration step, the add-on's models are not yet loaded, and also, in the post-migration step, the models defined by add-ons that depend on the current add-on are not yet loaded either. However, if this is not a problem for you, either because you want to use a model that your add-on doesn't touch or a model for which you know that this issue is not a problem, you can create the environment you're used to by writing the following:

```
from odoo import api, SUPERUSER_ID

def migrate(cr, version):
    env = api.Environment(cr, SUPERUSER_ID, {})
    # env holds all currently loaded models
```

See also

When writing migration scripts, you'll often be confronted with repetitive tasks, such as checking whether a column or table exists, renaming things, or mapping some old values to new values. It's frustrating and error-prone to reinvent the wheel here; consider using https://github.com/OCA/openupgradelib if you can afford the extra dependency.

Deleting records from XML files

In the previous recipes, we saw how we can create or update records from the XML file. Sometimes, from the dependent module, you want to delete the previously created records. This can be done with the `<delete>` tag.

Getting ready

In this recipe, we will add some categories from the XML file and then delete them. In real situations, you will create this record from another module. But for simplicity, we will just add some categories in the same XML file, as follows:

```xml
<record id="book_category_to_delete" model="library.book.category">
    <field name="name">Test Category</field>
</record>
<record id="book_category_not_delete" model="library.book.category">
    <field name="name">Test Category 2</field>
</record>
```

How to do it...

There are two ways to delete records from the XML file:

- With the XML ID of previously created records:

    ```xml
    <delete model="library.book.category" id="book_category_to_delete"/>
    ```

- With the search domain:

    ```xml
    <delete model="library.book.category" search="[('name', 'ilike', 'Test')]"/>
    ```

How it works...

You will need to use the `<delete>` tag. To delete a record from a model, you need to provide the name of the model in the `model` attribute. This is a compulsory attribute.

In the first method, you need to provide the XML ID of the records that were previously created from another module's data files. During the installation of the module, Odoo will try to find the record. If the record is found for the given XML ID, it will delete the record, otherwise, it will raise an error. You can delete only the records that are created from the XML files (or records that have XML IDs).

In the second method, you need to pass the domain in the `domain` attribute. During the installation of the module, Odoo will search the records by this domain. If records are found, it deletes them. This option will not raise an error if no records match the given domain. Use this option with extreme caution, because it might delete your user's data since the search option deletes all the records that match the domain.

> **Warning**
>
> `<delete>` is rarely used in Odoo as it is dangerous. If you are not careful with this, you might break the system. Avoid it if possible.

Invoking functions from XML files

You can create all types of records from XML files, but sometimes it is difficult to generate data that includes some business logic. You might want to modify records when a user installs a dependent module in production. For example, let's say you want to create a module to display books online. The `my_library` module already has an `image-cover` field. Imagine that, in the new module, you implemented logic to reduce the size of the image and stored it in the new thumbnail field. Now, when the user installs this module, they might already have books and images. It is not possible to generate thumbnails from the `<record>` tags in the XML file. In this case, you can invoke the `model` method through the `<function>` tag.

How to do it...

For this recipe, we will use the code from the previous recipe. As an example, we will increase the existing book price by $10 USD. Note that you might use another currency based on company configurations.

Follow these steps to invoke the Python method from the XML file:

1. Add the `_update_book_price()` method in the `library.book` model:

   ```
   @api.model
   def _update_book_price(self):
       all_books = self.search([])
       for book in all_books:
           book.cost_price += 10
   ```

2. Add `<function>` in the data XML file:

   ```
   <function model="library.book" name="_update_book_price"/>
   ```

How it works...

In *step 1*, we added the `_update_book_price()` method, which searches for all books and increases the price by $10 USD. We started the method name with `_` as this is considered private by ORM and cannot be invoked through RPC.

In *step 2*, we used the `<function>` tag with two attributes:

- `model`: The model name in which the method is declared
- `name`: The name of the method you want to invoke

When you install this module, `_update_book_price()` will be called and the price of books will be increased by $10 USD.

> **Important note**
> Always put this function with the `noupdate` options. Otherwise, it will be invoked every time you update your module.

There's more...

With `<function>`, it is also possible to send parameters to the functions. Let's say you only want to increase the price of books in a particular category and you want to send that amount as a parameter.

For that, you need to create a method that accepts the category as a parameter, as follows:

```
@api.model
def update_book_price(self, category, amount_to_increase):
    category_books = self.search([('category_id', '=', category.id)])
    for book in category_books:
        book.cost_price += amount_to_increase
```

To pass the category and amount as a parameter, you need to use the `eval` attribute, as follows:

```
<function model="library.book"
    name="update_book_price"
    eval="(ref('category_xml_id'), 20)"/>
```

When you install the module, it will increase the price of the books of the given category by $20 USD.

7
Debugging Modules

In *Chapter 5, Basic Server-Side Development*, we saw how to write model methods to implement the logic of our module. However, we may get stuck when we encounter errors or logical issues. In order to resolve these errors, we need to perform a detailed inspection and this may take time. Luckily, Odoo provides you with some debugging tools that can help you to find the root cause of various issues. In this chapter, we will look at various debugging tools and techniques in detail.

In this chapter, we will cover the following recipes:

- The auto-reload and --dev options
- Producing server logs to help debug methods
- Using the Odoo shell to interactively call methods
- Using the Python debugger to trace method execution
- Understanding the debug mode options

The auto-reload and --dev options

In the previous chapters, we saw how to add a model, fields, and views. Whenever we make changes to Python files, we need to restart the server to apply those changes. If we make changes in XML files, we need to restart the server and update the module to reflect those changes in the user interface. If you are developing a large application, this can be time-consuming and frustrating. Odoo provides a command-line option, --dev, to overcome these issues. The --dev option has several possible values, and, in this recipe, we will see each of them.

Getting ready

Install `inotify` in your developer environment with the following command in the shell. Without `inotify`, the auto-reload feature will not work:

```
$ pip3 install inotify
```

How to do it...

To enable the dev option, you need to use --dev=value from the command line. Possible values for this option are `all`, `reload`, `pudb|wdb|ipdb|pdb`, `qweb`, `werkzeug`, and `xml`. Take a look at the following example for more information:

```
$ odoo/odoo-bin -c ~/odoo-dev/my-instance.cfg --dev=all
```

If you want to enable only a few options, you can use comma-separated values, as follows:

```
$ odoo/odoo-bin -c ~/odoo-dev/my-instance.cfg --dev=reload,qweb
```

How it works...

Check the following list for all --dev options and their purposes:

- `reload`: Whenever you make changes in Python, you need to restart the server to reflect those changes in Odoo. The --dev=reload option will reload the Odoo server automatically when you make changes in any Python file. This feature will not work if you have not installed the Python `inotify` package. When you run Odoo server with this option server, you will see a log like this: `AutoReload watcher running with inotify`.

- qweb: You can create dynamic website pages in Odoo using QWeb templates. In *Chapter 14, CMS Website Development*, we will see how to develop a web page with the QWeb template. You can debug issues in the QWeb template with the `t-debug` attribute. The `t-debug` options will only work if you enable the dev mode with `--dev=qweb`.

- werkzeug: Odoo uses `werkzeug` to handle HTTP requests. Internally, Odoo will catch and suppress all exceptions generated by `werkzeug`. If you use `--dev=werkzeug`, werkzeug's interactive debugger will be displayed on the web page when an exception is generated.

- xml: Whenever you make changes in the view structure, you need to reload the server and update the module to apply those changes. With the `--dev=xml` option, you just need to reload Odoo from the browser. There is no need to restart the server or update the module.

- pudb|wdb|ipdb|pdb: You can use the **Python debugger** (**PDB**) to get more information about the errors. When you use the `--dev=pdb` option, it will activate the PDB whenever an exception is generated in Odoo. Odoo supports four Python debuggers: `pudb`, `wdb`, `ipdb`, and `pdb`.

- all: If you use `--dev=all`, all of the preceding options will be enabled.

> **Important note**
>
> If you have made changes to the database structure, such as if you have added new fields, the `--dev=reload` option will not reflect these in the database schema. You need to update the module manually; it only works for Python business logic.
>
> If you add a new view or menu, the `--dev=xml` option will not reflect this in the user interface. You need to update the module manually. This is very helpful when you are designing the structure of the view or the website page.
>
> If users have made changes in the view from the GUI, then `--dev=xml` will not load the XML from the file. Odoo will use the view structure, which the user changes.

Producing server logs to help debug methods

Server logs are useful when trying to figure out what has been happening at runtime before a crash. They can also be added to provide additional information when debugging is an issue. This recipe shows you how to add logging to an existing method.

Getting ready

We will add some logging statements to the following method, which saves the stock levels of products to a file (you will also need to add the dependencies of the `product` and `stock` modules to the manifest):

```python
from os.path import join
from odoo import models, api, exceptions
EXPORTS_DIR = '/srv/exports'


class ProductProduct(models.Model):
    _inherit = 'product.product'
    @api.model
    def export_stock_level(self, stock_location):
        products = self.with_context(
            location=stock_location.id
        ).search([])
        products = products.filtered('qty_available')
        fname = join(EXPORTS_DIR, 'stock_level.txt')
        try:
            with open(fname, 'w') as fobj:
                for prod in products:
                    fobj.write('%s\t%f\n' % (prod.name,
                                             prod.qty_available))
        except IOError:
            raise exceptions.UserError('unable to save file')
```

How to do it...

In order to get some logs when this method is being executed, perform the following steps:

1. At the beginning of the code, import the `logging` module:

    ```python
    import logging
    ```

2. Before the definition of the model class, get a logger for the module:

    ```python
    _logger = logging.getLogger(__name__)
    ```

3. Modify the code of the `export_stock_level()` method, as follows:

```python
    @api.model
    def export_stock_level(self, stock_location):
        _logger.info('export stock level for %s',
            stock_location.name)
        products = self.with_context(
            location=stock_location.id).search([])
        products = products.filtered('qty_available')
        _logger.debug('%d products in the location',
            len(products))
        fname = join(EXPORTS_DIR, 'stock_level.txt')
        try:
            with open(fname, 'w') as fobj:
                for prod in products:
                    fobj.write('%s\t%f\n' % (
                        prod.name, prod.qty_available))
        except IOError:
            _logger.exception(
                'Error while writing to %s in %s',
                'stock_level.txt', EXPORTS_DIR)
            raise exceptions.UserError('unable to save file')
```

How it works...

Step 1 imports the `logging` module from the Python standard library. Odoo uses this module to manage its logs.

Step 2 sets up a logger for the Python module. We use the common idiom __name__ in Odoo as an automatic variable for the name of the logger and to call the logger by _logger.

> **Important note**
>
> The __name__ variable is set automatically by the Python interpreter at module-import time, and its value is the full name of the module. Since Odoo does a little trick with the imports, the add-on modules are seen by Python as belonging to the `odoo.addons` Python package. So, if the code of the recipe is in `my_library/models/book.py`, __name__ will be `odoo.addons.my_library.models.book`.

By doing this, we get two benefits:

- The global logging configuration set on the `odoo` logger is applied to our logger because of the hierarchical structure of loggers in the `logging` module.
- The logs will be prefixed with the full module path, which is a great help when trying to find where a given log line is produced.

Step 3 uses the logger to produce log messages. The available methods for this are (by increasing log level) `debug`, `info`, `warning`, `error`, and `critical`. All these methods accept a message in which you can have `%` substitutions and additional arguments to be inserted into the message. You should not do the `%` substitution yourself; the logging module is smart enough to perform this operation if the log has to be produced. If you are running with a log level of `INFO`, then `DEBUG` logs will avoid substitutions that will consume CPU in the long run.

Another useful method shown in this recipe is `_logger.exception()`, which can be used in an exception handler. The message will be logged with a level of `ERROR`, and the stack trace is also printed in the application log.

There's more...

You can control the **logging level** of the application from the command line or from the configuration file. There are two main ways of doing this:

The first way is to use the `--log-handler` option. Its basic syntax is like this: `--log-handler=prefix:level`. In this case, the prefix is a piece of the path of the logger name, and the level is `DEBUG`, `INFO`, `WARNING`, `ERROR`, or `CRITICAL`. If you omit the prefix, you set the default level for all loggers. For instance, to set the logging level of `my_library` loggers to `DEBUG` and keep the default log level for the other add-ons, you can start Odoo as follows:

```
$ python odoo.py --log-handler=odoo.addons.my_library:DEBUG
```

It is possible to specify `--log-handler` multiple times on the command line. You can also configure the **log handler** in the configuration file of your Odoo instance. In that case, you can use a comma-separated list of `prefix:level` pairs. For example, the following line is the same configuration for a minimal logging output as before. We maintain the most important messages and the error messages by default, except for messages produced by `werkzeug`, for which we only want critical messages, and `odoo.service.server`, for which we keep info-level messages, including server startup notifications:

```
log_handler = :ERROR,werkzeug:CRITICAL,odoo.service.
 server:INFO
```

The second way is to use the `--log-level` option. To control the log level globally, you can use `--log-level` as the command-line option. Possible values for this option are `critical`, `error`, `warn`, `debug`, `debug_rpc`, `debug_rpc_answer`, `debug_sql`, and `test`.

There are some shortcuts for setting logging levels. Here is a list of them:

- `--log-request` is a shortcut for `--log-handler=odoo.http.rpc.request:DEBUG`.
- `--log-response` is a shortcut for `--log-handler=odoo.http.rpc.response:DEBUG`.
- `--log-web` is a shortcut for `--log-handler=odoo.http:DEBUG`.
- `--log-sql` is a shortcut for `--log-handler=odoo.sql_db:DEBUG`.

Using the Odoo shell to interactively call methods

The Odoo web interface is meant for end users, although the developer mode unlocks a number of powerful features. However, testing and debugging through the web interface is not the easiest way to do things, as you need to manually prepare the data, navigate in the menus to perform actions, and so on. The Odoo shell is a **command-line interface**, which you can use to issue calls. This recipe shows how to start the Odoo shell and perform actions such as calling a method inside the shell.

Getting ready

We will reuse the same code as in the previous recipe to produce server logs to help debug methods. This allows the `product.product` model to add a new method. We will assume that you have an instance with the add-on installed and available. In this recipe, we expect that you have an Odoo configuration file for this instance called `project.conf`.

How to do it...

In order to call the `export_stock_level()` method from the Odoo shell, perform the following steps:

1. Start the Odoo shell and specify your project configuration file:

   ```
   $ ./odoo-bin shell -c project.conf --log-level=error
   ```

2. Check for error messages and read the information text that's displayed before the usual Python command-line prompt:

   ```
   env: <odoo.api.Environment object at 0x10e3277f0>
   odoo: <module 'odoo' from '/home/parth/community/odoo/__init__.py'>
   openerp: <module 'odoo' from '/home/parth/community/odoo/__init__.py'>
   self: res.users(1,)
   Python 3.6.5 (default, Oct 30 2020, 14:23:58)
   [GCC 9.3.0] on linux
   Type "help", "copyright", "credits" or "license" for more information.
   >>>
   ```

3. Get a record set for `product.product`:

   ```
   >>> product = env['product.product']
   ```

4. Get the main stock location record:

   ```
   >>> location_stock = env.ref('stock.stock_location_stock')
   ```

5. Call the `export_stock_level()` method:

   ```
   >>> product.export_stock_level(location_stock)
   ```

6. Commit the transaction before exiting:

   ```
   >>> env.cr.commit()
   ```

7. Exit the shell by pressing *Ctrl + D*.

How it works...

Step 1 uses `odoo-bin shell` to start the Odoo shell. All the usual command-line arguments are available. We use `-c` to specify a project configuration file and `--log-level` to reduce the verbosity of the logs. When debugging, you may want to have a logging level of `DEBUG` for some specific add-ons.

Before providing you with a Python command-line prompt, `odoo-bin shell` starts an Odoo instance that does not listen on the network and initializes some global variables, which are mentioned in the output:

- `env` is an environment that's connected to the database and specified on the command line or in the configuration file.
- `odoo` is the `odoo` package that's imported for you. You get access to all the Python modules within that package to do what you want.
- `openerp` is an alias for the `odoo` package for backward compatibility.
- `self` is a record set of `res.users` that contains a single record for the Odoo superuser (administrator), which is linked to the `env` environment.

Steps 3 and *4* use `env` to get an empty record set and find a record according to the XML ID. *Step 5* calls the method on the `product.product` record set. These operations are identical to what you would use inside a method, with a minor difference being that we use `env` and not `self.env` (although we can have both, as they are identical). Take a look at *Chapter 5*, *Basic Server-Side Development*, for more information on what is available.

Step 6 commits the database transaction. This is not strictly necessary here because we did not modify any record in the database, but if we had done so and wanted these changes to persist, this is necessary; when you use Odoo through the web interface, each RPC call runs in its own database transaction, and Odoo manages these for you. When running in shell mode, this no longer happens and you have to call `env.cr.commit()` or `env.cr.rollback()` yourself. Otherwise, when you exit the shell, any transaction in progress is automatically rolled back. When testing, this is fine, but if you use the shell, for example, to script the configuration of an instance, don't forget to commit your work!

There's more...

In shell mode, by default, Odoo opens Python's REPL shell interface. You can use the REPL of your choice using the `--shell-interface` option. The supported REPLs are ipython, ptpython, bpython, and python:

```
$ ./odoo-bin shell -c project.conf  --shell-interface=ptpython
```

Using the Python debugger to trace method execution

Sometimes, application logs are not enough to figure out what is going wrong. Fortunately, we also have the Python debugger. This recipe shows us how to insert a breakpoint in a method and trace the execution by hand.

Getting ready

We will reuse the `export_stock_level()` method that was shown in the *Using the Odoo shell to interactively call methods* recipe of this chapter. Ensure that you have a copy to hand.

How to do it...

To trace the execution of `export_stock_level()` with pdb, perform the following steps:

1. Edit the code of the method, and insert the line highlighted here:

    ```
    def export_stock_level(self, stock_location):
        import pdb; pdb.set_trace()
        products = self.with_context( location=stock_location.id ).search([])
        fname = join(EXPORTS_DIR, 'stock_level.txt')
        try:
            with open(fname, 'w') as fobj:
                for prod in products.filtered('qty_available'):
                    fobj.write('%s\t%f\n' % (prod.name, prod.qty_available))
        except IOError:
            raise exceptions.UserError('unable to save file')
    ```

2. Run the method. We will use the Odoo shell, as explained in the *Using the Odoo shell to interactively call methods* recipe:

   ```
   $ ./odoo-bin shell -c project.cfg --log-level=error
   [...]
   >>> product = env['product.product']
   >>> location_stock = env.ref('stock.stock_location_stock')
   >>> product.export_stock_level(location_stock)
   > /home/cookbook/stock_level/models.py(18)export_stock_level()
   -> products = self.with_context(
   (Pdb)
   ```

3. At the (Pdb) prompt, issue the args command (the shortcut of which is a) to get the values of the arguments that were passed to the method:

   ```
   (Pdb) a
   self = product.product()
   stock_location = stock.location(14,)
   ```

4. Enter the list command to check where in the code you are standing:

   ```
   (Pdb) list
    13         @api.model
    14         def export_stock_level(self, stock_location):
    15             _logger.info('export stock level for %s',
    16                          stock_location.name)
    17             import pdb; pdb.set_trace()
    18  ->         products = self.with_context(
    19             location=stock_location.id).search([])
    20             products = products.filtered('qty_available')
    21             _logger.debug('%d products in the location',
    22                          len(products))
    23             fname = join(EXPORTS_DIR, 'stock_level.txt')
   (Pdb)
   ```

5. Enter the next command three times to walk through the first lines of the method. You may also use n, which is a shortcut:

   ```
   (Pdb) next
   > /home/cookbook/stock_level/models.py(19)export_stock_level()
   ```

```
    -> location=stock_location.id).search([])
    (Pdb) n
    > /home/cookbook/stock_level/models.py(20)export_stock_
    level()
    -> products = products.filtered('qty_available')
    (Pdb) n
    > /home/cookbook/stock_level/models.py(21)export_stock_
    level()
    -> _logger.debug('%d products in the location',
    (Pdb) n
    > /home/cookbook/stock_level/models.py(22)export_stock_
    level()
    -> len(products))
    (Pdb) n
    > /home/cookbook/stock_level/models.py(23)export_stock_
    level()
    -> fname = join(EXPORTS_DIR, 'stock_level.txt')
    (Pdb) n
    > /home/cookbook/stock_level/models.py(24)export_stock_
    level()
    -> try:
```

6. Use the p command to display the values of the products and fname variables:

```
(Pdb) p products
product.product(32, 14, 17, 19, 21, 22, 23, 29, 34, 33,
26, 27, 42)
(Pdb) p fname
'/srv/exports/stock_level.txt'
```

7. Change the value of fname to point to the /tmp directory:

```
(Pdb) !fname = '/tmp/stock_level.txt'
```

8. Use the return (shortcut: r) command to execute the current function:

```
(Pdb) return
--Return--
> /home/cookbook/stock_level/models.py(26)export_stock_
level()->None
-> for product in products:
```

9. Use the `cont` (shortcut: `c`) command to resume the execution of the program:

```
(Pdb) c
>>>
```

How it works...

In *step 1*, we hardcoded a breakpoint in the source code of the method by calling the `set_trace()` method of the `pdb` module from the Python standard library. When this method is executed, the normal flow of the program stops, and you get a (`Pdb`) prompt in which you can enter `pdb` commands.

Step 2 calls the `stock_level_export()` method using shell mode. It is also possible to restart the server normally and use the web interface to generate a call to the method you need to trace by clicking on the appropriate elements of the user interface.

When you need to manually step through some code using the Python debugger, here are a few tips that will make your life easier:

- Reduce the logging level to avoid having too many log lines, which pollutes the output of the debugger. Starting at the `ERROR` level is generally fine. You may want to enable some specific loggers with a higher verbosity, which you can do using the `--log-handler` command-line option (refer to the *Producing server logs to help debug methods* recipe).

- Run the server with `--workers=0` to avoid any multiprocessing issues that can cause the same breakpoint to be reached twice in two different processes.

- Run the server with `--max-cron-threads=0` to disable the processing of the `ir.cron` periodic tasks, which may otherwise trigger while you are stepping through the method, which produces unwanted logs and side effects.

Steps 3 to *8* use several `pdb` commands to step through the execution of the method. Here's a summary of the main commands of `pdb`. Most of these are also available using the first letter as a shortcut. We indicate this here by having the optional letters between parentheses:

- `h(elp)`: This displays help about the `pdb` commands.
- `a(rgs)`: This shows the value of the arguments of the current function/methods.
- `l(ist)`: This displays the source code being executed in chunks of 11 lines, initially centered on the current line. Successive calls will move further in the source code file. Optionally, you can pass two integers at the start and end, which specify the region to display.

- `p`: This prints a variable.
- `pp`: This pretty-prints a variable (useful with lists and dictionaries).
- `w(here)`: This shows the call stack, with the current line at the bottom and the Python interpreter at the top.
- `u(p)`: This moves up one level in the call stack.
- `d(own)`: This moves down one level in the call stack.
- `n(ext)`: This executes the current line of code and then stops.
- `s(tep)`: This is to step inside the execution of a method call.
- `r(eturn)`: This resumes the execution of the current method until it returns.
- `c(ont(inue))`: This resumes the execution of the program until the next breakpoint is hit.
- `b(reak) <args>`: This creates a new breakpoint and displays its identifier; `args` can be one of the following:
- `<empty>`: This lists all breakpoints.
- `line_number`: This breaks at the specified line in the current file.
- `filename:line_number`: This breaks at the specified line of the specified file (which is searched for in the directories of `sys.path`).
- `function_name`: This breaks at the first line of the specified function.
- `tbreak <args>`: This is similar to break, but the breakpoint will be canceled after it has been reached, so successive execution of the line won't trigger it twice.
- `disable bp_id`: This disables a breakpoint by ID.
- `enable bl_id`: This enables a disabled breakpoint by ID.
- `j(ump) lineno`: The next line to execute will be the one specified. This can be used to rerun or skip some lines.
- `(!) statement`: This executes a Python statement. The `!` character can be omitted if the command does not look like a `pdb` command. For instance, you need it if you want to set the value of a variable named `a`, because `a` is the shortcut for the `args` command.

There's more...

In the recipe, we inserted a `pdb.set_trace()` statement to break into `pdb` for debugging. We can also start `pdb` directly from within the Odoo shell, which is very useful when you cannot easily modify the code of the project using `pdb.runcall()`. This function takes a method as the first argument and the arguments to pass to the function as the next arguments. So, inside the Odoo shell, you do this:

```
>>> import pdb
>>> product = env['product.product']
>>> location_stock = env.ref('stock.stock_location_stock')
>>> pdb.runcall(product.export_stock_level, location_stock)
> /home/cookbook/stock_level/models.py(16)export_stock_level()
-> products = self.with_context(
(Pdb)
```

In this recipe, we focused on the Python debugger from the Python standard library, pdb. It is very useful to know about this tool because it is guaranteed to be available on any Python distribution. There are other Python debuggers available, such as `ipdb` (https://pypi.python.org/pypi/ipdb) and pudb (https://pypi.python.org/pypi/pudb), which can be used as drop-in replacements for pdb. They share the same API, and most of the commands that you saw in this recipe were unchanged. Also, of course, if you develop for Odoo using a Python IDE, you will have access to a debugger that was integrated with it.

See also

If you want to learn more about the `pdb` debugger, refer to the full documentation of `pdb` at https://docs.python.org/3.5/library/pdb.html.

Understanding the debug mode options

In *Chapter 1*, *Installing the Odoo Development Environment*, we saw how to enable debug/developer options in Odoo. These options are very helpful in debugging and reveal some further technical information. In this chapter, we will look at these options in detail.

How to do it...

Check the *Activating the Odoo developer tools* recipe of *Chapter 1, Installing the Odoo Development Environment*, and activate developer mode. After activating developer mode, you will see a drop-down menu with a bug icon in the top bar, as shown here:

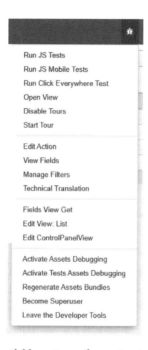

Figure 7.1 – Available options after activating debug mode

In this menu, you will see various options. Give them a go to see them in action. The next section will explain these options in more detail.

How it works...

Let's learn more about the options in the following points:

Run JS Tests: This option will redirect you to the JavaScript QUnit test case page, as shown in the following screenshot. It will start running all test cases one by one. Here, you can see the progress and the status of the test cases. In *Chapter 18, Automated Test Cases*, we will see how can we create our own QUnit JavaScript test cases:

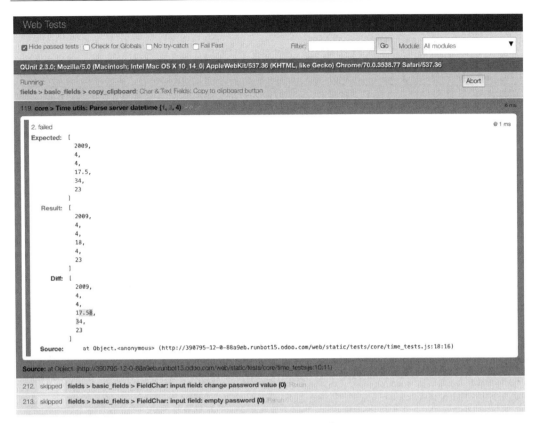

Figure 7.2 – QUnit test case result screen

- **Run JS Mobile Tests**: Similar to the preceding option, but this one runs a QUnit test case for a mobile environment.

- **Run Click Anywhere Tests**: This option will start clicking on all menus one by one. It will click in all the views and search filters. If something is broken or there is any regression, it will show the tracebacks. To stop this test, you will need to reload the page.

- **Open View**: This option will open a list of all available views. By selecting any of them, you can open that view without defining any menus or actions.

- **Disable Tours**: Odoo uses tours to improve the onboarding of new users. If you want to disable it, you can do it by using this option.

- **Start Tour**: Odoo also uses tours for automated testing. We will create a custom onboarding tour in *Chapter 15, Web Client Development*. This option will open a dialog box with a list of all tours, as shown in the following screenshot. By clicking on the play button next to a tour, Odoo will automatically perform all the steps of the tour:

Tours

Name	Path
website_crm_tour	/contactus
website_hr_recruitment_tour	/jobs/apply/3
shop	/shop
mail_tour	
widget_x2many	/web?debug=assets#action=test_new_api.action_discussions
stock	/web?debug=assets#action=stock.action_stock_config_settings
rte_translator	
bank_statement_reconciliation	
account_tour	
crm_tour	/web

Figure 7.3 – Dialog to manually launch tours

- **Edit Action**: In the *Adding menu items and views* recipe of *Chapter 3, Creating Odoo Add-On Modules*, we added a menu item and an action to open views in Odoo. Details of these actions are also stored in the database as a record. This option will open the record details of the action we open to display the current view.

- **View Fields**: This option will help you when you want to see the details of fields from the user interface. It will show a list of fields for the current model. For example, if you open a tree or form view for a `library.book` model, this option will show a list of fields for the `library.book` model.

- **Manage Filters**: In Odoo, users can create custom filters from the search view. This option will open a list of custom filters for the current model. Here, you can modify the custom filters.

- **Technical Translations**: This option will open a list of translated terms for the current model. You can modify the technical translation terms for your model from here. You can refer to *Chapter 11, Internationalization,* to learn more about translations.

- **View Access Rights**: This option will show a list of security access rights for the current model.

- **View Record Rules**: This option will show a list of security record rules for the current model.

- **Fields View Get**: You can extend and modify an existing view from other add-on modules. In some applications, these views are inherited by several add-on modules. Because of this, it is very difficult to get a clear idea of the whole view definition. With this option, you will get the final view definition after applying all view inheritances. Internally, it uses the `fields_view_get()` method.

- **Edit View: <view type>**: This option will open the dialog with the `ir.ui.view` record of the current view. This option is dynamic and it will show an option based on the view that is currently open. This means that if you open **Kanban View**, you will get an **Edit View: Kanban** option, and if you open **Form View**, you will get an **Edit View: Form** option.

> **Important tip**
> You can modify the view definition from the **Edit View** option. This updated definition will be applicable on the current database and these changes will be removed when you update the module. It's therefore better to modify views from modules.

- **Edit ControlPanelView**: This option is the same as the preceding one, but it will open the `ir.ui.view` record of the current model's search view.

- **Activate Assets Debugging**: Odoo provides two types of developer mode: *Developer mode* and *Developer mode with assets*. With this option, you can switch from *Developer* mode to *Developer mode with assets* mode. Check the *Activating the Odoo developer tools* recipe in *Chapter 1, Installing the Odoo Development Environment,* for more details.

- **Activate Test Assets Debugging**: As we know, Odoo uses tours for testing. Enabling this mode will load test assets in Odoo. This option will show some more tours in the **Start tour** dialog.

- **Regenerate Assets Bundles**: Odoo manages all CSS and JavaScript through asset bundles. This option deletes the old JavaScript and CSS assets and generates new ones. This option is helpful when you are getting issues because of asset caching. We will learn more about asset bundles in *Chapter 14, CMS Website Development*.

- **Become Super User**: This is a new option added from version 12. By activating this option, you switch to a super user. You can access the records even if you don't have access rights. This option is not available for all users; it is only available for users who have **Administration: settings** access rights. After activating this mode, you will see a striped top menu, as shown here:

Figure 7.4 – Menu after activating a super user

- **Leave Developer Tools**: This option allows you to leave developer mode.

We have seen all of the options that are available under the debug menu. These options can be used in several ways, such as debugging, testing, and fixing issues. They can also be used to explore the source code for views.

8
Advanced Server-Side Development Techniques

In *Chapter 5*, *Basic Server-Side Development*, you saw how to write methods for a model class, how to extend methods from inherited models, and how to work with recordsets. This chapter will deal with more advanced topics, such as working with the environment of a recordset, calling a method upon a button click, and working with `onchange` methods. The recipes in this chapter will help you manage more complex business problems. You will learn how to create more interactive apps.

In this chapter, we will look at the following recipes:

- Changing the user that performs an action
- Calling a method with a modified context
- Executing raw SQL queries
- Writing a wizard to guide the user
- Defining `onchange` methods
- Calling `onchange` methods on the server side

- Defining onchange with the compute method
- Defining a model based on a SQL view
- Adding custom settings options
- Implementing init hooks

Technical requirements

The technical requirement for this chapter is the Odoo online platform.

All the code used in this chapter can be downloaded from the GitHub repository at https://github.com/PacktPublishing/Odoo-14-Development-Cookbook-Fourth-Edition/tree/master/Chapter08.

Changing the user that performs an action

When writing business logic code, you may have to perform some actions with a different security context. A typical case is performing an action with **superuser** rights, bypassing security checks. Such a requirement arises when business requirements necessitate operating on records for which users do not have security access rights.

This recipe will show you how to allow normal users to modify the **rent** status of a book by using sudo(). Put simply, we will allow users to rent books by themselves even if they do not have the right to create a rent record.

Getting ready

For easier understanding, we will add a new model to manage the book rantings. We will add a new model called library.book.rent. You can refer to the following definition to add this model:

```
class LibraryBookRent(models.Model):
    _name = 'library.book.rent'

    book_id = fields.Many2one('library.book', 'Book', required=True)
    borrower_id = fields.Many2one('res.partner', 'Borrower', required=True)
    state = fields.Selection([('ongoing', 'Ongoing'), ('returned', 'Returned')],
                              'State', default='ongoing', required=True)
```

```
rent_date = fields.Date(default=fields.Date.today)
return_date = fields.Date()
```

You will need to add a form view, an action, and a menu item to see this new model from the user interface. You will also need to add security rules for the librarian, so they can issue the book for rent. Please refer to *Chapter 3, Creating Odoo Add-On Modules,* if you don't know how to add these things.

Alternatively, you can use the ready-made initial module from our GitHub code examples to save time. This module will be available in the Chapter08/r0_initial_module folder. The GitHub code examples are available at https://github.com/PacktPublishing/Odoo-14-Development-Cookbook-Fourth-Edition/tree/master/Chapter08/00_initial_module/my_library.

How to do it...

If you have tested the module, you will find that only users who have librarian access rights can mark a book as borrowed. Non-librarian users cannot borrow a book by themselves; they need to ask a librarian user. Suppose that we want to add a new feature so that non-librarian users can borrow books by themselves, for themselves. We will do this without giving them the access rights for the library.book.rent model.

In order to let normal users borrow books, you need to perform the following steps:

1. Add the book_rent() method in the library.book model:

    ```
    class LibraryBook(models.Model):
        _name = 'library.book'
        ...
        def book_rent(self):
    ```

2. In the method, ensure that we are acting on a single record:

    ```
    self.ensure_one()
    ```

3. Raise a warning if a book is not available to borrow (make sure you have imported UserError at the top):

    ```
    if self.state != 'available':
        raise UserError(_('Book is not available for renting'))
    ```

4. Get the empty recordset of `library.book.rent` as a superuser:

```
rent_as_superuser = self.env['library.book.rent'].sudo()
```

5. Create a new book borrow record with the appropriate values:

```
rent_as_superuser.create({
    'book_id': self.id,
    'borrower_id': self.env.user.partner_id.id,
})
```

6. To trigger this method from the user interface, add the button to the book's form view:

```
<button name="book_rent"
        string="Rent this book"
        type="object"
        class="btn-primary"/>
```

Restart the server and update `my_library` to apply the given changes. After the update, you will see a **Rent this book** button on the book form view. When you click on that, a new rent record will be created. This will also work for non-librarian users. You can test this by accessing Odoo as a demo user.

How it works...

In the first three steps, we have added new method called `book_rent()`. This method will be called when the user clicks on the **Rent this book** button on the book form view.

In *step 4*, we used `sudo()`. This method returns a new recordset with a modified **environment** in which the user has **superuser** rights. When `recordset` is called with `sudo()`, the environment will modify the `environment` attribute to `su`, which indicates the **superuser** state of the environment. You can access its status via `recordset.env.su`. All method calls through this `sudo` recordset are made with superuser privileges. To get a better idea of this, remove `.sudo()` from the method and then click on the **Rent this book** button. It will raise **Access Error** and the user will no longer have access to the model. Simply using `sudo()` will bypass all security rules.

If you need a specific user, you can pass a recordset containing either that user or the database ID of the user as follows:

```
public_user = self.env.ref('base.public_user')
public_book = self.env['library.book'].with_user(public_user)
public_book.search([('name', 'ilike', 'cookbook')])
```

This code snippet allows you to search for books that are visible, using the `public` user.

There's more...

Using `sudo()`, you can bypass the access rights and security record rules. Sometimes you can access multiple records that are meant to be isolated, such as records from different companies in multi-company environments. The `sudo()` recordset bypasses all the security rules of Odoo.

If you are not careful, records searched in this environment may be linked to any company present in the database, which means that you may be leaking information to a user; worse, you may be silently corrupting the database by linking records that belong to different companies.

> **Important tip**
> When using `sudo()`, always double-check to ensure that your calls to `search()` do not rely on the standard record rules to filter the results.

See also

Check out these references for more information:

- If you want to learn more about environments, refer to the *Obtaining an empty recordset for a model* recipe in *Chapter 5*, *Basic Server-Side Development*.
- For more information about access-control lists and record rules, check out *Chapter 10*, *Security Access*.

Calling a method with a modified context

The **context** is part of the environment of a recordset. It is used to pass extra information such as the time zone and the language of the user from the user interface. You can also use the context to pass the parameters specified in the actions. A number of methods in the standard Odoo add-ons use the context to adapt their business logic based on these context values. It is sometimes necessary to modify the context on a recordset to get the desired results from a method call or the desired value for a computed field.

This recipe will show how to change the behavior of a method based on values in the environmental context.

Getting ready

For this recipe, we will use the `my_library` module from the previous recipe. On the form view of the `library.book.rent` model, we will add a button to mark the book as lost, in case a normal user loses a book. Note that we already have the same button in the form view of the book, but here, we will have a slightly different behavior to understand the use of contexts in Odoo.

How to do it...

In order to add a button, you need to perform the following steps:

1. Update the definition of the `state` field to have a `lost` state:

    ```
    state = fields.Selection([
            ('ongoing', 'Ongoing'),
            ('returned', 'Returned'),
            ('lost', 'Lost')],
        'State', default='ongoing', required=True)
    ```

2. Add a **Mark as lost** button in the form view of `library.book.rent`:

    ```
    <button name="book_lost"
            string="Lost the Book"
            states="ongoing"
            type="object"/>
    ```

3. Add the `book_lost()` method in the `library.book.rent` model:

    ```
    def book_lost(self):
        ...
    ```

4. In the method, make sure that we are acting on a single record, and then change the state:

    ```
    self.ensure_one()
    self.sudo().state = 'lost'
    ```

5. Add the following code in the method to change the context of the environment and call the method to change the book's state to `lost`:

    ```
    book_with_different_context = self.book_id.with_context(avoid_deactivate=True)
    book_with_different_context.sudo().make_lost()
    ```

6. Update the `make_lost()` method of the `library.book` model to have a different behavior:

```
def make_lost(self):
    self.ensure_one()
    self.state = 'lost'
    if not self.env.context.get('avoid_deactivate'):
        self.active = False
```

How it works...

In *step 1*, we have added a new state for the book. This new state will indicate lost books.

In *step 2*, we have added a new button, **Mark as lost**. The user will use this button to report **lost books**.

In *step 3 and 4*, we have added method that will be called when user clicks on the **Mark as lost** button.

Step 5 calls `self.book_id.with_context()` with some keyword arguments. This returns a new version of the `book_id` recordset with an updated context. We are adding one key in the context here, `avoid_deactivate=True`, but you can add multiple keys if you want. We have used `sudo()` here, so non-librarian users can report books as lost.

In *step 6*, we checked whether the context has a positive value for the `avoid_deactivate` key. We avoid deactivating books, so the librarian can see them even if they are lost.

Now, when librarians report lost books in the book form view, the book record status will be changed to **lost**, and the book will be archived. But when non-librarian users report lost books in their rent records, the book record status will be changed to lost; the book will not be archived, so that librarians can take a look at them later.

This is just a simple example of a modified context, but you can use it anywhere in an **ORM**, short for **Object Relational Mapping**, based on your requirements.

There's more...

It is also possible to pass a dictionary to `with_context()`. In this case, the dictionary is used as the new context, which overwrites the current one. So, *step 5* can also be written as follows:

```
new_context = self.env.context.copy()
new_context.update({'avoid_deactivate': True})
```

```
book_with_different_context = self.book_id.with_context(new_
context)
book_with_different_context.make_lost()
```

See also

Refer to the following recipes to learn more about contexts in Odoo:

- The *Obtaining an empty recordset for a model* recipe in *Chapter 5, Basic Server-Side Development*, explains what the environment is.

- The *Passing parameters to forms and actions – context* recipe in *Chapter 9, Backend Views*, explains how to modify the context in action definitions.

- The *Search for records* recipe in *Chapter 5, Basic Server-Side Development*, explains active records.

Executing raw SQL queries

Most of the time, you can perform the operations you want by using Odoo's ORM. For example, you can use the `search()` method to fetch records. However, sometimes, you need more; either you cannot express what you want using the domain syntax (for which some operations are tricky, if not downright impossible) or your query requires several calls to `search()`, which ends up being inefficient.

This recipe shows you how to use raw SQL queries to get the average number of days a user keeps a particular book.

Getting ready

For this recipe, we will use the `my_library` module from the previous recipe. For simplicity, we will just print the results in a log, but in real scenarios, you will need to use the query result in your business logic. In *Chapter 9, Backend Views*, we will display the result of this query in the user interface.

How to do it...

To get the information about the average number of days a user keeps a particular book, you need to perform the following steps:

1. Add the `average_book_occupation()` method to `library.book`:

    ```
    def average_book_occupation(self):
        ...
    ```

2. Add this code to the method to push all pending updates:

   ```
   self.flush()
   ```

3. In the method, write the following SQL query:

   ```
   sql_query = """
       SELECT
           lb.name,
           avg((EXTRACT(epoch from age(return_date, rent_date)) / 86400))::int
       FROM
           library_book_rent AS lbr
       JOIN
           library_book as lb ON lb.id = lbr.book_id
       WHERE lbr.state = 'returned'
       GROUP BY lb.name;"""
   ```

4. Execute the query:

   ```
   self.env.cr.execute(sql_query)
   ```

5. Fetch the result and log it (make sure you have imported `logger`):

   ```
   result = self.env.cr.fetchall()
   logger.info("Average book occupation: %s", result)
   ```

6. Add a button in the form view of the `library.book` mode to trigger our method:

   ```
   <button name="average_book_occupation" string="Log Average Occ." type="object" />
   ```

Do not forget to import `logger` in this file. Then, restart and update the `my_library` module.

How it works...

In *step 1*, we added the `average_book_occupation()` method, which will be called when the user clicks on the **Log Average Occ.** button.

In *step 2*, we have used the `flush()` method. Starting from, Odoo v13 ORM uses cache excessively. The ORM uses one global cache per transaction. So, it might be possible that records in the database and records in the ORM cache have different data. Using the `flush()` method before the executing query will make sure all the changes in the cache are pushed to the database.

In *step 3*, we declare a SQL `SELECT` query. This will return the average number of days a user holds a particular book. If you run this query in the PostgreSQL CLI, you will get a result based on your book data. Here is the sample date based on my database:

```
+-------------------------------------------+-------+
| name                                      | avg   |
|-------------------------------------------+-------|
| Odoo 12 Development Cookbook              | 33    |
| PostgreSQL 10 Administration Cookbook     | 81    |
+-------------------------------------------+-------+
```

Step 4 calls the `execute()` method on the database cursor stored in `self.env.cr`. This sends the query to PostgreSQL and executes it.

Step 5 uses the `fetchall()` method of the cursor to retrieve a list of rows selected by the query. This method returns a list of rows. In my case, this is `[('Odoo 12 Development Cookbook', 33), ('PostgreSQL 10 Administration Cookbook', 81)]`. From the form of the query we execute, we know that each row will have exactly two values, the first being `name` and the other being the average number of days a user holds a particular book. Then, we simply log it.

In *step 6*, we have just an **Add** button to handle user actions.

> **Important Note**
> If you are executing an UPDATE query, you need to manually invalidate the cache, because Odoo ORM's cache is unaware of the changes you made with the UPDATE query. To invalidate the cache, you can use `self.invalidate_cache()`.

There's more...

The object in `self.env.cr` is a thin wrapper around a `psycopg2` cursor. The following methods are the ones that you will want to use most of the time:

- `execute(query, params)`: This executes the SQL query with the parameters marked as `%s` in the query substituted with the values in `params`, which is a tuple.

> **Warning**
> Never do the substitution yourself; always use formatting options such as `%s`, because if you use a technique such as string concatenation, it can make the code vulnerable to SQL injection.

- `fetchone()`: This returns one row from the database, wrapped in a tuple (even if there is only one column selected by the query).
- `fetchall()`: This returns all the rows from the database as a list of tuples.
- `dictfetchall()`: This returns all the rows from the database as a list of dictionaries mapping column names to values.

Be very careful when dealing with raw SQL queries:

- You are bypassing all the security of the application. Ensure that you call `search([('id', 'in', tuple(ids))])` with any list of IDs you are retrieving to filter out records to which the user has no access.
- Any modifications you are making are bypassing the constraints set by the add-on modules, except the `NOT NULL`, `UNIQUE`, and `FOREIGN KEY` constraints, which are enforced at the database level. This is also the case for any computed field recomputation triggers, so you may end up corrupting the database.
- Avoid the `INSERT/UPDATE` query, because inserting or updating records via queries will not run any business logic written by overriding the `create()` and `write()` methods. It will not update stored compute fields and the ORM constraints will be bypassed too.

See also

- For access-rights management, refer to *Chapter 10*, *Security Access*.

Writing a wizard to guide the user

In the *Using abstract models for reusable model features* recipe in *Chapter 4, Application Models*, the `models.TransientModel` base class was introduced. This class shares a lot with normal models, except that the records of transient models are periodically cleaned up in the database, hence the name transient. These are used to create wizards or dialog boxes, which are filled in the user interface by the users and are generally used to perform actions on the persistent records of the database.

Getting ready

For this recipe, we will use the `my_library` module from the previous recipes. This recipe will add a new wizard. With this wizard, librarians will be able to issue multiple books at the same time.

How to do it...

Follow the given steps to add a new wizard for creating book rent records:

1. Add a new transient model to the module, with the following definition:

   ```python
   class LibraryRentWizard(models.TransientModel):
       _name = 'library.rent.wizard'

       borrower_id = fields.Many2one('res.partner',
           string='Borrower')
       book_ids = fields.Many2many('library.book',
           string='Books')
   ```

2. Add the `callback` method that performs the action on the transient model. Add the following code to the `LibraryRentWizard` class:

   ```python
   def add_book_rents(self):
       rentModel = self.env['library.book.rent']
       for wiz in self:
           for book in wiz.book_ids:
               rentModel.create({
                   'borrower_id': wiz.borrower_id.id,
                   'book_id': book.id
               })
   ```

3. Create a form view for the model. Add the following view definition to the module views:

   ```xml
   <record id='library_rent_wizard_form' model='ir.ui.view'>
       <field name='name'>library rent wizard form view</field>
       <field name='model'>library.rent.wizard</field>
       <field name='arch' type='xml'>
           <form string="Borrow books">
               <sheet>
                   <group>
                       <field name='borrower_id'/>
                   </group>
                   <group>
                       <field name='book_ids'/>
                   </group>
               </sheet>
               <footer>
                   <button string='Rent' type='object'
   ```

```
                             name='add_book_rents'
                             class='btn-primary'/>
                 <button string='Cancel' class='btn-
default' special='cancel'/>
             </footer>
         </form>
     </field>
 </record>
```

4. Create an action and a menu entry to display the wizard. Add the following declarations to the module menu file:

```
<act_window id="action_wizard_rent_books"
            name="Give on Rent"
            res_model="library.rent.wizard"
            view_mode="form" target="new" />
<menuitem id="menu_wizard_rent_books"
          parent="library_base_menu"
          action="action_wizard_rent_books"
          sequence="20" />
```

5. Add access rights for `library.rent.wizard` in the `ir.model.access.csv` file:

```
acl_library_rent_wizard,library.library_rent_
wizard,model_library_rent_wizard,group_librarian,1,1,1,1
```

Update the `my_library` module to apply the changes.

How it works...

Step 1 defines a new model. It is no different from other models, apart from the base class, which is `TransientModel` instead of `Model`. Both `TransientModel` and `Model` share a common base class, called `BaseModel`, and if you check the source code of Odoo, you will see that 99% of the work is in `BaseModel`, and that both `Model` and `TransientModel` are almost empty.

The only things that change for the `TransientModel` records are as follows:

- Records are periodically removed from the database so that the tables for transient models do not grow over time.
- You are not allowed to define `one2many` fields on a `TransientModel` instance that refers to a normal model as this will add a column on the persistent model that links to transient data. Use `many2many` relations in this case. You can, of course, use `one2many` fields if the related model in `one2many` is also `TransientModel`.

We define two fields in the model: one to store the member borrowing the books and one to store the list of books being borrowed. We can add other scalar fields, to record a scheduled return date, for instance.

Step 2 adds the code to the wizard class that will be called when the button defined in *step 3* is clicked on. This code reads the values from the wizard and creates `library.book.rent` records for each book.

Step 3 defines a view for our wizard. Refer to the *Document-style forms* recipe in *Chapter 9, Backend Views*, for details. The important point here is the button in the footer; the `type` attribute is set to `'object'`, which means that when the user clicks on the button, the method with the name specified by the name attribute of the button will be called.

Step 4 ensures that we have an entry point for our wizard in the menu of the application. We use `target='new'` in the action so that the form view is displayed as a dialog box over the current form. Refer to the *Adding a menu item and window action* recipe in *Chapter 9, Backend Views*, for details.

Step 5 we have added access rights for the `library.rent.wizard` model. With this, the librarian user will get full rights of the `library.rent.wizard` model.

> **Note**
> Prior to Odoo v14, `TransientModel` does not require any access rules. Anyone can create a record, and they can only access records created by themselves. With Odoo v14, access rights are compulsory for `TransientModel`.

There's more...

Here are some tips to enhance your wizards.

Using the context to compute default values

The wizard we are presenting requires the user to fill in the name of the member in the form. There is a feature of the web client that we can use to save some typing. When an action is executed, the **context** is updated with some values that can be used by wizards:

- `active_model`: This is the name of the model related to the action. This is generally the model being displayed onscreen.
- `active_id`: This indicates that a single record is active and provides the ID of that record.
- `active_ids`: If several records are selected, this will be a list with the IDs. This happens when several items are selected in a tree view when the action is triggered. In a form view, you get `[active_id]`.
- `active_domain`: This is an additional domain on which the wizard will operate.

These values can be used to compute the default values of the model or even directly in the method called by the button. To improve on the example in this recipe, if we had a button displayed on the form view of a `res.partner` model to launch the wizard, the context of the creation of the wizard would contain `{'active_model': 'res.partner', 'active_id': <partner id>}`. In that case, you could define the `member_id` field to get a default value computed by the following method:

```
def _default_member(self):
    if self.context.get('active_model') == 'res.partner':
        return self.context.get('active_id', False)
```

Wizards and code reuse

In *step 2*, we could have removed the `for` loop in the wizard, and by assuming that `len(self)` will be 1, we can add `self.ensure_one()` at the beginning of the method, as follows:

```
def add_book_rents(self):
    self.ensure_one()
    rentModel = self.env['library.book.rent']
    for book in self.book_ids:
        rentModel.create({
            'borrower_id': self.borrower_id.id,
            'book_id': book.id
        })
```

Adding `self.ensure_one()` at the beginning of the method will ensure that the number of records in `self` is one. An error will be raised if there is more than one record in `self`.

We recommend using the version in the recipe. It will allow us to reuse the wizard from other parts of the code by creating records for the wizard, putting them in a single recordset (refer to the *Combining recordsets* recipe in *Chapter 5*, *Basic Server-Side Development*, to see how to do this), and then calling `add_book_rents()` on the recordset. Here, the code is trivial, and you do not really need to jump through all those hoops to record that some books have been borrowed by different members. However, in an Odoo instance, some operations are much more complex, and it is always nice to have a wizard available that does the right thing. When using these wizards, ensure that you check the source code for any possible use of the `active_model/active_id/active_ids` keys from the context. If this is the case, you need to pass a custom context (refer to the *Calling a method with a modified context* recipe).

Redirecting the user

The method in *step 2* does not return anything. This will cause the wizard dialog to be closed after the action is performed. Another possibility is to have the method return a dictionary with the fields of `ir.action`. In this case, the web client will process the action as if a menu entry had been clicked on by the user. The `get_formview_action()` method defined in the `BaseModel` class can be used to achieve this. For instance, if we wanted to display the form view of the member who has just borrowed the books, we could have written the following:

```python
def add_book_rents(self):
    rentModel = self.env['library.book.rent']
    for wiz in self:
        for book in wiz.book_ids:
            rentModel.create({
                'borrower_id': wiz.borrower_id.id,
                'book_id': book.id
            })
    borrowers = self.mapped('borrower_id')
    action = borrowers.get_formview_action()
    if len(borrowers.ids) > 1:
        action['domain'] = [('id', 'in', tuple(borrowers.ids))]
    action['view_mode'] = 'tree,form'
    return action
```

This builds a list of borrowers who have borrowed books from this wizard (in practice, there will only be one such member when the wizard is called from the user interface) and creates a dynamic action, which displays the members with the specified IDs.

The *redirecting the user* technique can be used to create a wizard that has several steps to be performed one after the other. Each step in the wizard can use the values of the previous steps, by providing a **Next** button that calls a method defined on the wizard that updates some fields on the wizard and returning an action that will redisplay the same updated wizard and get ready for the next step.

See also

- Refer to the *Document-style forms* recipe in *Chapter 9, Backend Views,* for more details on defining a view for a wizard.
- To understand more about views and calling server-side methods, refer to the *Adding a menu item and window action* recipe in *Chapter 9, Backend Views.*
- For more details on creating records for the wizard and putting them in a single recordset, refer to the *Combining recordsets* recipe in *Chapter 5, Basic Server-Side Development.*

Defining onchange methods

When writing business logic, it is often the case that some fields are interrelated. We looked at how to specify constraints between fields in the *Adding constraint validations to a model* recipe in *Chapter 4, Application Models.* This recipe illustrates a slightly different concept. Here, `onchange` methods are called when a field is modified in the user interface to update the values of other fields of the record in the web client, usually in a form view.

We will illustrate this by providing a wizard similar to the one defined in the *Writing a wizard to guide the user* recipe, but that can be used to record book returns. When a member is set in the wizard, the list of books is updated to the books that are currently borrowed by the member. While we are demonstrating `onchange` methods on `TransientModel`, these features are also available on normal models.

Getting ready

For this recipe, we will use the `my_library` module from the *Writing a wizard to guide the user* recipe of this chapter. We will create a wizard to return a borrowed book. We will add an `onchange` method, which will auto-fill books when a librarian selects a member field.

You will also want to prepare your work by defining the following transient model for the wizard:

```python
class LibraryReturnWizard(models.TransientModel):
    _name = 'library.return.wizard'

    borrower_id = fields.Many2one('res.partner', string='Member')
    book_ids = fields.Many2many('library.book', string='Books')

    def books_returns(self):
        loanModal = self.env['library.book.rent']
        for rec in self:
            loans = loanModal.search(
                [('state', '=', 'ongoing'),
                ('book_id', 'in', rec.book_ids.ids),
                ('borrower_id', '=', rec.borrower_id.id)]
            )
            for loan in loans:
                loan.book_return()
```

Finally, you will need to define a view, an action, and a menu entry for the wizard. These steps will be left as an exercise for you to carry out.

How to do it...

To automatically populate the list of books to return when the user is changed, you need to add an `onchange` method in the `LibraryReturnsWizard` step, with the following definition:

```python
    @api.onchange('borrower_id')
    def onchange_member(self):
        rentModel = self.env['library.book.rent']
        books_on_rent = rentModel.search(
            [('state', '=', 'ongoing'),
            ('borrower_id', '=', self.borrower_id.id)]
        )
        self.book_ids = books_on_rent.mapped('book_id')
```

How it works...

An onchange method uses the `@api.onchange` decorator, which is passed the names of the fields that change and will thus trigger the call to the method. In our case, we say that whenever `borrower_id` is modified in the user interface, the method must be called.

In the body of the method, we search the books currently borrowed by the member, and we use an attribute assignment to update the `book_ids` attribute of the wizard.

There's more...

The basic use of `onchange` methods is to compute new values for fields when some other fields are changed in the user interface, as we have seen in the recipe.

Inside the body of the method, you get access to the fields displayed in the current view of the record, but not necessarily all the fields of the model. This is because `onchange` methods can be called while the record is being created in the user interface before it is stored in the database! Inside an `onchange` method, `self` is in a special state, denoted by the fact that `self.id` is not an integer, but an instance of `odoo.models.NewId`. Therefore, you must not make any changes to the database in an `onchange` method, because the user may end up canceling the creation of the record, which will not roll back any changes made by the `onchange` method during the process of editing.

Additionally, `onchange` methods can return a Python dictionary. This dictionary can have the following keys:

- `warning`: The value must be another dictionary with the `title` and `message` keys containing the title and the content of a dialog box, respectively, which will be displayed when the `onchange` method is run. This is useful for drawing the attention of the user to inconsistencies or to potential problems.

- `domain`: The value must be another dictionary that maps field names to domains. This is useful when you want to change the domain of a `one2many` field, depending on the value of another field.

For instance, suppose that we have a fixed value set for `expected_return_date` in our `library.book.rent` model, and we want to display a warning when a member has some books that are late. We also want to restrict the choice of books to the ones currently borrowed by the user. We can rewrite the `onchange` method, as follows:

```
@api.onchange('member_id')
def onchange_member(self):
    rentModel = self.env['library.book.rent']
```

```python
        books_on_rent = rentModel.search(
            [('state', '=', 'ongoing'),
             ('borrower_id', '=', self.borrower_id.id)]
        )
        self.book_ids = books_on_rent.mapped('book_id')
        result = {
            'domain': {'book_ids': [
                        ('id', 'in', self.book_ids.ids)]
            }
        }
        late_domain = [
            ('id', 'in', books_on_rent.ids),
            ('expected_return_date', '<', fields.Date.today())
        ]
        late_books = loans.search(late_domain)
        if late_books:
            message = ('Warn the member that the following '
                       'books are late:\n')
            titles = late_books.mapped('book_id.name')
            result['warning'] = {
                'title': 'Late books',
                'message': message + '\n'.join(titles)
            }
        return result
```

This code will show a warning about the borrower's late books, but such warnings are like notifications. They cannot be used for validation purposes because they do not stop the business flow.

Calling onchange methods on the server side

The *onchange* method has a limitation: it will not be invoked when you are performing operations on the server side. onchange is invoked automatically only when the dependent operations are performed through the Odoo user interface. Yet, in a number of cases, it is important that these *onchange* methods are called, because they update important fields in the created or updated record. Of course, you can do the required computation yourself, but this is not always possible, as the *onchange* method can be added or modified by a third-party add-on module installed on the instance that you don't know about.

This recipe explains how to call the *onchange* methods on a record by manually invoking the *onchange* method before creating a record.

Getting ready

In the *Changing the user that performs an action* recipe, we added a **Rent this book** button so non-librarian users can borrow books by themselves. We now want to do the same for returning the books, but instead of writing the logic for returning the book, we will just use the book return wizard that we created in the *Defining onchange methods* recipe.

How to do it...

In this recipe, we will manually create a record of the `library.return.wizard` model. We want the *onchange* method to compute the returned books for us. To do this, you need to perform the following steps:

1. Import `Form` from the `tests` utility in the `library_book.py` file:

    ```
    from odoo.tests.common import Form
    ```

2. Create the `return_this_books` method in the `library.book` model:

    ```
    def return_all_books(self):
        self.ensure_one()
    ```

3. Get an empty recordset for `library.return.wizard`:

    ```
    wizard = self.env['library.return.wizard']
    ```

4. Create wizard `Form` block like this:

    ```
    with Form(wizard) as return_form:
    ```

5. Trigger onchange by assigning a borrower and then return the books:

    ```
        return_form.borrower_id = self.env.user.partner_id
        record = return_form.save()
        record.books_returns()
    ```

How it works...

For an explanation of *step 1* to *step 3*, refer to the *Creating new records* recipe in *Chapter 5, Basic Server-Side Development*.

Step 4 creates a virtual form to handle onchange specifications, such as the GUI.

Step 5 contains the full logic to return all books. In the first line, we have assigned `borrower_id` in the wizard. This will trigger the *onchange* method defined in the `library.return.wizard` model. The onchange method will assign the books in the many2many field `book_ids` (to learn more about the onchange method, refer to the onchange method definition in the previous recipe). Then, we call the `save()` method of the form, which will return a wizard record. After that, we call the `books_returns()` method to execute the logic to return all books.

The onchange method is mostly invoked from the user interface. But in this recipe, we have learned how you can use/trigger the business logic of the onchange method on the server side. This way, you can create records without bypassing any business logic.

See also

If you want to learn more about creating and updating records, refer to the *Creating new records* and *Updating the values of recordset records* recipes in *Chapter 5, Basic Server-Side Development*.

Defining onchange with the compute method

In the last two recipes, we have seen how to define and call the *onchange* method. We have also seen its limitation, which is that it can be invoked automatically only from the user interface. As a solution to this problem, Odoo v13 introduced a new way to define `onchange` behavior. In this recipe, we will see how you can use the `compute` method to produce behavior like the `onchange` method's.

Getting ready

For this recipe, we will use the `my_library` module from the previous recipe. We will replace the `onchange` method of `library.return.wizard` with the *compute* method.

How to do it...

Follow these steps to modify the onchange method with the compute method:

1. Replace api.onchange in the onchange_member() method with compute like this:

   ```
   @api.depends('borrower_id')
   def onchange_member(self):
       ...
   ```

2. Add the compute parameter in the definition of the field like this:

   ```
   book_ids = fields.Many2many('library.book',
       string='Books',
       compute="onchange_member",
       readonly=False)
   ```

Upgrade the my_library module to apply the code, then test the return book wizard to see the change.

How it works...

Functionally, our computed onchange works like the normal onchange method. The only difference is now onchange will be trigged upon backend changes too.

In *step 1*, we replaced @api.onchange with @api.compute. This is required to recompute the method when the field value changes.

In *step 2*, we registered the compute method with the field. If you notice, we have used readonly=False with the compute field definition. By default, compute methods are **read-only**, but by setting readonly=False, we are making sure that the field is editable and stored.

Refer to the *Adding computed fields to a model* recipe in *Chapter 4, Application Models*, to learn more about computed fields.

There's more...

As computed onchange works in the backend too, we no longer need to use the Form class in the return_all_books() method. You can replace the code as follows:

```
def return_all_books(self):
    self.ensure_one()
    wizard = self.env['library.return.wizard']
```

```
wizard.create({
    'borrower_id': self.env.user.partner_id.id
}).books_returns()
```

This code will return all the rented books of a user without using the Form class. With the normal onchange method, you need to create the Form object, but with computed onchange, you no longer need to create a Form object. The correct onchange method will be called when a record is created.

See also

- To learn more about computed fields, refer to the *Adding computed fields to a model* recipe in *Chapter 4, Application Models*.

Defining a model based on a SQL view

When working on the design of an **add-on** module, we model the data in classes that are then mapped to database tables by Odoo's ORM. We apply some well-known design principles, such as **separation of concerns** and **data normalization**. However, at later stages of the module design, it can be useful to aggregate data from several models in a single table, and to maybe perform some operations on them on the way, especially for reporting or producing dashboards. To make this easier, and to make use of the full power of the underlying **PostgreSQL** database engine in Odoo, it is possible to define a read-only model backed by a PostgreSQL view, rather than a table.

In this recipe, we will reuse the rent model from the *Writing a wizard to guide the user* recipe in this chapter, and we will create a new model to make it easier to gather statistics about books and authors.

Getting ready

For this recipe, we will use the `my_library` module from the previous recipe. We will create a new model called `library.book.rent.statistics` to hold the statistics data.

How to do it...

To create a new model backed by a PostgreSQL view, follow these instructions:

1. Create a new model with the _auto class attribute set to `False`:

   ```
   class LibraryBookRentStatistics(models.Model):
       _name = 'library.book.rent.statistics'
       _auto = False
   ```

2. Declare the fields you want to see in the model, setting them as `readonly`:

   ```
   book_id = fields.Many2one('library.book',
       string='Book',
       readonly=True)
   rent_count = fields.Integer(
       string="Times borrowed",
       readonly=True)
   average_occupation = fields.Integer(
       string="Average Occupation (DAYS)",
       readonly=True)
   ```

3. Define the init() method to create the view:

   ```
   def init(self):
       tools.drop_view_if_exists(self.env.cr, self._table)
       query = """
       CREATE OR REPLACE VIEW library_book_rent_statistics AS (
       SELECT
               min(lbr.id) as id,
               lbr.book_id as book_id,
               count(lbr.id) as rent_count,
               avg((EXTRACT(epoch from age(return_date, rent_date)) / 86400))::int as average_occupation

           FROM
               library_book_rent AS lbr
           JOIN
               library_book as lb ON lb.id = lbr.book_id
           WHERE lbr.state = 'returned'
           GROUP BY lbr.book_id
       );
       """
       self.env.cr.execute(query)
   ```

4. You can now define views for the new model. A pivot view is especially useful to explore data (refer to *Chapter 9, Backend Views*).

5. Do not forget to define some access rules for the new model (take a look at *Chapter 10, Security Access*).

How it works...

Normally, Odoo will create a new table for the model you are defining by using the field definitions for the columns. This is because in the `BaseModel` class, the `_auto` attribute defaults to `True`. In *step 1*, by positioning this class attribute to `False`, we tell Odoo that we will manage this by ourselves.

In *step 2*, we define some fields that will be used by Odoo to generate a table. We take care to flag them as `readonly=True`, so that the views do not enable modifications that you will not be able to save, since PostgreSQL views are read-only.

Step 3 defines the `init()` method. This method normally does nothing; it is called after `_auto_init()` (which is responsible for the table creation when `_auto = True`, but does nothing otherwise), and we use it to create a new SQL view (or to update the existing view in the case of a module upgrade). The view creation query must create a view with column names that match the field names of the model.

> **Important tip**
>
> It is a common mistake, in this case, to forget to rename the columns in the view definition query, and this will cause an error message when Odoo cannot find the column.

Note that we also need to provide an **integer column** called **ID** that contains unique values.

There's more...

It is also possible to have some computed and related fields on such models. The only restriction is that the fields cannot be stored (and therefore, you cannot use them to group records or to search). However, in the preceding example, we could have made the editor of the book available by adding a column, defined as follows:

```
publisher_id = fields.Many2one('res.partner', related='book_id.publisher_id', readonly=True)
```

If you need to group by publisher, you need to store the field by adding it in the view definition, rather than using a related field.

See also

- To learn more about UI views for user actions, refer to *Chapter 9, Backend Views*.
- For a better understanding of access control and record rules, take a look at *Chapter 10, Security Access*.

Adding custom settings options

In Odoo, you can provide optional features through the **Settings** options. The user can enable or disable this option at any time. We will illustrate how to create **Settings** options in this recipe.

Getting ready

In previous recipes, we have added buttons so that non-librarian users can borrow and return books. This is not the case for every library; however, we will create a settings option to enable and disable this feature. We will do this by hiding these buttons. In this recipe, we will use the same `my_library` module from the previous recipes.

How to do it...

In order to create **custom settings** options, follow these steps:

1. Add a new group in the `my_library/security/groups.xml` file:

    ```xml
    <record id="group_self_borrow" model="res.groups">
        <field name="name">Self borrow</field>
        <field name="users" eval="[(4, ref('base.user_admin'))]"/>
    </record>
    ```

2. Add a new field by inheriting the `res.config.settings` model:

```
class ResConfigSettings(models.TransientModel):
    _inherit = 'res.config.settings'

    group_self_borrow = fields.Boolean(string="Self borrow",
                                       implied_group='my_library.group_self_borrow')
```

3. Add this field in the existing `settings` view with `xpath` (for more details, refer to *Chapter 9, Backend Views*):

```
<record id="res_config_settings_view_form" model="ir.ui.view">
    <field name="name">res.config.settings.view.form.inherit.library</field>
    <field name="model">res.config.settings</field>
    <field name="priority" eval="5"/>
    <field name="inherit_id" ref="base.res_config_settings_view_form"/>
    <field name="arch" type="xml">
        <xpath expr="//div[hasclass('settings')]" position="inside">
            <div class="app_settings_block"
                data-string="Library" string="Library" data-key="my_library"
                groups="my_library.group_librarian">
                <h2>Library</h2>
                <div class="row mt16 o_settings_container">
                    <div class="col-12 col-lg-6 o_setting_box" id="library">
                        <div class="o_setting_left_pane">
                            <field name="group_self_borrow"/>
                        </div>
                        <div class="o_setting_right_pane">
                            <label for="group_self_borrow"/>
                            <div class="text-muted">
                                Allow users to borrow and return books by themself
                            </div>
```

```
                    </div>
                </div>
            </div>
        </div>
    </xpath>
</field>
</record>
```

4. Add some actions and a menu for Settings:

```
<record id="library_config_settings_action" model="ir.
actions.act_window">
    <field name="name">Settings</field>
    <field name="type">ir.actions.act_window</field>
    <field name="res_model">res.config.settings</field>
    <field name="view_id" ref="res_config_settings_view_
form"/>
    <field name="view_mode">form</field>
    <field name="target">inline</field>
    <field name="context">{'module' : 'my_library'}</
field>
</record>

<menuitem name="Settings"
    id="library_book_setting_menu"
    parent="library_base_menu"
    action="library_config_settings_action"
    sequence="50"/>
```

5. Modify the buttons in the book's form view and add a my_library.group_self_borrow group:

```
<button name="book_rent"
    string="Rent this book"
    type="object" class="btn-primary"
    groups="my_library.group_self_borrow"/>
<button
    name="return_all_books"
    string="Return all book"
    type="object" class="btn-primary"
    groups="my_library.group_self_borrow"/>
```

Restart the server and update the my_library module to apply the changes.

How it works...

In Odoo, all settings options are added in the `res.config.settings` model. `res.config.settings` is a transient model. In *step 1*, we created a new security group. We will use this group to create the **hide** and **show** buttons.

In *step 2*, we added a new `Boolean` field in the `res.config.settings` model by inheriting it. We added an `implied_group` attribute with the value of `my_library.group_self_borrow`. This group will be assigned to all `odoo` users when the admin enables or disables options with the `Boolean` field.

Odoo settings use a form view to display settings options on a user interface. All of these options are added in a single form view with the external ID, `base.res_config_settings_view_form`. In *step 3*, we added our option in the user interface by inheriting this setting form view. We used `xpath` to add our `setting` option. In *Chapter 9, Backend Views*, we will see this in detail. In the form definition, you will find that the attribute data-key value of this option will be your module name. This is only needed when you are adding a whole new tab in **Settings**. Otherwise, you can just add your option in the **Settings** tab of the existing module with `xpath`.

In *step 4*, we added an action and a menu to access the configuration options from the user interface. You will need to pass the `{'module' : 'my_library'}` context from the action to open the **Settings** tab of the `my_library` module by default when the menu is clicked.

In *step 5*, we added `my_library.group_self_borrow` groups to the buttons. Because of this group, the **Borrow** and **Return** buttons will be hidden or shown, based on the settings options.

After this, you will see a separate **Settings** tab for the library, and, in the tab, you will see a `Boolean` field to enable or disable the self-borrowing option. When you enable or disable this option, in the background, Odoo will apply or remove `implied_group` to or from all `odoo` users. Because we added the groups on buttons, the buttons will be displayed if the user has groups and will be hidden if the user doesn't have groups. In *Chapter 10, Security Access,* we will look at security groups in detail.

There's more...

There are a few other ways to manage the **Settings** options. One of them is to separate features in the new module and **install** or **uninstall** them through options. To do this, you will need to add a `Boolean` field with the name of the module prefixed with `module_`. If, for example, we create a new module called `my_library_extras`, you will need to add a `Boolean` field, as follows:

```
module_my_library_extras = fields.Boolean(
    string='Library Extra Features')
```

When you enable or disable this option, `odoo` will **install** or **uninstall** the `my_libarary_extras` module.

Another way to manage settings is to use system parameters. Such data is stored in the `ir.config_parameter` model. Here's how you to create system-wide global parameters:

```
digest_emails = fields.Boolean(
    string="Digest Emails",
    config_parameter='digest.default_digest_emails')
```

The `config_parameter` attribute in the fields will make sure the user data is stored in **System Parameters**, at **Settings | Technical | Parameters | System Parameters** menu. The data will be stored with the `digest.default_digest_emails` key.

Settings options are used to make your application generic. These options give freedom to users and allow them to enable or disable features on the fly. When you convert a feature into options, you can serve more customers with one module and your customers can enable the feature whenever they like.

Implementing init hooks

In *Chapter 6*, *Managing Module Data*, you saw how to add, update, and delete records from XML or CSV files. Sometimes, however, the business case is complex, and it can't be solved using data files. In such cases, you can use the `init` hook from the manifest file to perform the operations you want.

Getting ready

We will use the same `my_library` module from the previous recipe. For simplicity, in this recipe, we will just create some book records through `post_init_hook`.

How to do it...

In order to add `post_init_hook`, follow these steps:

1. Register the hook in the `__manifest__.py` file with the `post_init_hook` key:

   ```
   ...
   'post_init_hook': 'add_book_hook',
   ...
   ```

2. Add the `add_book_hook()` method in the `__init__.py` file:

   ```
   from odoo import api, fields, SUPERUSER_ID

   def add_book_hook(cr, registry):
       env = api.Environment(cr, SUPERUSER_ID, {})
       book_data1 = {'name': 'Book 1', 'date_release': fields.Date.today()}
       book_data2 = {'name': 'Book 2', 'date_release': fields.Date.today()}
       env['library.book'].create([book_data1, book_data2])
   ```

How it works...

In the first step, we registered `post_init_hook` in the manifest file with the `add_book_hook` value. This means that after the installation of the module, Odoo will look for the `add_book_hook` method in `__init__.py`. If it's found, it will call the method with the database cursor and registry.

In *step 2*, we declared the `add_book_hook()` method, which will be called after the module is installed. We created two records from this method. In real situations, you can write complex business logic here.

In the example, we looked at `post_init_hook`, but Odoo supports two more hooks:

- `pre_init_hook`: This hook will be invoked when you start installing a module. It is the opposite of `post_init_hook`; it will be invoked before installing the current module.

- `uninstall_hook`: This hook will be invoked when you uninstall the module. This is mostly used when your module needs a garbage-collection mechanism.

9
Backend Views

In all previous chapters, you have seen the server and database side of Odoo. In this chapter, you will see the UI side of Odoo. You will learn how to create different types of views. Aside from the views, this chapter also covers other components, such as action buttons, menu, and widgets, which will help you make your application more user-friendly. After completing this chapter, you will be able to design the UI of an Odoo backend. Note that this chapter does not cover the website part of Odoo; we have a separate chapter for that.

In this chapter, we will cover the following recipes:

- Adding a menu item and window actions
- Having an action open a specific view
- Adding content and widgets to a form view
- Adding buttons to forms
- Passing parameters to forms and actions – context
- Defining filters on record lists – domain
- Defining list views
- Defining search views
- Adding a search filter side panel
- Changing existing views – view inheritance

- Defining document-style forms
- Dynamic form elements using `attrs`
- Defining embedded views
- Displaying attachments on the side of the form view
- Defining kanban views
- Showing kanban cards in columns according to their state
- Defining calendar views
- Defining graph view and pivot view
- Defining the cohort view
- Defining the dashboard view
- Defining the gantt view
- Defining the activity view
- Defining the map view
- Show Banner on tree view

Technical requirements

Throughout this chapter, we will assume that you have a database with the base add-on installed and an empty Odoo add-on module where you can add XML code from the recipes to a data file referenced in the add-on's manifest. Refer to *Chapter 3*, *Creating Odoo Add-On Modules*, for more information on how to activate changes in your add-on.

The technical requirements for this chapter include an online Odoo platform.

All of the code used in this chapter can be downloaded from the GitHub repository at `https://github.com/PacktPublishing/Odoo-14-Development-Cookbook-Fourth-Edition/tree/master/Chapter09`.

Adding a menu item and window actions

The most obvious way to make a new feature available to users is by adding a menu item. When you click on a **menu** item, something happens. This recipe walks you through how to define that something.

We will create a top-level menu and its sub-menu, which will open a list of all customers.

This can also be done using the *web user interface*, through the **settings** menu, but we prefer to use XML data files since this is what we'll have to use when creating our add-on modules.

Getting ready

In this recipe, we will need a module with a dependency on the `account` module, as the account module adds new fields to the `res.partner` model to differentiate between customer and supplier records. So, if you are using an existing module, please add the `account` dependency in the manifest. Alternatively, you can grab the initial module from https://github.com/PacktPublishing/Odoo-14-Development-Cookbook-Fourth-Edition/tree/master/Chapter09/00_initial_module.

How to do it...

In an XML data file of our add-on module, perform the following steps:

1. Define an action to be executed:

    ```xml
    <act_window
        id="action_all_customers"
        name="All customers"
        res_model="res.partner"
        view_mode="tree,form"
        domain="[('customer_rank', '>', 0)]"
        context="{'default_customer_rank': 1}"
        limit="20"/>
    ```

2. Create the top-level menu, which will be as follows:

    ```xml
    <menuitem id="menu_custom_top_level"
        name="My App menu"
        web_icon="my_module,static/description/icon.png"/>
    ```

3. Refer to our action in the menu:

```xml
<menuitem id="menu_all_customers"
    parent="menu_custom_top_level"
    action="action_all_customers"
    sequence="10"/>
```

If we now upgrade the module, we will see a top-level menu with the label **My App menu** that opens a sub-menu called **All Customers**. Clicking on that menu item will open a list of all customers.

How it works...

The first XML element, `act_window`, declares a window action to display a list view with all the customers. We used the most important attributes:

- `name`: To be used as the title for views opened by the action.
- `res_model`: This is the model to be used. We are using `res.partner`, where Odoo stores all the partners and addresses, including customers.
- `view_mode`: This lists the view types to make available. It is a comma-separated values file of the views type. The default value is `tree, form`, which makes list and form views available. If you just want to show calendar and form views, then the value of `view_mode` should be `calendar, form`. Other possible view choices are `kanban`, `graph`, `pivot`, `calendar`, `cohort`, and `dashboard`. You will learn more about these views in forthcoming recipes.
- `domain`: This is optional and allows you to set a filter on the records to be made available in the views. In this case, we want to limit the partners to only those who are customers. We will see all of these views in more detail in the *Defining filters on record lists – Domain* recipe of this chapter.
- `context`: This can set values made available to the opened views, affecting their behavior. In our example, on new records, we want the customer rank's default value to be 1. This will be covered in more depth in the *Passing parameters to forms and actions – Context* recipe of this chapter.
- `limit`: This sets the default amount of records that can be seen on list views. In our example, we have given a limit of 20, but if you don't give a `limit` value, Odoo will use the default value of 80.

Next, we create the menu item hierarchy from the top-level menu to the clickable end menu item. The most important attributes for the `menuitem` element are as follows:

- `name`: This is used as the text that the menu items display. If your menu item links to an action, you can leave this out, because the action's name will be used in that case.
- `parent` (`parent_id` if using the `record` element): This is the XML ID that references the parent menu item. Items with no parents are top-level menus.
- `action`: This is the XML ID that references the action to be called.
- `sequence`: This is used to order the sibling menu items.
- `groups` (`groups_id` with the `record` tag): This is an optional list of user groups that can access the menu item. If empty, it will be available to all users.
- `web_icon`: This option only works on the top-level menu. It will display an icon of your application in the Enterprise edition.

Window actions automatically determine the view to be used by looking up views for the target model with the intended type (`form`, `tree`, and so on) and picking the one with the lowest sequence number. `act_window` and `menuitem` are convenient shortcut XML tags that hide what you're actually doing. If you don't want to use the shortcut XML tags, then you can create a record of the `ir.actions.act_window` and `ir.ui.menu` models via the `<record>` tag. For example, if you want to load `act_window` with `<record>`, you can do so as follows:

```xml
<record id='action_all_customers' model='ir.actions.act_window'>
    <field name="name">All customers</field>
    <field name="res_model">res.partner</field>
    <field name="view_mode">tree,form</field>
    <field name="domain">[('customer_rank','>', 0)]</field>
    <field name="context">{'default_customer_rank': 1}</field>
    <field name="limit">20</field>
</record>
```

In the same way, you can create a `menuitem` instance through `<record>`.

> **Important information**
>
> Be aware that names used with the `menuitem` shortcut may not map to the field names that are used when using a `record` element – `parent` should be `parent_id` and `groups` should be `groups_id`.

To build the menu, the web client reads all the records from `ir.ui.menu` and infers their hierarchy from the `parent_id` field. Menus are also filtered based on user permissions to models and groups assigned to menus and actions. When a user clicks on a menu item, its `action` is executed.

There's more...

Window actions also support a `target` attribute to specify how the view is to be presented. The possible choices are as follows:

- **current**: This is the default and opens the view in the web client main content area.
- **new**: This opens the view in a popup.
- **inline**: Like **current** but opens a form in edit mode and disables the **Action** menu.
- **fullscreen**: The action will cover the whole browser window, so this will overlay the menus too. Sometimes, this is called **tablet mode**.
- **main**: Like **current**, but also clears out the breadcrumbs.

There are also some additional attributes available for window actions that are not supported by the `act_window` shortcut tag. To use them, we must use the `record` element with the following fields:

- `res_id`: If opening a form, you can have it open a specific record by setting its ID here. This can be useful for multi-step wizards, or in cases when you have to view or edit a specific record frequently.
- `search_view_id`: This specifies a specific search view to use for tree and graph views.

Keep in mind that the menu in the top left (or the apps icon in the Enterprise version) and the menu in the bar at the top are both made up of menu items. The only difference is that the items in the menu in the top left don't have any parent menus, while the ones on the top bar have the respective menu item from the top bar as a parent. In the left bar, the hierarchical structure is more obvious.

Also bear in mind that for design reasons, the first-level menus will open the dropdown menu if your second-level menu has child menus. In any case, Odoo will open the first menu item's action based on the sequence of child menu items.

Refer to the following to learn more about menus and views:

- The `ir.actions.act_window` action type is the most common action type, but a menu can refer to any type of action. Technically, it is the same if you link to a client action, a server action, or any other model defined in the `ir.actions.*` namespace. It just differs in what the backend makes of the action.
- If you need just a tiny bit more flexibility in the concrete action to be called, look into server actions that return a window action. If you need complete flexibility, take a look at the client actions (`ir.actions.client`), which allow you to have a completely custom user interface. However, only do this as a last resort as you lose a lot of Odoo's convenient helpers when using them.

See also

- For detailed explanation filters on all of the views have a look at the *Defining filters on record lists – Domain* recipe of this chapter.

Having an action open a specific view

Window actions automatically determine the view to be used if none is given, but sometimes we want an action to open a specific view.

We will create a basic form view for the `res.partner` model, and then we will create a new window action specifically open that form view.

How to do it...

1. Define the `partner` minimal tree and form view:

```xml
    <record id="view_all_customers_tree" model="ir.ui.view">
        <field name="name">All customers</field>
        <field name="model">res.partner</field>
        <field name="arch" type="xml">
            <tree>
                <field name="name" />
            </tree>
        </field>
    </record>

    <record id="view_all_customers_form" model="ir.ui.view">
        <field name="name">All customers</field>
```

```xml
            <field name="model">res.partner</field>
            <field name="arch" type="xml">
                <form>
                    <group>
                        <field name="name" />
                    </group>
                </form>
            </field>
        </record>
```

2. Update the action from the *Adding a menu item and window action* recipe to use a new form view:

```xml
        <record id="action_all_customers_tree" model="ir.actions.act_window.view">
            <field name="act_window_id" ref="action_all_customers" />
            <field name="view_id" ref="view_all_customers_tree" />
            <field name="view_mode">tree</field>
            <field name="sequence" eval="2"/>
        </record>

        <record id="action_all_customers_form" model="ir.actions.act_window.view">
            <field name="act_window_id" ref="action_all_customers" />
            <field name="view_id" ref="view_all_customers_form" />
            <field name="view_mode">form</field>
            <field name="sequence" eval="2"/>
        </record>
```

Now, if you open your menu and click on a **partner** in the list, you should see the very minimal form and tree that we just defined.

How it works...

This time, we used the generic XML code for any type of record, that is, the `record` element with the required `id` and `model` attributes. The `id` attribute on the `record` element is an arbitrary string that must be unique for your add-on. The `model` attribute refers to the name of the model you want to create. Given that we want to create a view, we need to create a record of the `ir.ui.view` model. Within this element, you set fields as defined in the model you chose through the `model` attribute. For `ir.ui.view`, the crucial fields are `model` and `arch`. The `model` field contains the model you want to define a view for, while the `arch` field contains the definition of the view itself. We'll come to its contents in a short while.

The `name` field, while not strictly necessary, is helpful when debugging problems with views. So, set it to a string that tells you what this view is intended to do. This field's content is not shown to the user, so you can fill in any technical hints that you deem sensible. If you set nothing here, you'll get a default name that contains the model name and view type.

ir.actions.act_window.view

The second record we defined works in tandem with `act_window`, which we defined earlier in the *Adding a menu item and window action* recipe. We already know that by setting the `view_id` field there, we can select which view is used for the first view mode. However, given that we set the `view_mode` field to the `tree, form` view, `view_id` would have to pick a tree view, but we want to set the form view, which comes second here.

If you find yourself in a situation like this, use the `ir.actions.act_window.view` model, which gives you fine-grained control over which views to load for which view type. The first two fields defined here are examples of the generic way to refer to other objects; you keep the element's body empty but add an attribute called `ref`, which contains the XML ID of the object you want to reference. So, what happens here is we refer to our action from the previous recipe in the `act_window_id` field, and refer to the view we just created in the `view_id` field. Then, though not strictly necessary, we add a sequence number to position this view assignment relative to the other view assignments, for the same action. This is only relevant if you assign views for different view modes by creating multiple `ir.actions.act_window.view` records.

> **Important information**
>
> Once you define the `ir.actions.act_window.view` records, they take precedence over what you filled in the action's `view_mode` field. So, with the preceding records, you won't see a list at all, but only a form. You should add another `ir.actions.act_window.view` record that points to a list view for the `res.partner` model.

There's more...

As we saw in the *Adding a menu item and window action* recipe, we can replace `act_window` with `<record>`. If you want to use a custom view, you can follow the given syntax:

```xml
<record id='action_all_customers' model='ir.actions.act_window'>
    <field name="name">All customers</field>
    <field name="res_model">res.partner</field>
    <field name="view_mode">tree,form</field>
    <field name="domain">[('customer_rank', '>', 0)]</field>
    <field name="context">{'default_customer_rank': 1,
        'tree_view_ref': 'my_module.view_all_customers_tree',
        'form_view_ref': 'my_module.view_all_customers_form'
    }</field>
    <field name="limit">20</field>
</record>
```

This example is just an alternative of `act_window`. In the code base of Odoo, you will find both types of action.

Adding content and widgets to a form view

The preceding recipe showed how to pick a specific view for an action. Now, we'll demonstrate how to make the form view more useful. In this recipe, we will use the *form view* that we defined earlier in the *Having an action open a specific view* recipe. In the *form view*, we will add the widgets and content.

How to do it...

1. Define the basic structure of the form view:

```xml
<record id="form_all_customers" model="ir.ui.view">
    <field name="name">All customers</field>
    <field name="model">res.partner</field>
    <field name="arch" type="xml">
        <form>
            <!--form content goes here -->
        </form>
    </field>
</record>
```

2. To add a head bar, which is usually used for action buttons and stage pipeline, add this inside the form:

```xml
<header>
<button type="object" name="open_commercial_entity"
        string="Open commercial partner"
class="btn-primary" />
</header>
```

3. Add fields to the form, using `group` tags to organize them visually:

```xml
<group string="Content" name="my_content">
    <field name="name" />
    <field name="category_id" widget="many2many_tags" />
</group>
```

Now, the form should display a top bar with a button and two vertically aligned fields as shown in the following screenshot:

Figure 9.1 – Screenshot of the form view

How it works...

We'll look at the `arch` field of the `ir.ui.view` model first. First, note that views are defined in XML, so you need to pass the `type="xml"` attribute for the `arch` field, otherwise the parser will be confused. It is also mandatory that your view definition contains well-formed XML, otherwise you'll get in trouble when loading this snippet.

We'll now walk through the tags that we used previously and summarize the others that are available.

form

When you define a form view, it is mandatory that the first element within the `arch` field is a `form` element. This is used internally to derive the record's `type` field.

In addition to the following elements, you can use arbitrary HTML within the form tag. The algorithm has it that every element unknown to Odoo is considered plain HTML and is simply passed through to the browser. Be careful with that, as the HTML you fill in can interact with the HTML code the Odoo elements generates, which might distort the rendering.

header

This element is a container for elements that should be shown in a form's header, which is rendered as a white bar. Usually, as in this example, you place action buttons here. Alternatively, if your model has a `state` field, you could opt for a **status bar**.

button

The `button` element is used to allow the user to trigger an action. Refer to the *Adding buttons to forms* recipe for details.

group

The `<group>` element is Odoo's main element and is used for organizing content. Fields placed within a `<group>` element are rendered with their title, and all fields within the same group are aligned so that there's also a visual indicator that they belong together. You can also nest `<group>` elements; this causes Odoo to render the contained fields in adjacent columns.

In general, you should use the `<group>` mechanism to display all of your fields in the form view and only revert to the other elements, such as `<notebook>`, `<label>`, `<newline>`, and more, when necessary.

If you assign the `string` attribute on a group, its content will be rendered as a heading for the group.

You should develop the habit of assigning a name to every logical group of fields, too. This name is not visible to the user but is very helpful when we override views in the following recipes. Keep the name unique within the form definition to avoid confusion about which group you refer to. Don't use the `string` attribute for this, because the value of the string will change eventually because of translations.

field

In order to actually show and manipulate data, your form view should contain some `field` elements. Here is an example:

```
<field name="category_id" widget="many2many_tags"
    readonly="1"/>
```

These have one mandatory attribute, called `name`, which refers to the field's name in the model. Earlier, we offered the user the ability to edit the partner's categories. If we only want to disable the editing feature on a field, we can set the `readonly` attribute to `1` or `True`. This attribute may actually contain a small subset of Python code, so `readonly="2>1"` will make the field read-only too. This also applies to the `invisible` attribute, for which you used to have a value that is read from the database but not shown to the user. Later, we'll take a look at which situations this can be used in.

You must have noticed the `widget` attribute in the `categories` field. This defines how the data in the field is supposed to be presented to the user. Every type of field has a standard widget, so you don't have to explicitly choose a widget. However, several types provide multiple ways of representation, in which case you might opt for something other than the default. As a complete list of available widgets would exceed the scope of this recipe, consult **Odoo's source code** to try them out. Take a look at *Chapter 14, CMS Website Development*, for details on how to make your own.

notebook and page

If your model has too many fields, then you can use the `<notebook>` and `<page>` tags to create tabs. Each `<page>` in the `<notebook>` tag will create a new tab, and content inside the page will be the tab content. The following example will create two tabs with three fields in each tab:

```
<notebook>
    <page string="Tab 1">
        <field name="field1"/>
```

```
            <field name="field2"/>
            <field name="field3"/>
        </page>
        <page string="Tab 2">
            <field name="field4"/>
            <field name="field5"/>
            <field name="field6"/>
        </page>
    </notebook>
```

The `string` attribute in the `<page>` tag will be the name of the tab. You can only use `<page>` tags in the `<notebook>` tag, but in the `<page>` tag, you can use any other elements.

General attributes

On most elements (this includes `group`, `field`, and `button`), you can set the `attrs` and `groups` attributes. Here is a small example:

```
<field name="category_id"
        attrs="{'readpnly': [('state', '='. 'done')]}"
        groups="base.group_no_one"/>
```

While `attrs` is discussed in the *Dynamic form elements using attrs* recipe, the `groups` attribute gives you the possibility to show some elements only to members of certain groups. Simply put, the group's full XML ID (separated by commas for multiple groups) is the attribute, and the element will be hidden for everyone who is not a member of at least one of the groups mentioned.

Other tags

There are situations in which you might want to deviate from the strict layout groups prescribed. For example, if you want the `name` field of a record to be rendered as a heading, the field's label will interfere with the appearance. In this case, don't put your field into a `group` element, but instead into a plain HTML `h1` element. Then, before the `h1` element, put a `label` element with the `for` attribute set to your `field name`:

```
<label for="name" />
```
```
<h1><field name="name" /></h1>
```

This will be rendered with the field's content as a big heading, but the field's name will be written in a smaller type, above the big heading. This is basically what the standard partner form does.

If you need a line break within a group, use the `newline` element. It's always empty:

```
<newline />
```

Another useful element is `footer`. When you open a form as a popup, this is a good place to put the action buttons. It will be rendered as a separate bar too, analogous to the `header` element.

The form view also has special widgets such as `web_ribbon`. You can use it with the `<widget>` tag as follows:

```
<widget name="web_ribbon" title="Archived" bg_color="bg-danger"
    attrs="{'invisible': [('active', '=', True)]}"/>
```

You can use `attrs` to hide and show the ribbon based on a condition. Don't worry if you are not aware of `attrs`. It will be covered in the *Dynamic form elements using attrs* recipe of this chapter.

> **Important tip**
>
> Don't address **XML nodes** with their `string` attribute (or any other translated attribute, for that matter), as your view overrides will break for other languages because views are translated before inheritance is applied.

There's more...

Since form views are basically HTML with some extensions, Odoo also makes extensive use of CSS classes. Two very useful ones are `oe_read_only` and `oe_edit_only`. Elements with these classes will be visible only in *read-only mode* or *edit mode* respectively. For example, to have the label visible only in edit mode, use the following:

```
<label for="name" class="oe_edit_only" />
```

Another very useful class is `oe_inline`, which you can use on fields to make them render as an inline element, to avoid causing unwanted line breaks. Use this class when you embed a field into text or other markup tags.

Furthermore, the `form` element can have the `create`, `edit`, and `delete` attributes. If you set one of these to `false`, the corresponding action won't be available for this form. Without this being explicitly set, the availability of the action is inferred from the user's permissions. Note that this is purely for straightening up the UI; don't use this for security.

See also

The widgets and views already offer a lot of functionality, but sooner or later, you will have requirements that cannot be fulfilled with the exiting widgets and views. Refer to the following recipes to create your own views and widgets:

- Refer to the *Adding buttons to forms* recipe in this chapter for more details about using the `button` element to trigger an action.
- To define your own widgets, refer to the *Creating custom widgets* recipe of *Chapter 15, Web Client Development*.
- Refer to the *Creating a new view* recipe of *Chapter 15, Web Client Development*, to create your own view.

Adding buttons to forms

Buttons are used on form view to handle user actions. We added a button in the form view in the previous recipe, but there are quite a few different types of buttons that we can use. This recipe will add another button that will help the user to open another view. It will also put the following code in the recipe's `header` element.

How to do it...

Add a button that refers to an action:

```
<button type="action"
  name="%(base.action_partner_category_form)d"
  string="Open partner categories" />
```

How it works...

The button's `type` attribute determines the semantics of the other fields, so we'll first take a look at the possible values:

- `action`: This makes the button call an action as defined in the `ir.actions.*` namespace. The `name` attribute needs to contain the action's database ID, which you can conveniently have Odoo look up with a Python-format string that contains the XML ID of the action in question.
- `object`: This calls a method of the current model. The `name` attribute contains the function's name.
- `string`: The `string` attribute is used to assign the text the user sees.

There's more...

Use the `btn-primary` CSS classes to render a button that is highlighted and `btn-default` to render a normal button. This is commonly used for cancel buttons in wizards or to offer secondary actions in a visually unobtrusive way. Setting the `oe_link` class causes the button to look like a link. You can also use other bootstrap button classes to get different button colors.

A call with a button of the **object** type can return a dictionary that describes an action, which will then be executed on the client side. This way, you can implement multiscreen wizards or just open another record.

> **Note**
> Note that clicking on a button always causes the client to issue a `write` or `create` call before running the method.

You can also have content within the `button` tag by replacing the `string` attribute. This is commonly used in button boxes, as described in the *Document style forms* recipe.

Passing parameters to forms and actions – context

Internally, every method in Odoo has access to a dictionary, called **context**, that is propagated from every action to the methods involved in delivering that action. The UI also has access to it, and it can be modified in various ways by setting values in the context. In this recipe, we'll explore some of the applications of this mechanism by toying with the language, default values, and implicit filters.

Getting ready

While not strictly necessary, this recipe will be more fun if you install the French language, if you haven't got this already. Consult *Chapter 11, Internationalization*, for how to do it. If you have a French database, change `fr_FR` to some other language; `en_US` will do for English. Also, click on the **Active** button (changing to **Archive** when you hover over it) for one of your customers in order to archive it and verify that this partner doesn't show up anymore in the list.

How to do it...

1. Create a new action, very similar to the one from the *Adding a menu item and window action* recipe:

   ```xml
   <act_window id="action_all_customers_fr"
       name="Tous les clients"
       res_model="res.partner"
       domain="[('customer_rank', '<', 1)]"
       context="{'lang': 'fr_FR', 'default_lang': 'fr_FR',
           'active_test': False, 'default_customer_rank':
   1}" />
   ```

2. Add a menu that calls this action. This is left as an exercise for the reader.

When you open this menu, the views will show up in French, and if you create a new partner, they will have French as their pre-selected language. A less obvious difference is that you will also see the **deactivated (archived) partner records**.

How it works...

The context dictionary is populated from several sources. First, some values from the current user's record (`lang` and `tz`, for the user's language and the user's time zone) are read. Then, we have some add-ons that add keys for their own purposes. Furthermore, the UI adds keys about which model and which record we're busy with at the moment (`active_id`, `active_ids`, `active_model`). Also, as seen in the *Having an action open a specific view* recipe, we can add our own keys in actions. These are merged together and passed to the underlying server functions, and also to the client-side UI.

So, by setting the `lang` context key, we force the display language to be **French**. You will note that this doesn't change the whole UI language, which is because only the list view that we open lies within the scope of this context. The rest of the UI was loaded already with another context that contained the user's original language. However, if you open a record in this list view, it will be presented in French too, and if you open a linked record on the form or press a button that executes an action, the language will be propagated too.

By setting `default_lang`, we set a default value for every record created within the scope of this context. The general pattern is `default_$fieldname: my_default_value`, which enables you to set default values for newly created partners, in this case. Given that our menu is about customers, we have added `default_customer_rank: 1` as the value for the **Customer rank** field by default. However, this is a model-wide default for `res.partner`, so this wouldn't have changed anything. For scalar fields, the syntax for this is as you would write it in Python code: `string` fields go in quotes, `number` fields stay as they are, and `Boolean` fields are either `True` or `False`. For relational fields, the syntax is slightly more complicated; refer to *Chapter 6, Managing Module Data*, to learn how to write them.

> **Note**
> Note that the default values set in the context override the default values set in the model definition, so you can have different default values in different situations.

The last key is `active_test`, which has very special semantics. For every model that has a field called `active`, Odoo automatically filters out records where this field is `False`. This is why the partner where you unchecked this field disappeared from the list. By setting this key, we can suppress this behavior.

> **Important information**
> This is useful for the UI in its own right but even more useful in your Python code when you need to ensure that an operation is applied to all the records, not just the active ones.

There's more...

When defining a context, you have access to some variables, the most important one being `uid`, which evaluates to the current user's ID. You'll need this to set default filters (refer to the next recipe, *Defining filters on record lists – domain*). Furthermore, you have access to the `context_today` function and the `current_date` variable, where the first is a `date` object that represents the current date, as seen from the user's time zone, and the latter is the current date as seen in UTC, formatted as `YYYY-MM-DD`. To set a default value for a `date` field to the current date, use `current_date`, and, for default filters, use `context_today()`.

Furthermore, you can do some date calculations with a subset of Python's `datetime`, `time`, and `relativedelta` classes.

> **Important tips**
>
> Most of the domains are evaluated on the client side. The server-side domain evaluation is restricted for security reasons. When client-side evaluation was introduced, the best option in order to not break the whole system was to implement a part of Python in JavaScript. There is a small JavaScript Python interpreter built into Odoo that works well for simple expressions, and that is usually enough.
>
> Beware of the use of the `context` variable in the `<act_window />` shortcut. These are evaluated at installation time, which is nearly never what you want. If you need variables in your context, use the `<record />` syntax.

We can also add different contexts for the buttons. It works the same way as how we added context keys in our action. This causes the function or action that the button calls to be run in the context given.

Most form element attributes that are evaluated as Python also have access to the context dictionary. The `invisible` and `readonly` attributes are examples of these. So, in cases where you want an element to show up in a form sometimes, but not at other times, set the `invisible` attribute to `context.get('my_key')`. For actions that lead to a case in which the field is supposed to be invisible, set the context key to `my_key: True`. This strategy enables you to adapt your form without having to rewrite it for different occasions.

You can also set a context on relational fields, which influences how the field is loaded. By setting the `form_view_ref` or `tree_view_ref` keys to the full XML ID of a view, you can select a specific view for this field. This is necessary when you have multiple views of the same type for the same object. Without this key, you get the view with the lowest sequence number, which might not always be desirable.

See also

- The context is also used to set a default search filter. You can learn more about the default search filter in the *Defining search views* recipe of this chapter.
- For more details on setting default recipe refer to the next recipe, *Defining filters on record lists – domain*.
- To learn how to install the French language, consult *Chapter 11, Internationalization*.
- You can refer to learn how to write the syntax for relational fields in *Chapter 6, Managing Module Data*.

Defining filters on record lists – domain

We've already seen an example of a domain in the first recipe of this chapter, which was `[('customer_rank', '>', 0)]`. Often, you need to display a subset of all available records from an action or allow only a subset of possible records to be the target of a many2one relation. The way to describe these filters in Odoo is by using domains. This recipe illustrates how to use a domain to display a selection of partners.

How to do it...

To display a subset of partners from your action, you need to perform the following steps:

1. Add an action for non-French speaking customers:

    ```xml
    <record id="action_my_customers" model="ir.actions.act_window">
        <field name="name">
            All my customers who don't speak French
        </field>
        <field name="res_model">res.partner</field>
        <field name="domain">
            [('type', '=', 'contact'), ('user_id', '=', uid), ('lang', '!=', 'fr_FR')]
        </field>
    </record>
    ```

2. Add an action for customers who are customers or suppliers:

    ```xml
    <record id="action_no_email_or_phone" model="ir.actions.act_window">
        <field name="name">Customers with no email or phone</field>
        <field name="res_model">res.partner</field>
        <field name="domain">
            ['|', ('phone', '=', False), ('email', '=', False)]
        </field>
    </record>
    ```

3. Add menus that call these actions. This is left as an exercise for the reader.

How it works...

The simplest form of domain is a list of three tuples that contain a field name of the model in question as `string` in the first element, an operator as `string` in the second element, and the value that the field is to be checked against as the third element. This is what we did before, and this is interpreted as, "*All those conditions have to apply to the records we're interested in.*" This is actually a shortcut, because the domains know the two prefix operators – `&` and `|` – where `&` is the default. So, in normalized form, the first domain will be written as follows:

```
['&', '&', ('type', '=', 'contact'), ('user_id', '=', uid),
('lang', '!=', 'fr_FR')]
```

While they can be a bit hard to read for bigger expressions, the advantage of prefix operators is that their scope is rigidly defined, which saves you from having to worry about operator precedence and brackets. It's always two expressions: the first `&` applies to `'&', ('type', '=', 'contact')`, with `('user_id', '=', uid)` as the first operand and `('lang', '!=', 'fr_FR')` as the second. Then, the second `&` applies to `('customer', '=', True)` as the first operand and `('user_id', '=', uid)` as the second.

In the second step, we have to write out the full form because we need the `|` operator.

For example, say we have a complex domain such as this: `['|', ('user_id', '=', uid), '&', ('lang', '!=', 'fr_FR'), '|', ('phone', '=', False), ('email', '=', False)]`. See the following figure to learn about how this domain is evaluated:

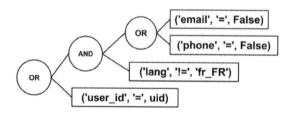

Figure 9.2 – The evaluation of a domain

There is also a `!` operator for negation, but, given logical equivalences and negated comparison operators such as `!=` and `not in`, it is not really necessary.

> **Note**
> Note that this is a unary prefix operator, so it only applies to the following expression in the domain and not to everything that follows.

Note that the right operand doesn't need to be a fixed value when you write a domain for a window action or other client-side domains. You can use the same minimal Python as in the *Passing parameters to forms and actions – context* recipe, so you can write filters such as *changed last week* or *my partners*.

There's more...

The preceding domains work only on fields of the model itself, while we often need to filter based on properties of linked records. To do this, you can use the notation that's also used in `@api.depends` definitions or related fields: create a dotted path from the current model to the model you want to filter for. To search partners that have a salesperson who is a member of a group starting with the letter G, you would use the `[('user_id.groups_id.name', '=like', 'G%')]` domain. The path can be long, so you only have to be sure that there are relation fields between the current model and the model you want to filter for.

Operators

The following table lists the available operators and their semantics:

Operator (equivalent)	Semantics
=, !=, <>	The first one is for an exact match, the second one is for not equal, and the last one is the deprecated notation of not equal.
in, not in	This checks whether the value is one of the values named in a list in the right operand. It is given as a Python list: `[('uid', 'in', [1, 2, 3])]` or `[('uid', 'not in', [1, 2, 3])]`.
<, <=	Greater than, greater than or equal to.
>, >=	Less than, less than or equal to.
like, not like	Checks whether the right operand is contained (as a substring) in the value.
ilike, not ilike	The same as the preceding one, but case insensitive.
=like, =ilike	You can search for patterns here: % matches any string and _ matches one character. This is the equivalent of PostgreSQL's `like`.
child_of	For models with a `parent_id` field, this searches for children of the right operand. The right operand is included in the results.
=?	Evaluates to `true` if the right operand is `false`; otherwise, it behaves like =. This is useful when you generate domains programmatically and want to filter by a value if one is set but ignore the value otherwise.

Table 9.1

Note that some of the operators work only with certain fields and values. For example, the domain [('category_id', 'in', 1)] is invalid and will generate an error, while the domain [('category_id', 'in', [1])] is valid.

Pitfalls of searching using domains

This all works fine for traditional fields, but a notorious problem is searching for the value of a non-stored function field. People often omit the search function. This is simple enough to fix by providing the search function in your own code, as described in *Chapter 4, Application Models*.

Another issue that might baffle developers is Odoo's behavior when searching through one2many or many2many fields with a negative operator. Imagine that you have a partner with the A tag and you search for [('category_id.name', '!=', 'B')]. Your partner shows up in the result and this is what you expected, but if you add the B tag to this partner, it still shows up in your results, because for the search algorithm, it is enough that there is one linked record (A in this case) that does not fulfill the criterion. Now, if you remove the A tag so that B is the only tag, the partner will be filtered out. If you also remove the B tag so that the partner has no tags, it is still filtered out, because conditions on the linked records presuppose the existence of this record. In other situations, though, this is the behavior you want, so it is not really an option to change the standard behavior. If you need a different behavior here, provide a search function that interprets the negation the way you need.

> **Important information**
> People often forget that they are writing XML files when it comes to domains. You need to escape the less-than operator. Searching for records that have been created before the current day will have to be written as [('create_date', '<', current_date)] in XML.

Domains are used widely in Odoo. You will find them everywhere in Odoo; they are used for searching, filtering, security rules, search views, user actions, and more.

If you ever need to manipulate a domain you didn't create programmatically, use the utility functions provided in odoo.osv.expression. The is_leaf, normalize_domain, AND, and OR functions will allow you to combine domains exactly the way that Odoo does. Don't do this yourself, because there are many corner cases that you have to take into account, and it is likely that you'll overlook one.

See also

- For the standard application of domains, see the *Search views* recipe.

Defining list views

After having spent quite some time on the form view, we'll now take a quick look at how to define list views. Internally, these are called tree views in some places and list views in others, but given that there is another construction within the Odoo view framework called **tree**, we'll stick to **list** here.

How to do it...

1. Define your list view:

   ```xml
   <record id="tree_all_contacts" model="ir.ui.view">
       <field name="model">res.partner</field>
       <field name="arch" type="xml">
           <tree
               decoration-bf="customer_rank &gt; 0"
               decoration-danger="supplier_rank &gt; 0"
               decoration-warning="customer_rank &gt; 0
                   and supplier_rank &gt; 0">
               <field name="name" />
               <field name="user_id" widget="many2one_avatar_user"/>
               <field name="state_id" optional="hide" />
               <field name="country_id" optional="show" />
               <field name="customer_rank" invisible="1" />
               <field name="supplier_rank" invisible="1" />
           </tree>
       </field>
   </record>
   ```

2. Register a tree view in the action we created in the *Adding a menu item and window action* recipe of this chapter:

   ```xml
   <record id='action_all_contacts' model='ir.actions.act_window'>
       <field name="name">All Contacts</field>
       <field name="res_model">res.partner</field>
       <field name="view_mode">tree,form</field>
       <field name="context">
           {'tree_view_ref': 'my_module.tree_all_contacts'}
   ```

```
        </field>
        <field name="limit">20</field>
    </record>
```

3. Add menus that call these actions. This is left as an exercise for the reader.

Install/Upgrade the module. After that, you will see our tree view for the customers. And if you check it, it will show different row styles based on our conditions.

How it works...

You already know most of what happens here. We define a view, of the `tree` type this time, and attach it to our action with an `ir.actions.act_window.view` element. So, the only thing left to discuss is the `tree` element and its semantics. With a list, you don't have many design choices, so the only valid children of this element are the `field` and `button` elements. You can also use some widgets in list view; in our example, we have used the `many2one_avatar_user` widget. The tree view has the support of a special widget called `handle`. This is specific to list views. It is meant for integer fields and renders a drag handle that the user can use to drag a row to a different position in the list, thereby updating the field's value. This is useful for sequence or priority fields.

By using the `optional` attribute, you can show fields optionally. Adding the `optional` attribute to a field will allow the user to hide and show the column at any time from the UI. In our example, we have used it for the `country` and `state` fields.

What is new here are the `decoration` attributes in the `tree` element. This contains rules as to which font and/or color is chosen for the row, given in the form of `decoration-$name="Python code"`. All matches turn into the corresponding CSS class, so the previous view renders partners that are **both suppliers and customers in brown**, **customers only in bold**, and **suppliers only in red**. In your Python code, you can only use the fields you named in the view definition, which is why we have to pull the `customer` and `supplier` fields too. We made these invisible because we only need the data and don't want to bother our users with the two extra columns. The possible classes are `decoration-bf` (bold), `decoration-it` (italic), and the semantic bootstrap classes, `decoration-danger`, `decoration-info`, `decoration-muted`, `decoration-primary`, `decoration-success`, and `decoration-warning`.

There's more...

For numeric fields, you can add a `sum` attribute that causes this column to be summed up with the text you set in the attribute as a tooltip. Less common are the `avg`, `min`, and `max` attributes, which display the average, minimum, and maximum, respectively. Note that these four only work on the records that are currently visible, so you might want to adjust the action's `limit` (covered earlier in the *Adding a menu item and window action* recipe) in order for the user to see all the records immediately.

A very interesting attribute for the `tree` element is `editable`. If you set this to top or bottom, the list behaves entirely differently. Without it, clicking on a row opens a form view for the row. With it, clicking on a row makes it editable inline, with the visible fields rendered as form fields. This is particularly useful in embedded list views, which are discussed later in the *Defining embedded views* recipe of this chapter. The choice of top or bottom relates to whether new lines will be added to the top or bottom of the list.

By default, records are ordered according to the `_order` property of the displayed model. The user can change the ordering by clicking on a column header, but you can also set a different initial order by setting the `default_order` property in the `tree` element. The syntax is the same as in `_order`.

> **Important tip**
>
> Ordering is often a source of frustration for new developers. As Odoo lets PostgreSQL do the work here, you can only order by fields that PostgreSQL knows about, and only the fields that live in the same database table. So, if you want to order by a function or a related field, ensure that you set `store=True`. If you need to order by a field inherited from another model, declare a stored related field.

The `create`, `edit`, and `delete` attributes of the `tree` element work the same as for the `form` element we described earlier in the *Adding content and widgets to a form view* recipe of this chapter. They also determine the available controls if the `editable` attribute is set.

Defining search views

When opening your list view, you'll notice the search field to the upper right. If you type something there, you get suggestions about what to search for, and there is also a set of predefined filters to choose from. This recipe will walk you through how to define these suggestions and options.

How to do it...

1. Define your search view:

```xml
<record id="search_all_customers" model="ir.ui.view">
    <field name="model">res.partner</field>
    <field name="arch" type="xml">
        <search>
            <field name="name" />
            <field name="category_id"
                    filter_domain="[('category_id', 'child_of', self)]" />
            <field name="bank_ids" widget="many2one" />
            <filter name="suppliers" string="Suppliers"
                    domain="[('supplier_rank', '>', 0)]" />
            <group expand="0" string="Group By">
                <filter string="Country" name="country"
                        context="{'group_by':'country_id'}"/>
            </group>
        </search>
    </field>
</record>
```

2. Tell your action to use it:

```xml
<record id="action_all_customers" model="ir.actions.act_window">
    <field name="name">All customers</field>
    <field name="res_model">res.partner</field>
    <field name="view_mode">tree,form</field>
    <field name="search_view_id" ref="search_all_customers" />
</record>
```

When you type something into the search bar now, you'll be offered the ability to search for this term in the name, categories, and bank account fields. If your term happens to be a substring of a bank account number in your system, you'll even be offered to search exactly for this bank account.

How it works...

In the case of name, we simply listed the field as the one to be offered to the user to search for. We left the semantics at the default, which is a substring search for character fields.

For categories, we do something more interesting. By default, your search term is applied to a many2many field trigger, name_search, which would be a substring search in the category names in this case. However, depending on your category structure, it can be very convenient to search for partners who have the category you're interested in or a child of it. Think of a main category, *Newsletter subscribers*, with the subcategories *Weekly newsletter*, *Monthly newsletter*, and a couple of other newsletter types. Searching for *newsletter subscribers* with the preceding search view definition will give you everyone who is subscribed to any of those newsletters in one go, which is a lot more convenient than searching for every single type and combining the results.

The filter_domain attribute can contain an arbitrary domain, so you're restricted neither to searching for the same field you named in the name attribute nor to using only one term. The self variable is what the user filled in, and also the only variable that you can use here.

Here's a more elaborate example from the default search view for partners:

```
<field name="name"
       filter_domain="[
           '|', '|',
           ('display_name', 'ilike', self),
           ('ref', '=', self),
           ('email', 'ilike', self)]"/>
```

This means that the user doesn't have to think about what to search for. All they need to do is type in some letters, press *Enter*, and, with a bit of luck, one of the fields mentioned contains the string we're looking for.

For the bank_ids field, we used another trick. The type of field not only decides the default way of searching for the user's input, but it also defines the way in which Odoo presents the suggestions. Also, given that many2one fields are the only ones that offer auto-completion, we force Odoo to do that, even though bank_ids is a one2many field, by setting the widget attribute. Without this, we will have to search in this field, without completion suggestions. The same applies to many2many fields.

> **Note**
> Note that every field with a many2one widget set will trigger a search on its model for every one of the user's keystrokes; don't use too many of them.

You should also put the most-used fields on the top, because the first field is what is searched if the user just types something and presses *Enter*. The search bar can also be used with the keyboard; select a suggestion by pressing the down arrow and open the completion suggestion of a `many2one` by pressing the right arrow. If you educate your users in this and pay attention to the sensible ordering of fields in the search view, this will be much more efficient than typing something first, grabbing the mouse, and selecting an option.

The `filter` element creates a button that adds the content of the filter's `domain` attribute to the search domain. You should add a logical internal `name` and a `string` attribute to describe the filter to your users.

The `<group>` tag is used to provide a grouping option under the **Group by** button. In this recipe, we have added an option to group records based on the `country_id` field.

There's more...

You can group filters with the `group` tag, which causes them to be rendered slightly closer together than the other filters, but this has semantic implications, too. If you put multiple filters in the same group and activate more than one of them, their domains will be combined with the `|` operator, while filters and fields not in the same group are combined with the `&` operator. Sometimes, you might want disjunction for your filters, which is where they filter for mutually exclusive sets, in which case selecting both of them will always lead to an empty result set. Within the same group, you can achieve the same effect with the `separator` element.

> **Note**
> Note that if the user fills in multiple queries for the same field, they will be combined with `|` too, so you don't need to worry about that.

Apart from the `field` attribute, the `filter` element can have a `context` attribute, whose content will be merged with the current context and eventually other context attributes in the search view. This is essential for views that support grouping (refer to the *Defining kanban view* and *Defining graph view* recipes), because the resulting context determines the field(s) to be grouped with the `group_by` key. We'll look into the details of grouping in the appropriate recipes, but the context has other uses, too. For example, you can write a function field that returns different values depending on the context, and then you can change the values by activating a filter.

The search view itself also responds to context keys. In a very similar way to default values when creating records, you can pass default values for a search view through the context. If we had set a context of `{'search_default_suppliers': 1}` in our previous action, the `suppliers` filter would have been preselected in the search view. This works only if the filter has a name, though, which is why you should always set it. To set defaults for fields in the search view, use `search_default_$fieldname`.

Furthermore, the `field` and `filter` elements can have a `groups` property with the same semantics as in the form views in order to make the element only visible to certain groups.

See also

- For further details about manipulating the context, see the *Passing parameters to forms and actions – context* recipe.
- Users who speak languages with heavy use of diacritical marks will probably want to have Odoo search for *e, è, é,* and *ê* when filling in the *e* character. This is a configuration of the *PostgreSQL server*, called **unaccent**, which Odoo has special support for, but is outside the scope of this book. Refer to `https://www.postgresql.org/docs/10/unaccent.html` for more information about unaccent.

Adding a search filter side panel

Odoo provides one more way to display search filters, which is a **search filter side panel**. This panel shows a list of filters on the side of the view. A search panel is very useful when search filters are used frequently by the end user.

Getting ready

The search panel is part of the search view. So, for this recipe, we will continue using the `my_module` add-on from the previous recipe. We will add our search panel to the previously designed search view.

How to do it...

Add `<searchpanel>` in the search view, as shown here:

```xml
<record id="search_all_customers" model="ir.ui.view">
    <field name="model">res.partner</field>
    <field name="arch" type="xml">
```

```xml
            <search>
                <field name="name" />
                <field name="category_id"
                    filter_domain="[('category_id', 'child_of', self)]" />
                <field name="bank_ids" widget="many2one" />
                <filter name="suppliers"
                    string="Suppliers"
                    domain="[('supplier_rank', '>', 0)]" />
                <group expand="0" string="Group By">
                    <filter string="Country" name="country"
                        context="{'group_by':'country_id'}"/>
                </group>
                <!-- Search Panel code -->
                <searchpanel>
                    <field name="user_id" icon="fa fa-users"/>
                    <field name="category_id" icon="fa fa-list"
                    select="multi"/>
                </searchpanel>
            </search>
        </field>
</record>
```

Update the module to apply the modification. After the update, you will see the search panel on the left side of the view.

How it works...

To add the search panel, you will need to use the `<searchpanel>` tag in the search view. To add your filter, you will need to add a field in the search panel.

In our example, first we added a `user_id` field. You also need to add an `icon` attribute to the field. This icon will be displayed before the title of the filter. Once you add the field in the search panel, it will display the title with an icon, and below that, a list of all the users. Upon clicking on a user, the records in the list view will be filtered and you will only see the contacts for the selected user. In this filter, only one item can be active, meaning once you click on another user's filter, the previous user's filter will be removed. If you want to activate multi-user filters, you can use the `select="multi"` attribute. If you use that attribute, you will find the checkbox for each filter option, and you will be able to activate multiple filters at a time. We have used the `select="multi"` attribute on the `category_id` filter. This will allow us to select and filter by multiple categories at once.

> **Note**
>
> Be careful when you are using the side panel filter on `many2one` or `many2many`. If the relation model has too many records, only the **top 200 records** will be displayed, to avoid performance issues.

There's more...

If you want to display search panel items in groups, you can use the `groupby` attribute on a field. For example, if you want to group a category based on its parent hierarchy, you can add the `groupby` attribute with the `parent_id` field, as here:

```
<field name="category_id"
       icon="fa fa-list"
       select="multi"
       groupby="parent_id"/>
```

This will show the category filters grouping by the parent category of the record.

Changing existing views – view inheritance

So far, we have ignored the existing views and declared completely new ones. While this is didactically sensible, you'll rarely be in situations where you'll want to define a new view for an existing model. Instead, you'll want to slightly modify the existing views, be it to simply have them show a field you added to the model in your add-on, or to customize them according to your needs or your customers' needs.

In this recipe, we'll change the default partner form to show the record's last modification date and make the `mobile` field searchable by modifying the search view. Then, we'll change the position of one column in the partners' list view.

How to do it...

1. Inject the field into the default form view:

```
<record id="view_partner_form" model="ir.ui.view">
    <field name="model">res.partner</field>
    <field name="inherit_id" ref="base.view_partner_form"/>
    <field name="arch" type="xml">
        <field name="website" position="after">
            <field name="write_date" />
        </field>
```

```xml
            </field>
        </record>
```

2. Add the field to the default search view:

```xml
<record id="view_res_partner_filter" model="ir.ui.view">
    <field name="model">res.partner</field>
    <field name="inherit_id" ref="base.view_res_partner_filter" />
    <field name="arch" type="xml">
        <xpath expr="." position="inside">
            <field name="mobile" />
        </xpath>
    </field>
</record>
```

3. Add the field to the default list view:

```xml
<record id="view_partner_tree" model="ir.ui.view">
    <field name="model">res.partner</field>
    <field name="inherit_id" ref="base.view_partner_tree" />
    <field name="arch" type="xml">
        <field name="email" position="after">
            <field name="phone" position="move"/>
        </field>
    </field>
</record>
```

After updating your module, you should see the **Last updated on** field beneath the website field on the partner form. When you type something into the search box, it should suggest that you search for the partners on the mobile field, and in the partner's list view, you will see that the order of the phone number and email has changed.

How it works...

In *step 1*, we added a basic structure for the form inheritance. The crucial field here is, as you've probably guessed, `inherit_id`. You need to pass it the XML ID of the view you want to modify (inherit from). The `arch` field contains instructions on how to modify the existing XML nodes within the view you're inheriting from. You should actually think of the whole process as simple XML processing, because all the semantic parts only come a lot later.

The most canonical instruction within the `arch` field of an inherited view is the `field` element, which has the required attributes, `name` and `position`. As you can have every field only once on a form, the name already uniquely identifies a field. With the `position` attribute, we can place whatever we put within the field element, either `before`, `inside`, or `after` the field we named. The default is `inside`, but for readability, you should always name the position you require. Remember that we're not talking semantics here; this is about the position in the XML tree relative to the field we have named. How this will be rendered afterward is a completely different matter.

Step 2 demonstrates a different approach. The `xpath` element selects the first element that matches the XPath expression named in the `expr` attribute. Here, the `position` attribute tells the processor where to put the contents of the `xpath` element.

> **Note**
> If you want to create an XPath expression based on a CSS class, Odoo provides a special function called `hasclass`. For example, if you want to select a `<div>` element with the `test_class` CSS class, then the expression will be `expr="//div[hasclass('test_class')]"`.

Step 3 shows how you can change the position of an element. This option was introduced in *version 12* and it is rarely used. In our example, we moved the `phone` field to come after the `email` field with the `position=move` option.

XPath might look somewhat scary but it is a very efficient means of selecting the node you need to work on. Take the time to look through some simple expressions; it's worth it. You'll likely stumble upon the term **context node**, to which some expressions are relative. In Odoo's view inheritance system, this is always the root element of the view you're inheriting from.

For all the other elements found in the `arch` field of an inheriting view, the processor looks for the first element with the same node name and matching attributes (with the attribute position excluded, as this is part of the instruction). Use this only in cases where it is very unlikely that this combination is not unique, such as a group element combined with a `name` attribute.

> **Important tip**
> Note that you can have as many instruction elements within the `arch` field as you need. We only used one per inherited view because there's nothing else we want to change currently.

There's more...

The `position` attribute has two other possible values: `replace` and `attributes`. Using `replace` causes the selected element to be replaced with the content of the instruction element. Consequently, if you don't have any content, the selected element can simply be removed. The preceding list or form view would cause the `email` field to be removed:

```
<field name="email" position="replace" />
```

> **Warning**
> Removing fields can cause other inheriting views to break and several other undesirable side effects, so avoid that if possible. If you really need to remove fields, do so in a view that comes late in the order of evaluation (refer to the next section, *Order of evaluation in view* inheritance, for more information).

`attributes` has very different semantics from the preceding examples. The processor expects the element to contain the `attribute` elements with a `name` attribute. These elements will then be used to set attributes on the selected element. If you want to heed the earlier warning, you should set the `invisible` attribute to 1 for the `email` field:

```
<field name="email" position="attributes">
    <attribute name="invisible">1</attribute>
</field>
```

An `attribute` node can have `add` and `remove` attributes, which in turn should contain the value to be removed from or added to the space-separated list. This is very useful for the `class` attribute, where you'd add a class (instead of overwriting the whole attribute) by using the following:

```
<field name="email" position="attributes">
    <attribute name="class" add="oe_inline" separator=" "/>
</field>
```

This code adds the `oe_inline` class to the `email` field. If the field already has a class attribute present, Odoo will join the value with the value of the `separator` attribute.

Order of evaluation in view inheritance

As we have only one parent view and one inheriting view currently, we don't run into any problems with conflicting view overrides. When you have installed a couple of modules, you'll find a lot of overrides for the partner form. This is fine as long as they change different things in a view, but there are occasions where it is important to understand how overriding works in order to avoid conflicts.

Direct descendants of a view are evaluated in ascending order of their `priority` field, so views with a lower priority are applied first. Every step of inheritance is applied to the result of the first, so if a view with priority 3 changes a field and another one with priority 5 removes it, this is fine. This does not work, however, if the priorities are reversed.

You can also inherit from a view that is an inheriting view itself. In this case, the second-level inheriting view is applied to the result of the view it inherits from. So, if you have four views, A, B, C, and D, where A is a standalone form, B and C inherit from A, and D inherits from B, the order of evaluation is A, B, D, C. Use this to enforce an order without having to rely on priorities; this is safer in general. If an inheriting view adds a field and you need to apply changes to this field, inherit from the inheriting view and not from the standalone one.

> **Important information**
> This kind of inheritance always works on the complete XML tree from the original view, with modifications from the previous inheriting views applied.

The following points provide information on some advanced tricks that are used to tweak the behavior of view inheritance:

- For inheriting views, a very useful and not very well-known field is `groups_id`. This field causes the inheritance to take place only if the user requesting the parent view is a member of one of the groups mentioned there. This can save you a lot of work when adapting the user interface for different levels of access, because with inheritance, you can have more complex operations than just showing or not showing the elements based on group membership, as is possible with the `groups` attribute on form elements.

- You can, for example, remove elements if the user is a member of a group (which is the inverse of what the `groups` attribute does). You can also carry out some elaborate tricks, such as adding attributes based on group membership. Think about simple things such as making a field read-only for certain groups, or more interesting concepts such as using different widgets for different groups.

- What was described in this recipe has the mode field of the original view set to primary, while the inheriting views have the mode extension, which is the default. We will investigate the case that the mode of an inheriting view is set to `primary` later, where the rules are slightly different.

Defining document-style forms

In this recipe, we'll review some design guidelines in order to present a uniform user experience.

How to do it...

1. Start your form with a `header` element:

   ```
   <header>
       <button type="object" name="open_commercial_entity"
           string="Open commercial partner"
           class="btn-primary" />
   </header>
   ```

2. Add a `sheet` element for content:

   ```
   <sheet>
   ```

3. Put in the `stat` button, which will be used to show total invoiced amount and redirect to invoices:

   ```
   <div class="oe_button_box" name="button_box">
       <button type="object" class="oe_stat_button"
               icon="fa-pencil-square-o"
               name="action_view_partner_invoices">
           <div class="o_form_field o_stat_info">
               <span class="o_stat_value">
                   <field name="total_invoiced"/>
               </span>
               <span class="o_stat_text">Invoiced</span>
           </div>
       </button>
   </div>
   ```

4. Add some prominent field(s):

```xml
<div class="oe_left oe_title">
    <label for="name" />
    <h1>
        <field name="name" />
    </h1>
</div>
```

5. Add your content; you can use a notebook if there are a lot of fields:

```xml
<group>
    <field name="category_id" widget="many2many_tags" />
    <field name="email"/>
    <field name="mobile"/>
</group>
```

6. After the sheet, add the `chatter` widget (if applicable):

```xml
</sheet>
<div class="oe_chatter">
    <field name="message_follower_ids" widget="mail_followers"/>
    <field name="activity_ids" widget="mail_activity"/>
    <field name="message_ids" widget="mail_thread"/>
</div>
```

Let's have a look at how this recipe works.

How it works...

The header should contain buttons that execute actions on the object that the user currently sees. Use the `btn-primary` class to make buttons visually stand out (in purple at the time of writing), which is a good way to guide the user regarding which is the most logical action to execute at the moment. Try to have all the highlighted buttons to the left of the non-highlighted buttons and hide the buttons that are not relevant in the current state (if applicable). If the model has a state, show it in the header using the `statusbar` widget. This will be rendered as right-aligned in the header.

The `sheet` element is rendered as a stylized sheet, and the most important fields should be the first thing the user sees when looking at it. Use the `oe_title` and `oe_left` classes to have them rendered in a prominent place (floating left with slightly adjusted font sizes at the time of writing).

If there are other records of interest concerning the record the user currently sees (such as the partner's invoices on a partner form), put them in an element with the oe_right and oe_button_box classes; this aligns the buttons in it to the right. On the buttons themselves, use the oe_stat_button class to enforce a uniform rendering of the buttons. It's also customary to assign an icon class from the Font Awesome icons for the icon attribute. You can learn more about Font Awesome at https://fontawesome.com/v4.7.0/icons/.

You can use the oe_chatter class and **Chatter widgets** to get the default chatter at the bottom of the form view. For this, you need to use the mail.thread mixin. We will see this in detail in *Chapter 23, Managing Emails in Odoo*.

> **Important information**
> Even if you do not like this layout, stick to the element and class names described here, and adjust what you need with CSS and possibly JavaScript. This will make the user interface more compatible with existing add-ons and allow you to integrate better with core add-ons.

See also

- To find out more about Font Awesome, go to https://fontawesome.com/v4.7.0/icons/.
- For more details on the mail.thread mixin, refer to *Chapter 23, Managing Emails in Odoo*.

Dynamic form elements using attrs

So far, we have only looked into changing forms depending on the user's groups (the groups attribute on elements and the groups_id field on inherited views) and nothing more. This recipe will show you how to modify the form view based on the value of the fields in it.

How to do it...

1. Define an attribute called `attrs` on a form element:

   ```
   <field name="parent_id"
     attrs="{
     'invisible': [('is_company', '=', True)],
     'required': [('is_company', '=', False)]
     }" />
   ```

2. Ensure that all the fields you refer to are available in your form:

   ```
   <field name="is_company"/>
   ```

This will make the `parent_id` field invisible if the partner is a company and required if it's not a company.

How it works...

The `attrs` attribute contains a dictionary with `invisible`, `required`, and `readonly` keys (all of which are optional). The values are domains that may refer to the fields that exist on the form (and really only those, so there are no dotted paths), and the whole dictionary is evaluated according to the rules for client-side Python, as described earlier in the *Passing parameters to forms and actions – context* recipe of this chapter. So, for example, you can access the context in the right-hand operand.

There's more...

While this mechanism is quite straightforward for scalar fields, it's less obvious how to handle the `one2many` and `many2many` fields. In fact, in standard Odoo, you can't do much with those fields within an `attrs` attribute. However, if you only need to check whether such a field is empty, use `[[6, False, []]]` as your right-hand operand.

Defining embedded views

When you show a `one2many` or a `many2many` field on a form, you don't have much control over how it is rendered if you haven't used one of the specialized widgets. Also, in the case of the `many2one` fields, it is sometimes desirable to be able to influence the way the linked record is opened. In this recipe, we'll look at how to define private views for those fields.

How to do it...

1. Define your field as usual, but don't close the tag:

   ```
   <field name="child_ids">
   ```

2. Write the view definition(s) into the tag:

   ```
   <tree>
       <field name="name" />
       <field name="email" />
       <field name="phone" />
   </tree>
   <form>
       <group>
           <field name="name" />
           <field name="function" />
       </group>
   </form>
   ```

3. Close the tag:

   ```
   </field>
   ```

How it works...

When Odoo loads a form view, it first checks whether the `relational` type fields have embedded views in the field, as outlined previously. Those embedded views can have the exact same elements as the views we defined before. Only if Odoo doesn't find an embedded view of some type does it use the model's default view of this type.

There's more...

While embedded views might seem like a great feature, they complicate view inheritance a lot. For example, as soon as embedded views are involved, field names are not guaranteed to be unique, and you'll usually have to use some elaborate XPaths to select elements within an embedded view.

So, in general, you should better define standalone views and use the `form_view_ref` and `tree_view_ref` keys, as described earlier in the *Having an action open a specific view* recipe of this chapter.

Displaying attachments on the side of the form view

In some applications, such as invoicing, you need to fill in data based on a document. To ease the data-filling process, a new feature was added to Odoo version 12 to display the document on the side of the form view.

In this recipe, we will learn how to display the form view and the document side by side:

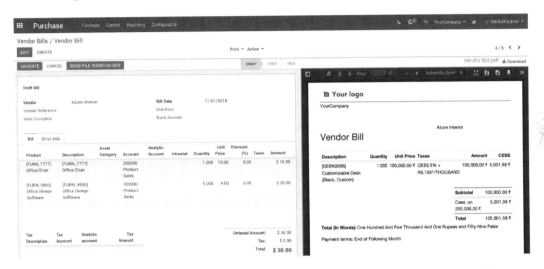

Figure 9.3 – Cascading attachments and the form view

> **Important information**
> This feature is only meant for large displays (>1534px), so if you have a small viewport, this feature will be hidden.
> Internally, this feature uses some responsive utilities, so this feature only works in the **Enterprise edition**. However, you can still use this code in your module. Odoo will automatically handle this, so if the module is installed in the Enterprise edition, it will show the document, while in the Community edition, it will hide everything without any side effects.

How to do it...

We will enable this feature to modify a form view for the `res.partner` model, as follows:

```xml
<record id="view_all_customers_form" model="ir.ui.view">
    <field name="name">All customers</field>
    <field name="model">res.partner</field>
    <field name="arch" type="xml">
        <form>
            <sheet>
                <group>
                    <field name="name" />
                    <field name="email"/>
                </group>
            </sheet>
            <div class="o_attachment_preview"
                 options="{types: ['image', 'pdf'], 'order': 'desc'}" />
            <div class="oe_chatter">
                <field name="message_follower_ids" widget="mail_followers"/>
                <field name="activity_ids" widget="mail_activity"/>
                <field name="message_ids" widget="mail_thread"/>
            </div>
        </form>
    </field>
</record>
```

Update the module to apply the changes. You need to upload a PDF or image via the record chatter. When you upload it, Odoo will display the attachment on the side.

How it works...

This feature only works if your model has inherited the `mail.thread` model. To show the document on the side of any form view, you will need to add an empty `<div>` with the `o_attachment_preview` class before the chatter elements. That's it – the documents attached in the chatter will be displayed on the side of the form view.

By default, `pdf` and `image` documents will be displayed in ascending order by date. You can change this behavior by providing extra options, which include the following:

- `type`: You need to pass the list of document types you want to allow. Only two values are possible: `pdf` and `image`. For example, if you want to display only `pdf` type images, you can pass `{ 'type': ['pdf'] }`.
- `order`: Possible values are `asc` and `desc`. These allow you to show documents in ascending order or descending order of the document creation date.

There's more...

In most cases, you want to display documents on the side of the initial state of any record. If you want to hide the attachment preview based on domain, you can use `attrs` on the `<div>` tag to hide the preview.

Take a look at the following example: it will hide the PDF preview if the value of the `state` field is not `draft`:

```
<div class="o_attachment_preview"
    attrs="{'invisible': [('state', '!=', 'draft')]}/>
```

This is how you can hide attachments when they are not needed. Usually, this feature is used to fill data from PDFs and is only activated in draft mode.

Defining kanban views

So far, we have presented you with a list of records that can be opened to show a form. While those lists are efficient when presenting a lot of information, they tend to be slightly boring, given the lack of design possibilities. In this recipe, we'll take a look at *kanban views*, which allow us to present lists of records in a more appealing way.

How to do it...

1. Define a view of the `kanban` type:

```
<record id="view_all_customers_kanban" model="ir.ui.view">
    <field name="model">res.partner</field>
    <field name="arch" type="xml">
        <kanban>
```

2. List the fields you'll use in your view:

```xml
<field name="name" />
<field name="supplier_rank" />
<field name="customer_rank" />
```

3. Implement a design:

```xml
<templates>
    <t t-name="kanban-box">
        <div class="oe_kanban_card">
            <a type="open">
                <field name="name" />
            </a>
            <t t-if="record.supplier_rank.raw_value or
                     record.customer_rank.raw_value">
                is
                <t t-if="record.customer_rank.raw_value">
                    a customer
                </t>
                <t t-if="record.customer_rank.raw_value and
                         record.supplier_rank.raw_value">
                    and
                </t>
                <t t-if="record.supplier_rank.raw_value">
                    a supplier
                </t>
            </t>
        </div>
    </t>
</templates>
```

4. Close all the tags:

```
        </kanban>
    </field>
</record>
```

5. Add this view to one of your actions. This is left as an exercise for the reader. You will find a full working example in the GitHub example files: `https://github.com/PacktPublishing/Odoo-13-Development-Cookbook-Fourth-Edition/tree/master/Chapter09/15_kanban_view/my_module`.

How it works...

We need to give a list of fields to load in *step 2* in order to be able to access them later. The content of the `templates` element must be a single `t` element with the `t-name` attribute set to `kanban-box`.

What you write inside this element will be repeated for each record, with special semantics for `t` elements and `t-*` attributes. For details about that, refer to the *Using client-side QWeb templates* recipe from *Chapter 15, Web Client Development*, because technically kanban views are just an application of QWeb templates.

There are a few modifications that are particular to kanban views. You have access to the `read_only_mode`, `record`, and `widget` variables during evaluation. Fields can be accessed using `record.fieldname`, which is an object with the `value` and `raw_value` properties, where `value` is the field's value that has been formatted in a way that is presentable to the user, and `raw_value` is the field's value as it comes from the database.

> **Important information**
> `many2many` fields make an exception here. You'll only get an ID list through the `record` variable. For a user-readable representation, you must use the `field` element.

Note the `type` attribute of the link at the top of the template. This attribute makes Odoo generate a link that opens the record in view mode (**open**) or edit mode (**edit**), or it deletes the record (**delete**). The `type` attribute can also be `object` or `action`, which will render links that call a function of the model or an action. In both cases, you need to supplement the attributes for buttons in form views, as outlined in the *Adding buttons to forms* recipe of this chapter. Instead of the `a` element, you can also use the `button` element; the `type` attribute has the same semantics there.

There's more…

There are a few more helper functions worth mentioning. If you need to generate a pseudo-random color for an element, use the `kanban_color(some_variable)` function, which will return a CSS class that sets the `background` and `color` properties. This is usually used in the `t-att-class` elements.

If you want to display an image stored in a binary field, use `kanban_image(modelname, fieldname, record.id.raw_value)`, which returns a data URI if you included the field in your fields list and the field is set, a placeholder if the field is not set, or a URL that makes Odoo stream the field's contents if you didn't include the field in your fields list. Do not include the field in the fields list if you need to display a lot of records simultaneously or you expect very big images. Usually, you'd use this in a `t-att-src` attribute of an `img` element.

> **Important tip**
>
> Doing design in kanban views can be a bit trying. What often works better is generating HTML using a function field of the HTML type and generating this HTML from a QWeb view. This way, you're still doing QWeb, but on the server side, which is a lot more convenient when you need to work on a lot of data.

See also

- To know more about template elements, refer to the *Using client-side QWeb templates* recipe from *Chapter 15, Web Client Development*.

Showing kanban cards in columns according to their state

This recipe shows you how to set up a kanban view where the user can drag and drop a record from one column to the other, thereby pushing the record in question into another state.

Getting ready

From now on, we'll make use of the project module here, as this defines models that lend themselves better to date- and state-based views than those defined in the base module. So, before proceeding, add `project` to the dependencies list of your add-on.

How to do it...

1. Define a kanban view for the tasks:

   ```xml
   <record id="kanban_tasks" model="ir.ui.view">
       <field name="name">project.task.kanban</field>
       <field name="model">project.task</field>
       <field name="sequence">20</field>
       <field name="arch" type="xml">
           <kanban default_group_by="stage_id">
               <field name="stage_id" />
               <field name="name" />
               <templates>
                   <t t-name="kanban-box">
                       <div class="oe_kanban_card oe_kanban_global_click">
                           <field name="name" />
                       </div>
                   </t>
               </templates>
           </kanban>
       </field>
   </record>
   ```

2. Add a menu and an action using this view. This is left as an exercise for the reader.

How it works...

Kanban views support grouping, which allows you to display records that have a group field in common in the same column. This is commonly used for a `state` or `stage_id` field, because it allows the user to change this field's value for a record by simply dragging it into another column. Set the `default_group_by` attribute on the `kanban` element to the name of the field you want to group by in order to make use of this functionality.

To control the behavior of kanban grouping, there are a few options available in Odoo:

- `group_create`: This option is used to hide or show the **Add a new column** option in grouped kanban. The default value is `true`.

- `group_delete`: This option enables or disables the **Column delete** option in the kanban group context menu. The default value is `true`.

- `group_edit`: This option enables or disables the **Column edit** option in the kanban group context menu. The default value is `true`.

- **archivable**: This option enables or disables the option to archive and restore the records from the kanban group context menu. This only works if the active Boolean field is present in your model.
- **quick_create**: With this option, you can create records directly from the kanban view.
- **quick_create_view**: By default, the quick_create option displays only the name field in kanban. But with the quick_create_view option, you can give the reference of the minimal form view to display it in kanban.
- **on_create**: If you don't want to use quick_create when creating a new record and you don't want to redirect the user to the form view either, you can give the reference of the wizard so it will open the wizard on a click of the **Create** button.

There's more...

If not defined in the dedicated attribute, any search filter can add grouping by setting a context key named group_by to the field name(s) to group by.

Defining calendar views

This recipe walks you through how to display and edit information about dates and duration in your records in a visual way.

How to do it...

Follow these steps to add a calendar view for the project.task model:

1. Define a calendar view:

   ```xml
   <record id="view_project_task_calendar" model="ir.ui.view">
       <field name="model">project.task</field>
       <field name="arch" type="xml">
           <calendar date_start="date_assign" date_stop="date_end" color="project_id">
               <field name="name" />
               <field name="user_id" />
           </calendar>
       </field>
   </record>
   ```

2. Add menus and actions using this view. This is left as an exercise for the reader.

How it works...

The `calendar` view needs to be passed the field names in the `date_start` and `date_stop` attributes to indicate which fields to look at when building the visual representation. Only use fields with the `Datetime` or `Date` type; other types of fields will not work and will instead generate an error. While `date_start` is required, you can leave out `date_stop` and set the `date_delay` attribute instead, which is expected to be a `Float` field that represents the duration in hours.

The `calendar` view allows you to give records that have the same value in a field the same (arbitrarily assigned) color. To use this functionality, set the `color` attribute to the name of the field you need. In our example, we can see at a glance which tasks belong to the same project, because we assigned `project_id` as the field to determine the color groups.

The fields you name in the `calendar` element's body are shown within the block that represents the time interval covered, separated by commas.

There's more...

The `calendar` view has some other helpful attributes. If you want to open calendar entries in a popup instead of the standard form view, set `event_open_popup` to `1`. By default, you create a new entry by just filling in some text, which internally calls the model's `name_create` function to actually create the record. If you want to disable this behavior, set `quick_add` to `0`.

If your model covers a whole day, set `all_day` to a field's name that is `true` if the record covers the whole day, and `false` otherwise.

Defining graph view and pivot view

In this recipe, we'll take a look at Odoo's business intelligence views. These are read-only views that are meant to present data.

Getting ready

We're still making use of the `project` module here. You can configure a graph and pivot views to get different statistics. For our example, we will focus on the assigned user. We will generate a graph and pivot view to see the users of the tasks per user. By the way, the end user can generate statistics of their choice by modifying the view options.

How to do it...

1. Define a graph view using bars:

   ```xml
   <record id="view_project_tasks_graph" model="ir.ui.view">
       <field name="model">project.task</field>
       <field name="arch" type="xml">
           <graph type="bar">
               <field name="user_id"/>
               <field name="stage_id"/>
           </graph>
       </field>
   </record>
   ```

2. Define a pivot view:

   ```xml
   <record id="view_project_tasks_pivot" model="ir.ui.view">
       <field name="model">project.task</field>
       <field name="arch" type="xml">
           <pivot>
               <field name="user_id" type="row"/>
               <field name="project_id" type="col"/>
               <field name="stage_id" type="col"/>
           </pivot>
       </field>
   </record>
   ```

3. Add menus and actions using this view. This is left as an exercise for the reader.

If everything went well, you should see graphs that show how many tasks are assigned to which user and the state of those tasks.

How it works...

The graph view is declared with a root element, `graph`. The `type` attribute on a `graph` element determines the initial mode of a graph view. The possible values are `bar`, `line`, and `chart`, but `bar` is the default. The graph view is highly interactive, so the user can switch between the different modes and also add and remove fields. If you use `type="bar"`, you can also use `stacked="1"` to show a stacked bar chart during grouping.

The `field` elements tell Odoo what to display on which axis. For all graph modes, you need at least one field with the `row` type and one with the `measure` type to see anything useful. Fields of the `row` type determine the grouping, while those of the `measure` type stand for the value(s) to be shown. Line graphs only support one field of each type, while charts and bars handle two group fields with one measure nicely.

Pivot views have their own root element, `pivot`. The pivot view supports an arbitrary amount of group and measure fields. Nothing will break if you switch to a mode that doesn't support the number of groups and measures you defined; some fields will just be ignored and the result might not be as interesting as it could be.

There's more...

For all graph types, `Datetime` fields are tricky to group, because you'll rarely encounter the same field value here. So, if you have a `Datetime` field of the `row` type, also specify the `interval` attribute with one of the following values: `day`, `week`, `month`, `quarter`, or `year`. This will cause the grouping to take place in the given interval.

> **Important information**
>
> Grouping, like sorting, relies heavily on PostgreSQL. So, here also, the rule applies that a field must live in the database and in the current table in order to be usable.
>
> It is a common practice to define database views that collect all the data you need and define a model on top of this view in order to have all the necessary fields available.
>
> Depending on the complexity of your view and the grouping, building the graph can be quite an expensive exercise. Consider setting the `auto_search` attribute to `False` in these cases, so that the user can first adjust all the parameters and only then trigger a search.

The pivot table also supports grouping in columns. Use the `col` type for the fields you want to have there.

Defining the cohort view

For the cohort analysis of records, the new cohort view was added in Odoo version 12. The cohort view is used to find out the life cycle of a record over a particular time span. With the cohort view, you can see the churn and retention rate of any object for a particular time.

Getting ready

The `cohort` view is part of the **Odoo Enterprise edition**, so you cannot use it with only the Community edition. If you are using the Enterprise edition, you need to add `web_cohort` in the manifest file of your module. For our example, we will create a view to see the cohort analysis for tasks.

How to do it...

Follow these steps to add the `cohort` view for the `project.task` model:

1. Define a `cohort` view:

```xml
<record id="view_project_tasks_graph" model="ir.ui.view">
    <field name="name">project task cohort</field>
    <field name="model">project.task</field>
    <field name="arch" type="xml">
        <cohort date_start="date_start"
            date_stop="date_deadline"
            interval="month"
            string="Task Cohort" />
    </field>
</record>
```

2. Add menus and actions using this view. This is left as an exercise for the reader.

How it works...

To create a cohort view, you need to provide `date_start` and `date_stop`. These will be used in the view to determine the time span of any record. For example, if you are managing the subscription of a service, the start date of the subscription will be `date_start` and the date when the subscription is going to expire will be `date_stop`.

By default, the `cohort` view will be displayed in `retention` mode by intervals of a month. You can use the given options to get different behaviors in the `cohort` view:

- `mode`: You can use cohort with two modes, `retention (default)` or `churn`. `retention` mode starts with 100% and decreases with time, while `churn` mode starts at 0% and increases with time.

- `timeline`: This option accepts two values: `forward (default)` or `backward`. In most cases, you need to use the forward timeline. But if `date_start` is in the future, you will need to use the backward timeline. An example of when we would use the backward timeline would be for the registration of an event attendee where the event date is in the future and the registration date is in the past.

- `interval`: By default, the cohort is grouped by month, but you can change this in the interval options. Other than months, cohort also supports day, week, and year intervals.
- `measure`: Just like graph and pivot, measure is used to display the aggregated value of a given field. If no option is given, cohort will display the count of records.

Defining the dashboard view

A new view called **dashboard** was introduced with Odoo version 12. This is used to display multiple views and the various business KPIs in a single screen.

Getting ready

The `dashboard` view is part of the Odoo Enterprise edition, so you can't use it with Community edition. If you are using the Enterprise edition, you need to add the dependency of the `web_dashboard` in the manifest file of your module.

In our example, we will display a few KPIs and a few existing views. We will display the `graph` and the `pivot` view in the same screen, so follow the *Defining graph views* recipe, if you haven't created the `pivot` and `graph` views. We will use the ID of these views in the `dashboard` view.

How to do it...

1. Define a `dashboard` view:

```xml
<record id="view_project_tasks_dashboard" model="ir.ui.view">
    <field name="name">project task dashbaord</field>
    <field name="model">project.task</field>
    <field name="arch" type="xml">
        <dashboard>
            <view ref="my_project.view_project_tasks_graph"
                type="graph" />
            <group>
                <aggregate name="all_task"
                    string="Total Tasks"
                    group_operator="count"
                    field="id" measure="__count__"/>
                <aggregate name="progress_task"
                    string="In Progress Tasks"
```

```xml
                        domain="[('stage_id.name', 'ilike',
'In Progress')]"
                        group_operator="count"
                        field="id" measure="__count__"/>
                <aggregate name="done_task"
                        string="Completed Tasks"
                        domain="[('stage_id.name', 'ilike',
'Done')]"
                        group_operator="count" field="id"
                        measure="__count__"/>
                <formula name="price_average"
                        string="Overall Progress"
                        value="record.done_task / record.all_
task"
                        widget="percentage"/>
            </group>
            <view ref="my_project.view_project_tasks_
pivot"
                    type="pivot"/>
        </dashboard>
    </field>
</record>
```

2. Add menus and actions using this view. This is left as an exercise for the reader.

How it works...

With the `dashboard` view, you can display KPIs with `aggregate` and `formula`. You can display multiple views on the same screen. If you look at the definition of the view, you will see that we have added two views: `graph` at the beginning and `pivot` at the end. To display the views, you just need to use the `<view>` tag with the XML reference and the type of view.

We have displayed various KPIs, including the total tasks, the tasks in progress, and the completed tasks, with the `<aggregate>` tag. This tag will display the aggregated result for the records of the current domain in the search view. In the `<aggregate>` tag, you can use the optional `domain` attribute to display aggregates for a particular set of records. By default, the `aggregate` function displays the count of records, but you can provide a *SQL aggregate function* using a `group_operator` attribute, such as `avg` or `max`.

Sometimes, it is not possible to display the KPI with `<aggregate>`; it needs some extra computation. With the help of `<formula>`, you can define the formula for any KPI. In our example, we have displayed the progress of all tasks and we have used the optional `widget` attribute to display the value as a percentage.

There's more....

Another useful element is the `<widget>` tag. With this, you can display data with the UI of your choice. In *Chapter 15*, *Web Client Development*, we will look at how to create a custom widget.

Defining the gantt view

Odoo version 13 added a new `gantt` view with new options. The `gantt` view is useful for seeing overall progress and scheduling business processes. In this recipe, we will create a new `gantt` view and look at its options.

Getting ready

The `gantt` view is part of the Odoo Enterprise edition, so you can't use it with the Community edition. If you are using the Enterprise edition, you need to add the `web_gantt` dependency in the manifest file of your module.

In our example, we will continue using the `my_project` module from the previous recipe. We will create a new `gantt` view for the tasks of the project.

How to do it...

1. Define a `gantt` view for the task model as follows:

```xml
<record id="view_project_tasks_gantt" model="ir.ui.view">
    <field name="name">project task gantt</field>
    <field name="model">project.task</field>
    <field name="arch" type="xml">
        <gantt date_start="date_assign" date_stop="date_end"
               string="Tasks" default_group_by="project_id"
               color="project_id" progress="sequence">
            <field name="name"/>
            <field name="stage_id"/>
        </gantt>
    </field>
</record>
```

2. Add menus and actions using this view. This is left as an exercise for the reader.

Install and update the module to apply the changes; after the update, you will see the `gantt` view on the project tasks.

How it works...

With the `gantt` view, you can display an overall schedule on one screen. In our example, we have created a gannt view for tasks grouped by project. Typically, you need two attributes to create a `gantt` view, `start_date` and `stop_date`, but there are some other attributes that extend the functionality of the `gantt` view. Let's see all the options:

- `start_date`: Defines the starting time of the `gantt` item. It must be a date or date-time field.
- `stop_date`: Defines the starting time of the `gantt` item. It must be a date or date-time field.
- `default_group_by`: Use this attribute if you want to group the `gantt` items based on field.
- `color`: This attribute is used to decide the color of a `gantt` item.
- `progress`: This attribute is used to indicate the progress of a `gantt` item.
- `decoration-*` : Decoration attributes are used to decide the color of a gantt item based on conditions. It can be used like this: `decoration-danger="state == 'lost'"`. Its other values are `decoration-success`, `decoration-info`, `decoration-warning`, and `decoration-secondary`.
- `scales`: Use the `scales` attribute if you want to enable the `gantt` view only for few scales. For example, if you only want day and week scales, you can use `scales="day,week"`.
- By default, `gantt` view items are resizable and draggable, but if you want to disable that, you can use the `edit="0"` attribute.

There's more...

When you hover over a `gantt` view item, you will see the name and date for the item. If you want to customize that popup, you can define a *QWeb template* in the `gantt` view definition like this:

```
<gantt date_start="date_assign" date_stop="date_end"
string="Tasks">
    <field name="name"/>
    <field name="stage_id"/>
    <templates>
        <div t-name="gantt-popover">
            <ul class="pl-1 mb-0 list-unstyled">
                <li>
                    <strong>Name: </strong> <t t-esc="name"/>
```

```
                </li>
                <li>
                    <strong>Stage: </strong> <t t-esc="stage_id[1]"/>
                </li>
            </ul>
        </div>
    </templates>
</gantt>
```

Note that you will need to add the fields that you want to use in the template via the `<field>` tag.

Defining the activity view

Activities are an important part of Odoo apps. They are used to schedule to-do actions for different business objects. The `activity` view helps you to see the statuses and schedules of all activities on the model.

Getting ready

In our example, we will continue using the `my_project` module from the previous recipe. We will create a new `activity` view for the tasks of the project.

How to do it...

1. Define a `gantt` view for the `task` model as follow:

   ```
   <record id="view_project_tasks_activity" model="ir.ui.view">
       <field name="name">project task activity</field>
       <field name="model">project.task</field>
       <field name="arch" type="xml">
           <activity string="Tasks">
               <templates>
                   <div t-name="activity-box">
                       <div>
                           <field name="name" display="full"/>
                           <field name="project_id"
                                  muted="1" display="full"/>
                       </div>
                   </div>
               </templates>
   ```

```
            </activity>
        </field>
</record>
```

2. Add menus and actions using this view. This is left as an exercise for the reader.

How it works...

The `activity` view is simplistic; most of the things are managed automatically. You just have the option to customize the first column. To display your data in the first column, you need to crate QWeb template with the name `activity-box` and that's it. Odoo will manage the rest.

The `activity` view will display your template in the first column and other columns will show the scheduled activities grouped by activity type.

Defining the map view

Odoo version 13 adds a new view called a `map` view. As its name suggests, it is used to show a map with a marker. They are very useful for on-site services.

Getting ready

In our example, we will continue using the `my_project` module from the previous recipe. We will create the new `map` view on for the customer of the task.
The map view is part of the **Odoo Enterprise edition**, so you can't use it with the Community edition. If you are using the Enterprise edition, you need to add the `web_map` dependency in the manifest file of your module.

Odoo uses the API from `https://www.mapbox.com/` to display maps in the view. In order to see the map in Odoo, you will need to generate the access token from the **mapbox**. Make sure you have generated an access token and set it in the Odoo configuration.

How to do it...

1. Define a `map` view for the task model as follows:

```xml
<record id="view_project_tasks_map" model="ir.ui.view">
    <field name="name">project task map</field>
    <field name="model">project.task</field>
    <field name="arch" type="xml">
        <map res_partner="partner_id">
            <marker-popup>
                <field name="name" string="Title "/>
                <field name="partner_id" string="Customer "/>
            </marker-popup>
        </map>
    </field>
</record>
```

2. Add menus and actions using this view. This is left as an exercise for the reader.

How it works...

Creating a map view is pretty simple: you just need a `many2one` field that refers to the `res.partner` model. The `res.partner` model has `address` fields, which are used by the map view to display the marker for the address. You will need to use the `res_partner` attribute to map the address for the map view. In our case, we have used the `partner_id` field as the customer record is set in the `partner_id` field.

Additionally, you can customize the fields that are displayed on the marker popup when the user clicks on the `marker`. To display data in a marker popup, you will need to use the `<marker-popup>` tag and place the fields inside it.

10
Security Access

In most cases, Odoo is used by multi-user organizations. In every organization, each user has different roles, and they have different access based on their role. For example, the HR manager does not have access to the company's accounting information. With access rights and record rules, you can specify which information the user can access in Odoo. In this chapter, we will learn how to specify access rights rules and record rules.

Such compartmentalization of access and security requires that we provide access to roles as per their permission levels. We will learn about this in this chapter.

In this chapter, we will cover the following recipes:

- Creating security groups and assigning them to users
- Adding security access to models
- Limiting access to fields in models
- Limiting record access using record rules
- Using security groups to activate features
- Accessing recordsets as a superuser
- Hiding view elements and menus based on groups

In order to concisely get the point across, the recipes in this chapter make small additions to an example existing module.

Technical requirements

The technical requirements for this chapter include using the module that we created by following the recipes in *Chapter 3*, *Creating Odoo Add-On Modules*. To follow the examples here, you should have that module created and ready to use.

All the code that will be used in this chapter can be downloaded from this book's GitHub repository at https://github.com/PacktPublishing/Odoo-14-Development-Cookbook-Fourth-Edition/tree/master/Chapter10.

Creating security groups and assigning them to users

Security access in Odoo is configured through security groups: permissions are given to groups and then groups are assigned to users. Each functional area has base security groups provided by a central application.

When add-on modules extend an existing *application*, they should add permissions to the corresponding groups, as shown in the *Adding security access to models* recipe later.

When add-on modules add a new functional area not yet covered by an existing central *application*, they should add the corresponding security groups. Usually, we should have at least *user* and *manager* roles.

Taking the Library example we introduced in *Chapter 3*, *Creating Odoo Add-On Modules*, it doesn't fit neatly into any of the Odoo core apps, so we will add security groups for it.

Getting ready

This recipe assumes that you have an Odoo instance ready with `my_library` available, as described in *Chapter 3*, *Creating Odoo Add-On Modules*.

How to do it...

To add new access security groups to a module, perform the following steps:

1. Ensure that the `__manifest__.py` add-on module manifest has the `category` key defined:

    ```
    'category': 'Library',
    ```

2. Add the new `security/groups.xml` file to the manifest `data` key:

```
'data': [
    'security/groups.xml',
    'views/library_book.xml',
],
```

3. Add the new XML file for the data records to the `security/library_security.xml` file, starting with an empty structure:

```xml
<?xml version="1.0" encoding="utf-8"?>
<odoo>
    <!-- Add step 4 goes here -->
</odoo>
```

4. Add the `<record>` tags for the two new groups inside the data XML element:

```xml
<record id="group_library_user" model="res.groups">
    <field name="name">User</field>
    <field name="category_id"
           ref="base.module_category_library"/>
    <field name="implied_ids"
           eval="[(4, ref('base.group_user'))]"/>
</record>

<record id="group_library_librarian" model="res.groups">
    <field name="name">Librarians</field>
    <field name="category_id"
           ref="base.module_category_library"/>
    <field name="implied_ids"
           eval="[(4, ref('group_library_user'))]"/>
    <field name="users" eval="[(4, ref('base.user_
admin'))]"/> </record>
```

If we upgrade the add-on module, these two records will be loaded. To see these groups in the UI, you need to activate developer mode. You'll then be able to see them through the **Settings | Users | Groups** menu option, like so:

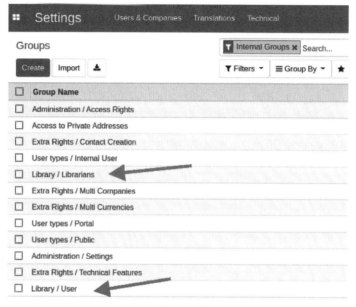

Figure 10.1 – Newly added security groups

> **Important Information**
>
> If you are adding a new model, the admin user doesn't get access rights for that model. This means that the menus and views that have been added for that model are not visible to the admin user. In order to display it, you need to add access rules for that model, which we will do in the *Adding security access to models* recipe. By the way, you can access newly added models through the superuser; to learn more about this, please refer to the *Accessing Odoo as a superuser* recipe in *Chapter 3, Creating Odoo Add-On Modules*.

How it works...

Add-on modules are organized into functional areas, or major *applications*, such as *Accounting and Finance*, *Sales*, or *Human Resources*. These are defined by the `category` key in the manifest file.

If a category name does not exist yet, it will be automatically created. For convenience, a `base.module_category_<category_name_in_manifest>` XML ID will also be generated for the new category name in lowercase letters, replacing the spaces with underscores. This is useful for relating security groups to application categories.

In our example, we used the **Library** category name in the manifest, and it generated a `base.module_category_library` XML identifier.

By convention, data files that contain security-related elements should be placed inside a `security` subdirectory.

You also need to register security files in a manifest file. The order in which files are declared in the `data` key of the module manifest is important, since you can't use a reference of security groups in other views or `ACL` files before the group has been defined. It's best to place the security data file at the top of the list before the ACL files and the other user interface data files.

In our example, we created groups with the `<record>` tag, which will create a record of the `res.groups` model. The most important columns of the *res.group* model are as follows:

- `name`: This is the group's display name.
- `category_id`: This is a reference to the application category and is used to organize the groups in the user's form.
- `implied_ids`: These are other groups to inherit permissions from.
- `users`: This is the list of users that belong to this group. In new add-on modules, we usually want the admin user to belong to the application's manager group.

The first security group uses `implied_ids` as the `base.group_user` group. This is the `Employee` user group and is the basic security group all the backend users are expected to share.

The second security group sets a value on the `users` field to assign it to the administrator user, which has the `base.user_admin` XML ID.

Users that belong to a security group will automatically belong to its implied groups. For example, if you assign a *Librarians* group to any user, that user will also be included in the *User* group. This is because the *Librarians* group has the *User* group in its `implied_ids` column.

Also, access permissions granted by security groups are cumulative. A user has permission if any of the groups they belong to (directly or implied) grant that permission.

Some security groups are shown in the user form as a selection box instead of individual check boxes. This happens when the involved groups are in the same application category and are linearly interrelated through `implied_ids`. For example, Group *A* has implied Group *B*, and Group *B* has implied Group *C*. If a group is not related to any other groups through `implied_ids`, instead of a selection box, you will see a checkbox.

> **Note**
>
> Note that the relationships that were defined in the preceding fields also have reverse relationships that can be edited in the related models, such as security groups and users.

Setting values on reference fields, such as `category_id` and `implied_ids`, is done using the related records' XML IDs and some special syntax. This syntax was explained in detail in *Chapter 6, Managing Module Data*.

There's more...

The special `base.group_no_one` security group called **Extra Rights** is also noteworthy. In previous Odoo versions, it was used for advanced features hidden by default, and was only made visible when the `Technical Features` flag was activated. From version 9.0, this has changed, and the features are visible as long as `Developer Mode` is active.

Access permissions granted by security groups are cumulative only. There is no way to deny access given by a group. This means that a manually created group used to customize permissions should inherit from the closest group with fewer permissions than those intended (if any), and then add all the remaining permissions needed.

Groups also have these additional fields available:

- **Menus (the `menu_access` field)**: These are the menu items the group has access to.
- **Views (the `view_access` field)**: These are the UI views the group has access to.
- **Access rights (the `model_access` field)**: This is the access it has to models, as detailed in the *Adding security access to models* recipe.
- **Rules (the `rule_groups` field)**: These are the record-level access rules that apply to the group, as detailed in the *Limiting record access using record rules* recipe.
- **Notes (the `comment` field)**: This is a description or commented piece of text for the group.

In this recipe, we have learned to how create security groups and assign them from the GUI. In the next few recipes, we will use these groups to create an access control list and record rules.

See also

To learn how to access newly added models through the *superuser*, please refer to the *Accessing Odoo as a superuser* recipe in *Chapter 3, Creating Odoo Add-On Modules*.

Adding security access to models

It's common for add-on modules to add new models. For example, in *Chapter 3, Creating Odoo Add-On Modules*, we added a new Library Books model. It is easy to miss out on creating security access for new models during development, and you might find it hard to see menus and views that have been created. This is because, from *Odoo version 12*, admin users don't get default access rights to new models. To see the views and menus for the new model, you to need to add security **access-control lists** (**ACLs**).

However, models with no ACLs will trigger a warning log message upon loading, informing the user about the missing ACL definitions:

```
WARNING The model library.book has no access rules, consider
adding one example, access_library_book, access_library_book,
model_library_book, base.group_user,1,0,0,0
```

You can also access newly added models through a superuser since this bypasses all security rules. To learn more about this, please refer to the *Accessing Odoo as a superuser* recipe in *Chapter 3, Creating Odoo Add-On Modules*. The superuser feature is only available for administrator users. So, for new models to be usable by non-admin users, we need to define their access control lists so that Odoo knows how it should access them, as well as what operations each user group should be allowed to perform.

Getting ready

We will continue using the `my_library` module from the previous recipe and add the missing ACLs to it.

How to do it...

`my_library` should already contain the `models/library_book.py` Python file that creates the `library.book` model. We will now add a data file that describes this model's security access control by performing the following steps:

1. Edit the `__manifest__.py` file to declare a new data file:

   ```
   data: [
       # ...Security Groups
       'security/ir.model.access.csv',
       # ...Other data files
   ]
   ```

2. Add a new `security/ir.model.access.csv` file to the module with the following lines:

   ```
   id,name,model_id:id,group_id:id,perm_read,perm_write,perm_create,perm_unlink
   acl_book,library.book_default,model_library_book,base_group_user,1,0,0,0
   acl_book_librarian,library.book_librarian,model_library_book,group_library_librarian,1,1,1,1
   ```

We should then upgrade the module so that it these ACL records are added to our Odoo database. More importantly, if we sign into a demonstration database using the `demo` user, we should be able to access the **Library** menu option without receiving any security errors.

How it works...

Security ACLs are stored in the core `ir.model.access` model. We just need to add the records that describe the intended access rights for each user group.

Any type of data file would do, but the common practice is to use a CSV file. The file can be placed anywhere inside the add-on module directory, but the convention is to have all the security-related files inside a `security` subdirectory.

The first step in our recipe adds this new data file to the manifest. The second step adds the files that describe the security access control rules. The CSV file must be named after the model where the records will be loaded, so the name we've used is not just a convention – it is mandatory. Please refer to *Chapter 6, Managing Module Data*, for details.

If the module also creates new security groups, its data file should be declared in the manifest before the ACLs' data files, since you may want to use them for the ACLs. They must already be created when the ACL file is processed.

The columns in the CSV file are as follows:

- `id`: This is the XML ID internal identifier for this rule. Any unique name inside the module will do, but the convention is to use `access_<model>_<group>`.
- `name`: This is a title for the access rule. It is a common practice to use a `access.<model>.<group>` name.
- `model_id:id`: This is the XML ID for the model. Odoo automatically assigns this kind of ID to models with a `model_<name>` format, using the model's _name with underscores instead of dots. If the model was created in a different add-on module, a fully qualified XML ID that includes the module name is needed.
- `group_id:id`: This is the XML ID for the user group. If left empty, it applies to all users. The base module provides some basic groups, such as `base.group_user` for all employees and `base.group_system` for the administration user. Other apps can add their own user groups.
- `perm_read`: Members of the preceding group can read the model's records. It accepts two values: 0 or 1. Use 0 to restrict read access on the model and 1 to provide read access.
- `perm_write`: Members of the preceding group can update the model's records. It accepts two values: 0 or 1. Use 0 to restrict write access on the model and 1 to provide write access.
- `perm_create`: Members of the preceding group can add new records of this model. It accepts two values: 0 or 1. Use 0 to restrict create access on the model and 1 to provide create access.
- `perm_unlink`: Members of the preceding group can delete records of this model. It accepts two values: 0 or 1. Use 0 to restrict unlink access on the model and 1 to provide unlink access.

The CSV file we used adds read-only access to the **Employees | Employee** standard security group and full write access to the **Administration | Settings** group.

The **Employee** user group, `base.group_user`, is particularly important because the user groups that are added by the Odoo standard apps inherit from it. This means that if we need a new model to be accessible by all the backend users, regardless of the specific apps they work with, we should add that permission to the **Employee** group.

The resulting ACLs can be viewed from the GUI in debug mode by navigating to **Settings | Technical | Security | Access Controls List**, as shown in the following screenshot:

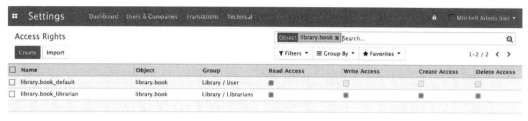

Figure 10.2 – ACL list view

Some people find it easier to use this user interface to define ACLs and then use the export feature to produce a CSV file.

There's more...

It would make sense for us to give this permission to the Library user and the Librarian groups we defined in the *Creating security groups and assigning them to users* recipe. If you followed that recipe, then it's a good exercise to follow this one while adapting the group identifiers to the Library ones.

It's important to note that access lists provided by add-on modules should not be directly customized, since they will be reloaded on the next module upgrade, destroying any customization that could have been done from the GUI.

To customize ACLs, two approaches can be used. One is to create new security groups that inherit from the one provided by the module and add additional permissions on it, but this only allows us to add permissions, not remove them. A more flexible approach would be to uncheck the **Active** flag on particular ACL lines to disable them. The active field is not visible by default, so we need to edit the tree view to add the `<field name="active" />` column. We can also add new ACL lines for additional or replacement permissions. On a module upgrade, the deactivated ACLs won't be reactivated, and the added ACL lines won't be affected.

It's also worth noting that ACLs only apply to regular models and don't need to be defined for *Abstract* or *Transient* models. If defined, these will be disregarded, and a warning message will be triggered in the server log.

See also

You can also access newly added models through a superuser since this bypasses all security rules. To learn more about this, please refer to the *Accessing Odoo as a superuser* recipe in *Chapter 3, Creating Odoo Add-On Modules*.

Limiting access to fields in models

In some cases, we may need more fine-grained access control, and we may also need to limit access to specific fields in a model.

It is possible for a field to only be accessed by specific security groups, using the `groups` attribute. In this recipe, we will show you how to add a field with limited access to the *Library Books* model.

Getting ready

We will continue using the `my_library` module from the previous recipe.

How to do it...

To add a field with access that's limited to specific security groups, perform the following steps:

1. Edit the model file to add the field:

    ```
    is_public = fields.Boolean(groups='my_library.group_
    library_librarian')
    private_notes = fields.Text(groups='my_library.group_
    library_librarian')
    ```

2. Edit the view in the XML file to add the field:

    ```
    <field name="is_public" />
    <field name="private_notes" />
    ```

That's it. Now, upgrade the add-on module for the changes in the model to take place. If you sign in with a user with no system configuration access, such as `demo` in a database with demonstration data, the Library Books form won't display the field.

How it works...

Fields with the `groups` attribute are specially handled to check whether the user belongs to any of the security groups indicated in the attribute. If a user doesn't belong to a particular group, Odoo will remove the field from the UI and restrict ORM operations on that field.

Note that this security is not superficial. The field is not only hidden in the UI but is also made unavailable to the user in the other ORM operations, such as `read` and `write`. This is also true for *XML-RPC* or *JSON-RPC* calls.

Be careful when using these fields in business logic or in on-change UI events (`@api.onchange` methods); they can raise errors for users with no access to the field. One workaround for this is to use privilege elevation, such as the `sudo()` model method or the `compute_sudo` field attribute for computed fields.

The `groups` value is a string that contains a comma-separated list of valid XML IDs for security groups. The simplest way to find the XML ID for a particular group is to activate developer mode and navigate to the group's form, at **Settings | Users | Groups**, and then access the **View Metadata** option from the debug menu, as shown in the following screenshot:

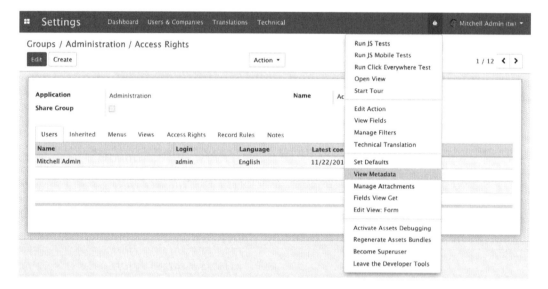

Figure 10.3 – Menu for viewing a group's XML ID

You can also view the XML ID of a security group via code by using the `<record>` tag that created the group. However, the most convenient way to find out a group's XML ID is by looking at the metadata, as shown in the previous screenshot.

There's more...

In some cases, we need a field to be available or unavailable, depending on particular conditions, such as the values in a field; for example, `stage_id` or `state`. This is usually handled at the view level using attributes such as `states` or `attrs` to dynamically display or hide the field according to certain conditions. Please refer to *Chapter 9, Backend Views*, for a detailed description.

Note that these techniques work at the user interface level only and don't provide actual access security. To do this, you should add checks to the business logic layer. Either add model methods decorated with `@constrains`, implementing the specific validations intended, or extend the `create`, `write`, or `unlink` methods to add validation logic. You can get further insights into how to do this by going back to *Chapter 5, Basic Server-Side Development*.

See also

For more details on how to hide and display a field using conditions, please refer to *Chapter 9, Backend Views*.

For further insights into the business logic layer, please refer to *Chapter 5, Basic Server-Side Development*.

Limiting record access using record rules

A common need for any application is it to have the ability to limit which records are available to each user on a specific model.

This is achieved using record rules. A **record rule** is a domain filter expression that's defined on a model that will then be added to every data query that's made by the affected users.

As an example, we will add a record rule to the *Library Books* model so that users in the `Employee` group will only have access to public books.

Getting ready

We will continue using the `my_library` module from the previous recipe.

How to do it...

Record rules are added using a data XML file. To do this, perform the following steps:

1. Ensure that the `security/security_rules.xml` file is referenced by the manifest `data` key:

    ```
    'data': [
        'security/security_rules.xml',
        # ...
    ],
    ```

2. We should have a `security/security_rules.xml` data file with a `<odoo>` section that creates the security group:

    ```xml
    <odoo noupdate="1">
        <record model="ir.rule" id="library_book_user_rule">
            <field name="name">Library: see only own books</field>
            <field name="model_id" ref="model_library_book"/>
            <field name="groups"
                eval="[(4, ref('my_library.group_library_user'))]"/>
            <field name="domain_force">
                [('is_public', '=', True)]
            </field>
        </record>

        <record model="ir.rule" id="library_book_all_rule">
            <field name="name">Library: see all books</field>
            <field name="model_id" ref="model_library_book"/>
            <field name="groups"
                eval="[(4, ref('my_library.group_library_librarian'))]"/>
            <field name="domain_force">[(1, '=', 1)]</field>
        </record>
    </odoo>
    ```

Upgrading the add-on module will load the record rules inside the Odoo instance. If you are using demo data, you can test it through the default `demo` user to give library user rights to the demo user. If you are not using demo data, you can create a new user with library user rights.

How it works...

Record rules are just data records that are loaded into the `ir.rule` core model. While the file adding them can be anywhere in the module, the convention is for it to be in the `security` subdirectory. It is common to have a single XML file with both security groups and record rules.

Unlike groups, in the standard modules, the record rules are loaded into an `odoo` section with the `noupdate="1"` attribute. With this, those records will not be reloaded on a module upgrade, meaning that manually customizing them is safe and they will survive later upgrades.

To stay consistent with the official modules, we should also have our record rules inside a <odoo noupdate="1"> section.

Record rules can be seen from the GUI via the **Settings| Technical | Security | Record Rules** menu option, as shown in the following screenshot:

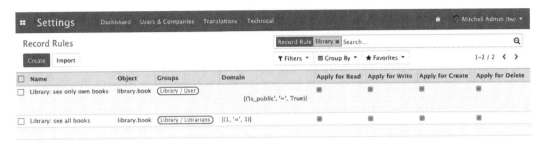

Figure 10.4 – ACLs for the book's model

The following are the most important record rule fields that were used in this example:

- **Name** (name): A descriptive title for the rule.
- **Object** (model_id): A reference to the model the rule applies to.
- **Groups** (groups): The security groups that the rule applies to. If no security group is specified, the rule is considered *global* and is applied in a different way (continue with this recipe to learn more about these groups).
- **Domain** (domain): A domain expression that is used to filter the records. The rule is only going to applied to these filtered records.

The first record rule we created was for the *Library User* security group. It uses the [('is_public', '=', True)] domain expression to select only the books that are available publicly. Thus, users with the *Library User* security group will only be able to see public books.

The domain expressions that are used in the record rules run on the server side using ORM objects. Due to this, dot notation can be used on the fields on the left-hand side (the first tuple element). For example, the [('country_id.code', '=', 'IN')] domain expression will only show records that contain the country of *India*.

Since record rules are mostly based on the current user, you can use the user recordset in the right-hand side (the third tuple element) of the domain. So, if you want to show the records for the company of the current user, you can use the [('conpany_id', '=', user.company_id.id)] domain. Alternatively, if you want to show the records that are created by the current user, you can use the [('user_id', '=', user.id)] domain.

We want the *Librarian* security group to be able to see all the books, independent of whether they are public or private. Since it inherits from the *Library User* group, unless we do something about it, it will also be able to see only public books.

The non-global record rules are joined using the OR logical operator; each rule adds access and never removes this access. For the `Librarian` security group to have access to all the books, we must add a record rule to it so that it can add access for all books, as follows:

```
[('is_public', 'in', [True, False])]
```

We chose to do this differently here and use the `[(1, '=', 1)]` special rule instead to unconditionally give access to all book records. While this may seem redundant, remember that if we don't do this, the Library user rule can be customized in a way that will keep some books out of reach from the Settings user. The domain is special because the first element of a domain tuple must be a field name; this exact case is one of two cases where that is not true. The special domain of `[(1, '=', 0)]` is never true, but also not very useful in the case of record rules. This is because this type of rule is used to restrict access to all the records. The same thing is also possible with access lists.

> **Important Information**
> Record rules are ignored if you've activated SUPERUSER mode. When testing your record rules, ensure that you use another user for that.

There's more...

When a record rule is not assigned to any security group, it is marked as **global** and is handled differently from the other rules.

Global record rules have a stronger effect than group-level record rules and set access restrictions that those can't override. Technically, they are joined with an AND operator. In standard modules, they are used to implement multi-company security access so that each user can only see their company's data.

In summary, regular non-global record rules are joined with an OR operator; they are added together, and a record is accessible if any of the rules grant that access. Global record rules then add restrictions to the access given by regular record rules using an AND operator. Restrictions that have been added by global record rules can't be overridden by regular record rules.

Using security groups to activate features

Security groups can restrict some features so that they can only be accessed by users that belong to these groups. Security groups can also inherit other groups, so they also grant their permissions.

These two features are used to implement a usability feature in Odoo: *feature toggling*. Security groups can also be used to enable or disable features for some or all the users in an Odoo instance.

This recipe shows how to add options to configuration settings and showcases the two methods you can use to enable additional features: making them visible using security groups or adding them by installing an additional module.

For the first case, we will make the book-release dates an optional additional feature and for the second, as an example, we will provide an option for installing the *Notes* module.

Getting ready

This recipe uses the `my_library` module, which was described in *Chapter 3, Creating Odoo Add-On Modules*. We will need security groups to work with, so you also need to have followed the *Adding security access to models* recipe in this chapter.

In this recipe, some identifiers need to refer to the add-on module's technical name. We will assume that this is `my_library`. In case you are using a different name, replace `my_library` with the actual technical name of your add-on module.

How to do it...

To add the configuration options, follow these steps:

1. To add the needed dependency and the new XML data files, edit the `__manifest__.py` file like this and check that it depends on `base_setup`:

    ```python
    {   'name': 'Cookbook code',
        'category': 'Library',
        'depends': ['base_setup'],
        'data': [
            'security/ir.model.access.csv',
            'security/groups.xml',
            'views/library_book.xml',
            'views/res_config_settings.xml',
    ```

```
        ],
    }
```

2. To add the new security group that's used for feature activation, edit the security/groups.xml file and add the following record to it:

```xml
    <record id="group_release_dates" model="res.groups">
        <field name="name">Library: release date feature</field>
        <field name="category_id" ref="base.module_category_hidden" />
    </record>
```

3. To make the book-release date visible only when this option is enabled, edit the field definition in the models/library_book.py file:

```python
class LibraryBook(models.Model):
    # ...
    date_release = fields.Date(
        'Release Date',
        groups='my_library.group_release_dates',
    )
```

4. Edit the models/__init__.py file in order to add a new Python file for the configuration settings model:

```python
from . import library_book
from . import res_config_settings
```

5. To extend the core configuration wizard by adding new options to it, add the models/res_config_settings.py file with the following code:

```python
from odoo import models, fields

class ConfigSettings(models.TransientModel):
    _inherit = 'res.config.settings'
    group_release_dates = fields.Boolean(
        "Manage book release dates",
        group='base.group_user',
        implied_group='my_library.group_release_dates',
```

```
        )
        module_note = fields.Boolean("Install Notes app")
```

6. To make the options available in the UI, add `views/res_config_settings.xml`, which extends the settings form view:

```xml
<?xml version="1.0" encoding="utf-8"?>
<odoo>
    <record id="view_general_config_library" model="ir.ui.view">
        <field name="name">Configuration: add Library options</field>
        <field name="model">res.config.settings</field>
        <field name="inherit_id" ref="base_setup.res_config_settings_view_form" />
        <field name="arch" type="xml">
            <div id="business_documents" position="before">
                <h2>Library</h2>
                <div class="row mt16 o_settings_container">
                    <!-- Add Step 7 and 8 goes here -->
                </div>
            </div>
        </field>
    </record>
</odoo>
```

7. In the settings form view, add the option to add a release date feature:

```xml
    <!-- Release Dates option -->
<div class="col-12 col-lg-6 o_setting_box">
    <div class="o_setting_left_pane">
        <field name="group_release_dates" class="oe_inline"/>
    </div>
    <div class="o_setting_right_pane">
        <label for="group_release_dates"/>
        <div class="text-muted">
            Enable relase date feature on books
        </div>
```

8. In the settings form view, add the option to install the note module:

```
<!-- Note module option -->
<div class="col-12 col-lg-6 o_setting_box">
    <div class="o_setting_left_pane">
        <field name="module_note" class="oe_inline"/>
    </div>
    <div class="o_setting_right_pane">
        <label for="module_note"/>
        <div class="text-muted">
            Install note module
        </div>
    </div>
</div>
```

After upgrading the add-on module, the two new configuration options should be available at **Settings | General Settings**. The screen should look like this:

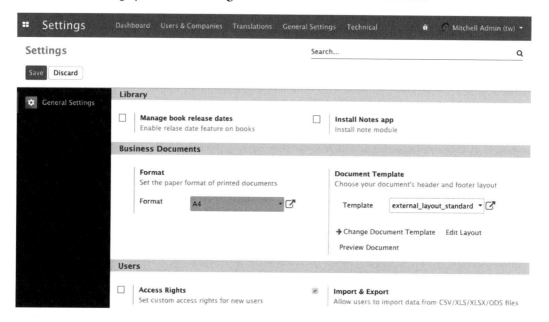

Figure 10.5 – Library config in general settings

As shown in the preceding screenshot, you will have new settings in the **Library** section. The first option, **Manage book release dates**, will enable the release date feature for the books record. The second option, **Install Notes app**, will install Odoo's Notes app.

How it works...

The core `base` module provides the `res.config.settings` model, which provides the business logic behind the activation option. The `base_setup` add-on module uses the `res.config.settings` model to provide several basic configuration options that can be made available inside a new database. It also makes the **Settings | General Settings** menu available.

The `base_setup` module adapts `res.config.settings` to a central management dashboard, so we need to extend it to add our own configuration settings.

If we decide to create a specific settings form for the Library app, we can still inherit from the `res.config.settings` model with a different `_name`, and then for the new model, provide the menu option and form view for just those settings. We already saw this method in the *Adding your own settings options* recipe of *Chapter 8, Advanced Server-Side Development Techniques*.

We used two different methods to activate these features: one by enabling a security group and making the feature visible to the user, and the other by installing an add-on module that provides this feature. The logic that's used to handle both these cases is provided by the base `res.config.settings` model.

The first step in this recipe adds the `base_setup` add-on module to the dependencies, since it provides extensions to the `res.config.settings` model we want to use. It also adds an additional XML data file that we will need to add the new options to the **General Settings** form.

In the second step, we created a new security group, **Library: release date feature**. The feature that needs to be activated should only be visible to that group, so it will be hidden until the group is enabled.

In our example, we want the book release date to only be available when the corresponding configuration option is enabled. To achieve this, we can use the `groups` attribute on the field so that it is made available only for this security group. We did this at the model level so that it is automatically applied to all the UI views where the field is used.

Finally, we extended the `res.config.settings` model to add the new options. Each option is a Boolean field, and its name must begin either with `group_` or `module_`, according to what we want it to do.

The `group_` option field should have an `implied_group` attribute and should be a string that contains a comma-separated list of XML IDs for the security groups to activate when it is enabled. The XML IDs must be complete, with the module name, dot, and identifier name provided; for example, `module_name.identifier`.

We can also provide a `group` attribute to specify which security groups the feature will be enabled for. It will be enabled for all the Employee-based groups if no groups are defined. Thus, the related groups won't apply to portal security groups, since these don't inherit from the Employee base security group like the other regular security groups do.

The mechanism behind the activation is quite simple: it adds the security group in the `group` attribute to `implied_group`, thus making the related feature visible to the corresponding users.

The `module_` option field does not require any additional attributes. The remaining part of the field name identifies the module to be installed when this option has been activated. In our example, `module_note` will install the note module.

> **Important Information**
> Unchecking the box will uninstall the module without warning, which can cause data loss (models or fields and module data will be removed as a consequence). To avoid unchecking the box by accident, the `secure_uninstall` community module (from https://github.com/OCA/server-tools) prompts the user for a password before they uninstall the add-on module.

The last step of this recipe is added to the **General Settings** form view, just before the **Business documents** group, which has `id="business_documents"`. We used this `id` for view inheritance. It creates its own `div` with the module name as the ID, which is good practice because then, other modules that extend `my_library` can easily add their own configuration items to this `div`.

There's more...

Configuration settings can also have fields named with the `default_` prefix. When one of these has a value, the ORM will set it as a global default. The `settings` field should have a `default_model` attribute to identify the model that's been affected, and the field name after the `default_` prefix identifies the `model` field that will have the default value set.

Additionally, fields with none of the three prefixes mentioned can be used for other settings, but you will need to implement the logic to populate their values, using the `get_default_` name prefixed methods, and have them act when their values are edited using the `set_` name prefixed methods.

For those who would like to go deeper into the details of the configuration settings, take a look at Odoo's source code in `./odoo/addons/base/models/res_config.py`, which is extensively commented on.

Accessing recordsets as a superuser

In the previous recipes, we looked at security techniques such as access rules, security groups, and record rules. With these techniques, you can avoid unauthorized access. Sometimes, however, you have complex business cases in which you want to access or modify records, even if the user doesn't have access to them. For example, let's say the public user doesn't have access to the leads records, but by submitting the website form, the user can generate leads records in the backend.

Using `sudo()`, you can access recordsets as a superuser. We already saw `sudo()` in the *Changing the user that performs an action* recipe of *Chapter 8, Advanced Server-Side Development Techniques*. Here, we will see that even if you have given ACL rules or have added a security group to the field, you can still get access through `sudo()`.

How to do it...

We will use the same `my_library` module from the previous recipe. We already have an ALC rule that gives read-only access to normal users. We will add a new field with security groups so that only the Librarian has access to it. After that, we will modify the field value for the normal user. Follow these steps to achieve this:

1. Add the new field to the `library.book` model:

   ```
   report_missing = fields.Text(
       string="Book is missing",
       groups='my_library.group_library_librarian')
   ```

2. Add the field to the form view:

   ```
   <field name="report_missing"/>
   ```

3. Add the `report_missing_book()` method to the `library.book` model:

   ```
   def report_missing_book(self):
       self.ensure_one()
   ```

```
            message = "Book is missing (Reported by: %s)" %
self.env.user.name
        self.sudo().write({
            'report_missing': message
        })
```

4. Add the button to the form view so that we can trigger our method from the user interface. This should be placed inside the `<header>` tag:

```
<button name="report_missing_book"
    string="Report Missing Book"
    type="object"/>
```

Restart the server and update the module to apply these changes.

How it works...

In *steps 1* and *2*, we added a new field called `report_missing` to the model and form view. Note that we put the `my_library.group_library_librarian` group on the field in Python, so this field can only be accessed by the Librarian user.

In the next step, we added the `report_missing_book()` method. We updated the value of the `report_missing` field inside this method's body. Note that we used `sudo()` before calling the write method.

Finally, we added a button in the form view to trigger the method from the user interface.

To test this implementation, you need to log in with the non-librarian user. If you have loaded the database with demonstration data, you can log in with the demo user and then click on the **Missing book** report button in the form view of the book. Upon clicking that button, the `report_missing_book()` method will be called, and this will write the message into the `report_missing` field, even if the user doesn't have proper rights. You can check the value of the field through the admin user because this field will be hidden from the demo user.

Upon clicking the **Report Missing Book** button, we will get the recordset of the current book in the `report_missing_book()` method as an argument, `self`. Before we wrote the values into the book recordset, we used `self.sudo()`. This returns the same recordset but with super user rights. This recordset will have the `su=True` environment attribute, and it will bypass all access rules and record rules. Because of that, the non-librarian user will be able to write in the book record.

There's more...

You need to be extra careful when you use `sudo()` because it bypasses all access rights. If you want to access the record set as another user, you can pass the ID of that user inside `sudo`; for example, `self.sudo(uid)`. This will return a recordset containing the environment of that user. This way, it will not bypass all the access rules and record rules, but you can perform all the actions that are allowed for that user.

Hiding view elements and menus based on groups

In the previous recipes, we've learned how to hide fields from some users with group arguments in the Python field definition. There is another way to hide fields in the user interface: by adding security groups to the XML tags in the view definition. You can also use security groups with menus to hide them from a particular user.

Getting ready

For this recipe, we will reuse the `my_library` add-on module from the previous recipe. In the previous recipe, we added a button to the `<header>` tag. We will hide that whole header from a few users by adding a groups attribute to it.

Add the model, the views, and the menus for the `book.category` model. We will hide the category menus from a user. Please refer to *Chapter 4*, *Application Models*, to learn how to add model views and menus.

How to do it...

Follow these steps to hide elements based in security groups:

1. Add a groups attribute to the `<header>` tag to hide it from other users:

    ```
    ...
    <header groups="my_library.group_library_user">
    ...
    ```

2. Add the groups attribute to the `<menuitem>` book category so that it's only displayed for librarian users:

```xml
<menuitem name="Book Categories"
    id="library_book_category_menu"
    parent="library_base_menu"
    action="library_book_category_action"
    groups="my_library.group_library_librarian"/>
```

Restart the server and update the module to apply these changes.

How it works...

In the first step, we added `groups="my_library.group_library_user"` to the `<header>` tag. This means that the whole header part will only be visible to library users and librarians. Normal backend users who don't have `group_library_user` will not see the header part.

In *step 2*, we added the `groups="my_library.group_library_librarian"` attribute to `menuitem`. This means that this menu is only visible to librarian users.

You can use the groups attribute almost everywhere, including `<field>`, `<notebook>`, `<group>`, and `<menuitems>`, or on any tag from the view architecture. Odoo will hide those elements if the user doesn't have that group. You can use the same group attributes in web pages and *QWeb reports*, which will be covered in *Chapter 12, Automation, Workflows, Emails, and Printing*, and *Chapter 14, CMS Website Development*.

As we saw in the *Accessing recordsets as a superuser* recipe of this chapter, we can hide fields from some users using the groups argument in the Python field definition. Note that there is a big difference between using security groups on fields and using Python security groups in views. Security groups in Python provide real security; unauthorized users can't even access the fields through ORM or through RPC calls. However, the groups in views are just for improving usability. Fields that are hidden through groups in the XML file can still be accessed through RPC or ORM.

See also

Please refer to *Chapter 4, Application Models*, to learn how to add model views and menus.

11
Internationalization

Odoo supports multiple languages and allows different users to use different languages according to what they're most comfortable with. This is done through the built-in i18n features of Odoo. With string translations, Odoo also supports number format of date and time formatting too.

In this chapter, you will learn how you can enable multiple languages in Odoo and how to add translation files in your custom modules. This will improve the user experience of Odoo when understanding these new features.

In this chapter, we will cover the following recipes:

- Installing a language and configuring user preferences
- Configuring language-related settings
- Translating texts through a web client user interface
- Exporting translation strings to a file
- Using `gettext` tools to make translations easier
- Importing translation files into Odoo
- Changing the custom language URL code for a website

Many of these actions can be done either from the web client user interface or from the command line. Wherever possible, we will see how to use both of these options.

Installing a language and configuring user preferences

Odoo is localization-ready, meaning that it supports several languages and locale settings, such as date and number formats.

When first installed, only the default English language is available. To have other languages and locales available to users, we need to install them. In this recipe, we will see how to set user preferences and how they are applied.

How to do it...

Activate developer mode and follow these steps to install a new language in an Odoo instance:

1. Go to **Settings | General Settings | Language**. Here you will see the **Add Language** link, as shown in the following screenshot. Click on that link and it will open a dialog box to load languages:

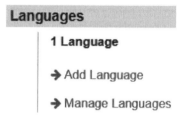

Figure 11.1 – Language options in the general settings

2. Select the language you want to load:

Figure 11.2 – Dialog to load a language

3. Clicking on **Add** will load the selected language, and the confirmation dialog box will open, shown as follows:

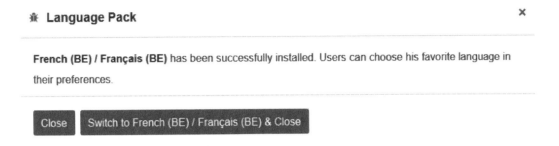

Figure 11.3 – Dialog that shows a language is loaded

4. New languages can also be installed from the command line. The equivalent command for the preceding steps is as follows:

```
$ ./odoo-bin -d mydb --load-language=es_ES
```

5. To set the language used by a user, go to **Settings | Users & Companies | Users**, and, in the **Preferences** tab of the **User** form, set the **Language** field value:

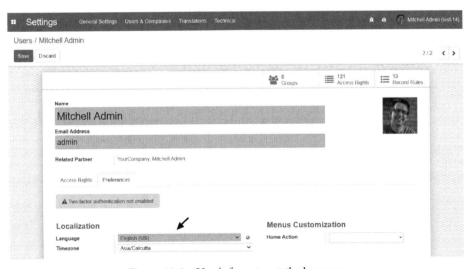

Figure 11.4 – User's form to set the language

Users can also set these configurations themselves through the **Preferences** menu option. This is available when they click on the username at the top-right of the web client window.

How it works...

Users can have their own language and time zone preferences. The language settings are used to translate user interface text into the chosen language and apply local conventions for float and monetary fields.

Before a language is made available for the user to select, it must be installed with the **Add language** option. The list of available languages can be seen with the **Settings | Translations | Languages** menu option in developer mode. The ones with the active flag set are installed.

Each Odoo add-on module is responsible for providing its own translation resources, which should be placed inside an `i18n` subdirectory. Each language's data should be in a `.po` file. In our example, for the Spanish language, the translation data is loaded from the `es_ES.po` data file.

Odoo also supports the notion of a **base language**. For example, if we have an `es.po` file for Spanish and an `es_MX.po` file for Mexican Spanish, then `es.po` is detected as the base language for `es_MX.po`. When the Mexican Spanish language is installed, both data files are loaded; first the one for the base language and then the specific language. Thus, the specific language translation file only needs to contain the strings that are specific to the language variant, which is Mexican Spanish in our example.

The `i18n` subdirectory is also expected to have a `<module_name>.pot` file, providing a template for translations and containing all the translatable strings. The *Exporting translation strings to a file* recipe of this chapter explains how to export the translatable strings to generate this file.

When an additional language is installed, the corresponding resources are loaded from all installed add-on modules and stored in the **Translated Terms** model. Its data can be viewed (and edited) within the **Settings | Translations | Application Terms | Translated Terms** menu option (note that this menu is only visible in developer mode).

Translation files for the installed languages are also loaded when a new add-on module is installed or an existing add-on module is upgraded.

There's more...

Translation files can be reloaded without upgrading the add-on modules by clicking again on the refresh icon on the languages. This can be used if you have updated translation files and don't want to go through the trouble of upgrading the modules (and all their dependencies).

If the **Overwrite Existing Terms** checkbox is left empty, only the newly translated strings are loaded. Thus, the changed translated strings won't be loaded. Check the box if you want the already-existing translations to also be loaded and overwrite the currently loaded translations. Note that this can potentially be problematic if someone changes the translations manually through the interface.

The **Overwrite Existing Terms** checkbox exists because we can edit specific translations by going to the **Settings** | **Translations** | **Application Terms** | **Translated Terms** menu item, or by using the **Technical Translation** shortcut option in the **Debug** menu. Translations that are added or modified in this way won't be overwritten unless the language is reloaded with the **Overwrite Existing Terms** checkbox enabled.

It can be useful to know that add-on modules can also have an `i18n_extra` subdirectory with extra translations. First, the `.po` files in the `i18n` subdirectory are downloaded. Then, Odoo ORM downloads files for the base language and, after that, for the language variant. Following this, the `.po` files in the `i18n_extra` subdirectory are downloaded, first for the base language and then for the language variant. The last string translation that's loaded is the one that prevails.

Configuring language-related settings

Languages and their variations (such as `es_MX` for Mexican Spanish) also provide locale settings, such as date and number formats.

They come with appropriate defaults, so as long as the user is using the correct language, the locale settings should be the correct ones.

However, you might still want to modify a language's settings. For example, you might prefer to have the user interface in the default English but want to change the American default date and number formats to match your requirements.

Getting ready

We will need to have developer mode activated. If it's not already activated, activate it as shown in the *Activating the Odoo developer tools* recipe from *Chapter 1, Installing the Odoo Development Environment*.

How to do it...

To modify a language's locale settings, follow these steps:

1. To check the installed languages and their configurations, select the **Settings | Translations | Languages** menu option. Clicking on one of the installed languages will open a form with the corresponding settings:

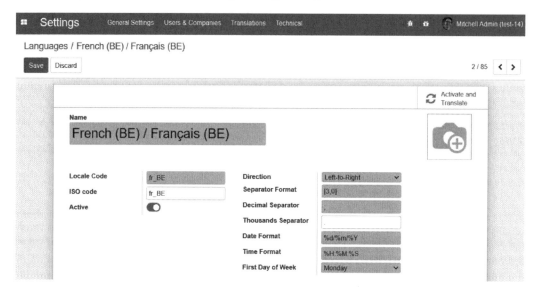

Figure 11.5 – Form to configure language settings

2. Edit the language settings. To change the date to the ISO format, change the **Date Format** to `%Y-%m-%d`. To change the number format to use a comma as a decimal separator, modify the **Decimal Separator** and **Thousands Separator** fields accordingly.

How it works...

When signing in and creating a new Odoo user session, the user language is checked in the user preferences and set in the `lang` context key. This is then used to format the output appropriately—the source texts are translated into the user language, and the dates and numbers are formatted according to the language's current locale settings.

There's more...

Server-side processes are able to modify the context in which actions are run. For example, to get a recordset where the dates are formatted according to the American English format, independent of the current user's language preference, you can do the following:

```
en_records = self.with_context(lang='en_US').search([])
```

For more details, refer to the *Calling a method with a modified context* recipe from *Chapter 8, Advanced Server-Side Development Techniques*.

Translating texts through the web client user interface

The simplest way to translate is to use the translation feature provided by the web client. These translation strings are stored in the database and can later be exported to a .po file, either to be included in an add-on module or just to later be imported back manually.

Text fields can have translatable content, meaning that their value will depend on the current user's language. We will also see how to set the language-dependent values on these fields.

Getting ready

We will need to have developer mode activated. If it's not, activate it as shown in the *Activating the Odoo developer tools* recipe in *Chapter 1, Installing the Odoo Development Environment*.

How to do it...

We will demonstrate how to translate terms through the web client using the **User Groups** feature as an example:

1. Navigate to the screen you want to translate. As an example, we will open the **Groups** view via the **Settings | Users & Companies | Groups** menu item.

2. In the top menu bar, click on the **Debug** menu icon and select the **Technical Translation** option:

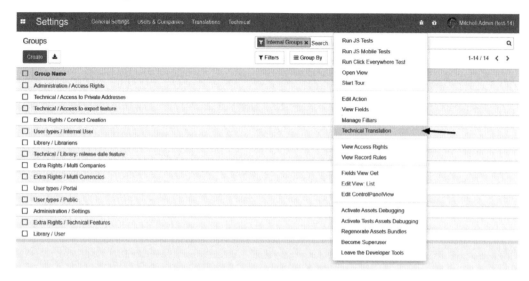

Figure 11.6 – Option to open translation for the current view

3. A list of the available translation terms for that view will be shown. Edit **Translation Value** in a line to change (or add) its translation text. If you are looking for a particular source string, use the listed filters to narrow down the displayed text:

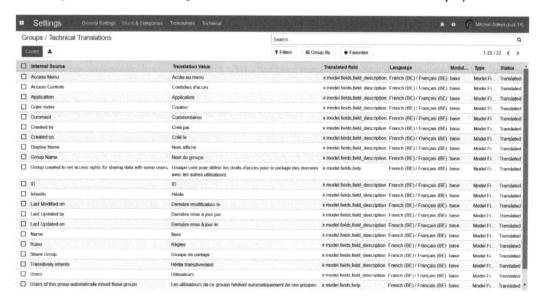

Figure 11.7 – Translation terms for the view

Group Name is a translatable field. Let's translate a record's value to the several languages installed.

4. Navigate to the **User Groups** menu option once more, open one of the group records in the form view, and click on **Edit**:

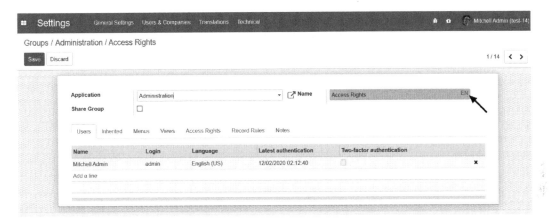

Figure 11.8 – Translation for the field values

5. Note that the **Name** field has a special icon on the far right. This indicates that it is a translatable field. Clicking on the icon opens a **Translate** list with the different installed languages. This allows us to set the translation for each of those languages.

How it works...

Translated terms are stored in the database table for the `ir.translation` model. The **Technical Translation** option in the **Debug** menu provides quick access to those terms, in context with the currently selected view.

Similarly, model fields with translatable content will feature an icon to access a list of the installed languages and to set the appropriate value for each language.

Alternatively, the translation terms can be accessed from the **Settings** top menu using the **Translations | Application Terms | Translated Terms** menu option. Here, we can see all the terms that are available for our instance. We should use data filters to locate the terms we might be interested in.

There's more...

Alongside the **Translated Terms** menu option, we can also find the **Generate Missing Terms** option. Selecting this will display a dialog window to provide the desired language, and then launch a process to extract translatable strings from the installed add-on modules and add any new ones to the **Translated Terms** table. It is equivalent to performing the **Export Translation** steps, as described in the *Exporting translation strings to a file* recipe of this chapter.

This can be useful after changing some models or views. By doing this, the new strings will be added so that we can translate them.

It can also be used to populate the strings from the en_US default language. We can then make use of the translation terms to replace the original English text with new text that is better for the end user's specific business vocabulary.

> **Important note**
> When editing a QWeb view in a language other than the main website language, you'll notice that you can only change strings. This is because, for other languages, you actually only add translations to the text content of nodes using Odoo's i18n mechanism.

Exporting translation strings to a file

Translation strings can be exported with or without the translated texts for a selected language. This can either be to include i18n data in a module or to later perform translations with a text editor or perhaps with a specialized tool.

We will demonstrate how to do this using the standard mail module, so feel free to replace mail with your own module.

Getting ready

We will need to have developer mode activated. If it's not already activated, activate it as demonstrated in the *Activating the Odoo developer tools* recipe in *Chapter 1, Installing the Odoo Development Environment*.

How to do it...

To export the translation terms for the `mail` add-on module, follow these steps:

1. In the web client user interface, from the **Settings** top menu, select the **Translations | Import/Export | Export Translation** menu option.

2. In the **Export Translations** dialog box, choose the language translation to export, the file format, and the modules to export. To export a translation template file, select **New Language (Empty translation template)** from the **Language** selection list. It's recommended to use the `.po` format and to export only one add-on module at a time—the **Discuss** module (`mail` is the technical name for the Discuss app), in our example:

Figure 11.9 – Dialog to export translation terms

3. Once the export process is complete, a new window will be displayed, with a link to download the file and some additional advice.

4. To export a translation template file for the `mail` add-on module from the Odoo command-line interface, enter the following command:

```
$ ./odoo-bin -d mydb --i18n-export=mail.po --modules=mail
$ mv mail.po ./addons/mail/i18n/mail.pot
```

5. To export the translation template file for a language—`es_ES` for Spanish, for example—from the Odoo command-line interface, enter the following command:

```
$ ./odoo-bin -d mydb --i18n-export=es_ES.po
--modules=mail
--language=es_ES
$ mv es_ES.po ./addons/mail/i18n
```

How it works...

The **Export Translation** feature does two things: extracts the translatable strings from the target modules, adding the new ones in the `ir.translation` model, and then creates a file with the translation terms. This can be done both from the web client and the command-line interface.

When exporting from the web client, we can choose to either export an empty translation template, that is, a file with the strings to translate along with empty translations, or export a language, resulting in a file with the strings to translate, along with the translation for the selected language.

The file formats that are available are CSV, PO, and TGZ. The TGZ file format exports a compressed file that contains a `<name>/i18n/` directory structure with the PO or POT file.

The CSV format can be useful for performing translations using a spreadsheet, but the format to use in the add-on modules is PO files. These are expected to be placed inside the `i18n` subdirectory. They are then automatically loaded once the corresponding language is installed. When exporting these PO files, we should export only one module at a time. The PO file is also a popular format supported by translation tools, such as Poedit.

Translations can also be exported directly from the command line, using the `--i18n-export` option. This recipe shows how to extract both the template files and the translated language files.

In *step 4* of this recipe, we exported a template file. The `--i18n-export` option expects the path and the file name to export. Bear in mind that the file extension is required to be either CSV, PO, or TGZ. This option requires the `-d` option, which specifies the database to use. The `--modules` option is also needed to indicate the add-on modules to export. Note that the `--stop-after-init` option is not needed, since the `export` command automatically returns to the command line when finished.

This exports a template file. The Odoo module expects this exported template in the `i18n` folder with the `.pot` extension. When working on a module, after the export operation, we usually want to move the exported PO file to the module's `i18n` directory with a `<module>.pot` name.

In *step 5*, the `--language` option was also used. With it, instead of an empty translation file, the translated terms for the selected language were also exported. One use case for this is to perform some translations through the web client user interface using the **Technical Translation** feature, and then export and include them in the module.

There's more...

Text strings in view and model definitions are automatically extracted for translation. For models, the `_description` attribute, the field names (the `string` attribute), help text, and selection field options are extracted, as well as the user texts for model constraints (`_constraints` and `_sql_constraints`).

Text strings to translate inside Python or JavaScript code can't be automatically detected, so the code should identify those strings, wrapping them inside the underscore function.

In Python's module file, we should ensure that the file is imported with the following:

```
from odoo import _
```

This file can then be used wherever a translatable text is used with something like this:

```
_('Hello World')
```

For strings that use additional context information, we should use Python string interpolation, as shown here:

```
_('Hello %s') % 'World'
```

Note that the interpolation should go outside the translation function. For example, `_("Hello %s" % 'World')` is wrong. String interpolations should also be preferred to string concatenation so that each interface text is just one translation string.

Be careful with the `Selection` fields! If you pass an explicit list of values to the field definition, the displayed strings are automatically flagged for translation. On the other hand, if you pass a method that returns the list of values, the display strings must be explicitly marked for translation.

Regarding manual translation work, any text file editor will do, but using an editor that specifically supports the PO file syntax makes the work easier by reducing the risk of formatting errors. Such editors include those listed here:

- **POEDIT**: `https://poedit.net/`
- **Emacs (PO-mode)**: `https://www.gnu.org/software/gettext/manual/html_node/PO-Mode.html`
- **Lokalize**: `http://i18n.kde.org/tools`
- **Gtranslator**: `https://wiki.gnome.org/Apps/Gtranslator`

Using gettext tools to make translations easier

The PO file format is part of the `gettext` i18n and localization system that's commonly used in Unix-like systems. This system includes tools to ease translation work.

This recipe demonstrates how to use these tools to help translate our add-on modules. We want to use it on a custom module, so the `my_library` we created in *Chapter 3, Creating Odoo Add-On Modules*, is a good candidate. However, feel free to replace it with some other custom module you have at hand, replacing the recipe's `my_library` references as appropriate.

How to do it...

To manage translations from the command line, assuming that your Odoo installation is at `~/odoo-work/odoo`, follow these steps:

1. Create a compendium of translation terms for the target language, for example, Spanish. If we name our compendium file `odoo_es.po`, we should write the following code:

   ```
   $ cd ~/odoo-work/odoo  # Use the path to your Odoo installation
   $ find ./ -name es_ES.po | xargs msgcat --use-first | msgattrib
   -- translated --no-fuzzy \ -o ./odoo_es.po
   ```

2. Export the translation template file for the add-on module from the Odoo command-line interface and place it in the module's expected location:

   ```
   $ ./odoo-bin -d mydb --i18n-export=my_module.po
   --modules=my_module
   $ mv my_module.po ./addons/my_module/i18n/my_module.pot
   ```

3. If no translation file is available yet for the target language, create the PO translation file, reusing the terms that have been already found and translated in the compendium:

   ```
   $ msgmerge --compendium ./odoo_es.po -o
   ./addons/my_module/i18n/es_ES.po \
   /dev/null ./addons/my_module/i18n/my_module.pot
   ```

4. If a translation file exists, add the translations that can be found in the compendium:

   ```
   $ mv ./addons/my_module/i18n/es_ES.po /tmp/my_module_es_old.po
   $ msgmerge --compendium ./odoo_es.po -o ./addons/my_module/i18n/es_ES.po
   \ /tmp/my_module_es_old.po ./addons/my_module/i18n/my_module.pot
   $ rm /tmp/my_module_es_old.po
   ```

5. To take a peek at the untranslated terms in a PO file, use this:

   ```
   $ msgattrib --untranslated ./addons/my_module/i18n/es_ES.po
   ```

6. Use your favorite editor to complete the translation.

How it works...

Step 1 uses commands from the `gettext` toolbox to create a translation compendium for the chosen language—Spanish, in our case. It works by finding all the `es_ES.po` files in the Odoo code base, and passing them to the `msgcat` command. We use the `--use-first` flag to avoid conflicting translations (there are a few in the Odoo code base). The result is passed to the `msgattrib` filter. We use the `--translated` option to filter out the untranslated entries and the `--no-fuzzy` option to remove fuzzy translations. We then save the result in `odoo_es.po`.

Step 2 of the preceding section calls `odoo.py` with the `--i18n-export` option. You need to specify a database on the command line, even if one is specified in the configuration file and the `--modules` option, with a comma-separated list of modules to export the translation.

In the `gettext` world, fuzzy translations are those created automatically by the `msgmerge` command (or other tools) using a proximity match on the source string. We want to avoid these in the compendium.

Step 3 creates a new translation file by using existing translated values found in the compendium. The `msgmerge` command is used with the `--compendium` option to find the `msgid` lines in the compendium files, matching those in the translation template file generated in *step 2*. The result is saved in the `es_ES.po` file.

If you have a preexisting `.po` file for your add-on with translations that you would like to preserve, you should rename it and replace the `/dev/null` argument with this file. The renaming procedure is required to avoid using the same file for input and output.

There's more...

This recipe only skims the surface of the rich tools that are available with the GNU `gettext` toolbox. Full coverage is well beyond the scope of this book. If you are interested, the GNU `gettext` documentation contains a wealth of precious information about PO file manipulation and is available at http://www.gnu.org/software/gettext/manual/gettext.html.

Importing translation files into Odoo

The usual practice to load translations is to place PO files inside the module's `i18n` subdirectory. Whenever the add-on module is installed or upgraded, the translation files are loaded and the newly translated strings are added.

However, there may be cases where we want to directly import a translation file. In this recipe, we will see how to load a translation file, either from the web client or from the command line.

Getting ready

We need to have developer mode activated. If it's not activated already, activate it as demonstrated in the *Activating the Odoo developer tools* recipe from *Chapter 1, Installing the Odoo Development Environment*. We will also need a translation po file, which we are going import in this recipe, for example, the `myfile.po` file.

How to do it...

To import the translation terms, follow these steps:

1. In the web client user interface, from the **Settings** top menu, select the **Translations | Import/Export | Import Translation** menu option.

2. In the **Import Translations** dialog box, fill out the language name and the language code, and select the file to import. Finally, click on the **Import** button to perform the action:

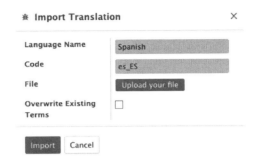

Figure 11.10 – Dialog to import a translation file

3. To import a translation file from the Odoo command-line interface, we must place it inside the server add-ons path and then perform the import:

```
$ mv myfile.po ./addons/
$ ./odoo.py -d mydb --i18n-import="myfile.po" --lang=es_ES
```

How it works...

Import Translation takes a PO or CSV file and loads the translation strings into the `ir.translation` table.

The web client feature asks for the language name, but this is not used in the import process. It also has an overwrite option. If selected, it forces all the translation strings to be imported, even the ones that already exist, overwriting them in the process.

On the command line, the import can be done using the `--i18n-import` option. It must be provided with the path to the file, relative to an add-ons' path directory; `-d` and `--language` (or `-l`) are mandatory. Overwriting can also be achieved by adding the `--i18n-overwrite` option to the command. Note that we didn't use the `--stop-after-init` option here. It is not needed, since the import action stops the server when it finishes.

Changing the custom language URL code for a website

Odoo supports multiple languages for websites too. On a website, the current language is identified as a language string. In this recipe, you will see how to change the language code in a URL.

Getting ready

Before following this recipe, make sure you have installed the `website` module and enabled multiple languages for the website.

How to do it...

To modify a language's URL code, follow these steps:

1. Open the language list from the **Settings | Translations | Languages** menu option. Clicking on one of the installed languages will open a form like this:

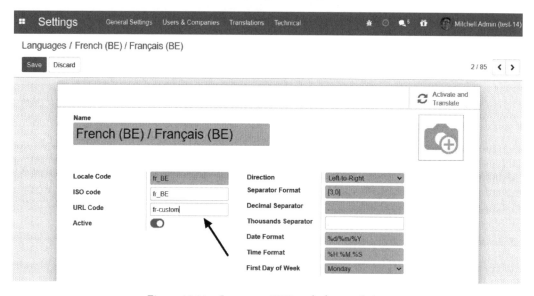

Figure 11.11 – Language URL code for a website

2. Here you will see the **URL Code** field. Set the value that you want. Make sure you don't add spaces or special characters here.

After configuring this, you can test the results on your website. Open the home page and change the language; you will see the custom language code in the URL.

How it works...

Odoo identifies the languages for a website via the URL path. For example, www.odoo.com/fr_FR is used for the French language and www.odoo.com/es_ES is used for the Spanish language. Here, the fr_FR and es_ES parts of the URL are the language ISO codes, and they are used by Odoo to detect the requested language. But sometimes, you want to set the language in a more user-friendly way. In that case, you can update the **URL Code** field. Once you have changed that, the Odoo website will use the **URL Code** value to identify the language. For example, you could set **URL Code** to fr for the French language. Then, www.odoo.com/fr_FR would be converted into www.odoo.com/fr.

> **Note**
> It is no issue if you change the URL code in production; Odoo will redirect the URL with the language ISO code to your custom URL.

12
Automation, Workflows, Emails, and Printing

Business applications are expected not only to store records but also to manage business workflows. Some objects, such as leads or project tasks, have a lot of records that run in parallel. Having too many records for an object makes it harder to have a clear picture of the business. Odoo has several techniques that can deal with this problem. In this chapter, we will look at how we can set a business workflow with dynamic stages and kanban groups. This will help the user to get an idea about how their business is running.

We will also look at techniques, such as server actions and automated actions, that can be used by power users or functional consultants to add simpler process automation without the need to create custom add-ons. Finally, we will create **QWeb-based PDF reports** to print out.

In this chapter, we will cover the following recipes:

- Managing dynamic record stages
- Managing kanban stages
- Adding a quick create form to a kanban card

- Creating interactive kanban cards
- Adding a progress bar in kanban views
- Creating server actions
- Using Python code server actions
- Using automated actions on time conditions
- Using automated actions on event conditions
- Creating QWeb-based PDF reports
- Managing activities from a kanban card
- Adding a stat button to a form view
- Enabling the archive option for records

Technical requirements

The technical requirement for this chapter is having an online Odoo platform.

All the code used in this chapter can be downloaded from the GitHub repository at `https://github.com/PacktPublishing/Odoo-14-Development-Cookbook-Fourth-Edition/tree/master/Chapter12`.

Managing dynamic record stages

In `my_library`, we have a `state` field to indicate the current status of a book rent record. This `state` field is limited to the `ongoing` or `returned` statuses and it is not possible to add a new state to the business process. To avoid this, we can use the `many2one` field to give flexibility when designing the kanban workflow of a user's choice, and you can add/remove a new state any time.

Getting ready

For this recipe, we will be using the `my_library` module from *Chapter 8, Advanced Server-Side Development Techniques*. That module manages books and their categories. It also records book rents. We added an initial module, `Chapter12/00_initial_module/my_library`, to the GitHub repository for this book to help you get started: `https://github.com/PacktPublishing/Odoo-14-Development-Cookbook-Fourth-Edition/tree/master/Chapter12`.

How to do it...

Follow these simple steps to add stages to the `library.book.rent` module:

1. Add a new model called `library.rent.stage`, as follows:

   ```
   class LibraryRentStage(models.Model):
       _name = 'library.rent.stage'
       _order = 'sequence,name'

       name = fields.Char()
       sequence = fields.Integer()
       fold = fields.Boolean()
       book_state = fields.Selection(
           [('available', 'Available'),
            ('borrowed', 'Borrowed'),
            ('lost', 'Lost')],
           'State', default="available")
   ```

2. Add access rights for this new module in the `security/ir.model.access.csv` file, as follows:

   ```
   acl_book_rent_stage,library.book_rent_stage_default,model_library_rent_stage,,1,0,0,0
   acl_book_rent_librarian_stage,library.book_rent_stage_librarian,model_library_rent_stage,group_librarian,1,1,1,1
   ```

3. Remove the `state` field from the `library.book.rent` model and replace it with a new `stage_id` field, which is a `many2one` field, and its methods, as shown in the following example:

   ```
   @api.model
   def _default_rent_stage(self):
       Stage = self.env['library.rent.stage']
       return Stage.search([], limit=1)

   stage_id = fields.Many2one(
       'library.rent.stage',
       default=_default_rent_stage
   )
   ```

4. Replace the state field in the form view with the stage_id field, as shown in the following example:

```xml
<header>
    <field name="stage_id" widget="statusbar"
        options="{'clickable': 1, 'fold_field':
'fold'}"/>
</header>
```

5. Replace the state field in the tree view with the stage_id field, as follows:

```xml
<tree>
    <field name="book_id"/>
    <field name="borrower_id"/>
    <field name="stage_id"/>
</tree>
```

6. Add some initial stages from the data/library_stage.xml file. Don't forget to add this file to the manifest, as shown in the following example:

```xml
<?xml version="1.0" encoding="utf-8"?>
<odoo noupdate="1">
    <record id="stage_draft" model="library.rent.stage">
        <field name="name">Draft</field>
        <field name="sequence">1</field>
        <field name="book_state">available</field>
    </record>
    <record id="stage_rent" model="library.rent.stage">
        <field name="name">On rent</field>
        <field name="sequence">5</field>
        <field name="book_state">borrowed</field>
    </record>
    <record id="stage_due" model="library.rent.stage">
        <field name="name">Due</field>
        <field name="sequence">15</field>
        <field name="book_state">borrowed</field>
    </record>
    <record id="stage_returned" model="library.rent.stage">
        <field name="name">Completed</field>
        <field name="sequence">25</field>
        <field name="book_state">available</field>
    </record>
    <record id="stage_lost" model="library.rent.stage">
        <field name="name">Lost</field>
```

```xml
            <field name="sequence">35</field>
            <field name="fold" eval="True"/>
            <field name="book_state">lost</field>
    </record>
</odoo>
```

After installing the module, you will see stages in the form view, as shown in the following screenshot:

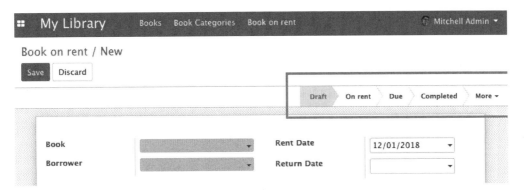

Figure 12.1 – Stage selector in the form view

As you can see in the preceding screenshot, you will see the stages on the book rent record. These stages are clickable, so you will be able to change the stage by clicking on it. Folded stages will be displayed under the **More** dropdown.

How it works...

As we want to manage the record stages dynamically, we need to create a new model. In *step 1*, we created a new model called `library.rent.stage` to store the dynamic stages. In this model, we added a few fields. One of these was the `sequence` field, which is used to determine the order of the stages. We also added the `fold` Boolean field, which is used to collapse the stages and put them in a drop-down list. This is very helpful when your business process has lots of stages because it means that you can hide insignificant stages in the drop-down menu by setting this field. We added a `book_state` field to map the dynamic stage to the state of the book. We will use this field in the upcoming section.

The `fold` field is also used in kanban views to display folded kanban columns. Usually, **Work in Progress** items are expected to be in the **Unfolded** stage, and terminated items that are marked as either **Done** or **Cancelled** should be in the **Folded** stage.

By default, `fold` is the name of the field that is used to hold the value of the stage fold. You can change this, however, by adding the `_fold_name = 'is_fold'` class attribute.

In *step 2*, we added the basic access right rules for the new model.

In *step 3*, we added the `stage_id` many2one field to the `library.book.rent` model. While creating a new loan record, we wanted to set the default stage value to `Draft`. To accomplish this, we added a `_default_rent_stage()` method. This method will fetch the record of the `library.rent.stage` model with the lowest sequence number, so, while creating a new record, the stage with the lowest sequence will be displayed as active in the form view.

In *step 4*, we added the `stage_id` field to the form view. By adding the `clickable` option, we made the status bar clickable. We also added an option for the `fold` field, which will allow us to display insignificant stages in the drop-down menu.

In *step 5*, we added `stage_id` to the tree view.

In *step 6*, we added the default data for the stages. Users will see these basic stages after installing our module. If you want to learn more about XML data syntax, refer to the *Loading data using XML files* recipe in *Chapter 6, Managing Module Data*.

> **Important note**
>
> With this implementation, the user can define new stages on the fly. You will need to add views and menus for `library.rent.stage` so that you can add new stages from the user interface. Refer to *Chapter 9, Backend Views*, if you don't know how to add views and menus.
>
> If you don't want to do this, the kanban view provides inbuilt features for adding, removing, or modifying stages from the kanban view itself, which is coming up in the next recipe.

There's more...

Notice that we have the `state` field in the `library.book` model. This field is used to represent the status of the book, or, in other words, whether it is available or not. We have added a `book_state` field to map the state of the book with the dynamic stages.

In order to reflect the book state from the stage, we need to override the create and write methods in the `library.book.rent` model, as follows:

```
@api.model
def create(self, vals):
    rent = super(LibraryBookRent, self).create(vals)
    if rent.stage_id.book_state:
        rent.book_id.state = rent.stage_id.book_state
    return rent
```

```python
@api.multi
def write(self, vals):
    rent = super(LibraryBookRent, self).write(vals)
    if self.stage_id.book_state:
        self.book_id.state = self.stage_id.book_state
    return rent
```

After this, whenever the user changes the stage of any rent record, it will be reflected in the book record.

See more

- Refer to *Chapter 9*, *Backend Views*, to learn about adding views and menus.

Managing kanban stages

Using a **kanban board** is a simple method to manage workflows. It is organized in columns, each corresponding to stages, and the work items progress from left to right until they are finished. A kanban view, with the stages, provides flexibility because it allows users to choose their own workflows. It provides a full overview of the records on a single screen.

Getting started

For this recipe, we will be using the `my_library` module from the previous recipe. We will add kanban for the `libary.book.rent` model and we will group kanban cards by stage.

How to do it...

Perform the following steps to enable workflows such as kanban for the book rent model:

1. Add a kanban view for `libary.book.rent`, as follows:

   ```xml
   <record id="library_book_rent_view_kanban" model="ir.ui.view">
       <field name="name">Rent Kanban</field>
       <field name="model">library.book.rent</field>
       <field name="arch" type="xml">
           <kanban default_group_by="stage_id">
               <field name="stage_id" />
               <templates>
   ```

```xml
                        <t t-name="kanban-box">
                            <div class="oe_kanban_global_click">
                                <div class="oe_kanban_content">
                                    <div class="oe_kanban_card">
                                        <div>
                                            <i class="fa fa-user"/>
                                            <b>
                                                <field name="borrower_id" />
                                            </b>
                                        </div>
                                        <div class="text-muted">
                                            <i class="fa fa-book"/>
                                            <field name="book_id" />
                                        </div>
                                    </div>
                                </div>
                            </div>
                        </t>
                    </templates>
                </kanban>
            </field>
        </record>
```

2. Add kanban to the `library_book_rent_action` action, as follows:

   ```xml
   ...
   <field name="view_mode">kanban,tree,form</field>
   ...
   ```

3. Add the `_group_expand_stages()` method and the `group_expand` attribute to the `stage_id` field, as follows:

   ```python
   @api.model
   def _group_expand_stages(self, stages, domain, order):
       return stages.search([], order=order)

   stage_id = fields.Many2one(
       'library.rent.stage',
       default=_default_rent_stage,
       group_expand='_group_expand_stages'
   )
   ```

Restart the server and update the module to apply the changes. This will enable a kanban board, as shown in the following screenshot:

Figure 12.2 – Kanban view with groups by stage

As you can see in the preceding screenshot, the kanban will show the rent records grouped by stage. You will be able to drag and drop cards to another stage column. Moving cards to another column will change the stage value in the database too.

How it works...

In *step 1*, we added a kanban view for the `library.book.rent` model. Note that we used `stage_id` as the default group for kanban, so, when the user opens kanban, the kanban cards will be grouped by stage. To find out more about kanban, please refer to *Chapter 9*, *Backend Views*.

In *step 2*, we added the `kanban` keyword to the existing action.

In *step 3*, we added the `group_expand` attribute to the `stage_id` field. We also added a new `_group_expand_stages()` method. `group_expand` changes the behavior of the field grouping. By default, field grouping shows the stages that are being used. For example, if there is no rent record that has the `lost` stage, the grouping will not return that stage, so kanban will not display the `lost` column. But in our case, we want to display all of the stages, regardless of whether or not they are being used.

The `_group_expand_stages()` function is used to return all the records for the stages. Because of this, the kanban view will display all the stages and you will be able to use workflows by dragging and dropping them.

There's more...

If you play around with the kanban board created in this recipe, you will find lots of different features. Some of these are as follows:

- You can create a new stage by clicking on the **Add new column** option. The `group_create` option can be used to disable the **Add column** option from the kanban board.
- You can arrange columns into a different order by dragging them by their headers. This will update the sequence field of the `library.rent.stage` model.
- You can edit or delete columns with the gear icon in the header of a kanban column. The `group_edit` and `group_delete` options can be used to disable this feature.
- The stages that have a `true` value in the `fold` field will collapse and the column will be displayed like a slim bar. If you click on this slim bar, it will expand and display the kanban cards.
- If the model has an `active` Boolean field, it will display the option to archive and unarchive records in the kanban column. The `archivable` option can be used to disable this feature.
- The plus icon on the kanban column can be used to create records directly from the kanban view. The `quick_create` option can be used to disable this feature. For the moment, this feature will not work in our example. This will be solved in the next recipe.

See more

- To learn more about kanban, please refer to *Chapter 9, Backend Views*.

Adding a quick create form to a kanban card

Grouped kanban views provide the quick create feature, which allows us to generate records directly from the kanban view. The plus icon on a column will display an editable kanban card on the column, using which you can create a record. In this recipe, we will see how we can design a quick create kanban form of our choice.

Getting started

For this recipe, we will be using the `my_library` module from the previous recipe. We will use the quick create option in kanban for the `library.book.rent` model.

How to do it...

Follow these steps to add a custom quick create form for kanban:

1. Create a new minimal form view for the `library.book.rent` model, as follows:

```xml
<record id="library_book_rent_view_form_minimal" model="ir.ui.view">
    <field name="name">Library Rent Form</field>
    <field name="model">library.book.rent</field>
    <field name="arch" type="xml">
        <form>
            <group>
                <field name="book_id" domain="[('state', '=', 'available')]"/>
                <field name="borrower_id"/>
            </group>
        </form>
    </field>
</record>
```

2. Add quick create options to the `<kanban>` tag, as follows:

```xml
<kanban default_group_by="stage_id"
        quick_create_view="my_library.library_book_rent_view_form_minimal"
        on_create="quick_create">
```

3. Restart the server and update the module to apply the changes. Then, click on the plus icon in the column. This will enable kanban forms, as shown in the following screenshot:

Figure 12.3 – Quickly creating a record directly from the kanban view

When you click on the **Create** button in the Kanban view, you will see a small card with input instead of redirecting to the form view. You can fill in the values and click on **Add**, which will create a book rent record.

How it works...

In order to create a custom quick create option, we need to create a minimal form view. We did this in *step 1*. We added two required fields, because you cannot create a record without filling in the required fields. If you do so, Odoo will generate an error and open the default form view in the dialog so that you can enter all the required values.

In *step 2*, we added this new form view to the kanban view. Using the `quick_create_view` option, you can map the custom form view to the kanban view. We also added one extra option – `on_create="quick_create"`. This option will display a quick create form in the first column when you click on the **Create** button in the control panel. Without this option, the **Create** button will open a form view in editable mode.

You can disable the quick create feature by adding `quick_create="false"` to the kanban tag.

Creating interactive kanban cards

Kanban cards support all HTML tags, which means you can design them however you like. Odoo provides some built-in ways to make kanban cards more interactive. In this recipe, we will add color options, the star widget, and `many2many` tags to the kanban card.

Getting started

For this recipe, we will be using the `my_library` module from the previous recipe.

How to do it...

Follow these steps to create an attractive kanban card:

1. Add a new model to manage the tags for the `library.book.rent` model, as follows:

    ```python
    class LibraryRentTags(models.Model):
        _name = 'library.rent.tag'
        name = fields.Char()
        color = fields.Integer()
    ```

2. Add basic access rights for the `library.rent.tag` model, as follows:

   ```
   acl_book_rent_tags,library.book_rent_tags_default,model_
   library_rent_tag,,1,0,0,0
   acl_book_rent_librarian_tags,library.book_rent_tags_
   librarian,model_library_rent_tag,group_librarian,1,1,1,1
   ```

3. Add new fields to the `library.book.rent` model, as follows:

   ```
   color = fields.Integer()
   popularity = fields.Selection([
       ('no', 'No Demand'),
       ('low', 'Low Demand'),
       ('medium', 'Average Demand'),
       ('high', 'High Demand')], default="no")
   tag_ids = fields.Many2many('library.rent.tag')
   ```

4. Add fields in the form view, as follows:

   ```
   <field name="popularity" widget="priority"/>
   <field name="tag_ids" widget="many2many_tags"
       options="{'color_field': 'color', 'no_create_edit':
   True}"/>
   ```

   In the next few steps, we will update an existing kanban view. The code in bold text is newly added code.

5. Add a `color` field to the kanban view:

   ```
   ...
   <field name="stage_id" />
   <field name="color" />
   ...
   ```

6. Add a dropdown to choose a color on the kanban view:

   ```
   ...
   <t t-name="kanban-box">
       <div t-attf-class="#{kanban_color(record.color.raw_value)} oe_kanban_global_click">
           <div class="o_dropdown_kanban dropdown">
               <a class="dropdown-toggle o-no-caret btn" role="button" data-toggle="dropdown">
                   <span class="fa fa-ellipsis-v"/>
               </a>
   ```

```xml
                <div class="dropdown-menu" role="menu">
                    <t t-if="widget.editable">
                        <a role="menuitem" type="edit" class="dropdown-item">Edit</a>
                    </t>
                    <t t-if="widget.deletable">
                        <a role="menuitem" type="delete" class="dropdown-item">Delete</a>
                    </t>
                    <ul class="oe_kanban_colorpicker" data-field="color"/>
                </div>
            </div>
...
```

7. Add tags and a `popularity` field to the kanban view:

```xml
...
<div class="text-muted">
    <i class="fa fa-book"/>
    <field name="book_id" />
</div>
<span class="oe_kanban_list_many2many">
    <field name="tag_ids" widget="many2many_tags" options="{'color_field': 'color'}"/>
</span>
<div>
    <field name="popularity" widget="priority"/>
</div>
...
```

> **Important note**
> The code in bold should be added to the existing kanban view.

Restart the server and update the module to apply the changes. Then, click on the plus icon on a column. It will display the kanban, as shown in the following figure:

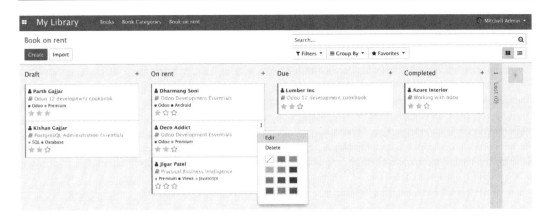

Figure 12.4 – Kanban cards with new options

Our changes in the kanban structure will enable extra options in the kanban card. Now you will be able to choose the color on kanban itself. Also, you will be able to prioritize cards with stars.

How it works...

In the first two steps, we added a new model and security rules for tags. In the third step, we added a few fields to the rent model.

In *step 4*, we added those fields to the form view. Note that we used the `priority` widget on the `popularity` field, which displays the selection field with star icons. In the `tag_ids` field, we used the `many2many_tags` widget, which displays the many2many field in the form of tags. The `color_field` option is passed to enable the color feature on tags. The value of this option is the field name where the color index is stored. The `no_create_edit` option will disable the feature of creating new tags via the form view.

In *step 5*, we improved lots of things. To the kanban card, we added `t-attf-class="#{kanban_color(record.color.raw_value)}`. This will be used to display the color of the kanban card. It uses the value of the `color` field and generates a class based on that value. For example, if a kanban record has a value of 2 in the `color` field, it will add `kanban_color_2` to the class. After that, we added a drop-down menu to add options such as **Edit**, **Delete**, and the kanban color picker. The **Edit** and **Delete** options are only displayed if the user has proper access rights.

Finally, we added tags and priority to the kanban card. After adding all of this, the kanban card will look as in the following screenshot:

Figure 12.5 – Kanban card options

With this card design, you will be able to set popularity stars and colors directly from the kanban card.

Adding a progress bar in kanban views

Sometimes, you have tons of records in columns and it is very difficult to get a clear picture of the particular stages. A progress bar can be used to display the status of any column. In this recipe, we will display a progress bar on kanban, based on the field named `popularity`.

Getting started

For this recipe, we will be using the `my_library` module from the previous recipe.

How to do it...

In order to add a progress bar to the kanban columns, you will need to add a `progressbar` tag to the kanban view definition, as follows:

```
<progressbar
    field="popularity"
    colors='{"low": "success", "medium": "warning", "high": "danger"}'/>
```

Note that kanban column progress bars were introduced in Odoo version 11. Versions prior to that will not display column progress bars.

Restart the server and update the module to apply the changes. Then, click on the plus icon on a column. This will display the progress bar on the kanban columns, as shown in the following screenshot:

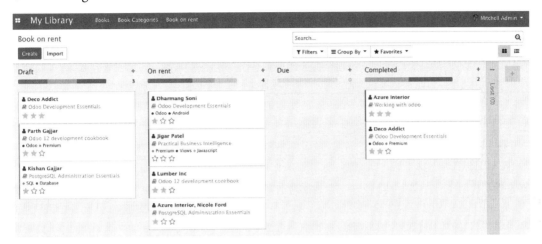

Figure 12.6 – Kanban view with a progress bar

Once you update the module, you have added a progress bar to the kanban columns. The color of the progress bar shows the number of records based on the record state. You will be able to click on one of the progress bars to filter records based on that state.

How it works...

Progress bars on kanban columns are displayed based on the values of the field. Progress bars support four colors, so you cannot display more than four states. The available colors are green (success), blue (information), red (danger), and yellow (warning). Then, you need to map colors to the field states. In our example, we mapped three states of the priority field because we didn't want any progress bars for the books that are not in demand.

By default, progress bars show a count of the records on the side. You can see the total of a particular state by clicking on it in the progress bar. Clicking on the progress bar will also highlight the cards for that state. Instead of the count of records, you can also display the sum of the integer or float field. To do this, you need to add the `sum_field` attribute with the field value, such as `sum_field="field_name"`.

Creating server actions

Server actions underpin Odoo's automation tools. They allow us to describe the actions to perform. These actions are then available to be called by **event triggers,** or to be triggered automatically when certain time conditions are met.

The simplest case is to let the end user perform an action on a document by selecting it from the **More** button. We will create this kind of action for project tasks, to **Set Priority** by starring the currently selected task and setting a deadline on it for 3 days from now.

Getting ready

We will need an Odoo instance with the Project app installed. We will also need **Developer Mode** activated. If it's not already activated, activate it in the Odoo **Settings** dashboard.

How to do it...

To create a server action and use it from the **More** menu, follow these steps:

1. On the **Settings** top menu, select the **Technical | Actions | Server Actions** menu item, and click on the **Create Contextual Action** button at the top of the record list, as shown in the following screenshot:

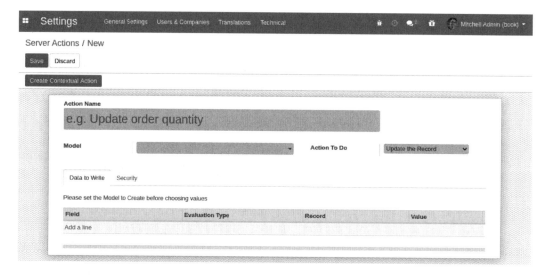

Figure 12.7 – Server action form view

2. Fill out the server action form with these values:

   Action Name: Set as Priority

   Model: Task

   Action To Do: Update the Record

3. In the server action, under the **Data to Write** tab, add the following:

   - As the first value, we will enter the following parameters:

     Field: `Deadline`

     Evaluation Type: `Python expression`

     Value: `datetime.date.today() + datetime.timedelta(days=3)`

   - As the second value, we will enter the following parameters:

     Field: `Priority`

     Evaluation Type: `Value`

     Value: `1`

The following screenshot shows the entered values:

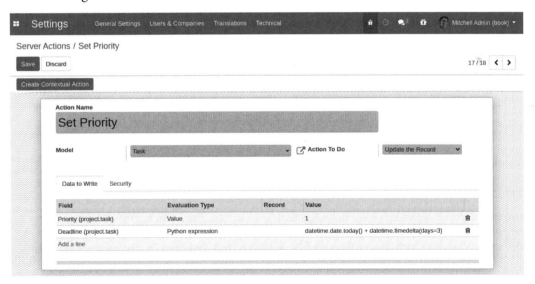

Figure 12.8 – Set lines to write

4. Save the server action and click on the **Create Contextual Action** button at the top left to make it available under the project task's **More** button.

5. To try it out, go to the **Project** top menu, select the **Search | Tasks** menu item, and open a random task. By clicking on the **More** button, we should see the **Set Priority** option, as shown in the following screenshot. Selecting this will star the task and change the deadline date to three days from now:

Figure 12.9 – Set Priority server action

Once you add the server action, you will have set the priority option on the task. Upon clicking on it, the server action star will turn yellow, meaning the priority of the task has increased. Also, the server action will change the deadline.

How it works...

Server actions work on a model, so one of the first things to do is to pick the model we want to work with. In our example, we used project tasks.

Next, we should select the type of action to perform. There are a few options available:

- **Execute Python Code** allows you to write arbitrary code to execute when none of the other options are flexible enough for what we need.
- **Create a new Record** allows you to create a new record to the current model or on another model.
- **Update the Record** allows you to set values on the current record or on another record.
- **Send Email** allows you to choose an email template. This will be used to send out an email when the action is triggered.
- **Execute several actions** can be used to trigger a client or window action, just like when a menu item is clicked on.
- **Add Followers** allows users or channels to subscribe to the record.

- **Create Next Activity** allows you to create a new activity. This will be displayed in the chatter.
- **Send SMS Text Message** allows you to send an SMS. You need to select the SMS template.

> **Note**
> **Send SMS Text Message** is a chargeable service from Odoo. You need to purchase credit for SMS if you want to send an SMS.

For our example, we used **Update the Record** to set some values on the current record. We set **Priority** to 1 to star the task, and set a value on the **Deadline** field. This one is more interesting, because the value to use is evaluated from a Python expression. Our example makes use of the `datetime` Python module (https://docs.python.org/2/library/datetime.html) to compute the date three days from today.

Arbitrary Python expressions can be used there, as well as in several of the other action types available. For security reasons, the code is checked by the `safe_eval` function implemented in the `odoo/tools/safe_eval.py` file. This means that some Python operations may not be allowed, but this rarely proves to be a problem.

When you add a drop-down option to the server action, usually it is available for all internal users. But if you just want to show this option to selected users, you can assign a group to the server action. This is available under the **Security** tab in the server action form view.

There's more...

The Python code is evaluated in a restricted context, where the following objects are available to use:

- `env`: This is a reference for the `Environment` object, just like `self.env` in a class method.
- `model`: This is a reference to the `model` class that the server action acts upon. In our example, it is equivalent to `self.env['project.task]`.
- `Warning`: This is a reference to `openerp.exceptions.Warning`, allowing validations that block unintended actions. It can be used as `raise Warning('Message!')`.
- `Record` or `records`: This provides references to the current record or records, allowing you to access their field values and methods.

- **log**: This is a function to log messages in the `ir.logging` model, allowing database-side logging-on actions.
- **datetime**, **dateutil**, and **time**: These provide access to the Python libraries.

Using Python code server actions

Server actions have several types available, but executing arbitrary Python code is the most flexible option. When used wisely, it empowers users with the capability to implement advanced business rules from the user interface, without the need to create specific add-on modules to install that code.

We will demonstrate using this type of server action by implementing a server action that sends reminder notifications to the followers of a project task.

Getting ready

We will need an Odoo instance with the Project app installed.

How to do it...

To create a Python code server action, follow these steps:

1. Create a new server action. In the **Settings** menu, select the **Technical | Actions | Server Actions** menu item, and click on the **Create** button at the top of the record list.

2. Fill out the **Server Action** form with the following values:

   Action Name: **Send Reminder**

   Base Model: **Task**

   Action To Do: **Execute Python Code**

3. In the **Python Code** text area, remove the default text and replace it with the following code:

   ```
   if not record.date_deadline:
       raise Warning('Task has no deadline!')
   delta = record.date_deadline - datetime.date.today()
   days = delta.days
   if days==0:
       msg = 'Task is due today.'
   elif days < 0:
       msg = 'Task is %d day(s) late.' % abs(days)
   ```

```
    else:
        msg = 'Task will be due in %d day(s).' % days
    record.message_post(body=msg, subject='Reminder',
    subtype='mt_comment')
```

The following screenshot shows the entered values:

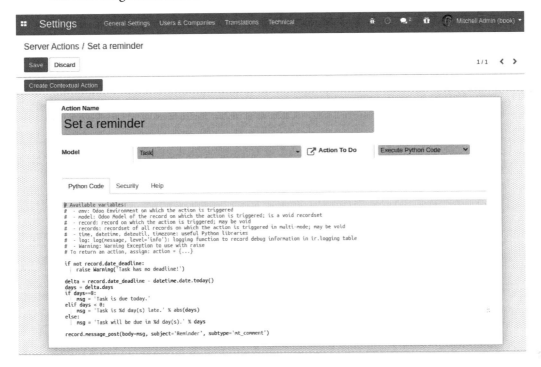

Figure 12.10 – Python code with the values entered

4. Save the server action and click on **Create Contextual Action** at the top left to make it available under the project task's **More** button.

5. Now, click on the **Project** top menu and select the **Search | Tasks** menu item. Pick a random task, set a deadline date on it, and then try the **Send Reminder** option under the **More** button.

This works just like the previous recipe; the only difference is, this server action will run your Python code. Once you run the server action on a task, it will put a message in the chatter.

How it works...

The *Creating server actions* recipe of this chapter provides a detailed explanation of how to create a server action in general. For this particular type of action, we need to pick the **Execute Python Code** option and then write the code to run the text area.

The code can have multiple lines, as is the case in our recipe, and it runs in a context that has references to objects such as the current record object or the session user. The references available are described in the *Creating server actions* recipe.

The code we used computes the number of days from the current date until the deadline date and uses that to prepare an appropriate notification message. The last line does the actual posting of the message in the task's message wall. The `subtype='mt_comment'` argument is needed for email notifications to be sent to the followers, just like when we use the **New Message** button. If no subtype is given, `mt_note` is used as a default, posting an internal note without notification, as if we had used the **Log an internal note** button. Refer to *Chapter 23, Managing Emails in Odoo*, to learn more about mailing in Odoo.

There's more...

Python code server actions are a powerful and flexible resource, but they do have some limitations compared to the custom add-on modules.

Because the Python code is evaluated at runtime, if an error occurs, the stack trace is not as informative and can be harder to debug. It is also not possible to insert a breakpoint in the code of a server action using the techniques shown in *Chapter 7, Debugging Modules*, so debugging needs to be done using logging statements. Another concern is that, when trying to track down the cause of behavior in the module code, you may not find anything relevant. In this case, it's probably caused by a server action.

When carrying out a more intensive use of server actions, the interactions can be quite complex, so it is advisable to plan properly and keep them organized.

See more

- Refer to *Chapter 23, Managing Emails in Odoo*, to learn more about mailing in Odoo.

Using automated actions on time conditions

Automated actions can be used to automatically trigger actions based on time conditions. We can use them to automatically perform some operations on records that meet certain criteria and time conditions.

As an example, we can trigger a reminder notification for project tasks one day before their deadline, if they have one. Let's see how this can be done.

Getting ready

To follow this recipe, we will need to have both the *project management* app (which has the technical name `project`) and the **Automated Action Rules** add-on (which has the technical name `base_automation`) already installed, and have **Developer Mode** activated. We will also need the server action created in the *Using Python code server actions* recipe of this chapter.

How to do it...

To create an automated action with a timed condition on tasks, follow these steps:

1. In the **Settings** menu, select the **Technical | Automation | Automated Actions** menu item, and click on the **Create** button.

2. Fill out the basic information on the **Automated Actions** form:

   Rule Name: `Send notification near deadline`.

   Model: **Task**.

   Select **Based on Time Condition** in the **Trigger Condition** field.

   In **Action To Do**, select **Execute several actions**.

3. To set the record criteria, click on the **Edit Domain** button in the **Apply on** section. In the pop-up dialog, set a valid domain expression in the code editor, `["&",["date_deadline","!=",False],["stage_id.fold","=",False]]`, and click on the **Save** button. When changing to another field, the information on the number of records meeting the criteria is updated and displays **Record(s)** buttons. By clicking on the **Records** button, we can check the records list of the records meeting the domain expression.

4. To set the time condition for **Trigger Date**, select the field to use, which is **Deadline**, and set **Delay after trigger date** to `-1` **Days**.

5. On the **Actions** tab, under **Server actions to run**, click on **Add an item** and pick **Send Reminder** from the list, which should have been created previously. Refer to the following screenshot:

Figure 12.11 – Automated action form view

If not, we can still create the server action to run using the **Create** button.

6. Click on **Save** to save the automated action.

7. Perform the following steps to try it out:

   - Go to the **Project** menu, go to **Search | Tasks**, and set a deadline on a task with the date in the past.

   - Go to the **Settings** menu, click on the **Technical | Automation | Scheduled Actions** menu item, find the **Base Action Rule: check and execute** action in the list, open its form view, and press on the **Run Manually** button at the top left. This forces timed automated actions to be checked now. This is shown in the following screenshot. Note that this should work on a newly created demo database, but might not work this way in an existing database:

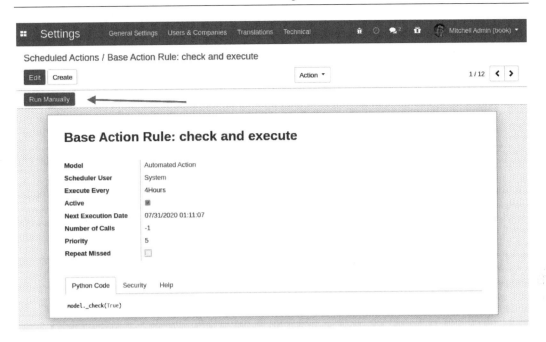

Figure 12.12 – Run automated action (for test)

8. Again, go to the **Project** menu and open the same task you previously set a deadline date on. Check the message board; you should see the notification generated by the server action triggered by our automated action.

After adding add the time-based automated action for the deadline, a reminder message will be added to the task one day before the deadline.

How it works...

Automated actions act on a model, and can be triggered either by events or time conditions. The first steps are to set the **Model** and **When to Run** values.

Both methods can use a filter to narrow down the records that are eligible to perform the action on. We can use a domain expression for this. You can find further information about writing domain expressions in *Chapter 9, Backend Views*. Alternatively, you can create and save a filter on project tasks, using the user interface features, and then copy the automatically generated domain expression, selecting it from the **Set selection based on a search filter** list.

The domain expression we used selects all the records with a non-empty **Deadline** date, in a stage where the **Fold** flag is not checked. Stages without the **Fold** flag are considered to be work-in-progress. This way, we avoid triggering notifications on tasks that are in the **Done**, **Canceled**, or **Closed** stages.

Then, we should define the time condition – the date field to use and when the action should be triggered. The time period can be in minutes, hours, days, or months, and the number set for the period can be positive, indicating the time after the date, or negative, indicating the time before the date. When using a time period in days, we can provide a resource calendar that defines the working days and that can be used by the day count.

These actions are checked by the **Check Action Rules** scheduled job. Note that, by default, this is run every 4 hours. This is appropriate for actions that work on a day or month scale, but if you need actions that work on smaller timescales, you need to change the running interval to a smaller value.

Actions will be triggered for records that meet all the criteria and whose triggering date condition (the field date plus the interval) is after the last action execution. This is to avoid repeatedly triggering the same action. Also, this is why manually running the preceding action will work in a database in which the scheduled action has not yet been triggered, but why it might not work immediately in a database where it was already run by the scheduler.

Once an automated action is triggered, the **Actions** tab tells you what should happen. This might be a list of server actions that do things such as changing values on the record, posting notifications, or sending out emails.

There's more...

These types of automated actions are triggered once a certain time condition is reached. This is not the same as regularly repeating an action while a condition is still true. For example, an automated action will not be capable of posting a reminder for every day after the deadline has been exceeded.

This type of action can, instead, be performed by scheduled actions, which are stored in the `ir.cron` model. However, scheduled actions do not support server actions; they can only call an existing method of a model object. So, to implement a custom action, we need to write an add-on module, adding the underlying Python method.

For reference, the technical name for the model is `base.action.rule`.

See more

- For further details about writing domain expressions, refer to *Chapter 9, Backend Views*.

Using automated actions on event conditions

Business applications provide systems with records for business operations but are also expected to support dynamic business rules that are specific to the organization's use cases.

Carving these rules into custom add-on modules can be inflexible and out of the reach of functional users. Automated actions triggered by event conditions can bridge this gap and provide a powerful tool to automate or enforce the organization's procedures. As an example, we will enforce validation on project tasks so that only the project manager can change tasks to the **Done** stage.

Getting ready

To follow this recipe, you will need to have the project management app already installed. We also need to have **Developer Mode** activated. If it's not activated already, activate it in the Odoo **About** dialog.

How to do it...

To create an automated action with an event condition on tasks, follow these steps:

1. In the **Settings** menu, select the **Technical | Automation | Automated Actions** menu item, and click on the **Create** button

2. Fill out the basic information in the **Automated Actions** form:

   Action Name: `Validate Closing Tasks`

   Model: **Task**

   Trigger Condition: **On Update**

   Action To Do: **Execute several actions**

   Watched fields: `Stage id`

3. The **On Update** rules allow you to set two record filters, before and after the update operation:

   For the **Before Update Filter** field, click on the **Edit Domain** button, set a valid domain expression – `[('stage_id.name', '!=', 'Done')]` – in the code editor, and save.

For the **Apply on** field, click on the **Edit Domain** button, set the `[('stage_id.name', '=', 'Done')]` domain in the code editor, and save, as shown in the following screenshot:

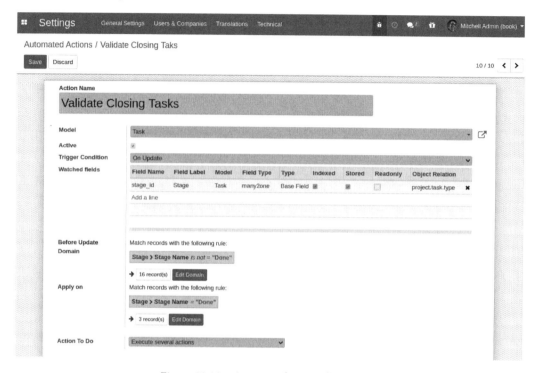

Figure 12.13 – Automated action form view

4. In the **Actions** tab, click on **Add an item**. In the list dialog, click on the **Create** button to create a new server action.

5. Fill out the server action form with the following values, and then click on the **Save** button:

    Action Name: `Validate Closing tasks`

    Model: **Task**

    Action To Do: **Execute Python Code**

    Python Code: Enter the following code:

    ```
    if user != record.project_id.user_id:
        raise Warning('Only the Project Manager can close Tasks')
    ```

The following screenshot shows the entered values:

```
Add: Child Actions                                                                    ×

 Create Contextual Action

Action Name
 Validate Closing tasks

Model          Task                              ↗ Action To Do    Execute Python Code  ◊

 Python Code   Help
# Available variables:
#  - env: Odoo Environment on which the action is triggered
#  - model: Odoo Model of the record on which the action is triggered; is a void recordset
#  - record: record on which the action is triggered; may be void
#  - records: recordset of all records on which the action is triggered in multi-mode; may be void
#  - time, datetime, dateutil, timezone: useful Python libraries
#  - log(message, level='info'): logging function to record debug information in ir.logging table
#  - Warning: Warning Exception to use with raise
# To return an action, assign: action = {...}

if user != record.project_id.user_id:
    raise Warning('Only the Project Manager can close Tasks')


 Save & Close    Save & New    Discard
```

Figure 12.14 – Add child action

6. Click on **Save & Close** to save the automated action and try it out:

- On a database with demo data and where you're logged in as an administrator, go to the **Project** menu and click on the project to open the kanban view of the tasks.

- Then, try dragging one of the tasks into the **Done** stage column. Since this project's manager is the `Demo` user and we are working with the `Administrator` user, our automated action should be triggered, and our warning message should block the change.

How it works...

We start by giving a name to our automated actions and setting the model it should work with. For the type of action we require, we should choose **On Update**, but the **On Creation**, **On Creation & Update**, **On Deletion**, and **Based On Form Modification** options are also possible.

Next, we define the filters to determine when our action should be triggered. The **On Update** actions allow us to define two filters – one to check before and the other after the changes are made to the record. This can be used to express transitions – to detect when a record changes from *state A* to *state B*. In our example, we want to trigger the action when a *not-done* task changes to the *done* stage. The **On Update** action is the only one that allows these two filters; the other action types only allow one filter.

> **Important note**
> It is important to note that our example condition will only work correctly for English language users. This is because **Stage Name** is a translatable field that can have different values for different languages. So, the filters on the translatable fields should be avoided or used with care.

Finally, we create and add one (or more) server actions with whatever we want to be done when the automated action is triggered. In this case, we chose to demonstrate how to implement custom validation, making use of a Python code server action that used the `Warning` exception to block the user's changes.

There's more...

In *Chapter 5, Basic Server-Side Development*, we saw how to redefine the `write()` methods of a model to perform actions on record updates. Automated actions on record updates provide another way to achieve this, with some benefits and drawbacks.

Among the benefits, it is easy to define an action triggered by the update of a stored computed field, which is tricky to do in pure code. It is also possible to define filters on records and have different rules for different records, or for records matching different conditions that can be expressed with search domains.

However, automated actions can have disadvantages when compared to Python business logic code inside modules. With poor planning, the flexibility provided can lead to complex interactions that are difficult to maintain and debug. Also, the before-and-after write filter operations bring some overhead, which can be an issue if you are performing sensitive actions.

Creating QWeb-based PDF reports

When communicating with the outside world, it is often necessary to produce a PDF document from a record in the database. Odoo uses the same template language as that used for form views: QWeb.

In this recipe, we will create a QWeb report to print information about a book that is currently being borrowed by a partner. This recipe will reuse the models presented in the *Adding a progress bar in kanban views* recipe from earlier on in this chapter.

Getting ready

If you haven't done so already, install `wkhtmltopdf` as described in *Chapter 1, Installing the Odoo Development Environment*; otherwise, you won't get shiny PDFs as a result of your efforts.

Also, double-check that the `web.base.url` configuration parameter (or, alternatively, `report.url`) is a URL that is accessible from your Odoo instance; otherwise, the report will take a long time to generate and the result will look strange.

How to do it...

1. In this recipe, we will add a report to `res.partner` that prints a list of books that the partner borrowed. We need to add a `one2many` field to the partner model with relation to the `library.book.rent` model, as shown in the following example:

   ```python
   class ResPartner(models.Model):
       _inherit = 'res.partner'

       rent_ids = fields.One2many('library.book.rent',
   'borrower_id')
   ```

2. Define a view for your report in `reports/book_rent_templates.xml`, as follows:

   ```xml
   <?xml version="1.0" encoding="utf-8"?>
   <odoo>
   <template id="book_rents_template">
       <t t-call="web.html_container">
           <t t-foreach="docs" t-as="doc">
               <t t-call="web.internal_layout">
                   <div class="page">
                       <h1>Book Rent for <t t-esc="doc.name"/></h1>
                       <table class="table table-condensed">
                           <thead>
                               <tr>
                                   <th>Title</th>
                                   <th>Expected return date</th>
                               </tr>
                           </thead>
                           <tbody>
                               <tr t-foreach="doc.rent_ids" t-as="rent" >
   ```

```xml
                                    <td><t t-esc="rent.book_id.name" /></td>
                                    <td><t t-esc="rent.return_date" /></td>
                                </tr>
                            </tbody>
                        </table>
                    </div>
                </t>
            </t>
        </t>
    </template>
</odoo>
```

3. Add a tag in `reports/book_rent_report.xml`, as shown in the following example:

```xml
<?xml version="1.0" encoding="utf-8"?>
<odoo>
    <record id="report_book_rent" model="ir.actions.report">
        <field name="name">Book Rents</field>
        <field name="model">res.partner</field>
        <field name="report_type">qweb-pdf</field>
        <field name="report_name">my_library.book_rents_template</field>
        <field name="report_file">my_library.book_rents_template</field>
        <field name="binding_model_id" ref="model_res_partner"/>
        <field name="binding_type">report</field>
    </record>
</odoo>
```

4. Add both files to the manifest of the add-on and add `contacts` to `depends`, so that you can open the form view of the partner, as shown in the following example:

```
...
    'depends': ['base', 'contacts'],
    'data': [
        'views/library_book.xml',
        'views/library_member.xml',
        ...
```

```
            'reports/book_rent_report.xml',
            'reports/book_rent_templates.xml',
    ],
    ...
```

Now, when opening the partner form view, or when selecting partners in the list view, you should be offered the option to print the book loans in a drop-down menu, as shown in the following screenshot:

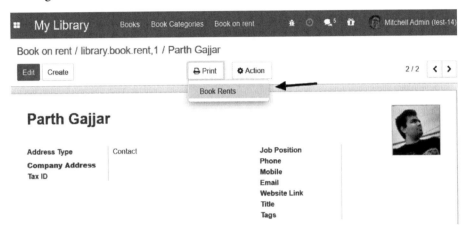

Figure 12.15 – Print action for report

How it works...

In *step 1*, we added a `one2many rent_ids` field. This field will contain rent records for the customer. We will use it in the QWeb report to list the books that the customer has rented.

In *step 2*, we defined the QWeb template. The content of the template will be used to generate the PDF. In our example, we have used some basic HTML structure. We have also used some attributes such as `t-esc` and `t-foreach`, which are used to generate dynamic content in the report. Don't worry about this syntax within the `template` element for now. This topic will be addressed extensively in the *Creating or modifying templates – QWeb* recipe in *Chapter 14, CMS Website Development*. Another important thing to notice in the template is the layout. In our example, we have used `web.internal_layout` in our template, which will generate the final PDF with a minimal header and footer. If you want an informative header and footer with the company logo and company information, use the `web.external_layout` layout. We have also added one `for` loop to the `docs` parameter that will be used to generate a report for multiple records when the user prints it from the list view.

In *step 3*, we declared the report in another XML file via the `<record>` tag. It will register the report's `ir.actions.report` model. The crucial part here is that you set the `report_name` field to the complete XML ID (that is, `modulename.record_id`) of the template you defined, or the report generation will fail. The `model` field determines which type of record the report operates, and the `name` field is the name shown to the user in the print menu.

> **Note**
>
> In previous versions of Odoo, a `<report>` tag was used to register a report. But from version v14, it is deprecated and you need to create a record of `ir.actions.report` with the `<record>` tag. The `<report>` tag is still supported in Odoo v14 for backward compatibility but using it will show a warning in the log.

By setting `report_type` to `qweb-pdf`, we requested that the HTML generated by our view is run through `wkhtmltopdf` in order to deliver a PDF to the user. In some cases, you may want to use `qweb-html` to render the HTML within the browser.

There's more...

There are some marker classes in a report's HTML that are crucial for the layout. Ensure that you wrap all your content in an element with the `page` class set. If you forget that, you'll see nothing at all. To add a header or footer to your record, use the `header` or `footer` class.

Also, remember that this is HTML, so make use of *CSS attributes* such as `page-break-before`, `page-break-after`, and `page-break-inside`.

You'll have noted that all of our template body is wrapped in two elements with the `t-call` attribute set. We'll examine the mechanics of this attribute later in *Chapter 14, CMS Website Development*, but it is crucial that you do the same in your reports. These elements ensure that the HTML generates links to all the necessary CSS files and contains some other data that is needed for the report generation. While `web.html_container` doesn't really have an alternative, the second `t-call` can be `web.external_layout`. The difference is that the external layout already comes with a header and footer displaying the company logo, the company's name, and some other information you expect from a company's external communication, while the internal layout just gives you a header with pagination, the print date, and the company's name. For the sake of consistency, always use one of the two.

> **Important note**
>
> Note that `web.internal_layout`, `web.external_layout`, `web.external_layout_header`, and `web.external_layout_footer` (the last two are called by the *external layout*) are just views by themselves, and you already know how to change them by inheritance. To inherit with the template element, use the `inherit_id` attribute.

Managing activities from a kanban card

Odoo uses activities to schedule actions on records. These activities can be managed in form view and the kanban view. In this recipe, we will see how you can manage activities from the kanban view card. We will add an activity widget to the cards of the rent kanban.

Getting started

For this recipe, we will be using the `my_library` module from the previous recipe.

How to do it...

Follow these steps to add and mange activity from the kanban view:

1. Add mail dependencies to the `manifest` file:

    ```
    'depends': ['base', 'mail'],
    ```

2. Inherit `activity mixin` in the `library.book.rent` model:

    ```
    class LibraryBookRent(models.Model):
        _name = 'library.book.rent'
        _inherit = ['mail.thread', 'mail.activity.mixin']
    ```

3. Add the `activity_state` field to the kanban view under the `color` field:

    ```xml
    <field name="color" />
    <field name="activity_state"/>
    ```

4. Add the `activity_ids` field inside the kanban template. Add this field under the `popularity` field as in the given code:

    ```xml
    <div>
        <field name="popularity" widget="priority"/>
    </div>
    ```

```xml
<div>
    <field name="activity_ids" widget="kanban_activity"/>
</div>
```

Update the `my_library` module to apply the change. Open the kanban view of book rents and you will see the activity manger on the kanban card, as in the following screenshot:

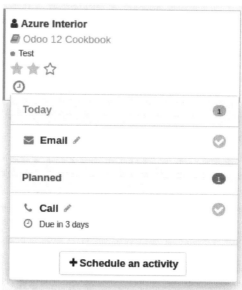

Figure 12.16 – Activity manager in a kanban card

As you can see in the preceding screenshot, after applying the code from this recipe, you will be able to manage activity from a kanban card. Also, you can process or create an activity from a kanban card.

How it works...

In *step 1*, we added a dependency to the manifest of our module. The reason behind this is, all the implementation associated with the activity is part of the `mail` module. Without installing `mail`, we cannot use activities in our model.

In *step 2*, we added `activity mixin` to the `library.book.rent` model. This will enable activities for the book rent records. Adding `mail.activity.mixin` will add all the fields and methods required for activities. We have also added the `mail.thread` mixin because the activity logs the message when the user processes the activity. If you want to learn more about this activity, please refer to the *Managing activities on documents* recipe of *Chapter 23, Managing Emails in Odoo*.

In *step 3*, we added the `activity_state` field to the kanban view. This field is used by the activity widget to display the color widget. The color will represent the current state of the upcoming activity.

In *step 4*, we added the activity widget itself. It uses the `activity_ids` field. In our example, we have added the activity widget in a separate `<div>` tag, but you can put it anywhere according to your design requirements. With the activity widget, you can schedule, edit, and process the activity directly from the kanban card.

There's more...

In the *Adding a progress bar in kanban views* recipe of this chapter, we displayed a kanban progress bar based on the `popularity` field. But we can also show a progress bar based on the state of the upcoming activity:

```
<progressbar field="activity_state"
    colors='{"planned": "success",
            "today": "warning",
            "overdue": "danger"}'/>
```

This will show the progress bar based on the state of the upcoming activity. A state-based progress bar is used in several views in Odoo.

See also

- If you want to learn more about the mail thread, refer to the *Managing chatter on documents* recipe of *Chapter 23, Managing Emails in Odoo*.
- If you want to learn more about activities, refer to the *Managing activities on documents* recipe of *Chapter 23, Managing Emails in Odoo*.

Adding a stat button to a form view

Odoo uses a stat button to relate two different objects visually on the form view. It is used to show some basic KPIs for related records. It is also used to redirect and open another view. In this recipe, we will add a stat button to the form view of a book. This stat button will display the count of rent records and on clicking it, we will be redirected to the list of kanban views.

Getting started

For this recipe, we will be using the `my_library` module from the previous recipe.

How to do it...

Follow these steps to add a stat button to the book's form view:

1. Add the `rent_count` compute field to the `library.book` model. This field will count the number of rent orders for a book:

```python
rent_count = fields.Integer(compute="_compute_rent_count")
def _compute_rent_count(self):
    BookRent = self.env['library.book.rent']
    for book in self:
        book.rent_count = BookRent.search_count(
            [('book_id', '=', book.id)]
        )
```

2. Add a stat button to the form view of the `library.book` model. Prepend it just inside the `<sheet>` tag:

```xml
<div class="oe_button_box" name="button_box">
    <button class="oe_stat_button"
            name="%(library_book_rent_action)d"
            type="action" icon="fa-book"
            context="{'search_default_book_id': active_id}">
        <field string="Rent Orders"
               name="rent_count"
               widget="statinfo"/>
    </button>
</div>
```

Update the `my_library` module to apply the changes. Open the form view of any book and you will find the stat button, as in the following screenshot:

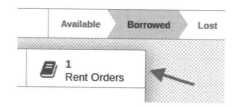

Figure 12.17 – Stat button in a book's form view

On clicking the stat button, you will be redirected to the rent orders kanban view. Here, in kanban, you will see orders only from the current book.

How it works...

In *step 1*, we added a compute field that calculates the number of rent records for the current book. The value of this field will be used for a stat button to show the count. If you want to learn more about compute, refer to the *Adding computed fields to a model* recipe in *Chapter 4*, *Application Models*.

In *step 2*, we added the stat button in the form view of the `library.book` model. There are a specific syntax and location for the stat button. All the stat button needs to do is wrap under `<div>` with the `oe_button_box` class. The stat button box needs to be placed inside the `<sheet>` tag. Note that we have used a `name` attribute on the button box. This `name` attribute is useful when you want to add a new stat, but then you will need to add a stat button with the `<button>` tag with the `oe_stat_button` class. Internally, the stat button is just a form view button with a different user interface. This means it supports all of the attributes that are supported by a normal button, such as an action, icon, and context.

In our example, we have used the action of rent orders, which means when the user clicks on the stat button, they will be redirected to the rent records but it will show all the rent records. We want to show the rent records only for the current book. To do so, we have to pass `search_default_book_id`. This will apply a default filter for the current book. Note that `book_id` is the `many2one` field on the `library.book.rent` model. If you want to filter by another field, use it by prefixing it with `search_default_` in context.

Stat buttons are used often as they are very useful and show the overall statistics related to a record. You could use them to show all the information that relates to the current record. For example, on the contact record, Odoo shows stat buttons that show information related to the current contact total of the invoice, the number of leads, the number of orders, and so on.

See also

- To learn more about buttons, refer to the *Adding buttons to forms* recipe in *Chapter 9*, *Backend Views*
- To learn more about actions, refer to the *Adding a menu item and window action* recipe in *Chapter 9*, *Backend Views*

Enabling the archive option for records

Odoo provides inbuilt features to enable archive and unarchive options for records. This will help the user to hide records that are no longer important. In this recipe, we will add an archive/unarchive option for a book. We can archive a book once it is not available.

Getting started

For this recipe, we will be using the `my_library` module from the previous recipe.

How to do it...

Archive and unarchive mostly work automatically. The options are available on a record if the model has a Boolean field named `active`. We already have an `active` field in the `library.book` model. But if you have not added it, follow these steps to add the `active` field:

1. Add an `active` Boolean field to the `library.book` model like this:

   ```
   active = fields.Boolean(default=True)
   ```

2. Add an `active` field in the form view:

   ```
   <field name="active" invisible="1"/>
   ```

Update the `my_library` module to apply the changes. Now, you will be able to archive books. The archive option is available in the **Action** dropdown, as in the following screenshot:

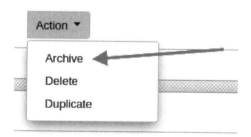

Figure 12.18 – Archive option on the form view

Once you archive a record, you want to see that record anywhere in Odoo. In order to see it, you need to apply a filter from the search view.

How it works...

A Boolean field named `active` has a special purpose in Odoo. If you add an `active` field to your model, records with a `false` value in the `active` field won't be displayed anywhere in Odoo.

In *step 1*, we added an `active` field to the `library.book` model. Note that we kept the default value of `True` here. If we don't add this default value, the new records will be created in archive mode by default and won't be displayed in views, even if we have recently created them.

In *step 2*, we added the `active` field in the form view. If you don't add an `active` field in the form view, the archive/unarchive option won't be displayed in the **Action** drop-down menu. If you don't want to show the field in the form view, you can use the `invisible` attribute to hide it from the form view.

In our example, once you archive a book, then that book will not be displayed in the tree view or any other view. The book won't even be displayed in the `many2one` dropdown in the rent order record. If you want to unarchive that book, then you need to apply a filter to display archived records from the search view, then restore the book.

There's more...

If your model has an `active` Boolean field, the `search` method will not return an archived record. If you want to search all the records, whether they are archived or not, then pass `active_test` in context like this:

```
self.env['library.book'].with_context(active_test=False).search([])
```

Note that if the archive record is linked to another record, then it will be displayed in the related form view. For example, say you have rent *Order A* for *Book A*. Then, you archive *Book A*, which means from now on, you cannot select *Book A* in the rent order. But if you open *Order A*, you will see the archived *Book A*.

13
Web Server Development

We'll introduce the basics of the web server part of Odoo in this chapter. Note that this will cover the fundamental aspects. For high-level functionality, you should refer to *Chapter 14, CMS Website Development*.

All of Odoo's web request handling is driven by the Python library `werkzeug` (https://werkzeug.palletsprojects.com/en/1.0.x/). While the complexity of `werkzeug` is mostly hidden by Odoo's convenient wrappers, it is interesting to see how things work under the hood, if you want to read up on it.

In this chapter, we'll cover the following topics:

- Making a path accessible from the network
- Restricting access to web-accessible paths
- Consuming parameters passed to your handlers
- Modifying an existing handler
- Serving static resources

Technical requirements

The technical requirements for this chapter include the online Odoo platform.

All the code used in this chapter can be downloaded from the GitHub repository at `https://github.com/PacktPublishing/Odoo-14-Development-Cookbook-Fourth-Edition/tree/master/Chapter13`.

Making a path accessible from the network

In this recipe, we'll look at how to make a URL of the `http://yourserver/path1/path2` form accessible to users. This can be either a web page or a path returning arbitrary data to be consumed by other programs. In the latter case, you would usually use JSON format to consume parameters and offer your data.

Getting ready

We'll make use of the `library.book` model, which we looked at in *Chapter 4, Application Models*; so, if you haven't done so yet, grab the initial module from `https://github.com/PacktPublishing/Odoo-14-Development-Cookbook-Fourth-Edition/tree/master/Chapter13/00_initial_module`, so that you will be able to follow the examples.

We want to allow any user to query the full list of books. Furthermore, we want to provide the same information to programs through a JSON request.

How to do it...

We'll need to add controllers, which go into a folder called `controllers` by convention:

1. Add a `controllers/main.py` file with the HTML version of our page, as follows:

```python
from odoo import http
from odoo.http import request

class Main(http.Controller):
    @http.route('/my_library/books', type='http',
auth='none')
    def books(self):
        books = request.env['library.book'].sudo().search([])
        html_result = '<html><body><ul>'
        for book in books:
```

```
        html_result += "<li> %s </li>" % book.name
    html_result += '</ul></body></html>'
    return html_result
```

2. Add a function to serve the same information in JSON format, as shown in the following example:

```
    @http.route('/my_library/books/json', type='json', auth='none')
    def books_json(self):
        records = request.env['library.book'].sudo().search([])
        return records.read(['name'])
```

3. Add the `controllers/__init__.py` file, as follows:

```
from . import main
```

4. Import `controllers` to your `my_library/__init__.py` file, as follows:

```
from . import controllers
```

After restarting your server, you can visit `/my_library/books` in your browser and you'll be presented with a flat list of book names. To test the JSON-RPC part, you'll have to craft a JSON request. A simple way to do that would be by using the following command to receive the output on the command line:

```
curl -i -X POST -H "Content-Type: application/json" -d "{}" localhost:8069/my_library/books/json
```

If you get 404 errors at this point, you probably have more than one database available on your instance. In that case, it's impossible for Odoo to determine which database is meant to serve the request.

Use the `--db-filter='^yourdatabasename$'` parameter to force Odoo to use the exact database you installed the module in. The path should now be accessible.

How it works...

The two crucial parts here are that our controller is derived from `odoo.http.Controller`, and the methods we use to serve content are decorated with `odoo.http.route`. Inheriting from `odoo.http.Controller` registers the controller with Odoo's routing system in a similar way to how the models are registered, by inheriting from `odoo.models.Model`. Also, `Controller` has a metaclass that takes care of this.

In general, paths handled by your add-on should start with your add-on's name, to avoid name clashes. Of course, if you extend some of the add-on's functionality, you'll use this add-on's name.

odoo.http.route

The `route` decorator allows us to tell Odoo that a method should be web-accessible in the first place, and the first parameter determines on which path it is accessible. Instead of a string, you can also pass a list of strings, in case you use the same function to serve multiple paths.

The `type` argument defaults to `http` and determines what type of request is to be served. While, strictly speaking, JSON is HTTP, declaring the second function as `type='json'` makes life a lot easier, because Odoo then handles type conversions for us.

Don't worry about the `auth` parameter for now; it will be addressed in the *Restricting access to web-accessible paths* recipe in this chapter.

Return values

Odoo's treatment of the functions' return values is determined by the `type` argument of the `route` decorator. For `type='http'`, we usually want to deliver some HTML, so the first function simply returns a string containing it. An alternative is to use `request.make_response()`, which gives you control over the headers to send in the response. So, to indicate when our page was last updated, we might change the last line in `books()` to the following code:

```
return request.make_response(
  html_result, headers=[
    ('Last-modified', email.utils.formatdate(
      (
        fields.Datetime.from_string(
          request.env['library.book'].sudo()
          .search([], order='write_date desc', limit=1)
          .write_date) -
```

```
            datetime.datetime(1970, 1, 1)
        ).total_seconds(),
        usegmt=True)),
])
```

This code sends a `Last-modified` header along with the HTML we generated, telling the browser when the list was modified for the last time. We can extract this information from the `write_date` field of the `library.book` model.

In order for the preceding snippet to work, you'll have to add some imports at the top of the file, as follows:

```
import email
import datetime
from odoo import fields
```

You can also create a `Response` object of `werkzeug` manually and return that, but there's little to gain for the effort.

> **Important information**
>
> Generating HTML manually is nice for demonstration purposes, but you should never do this in production code. Always use templates, as demonstrated in the *Creating or modifying templates – QWeb* recipe in *Chapter 15, Web Client Development*, and return them by calling `request.render()`.
>
> This will give you localization for free and will make your code better by separating business logic from the presentation layer. Also, templates provide you with functions to escape data before outputting HTML. The preceding code is vulnerable to cross-site scripting attacks (if a user manages to slip a `script` tag into the book name, for example).

For a JSON request, simply return the data structure you want to hand over to the client; Odoo takes care of serialization. For this to work, you should restrict yourself to data types that are JSON serializable, which generally means dictionaries, lists, strings, floats, and integers.

odoo.http.request

The `request` object is a static object referring to the currently handled request, which contains everything you need in order to take action. The most important aspect here is the `request.env` property, which contains an `Environment` object that is just the same as `self.env` for models. This environment is bound to the current user, which is not in the preceding example, because we used `auth='none'`. The lack of a user is also why we have to `sudo()` all our calls to model methods in the example code.

If you're used to web development, you'll expect session handling, which is perfectly correct. Use `request.session` for an `OpenERPSession` object (which is quite a thin wrapper around the `Session` object of werkzeug), and `request.session.sid` to access the session ID. To store session values, just treat `request.session` as a dictionary, as shown in the following example:

```
request.session['hello'] = 'world'
request.session.get('hello')
```

> **Important note**
>
> Note that storing data in the session is no different from using global variables. Only use it if you must. This is usually the case for multi-request actions, such as a checkout in the `website_sale` module.

There's more...

The `route` decorator can have some extra parameters, in order to customize its behavior further. By default, all HTTP methods are allowed, and Odoo intermingles the parameters passed. Using the `methods` parameter, you can pass a list of methods to accept, which would usually be one of either `['GET']` or `['POST']`.

To allow cross-origin requests (browsers block AJAX and some other types of requests to domains other than where the script was loaded from, for security and privacy reasons), set the `cors` parameter to `*` to allow requests from all origins, or a URI to restrict requests to ones originating from this URI. If this parameter is unset, which is the default, the `Access-Control-Allow-Origin` header is not set, leaving you with the browser's standard behavior. In our example, we might want to set it on `/my_module/books/json`, in order to allow scripts pulled from other websites to access the list of books.

By default, Odoo protects certain types of requests from an attack known as cross-site request forgery, by passing a token along on every request. If you want to turn that off, set the `csrf` parameter to `False`, but note that this is a bad idea, in general.

See also

Refer to the following points to learn more about the HTTP routes:

- If you host multiple Odoo databases on the same instance, then different databases might be running on different domains. In that case, you can use `--db-filter` options, or you can use the `dbfilter_from_header` module from https://github.com/OCA/server-tools, which helps you filter databases based on domain. This module was not migrated to version 12 at the time of writing this book, but by the time of publication, it probably will have been.
- To see how using templates makes modularity possible, check out the *Modifying an existing handler* recipe later in the chapter.

Restricting access to web-accessible paths

We'll explore the three authentication mechanisms Odoo provides for routes in this recipe. We'll define routes with different authentication mechanisms, in order to show their differences.

Getting ready

As we extend the code from the previous recipe, we'll also depend on the `library.book` model of *Chapter 4, Application Models*, so you should get its code in order to proceed.

How to do it...

Define the handlers in `controllers/main.py`:

1. Add a path that shows all the books, as shown in the following example:

    ```
    @http.route('/my_library/all-books', type='http',
    auth='none')
    def all_books(self):
        books = request.env['library.book'].sudo().search([])
        html_result = '<html><body><ul>'
        for book in books:
            html_result += "<li> %s </li>" % book.name
        html_result += '</ul></body></html>'
        return html_result
    ```

2. Add a path that shows all the books and indicates which were written by the current user, if any. This is shown in the following example:

```
@http.route('/my_library/all-books/mark-mine',
type='http', auth='public')
def all_books_mark_mine(self):
    books = request.env['library.book'].sudo().search([])
    html_result = '<html><body><ul>'
    for book in books:
        if request.env.user.partner_id.id in book.author_ids.ids:
            html_result += "<li> <b>%s</b> </li>" % book.name
        else:
            html_result += "<li> %s </li>" % book.name
    html_result += '</ul></body></html>'
    return html_result
```

3. Add a path that shows the current user's books, as follows:

```
@http.route('/my_library/all-books/mine', type='http',
auth='user')
def all_books_mine(self):
    books = request.env['library.book'].search([
        ('author_ids', 'in', request.env.user.partner_id.ids),
    ])
    html_result = '<html><body><ul>'
    for book in books:
        html_result += "<li> %s </li>" % book.name
    html_result += '</ul></body></html>'
    return html_result
```

With this code, the `/my_library/all-books` and `/my_library/all-books/mark-mine` paths look the same for unauthenticated users, while a logged-in user sees their books in bold font on the latter path. The `/my_library/all-books/mine` path is not accessible at all for unauthenticated users. If you try to access it without being authenticated, you'll be redirected to the login screen in order to do so.

How it works...

The difference between authentication methods is basically what you can expect from the content of `request.env.user`.

For `auth='none'`, the user record is always empty, even if an authenticated user is accessing the path. Use this if you want to serve content that has no dependencies on users, or if you want to provide database-agnostic functionality in a server-wide module.

The `auth='public'` value sets the user record to a special user with an XML ID of `base.public_user` for unauthenticated users, and to the user's record for authenticated ones. This is the right choice if you want to offer functionality to both unauthenticated and authenticated users, while the authenticated ones get some extras, as demonstrated in the preceding code.

Use `auth='user'` to ensure that only authenticated users have access to what you've got to offer. With this method, you can be sure that `request.env.user` points to an existing user.

There's more...

The magic of authentication methods happens in the `ir.http` model from the base add-on. For whatever value you pass to the `auth` parameter in your route, Odoo searches for a function called `_auth_method_<yourvalue>` on this model, so you can easily customize it by inheriting it and declaring a method that takes care of your authentication method of choice.

As an example, we will provide an authentication method called `base_group_user`, which will only authorize the user if the currently logged-in user is part of the `base.group_user` group, as shown in the following example:

```
from odoo import exceptions, http, models
from odoo.http import request

class IrHttp(models.Model):
    _inherit = 'ir.http'

    def _auth_method_base_group_user(self):
        self._auth_method_user()
        if not request.env.user.has_group('base.group_user'):
            raise exceptions.AccessDenied()
```

Now you can say `auth='base_group_user'` in your decorator and be sure that users running this route's handler are members of the group. With a little trickery, you can extend this to `auth='groups(xmlid1,...)'`; its implementation is left as an exercise to the reader but is included in the GitHub repository example code at `Chapter13/r2_paths_auth/my_library/models/sample_auth_http.py`.

Consuming parameters passed to your handlers

It's nice to be able to show content, but it's better to show content as a result of user input. This recipe will demonstrate the different ways to receive this input and react to it. As in the previous recipes, we'll make use of the `library.book` model.

How to do it...

First, we'll add a route that expects a traditional parameter with a book's ID to show some details about it. Then, we'll do the same, but we'll incorporate our parameter into the path itself:

1. Add a path that expects a book's ID as a parameter, as shown in the following example:

    ```python
    @http.route('/my_library/book_details', type='http', auth='none')
    def book_details(self, book_id):
        record = request.env['library.book'].sudo().browse(int(book_id))
        return u'<html><body><h1>%s</h1>Authors: %s' % (
            record.name,
            u', '.join(record.author_ids.mapped('name'))
            or 'none',
            )
    ```

2. Add a path where we can pass the book's ID in the path, as follows:

    ```python
    @http.route("/my_library/book_details/<model('library.book'):book>",
                type='http', auth='none')
    def book_details_in_path(self, book):
        return self.book_details(book.id)
    ```

If you point your browser to `/my_library/book_details?book_id=1`, you should see a detailed page of the book with ID 1. If this doesn't exist, you'll receive an error page.

The second handler allows you to go to `/my_library/book_details/1` and view the same page.

How it works...

By default, Odoo (actually, `werkzeug`) intermingles the `GET` and `POST` parameters and passes them as keyword arguments to your handler. So, by simply declaring your function as expecting a parameter called `book_id`, you introduce this parameter as either `GET` (the parameter in the URL) or `POST` (usually passed by the `<form>` element with your handler as the `action` attribute). Given that we didn't add a default value for this parameter, the runtime will raise an error if you try to access this path without setting the parameter.

The second example makes use of the fact that in a `werkzeug` environment, most paths are virtual, anyway. So, we can simply define our path as containing some input. In this case, we say we expect the ID of a `library.book` instance as the last component of the path. The name after the colon is the name of a keyword argument. Our function will be called with this parameter passed as a keyword argument. Here, Odoo takes care of looking up this ID and delivering a browse record, which, of course, only works if the user accessing this path has appropriate permissions. Given that `book` is a browse record, we can simply recycle the first example's function by passing `book.id` as a `book_id` parameter, to give out the same content.

There's more...

Defining parameters within the path is a functionality delivered by `werkzeug`, called **converters**. The `model` converter is added by Odoo, which also defines the converter models that accept a comma-separated list of IDs and pass a recordset containing those IDs to your handler.

The beauty of converters is that the runtime coerces parameters to the expected type, whereas you're on your own with normal keyword parameters. These are delivered as strings, and you have to take care of the necessary type conversions yourself, as seen in the first example.

Built-in `werkzeug` converters include `int`, `float`, and `string`, but also more intricate ones, such as `path`, `any`, and `uuid`. You can look up their semantics at https://werkzeug.palletsprojects.com/en/1.0.x/.

See also

If you want to learn more about the HTTP routes, refer to the following points:

- Odoo's custom converters are defined in `ir_http.py` in the base module and registered in the `_get_converters` class method of `ir.http`. As an exercise, you can create your own converter, which allows you to visit the `/my_library/book_details/Odoo+cookbook` page to receive the details of this book (if you added it to your library earlier).
- If you want to learn more about the form submission on the route, refer to the *Getting input from users* recipe from *Chapter 14, CMS Website Development*.

Modifying an existing handler

When you install the website module, the `/website/info` path displays some information about your Odoo instance. In this recipe, we will override this in order to change this information page's layout, and to also change what is displayed.

Getting ready

Install the `website` module and inspect the `/website/info` path. In this recipe, we will update the `/website/info` route to provide more information.

How to do it...

We'll have to adapt the existing template and override the existing handler. We can do this as follows:

1. Override the qweb template in a file called `views/templates.xml`, as follows:

```xml
<?xml version="1.0" encoding="UTF-8"?>
<odoo>
    <template id="show_website_info"
              inherit_id="website.show_website_info">
      <xpath expr="//dl[@t-foreach='apps']" position="replace">
        <table class="table">
          <tr t-foreach="apps" t-as="app">
            <th>
              <a t-att-href="app.website">
                <t t-esc="app.name" /></a>
```

```
            </th>
            <td><t t-esc="app.summary" /></td>
        </tr>
    </table>
</xpath>
</template>
</odoo>
```

2. Override the handler in a file called `controllers/main.py`, as shown in the following example:

```
from odoo import http
from odoo.addons.website.controllers.main import Website
class WebsiteInfo(Website):
    @http.route()
    def website_info(self):
        result = super(WebsiteInfo, self).website_info()
        result.qcontext['apps'] = result.qcontext['apps'].filtered(
            lambda x: x.name != 'website'
        )
        return result
```

Now, when visiting the info page, we'll only see a filtered list of installed applications in a table, as opposed to the original definition list.

How it works...

In the first step, we overrode an existing QWeb template. In order to find out which one it is, you'll have to consult the code of the original handler. Usually, this will give you something similar to the following line, which tells you that you need to override `template.name`:

```
return request.render('template.name', values)
```

In our case, the handler used a template called `website_info`, but this one was immediately extended by another template called `website.show_website_info`, so it's more convenient to override this one. Here, we replaced the definition list showing installed apps with a table. For details on how QWeb inheritance works, consult *Chapter 15, Web Client Development*.

In order to override the handler method, we must identify the class that defines the handler, which is `odoo.addons.website.controllers.main.Website`, in this case. We need to import the class to be able to inherit from it. Now, we can override the method and change the data passed to the response. Note that what the overridden handler returns here is a `Response` object and not a string of HTML like the previous recipes did, for the sake of brevity. This object contains a reference to the template to be used and the values accessible to the template, but it is only evaluated at the very end of the request.

In general, there are three ways to change an existing handler:

- If it uses a QWeb template, the simplest way to change it is to override the template. This is the right choice for layout changes and small logic changes.
- QWeb templates get a context passed, which is available in the response as the `qcontext` member. This is usually a dictionary where you can add or remove values to suit your needs. In the preceding example, we filtered the list of apps to the website only.
- If the handler receives parameters, you can also preprocess those, in order to have the overridden handler behave in the way you want.

There's more...

As seen in the preceding section, inheritance with controllers works slightly differently than model inheritance; you actually need a reference to the base class and to use Python inheritance on it.

Don't forget to decorate your new handler with the `@http.route` decorator; Odoo uses it as a marker, for which methods are exposed to the network layer. If you omit the decorator, you actually make the handler's path inaccessible.

The `@http.route` decorator itself behaves similarly to field declarations: every value you don't set will be derived from the decorator of the function you're overriding, so we don't have to repeat values we don't want to change.

After receiving a `response` object from the function you override, you can do a lot more than just change the QWeb context:

- You can add or remove HTTP headers by manipulating `response.headers`.
- If you want to render an entirely different template, you can overwrite `response.template`.

- To detect whether a response is based on QWeb in the first place, query `response.is_qweb`.
- The resulting HTML code is available by calling `response.render()`.

See also
- Details on QWeb templates will be given in *Chapter 15, Web Client Development*.

Serving static resources

Web pages contain several types of static resources, such as images, videos, CSS, and so on. In this recipe, we will see how you can manage such static resources for your module.

Getting ready

For this recipe, we will display an image on the page. So, get one image ready. Also, grab the `my_library` module from the previous recipe.

How to do it...

Follow these steps to show an image on the page:

1. Add your image to the `/my_library/static/src/img` directory.
2. Define the new route in `controller`. In the code, replace the image URL with the URL of your image:

```python
@http.route('/demo_page', type='http', auth='none')
def books(self):
    image_url = '/my_library/static/src/image/odoo.png'
    html_result = """<html>
        <body>
            <img src="%s"/>
        </body>
    </html>""" % image_url
    return html_result
```

Restart the server and update the module to apply the changes. Now visit `/demo_page` to see the image on the page.

How it works...

All the files placed under the /static folder are considered static resources and are publicly accessible. In our example, we have put our image in the /static/src/img directory. You can place the static resource anywhere under the static directory, but there is a recommended directory structure based on the type of file:

- /static/src/img is the directory used for images.
- /static/src/css is the directory used for CSS files.
- /static/src/scss is the directory used for SCSS files.
- /static/src/fonts is the directory used for font files.
- /static/src/js is the directory used for JavaScript files.
- /static/src/xml is the directory used for XML files for client-side QWeb templates.
- /static/lib is the directory used for files of external libraries.

In our example, we have displayed an image on the page. You can also access the image directly from /my_library/static/src/image/odoo.png.

In this recipe, we displayed a static resource (an image) on the page and we saw the recommended directories for different static resources. There are more simple ways to present page content and static resources, which we will see in the next chapter.

14
CMS Website Development

Odoo comes with a fully featured **Content Management System** (**CMS**). With drag-and-drop features, your end user can design a page in a few minutes, but it is not so simple to develop a new feature or building block in the Odoo CMS. In this chapter, you will explore the frontend side of Odoo. You will learn how to create web pages. You will also learn how to create building blocks that users can drag and drop on a page. Advanced things such as **Urchin Tracking Modules** (**UTMs**), **Search Engine Optimization** (**SEO**), multi-website, GeoIP, and sitemaps are also covered in this chapter. In short, you will learn everything that is required to develop interactive websites.

> **Important information**
>
> All of the Odoo CMS features are implemented by the `website` and `web_editor` modules. If you want to learn how the CMS works under the hood, take a look at both of these modules. You may find the Code in Action video here: `http://bit.ly/2UH0eMM`.

In this chapter, we will cover the following recipes:

- Managing static assets
- Adding CSS and JavaScript for a website
- Creating or modifying templates – QWeb
- Managing dynamic routes
- Offering static snippets to the user
- Offering dynamic snippets to the user
- Getting input from website users
- Managing SEO options
- Managing sitemaps for the website
- Getting a visitor's country information
- Tracking a marketing campaign
- Managing multiple websites
- Redirecting old URLs
- Publish management for website-related records

Managing static assets

Modern websites contain a lot of JavaScript and CSS files. When a page is loaded in the browser, these static files make a separate request to the server. The higher the number of requests, the lower the website speed. To avoid this issue, most websites serve **static assets** by combining multiple files. There are several tools on the market to manage these sorts of things, but Odoo has its own implementation for managing static assets.

What are asset bundles and different assets in Odoo?

In Odoo, static asset management is not as simple as it is in other apps. Odoo has a lot of different applications and code bases. Different Odoo applications have different purposes and UIs. These apps do not share common code, so there are some cases in which we want to load some assets, but we don't want to do so for all cases. It is not a good practice to load unnecessary static assets on a page. To avoid loading extra assets in all applications, Odoo uses the concept of asset bundles. The job of an asset bundle is to combine all the JavaScript and CSS in a single file and reduce its size by minimizing it. There are asset bundles in the Odoo code base and also different asset bundles for different code bases.

Here are the different asset bundles used in Odoo:

- `web.assets_common`: This asset bundle includes all the basic utilities that are common to all applications, such as jQuery, Underscore.js, Font Awesome, and so on. This asset bundle is used in the frontend (website), backend, Point of Sale, reports, and so on. This common asset is loaded almost everywhere in Odoo. It also contains the `boot.js` file, which is used for the Odoo module system.

- `web.assets_backend`: This asset bundle is used in the backend of Odoo (the **Enterprise Resource Planning** (**ERP**) part). It contains all of the code related to the web client, views, field widgets, the action manager, and so on.

- `web.assets_frontend` or `website.assets_frontend`: This asset bundle is used in the frontend of Odoo (the website part). It contains all the code related to website-side applications, such as e-commerce, blogs, online events, forums, live chat, and so on. Note that this asset bundle does not contain code related to website editing or the drag-and-drop feature (the website builder). The reason behind this is that we don't want to load editor assets for the public use of the website.

- `website.assets_editor` and `web_editor.summernote`: This asset bundle contains code related to website-editing snippet options and the drag-and-drop feature (the website builder). It is loaded on a website only if the user has editing rights. It is also used in the mass-mailing designer.

- `web.report_assets_common`: QWeb reports are just PDF files generated from HTML. This asset is loaded in the report layout.

> **Important information**
> There are some other asset bundles used for specific applications: `point_of_sale.assets`, `survey.survey_assets`, `mass_mailing.layout`, and `website_slides.slide_embed_assets`.

Odoo manages its static assets through the `AssetBundle` class, which is located at `/odoo/addons/base/models/assetsbundle.py`. Now, `AssetBundle` not only combines multiple files; it is also packed with more features. Here is the list of features it provides:

- It combines multiple JavaScript and CSS files.
- It minifies the JavaScript and CSS files by removing comments, extra spaces, and carriage returns from the file content. Removing this extra data will reduce the size of static assets and improve the page loading speed.
- It has built-in support for CSS preprocessors, such as **SCSS** and **LESS**. This means you can add **SCSS** and **LESS** files and they will automatically be compiled and will get added to the bundle.

Custom assets

As we have seen, Odoo has different assets for different code bases. To get the right result, you will need to choose the right asset bundle in which to place your custom JavaScript and CSS files. For example, if you are designing a website, you need to put your file in `web.assets_frontend`. Although it is rare, sometimes, you need to create a whole new asset bundle. You can create your own asset bundle, as we will describe in the following section.

How to do it...

Follow these steps to create a custom assets bundle:

1. Create the QWeb template and add your JavaScript, CSS, or SCSS files there, as follows:

```
<template id="my_custom_assets" name="My Custom Assets">
    <link rel="stylesheet" type="text/scss"
          href="/my_module/static/src/scss/my_scss.scss"/>
    <link rel="stylesheet" type="text/css"
          href="/my_module/static/src/scss/my_css.css"/>
    <script type="text/JavaScript"
          src="/my_module/static/src/js/widgets/my_JavaScript.js"/>
</template>
```

2. Use `t-call-assets` in the QWeb template where you want to load this bundle, as follows:

```
<template id="some_page">
...
<head>
    <t t-call-assets="my_module.my_custom_assets" t-js="false"/>
    <t t-call-assets="my_module.my_custom_assets" t-css="false"/>
</head>
...
```

How it works...

In *step 1*, we created the new QWeb template with the `my_custom_assets` external ID. In this template, you will need to list all of your CSS, SCSS, and JavaScript files. First, Odoo will compile the SCSS files into CSS, then Odoo will combine all CSS and JavaScript files into an individual CSS and JavaScript file.

After declaring the assets, you need to load them into the QWeb template (web page). In *step 2*, we have loaded the CSS and JavaScript assets in the template. The `t-css` and `t-js` attributes are only used to load style sheets or scripts.

> **Important information**
>
> In most website development, you will need to add your JavaScript and CSS files in existing asset bundles. Adding a new asset bundle is very rare. It is only required when you want to develop pages/apps without Odoo CMS features. In the next recipe, you will learn about adding custom CSS/JavaScript to an existing asset bundle.

There's more...

The following are a few things you need to know if you are working with assets in Odoo.

Debugging JavaScript can be very hard in Odoo because `AssetBundle` merges multiple JavaScript files into a single file and also minifies them. By enabling developer mode with assets, you can skip asset bundling, and the page will load static assets separately so that you can debug easily.

Combined assets are generated once and stored in the `ir.attachment` model. After that, they are served from the attachment. If you want to regenerate assets, you can do so from the debug options, as shown in the following screenshot:

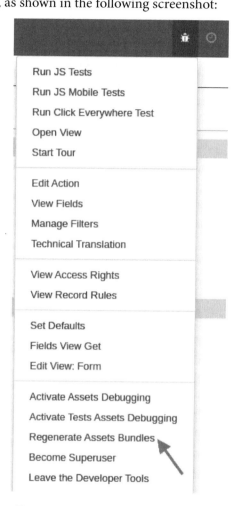

Figure 14.1 – Option to regenerate assets

> **Tip**
> As you know, Odoo will generate the asset only once. This behavior can be a headache during development, as it requires frequent server restarts. To overcome this issue, you can use `dev=xml` in the command line, which will load assets directly, so there will be no need for a server restart.

In the next recipe, you will see how you can include custom CSS/JavaScript in an existing asset bundle.

Adding CSS and JavaScript for a website

In this recipe, we'll cover how to add CSS and JavaScript to a website.

Getting ready

We will be using the `my_library` module from *Chapter 3, Creating Odoo Add-On Modules*, for this recipe. You can use the initial module from the `https://github.com/PacktPublishing/Odoo-14-Development-Cookbook-Fourth-Edition/tree/master/Chapter14/00_initial_module/my_library` GitHub repository. We will add CSS, SCSS, and JavaScript files, which will modify the website. As we are modifying the website, we will need to add `website` as a dependency. Modify the `manifest` file like this:

```
...
    'depends': ['base', 'website'],
...
```

How to do it...

Override the main website template to inject your code, as follows:

1. Add a file called `views/templates.xml` and add an empty view override, as follows (don't forget to list the file in `__manifest__.py`):

    ```xml
    <odoo>
        <template id="assets_frontend"
                  inherit_id="web.assets_frontend">
            <xpath expr="." position="inside">
                <!-- points 2 & 3 go here /-->
            </xpath>
        </template>
    </odoo>
    ```

2. Add the references of the CSS and SCSS files, as follows:

    ```xml
    <link href="/my_library/static/src/css/my_library.css"
          rel="stylesheet"
          type="text/css"/>
    <link href="/my_library/static/src/scss/my_library.scss"
          rel="stylesheet"
          type="text/scss"/>
    ```

3. Add a reference to your JavaScript file, as follows:

   ```
   <script src="/my_library/static/src/js/my_library.js"
           type="text/javascript" />
   ```

4. Add some CSS code to `static/src/css/my_library.css`, as follows:

   ```css
   body main {
       background: #b9ced8;
   }
   ```

5. Add some SCSS code to `static/src/scss/my_library.scss`, as follows:

   ```scss
   $my-bg-color: #1C2529;
   $my-text-color: #D3F4FF;

   nav.navbar {
       background-color: $my-bg-color !important;
       .navbar-nav .nav-link span{
           color: darken($my-text-color, 15);
           font-weight: 600;
       }
   }

   footer.o_footer {
       background-color: $my-bg-color !important;
       color: $my-text-color;
   }
   ```

6. Add some JavaScript code to `static/src/js/my_library.js`, as follows:

   ```javascript
   odoo.define('my_library', function (require) {
       var core = require('web.core');

       alert(core._t('Hello world'));
       return {
           // if you created functionality to export, add it here
       }
   });
   ```

After updating your module, you should see that the Odoo website has custom colors in the menu, body, and footer, and a somewhat annoying **Hello World** popup on each page load, as shown in the following screenshot:

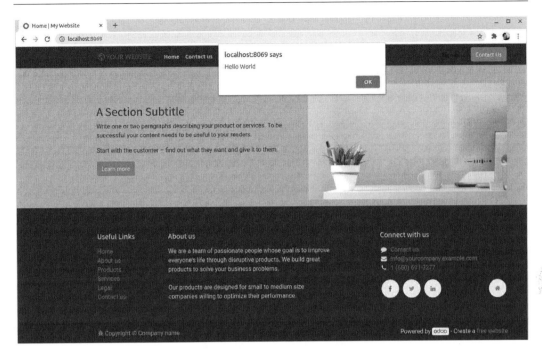

Figure 14.2 – Website page after adding custom CSS, SCSS, and JavaScript

How it works...

At the base of Odoo's CMS lies an XML templating engine called **QWeb**, which will be discussed in detail in the next recipe. Asset bundles are just created with such QWeb templates. In *steps 1*, *2*, and *3*, we have listed our style sheets and JavaScript file in `web.assets_frontend` by extending it. We have chosen `web.assets_frontend` because we want to update the website. These assets are loaded for every website page.

In *step 4*, we have added CSS, which sets the body background color of the website.

> **Tip**
> For CSS/SCSS files, sometimes, order matters. So, if you need to override a style defined in another add-on, you will have to ensure that your file is loaded after the original file you want to modify. This can be done by either adjusting your view's priority field or directly inheriting from the add-on's view that injects the reference to the CSS file. For details, refer to the *Changing the existing views – view inheritance* recipe in *Chapter 9, Backend Views*.

In *step 5*, we have added basic SCSS. Odoo has built-in support for the SCSS preprocessor. Odoo will automatically compile SCSS files into CSS. In our example, we have used basic SCSS with some variables and the `darken` function to make `$my-text-color` darker by 15%. The SCSS preprocessor has tons of other features; if you want to learn more about SCSS, refer to http://sass-lang.com/.

In *step 6*, we have added basic JavaScript, which just shows the `alert` message when the page is loaded. To avoid ordering issues with JavaScript, Odoo uses a mechanism very similar to **RequireJS** (http://requirejs.org). In our JavaScript file, we called `odoo.define()`, which needs two arguments: the namespace you want to define and a function that contains the actual implementation. If you're developing a complex product that uses JavaScript extensively, then you can divide the code into logically different parts and define them in different functions. This will be very useful because you can reuse functions by importing them via `require`. Also, to define the namespace of your module, add your add-on's name, making it prepended and separated by dots to avoid naming conflicts in the future. This is what the web module does, which defines, among other things, `web.core` and `web.data`.

With the second argument, the definition function receives only one parameter, `require`, which is a function you can use to obtain references to JavaScript namespaces defined in other modules. Use this for all interactions with Odoo, and never rely on the global `odoo` object.

Your own function can then return an object pointing to the references you want to make available for other add-ons, or nothing, if there are no such references. If you have returned some references from your function, you can use them in another function, as shown in the following example:

```
odoo.define('my_module', function (require) {
    var test = {
        key1: 'value1',
        key2: 'value2'
    };
    var square = function(number) {
        return 2*2;
    };

    return {
        test: test,
        square: square
    }
});

// In another file
```

```
odoo.define('another_module', function (require) {
    var my_module = require('my_module');

    console.log(my_module.test.key1);
    console.log('square of 5 is', my_module.square(5));

});
```

There's more...

To improve performance, Odoo only loads minimal JavaScript for the frontend. All other JavaScript from the assets will be loaded lazily once the page is fully loaded and the minimal assets available have the `web.assets_frontend_minimal_js` ID.

Creating or modifying templates – QWeb

We'll add website capabilities to the `my_library` add-on developed in *Chapter 4, Application Models*. What we're interested in is allowing users to browse through the library and, if they are logged in with the appropriate permissions, enabling them to edit book details right from the website interface.

Getting ready

For this recipe, we will be using `my_library` from the `https://github.com/PacktPublishing/Odoo-14-Development-Cookbook-Fourth-Edition/tree/master/Chapter14/00_initial_module/my_library` directory from the GitHub repository of this book.

How to do it...

We'll need to define the following couple of controllers and views:

1. Add a controller that serves the list of books in `controllers/main.py`, as follows:

    ```
    from odoo import http
    from odoo.http import request

    class Main(http.Controller):
        @http.route('/books', type='http', auth="user", website=True)
        def library_books(self):
            return request.render(
    ```

```
                    'my_library.books', {
                        'books': request.env['library.book'].
    search([]),
                    })
```

2. Add a minimal template in `views/templates.xml`, as follows (make sure you have added the `views/templates.xml` file in the manifest):

```xml
<?xml version="1.0" encoding="utf-8"?>
<odoo>

<template id="books">
    <t t-call="website.layout">
        <!-- Add page elements here -->
    </t>
</template>

</odoo>
```

3. Inside `website.layout`, add the droppable element with the `oe_structure` class, as follows:

```xml
<div class="oe_structure">
    <section class="pt32 pb32 bg-secondary oe_custom_bg">
        <div class="container text-center">
            <h1> Editable text and supports drag and drop.</h1>
        </div>
    </section>
</div>
```

4. Append the code block to `website.layout` to display the books' information, as follows:

```xml
<div class="container">
    <t t-foreach="books" t-as="book">
        <div t-attf-class="card mt-3 #{'bg-info' if book_odd else ''}">
            <div class="card-body" id="card_body">
                <h3 t-field="book.name"/>
                <t t-if="book.date_release">
                    <div t-field="book.date_release"
                        class="text-muted"/>
                </t>
                <b class="mt8"> Authors </b>
```

```
            <ul>
                <li t-foreach="book.author_ids"
                    t-as="author">
                    <span t-esc="author.name" />
                </li>
            </ul>
        </div>
    </div>
  </t>
</div>
```

5. Append a non-editable element into `website.layout`, as follows:

```
<section class="container mt16" contenteditable="False">
        This is a non-editable text after the list of books.
</section>
```

Open `http://your-server-url:8069/books` in a browser and you will be able to see a list of books, with authors. With this code, a user can see a list of books and their details. Given the appropriate permissions, users will also be able to change the book details and other text.

How it works...

In *step 1*, we have a controller to pass custom values. These custom values will be passed from the controller to the QWeb template.

In the following steps *(2, 3, 4, 5)*, we created a template called `books` that is used to generate the HTML code necessary to display a list of books. All of the code is wrapped in a t element with the `t-call` attribute set, which makes Odoo render the page with the `website.layout` template and insert our content inside the template. The `website.layout` template includes all of the required utilities, such as Bootstrap, jQuery, Font Awesome, and so on. These utilities are used for designing the web page. `website.layout` also includes the default header, footer, snippets, and page editing functionalities. This way, we get a full Odoo web page with the menus, footer, and page editing features, without having to repeat the code in all pages. If you don't use `t-call="website.layout"`, you will not get the default header, footers, and website editing features.

In *steps 3, 4,* and *5*, we have added HTML with some QWeb template attributes inside `website.layout`. This HTML code will be used to display a list of books. Let's take a look at different QWeb attributes and their usage.

Loops

To work on recordsets or iterable data types, you need a **construct** to *loop* through lists. In the QWeb template, this can be done with the `t-foreach` element. Iteration can happen in a `t` element, in which case its contents are repeated for every member of the iterable that was passed in the `t-foreach` attribute, as follows:

```
<t t-foreach="[1, 2, 3, 4, 5]" t-as="num">
    <p><t t-esc="num"/></p>
</t>
```

This will be rendered as follows:

```
<p>1</p>
<p>2</p>
<p>3</p>
<p>4</p>
<p>5</p>
```

You can also place the `t-foreach` and `t-as` attributes in some arbitrary element, at which point this element and its contents will be repeated for every item in the iterable. Take a look at the following code block. This will generate exactly the same result as the previous example:

```
<p t-foreach="[1, 2, 3, 4, 5]" t-as="num">
    <t t-esc="num"/>
</p>
```

In our example, take a look at the inside of the `t-call` element, where the actual content generation happens. The template expects to be rendered with a context that has a variable called `books` set that iterates through it in the `t-foreach` element. The `t-as` attribute is mandatory and will be used as the name of the iterator variable, to access the iterated data. While the most common use for this construction is to iterate over recordsets, you can use it on any Python object that is iterable.

Within `t-foreach` loops, you've got access to a couple of **extra variables**, whose names are derived from the accompanying `t-as` attribute. As it is `book` in the preceding example, we have access to the `book_odd` variable, which contains the value `True` for odd indices while iterating and `False` for even ones. In this example, we used this to be able to have alternating background colors for our cards.

The following are other available variables:

- `book_index`, which returns the current (zero-based) index in the iteration.
- `book_first` and `book_last`, which are `True` if this is the first or last iteration, respectively.
- `book_value`, which would contain the item's value if the `book` variable we iterate over were a dictionary; in this case, `book` would iterate through the dictionary's keys.
- `book_size`, which is the size of the collection (if available).
- `book_even` and `book_odd` get true values, based on the iteration index.
- `book_parity` contains the `even` value for even indices while iterating, and `odd` for odd ones.

> **Important note**
> The examples here are based on our scenario. In your case, you need to replace `book` with the value given for the `t-as` attribute.

Dynamic attributes

QWeb templates can set attribute values dynamically. This can be done in the following three ways.

The first way is through `t-att-$attr_name`. At the time of template rendering, an attribute, `$attr_name`, is created; its value can be any valid Python expression. This is computed with the current context and the result is set as the value of the attribute, like this:

```
<div t-att-total="10 + 5 + 5"/>
```

It will be rendered like this:

```
<div total="20"></div>
```

The second way is through `t-attf-$attr_name`. This is similar to the previous option. The only difference is that only strings between {{ .. }} and #{..} are evaluated. This is helpful when values are mixed with the strings. It is mostly used to evaluate classes, as in this example:

```
<t t-foreach="['info', 'danger', 'warning']" t-as="color">
    <div t-attf-class="alert alert-#{color}">
        Simple bootstrap alert
    </div>
</t>
```

It will be rendered like this:

```
<div class="alert alert-info">
    Simple bootstrap alert
</div>
<div class="alert alert-danger">
    Simple bootstrap alert
</div>
<div class="alert alert-warning">
    Simple bootstrap alert
</div>
```

The third way is through the `t-att=mapping` option. This option accepts the dictionary after the template rendering the dictionary's data is converted into attributes and values. Take a look at the following example:

```
<div t-att="{'id': 'my_el_id', 'class': 'alert alert-danger'}"/>
```

After rendering this template, it will be converted into the following:

```
<div id="my_el_id" class="alert alert-danger"/>
```

In our example, we have used `t-attf-class` to get a dynamic background based on index values.

Fields

The h3 and div tags use the t-field attribute. The value of the t-field attribute must be used with the recordset with a length of one; this allows the user to change the content of the web page when they open the website in edit mode. When you save the page, updated values will be stored in the database. Of course, this is subject to a permission check and is only allowed if the current user has write permissions for the displayed record. With an optional t-options attribute, you can give a dictionary option to be passed to the field renderer, including the widget to be used. Currently, there is not a vast collection of widgets for the backend, so the choices are a bit limited here. For example, if you want to display an image from the binary field, then you can use the image widget like this:

```
<span t-field="author.image_small" t-options="{'widget':
'image'}"/>
```

t-field has some limitations. It only works on recordsets and it cannot work on the <t> element. For this, you need to use some HTML elements, such as <span> or <div>. There is an alternative to the t-field attribute, which is t-esc. The t-esc attribute is not limited to recordsets; it can also be used on any data types, but it is not editable in a website.

Another difference between t-esc and t-field is that t-field shows values based on the user's language, while t-esc shows raw values from the database. For example, for users who configured the English language in their preferences and set the datetime field as used with t-field, the result will be rendered in 12/15/2018 17:12:13 format. In contrast, if the t-esc attribute is used, then the result will be in a rendered format like this: 2018-12-15 16:12:13.

Conditionals

Note that the division showing the publication date is wrapped by a t element with the t-if attribute set. This attribute is evaluated as Python code, and the element is only rendered if the result is a *truthy value*. In the following example, we only show the div class if there is actually a publication date set. However, in complex cases, you can use t-elif and t-else as in the following example:

```
<div t-if="state == 'new'">
    Text will be added of state is new.
</div>
<div t-elif="state == 'progress'">
    Text will be added of state is progress.
</div>
```

```
<div t-else="">
    Text will be added for all other stages.
</div>
```

Setting variables

The QWeb template is also capable of defining the variable in the template itself. After defining the template, you can use the variable in the subsequent template. You can set the variable like this:

```
<t t-set="my_var" t-value="5 + 1"/>
<t t-esc="my_var"/>
```

Subtemplates

If you are developing a big application, managing large templates can be difficult. The QWeb template supports subtemplates, so you can divide large templates into smaller subtemplates and you can reuse them in multiple templates. For subtemplates, you can use a `t-call` attribute, like in this example:

```
<template id="first_template">
    <div> Test Template </div>
</template>

<template id="second_template">
    <t t-call="first_template"/>
</template>
```

Inline editing

The user will be able to modify records directly from the website in edit mode. The data loaded with the `t-field` node will be editable by default. If the user changes the value in such a node and saves the page, the values will also be updated in the backend. Don't worry; in order to update the record, a user will need `write` permissions on the record. Note that `t-field` only works on a recordset. To display other types of data, you can use `t-esc`. This works exactly like `t-field`, but the only difference is that `t-esc` is not editable and can be used with any type of data.

If you want to enable snippet drag-and-drop support on the page, you can use the `oe_structure` class. In our example, we have added this at the top of the template. Using `oe_structure` will enable editing and snippet drag-and-drop support.

If you want to disable the website editing feature on a block, you can use the `contenteditable=False` attribute. This makes an element read-only. In *step 5*, we have used this attribute in the last `<section>` tag.

> **Note**
>
> To make the page multi-website-compatible, when you edit a page/view through the website editor, Odoo will create a separate copy of the page for that website. This means that subsequent code updates will never make it to the edited website page. In order to also get the ease of use of inline editing and the possibility of updating your HTML code in subsequent releases, create one view that contains the semantic HTML elements and a second one that injects editable elements. Then, only the latter view will be copied, and you can still have updates for the parent view.

For the other CSS classes used here, consult Bootstrap's documentation, as linked in this recipe's *See also* section.

In *step 1*, we have declared the route to render the template. If you noticed, we have used the `website=True` parameter in `route()`, which will pass some extra context in the template, such as menus, user language, company, and so on. This will be used in `website.layout` to render the menus and footers. The `website=True` parameter also enables multilanguage support in a website. It also displays exceptions in a better way.

At the function end, we returned the result by rendering the template; we then passed the recordset of all books that are being used in the template.

There's more...

To modify existing templates, you can use the `inherit_id` attribute on the template and then use an `xpath` element like view inheritance. For example, we want to display the count of authors near the `Authors` label by inheriting the `books` template. We can do this in the following way:

```
<template id="books_ids_inh" inherit_id="my_library.books">
    <xpath expr="//div[@id='card_body']/b" position="replace">
        <b class="mt8"> Authors (<t t-esc="len(book.author_ids)"/>) </b>
    </xpath>
</template>
```

Inheritance works exactly like views, because internally, QWeb templates are normal views with the `qweb` type. The `template` element is shorthand for a `record` element that sets some properties on the record for you. While there's never a reason to not use the convenience of the `template` element, you should know what happens under the hood: the element creates a record of the `ir.ui.view` model with the `qweb` type. Then, depending on the `template` element's `name` and `inherit_id` attributes, the `inherit_id` field on the view record will be set.

In the next recipe, we will learn about managing dynamic routes to handle dynamic URLs.

See also

Refer to the following to design QWeb templates effectively:

- Odoo, as a whole, makes extensive use of Bootstrap (http://getbootstrap.com), which you should use to get adaptive designs without much effort.
- For details on view inheritance, take a look at the *Changing the existing views – view inheritance* recipe in *Chapter 9, Backend Views*.
- For a more in-depth discussion of controllers, refer to the *Making a path accessible from the network* and *Restricting access to web-accessible paths* recipes in *Chapter 13, Web Server Development*.
- For more information about updating existing routes, refer to the *Modifying an existing handler* recipe in *Chapter 13, Web Server Development*.

Managing dynamic routes

In website development projects, it is often the case that we need to create pages with dynamic URLs. For example, in e-commerce, each product has a detailed page linked with a different URL. In this recipe, we will create a web page to display the book details.

Getting ready

We will be using the `my_library` module from the previous recipe. To make a book detail page attractive, we will need to add a few new fields. Please add the following two new fields in the `library.book` model and form a view, like this:

```
class LibraryBook(models.Model):
    _name = 'library.book'

    name = fields.Char('Title', required=True)
    date_release = fields.Date('Release Date')
```

```
        author_ids = fields.Many2many('res.partner',
string='Authors')
        image = fields.Binary(attachment=True)
        html_description = fields.Html()
```

If you want, add these fields into the form view. Anyway, you will also be able to edit it from the web page itself.

How to do it...

Follow these steps to generate a details page for books:

1. Add a new route for book details in `main.py`, as follows:

   ```
   @http.route('/books/<model("library.book"):book>',
   type='http', auth="user", website=True)
   def library_book_detail(self, book):
       return request.render(
           'my_library.book_detail', {
               'book': book,
           })
   ```

2. Add a new template for book details in `templates.xml`, as follows:

   ```
   <template id="book_detail" name="Books Detail">
       <t t-call="website.layout">
           <div class="container">
               <div class="row mt16">
                   <div class="col-5">
                       <span t-field="book.image" t-options="{
                           'widget': 'image',
                           'class': 'mx-auto d-block img-thumbnail'}"/>
                   </div>
                   <div class="offset-1 col-6">
                       <h1 t-field="book.name"/>
                       <t t-if="book.date_release">
                           <div t-field="book.date_release"
                           class="text-muted"/>
                       </t>
                       <b class="mt8"> Authors </b>
                       <ul>
                           <li t-foreach="book.author_ids" t-as="author">
   ```

```xml
                                        <span t-esc="author.name" />
                                </li>
                            </ul>
                        </div>
                    </div>
                </div>
                <div t-field="book.html_description"/>
        </t>
</template>
```

3. Add a button in the book list template, as follows. This button will redirect to the book details web page:

```xml
...
<div t-attf-class="card mt24 #{'bg-light' if book_odd else ''}">
    <div class="card-body">
        <h3 t-field="book.name"/>
        <t t-if="book.date_release">
            <div t-field="book.date_release" class="text-muted"/>
        </t>
        <b class="mt8"> Authors </b>
        <ul>
            <li t-foreach="book.author_ids" t-as="author">
                <span t-esc="author.name" />
            </li>
        </ul>
        <a t-attf-href="/books/#{book.id}" class="btn btn-primary btn-sm">
            <i class="fa fa-book"/> Book Detail
        </a>
    </div>
</div>
...
```

Update the `my_library` module to apply changes. After the update, you will see book details page links on the book card. Upon clicking those links, the book detail pages will open.

How it works...

In the *first step*, we created a dynamic route for the book details page. In this route, we added `<model("library.book"):book>`. This accepts URLs with integers, as in `/books/1`. Odoo considers this integer as the ID of the `library.book` model, and when this URL is accessed, Odoo fetches a recordset and passes it to the function as the argument. So, when `/books/1` is accessed from the browser, the `book` parameter in the `library_book_detail()` function will have a recordset of the `library.book` model with the ID 1. We passed this `book` recordset and rendered a new template called `my_library.book2_detail`.

In the *second step*, we created a new QWeb template called `book_detail` to render a book details page. This is simple and is created using the Bootstrap structure. If you check, we have added `html_description` in the detail page. The `html_description` field has a field type of HTML, so you can store HTML data in the field. Odoo automatically adds the snippet drag-and-drop support to the HTML types of fields. So, now we are able to use snippets in the book details page. The snippets dropped in the HTML fields are stored in a book's records, so you can design different content for different books.

In the *last step*, we added a link with the anchor tag so that a visitor can be redirected to the book details page.

> **Note**
>
> The model route also supports domain filtering. For example, if you want to restrict some books based on a condition, you can do so by passing the domain to the route as follows:
>
> `/books/<model("library.book", "[(name','!=', 'Book 1')]"):team>/submit`
>
> This will restrict access to the books that have the name `Book 1`.

There's more...

Odoo uses `werkzeug` to handle HTTP requests. Odoo adds a thin wrapper around `werkzeug` to easily handle routes. You saw the `<model("library.book"):book>` route in the last example. This is Odoo's own implementation, but it also supports all features from the `werkzeug` routing. Consequently, you can use routing like this:

- `/page/<int:page>` accepts integer values.
- `/page/<any(about, help):page_name>` accepts selected values.

- `/pages/<page>` accepts strings.
- `/pages/<category>/<int:page>` accepts multiple values.

There are lots of variations available for the routes, which you can read about at `http://werkzeug.pocoo.org/docs/0.14/routing/`.

Offering static snippets to the user

Odoo's website editor offers several editing building blocks, which can be dragged onto the page and edited according to your needs. This recipe will cover how to offer your own building blocks. These blocks are referred to as snippets. There are several types of snippets, but in general, we can categorize them into two types: **static** and **dynamic**. The static snippet is fixed and does not change until the user changes it. Dynamic snippets depend on database records and are changed based on record values. In this recipe, we will see how to create a static snippet.

Getting ready

For this recipe, we will be using the `my_library` module from the previous recipe.

How to do it...

A snippet is actually just a QWeb view that gets injected into the **Insert blocks** bar. We will create a small snippet that will show the book's image and book title. You will be able to drag and drop the snippet on the page and you will be able to edit the image and text. Follow these steps to add a new static snippet:

1. Add a file called `views/snippets.xml`, as follows (do not forget to register the file in the manifest):

    ```xml
    <?xml version="1.0" encoding="UTF-8"?>
    <odoo>

    <!-- Step 2 and 3 comes here -->

    </odoo>
    ```

2. Add a QWeb template for the snippet in `views/snippets.xml`, as follows:

    ```xml
    <template id="snippet_book_cover" name="Book Cover">
        <section class="pt-3 pb-3">
            <div class="container">
    ```

```xml
                <div class="row align-items-center">
                    <div class="col-lg-6 pt16 pb16">
                        <h1>Odoo 12 Development Cookbook</h1>
                        <p>
                            Learn with Odoo development
                            quicky with examples
                        </p>
                        <a class="btn btn-primary" href="#" >
                            Book Details
                        </a>
                    </div>
                    <div class="col-lg-6 pt16 pb16">
                        <img
                            src="/my_library/static/src/img/cover.jpeg"
                            class="mx-auto img-thumbnail w-50 img img-fluid shadow"/>
                    </div>
                </div>
            </div>
        </section>
</template>
```

3. List the template in the snippet list like this:

```xml
<template id="book_snippets_options" inherit_id="website.snippets">
    <xpath expr="//div[@id='snippet_structure']/div[hasclass('o_panel_body')]" position="inside">
        <t t-snippet="my_library.snippet_book_cover"
           t-thumbnail="/my_library/static/src/img/s_book_thumb.png"/>
    </xpath>
</template>
```

4. Add the cover image and snippet thumbnail image in the `/my_library/static/src/img` directory.

Restart the server and update the `my_library` module to apply the changes. When you open the website page in edit mode, you will be able to see our snippet in the snippets blocks panel.

How it works...

The static snippet is nothing but a block of HTML code. In *step 1*, we created a QWeb template with our HTML for the book block. In this HTML, we have just used a Bootstrap column structure, but you can use any HTML code. Note that the HTML code you add in the snippet's QWeb template will be added to the page when you drag and drop. In general, it is a good idea to use `section` elements and Bootstrap classes for snippets, because for them, Odoo's editor offers edit, background, and resize controls out of the box.

In *step 2*, we registered our snippet in the snippet list. You will need to inherit `website.snippets` to register a snippet. In the website editor GUI, snippets are divided into different sections based on their usage. In our example, we have registered our snippet in the **Structure** section via `xpath`. To list your snippet, you need to use a `<t>` tag with the `t-snippet` attribute. The `t-snippet` attribute will have the XML ID of the QWeb template, which is `my_library.snippet_book_cover` in our example. You will also need to use the `t-thumbnail` attribute, which is used to show a small snippet image in the website editor.

> **Note**
>
> The `website.snippets` template contains all the default snippets, and you can learn more about it by exploring the `/addons/website/views/snippets/snippets.xml` file.

Odoo will add some default options to your snippets when you have a proper Bootstrap structure. For example, in our snippet, you would be able to set a background color, a background image, width, height, and so on. Explore the `/addons/website/views/snippets/snippets.xml` file to see all the snippet options. In the next recipe, we will see how to add our own options.

In *step 3*, we have listed our snippet under the `structure` block. Once you update the module, you will be able to drag and drop the snippet. In *step 4*, we have just added an image for the snippet thumbnail.

There's more...

In such cases, there will be no need for extra JavaScript. Odoo's editor offers lots of options and controls out of the box, and they are more than enough for static snippets. You will find all existing snippets and options at `website/views/snippets.xml`.

Snippet options also support the `data-exclude`, `data-drop-near`, and `data-drop-in` attributes, which determine where a snippet can be placed when dragging it out of the snippet bar. These are also jQuery selectors, and in *step 3* of this recipe, we didn't use them, because we allow putting the snippet basically anywhere that content can go.

Offering dynamic snippets to the user

In this recipe, we will see how we can create dynamic snippets for Odoo. We will generate content based on database values.

Getting ready

For this recipe, we will be using the `my_library` module from the previous recipe.

How to do it...

Perform the following steps to add a dynamic snippet that shows a list of books:

1. Add a given QWeb template for the snippet in `views/snippets.xml`:

    ```xml
    <template id="snippet_book_dynamic" name="Latest Books">
        <section class="book_list">
            <div class="container">
                <h2>Latest books</h2>
                <table class="table book_snippet table-striped"
                    data-number-of-books="5">
                    <tr>
                        <th>Name</th>
                        <th>Release date</th>
                    </tr>
                </table>
            </div>
        </section>
    </template>
    ```

2. Register the snippet and add an option to change the snippet behavior:

```xml
<template id="book_snippets_options"
          inherit_id="website.snippets">
    <!-- register snippet -->
    <xpath expr="//div[@id='snippet_structure']/
                 div[hasclass('o_panel_body')]"
           position="inside">
        <t t-snippet="my_library.snippet_book_dynamic"
           t-thumbnail="/my_library/static/src/img/s_list.png"/>
    </xpath>

    <xpath expr="//div[@id='snippet_options']"
           position="inside">
        <!--Add step 3 here -->
    </xpath>
</template>
```

3. Then, add the snippet options for the book snippet:

```xml
<div data-selector=".book_snippet">
    <we-select string="Table Style">
        <we-button data-select-class="table-striped">
            Striped
        </we-button>
        <we-button data-select-class="table-dark">
            Dark
        </we-button>
        <we-button data-select-class="table-bordered">
            Bordered
        </we-button>
    </we-select>
    <we-button-group string="No of Books"
        data-attribute-name="numberOfBooks">
        <we-button data-select-data-attribute="5">
            5
        </we-button>
```

```xml
            <we-button data-select-data-attribute="10">
                10
            </we-button>
            <we-button data-select-data-attribute="15">
                15
            </we-button>
        </we-button-group>
    </div>
```

4. Add a new /static/src/snippets.js file and add code to render a dynamic snippet:

```javascript
odoo.define('book.dynamic.snippet', function (require) {
'use strict';

var publicWidget = require('web.public.widget');

// Add step 5 here

});
```

5. Add a public widget to render the book snippet dynamically:

```javascript
publicWidget.registry.books = publicWidget.Widget.extend({
    selector: '.book_snippet',
    disabledInEditableMode: false,
    start: function () {
        var self = this;
        var rows = this.$el[0].dataset.numberOfBooks || '5';
        this.$el.find('td').parents('tr').remove();
        this._rpc({
            model: 'library.book',
            method: 'search_read',
            domain: [],
            fields: ['name', 'date_release'],
            orderBy: [{ name: 'date_release', asc: false }],
```

```
                    limit: parseInt(rows)
            }).then(function (data) {
                _.each(data, function (book) {
                    self.$el.append(
                        $('<tr />').append(
                            $('<td />').text(book.name),
                            $('<td />').text(book.date_release)
                        ));
                });
            });
        },
    });

});
```

6. Add the JavaScript file to the module:

```
    <template id="assets_frontend"
            inherit_id="website.assets_frontend">
        <xpath expr="." position="inside">
            <script src="/my_library/static/src/js/snippets.js"
                    type="text/javascript" />
        </xpath>
    </template>
```

After updating the module, you will be offered a new snippet called **Latest books**, which has an option to change the number of recently added books. We have also added the option to change the table design, which can be displayed when you click on the table.

How it works...

In the *first step*, we added a QWeb template for the new snippet (it is just like the previous recipe). Note that we have added a basic structure for the table. We will dynamically add lines for books in the table.

In the *second step*, we have registered our dynamic snippet, and we have added custom options to change the behavior of our dynamic snippet. The first option we have added is **Table Style**. It will be used to change the style of the table. The second option we have added is **No of Books**. We have used the `<we-select>` and `<we-button-group>` tags for our options. These tags will provide different GUIs to the snippet option. The `<we-select>` tag will show the options as a dropdown while the `<we-button-group>` tag will show the options as a button group. There are several other GUI options, such as `<we-checkbox>` and `<we-colorpicker>`. You can explore more GUI options in the `/addons/website/views/snippets/snippets.xml` file.

If you look at the options closely, you will see we have `data-select-class` and `data-select-data-attribute` attributes for the option buttons. This will let Odoo know which attribute to change when the user chooses an option. `data-select-class` will set the class attribute on the element when the user chooses this option, while `data-select-data-attribute` will set the custom attribute and value on the element. Note that it will use the value of `data-attribute-name` to set the attribute.

Now, we have added the snippets and snippet options. If you drag and drop the snippet at this point, you will only see the table header and the snippet options. Changing the snippet options will change the table style, but there is no book data yet. For that, we need to write some JavaScript code that will fetch the data and display it in the table. In *step 3*, we have added JavaScript code that will render the book data in the table. To map a JavaScript object to an HTML element, Odoo uses `PublicWidget`. Now, `PublicWidget` is available through the `require('web.public.widget')` module. The key attribute in using `PublicWidget` is the `selector` attribute. In the `selector` attribute, you will need to use the CSS selector of the element, and Odoo will automatically bind the element with `PublicWidget`. You can access the related element in the `$el` attribute. The rest of the code is basic JavaScript and jQuery except `_rpc`. The `_rpc` method is used to make network requests and fetch book data. We will learn more about the `_rpc` method in the *Making RPC calls to the server* recipe of *Chapter 15, Web Client Development*.

In the *last step*, we have added a JavaScript file to the assets.

There's more...

If you want to create your own snippet option, you can use the `t-js` option on the snippet option. After that, you will need to define your own option in the JavaScript code. Explore the `addons/website/static/src/js/editor/snippets.options.js` file to learn more about snippet options.

Getting input from website users

In website development, often you need to create forms to take input from the website users (visitors). In this recipe, we will create an HTML form for the page for users to report issues related to books.

Getting ready

For this recipe, we will be using the `my_library` module from the previous recipe. We will need a new model to store issues submitted by users.

So, before starting this recipe, modify the previous code:

1. Add a field in the `library.book` model and the new `book.issues` model, as follows:

    ```
    class LibraryBook(models.Model):
        _name = 'library.book'

        name = fields.Char('Title', required=True)
        date_release = fields.Date('Release Date')
        author_ids = fields.Many2many('res.partner',
    string='Authors')
        image = fields.Binary(attachment=True)
        html_description = fields.Html()
        book_issue_id = fields.One2many('book.issue', 'book_id')


    class LibraryBookIssues(models.Model):
        _name = 'book.issue'

        book_id = fields.Many2one('library.book',
    required=True)
        submitted_by = fields.Many2one('res.users')
        isuue_description = fields.Text()
    ```

2. Add a `book_issues_id` field in the book form view, as follows:

    ```
    ...
    <group string="Book Issues">
        <field name="book_issue_id" nolabel="1">
            <tree>
                <field name="create_date"/>
                <field name="submitted_by"/>
    ```

```
                <field name="isuue_description"/>
            </tree>
        </field>
</group>
...
```

3. Add access rights for the new `book.issue` model in the `ir.model.access.csv` file, as follows:

```
acl_book_issues,library.book_issue,model_book_issue,group_librarian,1,1,1,1
```

We have added a new model for the book issues, and now, we will add a new template with an HTML form.

How to do it...

Follow these steps to create a new route and template page for the issue page:

1. Add a new route in `main.py`, as follows:

```
@http.route('/books/submit_issues', type='http',
auth="user", website=True)
def books_issues(self, **post):
    if post.get('book_id'):
        book_id = int(post.get('book_id'))
        issue_description = post.get('issue_description')
        request.env['book.issue'].sudo().create({
            'book_id': book_id,
            'issue_description': issue_description,
            'submitted_by': request.env.user.id
        })
        return request.redirect('/books/submit_issues?submitted=1')

    return request.render('my_library.books_issue_form',
{
        'books': request.env['library.book'].search([]),
        'submitted': post.get('submitted', False)
    })
```

2. Add a template with an HTML form in it, as follows:

```
<template id="books_issue_form" name="Book Issues Form">
    <t t-call="website.layout">
```

```
            <div class="container mt32">
                <!-- add the page elements here(step 3 and 4)
-->
            </div>
        </t>
</template>
```

3. Add the conditional header for the page, as follows:

```
<t t-if="submitted">
    <h3 class="alert alert-success mt16 mb16">
        <i class="fa fa-thumbs-up"/>
        Book submitted successfully
    </h3>
    <h1> Report the another book issue </h1>
</t>
<t t-else="">
    <h1> Report the book issue </h1>
</t>
```

4. Add `<form>` to submit the issues as follows:

```
<div class="row mt16">
    <div class="col-6">
        <form method="post">
            <input type="hidden" name="csrf_token"
                    t-att-value="request.csrf_token()"/>
            <div class="form-group">
                <label>Select Book</label>
                <select class="form-control" name="book_id">
                    <t t-foreach="books" t-as="book">
                        <option t-att-value="book.id">
                            <t t-esc="book.name"/>
                        </option>
                    </t>
                </select>
            </div>
            <div class="form-group">
                <label>Issue Description</label>
                <textarea name="issue_description"
                        class="form-control"
                        placeholder="e.g. pages are missing"/>
            </div>
```

```
                <button type="submit" class="btn
btn-primary">
                    Submit
                </button>
            </form>
        </div>
    </div>
```

Update the module and open the /books/submit_issues URL. From this page, you will be able to submit the issues for the book. After submission, you can check them into the respective book form view in the backend.

How it works...

In *step 1* of this recipe, we created a route to submit book issues. The **post argument in the function will accept all query parameters in the URL. You will also get the submitted form data in the **post argument. In our example, we have used the same controller to display the pages and submit the issue. If we find data in the post, we will create a new issue in the book.issue model and then redirect the user to the issue page with the submitted query parameters, so the user can see that the acknowledgment issue is submitted and can therefore submit another issue if he/she wants.

> **Note**
> We have used sudo() to create a book issue record because a normal user (visitor) does not have access rights to create the new book issue record. This is despite it being necessary to create the book issue record if a user has submitted an issue from a web page. This is a practical example of the usage of sudo().

In *step 2*, we have created the template for the issue page. In *step 3*, we have added the conditional headers. The success header will be displayed after submitting an issue.

In *step 4*, we have added <form> with three fields: csrf_token, book selection, and issue description. The last two fields are used to get input from the website user. However, csrf_token is used to avoid a **Cross-Site Request Forgery** (**CSRF**) attack. If you do not use it in the form, the user won't be able to submit the form. When you submit the form, you will get the submitted data as the **post parameter in the books_issues() method of *step 1*.

> **Tip**
>
> In some cases, if you want to disable `csrf` validation, you can use `csrf=False` in the route, like this:
> `@http.route('/url', type='http',auth="user", website=True, csrf=False )`

There's more...

If you want, you can use separate routes page, and for the post data, which you can do by adding `action` to the form as follows:

```
...
<form action="/my_url" method="post">
...
```

Additionally, you can restrict the `get` requests by adding the `method` parameter in the route like this:

```
@http.route('/my_url', type='http', method='POST' auth="user", website=True)
```

Managing SEO options

Odoo provides built-in support for SEO for templates (pages). However, some templates are used in multiple URLs. For example, in an online shop, product pages are rendered with the same template and different product data. For these kinds of cases, we want separate SEO options for each URL.

Getting ready

For this recipe, we will be using the `my_library` module from the previous recipe. We will store separate SEO data for each book details page. Before developing this recipe, you should test the SEO options in the different book pages. You can get an SEO dialog from the **Promote** drop-down menu on the top, as shown in the following figure:

Figure 14.3 – Opening the SEO configuration for a page

If you test SEO options in different book details pages, you will notice that changing the SEO data in one book page will reflect on all book pages. We will fix this issue in this recipe.

How to do it...

To manage separate SEO options for each book, follow these steps:

1. Inherit the `website.seo.metadata` mixin in the `library.book` model, as follows:

   ```
   ...
   class LibraryBook(models.Model):
       _name = 'library.book'
       _inherit = ['website.seo.metadata']

       name = fields.Char('Title', required=True)
       date_release = fields.Date('Release Date')
   ...
   ```

2. Pass the `book` object in the book details route as `main_object`, as follows:

   ```
   ...
   @http.route('/books/<model("library.book"):book>',
   type='http', auth="user", website=True)
   def library_book_detail(self, book):
       return request.render(
           'my_library.book_detail', {
               'book': book,
               'main_object': book
           })
   ...
   ```

Update the module and change the SEO on the different book pages. It can be changed through the **Optimize SEO** option. Now, you will be able to manage separate SEO details per book.

How it works...

To enable SEO on each record of the model, you will need to inherit the `website.seo.metadata` mixin in your model. This will add a few fields and methods in the `library.book` model. These fields and methods will be used from the website to store separate data for each book.

> **Tip**
> If you want to see fields and methods for the SEO mixin, search for the `website.seo.metadata` model in the `/addons/website/models/website.py` file.

All SEO-related code is written in `website.layout` and it gets all the SEO meta-information from the recordset passed as `main_object`. Consequently, in *step 2*, we have passed a `book` object with the `main_object` key, so the website layout will get all SEO information from the book. If you don't pass `main_object` from the controller, then the template recordset will be passed as `main_object`, and that's why you were getting the same SEO data in all books.

There's more...

In Odoo, you can add custom metatags for Open Graph and Twitter sharing. If you want to add your custom metatags to a page, you can override `_default_website_meta()` after adding the SEO mixin. For example, if we want to use the book cover as the social sharing image, then we can use the following code in our book model:

```
def _default_website_meta(self):
    res = super(LibraryBook, self)._default_website_meta()
    res['default_opengraph']['og:image'] = self.env['website'].image_url(self, 'image')
    res['default_twitter']['twitter:image'] = self.env['website'].image_url(self, 'image')
    return res
```

After this, the book cover will be displayed on social media when you share the book's URL. Additionally, you can also set the page title and the description from the same method.

Managing sitemaps for the website

A website's sitemaps are crucial for any website. The search engine will use website sitemaps to index the pages of a website. In this recipe, we will add book details pages to the sitemap.

Getting ready...

For this recipe, we will be using the `my_library` module from the previous recipe. If you want to check the current sitemap in Odoo, open `<your_odoo_server_url>/sitemap.xml` in your browser. This will not have the book's URL in it.

How to do it...

Follow these steps to add a book's page to `sitemap.xml`:

1. Import the methods in `main.py`, as follows:

    ```
    from odoo.addons.http_routing.models.ir_http import slug
    from odoo.addons.website.models.ir_http import sitemap_qs2dom
    ```

2. Add the `sitemap_books` method to `main.py`, as follows:

    ```
    class Main(http.Controller):
    ...
        def sitemap_books(env, rule, qs):
            Books = env['library.book']
            dom = sitemap_qs2dom(qs, '/books', Books._rec_name)
            for f in Books.search(dom):
                loc = '/books/%s' % slug(f)
                if not qs or qs.lower() in loc:
                    yield {'loc': loc}
    ...
    ```

3. Add the `sitemap_books` function reference in a book's detail routes as follows:

    ```
    ...
    @http.route('/books/<model("library.book"):book>',
    type='http', auth="user", website=True, sitemap=sitemap_books)
        def library_book_detail(self, book):
    ...
    ```

Update the module to apply the changes. The `sitemap.xml` file is generated and stored in attachments. Then, it is regenerated every few hours. To see our changes, you will need to remove the sitemap file from the attachment. To do this, visit **Settings | Technical | Database Structure | Attachments**, search for the sitemap, and delete the file. Now, access the `/sitemap.xml` URL in a browser, and you will see the book's pages in the sitemap.

How it works...

In the *first step*, we have imported a few required functions. `slug` is used to generate a clean, user-friendly URL, based on a record name. `sitemap_qs2dom` is used to generate a domain based on route and query strings.

In *step 2*, we have created a Python generator function, `sitemap_books()`. This function will be called whenever a sitemap is generated. During the call, it will receive three arguments—the `env` Odoo environment, the `rule` route rule, and the `qs` query string. In the function, we have generated a domain with `sitemap_qs2dom`. Then, we used the generated domain to search the book records, which are used to generate the location through the `slug()` method. With `slug`, you will get a user-friendly URL, such as `/books/odoo-12-development-cookbook-1`, instead of `books/1`. If you do not want to list all the books on the sitemap, you can just use a valid domain in the search to filter the books.

In *step 3*, we have passed the `sitemap_books()` function reference to the route with a `sitemap` keyword.

There's more...

In this recipe, we have seen how you can use a custom method to generate a URL for a sitemap. But if you do not want to filter books and you want to list all books in a sitemap, then instead of the function reference, just pass `True` as follows:

```
...
@http.route('/books/<model("library.book"):book>', type='http',
auth="user", website=True, sitemap=True)
...
```

Getting a visitor's country information

The Odoo CMS has built-in support for **GeoIP**. In a live environment, you can track a visitor's country based on the IP address. In this recipe, we will get the country of the visitor based on the visitor's IP address.

Getting ready

For this recipe, we will be using the `my_library` module from the previous recipe. In this recipe, we will hide some books on the web page based on the visitor's country. You will need to download the GeoIP database for this recipe. After that, you will need to pass the database location from the `cli` option, like this:

```
./odoo-bin -c config_file --geoip-db=location_of_geoip_DB
```

How to do it...

Follow these steps to restrict books based on country:

1. Add the `restrict_country_ids` Many2many field in the `library.book` model, as follows:

   ```python
   class LibraryBook(models.Model):
       _name = 'library.book'
       _inherit = ['website.seo.metadata']

       ...
       restrict_country_ids = fields.Many2many('res.country')
       ...
   ```

2. Add a `restrict_country_ids` field in the form view of the `library.books` model, as follows:

   ```xml
   ...
   <group>
       <field name="date_release"/>
       <field name="restrict_country_ids" widget="many2many_tags"/>
   </group>
   ...
   ```

3. Update the `/books` controller to restrict books based on country, as follows:

   ```python
   @http.route('/books', type='http', auth="user", website=True)
   def library_books(self):
       country_id = False
       country_code = request.session.geoip and request.session.geoip.get('country_code') or False
       if country_code:
   ```

```
            country_ids = request.env['res.country'].sudo().
search([('code', '=', country_code)])
            if country_ids:
                country_id = country_ids[0].id
        domain = ['|', ('restrict_country_ids', '=', False),
('restrict_country_ids', 'not in', [country_id])]
        return request.render(
            'my_library.books', {
                'books': request.env['library.book'].
search(domain),
            })
```

Update the module to apply the changes. Add your country in the restricted country field of the book, and access /book. Restricted books will not be shown on the list.

> **Warning**
>
> This recipe does not work with the local server. It will require a hosted server, because with the local machine, you will get the local IP, which is not related to any country.
>
> You will also need to configure NGINX properly.

How it works...

In the *first step*, we added a new `restricted_country_ids` many2many type field in the `library.book` model. We will hide the book if the website visitor is from a restricted country.

In *step 2*, we have just added a `restricted_country_ids` field in the book's form view. If GeoIP and NGINX are configured properly, Odoo will add GeoIP information to `request.session.geoip`, and then you can get the country code from that.

In the *third step*, we have fetched the country code from GeoIP, followed by the recordset of the country, based on `country_code`. After getting a visitor's country information, we filtered books with domains based on a restricted country.

> **Important information**
>
> If you don't have a real server and you want to test this anyway, you can add a default country code in the controller, like this:
> `country_code = request.session.geoip and request.session.geoip.get('country_code') or 'IN'`

The GeoIP database gets updated from time to time, so you will need to update your copy to get up-to-date country information.

Tracking a marketing campaign

In any business or service, it is really important to be familiar with the **Return on Investment** (**ROI**). The ROI is used to evaluate the effectiveness of an investment. Investments in ads can be tracked through **UTM** codes. A UTM code is a small string that you can add to a URL. This UTM code will help you to track campaigns, sources, and media.

Getting ready

For this recipe, we will be using the `my_library` module from the previous recipe. Odoo has built-in support for UTMs. With our library application, we don't have any practical case where UTMs can be used. However, in this recipe, we will add a UTM in the issues generated by `/books/submit_issues` in `my_library`.

How to do it...

Follow these steps to link UTMs in a book issue generated from our web page to the `/books/submit_issues` URL:

1. Add a `utm` module in the `depends` section of `manifest.py`, as follows:

    ```python
    'depends': ['base', 'website', 'utm'],
    ```

2. Inherit `utm.mixin` in the `book.issue` model, as follows:

    ```python
    class LibraryBookIssues(models.Model):
        _name = 'book.issue'
        _inherit = ['utm.mixin']

        book_id = fields.Many2one('library.book', required=True)
        submitted_by = fields.Many2one('res.users')
        issue_description = fields.Text()
    ```

3. Add a `campaign_id` field in the tree view of the `book_issue_ids` field, as follows:

```
...
<group string="Book Issues">
    <field name="book_issue_ids" nolabel="1">
        <tree name="Book isuues">
            <field name="create_date"/>
            <field name="submitted_by"/>
            <field name="issue_description"/>
            <field name="campaign_id"/>
        </tree>
    </field>
</group>
...
```

Update the module to apply the changes. To test the UTM, you need to perform the following steps:

1. In Odoo, a UTM is processed based on cookies, and some browsers do not support cookies in the localhost, so if you are testing it with the localhost, access the instance with `http://127.0.0.1:8069`.

   By default, UTM tracking is blocked for salespeople. Consequently, to test the UTM feature, you need to log in with a portal user.

2. Now, open the URL: `http://127.0.0.1:8069/books/submit_issues?utm_campaign=sale`.

3. Submit the book issue and check the book issue in the backend. This will display the campaign in the book's form view.

How it works...

In the first step, we have inherited `utm.mixin` in the `book.issue` model. This will add the following fields to the `book.issue` model:

- `campaign_id`: The Many2one field with the `utm.campaign` model. This is used to track different campaigns, such as the *Summer and Christmas Special*.
- `source_id`: The Many2one field with the `utm.source` model. This is used to track different sources, such as search engines and other domains.
- `medium_id`: The Many2one field with the `utm.medium` model. This is used to track different media, such as postcards, emails, and banner ads.

To track the campaign, medium, and source, you need to share a URL in the marketing media like this: `your_url?utm_campaign=campaign_name&utm_medium=medium_name&utm_source=source_name`.

If a visitor visits your website from any marketing media, then the `campaign_id`, `source_id`, and `medium_id` fields are automatically filled when records are created on the website page.

In our example, we have just tracked `campaign_id`, but you can also add `source_id` and `medium_id`.

> **Important note**
>
> In our test example, we have used `campaign_id=sale`. Now, `sale` is the name of the record in the `utm.campaign` model. By default, the `utm` module adds a few records of the campaign, medium, and source. The `sale` record is one of them. If you want to create a new campaign, medium, and source, you can do this by visiting the `Link Tracker > UTMs` menu in developer mode.

Managing multiple websites

Odoo has built-in support for multiple websites. This means that the same Odoo instance can be run on multiple domains as well as when displaying different records.

Getting ready

For this recipe, we will be using the `my_library` module from the previous recipe. In this recipe, we will hide books based on the website.

How to do it...

Follow these steps to make the online website multi-website-compatible:

1. Add `website.multi.mixin` in the `library.book` model, as follows:

    ```python
    class LibraryBook(models.Model):
        _name = 'library.book'
        _inherit = ['website.seo.metadata', 'website.multi.mixin']
        ...
    ```

2. Add `website_id` in the book form view, as follows:

    ```xml
    ...
    <group>
        <field name="author_ids" widget="many2many_tags"/>
        <field name="website_id"/>
    </group>
    ...
    ```

3. Modify the domain in the `/books` controller, as follows:

    ```python
    @http.route('/books', type='http', auth="user", website=True)
    def library_books(self, **post):
        ...
        domain = ['|', ('restrict_country_ids', '=', False), ('restrict_country_ids', 'not in', [country_id])]
        domain += request.website.website_domain()
        return request.render(
            'my_library.books', {
                'books': request.env['library.book'].search(domain),
            })
        ...
    ```

4. Import `werkzeug` and modify a book details controller to restrict book access from another website, as follows:

    ```python
    import werkzeug
    ...
    @http.route('/books/<model("library.book"):book>', type='http', auth="user", website=True, sitemap=sitemap_books)
    def library_book_detail(self, book, **post):
    ```

```
    if not book.can_access_from_current_website():
        raise werkzeug.exceptions.NotFound()
    return request.render(
        'my_library.book_detail', {
            'book': book,
            'main_object': book
    })
...
```

Update the module to apply the changes. To test this module, set different websites in some books. Now, open the /books URL and check the list of books. After this, change the website and check the list of books. For testing, you can change the website from the website switcher drop-down menu. Refer to the following screenshot to do that:

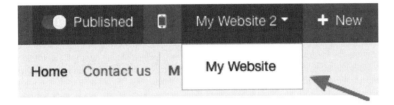

Figure 14.4 – Website switcher

You can also try to access the book details directly from the URL, such as for /books/1. If a book is not from that website, it will show as 404.

How it works...

In the *first step*, we added website.multi.mixin. This mixin adds a basic utility to handle multiple websites in the model. This mixin adds the website_id field in the model. This field is used to determine which website a record is meant for.

In *step 2*, we added the website_id field in the form view of the book, so the books will be filtered based on the website.

In *step 3*, we have modified the domain used to find a list of books. request.website.website_domain() will return the domain that filters out the books that are not from the website.

> **Important note**
> Notice that there are records that do not have any website_id set. Such records will be displayed on all websites. This means that if you don't have a website_id field on a particular book, then that book will be displayed on all websites.

Then, we added the domain in the web search, as follows:

- In *step 4*, we restricted book access. If the book is not meant for the current website, then we will raise a `not found` error. The `can_access_from_current_website()` method will return the value `True` if a book record is meant for the currently active website and `False` if a book record is meant for another website.

- If you noticed, we added `**post` in both controllers. This is because without it, `**post /books` and `/books/<model:library.book:book>` will not accept a query parameter. They will also generate an error while switching the website from the website switcher, so we added it. Normally, it is a good practice to add `**post` in every controller so that they can handle query parameters.

Redirecting old URLs

When you move to the Odoo website from an existing system or website, you must redirect your old URLs to new URLs. With proper redirection, all of your SEO rankings will be moved to new pages. In this recipe, we will see how to redirect old URLs to new URLs in Odoo.

Getting ready

For this recipe, we will be using the `my_library` module from the previous recipe. For this recipe, we are assuming that you used to have an website and have just moved to Odoo.

How to do it...

Imagine that, in your old website, books were listed at the `/library` URL, and as you know, the `my_library` module lists books on the `/books` URL as well. So, now we will add a **redirection** rule in Odoo that will redirect your old `/library` URL to the new `/books` URL. Perform the following steps to add the redirection rule:

1. Activate developer mode.
2. Open **Website | Configuration | Redirects**.
3. Click on **Create** to add a new rule.
4. Enter values in the form as shown in the following figure. In **URL from**, enter `/library`, and in **URL to**, enter `/books`.

5. Select the **Action** value of **301 Moved permanently**.
6. Save the record. Once you have filled in the data, your form will look like this:

Figure 14.5 – Redirection rule

Once you have added this rule, open the `/library` page. You will notice that the page gets redirected automatically to the `/books` page.

How it works...

Page redirection is simple; it's just part of the HTTP protocol. In our example, we have moved `/library` to `/books`. We have used a **301 Moved permanently** redirect for redirection. Here are all the redirection options that are available in Odoo:

- **404 Not Found**: This option is used if you want to give a `404 Not Found` response for a page. Note that Odoo will display the default `404` page for such requests.

- **301 Moved permanently**: This option redirects old URLs to new ones permanently. This type of redirection will move the SEO rankings to a new page.

- **302 Moved temporarily**: This option redirects old URLs to new ones temporarily. Use this option when you need to redirect a URL for a limited time. This type of redirection will not move the SEO rankings to a new page.

- **308 Redirect/Rewrite**: An interesting option – with this, you will be able to change/rewrite existing Odoo URLs to new ones. In this recipe, this would allow us to rewrite the old `/library` URL to the new `/books` URL. Hence, we would have no need to redirect the old URL by using the **301 Moved permanently** rule for `/library`.

There are a few more fields on the redirection rule form. One of them is the **Active** field, which can used if you want to enable/disable rules from time to time. The second important field is **Website**. The **Website** field is used when you are using the multi-website feature and you want to limit the redirection rule to one website only. By default, however, the rule will be applied to all websites.

Publish management for website-related records

In business flows, there are some cases where you need to allow or revoke page access to public users. One such case is e-commerce products, where you need to publish or unpublish products based on availability. In this recipe, we will see how you can publish and unpublish book records for public users.

Getting ready

For this recipe, we will be using the `my_library` module from the previous recipe.

> **Important note**
>
> If you notice, we have put `auth='user'` on the `/books` and `/books/<model("library.book"):book>` routes. Please change this to `auth='public'` to make those URLs accessible for public users.

How to do it...

Perform the following steps to enable a publish/unpublish option for book detail pages:

1. Add `website.published.mixin` to the `library.book` model like this:

    ```python
    class LibraryBook(models.Model):
        _name = 'library.book'
        _description = 'Library Book'
        _inherit = ['website.seo.metadata', 'website.published.mixin']
        ...
    ```

2. Add a new file to `my_library/security/rules.xml` and add a record rule for the books like this (make sure you register the file in the manifest):

    ```xml
    <?xml version="1.0" encoding="utf-8"?>
    <odoo noupdate="1">
        <record id="books_rule_portal_public" model="ir.rule">
            <field name="name">
                Portal/Public user: read published books
            </field>
    ```

```xml
            <field name="model_id"
                    ref="my_library.model_library_book"/>
            <field name="groups"
                    eval="[(4, ref('base.group_portal')),
                           (4, ref('base.group_public'))]"/>
            <field name="domain_force">
                [('website_published','=', True)]
            </field>
            <field name="perm_read" eval="True"/>
        </record>
</odoo>
```

3. Update the `my_library` module to apply the changes. Now you can publish and unpublish book pages:

Figure 14.6 – The publish/unpublish button

To publish/unpublish books, you can use the toggle shown in the preceding screenshot of a book detail page.

How it works...

Odoo provides a ready-made **mixin** to handle publish management for your records. It does most of the job for you. All you need to do is add `website.published.mixin` to your model. In *step 1*, we added `website.published.mixin` to our books model. This will add all the fields and methods required to publish and unpublish books. Once you add this mixin to the books model, you will be able to see the button to toggle the state on the book detail page, as shown in the preceding figure.

> **Note**
>
> We are sending a book record as `main_object` from our book details route. Without this, you will not be able to see the publish/unpublish button on the book detail page.

Adding the mixin will show the publish/unpublish button on the book's detail page, but it will not restrict a public user from accessing it. To do this, we need to add a record rule. In *step 2*, we added a record rule to restrict access to unpublished books. If you want to learn more about record rules, refer to *Chapter 10, Security Access*.

There's more...

The publish mixin will enable the publish/unpublish button on the website. But if you want to show a redirect button on the backend form view, the publish mixin can provide a means for that too. The following steps show how to add a redirect button to a book's form view:

1. Add a method in the `library.book` model to compute the URL for a book:

    ```python
    @api.depends('name')
    def _compute_website_url(self):
        for book in self:
            book.website_url = '/books/%s' % (slug(book))
    ```

2. Add a button in the form view to redirect to the website:

    ```xml
    ...
    <sheet>
        <div class="oe_button_box" name="button_box">
            <field name="is_published"
                widget="website_redirect_button"/>
        </div>
    ...
    ```

Once you add the button, you will be able to see the button in the book's form view, and by clicking on it, you will be redirected to the book's detail page.

15
Web Client Development

Odoo's web client, or backend, is where employees spend most of their time. In *Chapter 9, Backend Views,* you saw how to use the existing possibilities that backends offer. Here, we'll take a look at how to extend and customize those possibilities. The web module contains everything related to the user interface in Odoo.

All of the code in this chapter will depend on the web module. As you know, Odoo has two different editions (Enterprise and Community). Community uses the web module for user interfaces, while the Enterprise version uses an extended version of the Community web module, which is the web_enterprise module.

The Enterprise version provides some extra features compared with the Community web, including mobile compatibility, searchable menus, and material design. We'll work on the Community Edition here. Don't worry—the modules developed in Community work perfectly in the Enterprise Edition because, internally, web_enterprise depends on the Community web module and just adds some features to it.

> **Important information**
>
> Odoo 14 is a bit unique for the backend web client compared to other Odoo versions. It contains two different frameworks to maintain the GUI of the Odoo backend. The first one is the widget-based legacy framework, and the second one is the component-based modern framework called the **Odoo Web Library (OWL)**. OWL is the new UI framework introduced in Odoo v14. Both use QWeb templates for structure, but there are significant changes in the syntax and the way those frameworks work.
>
> Although Odoo 14 has a new framework OWL, Odoo does not use this new framework everywhere. Most of the web client is still written with the old widget-based framework. In this chapter, we will see how to customize the web client using a widget-based framework. In the next chapter, we will look at the OWL framework.

In this chapter, you will learn how to create new field widgets to get input from users. We will also be creating a new view from scratch. After reading this chapter, you will be able to create your own UI elements in the Odoo backend.

> **Note**
>
> Odoo's user interface heavily depends on JavaScript. Throughout this chapter, we will assume you have a basic knowledge of JavaScript, jQuery, Underscore.js, and SCSS.

In this chapter, we will cover the following recipes:

- Creating custom widgets
- Using client-side QWeb templates
- Making RPC calls to the server
- Creating a new view
- Debugging your client-side code
- Improving onboarding with tours
- Mobile app JavaScript

Technical requirements

The technical requirements for this chapter include the online Odoo platform.

All the code used in this chapter can be downloaded from the GitHub repository at `https://github.com/PacktPublishing/Odoo-14-Development-Cookbook-Fourth-Edition/tree/master/Chapter15`.

Creating custom widgets

As you saw in *Chapter 9*, *Backend Views*, we can use widgets to display certain data in different formats. For example, we used `widget='image'` to display a binary field as an image. To demonstrate how to create your own widget, we'll write one widget that lets the user choose an `integer` field, but we will display it differently. Instead of an input box, we will display a color picker so that we can select a color number. Here, each number will be mapped to its related color.

Getting ready

For this recipe, we will be using the `my_library` module with basic fields and views. You will find the basic `my_library` module in the `Chapter15/00_initial_module` directory in the GitHub repository.

How to do it...

We'll add a JavaScript file that contains our widget's logic, and an SCSS file to do some styling. Then, we will add one integer field to the books form to use our new widget. Perform the following steps to add a new field widget:

1. Add a `static/src/js/field_widget.js` file. For the syntax that's used here, refer to the *Extending CSS and JavaScript for the website* recipe from *Chapter 14*, *CMS Website Development*:

    ```
    odoo.define('my_field_widget', function (require) {
    "use strict";

    var AbstractField = require('web.AbstractField');
    var fieldRegistry = require('web.field_registry');
    ```

2. Create your widget by extending `AbstractField`:

    ```
    var colorField = AbstractField.extend({
    ```

3. Set the CSS class, root element tag, and supported field types for the widget:

   ```
   className: 'o_int_colorpicker',
   tagName: 'span',
   supportedFieldTypes: ['integer'],
   ```

4. Capture some JavaScript events:

   ```
   events: {
       'click .o_color_pill': 'clickPill',
   },
   ```

5. Override `init` to do some initialization:

   ```
   init: function () {
       this.totalColors = 10;
       this._super.apply(this, arguments);
   },
   ```

6. Override `_renderEdit` and `_renderReadonly` to set up the DOM elements:

   ```
   _renderEdit: function () {
       this.$el.empty();
       for (var i = 0; i < this.totalColors; i++ ) {
           var className = "o_color_pill o_color_" + i;
           if (this.value === i ) {
               className += ' active';
           }
           this.$el.append($('<span>', {
               'class': className,
               'data-val': i,
           }));
       }
   },
   _renderReadonly: function () {
       var className = "o_color_pill active readonly o_color_" + this.value;
       this.$el.append($('<span>', {
           'class': className,
       }));
   },
   ```

7. Define the handlers we referred to earlier:

   ```
   clickPill: function (ev) {
       var $target = $(ev.currentTarget);
   ```

```
                var data = $target.data();
                this._setValue(data.val.toString());
            }
    });      // closing AbstractField
```

8. Don't forget to register your widget:

   ```
   fieldRegistry.add('int_color', colorField);
   ```

9. Make it available for other add-ons:

   ```
   return {
       colorField: colorField,
   };
   });   // closing 'my_field_widget' namespace
   ```

10. Add some SCSS in `static/src/scss/field_widget.scss`:

    ```
    .o_int_colorpicker {
        .o_color_pill {
            display: inline-block;
            height: 25px;
            width: 25px;
            margin: 4px;
            border-radius: 25px;
            position: relative;
            @for $size from 1 through length($o-colors) {
                &.o_color_#{$size - 1} {
                    background-color: nth($o-colors, $size);
                    &:not(.readonly):hover {
                        transform: scale(1.2);
                        transition: 0.3s;
                        cursor: pointer;
                    }
                    &.active:after{
                        content: "\f00c";
                        display: inline-block;
                        font: normal 14px/1 FontAwesome;
                        font-size: inherit;
                        color: #fff;
                        position: absolute;
                        padding: 4px;
                        font-size: 16px;
                    }
    ```

```
            }
        }
    }
}
```

11. Register both files in the backend assets in `views/templates.xml`:

    ```xml
    <?xml version="1.0" encoding="UTF-8"?>
    <odoo>
        <template id="assets_end" inherit_id="web.assets_backend">
            <xpath expr="." position="inside">
                <script src="/my_library /static/src/js/field_widget.js"
                        type="text/javascript" />
                <link href="/my_library/static/src/scss/field_widget.scss"
                      rel="stylesheet" type="text/scss" />
            </xpath>
        </template>
    </odoo>
    ```

12. Finally, add the color `integer` field to the `library.book` model:

    ```
    color = fields.Integer()
    ```

13. Add the color field to the book's `form` view, and then add `widget="int_color"`:

    ```xml
    ...
    <group>
        <field name="date_release"/>
        <field name="color" widget="int_color"/>
    </group>
    ...
    ```

Update the module to apply the changes. After the update, open the book's `form` view and you will see the color picker, as shown in the following screenshot:

Figure 15.1 – How the custom widget is displayed

How it works...

So that you can understand our example, let's go over the life cycle of the widget by looking at its components:

- `init()`: This is the widget constructor. It is used for initialization purposes. When the widget is initialized, this method is called first.
- `willStart()`: This method is called when the widget is initialized and in the process of being appended in the DOM. It is used to initialize asynchronous data in the widget. It is also supposed to return a deferred object, which can be obtained simply from a `super()` call. We will use this method in the subsequent recipe.
- `start()`: This method is called after the widget has completed the rendering, but has not yet been added to the DOM. It is very useful for a post-rendering job and is supposed to return a deferred object. You can access a rendered element in `this.$el`.
- `destroy()`: This method is called when the widget is destroyed. It is mostly used for basic cleanup operations, such as event unbinding.

> **Important information**
> The fundamental base class for widgets is `Widget` (defined by `web.Widget`). If you want to dig further into this, you can study it at `/addons/web/static/src/js/core/widget.js`.

In *step 1*, we imported `AbstractField` and `fieldRegistry`.

In *step 2*, we created `colorField` by extending `AbstractField`. Through this, `colorField` will get all the properties and methods from `AbstractField`.

In *step 3*, we added three properties: `className` is used to define the class for the root element of the widget; `tagName` is used for the root element type; and `supportedFieldTypes` is used for deciding which type of fields are supported by this widget. In our case, we want to create a widget for the integer type field.

In *step 4*, we mapped the events of our widget. Usually, the key is a combination of the event name and the optional CSS selector. The event and CSS selector are separated by a space, and the value will be the name of the widget method. So, when the event is performed, the assigned method is called automatically. In this recipe, when a user clicks on the color pill, we want to set the integer value in the field. To manage click events, we have added a CSS selector and the method name to the `events` key.

In *step 5*, we overrode the `init` method and set the value of the `this.totalColors` attribute. We will use this variable to decide on the number of color pills. We want to display 10 color pills, so we assigned the value of `10`.

In *step 6*, we added two methods—`_renderEdit` and `_renderReadonly`. As their names suggest, `_renderEdit` was called when the widget was in edit mode, and `_renderReadonly` was called when the widget was in read-only mode. In the `edit` method, we added a few `<span>` tags, with each representing a separate color in the widget. Upon clicking the `<span>` tag, we will set the value in the field. We added them to `this.$el`. Here, $el is the root element of the widget, and it will be added in the form view. In read-only mode, we just want to display the active color, so we added a single pill via the `_renderReadonly()` method. For now, we have added pills in a hardcoded way, but in the next recipe, we will use a JavaScript QWeb template to render the pills. Note that in the `edit` method, we used the `totalColors` property, which was set from the `init()` method.

In *step 7*, we added the `clickPill` handler method to manage pill clicks. To set the field value, we used the `_setValue` method. This method is added from the `AbstractField` class. When you set the field value, the Odoo framework will rerender the widget and call the `_renderEdit` method again so that you can render the widget with the updated values.

In *step 8*, after we've defined our new widget, it's crucial to register it with the form widget registry, which lives in `web.field_registry`. Note that all view types look at this registry, so if you want to create another way of displaying a field in a list view, you can also add your widget here and set the widget attribute on the field in the view definition.

Finally, we exported our widget class so that other add-ons can extend it or inherit from it. Then, we added a new integer field called `color` to the `library.book` model. We also added the same field to the `form` view with the `widget="int_color"` attribute. This will display our widget in the form instead of the default integer widget.

There's more...

The `web.mixins` namespace defines a couple of very helpful `mixin` classes that you should not miss out on when developing form widgets. You have already used these mixins in this recipe. The `AbstractField` is created by inheriting from the `Widget` class, and the `Widget` class inherits two mixins. The first one is `EventDispatcherMixin`, which offers a simple interface for attaching event handlers and triggering them. The second one is `ServicesMixin`, which provides functions for RPC calls and actions..

> **Important tip**
> When you want to override a method, always study the base class to see what the function is supposed to return. A very common cause of bugs is forgetting to return the super user's deferred object, which causes trouble with asynchronous operations.

Widgets are responsible for validation. Use the `isValid` function to implement your customization of this aspect.

Using client-side QWeb templates

Just as it's a bad habit to programmatically create HTML code in JavaScript, you should only create the minimum amount of DOM elements in your client-side JavaScript code. Fortunately, there's a templating engine available for the client side, too, and even more fortunately, the client-side templating engine has the same syntax as the server-side templates.

Getting ready

For this recipe, we will be using the `my_library` module from the previous recipe. We will make this more modular by moving the DOM element creation to QWeb.

How to do it...

We need to add the QWeb definition to the manifest and change the JavaScript code so that we can use it. Perform the following steps to get started:

1. Import `web.core` and extract the `qweb` reference to a variable, as shown in the following code:

```javascript
odoo.define('my_field_widget', function (require) {
"use strict";

var AbstractField = require('web.AbstractField');
var fieldRegistry = require('web.field_registry');
var core = require('web.core');

var qweb = core.qweb;
...
```

2. Change the `_renderEdit` function to simply render the element (inherited from `widget`):

   ```
   _renderEdit: function () {
       this.$el.empty();
       var pills = qweb.render('FieldColorPills',
   {widget: this});
       this.$el.append(pills);
   },
   ```

3. Add the template file to `static/src/xml/qweb_template.xml`:

   ```
   <?xml version="1.0" encoding="UTF-8"?>
   <templates>
       <t t-name="FieldColorPills">
           <t t-foreach="widget.totalColors" t-as='pill_no'>
               <span t-attf-class="o_color_pill o_color_#{pill_no} #{widget.value === pill_no and 'active' or ''}"
                   t-att-data-val="pill_no"/>
           </t>
       </t>
   </templates>
   ```

4. Register the QWeb file in your manifest:

   ```
   "qweb": [
       'static/src/xml/qweb_template.xml',
   ],
   ```

Now, with other add-ons, it is much easier to change the HTML code our widget uses because they can simply override it with the usual QWeb patterns.

How it works...

As there is already a comprehensive discussion on the basics of QWeb in the *Creating or modifying templates – QWeb* recipe from *Chapter 14, CMS Website Development*, we'll focus on what is different here. First of all, you need to realize that we're dealing with the JavaScript QWeb implementation, as opposed to the Python implementation on the server side. This means that you don't have access to browsing records or the environment; you only have access to the parameters you have passed from the `qweb.render` function.

In our case, we have passed the current object via the `widget` key. This means that you should have all the intelligence in the widget's JavaScript code and have your template only access properties, or possibly functions. Given that we can access all the properties that are available on the widget, we can simply check the value in the template by checking the `totalColors` property.

As client-side QWeb has nothing to do with QWeb views, there's a different mechanism to make those templates known to the web client—add them via the `qweb` key to your add-on's manifest in a list of filenames relative to the add-on's root.

> **Note**
>
> If you do not want to list your QWeb template in the manifest, you can use the `xmlDependencies` key on the snippet to lazily load the template. With `xmlDependencies`, the QWeb template is only loaded when the widget is being initialized.

There's more...

The reason for going to the effort of using QWeb here was extensibility, and this is the second big difference between client-side and server-side QWeb. On the client side, you can't use XPath expressions; you need to use jQuery selectors and operations. If, for example, we want to add user icons to our widget from another module, we'll use the following code to have an icon in each pill:

```
<t t-extend="FieldColorPills">
    <t t-jquery="span" t-operation="prepend">
        <i class="fa fa-user" />
    </t>
</t>
```

If we also provided a `t-name` attribute here, we'd have made a copy of the original template and left that one untouched. Other possible values for the `t-operation` attribute are `append`, `before`, `after`, `inner`, and `replace`, which causes the content of the `t` element to either be appended to the content of the matched element via `append`, put before or after the matched element via `before` or `after`, the content of the matched element replaced via `inner`, or the complete element replaced via `replace`. There's also `t-operation='attributes'`, which allows you to set an attribute on the matched element, following the same rules as server-side QWeb.

Another difference is that the names in client-side QWeb are not namespaced by the module name, so you have to choose names for your templates that are probably unique over all add-ons you install, which is why developers tend to choose rather long names.

See also

If you want to learn more about the QWeb templates, refer to the following points:

- The client-side QWeb engine has less convenient error messages and handling than other parts of Odoo. A small error often means that nothing happens, and it's hard for beginners to continue from there.

- Fortunately, there are some debug statements for client-side QWeb templates that will be described later in this chapter, in the *Debugging your client-side code* recipe.

Making RPC calls to the server

Sooner or later, your widget will need to look up some data from the server. In this recipe, we will add a tooltip on the color pill. When the user hovers their cursor over the color pill element, the tooltip will show the number of books related to that color. We will make an RPC call to the server to fetch a book count of the data associated with that particular color.

Getting ready

For this recipe, we will be using the `my_library` module from the previous recipe.

How to do it...

Perform the following steps to make an RPC call to the server and display the result in a tooltip:

1. Add the `willStart` method and set `colorGroupData` in the RPC call:

    ```
    willStart: function () {
        var self = this;
        this.colorGroupData = {};
        var colorDataPromise = this._rpc({
            model: this.model,
            method: 'read_group',
            domain: [],
            fields: ['color'],
            groupBy: ['color'],
        }).then(function (result) {
            _.each(result, function (r) {
                self.colorGroupData[r.color] = r.color_count;
            });
    ```

```
            });
            return Promise.all([this._super.apply(this,
arguments), colorDataPromise]);
        },
```

2. Update `_renderEdit` and set up a bootstrap `tooltip` on `pills`:

```
        _renderEdit: function () {
            this.$el.empty();
            var pills = qweb.render('FieldColorPills',
{widget: this});
            this.$el.append(pills);
            this.$el.find('[data-toggle="tooltip"]').
tooltip();
        },
```

3. Update the `FieldColorPills` template and add the `tooltip` data:

```
<t t-name="FieldColorPills">
    <t t-foreach="widget.totalColors" t-as='pill_no'>
        <span t-attf-class="o_color_pill o_color_#{pill_
no} #{widget.value === pill_no and 'active' or ''}"
            t-att-data-val="pill_no"
            data-toggle="tooltip"
            data-placement="top"
            t-attf-title="This color is used in #{widget.
colorGroupData[pill_no] or 0 } books."
            />
    </t>
</t>
```

Update the module to apply the changes. After the update, you will be able to see a tooltip on the pills, as shown in the following screenshot:

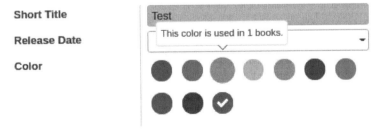

Figure 15.2 – Tooltip that uses the data obtained from RPC

How it works...

The `willStart` function is called before rendering and, more importantly, it returns a `Promise` object that must be resolved before the rendering starts. So, in a case like ours, where we need to run an asynchronous action before rendering can occur, this is the right function to do this.

When dealing with data access, we rely on the `_rpc` function provided by the `ServicesMixin` class, as we explained earlier. This function allows you to call any public function on models such as `search`, `read`, `write`, or, in this case, `read_group`.

In *step 1*, we made an RPC call and invoked the `read_group` method on the current model, which is `library.book` in our case. We grouped data based on the `color` field, so that the RPC call will return book data that was grouped by `color` and add an aggregate in the `color_count` key. We also mapped the `color_count` and `color` index in the `colorGroupData` so that we could use it in the QWeb template. In the last line of the function, we resolved `willStart` with `super` and our RPC call using `$.when`. Because of this, rendering only occurs after the values are fetched and after any asynchronous action `super` that was busy earlier, has finished, too.

Step 2 is nothing special. We just initialized the bootstrap tooltip.

In *step 3*, we used `colorGroupData` to set the attributes that are needed to display the tooltip. In the `willStart` method, we assigned a color map via `this.colorGroupData`, so that you can access them in the QWeb template via `widget.colorGroupData`. This is because we passed the widget reference; this is the `qweb.render` method.

> **Note**
>
> You can use `_rpc` anywhere in the widget. Note that it is an asynchronous call, and you need to manage a deferred object properly to get the desired result.

There's more...

The `AbstractField` class comes with a couple of interesting properties, one of which we just used. In our example, we used the `this.model` property, which holds the name of the current model (for example, `library.book`). Another property is `this.field`, which contains roughly the output of the model's `fields_get()` function for the field the widget is displaying. This will give all the information related to the current field. For example, for `x2x` fields, the `fields_get()` function gives you information about the co-model or the domain. You can also use this to query the field's string, size, or whatever other property you can set on the field during model definition.

Another helpful property is `nodeOptions`, which contains data passed via the `options` attribute in the `<form>` view definition. This is already JSON parsed, so you can access it like any object. For more information on such properties, dig further into the `abstract_field.js` file.

See also

Refer to the following documentation if you have issues managing asynchronous operations:

- Odoo's RPC returns JavaScript's native `Promise` object. You will get requested data once `Promise` is resolved. You can learn more about `Promise` here: https://developer.mozilla.org/en-US/docs/Web/JavaScript/Reference/Global_Objects/Promise.

Creating a new view

As you saw in *Chapter 9, Backend Views*, there are different kinds of views, such as form, list, and kanban. In this recipe, we will create a brand-new view. This view will display the list of authors, along with their books.

Getting ready

For this recipe, we will be using the `my_library` module from the previous recipe. Note that views are very complex structures, and each existing view has a different purpose and implementation. The purpose of this recipe is to make you aware of the MVC pattern view and how to create simple views. In this recipe, we will create a view called `m2m_group`, the purpose of which is to display records in groups. To divide records into different groups, the view will use the `many2many` field data. In the `my_library` module, we have the `author_ids` field. Here, we will group books based on authors and display them in cards.

In addition, we will add a new button to the control panel. With the help of this button, you will be able to add a new book record. We will also add a button to the author's card so that we can redirect users to another view.

How to do it...

Perform the following steps to add a new view called `m2m_group`:

1. Add a new view type in `ir.ui.view`:

   ```python
   class View(models.Model):
       _inherit = 'ir.ui.view'

       type = fields.Selection(selection_add=[('m2m_group', 'M2m Group')])
   ```

2. Add a new view mode in `ir.actions.act_window.view`:

   ```python
   class ActWindowView(models.Model):
       _inherit = 'ir.actions.act_window.view'

       view_mode = fields.Selection(selection_add=[('m2m_group', 'M2m group')], ondelete={'m2m_group': 'cascade'})
   ```

3. Add a new method by inheriting from the `base` model. This method will be called from the JavaScript model (see *step 4* for more details):

   ```python
   class Base(models.AbstractModel):
       _inherit = 'base'

       @api.model
       def get_m2m_group_data(self, domain, m2m_field):
           records = self.search(domain)
           result_dict = {}
           for record in records:
               for m2m_record in record[m2m_field]:
                   if m2m_record.id not in result_dict:
                       result_dict[m2m_record.id] = {
                           'name': m2m_record.display_name,
                           'children': [],
                           'model': m2m_record._name
                       }
                   result_dict[m2m_record.id]['children'].append({
                       'name': record.display_name,
                       'id': record.id,
                   })
           return result_dict
   ```

4. Add a new file called /static/src/js/m2m_group_model.js and add the following content to it:

```javascript
odoo.define('m2m_group.Model', function (require) {
    'use strict';

    var AbstractModel = require('web.AbstractModel');

    var M2mGroupModel = AbstractModel.extend({
        __get: function () {
            return this.data;
        },
        __load: function (params) {
            this.modelName = params.modelName;
            this.domain = params.domain;
            this.m2m_field = params.m2m_field;
            return this._fetchData();
        },
        __reload: function (handle, params) {
            if ('domain' in params) {
                this.domain = params.domain;
            }
            return this._fetchData();
        },
        _fetchData: function () {
            var self = this;
            return this._rpc({
                model: this.modelName,
                method: 'get_m2m_group_data',
                kwargs: {
                    domain: this.domain,
                    m2m_field: this.m2m_field
                }
            }).then(function (result) {
                self.data = result;
            });
        },
    });

    return M2mGroupModel;

});
```

5. Add a new file called /static/src/js/m2m_group_controller.js and add the following content to it:

```javascript
odoo.define('m2m_group.Controller', function (require) {
    'use strict';

    var AbstractController = require('web.AbstractController');
    var core = require('web.core');
    var qweb = core.qweb;

    var M2mGroupController = AbstractController.extend({
        custom_events: _.extend({}, AbstractController.prototype.custom_events, {
            'btn_clicked': '_onBtnClicked',
        }),
        renderButtons: function ($node) {
            if ($node) {
                this.$buttons = $(qweb.render('ViewM2mGroup.buttons'));
                this.$buttons.appendTo($node);
                this.$buttons.on('click', 'button', this._onAddButtonClick.bind(this));
            }
        },
        _onBtnClicked: function (ev) {
            this.do_action({
                type: 'ir.actions.act_window',
                name: this.title,
                res_model: this.modelName,
                views: [[false, 'list'], [false, 'form']],
                domain: ev.data.domain,
            });
        },
        _onAddButtonClick: function (ev) {
            this.do_action({
                type: 'ir.actions.act_window',
                name: this.title,
                res_model: this.modelName,
                views: [[false, 'form']],
                target: 'new'
            });
        },
```

```
    });

    return M2mGroupController;
});
```

6. Add a new file called `/static/src/js/m2m_group_renderer.js` and add the following content to it:

```
odoo.define('m2m_group.Renderer', function (require) {
    'use strict';

    var AbstractRenderer = require('web.AbstractRenderer');
    var core = require('web.core');

    var qweb = core.qweb;

    var M2mGroupRenderer = AbstractRenderer.extend({
        events: _.extend({}, AbstractRenderer.prototype.events, {
            'click .o_primay_button': '_onClickButton',
        }),
        _render: function () {
            var self = this;
            this.$el.empty();
            this.$el.append(qweb.render('ViewM2mGroup', {
                'groups': this.state,
            }));
            return this._super.apply(this, arguments);
        },
        _onClickButton: function (ev) {
            ev.preventDefault();
            var target = $(ev.currentTarget);
            var group_id = target.data('group');
            var children_ids = _.map(this.state[group_id].children, function (group_id) {
                return group_id.id;
            });
            this.trigger_up('btn_clicked', {
                'domain': [['id', 'in', children_ids]]
            });
        }
    });
```

```
        return M2mGroupRenderer;

});
```

7. Add a new file called /static/src/js/m2m_group_view.js and add the following content to it:

```
odoo.define('m2m_group.View', function (require) {
    'use strict';

    var AbstractView = require('web.AbstractView');
    var view_registry = require('web.view_registry');
    var M2mGroupController = require('m2m_group.Controller');
    var M2mGroupModel = require('m2m_group.Model');
    var M2mGroupRenderer = require('m2m_group.Renderer');

    var M2mGroupView = AbstractView.extend({
        display_name: 'Author',
        icon: 'fa-id-card-o',
        config: _.extend({}, AbstractView.prototype.config, {
            Model: M2mGroupModel,
            Controller: M2mGroupController,
            Renderer: M2mGroupRenderer,
        }),
        viewType: 'm2m_group',
        searchMenuTypes: ['filter', 'favorite'],
        accesskey: "a",
        init: function (viewInfo, params) {
            this._super.apply(this, arguments);
            var attrs = this.arch.attrs;

            if (!attrs.m2m_field) {
                throw new Error('M2m view has not defined "m2m_field" attribute.');
            }

            // Model Parameters
            this.loadParams.m2m_field = attrs.m2m_field;
```

```
        },
    });

    view_registry.add('m2m_group', M2mGroupView);

    return M2mGroupView;
});
```

8. Add the QWeb template for the view to the `/static/src/xml/qweb_template.xml` file:

```
<t t-name="ViewM2mGroup">
    <div class="row ml16 mr16">
        <div t-foreach="groups" t-as="group" class="col-3">
            <t t-set="group_data" t-value="groups[group]"/>
            <div class="card mt16">
                <img class="card-img-top" t-attf-src="/web/image/#{group_data.model}/#{group}/image_512"/>
                <div class="card-body">
                    <h5 class="card-title mt8"><t t-esc="group_data['name']"/></h5>
                </div>
                <ul class="list-group list-group-flush">
                    <t t-foreach="group_data['children']" t-as="child">
                        <li class="list-group-item"><i class="fa fa-book"/> <t t-esc="child.name"/></li>
                    </t>
                </ul>
                <div class="card-body">
                    <a href="#" class="btn btn-sm btn-primary o_primay_button" t-att-data-group="group">View books</a>
                </div>
            </div>
        </div>
    </div>
</t>

<div t-name="ViewM2mGroup.buttons">
    <button type="button" class="btn btn-primary">
        Add Record
```

```
        </button>
    </div>
```

9. Add all of the JavaScript files to the backend assets:

```
...
<script type="text/javascript" src="/my_library/static/
src/js/m2m_group_view.js" />
<script type="text/javascript" src="/my_library/static/
src/js/m2m_group_model.js" />
<script type="text/javascript" src="/my_library/static/
src/js/m2m_group_controller.js" />
<script type="text/javascript" src="/my_library/static/
src/js/m2m_group_renderer.js" />
...
```

10. Finally, add our new view for the `library.book` model:

```
    <record id="library_book_view_author" model="ir.
ui.view">
        <field name="name">Library Book Author</field>
        <field name="model">library.book</field>
        <field name="arch" type="xml">
            <m2m_group m2m_field="author_ids" color_
field="color">
            </m2m_group>
        </field>
    </record>
```

11. Add `m2m_group` to the `Book` action:

```
...
<field name="view_mode">tree,m2m_group,form</field>
...
```

Update the `my_library` module to open the `Book` view, and then, from the view switcher, open the new view that we just added. This will look as follows:

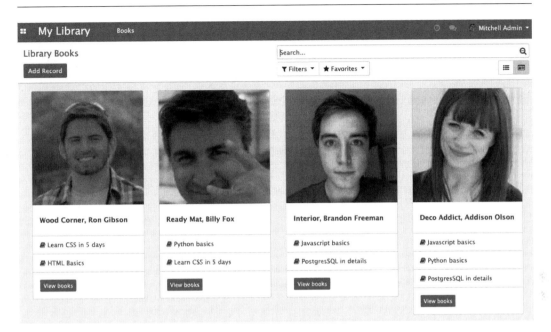

Figure 15.3 – Many2many group view

> **Important information**
> Odoo views are very easy to use and are very flexible. However, it is often the case that easy and flexible things have complex implementations under the hood. This is true of Odoo JavaScript views: they are easy to use, but complex to implement. They consist of lots of components, including the model, renderer, controller, view, and QWeb template. In the next section, we have added all of the required components for the views and have also used a new view for the `library.book` model. If you don't want to add everything manually, grab a module from the example file in this book's GitHub repository.

How it works...

In *steps 1* and *2*, we registered a new type of view, called m2m_group, in ir.ui.view and ir.actions.act_window.view.

In *step 3*, we added the get_m2m_group_data method to the base. Adding this method to the base will make that method available in every model. This method will be called via an RPC call from the JavaScript view. The view will pass two parameters—the domain and m2m_field. In the domain argument, the value of the domain will be the domain generated with a combination of the search view domain and the action domain. m2m_field is the field name by which we want to group the records. This field will be set on the view definition.

In the next few steps, we added the JavaScript files that are required to form the view. An Odoo JavaScript view consists of the view, model, renderer, and controller. The word *view* has historical meaning in the Odoo code base, so **model, view, controller** (**MVC**) becomes **model, renderer, controller** (**MRC**) in Odoo. In general, the view sets up the model, renderer, and controller, and sets the MVC hierarchy so that it looks similar to the following:

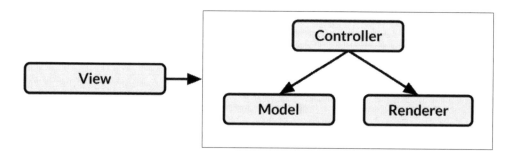

Figure 15.4 – View components

Let's look at the roles of **Model**, **Renderer**, **Controller**, and **View**. Abstract versions of **Model**, **Renderer**, **Controller**, and **View** have all the basic things that are needed to form a view. Consequently, in our example, we have created the model, renderer, controller, and view by inheriting them.

Here is an in-depth explanation of the different parts that are used to create a view:

- **Model:** The role of the **model** is to hold the state of the view. It sends an RPC request to the server for the data, and then passes the data to the controller and renderer. We then override the __load and __reload methods. When the view is being initialized, it calls the __load() method to fetch the data, and when the search conditions are changed and the view needs a new state, then the __reload() method is called. In our case, we have created the common _fetchData() method to make an RPC call for data. Note that we used the get_m2m_group_data method that we added in *step 3*. The __get() method will be called from the controller to get the state of the model.

- **Controller:** The role of the **Controller** is to manage coordination between the **Model** and the **Renderer**. When an action occurs in the **Renderer**, it passes that information to the controller and performs the action accordingly. Sometimes, it also calls some methods in the **Model**. In addition to this, it manages the buttons in the control panel. In our example, we added a button to add new records. To do so, we had to override the `renderButtons()` method of `AbstractController`. We also registered `custom_events` so that when a button in the author card is clicked, the renderer will trigger the event to the controller to make it perform the action.

- **Renderer:** The role of the **renderer** is to manage the DOM elements for the view. Every view can render data in a different way. In the renderer, you can get the state of the model in a state variable. It calls the `render()` method for the rendering. In our example, we rendered the `ViewM2mGroup` QWeb template with its current state to display our view. We also mapped the JavaScript events to take user actions. In this recipe, we have bound the click event for the buttons of the card. Upon clicking the author card button, it will trigger the `btn_clicked` event to the controller, and it will open the list of books for that author.

  > **Important note**
  > Note that events and `custom_events` are different. Events are normal JavaScript events, while `custom_events` events are from the Odoo JavaScript framework. Custom events can be invoked via the `trigger_up` method.

- **View:** The role of the **View** is to get all the basic things that are required to build views, such as a set of fields, a context, a view arch, and some other parameters. After that, the view will initialize the controller, renderer, and model triplet. It will set them in the MVC hierarchy. Usually, it sets up the parameters that are required in the model, view, and controller. In our example, we want the `m2m_field` name to get properly grouped data in the **Model**, so we have set the model parameter in it. In the same way, `this.controllerParams` and `this.rendererParams` can be used to set the parameters in the controller and renderer.

In *step 8*, we added a QWeb template for the views and control panel buttons. To learn more about the QWeb template, refer to the *Using client-side QWeb templates* recipe in this chapter.

> **Important information**
> Odoo views have tons of methods for different purposes; we looked at the most important one in this section. If you want to learn more about views, you can explore them further by going to the `/addons/web/static/src/js/views/` directory. This directory also includes code for the abstract model, controller, renderer, and view.

In *step 9*, we added JavaScript files to the assets.

Finally, in the last two steps, we added a view definition for the `book.library` model. In *step 10*, we used the `<m2m_group>` tag for the view, and we also passed the `m2m_field` attribute as the option. This will be passed to the model to fetch the data from the server.

There's more...

If you don't want to introduce the new view type and you just want to modify a few things in the view instead, you can use `js_class` on the view. For example, if we want a view similar to the kanban one that we created, then we can extend it as follows:

```javascript
var CustomRenderer = KanbanRenderer.extend({
    ...
});

var CustomRendererModel = KanbanModel.extend({
    ...
});

var CustomRendererController = KanbanController.extend({
    ...
});

var CustomDashboardView = KanbanView.extend({
    config: _.extend({}, KanbanView.prototype.config, {
        Model: CustomDashboardModel,
        Renderer: CustomDashboardRenderer,
        Controller: CustomDashboardController,
    }),
});

var viewRegistry = require('web.view_registry');
viewRegistry.add('my_custom_view', CustomDashboardView);
```

We can then use the kanban view with `js_class` (note that the server still thinks of this as a kanban view):

```
...
<field name="arch" type="xml">
    <kanban js_class="my_custom_view">
        ...
    </kanban>
</field>
...
```

Debugging your client-side code

For debugging server-side code, this book contains a whole chapter, that is, *Chapter 7, Debugging Modules*. For the client-side part, you'll get a kick-start in this recipe.

Getting ready

This recipe doesn't really rely on specific code, but if you want to be able to reproduce exactly what's going on, grab the previous recipe's code.

How to do it...

What makes debugging client-side script difficult is that the web client relies heavily on jQuery's asynchronous events. Given that breakpoints halt execution, there is a high chance that a bug caused by timing issues will not occur when debugging. We'll discuss some strategies for this later:

1. For the client-side debugging, you will need to activate debug mode with the assets. If you don't know how to activate debug mode with the assets, read the *Activating the Odoo developer tools* recipe from *Chapter 1, Installing the Odoo Development Environment*.

2. In the JavaScript function you're interested in, call `debugger`:

    ```
    debugger;
    ```

3. If you have timing problems, log in to the console through a JavaScript function:

    ```
    console.log("I'm in function X currently");
    ```

4. If you want to debug during template rendering, call the debugger from QWeb:

    ```
    <t t-debug="" />
    ```

5. You can also have QWeb log in to the console, as follows:

```
<t t-log="myvalue" />
```

All of this relies on your browser offering the appropriate functionality for debugging. While all major browsers do that, we'll only look at Chromium here, for demonstration purposes. To be able to use the debug tools, open them by clicking on the top-right menu button and selecting **More tools | Developer tools**:

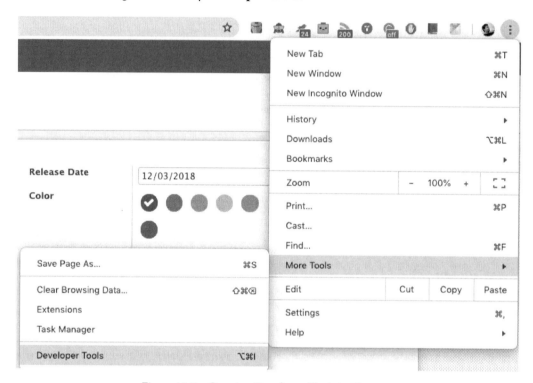

Figure 15.5 – Opening Developer Tools in Chrome

How it works...

When the debugger is open, you should see something similar to the following screenshot:

Debugging your client-side code

Figure 15.6 – Paused debugger

Here, you have access to a lot of different tools in the separate tabs. The currently active tab in the preceding screenshot is the JavaScript debugger, where we set a breakpoint in line **31** by clicking on the line number. Every time our widget fetches the list of users, the execution should stop at this line, and the debugger will allow you to inspect variables or change their values. Within the watch list to the right, you can also call functions to try out their effects without having to continuously save your script file and reload the page.

The debugger statements we described earlier will behave the same as soon as you have the developer tools open. The execution will then stop, and the browser will switch to the **Sources** tab, with the file in question opened and the line with the debugger statement highlighted.

The two logging possibilities from earlier will end up in the **Console** tab. This is the first tab you should inspect in case of problems in any case because, if some JavaScript code doesn't load at all because of syntax errors or similar fundamental problems, you'll see an error message there explaining what's going on.

There's more...

Use the **Elements** tab to inspect the DOM representation of the page the browser currently displays. This will prove helpful when it comes to familiarizing yourself with the HTML code the existing widgets produce, and it will also allow you to play with classes and CSS attributes, in general. This is a great resource for testing layout changes.

The **Network** tab gives you an overview of which requests the current page made and how long it took. This is helpful when it comes to debugging slow page loads as, in the **Network** tab, you will usually find the details of the requests. If you select a request, you can inspect the payload that was passed to the server and the result returned, which helps you to figure out the reason for unexpected behavior on the client side. You'll also see the status codes of requests made—for example, **404**—in case a resource can't be found because you misspelled a filename, for instance.

Improving onboarding with tours

After developing a large application, it is crucial to explain software flows to the end users. The Odoo framework includes a built-in tour manager. With this tour manager, you can guide an end user through learning specific flows. In this recipe, we will create a tour so that we can create a book in the library.

Getting ready

We will be using the `my_library` module from the previous recipe. Tours are only displayed in the database without demo data, so if you are using a database with demo data, create a new database without demo data for this recipe.

How to do it...

To add a tour to a library, perform the following steps:

1. Add a new `/static/src/js/my_library_tour.js` file with the following code:

```javascript
odoo.define('my_library.tour', function (require) {
"use strict";
var core = require('web.core');
var tour = require('web_tour.tour');
var _t = core._t;

tour.register('library_tour', {
    url: "/web",
    rainbowManMessage: _t("Congrats, you have listed a book."),
    sequence: 5,
```

```javascript
        }, [tour.stepUtils.showAppsMenuItem(), {
            trigger: '.o_app[data-menu-xmlid="my_library.library_base_menu"]',
            content: _t('Manage books and authors in <b>Library app</b>.'),
            position: 'right'
        }, {
            trigger: '.o_list_button_add',
            content: _t("Let's create new book."),
            position: 'bottom'
        }, {
            trigger: 'input[name="name"]',
            extra_trigger: '.o_form_editable',
            content: _t('Set the book title'),
            position: 'right',
        }, {
            trigger: '.o_form_button_save',
            content: _t('Save this book record'),
            position: 'bottom',
        }
    ]);
});
```

2. Add the tour JavaScript file in the backend assets:

```
...
<script type="text/javascript" src="/my_library/static/src/js/my_library_tour.js" />
...
```

Update the module and open the Odoo backend. At this point, you will see the tour, as shown in the following screenshot:

Figure 15.7 – Tour step for user onboarding

Make sure you have disabled demo data in your Odoo instance. An instance with demo data does not show tours.

How it works...

The tour manager is available under the `web_tour.tour` namespace.

In the first step, we imported `web_tour.tour`. We can then add a new tour with the `register()` function. We registered our tour with the `library_tour` name and passed the URL on which this tour should run.

The next parameter is a list of these tour steps. A tour step requires three values. The trigger is used to select the element on which the tour should be displayed. This is a JavaScript selector. We used the XML ID of the menu because it is available in the DOM.

The *first step*, `tour.stepUtils.showAppsMenuItem()`, is the predefined step from the tour for the main menu. The next key is the content, and this is displayed when the user hovers over the tour drop. We used the `_t()` function because we want to translate the string, while the position key is used to decide on the position of the tour drop. Possible values include top, right, left, or bottom.

> **Important information**
> The tours improve the onboarding experience of the user, as well as managing the integration tests. When you run Odoo with test mode internally, it also runs the tours and causes the test case to fail if a tour has not finished.

Mobile app JavaScript

Odoo v10 introduced the Odoo mobile application. It provides a few small utilities to perform mobile actions, such as vibrate phone, show toast message, and scan QR code.

Getting ready

We will be using the `my_library` module from the previous library. We will show you the toast when we change the value of the **color** field from the mobile app.

> **Warning**
> The Odoo mobile app only supports the Enterprise Edition, so if you don't have the Enterprise Edition, then you cannot test it.

How to do it...

Perform the following steps to show a toast message in the Odoo mobile app:

1. Import `web_mobile.rpc` in `field_widget.js`:

   ```
   var mobile = require('web_mobile.core');
   ```

2. Modify the `clickPill` method to display the toast when the user changes the color from the mobile device:

   ```
   clickPill: function (ev) {
       var $target = $(ev.currentTarget);
       var data = $target.data();
       if (mobile.methods.showToast) {
           mobile.methods.showToast({ 'message': 'Color changed' });
       }
       this._setValue(data.val.toString());
   }
   ```

Update the module and open the `form` view of the `library.book` model in the mobile app. When you change the color, you will see the toast, as shown in the following screenshot:

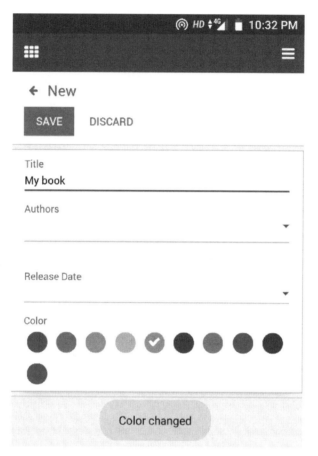

Figure 15.8 – Toast on color change

How it works...

`web_mobile.rpc` provides the bridge between a mobile device and Odoo JavaScript. It exposes a few basic mobile utilities. In our example, we used the `showToast` method to display toast in the mobile app. We also need to check the availability of the function. The reason behind this is that some mobile phones might not support a few features. For example, if devices don't have a camera, then you can't use the `scanBarcode()` method. In such cases, to avoid tracebacks, we need to wrap them with the `if` condition.

There's more...

The mobile utilities that are to be found in Odoo are as follows:

- `showToast()`: To display a toast message
- `vibrate()`: To make a phone vibrate
- `showSnackBar()`: To display a snack bar with a button
- `showNotification()`: To display a mobile notification
- `addContact()`: To add a new contact to the phonebook
- `scanBarcode()`: To scan QR codes
- `switchAccount()`: To open the account switcher in Android

To learn more about mobile JavaScript, refer to `https://www.odoo.com/documentation/14.0/reference/mobile.html`.

16
The Odoo Web Library (OWL)

Odoo v14 introduced a new JavaScript framework called **OWL** (short for **Odoo Web Library**). OWL is a component-based UI framework and uses QWeb templates for structure. OWL is very fast compared to Odoo's legacy widget system and introduces tons of new features, including hooks, reactivity, the autoinstantiation of subcomponents, and more besides. In this chapter, we will learn how to use an OWL component to generate interactive UI elements. We will start from the minimal OWL component and then we will learn about the component's life cycle. Finally, we will create a new field widget for the form view. In this chapter, we will cover the following recipes:

- Creating an OWL component
- Managing user actions in an OWL component
- Making OWL components reactive
- Understanding the OWL component life cycle
- Adding an OWL field to the form view

> **Note**
>
> The following question may occur to you: Why is Odoo not using some well-known JavaScript frameworks, such as React.js or Vue.js? You can refer to `https://github.com/odoo/owl` to learn more about the OWL framework.

Technical requirements

OWL components are defined with ES6 classes. In this chapter, we will be using some ES6 syntax. Also, some ES6 syntaxes are not supported by old browsers, so make sure you are using the latest version of Chrome or Firefox. You will find the code for this chapter at `https://github.com/PacktPublishing/Odoo-14-Development-Cookbook-Fourth-Edition/tree/master/Chapter16`.

Creating an OWL component

The goal of this recipe is to learn the basics of an OWL component. We will create a minimal OWL component and append it to the Odoo web client. In this recipe, we will create a component for a small horizontal bar with some text.

Getting ready

For this recipe, we will be using the `my_library` module with basic fields and views. You will find the basic `my_library` module in the `Chapter16/00_initial_module` directory in the GitHub repository.

How to do it...

We will add a small horizontal bar component to the Odoo web client. Perform the following steps to add your first component to the Odoo web client:

1. Add a `/my_library/static/src/js/component.js` JavaScript file and define the new module's namespace:

    ```js
    odoo.define('my.component', function (require) {
        "use strict";
        // Place steps 3, 4, 5 here

    });
    ```

2. Add the `/my_library/views/templates.xml` XML file and load the component JavaScript in assets such as these:

```xml
<template id="assets_end" inherit_id="web.assets_backend">
    <xpath expr="." position="inside">
        <script src="/my_library/static/src/js/component.js" type="text/javascript" />
    </xpath>
</template>
```

3. Define the OWL utilities in the `component.js` file added in *step 1*:

```javascript
const { Component } = owl;
const { xml } = owl.tags;
```

4. Add the OWL component and its basic template to the `component.js` file added in *step 1*:

```javascript
class MyComponent extends Component {
    static template = xml`
        <div class="bg-info text-center p-2">
            <b> Welcome to Odoo </b>
        </div>`
}
```

5. Initialize and append the component to the web client. Add this to the `component.js` file added in *step 1*:

```javascript
owl.utils.whenReady().then(() => {
    const app = new MyComponent();
    app.mount(document.body);
});
```

Install/upgrade the `my_library` module to apply our changes. Once our module is loaded in Odoo, you will see the horizontal bar, as in the following screenshot:

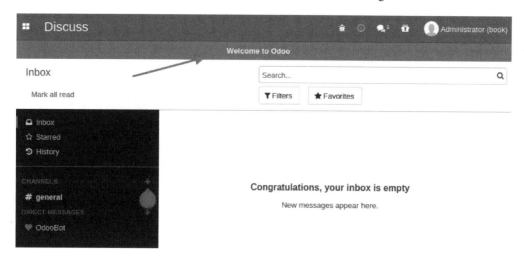

Figure 16.1 – OWL component

This is just a simple component. Right now, it will not handle any user events and you cannot remove it.

How it works...

In *step 1* and *step 2*, we added a JavaScript file and listed this in the backend assets. If you want to learn more about assets, refer to the *Static assets management* recipe in *Chapter 14, CMS Website Development*.

In *step 3*, we initialized a variable from OWL. All the utilities from OWL are available under a single global variable, `owl`. In our example, we pulled an OWL utility. First, we declared `Component`, and then we declared `xml` from `owl.tags`. `Component` is the main class for the OWL component and by extending it, we will create our own components.

In *step 4*, we created our component, `MyComponent`, by extending OWL's `Component` class. For the sake of simplicity, we have just added the QWeb template to the definition of the `MyComponent` class. If you notice here, we have used xml \`...\` to declare our template. This syntax is known as an **inline template**. However, you can load QWeb templates via separate files, which is usually the case. We will see examples of external QWeb templates in the upcoming recipes.

> **Note**
> Inline QWeb templates do not support translations or modifications via inheritance. So, always endeavor to load QWeb templates from a separate file.

In *step 5*, we instantiated the `MyComponent` component and appended it to the body. The OWL component is an ES6 class, so you can create an object via the `new` keyword. Then you can use the `mount()` method to add the component to the page. If you notice, we have placed our code inside the `whenReady()` callback. This will ensure that all OWL functionality is properly loaded before we start using OWL components.

There's more...

OWL is a separate library and loaded in Odoo as an external JavaScript library. You can use OWL in your other projects, too. The OWL library is listed at `https://github.com/odoo/owl`. There is also an online playground available in case you just want to test OWL without setting it in your local machine. You can play with OWL at `https://odoo.github.io/owl/playground/`.

Managing user actions in an OWL component

To make the user interface interactive, components need to handle user actions such as click, hover, and form submission. In this recipe, we will add a button to our component, and we will handle a click event.

Getting ready

For this recipe, we will continue using the `my_library` module from the previous recipe.

How to do it...

In this recipe, we will add a delete button to the component. Upon clicking the delete button, the component gets removed. Perform the following steps to add a delete button and its event in the component:

1. Update the QWeb template and add an icon to remove the bar:

    ```
    static template = xml`
        <div class="bg-info text-center p-2">
            <b> Welcome to Odoo </b>
            <i class="fa fa-close p-1 float-right"
    ```

```
                style="cursor: pointer;"
                t-on-click="onRemove"> </i>
    </div>`
```

2. To remove the component, add the `onRemove` method to the `MyComponent` class, as follows:

```
class MyComponent extends Component {
    static template = xml`
        <div class="bg-info text-center p-2">
            <b> Welcome to Odoo </b>
            <i class="fa fa-close p-1 float-right"
                style="cursor: pointer;"
                t-on-click="onRemove"> </i>
        </div>`
    onRemove(ev) {
        this.destroy();
    }
}
```

Update the module to apply the changes. Following the update, you will see a little cross icon on the right side of the bar, as in the following screenshot:

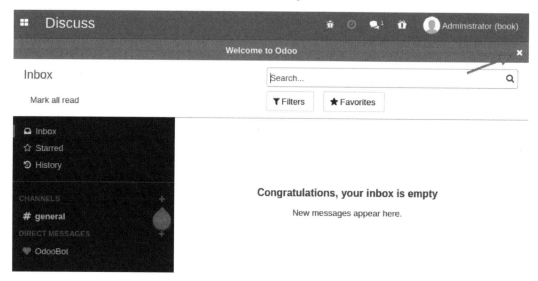

Figure 16.2 – The remove button on the top bar component

Upon clicking the remove icon, our OWL component will be removed. The bar will reappear when you reload the page.

How it works...

In *step 1*, we added a remove icon to the component. If you notice, we have added a `t-on-click` attribute. This will be used to bind a click event. The value of the attribute will be the method in the component. In our example, we have used `t-on-click="onRemove"`. This implies that when the user clicks on the remove icon, the `onRemove` method in the component will be called. The syntax to define the event is simple:

```
t-on-<name of event>="<method name in component>"
```

For example, if you want to call the method when the user moves the mouse over the component, you can do so by adding the following code:

```
t-on-mouseover="onMouseover"
```

After adding the preceding code, whenever the user moves the mouse cursor over the component, OWL will call the `onMouseover` method specified in the component.

In *step 2*, we have added the `onRemove` method. This method will be called when the user clicks on the remove icon. In the method, we have called the `destroy()` method, which will remove the component from the DOM. In the `destroy()` method, we are receiving the JavaScript event object. `destroy()` is one of the default methods of the OWL component. We will be seeing several default methods in the upcoming recipes.

There's more...

Event handling is not limited to the DOM events. You can use your custom events as well. For instance, if you are manually triggering the event called `my-custom-event`, you can use `t-on-my-custom-event` to catch custom triggered events.

Making OWL components reactive

OWL is a powerful framework and supports auto updates for the UI based on hooks. With update hooks, a component's UI will be automatically updated when the internal state of the component is changed. In this recipe, we will update the message in the component based on user actions.

Getting ready

For this recipe, we will continue using the `my_library` module from the previous recipe.

How to do it...

In this recipe, we will add arrows around the text in the component. Upon clicking the arrow, we will change the message. Perform the following steps to make the OWL component reactive:

1. Update the XML template of the component. Add two buttons with an event directive around the text. Also retrieve the message dynamically from the list:

   ```
   static template = xml`
       <div class="bg-info text-center p-2">

           <i class="fa fa-arrow-left p-1"
               style="cursor: pointer;"
               t-on-click="onPrevious"> </i>
           <b t-esc="messageList[Math.abs(
               state.currentIndex%4)]"/>
           <i class="fa fa-arrow-right p-1"
               style="cursor: pointer;"
               t-on-click="onNext"> </i>

           <i class="fa fa-close p-1 float-right"
               style="cursor: pointer;"
               t-on-click="onRemove"> </i>
       </div>`
   ```

2. In the JavaScript file of the component, import the `useState` hook as follows:

   ```
   const { Component, useState } = owl;
   ```

3. Add the `constructor` method to the component and initialize some variables as follows:

   ```
   constructor() {
       super(...arguments);
       this.messageList = [
   ```

```
            'Hello World',
            'Welcome to Odoo',
            'Odoo is awesome',
            'You are awesome too'
        ];
        this.state = useState({ currentIndex: 0 });
    }
```

4. In the Component class, add methods to handle the user's click event:

```
onNext(ev) {
    this.state.currentIndex++;
}
onPrevious(ev) {
    this.state.currentIndex--;
}
```

Restart and update the module to apply the changes to the module. Following the update, you will see the two arrow icons around the text like this:

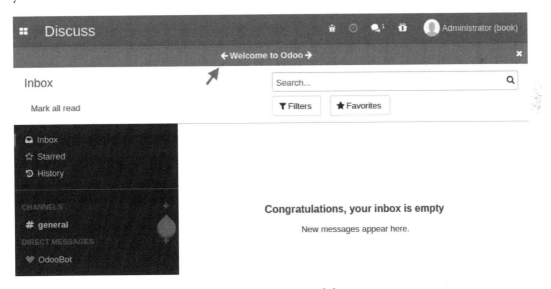

Figure 16.3 – Arrows around the text

If you click on the arrow, the message text will be changed based on the list of messages in the constructor.

How it works...

In *step 1*, we updated the XML template of our component. Basically, we made two changes to the template. We rendered the text message from the list of messages, and we selected the message based on the value of `currentIndex` in the state variable. We added two arrow icons around the text block. In the arrow icons, we added the `t-on-click` attribute to bind the click event to the arrow.

In *step 2*, we imported the `useState` hook from OWL. This hook is used to handle the state of the component. In *step 3*, we added a constructor. This constructor will be called when you create an instance of the object. In the constructor, we added a list of messages we want to show, and then we added the state variable using the `useState` hook. This will make the component reactive. When the state is changed, the UI will be updated based on the new state. In our example, we used `currentIndex` in the `useState` hook. This implies that whenever the value of `currentIndex` changes, the UI will be updated as well.

> **Important information**
> There is only one rule for defining hooks, which is, the hooks will only work if you have declared them in the constructor. Several other types of hooks are available, which you can find here: https://github.com/odoo/owl/blob/master/doc/reference/hooks.md.

In *step 4*, we added methods to handle the click events of the arrow. Upon clicking the arrow, we are changing the state of the component. As we are using a hook on the state, the UI of the component will be automatically updated.

Understanding the OWL component life cycle

OWL components have several methods that help developers to create powerful and interactive components. In this recipe, we will see important methods of the components and the life cycle when these methods are called. In this recipe, we will add several methods to the component, and we will log the message in the console to understand the life cycle of the component.

Getting ready

For this recipe, we will continue using the `my_library` module from the previous recipe.

How to do it…

To add life cycle methods to the component, you need to carry out the following steps:

1. As we already have a constructor in the component, let's add a message to the console like this:

   ```
   constructor() {
       console.log('CALLED:> constructor');
   ...
   ```

2. Add the `willStart` method to the component:

   ```
   async willStart() {
       console.log('CALLED:> willStart');
   }
   ```

3. Add the `mounted` method to the component:

   ```
   mounted() {
       console.log('CALLED:> mounted');
   }
   ```

4. Add the `willPatch` method to the component:

   ```
   willPatch() {
       console.log('CALLED:> willPatch');
   }
   ```

5. Add the `patched` method to the component:

   ```
   patched() {
       console.log('CALLED:> patched');
   }
   ```

6. Add the `willUnmount` method to the component:

   ```
   willUnmount() {
       console.log('CALLED:> willUnmount');
   }
   ```

Restart and update the module to apply the module changes. Following the update, perform some operations, such as changing the message via arrows, and removing the component. In the browser console, you will see the logs like this:

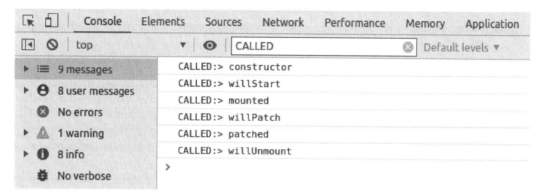

Figure 16.4 – Logs in the browser console

You may have different logs based on the operation you have performed on the component.

How it works...

In this recipe, we have added several methods and added logged messages to the method. You can use these methods based on your requirements. Let's see the life cycle of the component and when these methods are called.

`constructor()`: The constructor is called first in the component life cycle. It will be called when you initialize the component. You need to set the initial state of the component here.

`willStart()`: The `willStart` method is called after the constructor and before the rendering of the element. This is an asynchronous method; you can perform asynchronous operations such as RPC here.

`mounted()`: The `mounted` method is called after the component is rendered and the DOM added.

`willPatch()`: The `willPatch` method is called when the state of the component is changed. This method is called **before** the element is re-rendered based on a new state. In our example, this method will be called when you click on the arrow. But when this method is called, the DOM will be based on the **old** values.

`patched()`: The `patched` method works like the `willPatch` method. It will be called when the state of the component is changed, the only difference being that the `patched` method will be called **after** the element is re-rendered based on the new state.

`willUnmount()`: The `willUnmount` method is called just before the element is being removed from the DOM. In our example, this method will be called when you remove the component by clicking on the remove icon.

These are the life cycle methods of the component and you will need to use them as per your requirements. For instance, the `mounted` and `willUnmount` methods can be used to **bind** and **unbind** event listeners.

There's more...

There is one more method in the component life cycle, but it is used when you are using subcomponents. OWL passes the parent component state via the `props` parameter, and when `props` is changed, the `willUpdateProps` method is called. This is an asynchronous method, which means you can perform an asynchronous operation such as RPC here.

Adding an OWL field to the form view

Up to this point, we have learned about all the basics of OWL. Now we will move on to more advanced aspects and create a field widget that can be used in the form view, just like the field widget recipe from the previous chapter. In this recipe, we will create a color picker widget that will save integer values based on the color selected.

To make the example more informative, we will use some advanced concepts of OWL. We will use multiple components, custom events, external QWeb templates, and more.

Getting ready

For this recipe, we will continue using the `my_library` module from the previous recipe.

How to do it...

Perform the following steps to add a new OWL field component to choose the colors on the form view:

1. Add a color integer field to the `library.book` model as follows:

   ```
   color = fields.Integer()
   ```

2. Add the same field to the form view, with a widget attribute as well:

   ```
   <field name="color" widget="int_color"/>
   ```

3. Add the QWeb templates for the field at `static/src/xml/qweb_template.xml`:

   ```xml
   <?xml version="1.0" encoding="UTF-8"?>
   <templates>
       <t t-name="OWLColorPill" owl="1">
           <span t-attf-class="o_color_pill
                   o_color_{{props.pill_no}}
                   {{props.active and
                   'active' or ''}}"
               t-att-data-val="props.pill_no"
               t-on-click="pillClicked"
               t-attf-title="This color is used in
                   {{props.book_count or 0 }} books." />
       </t>

       <span t-name="OWLFieldColorPills" owl="1"
               class="o_int_colorpicker"
               t-on-color-updated="colorUpdated">
           <t t-foreach="totalColors" t-as='pill_no'>
               <ColorPill t-if="mode === 'edit'
                   or value == pill_no"
                   pill_no='pill_no' active='value ==
                   pill_no'
                   book_count="colorGroupData[pill_no]"/>
           </t>
       </span>
   </templates>
   ```

4. List the QWeb file in the module's `manifest` file:

```
"qweb": [
    'static/src/xml/qweb_template.xml',
],
```

5. Now we want to add some SCSS for the field at `static/src/scss/field_widget.scss`. As the content of SCSS is too long, please find the content of the SCSS file in this book's GitHub repository at https://github.com/PacktPublishing/Odoo-13-Development-Cookbook-Fourth-Edition/blob/master/Chapter16/05_owl_field/my_library/static/src/scss/field_widget.scss.

6. Add the `static/src/js/field_widget.js` JavaScript file with the following basic content:

```
odoo.define('my_field_widget', function (require) {
    "use strict";

    const { Component } = owl;
    const AbstractField = require(
        'web.AbstractFieldOwl');
    const fieldRegistry = require(
        'web.field_registry_owl');

    // Place steps 7 and 8 here
});
```

7. In `field_widget.js`, add the color pill component as follows:

```
class ColorPill extends Component {
    static template = 'OWLColorPill';
    pillClicked() {
        this.trigger('color-updated', {val:
            this.props.pill_no});
    }
}
```

8. In `field_widget.js`, add the field color component by extending `AbstractField` like this:

```
class FieldColor extends AbstractField {
    static supportedFieldTypes = ['integer'];
    static template = 'OWLFieldColorPills';
    static components = { ColorPill };

    // Add methods from step 9 here

}
fieldRegistry.add('int_color', FieldColor);
```

9. Add the given methods to `FieldComponent` created in *step 8*:

```
        constructor(...args) {
            super(...args);
            this.totalColors = Array.from({length: 10},
                (_, i) => (i + 1).toString());
        }
        async willStart() {
            this.colorGroupData = {};
            var colorData = await this.rpc({
                model: this.model, method: 'read_group',
                domain: [], fields: ['color'],
                groupBy: ['color'],
            });
            colorData.forEach(res => {
                this.colorGroupData[res.color] =
                    res.color_count;
            });
        }
        colorUpdated(ev) {
            this._setValue(ev.detail.val);
        }
```

10. Add JavaScript and an SCSS file to the backend assets as follows:

```xml
<template id="assets_backend" inherit_id="web.assets_backend">
    <xpath expr="." position="inside">
        <script src="/my_library/static/src/js
            /component.js" type="text/javascript" />
        <script src="/my_library/static/src/js
            /field_widget.js" type="text/javascript"
        />
        <link href="/my_library/static/src/scss
            /field_widget.scss" rel="stylesheet"
            type="text/scss" />
    </xpath>
</template>
```

Restart and update the module to apply the module changes. Open the book's form view in edit mode. You will be able to see the color picker widget as in the following screenshot:

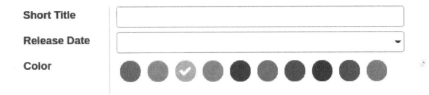

Figure 16.5 – Color picker OWL widget

This field looks just like the color widget from the last chapter, but the actual difference lies under the hood. This new field is built with OWL, while the previous one was built with widgets.

How it works...

In *step 1*, we added an integer field to the `library.book` model. In *step 2*, we added the field to the form view of the book.

In *step 3*, we added the QWeb template file. If you notice, we added two templates to the file, one for the color pill and the other for the field itself. We used two templates because we want to see the concept of the subcomponent. If you observe the template closely, you will find that we have used the `<ColorPill>` tag. This will be used to instantiate the subcomponent. On the `<ColorPill>` tag, we have passed the `active` and `pill_no` attributes. These attributes will be received as `props` in the template of the subcomponent. Also note that the `t-on-color-updated` attribute is used to listen to the custom event triggered from the subcomponent.

> **Important information**
>
> Odoo v14 uses both the widget system and the OWL framework. Both use QWeb templates, but to differentiate OWL QWeb templates from the legacy QWeb template, you will need to use the `owl="1"` attribute in the template definition.

In *step 4*, we listed our QWeb template in the manifest. This will automatically load our template in the browser.

In *step 5*, we added SCSS for the color. This will help us to have a beautiful UI for the color picker.

In *step 6*, we added JavaScript for the field component. We imported the OWL utility and we also imported `AbstractField` and `fieldRegistry`. `AbstractField` is the abstract OWL component for the fields. It contains all the basic elements that are required to create the field. `fieldRegistry` is used to list the OWL component as a field component.

In *step 7*, we created the `ColorPill` component. The `template` variable on the component is the name of the template that is loaded from the external XML file. The `ColorPill` component has the `pillClicked` method, which is called when the user clicks on the color pill. Inside the method body, we have triggered the `color-updated` event, which will be captured by the parent `FieldColor` component as we used `t-on-color-updated` on the `FieldColor` component.

In *step 8* and *step 9*, we created the `FieldColor` component by extending `AbstractField`. We used the `AbstractField` component because it will have all the utilities that are required to create the field widget. If you notice, we used the `components` static variable at the start. You need to list the components via the `components` static variable when you are using subcomponents in the template. We also added the `willStart` method in our example. The `willStart` method is an asynchronous method, so we have called RPC (network call) to fetch data regarding the number of books used for a particular color. Toward the end, we added the `colorUpdated` method, which will be called when the user clicks on the pill. So, we are changing the values of the field. The `setValue` method is used to set the field values (which will be saved in the database). Note here that the data triggered from the child component is available under the `detail` attribute in the `event` parameter. Finally, we registered our widget in `fieldRegistry`, implying that henceforth, we will be able to use our field via the `widget` attribute in the form view.

In *step 10*, we loaded JavaScript and SCSS files into the backend assets.

17
In-App Purchasing with Odoo

Odoo has had built-in support for **in-app purchasing** (**IAP**) since version 11. IAP is used to provide recurring services without any complex configurations. Usually, apps purchased from the app store only require a one-time payment from the customer, because they are normal modules and once the user has purchased and started using the module, it won't cost the developer anything. In contrast to this, IAP apps are used to provide services to users, and so there is an operational cost to providing the continuous service. In such cases, it is not possible to provide a service with just the single initial purchase. The service provider needs something that charges the user in a recurring manner, based on usage. Odoo's IAP fixes these issues and provides a way to charge based on usage.

In this chapter, we will cover the following recipes:

- IAP concepts
- Registering an IAP service in Odoo
- Creating an IAP service module
- Authorizing and charging IAP credits
- Creating an IAP client module
- Displaying offers when an account lacks credit

There are several use cases where you can use IAP, such as a fax service for sending documents or an SMS service. In this chapter, we will create a small IAP service that will provide us with information about books based on the ISBN numbers we enter.

Technical requirements

The technical requirement for this chapter is the online Odoo platform.

All the code used in this chapter can be downloaded from the GitHub repository at `https://github.com/PacktPublishing/Odoo-14-Development-Cookbook-Fourth-Edition/tree/master/Chapter17`.

IAP concepts

In this recipe, we will explore the different entities that are a part of the IAP process. We will also look at the role of each entity and how they combine to complete the IAP process.

How it works...

There are three main entities in the IAP process: the **customer**, the **service provider**, and **Odoo** itself. These are described as follows:

- The **customer** is the end user who wants to use the service. In order to use the service, the customer needs to install the application provided by the service provider. The customer then needs to purchase a service plan according to their usage requirements. With that, the customer can start to use the service straight away. This prevents difficulties for the customer, as it is not necessary to carry out complex configurations. Instead, they just pay for the service and start to use it.

- The **service provider** is the developer that wants to sell the service (probably you, as you are the developer). The customer will ask the provider for the service, at which point the service provider will check whether the customer purchased a valid plan and whether there is enough credit in the customer's account. If the customer has enough credit, the service provider will deduct the credit and provide the service to the customer.

- **Odoo** is a kind of broker in this. It provides the medium for handling payments, credits, plans, and so on. Customers purchase the service credit from Odoo, and the service provider draws this credit when serving the service. Odoo then bridges the gap between the customer and the service provider, so the customer has no need to do complex configurations and the service provider has no need to set up a payment gateway, customer account management, and so on. In return, Odoo takes a commission fee from the sale. At the time of writing this book, Odoo takes 25% commission from the packs.

There is also an optional entity in the process, which is the **external service**. In some cases, service providers use some external services. However, we will ignore external services here, as they are the secondary service provider. An example of this could be an SMS service. If you are providing an SMS IAP service to Odoo users, then you (the service provider) will use an SMS service internally.

The IAP service flow

Now, we will look at how all IAP entities work together to provide the service. The following diagram illustrates the IAP process:

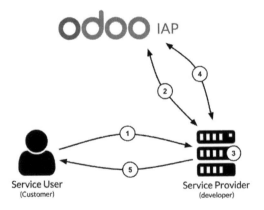

Figure 17.1 – IAP workflow

Here is an explanation of every step of the IAP service flow:

1. A **Customer** will make a request to the **Service Provider** for a service. With this request, the **Customer** will pass the account token, which will be used by the **Service Provider** to identify the user. (Note the customers will have your module installed on their server.)

2. After receiving a request from the **Customer**, the **Service Provider** will ask **Odoo** whether the **Customer** has enough credit in their account. If the **Customer** has enough credit, then it will create the transaction to reserve that credit before providing the service.

3. After reserving the credit, the **Service Provider** will perform the service. In some cases, the **Service Provider** will call an external service to perform the requested service.

4. After performing the service requested by the **Customer**, the **Service Provider** goes back to **Odoo** to capture the credit reserved in *step 2*; if the requested service cannot be served due to an error, the **Service Provider** will ask **Odoo** to release the reserved credit.

5. Finally, the **Service Provider** will get back to the **Customer** to notify them that the requested service has been served. Some services might return the resulting information; here, you will get the result of the service. This resulting information is used by the **Customer** based on their specifications (depending on the service).

There's more...

If the customer does not have enough credit, the service flow is as follows:

1. The customer requests the service (just like in the previous flow).

2. The service provider gets the request and asks Odoo whether the user has enough credit. Suppose that the customer does not have enough credit.

3. The service provider returns to the customer and informs them that there is not enough credit in the account, showing information (an Odoo service packs link) on where the user can purchase the service.

4. The customer is redirected to Odoo and purchases the credit for the service.

Registering an IAP service in Odoo

In order to draw credit from the customer account, the service providers need to register their services on Odoo. You also define plans for the services. The user will purchase your plans through this registered service. In this recipe, we will register our service on Odoo and define plans for our service.

Getting ready

To sell the services from the IAP platform, the service provider needs to register services and plans to Odoo. We are going to register our service on `https://iap-sandbox.odoo.com/`. This IAP endpoint is used for testing purposes. You can purchase a service pack for free. For production, you need to register for a service at `https://iap.odoo.com`. For this recipe, we will use the sandbox IAP endpoint.

How to do it...

Follow these steps to create an IAP service on Odoo:

1. Open `https://iap-sandbox.odoo.com/` and log in (sign up if you don't have an account).
2. Click on the **My Services** button on the home page.
3. Click on the **Add a Service** button to create a new service.

4. This will open a form like the one seen in the following screenshot. Here, fill in information, including the **Service Logo**, **Technical Name** (must be unique), **Unit Name**, and **Private Policy** fields:

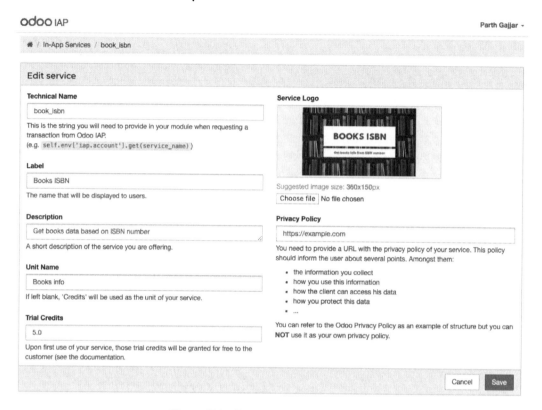

Figure 17.2 – Registering an IAP service

5. Saving a service will give you a service key, as shown in the following screenshot. Note the service key at this point, as it will not be displayed again:

Registering an IAP service in Odoo   543

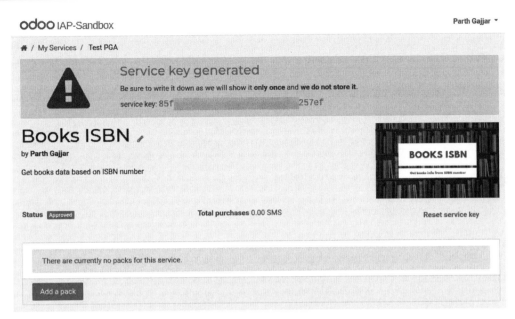

Figure 17.3 – A new IAP service

6. Create a few packs (plans) for the service by clicking on the **Add a pack** button in the **Packs** section – for example, Get 50 books info in 10 Euro. The following screenshot shows the page to create a new pack:

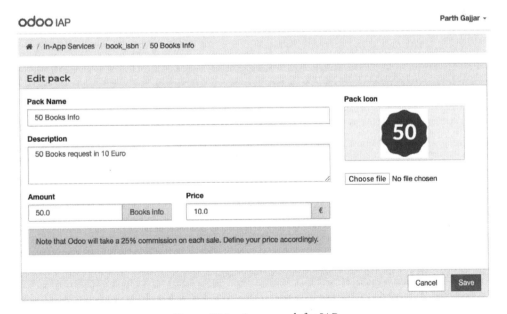

Figure 17.4 – A new pack for IAP

After the configuration is complete, your service page will look like this:

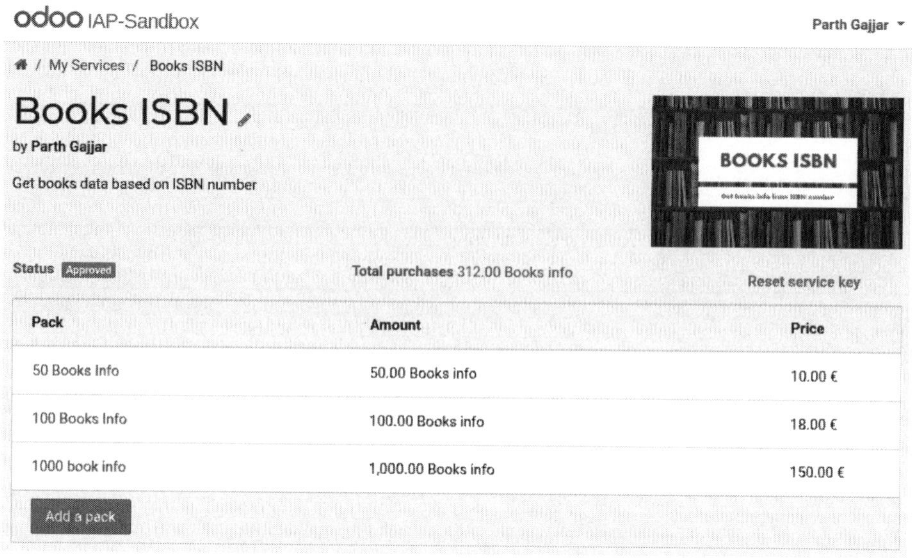

Figure 17.5 – The IAP service after configuring the packs

You can add a new pack at any time. You can also change the pack at any time, but at the time of writing this book, there is no option to delete a pack.

How it works...

We have created an IAP service at `https://iap-sandbox.odoo.com/`, as we want to test the IAP service before moving the service into production. Let's explore the use of the fields that we filled in while creating the service:

- The **Technical Name** value is used to identify your service, and it must be a unique name. We have added the `book_isbn` technical name here. (It is not possible to change this later.)

- The **Label**, **Description**, and **Service Logo** values are used for informational purposes. This information will be displayed on the web page when the user is purchasing the service.

- The **Unit Name** value is the unit by which your service is sold. For example, in an SMS service, your unit name will be `SMS` (for example, 100 SMS costs $5). In our case, we have used a unit name of `Books info`.

- **Trial Credit** is for the free credit provided to a customer for testing. This is only provided once per customer. Also, trial credit only works if the user has a valid enterprise contract so that any misuse of free credit can be avoided.
- **Privacy Policy** is for the URL of the privacy policy for your service.

After submitting these details, your service will be created, and it will display the service key. Refer to the screenshot shown in *step 5* of this recipe for more information. The service key will be used to capture customer credit during a service request. Store this key securely, because it won't be displayed again, although it is possible to generate a new key from the same page; but once you generate a new key, the old key will stop working.

We still need to create plans for our service. You need to provide the plan name, description, logo, amount, and price. The **Amount** field is used for the number of service units for that plan. The **Price** field is used for defining the amount that a user needs to pay to get this plan. In *step 6* of this recipe, we created a plan for 50 books info in 10 Euro. Here, **Books info** is the unit type that we submitted during the creation of the service. This means that if a user purchases this plan, they will be able to get the information for 50 books.

> **Note**
> Odoo takes a 25% commission from this price, so define your service plan price accordingly.

Now, we will create an IAP service and an IAP client module in the following sections.

Creating an IAP service module

In this recipe, we will create a service module to be used by the service provider. This module will accept the IAP request from the customer and return the service result in the response.

Getting ready

We will create the `iap_isbn_service` module. This service module will handle customer IAP requests. Customers will send book info requests with ISBN numbers. The service module will capture the credit from the customer account and return information such as the name, author, and cover image.

For ease of understanding, we will develop a service module by splitting it into two recipes. In this recipe, we will create a basic module that creates a table for the book's information. Upon customer request, the service provider will return the book information by searching in this table. In the next recipe, we will add the second part of the service module; in that module, we will add the code to capture the credits and return the book info.

How to do it...

Follow these steps to generate a basic service module:

1. Create a new `iap_isbn_service` module and add `__init__.py`:

   ```python
   from . import models
   from . import controllers
   ```

2. Add `__manifest__.py`, with the following content:

   ```python
   {
       'name': "IAP ISBN service",
       'summary': "Get books information by ISBN number",
       'website': "http://www.example.com",
       'category': 'Uncategorized',
       'version': '14.0.1',
       'author': "Parth Gajjar",
       'depends': ['iap', 'web', 'base_setup'],
       'data': [
           'security/ir.model.access.csv',
           'views/book_info_views.xml',
           'data/books_data.xml',
       ]
   }
   ```

3. Add a `book.info` model at `models/book_info.py`, with a method to fetch the book data:

   ```python
   from odoo import models, fields, api

   class BookInfo(models.Model):
       _name = 'book.info'

       name = fields.Char('Books Name', required=True)
       isbn = fields.Char('ISBN', required=True)
       date_release = fields.Date('Release Date')
   ```

```python
    cover_image = fields.Binary('BooksCover')
    author_ids = fields.Many2many('res.partner',
string='Authors')

    @api.model
    def _books_data_by_isbn(self, isbn):
        book = self.search([('isbn', '=', isbn)],
limit=1)
        if book:
            return {
                'status': 'found',
                'data': {
                    'name': book.name,
                    'isbn': book.isbn,
                    'date_release': book.date_release,
                    'cover_image': book.cover_image,
                    'authors': [a.name for a in book.
author_ids]
                }
            }
        else:
            return {
                'status': 'not found',
            }
```

4. Add an http controller in the controller/main.py file (don't forget to add the controllers/__init__.py file):

```python
from odoo import http
from odoo.http import request

class Main(http.Controller):
    @http.route('/get_book_data', type='json',
auth="public")
    def get_book_data(self):
        # We will capture credit here
        return {
            'test': 'data'
        }
```

5. Add access rules to `security/ir.model.access.csv` and list the file in the module `manifest` file:

```
id,name,model_id:id,group_id:id,perm_read,perm_write,perm_create,perm_unlink
acl_book_backend_user,book_info,model_book_info,base.group_user,1,1,1,1
```

6. Add views, menus, and actions to `views/book_info_views.xml`:

```xml
<?xml version="1.0" encoding="utf-8"?>
<odoo>
    <!-- Form View -->
    <record id="book_info_view_form" model="ir.ui.view">
        <field name="name">Book Info Form</field>
        <field name="model">book.info</field>
        <field name="arch" type="xml">
            <form>
                <sheet>
                    <field name="cover_image" widget='image' class="oe_avatar"/>
                    <div class="oe_title">
                        <label for="name" class="oe_edit_only"/>
                        <h1>
                            <field name="name" class="oe_inline"/>
                        </h1>
                    </div>
                    <group>
                        <group>
                            <field name="isbn"/>
                            <field name="author_ids" widget="many2many_tags"/>
                        </group>
                        <group>
                            <field name="date_release"/>
                        </group>
                    </group>
                </sheet>
            </form>
        </field>
    </record>
```

```
            <!-- Add step 7 and 8 here -->
</odoo>
```

7. Add a tree view for the book info:

```
            <!-- Tree(list) View -->
            <record id="books_info_view_tree" model="ir.ui.view">
                <field name="name">Book Info List</field>
                <field name="model">book.info</field>
                <field name="arch" type="xml">
                    <tree>
                        <field name="name"/>
                        <field name="date_release"/>
                    </tree>
                </field>
            </record>
```

8. Add actions and menu items:

```
    <!-- action and menus -->
        <record id='book_info_action' model='ir.actions.act_window'>
            <field name="name">Book info</field>
            <field name="res_model">book.info</field>
            <field name="view_mode">tree,form</field>
        </record>
        <menuitem name="Books Data" id="books_info_base_menu" />
        <menuitem name="Books" id="book_info_menu" parent="books_info_base_menu" action="book_info_action"/>
```

9. If you want, you can add some sample book data. We have added sample data to the module via the data/books_data.xml file (don't forget to add cover images to the given directory).

After installing the module, you will see a new menu with book data, as follows:

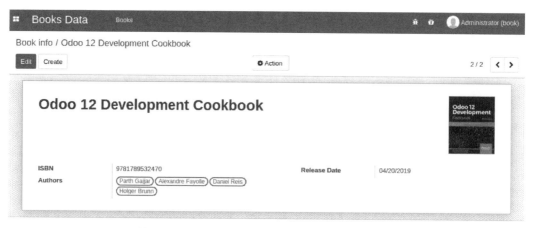

Figure 17.6 – Book data for the IAP service module

How it works...

We have now created the `iap_isbn_service` module. We have created a new `book.info` table. Consider this table the main table, where we will store data for all of the books. When the customer requests book data, we will search in this table. If the requested data is found, we will charge credits in exchange for book data.

> **Note**
> If you want to create this service for commercial purposes, you will need to have information about every book in the world. In the real world, you will need to have an external service as the book's information source. For our exercise, assume that we have the data of all of the books in the `book.info` table, and we will give book data from this table only.

In the model, we have also created the `_books_data_by_isbn()` method. This method will find a book given an ISBN number and generate the proper data so that it can be sent back to the customer. The `status` key in the result will be used to indicate whether the book data is found. It will be used to release reserved credit when the book data is not found.

We have also added a `/get_book_data` route. The IAP customer will make a request using this URL to get the book details. We still need to add the code for capturing IAP credit for the service, which will be done in the next recipe. However, for testing purposes, you can make a test request through `curl`, like this:

```
curl --header "Content-Type: application/json" \
     --request POST \
     --data "{}" \
     http://localhost:8069/get_book_data
```

This will return something like this:

```
{"jsonrpc": "2.0", "id": null, "result": {"test": "data"}}.
```

The rest of the steps in this recipe are from previous recipes and don't need detailed explanation. In the next recipe, we will update our module to capture the customer's credit and return the book data to them.

Authorizing and charging IAP credits

In this recipe, we will complete the IAP service module. We will use the IAP platform to authorize and capture credit from the customer account. We will also add an optional configuration to save the service key generated in the *Registering an IAP service in Odoo* recipe of this chapter.

Getting ready

For this recipe, we will be using the `iap_isbn_service` module.

As we are using the IAP sandbox service, we need to set an IAP endpoint in the system parameters. To set the IAP sandbox endpoint, follow these steps:

1. Activate developer mode.
2. Open **Technical | Parameters | System Parameters**.
3. Create a new record and add a key and a value, as follows:

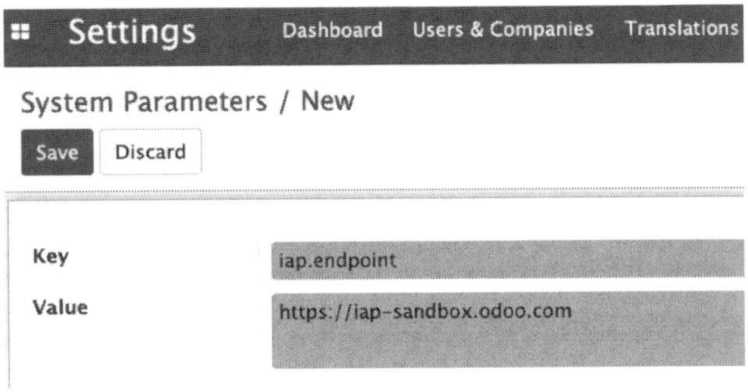

Figure 17.7 – Setting an endpoint for the IAP sandbox

How to do it...

In order to complete the service module, we will add a configuration option to the store service key. Follow these steps to add a new field to set `isbn_service_key` in the general settings:

1. Add an `isbn_service_key` field in `res.config.settings`:

   ```
   from odoo import models, fields

   class ConfigSettings(models.TransientModel):
       _inherit = 'res.config.settings'

       isbn_service_key = fields.Char("ISBN service key",
                                      config_parameter='iap.isbn_service_key')
   ```

2. Add an `isbn_service_key` field in the general settings view:

   ```
   <?xml version="1.0" encoding="utf-8"?>
   <odoo>
       <record id="view_general_config_isbn_service" model="ir.ui.view">
           <field name="name">Configuration: IAP service key</field>
           <field name="model">res.config.settings</field>
           <field name="inherit_id" ref="base_setup.res_config_settings_view_form" />
           <field name="arch" type="xml">
               <div id="business_documents" position="before">
                   <h2>IAP Books ISBN service</h2>
                   <div class="row mt16 o_settings_container">
                       <div class="col-12 col-lg-6 o_setting_box">
                           <div class="o_setting_right_pane">
                               <span class="o_form_label">IAP service key</span>
                               <div class="text-muted">
                                   Generate service in odoo IAP and add service key here
                               </div>
                               <div class="content-group">
   ```

```xml
                                <div class="mt16 row">
                                    <label for="isbn_service_key"
                                        class="col-3 col-lg-3 o_light_label"/>
                                    <field name="isbn_service_key"
                                        class="oe_inline" required="1"/>
                                </div>
                            </div>
                        </div>
                    </div>
                </div>
            </field>
        </record>
    </odoo>
```

3. Update the `iap_isbn_service` module. After the module updates, you will see a field in **General Settings** to store a service key, as shown in the following screenshot. If you remember, we generated the service key in the *Registering an IAP service in Odoo* recipe of this chapter. Add the generated service key in this field. See the following screenshot for more information:

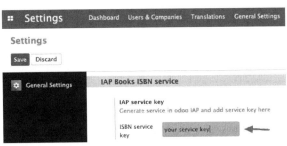

Figure 17.8 – Setting the service key in the configuration

4. Now, we will update the `/get_book_data` controller to capture the customer credit. Update the `main.py` file as follows:

```
from odoo import http
from odoo.http import request
from odoo.addons.iap.tools import iap_tools

class Main(http.Controller):
    @http.route('/get_book_data', type='json',
```

```
        auth="public")
    def get_book_data(self, account_token, isbn_number):
        service_key = request.env['ir.config_parameter'].sudo()
                             .get_param('iap.isbn_service_key', False)
        if not service_key:
            return {
                'status': 'service is not active'
            }
        credits_to_reserve = 1
        data = {}
        with iap_tools.iap_charge(request.env, service_key,
                                   account_token, credits_to_reserve):
            data = request.env['book.info'].sudo().books_data_by_isbn(isbn_number)
            if data['status'] == 'not found':
                raise Exception('Book not found')
        return data
```

Update the module to apply these changes.

How it works...

In order to draw credit from the customer's account, we will need a service key generated from the IAP platform. In the *Registering an IAP service in Odoo* recipe of this chapter, we generated a service key. (It's no problem if you have lost the service key; it can be regenerated from the service page.) We have added an `isbn_service_key` field in the general settings so that we can store a service key in Odoo. You may have noticed that we used the `config_parameter` attribute in the file definition.

The use of this attribute in the field will store the value in the `ir.config_parameter` model, also known as **System Parameters**. After saving it, you can check its value in the **Technical | Parameters | System Parameters** menu, in developer mode. While capturing IAP credits, we will retrieve the service key from **System Parameters**. To retrieve the values from **System Parameters**, you can use `get_param()`. For example, you can fetch a service key like this:

```
self.env['ir.config_parameter'].sudo().get_param('iap.isbn_service_key', False)
```

Here, the first argument is the key of the parameter that has a value you want to access, and the second argument is a default value. If the requested key is not present in the database, then the default value will be returned.

Next, we updated the `/get_book_data` route. Now, it is accepting two arguments:

- `account_token`, which is the customer token used to identify the user. The credit purchased by the customer for the service will be linked to this `account_token` on the IAP platform. Service providers will send this token while capturing credit.
- `isbn_number` is the ISBN number of the book whose information the customer wants in exchange for credit.

> **Note**
>
> These arguments are not fixed here. Our example service needs `isbn_number`, so we have passed it. However, you can pass any number of arguments that you want. Just make sure that you have passed `account_token`, because without it, you cannot capture credit from the customer account.

The IAP service provides the `iap_tools.iap_charge()` helper method, which handles the process of capturing credit from the customer account. The `iap_charge()` method accepts four parameters: the environment, the provider service key, the customer account token, and the amount of credit to capture. The `iap_charge()` method manages the following things:

- Creating the transaction object and reserving the specified number of credit. If a customer account doesn't have enough credit, then it will raise `InsufficientCreditError`.
- If enough credit is found in a customer account, it will run code in the `with` block.
- If the code in the `with` block runs successfully, it captures the received credit.
- If the code in the `with` block generates an exception, it will release the reserved credit, as the service request cannot be completed.

In the previous example, we used the same `iap_tools.iap_charge()` method to capture credit for a book request. We used our service key and customer account token to reserve one credit for the book info. Then, inside the `with` block, we used the `_books_data_by_isbn()` method to get book data based on the ISBN number. If the book data is found, then it will execute the `with` block without any errors and one reserved credit will be deducted from the customer account. Later, we will return this data to the customer. If the book data is not found, then we raise the exception so that the reserved credit is released.

There's more...

In our example, we are handling the request of only one book's data, and capturing the single credit is simple; but things get complicated with multiple credits. A complex pricing structure can introduce a few corner cases. Let's look at this issue through the following example. Suppose that we want to handle multiple book requests. In this case, a customer has requested the data of 10 books, but we only have the data of 5 books. Here, if we complete the `with` block without encountering any errors, `iap_charge()` will capture 10 credits, which is incorrect, because we only have the data for a certain number of books. Furthermore, if we raise the exception, then it will release all 10 credits and show the customer that the book info is not found. To fix this issue, Odoo provides the object of the transaction in the `with` block. In some cases, the services cannot fully serve a request. For example, say a user asked for the data of 10 books but you only have the data for 5 books. In such cases, you can change the actual credit amount on the go and capture partial credits. See the following example for a further explanation:

```
...
isbn_list = [<assume list of 10 isbn number>]
credits_to_reserve = len(isbn_list)
data_found = []
with iap_tools.iap_charge(request.env, service_key, account_token, credits_to_reserve) as transection:
    for isbn in isbn_list:
        data = request.env['books.info']._books_data_by_isbn(isbn)
        if data['status'] == 'found':
            data_found.appned(data)
    transection.credit = len(data_found)
return data_found
```

In the preceding code block, we have updated the value of the credit to capture on the fly, according to `transection.credit`; this is how we can only charge credit for the book data that is found.

See also

- IAP is not limited to the Odoo framework. You can develop a service provider module for any other platform or framework. Just make sure that it can handle JSON-RPC2 (`https://www.jsonrpc.org/specification`) requests.
- If you develop a service provider in any other platform, you will also need to manage the transaction manually by using IAP endpoints. You will need to authorize and capture credit by requesting IAP endpoints. You can get endpoint information at `https://www.odoo.com/documentation/12.0/webservices/iap.html#json-rpc2-transaction-api`.

Creating an IAP client module

In the previous recipe, we created the IAP service module. Now, we will create an IAP client module to complete the IAP service flow.

Getting ready

We will need the `my_library` module from *Chapter 3*, *Creating Odoo Add-On Modules*. We will add a new button in the book's form view and clicking that button will create a request to an IAP service and fetch the book data.

As per the IAP service flow, the customer makes the request to the service provider. Here, to register a customer's request, we need to run a separate server for the IAP service. If you want to test this on the same machine, you can run the service instance on a different port and different database, like this:

```
./odoo-bin -c server-config -d service_db --db-filter=^service_db$ --http-port=8070
```

This will run the Odoo server on port `8070`. Make sure that you have installed the service module in this database and have added the IAP service key. Note that this recipe is written assuming that you have an IAP service running on `http://localhost:8070`.

How to do it...

We will create a new `iap_isbn_client` module. This module will inherit the `my_library` module and add a button in the book's form view. Clicking on a button will send a request to our IAP service running on port 8090. The IAP service will capture the credit and return the information of the requested book. We will write this information in the book's record. Follow these steps to complete the IAP client module:

1. Create a new `iap_isbn_client` module and add `__init__.py`:

    ```
    from . import models
    ```

2. Add `__manifest__.py`, with the given content:

    ```
    {
        'name': "Books ISBN",
        'summary': "Get Books Data based on ISBN",
        'website': "http://www.example.com",
        'category': 'Uncategorized',
        'version': '14.0.1',
        'author': "Parth Gajjar",
        'depends': ['iap', 'my_library'],
        'data': [
            'views/library_books_views.xml',
        ]
    }
    ```

3. Add `models/library_book.py` and add a few fields by inheriting the `library.book` model:

    ```
    from odoo import models, fields, api
    from odoo.exceptions import UserError
    from odoo.addons.iap.tools import iap_tools


    class LibraryBook(models.Model):
        _inherit = 'library.book'

        cover_image = fields.Binary('Books Cover')
        isbn = fields.Char('ISBN')
    ```

4. Add the `fetch_book_data()` method in the same model. This will be called upon a button click:

```
def fetch_book_data(self):
    self.ensure_one()
    if not self.isbn:
        raise UserError("Please add ISBN number")

    user_token = self.env['iap.account'].get('book_isbn')
    params = {
        'account_token': user_token.account_token,
        'isbn_number': self.isbn
    }
    service_endpoint = 'http://localhost:8070'
    result = iap_tools.iap_jsonrpc(service_endpoint + '/get_book_data', params=params)
    if result.get('status') == 'found':
        self.write(self.process_result(result['data']))
    return True
```

5. Add the `process_result()` method to process the IAP service's response:

```
@api.model
def process_result(self, result):
    authors = []
    existing_author_ids = []
    for author_name in result['authors']:
        author = self.env['res.partner'].search([('name','=',author_name)], limit=1)
        if author:
            existing_author_ids.append(author.id)
        else:
            authors.append((0, 0, {'name': author_name}))
    if existing_author_ids:
        authors.append((6, 0, existing_author_ids))
    return {
        'author_ids': authors,
        'name': result.get('name'),
        'isbn': result.get('isbn'),
        'cover_image': result.get('cover_image'),
        'date_release': result.get('date_release'),
    }
```

6. Add `views/library_books_views.xml`, and add a button and fields by inheriting the book's form view:

```xml
<?xml version="1.0" encoding="utf-8"?>
<odoo>

    <record id="library_book_view_form_inh" model="ir.ui.view">
        <field name="name">Library Book Form</field>
        <field name="model">library.book</field>
        <field name="inherit_id" ref="my_library.library_book_view_form"/>
        <field name="arch" type="xml">
            <xpath expr="//group" position="before">
                <header>
                    <button name="fetch_book_data" string="Fetch Book Data" type="object"/>
                </header>
            </xpath>
            <field name="date_release" position="after">
                <field name="isbn"/>
                <field name="cover_image" widget="image" class="oe_avatar"/>
            </field>
        </field>
    </record>

</odoo>
```

Install the `iap_isbn_client` module. This will add a **Fetch Book Data** button to the book form. After doing this, add a valid **ISBN** number (for example, 1788392019) and click on the button. This will make a request and fetch the data from the service. If you are making the IAP service call for the first time, then your Odoo instance won't have information about the linked account, so Odoo will raise a popup to buy the credits, as follows:

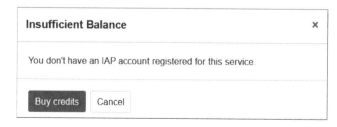

Figure 17.9 – Alert for insufficient balance

Upon clicking on the **Buy credits** at Odoo button, you will be redirected to the IAP service page, where you will see the information about the packs available to purchase. For our recipe, you will see the packs that we defined while registering our service in the *Registering an IAP service in Odoo* recipe of this chapter. Take a look at the following screenshot: there is a list of packs to purchase:

Figure 17.10 – IAP packs to purchase

As we are using the sandbox endpoint, you can buy any pack without any payment being necessary. After that, you can request the book information from the book's form view.

How it works...

We have created a /get_book_data route in the service module. This route is used to handle a customer's IAP requests. So, from this client module, we will make a JSON-RPC request to that route. This IAP request will capture the credit and fetch the book's data. Luckily, the IAP module provides an iap_jsonrpc wrapper to make the jsonrpc request, so we will use it.

The library.book model of the my_library module doesn't have the ISBN and cover_image field, so we have extra fields in the library.book model by inheritance. Refer to the *Adding features to a model using inheritance* recipe from *Chapter 4, Application Models*. We have added fields through inheritance because we don't want to use these fields when the iap_isbn_client module is not installed.

In order to initiate a request, we have added a button to the book's form view through inheritance. A button click will trigger the fetch_book_data() method, and in that method, we have made the jsonrpc request to the service endpoint. With the request, we have passed two parameters: the customer account tokens and the ISBN number for the book data.

You can get a customer account token from the `get()` method of the `iap.account` model. The token generation is automatic. You just need to call the `get()` method with the name of the service. In our case, the service name is `book_isbn`. This will return the record set of the customer IAP account, and you can grab the customer token's `account_token` field.

We have made a `jsonrpc` request to fetch the book info. If the customer doesn't have enough credit, the service module will generate `InsufficientCreditError`. Now, `jsonrpc` will handle this exception automatically, and it will display a popup to the customer to purchase the credit. The popup will have a link to the page where the customer can purchase the service plans. As we are using the sandbox, you can get any pack without payment being needed. However, in production, the customer needs to make a payment for the service.

Upon a button click, if everything goes well, the customer has enough credit, and our database has data for the requested ISBN, the credit will be deducted from the customer's account and `iap_jsonrpc` will return the book's data. Then, we simply pass the result to the `process_result()` method and write data to the book's record.

There's more...

If you want to find out the amount of credit remaining for the services, you can see it at the link provided on the dashboard:

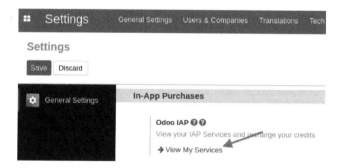

Figure 17.11 – View your active services and balance

Also, the `iap_tools.iap_charge()` method supports one more parameter, `description`, which you can pass as follows:

```
...
with iap_tools.iap_charge(request.env, service_key, account_token, credits_to_reserve, description="For the book info"):
...
```

If you pass `description` while capturing credits, the customer will be able to see the description for the deducted credit in the IAP portal.

Displaying offers when an account lacks credits

If you make an IAP service request after all of the purchased credits are consumed, then the service module will generate `InsufficientCreditError`, and the client-side module will handle this error automatically and display a popup. Whenever all of your IAP account credit is consumed, Odoo will display a popup as in the following screenshot to prompt the purchase of more credit:

Figure 17.12 – An alert shown for an insufficient balance

The default popup is too simple and does not provide enough information. In this recipe, we will look at how you can change the content of this popup with an attractive template.

Getting ready

We will be using the `iap_isbn_service` module for this recipe. The offer template is created on the IAP service provider module, so it can be changed at any time without updating the client module.

How to do it...

Follow these steps to add a custom credit template:

1. Add a template with service information at `views/templates.xml`:

```
<odoo>
<template id="no_credit_info" name="No credit info">
    <section class="jumbotron text-center bg-primary">
        <div class="container pb32 pt32">
            <h1 class="jumbotron-heading">Library ISBN</h1>
            <p class="lead text-muted">
                Get full book information with cover
```

```xml
                    image just by the ISBN number.
                </p>
                <span class="badge badge-warning" style="font-size: 30px;">
                    20% Off
                </span>
            </div>
        </section>
        <div class="container">
            <div class="row">
                <div class="col">
                    <div class="card mb-3">
                        <div class="card-header">
                            <i class="fa fa-database"/> Large books database
                        </div>
                        <div class="card-body">
                            <p class="card-text">
                                We have largest book database. It contains more
                                then 2500000+ books.
                            </p>
                        </div>
                    </div>
                </div>
                <div class="col">
                    <div class="card mb-3">
                        <div class="card-header">
                            <i class="fa fa-image"/>
                            With cover image
                        </div>
                        <div class="card-body">
                            <p class="card-text">
                                More than 95% of our books having high quality
                                book cover images.
                            </p>
                        </div>
                    </div>
                </div>
            </div>
        </div>
    </div>
</template>
</odoo>
```

2. Add a template to __manifest__.py:

```
...
    'data': [
        'security/ir.model.access.csv',
        'views/book_info_views.xml',
        'data/books_data.xml',
        'views/res_config_settings.xml',
        'views/templates.xml'
    ]
...
```

3. Add a template reference to iap.charge at controllers/main.py:

```
...
with iap_tools.iap_charge(request.env, service_key,
account_token, credits_to_reserve, credit_template='iap_
isbn_service.no_credit_info'):
    data = request.env['book.info'].sudo()._books_data_
by_isbn(isbn_number)
    if data['status'] == 'not found':
        raise Exception('Book not found')
```

Update the module to apply the changes.

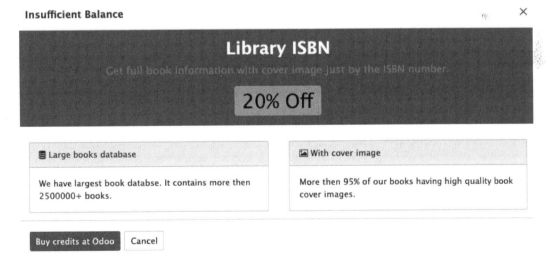

Figure 17.13 – Offers shown for an insufficient balance

After the update, you will see a credit popup if all of the customer's credit is consumed, as indicated in *Figure 17.13*.

How it works...

In order to display an attractive popup on the client side, we need to create a QWeb template. In *step 1*, we created the QWeb template, `no_credit_info`. This is made with simple bootstrap content. Note that it just contains static HTML content. In *step 2*, we added the template file to the app manifest.

After designing the template, you need to pass the template XML reference to the `iap_tools.iap_charge()` method. This can be passed through the optional `credit_template` parameter. In *step 3*, we passed a template reference to the `charge` method. After passing the template, if `InsufficientCreditError` is raised, then the template will be passed along with the error message to the customer. On the client side, if an error message is received with the template body, then this custom template will be displayed in a popup instead of the default popup.

There's more...

We don't have an image in the template, but if you want to use an image in the template, you need to be extra careful. The reason is that here, you cannot use an absolute image URL as you normally would. Because the service module is running on a separate server, the popup will not display the image. To fix this issue, you need to pass a full image URL with the domain, as this template is going to be displayed on the client screen.

18
Automated Test Cases

When it comes to developing large applications, using automated test cases is a good practice for improving the reliability of your module. This makes your module more robust. Every year, Odoo releases a new version of its software, and automated test cases are very helpful in detecting regression in your application, which may have been caused by a version upgrade. Luckily, any Odoo framework comes with different automated testing utilities. Odoo includes the following three main types of tests:

- **Python test case**: Used to test Python business logic
- **JavaScript QUnit test**: Used to test JavaScript implementation in Odoo
- **Tours**: Integration test to check that Python and JavaScript work with each other properly

In this chapter, we will cover the following recipes:

- Adding Python test cases
- Running tagged Python test cases
- Setting up Headless Chrome for client-side test cases
- Adding client-side QUnit test cases

- Adding tour test cases
- Running client-side test cases from the UI
- Debugging client-side test cases
- Generating videos/screenshots for failed test cases
- Populating random data for testing

Technical requirements

In this chapter, we will look at all of the test cases in detail. In order to cover all of the test cases in a single module, we have created a small module. Its Python definition is as follows:

```
class LibraryBook(models.Model):
    _name = 'library.book'
    name = fields.Char('Title', required=True)
    date_release = fields.Date('Release Date')
    author_ids = fields.Many2many('res.partner',
string='Authors')
    state = fields.Selection(
        [('draft', 'Not Available'),
         ('available', 'Available'),
         ('lost', 'Lost')],
        'State', default="draft")
    color = fields.Integer()

    def make_available(self):
        self.write({'state': 'available'})

    def make_lost(self):
        self.write({'state': 'lost'})
```

The Python code given here will help us to write test cases for Python business cases. For JavaScript test cases, we have added the `int_color` widget from the *Creating custom widgets recipe* in *Chapter 15, Web Client Development*.

You can grab this initial module from the GitHub repository of this book at the following link: https://github.com/PacktPublishing/Odoo-14-Development-Cookbook-Fourth-Edition/tree/master/Chapter18/00_initial_module.

Adding Python test cases

Python test cases are used to check the correctness of business logic. In *Chapter 5, Basic Server-Side Development*, you saw how you can modify the business logic of our existing app. This makes it even more important, as customization might break the app's functionality. In this chapter, we will write a test case to validate the business logic to change a book's state.

Getting ready

We will be using the `my_library` module from the `Chapter17/r0_initial_module` directory of the GitHub repository.

How to do it...

Follow these steps to add Python test cases to the `my_library` module:

1. Add a new file, `tests/__init__.py`, as follows:

   ```python
   from . import test_book_state
   ```

2. Add a `tests/test_book_state.py` file, and add the test case, as follows:

   ```python
   from odoo.tests.common import import TransactionCase

   class TestBookState(TransactionCase):

       def setUp(self, *args, **kwargs):
           super(TestBookState, self).setUp(*args, **kwargs)
           self.test_book = self.env['library.book'].create({'name': 'Book 1'})

       def test_button_available(self):
           """Make available button"""
           self.test_book.make_available()
           self.assertEqual(self.test_book.state, 'available',
                   'Book state should be changed to available')

       def test_button_lost(self):
           """Make lost button"""
           self.test_book.make_lost()
           self.assertEqual(self.test_book.state, 'lost',
                   'Book state should be changed to lost')
   ```

3. In order to run the test cases, start the Odoo server with the following option:

```
./odoo-bin -c server.conf -i my_library --test-enable
```

Now, check the server log. You will find the following logs if our test cases ran successfully:

```
... INFO test odoo.addons.my_library.tests.test_book_state:
Starting TestBookState.test_button_available ...
... INFO test odoo.addons.my_library.tests.test_book_state:
Starting TestBookState.test_button_lost ...
... INFO test odoo.modules.loading: Module my_library loaded in
0.79s (incl. 0.12s test), 179 queries (+10 test)
```

You will see the ERROR log instead of INFO if a test case fails or there is an error.

How it works...

In Odoo, Python test cases are added to the `tests/` directory of the module. Odoo will automatically identify this directory and run the test under the folder.

> **Note**
>
> You also need to list your test case files in `tests/__init__.py`. If you don't do that, that test case will not execute.

Odoo uses Python's `unittest` for Python test cases. To learn more about Python's `unittest`, refer to https://docs.python.org/3.5/library/unittest.html. Odoo provides some helper classes, wrapped over `unittest`. These classes simplify the process of developing test cases. In our case, we have used `TransactionCase`. Now, `TransactionCase` runs each test case method in a different transaction. Once a test case method runs successfully, a transaction is automatically rolled back. This means the next test case will not have any modification made by the previous test case.

The class method starts from `test_` and is considered a test case. In our example, we have added two test cases. This checks the methods that change the book's state. The `self.assertEqual` method is used to check whether the test case runs successfully. We have checked the book state after performing operations on the book's record. So, if the developer made a mistake and the method is not changing states as expected, the test case will fail.

> **Important information**
> Note that the `setUp()` method will automatically call for every test case we run, so in this recipe, we have added two test cases, so that `setUp()` will call twice. As per the code in this recipe, there will only be one record of the book present during testing, because with `TransactionCase`, the transaction is rolled back with every test case.

`docstrings` on the methods will be printed in the logger. This will be very helpful for checking the status of the particular test case.

There's more...

The test suite provides the following additional test utility classes:

- `SingleTransactionCase`: Test cases generated through this class will run all cases in a single transaction, so changes made from one test case will be available in a second test case. In this way, the transaction is begun with the first test method and is only rolled back at the end of the last test case.
- `SavepointCase`: This is the same as `SingleTransactionCase`, but in this case, test methods run inside a rolled-back save point, instead of having all test methods in a single transaction. This is used to create large test cases to make them faster by generating test data only once. Here, we use the `setUpClass()` method to generate the initial test data.

Running tagged Python test cases

When you run the Odoo server with the `--test-enabled` module, the test cases run immediately after the module is installed. If you want to run a test case after the installation of all the modules, or if you just want to run a test case for only one module, a `tagged()` decorator is the answer. In this recipe, we will illustrate how to use this decorator to mold test cases.

Getting ready

For this recipe, we will be using the `my_library` module from the last recipe. We will modify the sequence of the test case.

How to do it...

Follow these steps to add tags to the Python test cases:

1. Add a `tagged()` decorator (such as the following) to the test class to run it after the installation of all modules:

   ```
   from odoo.tests.common import import TransactionCase, tagged

   @tagged('-at_install', 'post_install')
   class TestBookState(TransactionCase):
       ...
   ```

2. After that, run the test case as follows, just like before:

   ```
   ./odoo-bin -c server.conf -i my_library --test-enable
   ```

3. Now check the server log. This time, you will see our test case log after the following logs, meaning that our test cases were run after all of the modules were installed, as follows:

   ```
   ... INFO book odoo.modules.loading: 9 modules loaded in 1.87s, 177 queries (+0 extra)
   ... INFO book odoo.modules.loading: Modules loaded.
   ... INFO book odoo.service.server: Starting post tests
   ... INFO book odoo.addons.my_library.tests.test_book_state: Starting TestBookState.test_button_available ...
   ... INFO book odoo.addons.my_library.tests.test_book_state: Starting TestBookState.test_button_lost ...
   ... INFO book odoo.service.server: 2 post-tests in 0.14s, 10 queries
   ```

In these logs, the first line shows that nine modules were loaded. The second line shows that all requested modules and their dependencies were installed successfully, and the third line shows that it will start running the test cases that are tagged as `post_install`.

How it works...

By default, all of the test cases are tagged with `standard`, `at_install`, and the current module's technical name (in our case, the technical name is `my_library`). Consequently, if you are not using a `tagged()` decorator, your test case will have these three tags.

In our case, we want to run the test case after installing all of the modules. To do so, we have added a `tagged()` decorator to the `TestBookState` class. By default, the test case has the `at_install` tag. Because of this tag, your test case will run immediately after the module is installed; it will not wait for other modules to be installed. We don't want this, so to remove the `at_install` tag, we have added `-at_install` to the tagged function. The tags that are prefixed by `-` will remove that tag.

By adding `-at_install` to the `tagged()` function, we stopped the test case execution after the module installation. As we haven't specified any other tag in this, the test case won't run.

So, we have added a `post_install` tag. This tag specifies that the test case needs to be run after the installation of all modules is completed.

As you have seen, all test cases are tagged with the `standard` tag, by default. Odoo will run all of the test cases tagged with the `standard` tag, in case you don't want to run the specific test case all of the time and you only want to run the test case when it is requested. To do so, you need to remove the `standard` tag by adding `-standard` to the `tagged()` decorator, and you need to add a custom tag like this:

```
@tagged('-standard', 'my_custom_tag')
class TestClass(TransactionCase):
    ...
```

All of the non-standard test cases will not run with the `--test-enable` option. To run the preceding test case, you need to use the `--test-tags` option, as follows (note that here, we do not need to pass the `--test-enable` option explicitly):

```
./odoo-bin -c server.conf -i my_library --test-tags=my_custom_tag
```

There's more...

During the development of the test case, it is important to run the test case for just one module. By default, the technical name of the module is added as a tag, so you can use the module's technical name with the `--test-tags` option. For example, if you want to run test cases for the `my_library` module, then you can run the server like this:

```
./odoo-bin -c server.conf -i my_library --test-tags=my_library
```

The command given here will run the test case in the `my_library` module, but it will still decide the sequence based on the `at_install` and `post_install` options.

Setting up Headless Chrome for client-side test cases

Odoo uses **Headless Chrome** to perform JavaScript test cases and tour test cases. Headless Chrome is a way to run Chrome without the full UI. This way, we can run JavaScript test cases in the same environment as the end user. In this recipe, we will install Headless Chrome and other packages in order to run JavaScript test cases.

How to do it...

You will need to install Chrome to enable a JavaScript test case. For the development of the modules, we mostly use the desktop OS. Consequently, if you have a Chrome browser installed on your system, then there is no need to install it separately. You can run client-side test cases with desktop Chrome. Make sure that you have a Chrome version higher than Chrome 59. Odoo also supports the Chromium browser.

> **Note**
> Headless Chrome client-side test cases work fine with macOS and Linux, but Odoo does not support Headless Chrome test cases on Windows.

Things change slightly when you want to run test cases in the production server or on Server OS. Server OS does not have a GUI, so you need to install Chrome differently. If you are using a Debian-based OS, you can install Chromium with the following command:

```
apt-get install chromium-browser
```

> **Important information**
> Ubuntu 18.04 Server Edition has not enabled the `universe` repository by default. So, it's possible that installing `chromium-browser` will show an installation candidate error. To fix this error, enable the `universe` repository with the following command: `sudo add-apt-repository universe`.

Odoo also uses **WebSockets** for JavaScript test cases. For that, Odoo uses the `websocket-client` Python library. To install it, use the following command:

```
pip3 install websocket-client
```

Now your system is ready to run client-side test cases.

How it works...

Odoo uses Headless Chrome for JavaScript test cases. The reason behind this is that it runs test cases in the background, so it can be run on Server OS, too. Headless Chrome prefers to run the Chrome browser in the background, without opening a GUI browser. Odoo opens a Chrome tab in the background and starts running the test cases in it. It also uses **jQuery's QUnit** for JavaScript test cases. In the next few recipes, we will create a **QUnit** test case for our custom JavaScript widgets.

For test cases, Odoo opens Headless Chrome in a separate process, so to find out the status of a test case running in that process, the Odoo server uses WebSockets. The `websocket-client` Python library is used to manage WebSockets to communicate with Chrome from the Odoo server.

Adding client-side QUnit test cases

Building new fields or views is very simple in Odoo. In just a few lines of XML, you can define a new view. However, under the hood, it uses a lot of JavaScript. Modifying/adding new features on the client side is complex, and it might break a few things. Most client-side issues go unnoticed, as most errors are only displayed in the console. So, QUnit test cases are used in Odoo to check the correctness of different JavaScript components.

Getting ready

For this recipe, we will continue using the `my_library` module from the previous recipe. We will add a QUnit test case for the `int_color` widget.

How to do it...

Follow these steps to add JavaScript test cases to the `int_color` widget:

1. Add `/static/tests/colorpicker_tests.js` with the following code:

    ```javascript
    odoo.define('colorpicker_tests', function (require) {
    "use strict";

    var FormView = require('web.FormView');
    var testUtils = require('web.test_utils');

    QUnit.module('Color Picker Tests', {
        beforeEach: function () {
            this.data = {
                book: {
    ```

```
                        fields: {
                            name: { string: "Name", type: "char"
},
                            color: { string: "color", type:
"integer"},
                        },
                        records: [{id: 1, name: "Book 1", color:
1},
                                    {id: 2, name: "Book 2",color:
3}]
                } };
        }
    }, function () {
        // Place step 2 here
    });
});
```

2. Add a `QUnit` test case for the color picker field like this:

```
QUnit.only('int_color field test cases', async function
(assert) {
    assert.expect(2);

    var form = await testUtils.createView({
        View: FormView,
        model: 'book',
        data: this.data,
        arch: '<form string="Books">' +
            '<group>' +
                '<field name="name"/>' +
                '<field name="color" widget="int_
color"/>' +
            '</group>' +
            '</form>',
        res_id: 1,
    });

    await testUtils.form.clickEdit(form);
    assert.strictEqual(form.$('.o_int_colorpicker .o_
color_pill').length, 10,
```

```
            "colorpicker should have 10 pills");
        await testUtils.dom.click(form.$('.o_int_colorpicker
.o_color_pill:eq(5)'));
        assert.strictEqual(form.$('.o_int_colorpicker .o_
color_5').hasClass('active'), true,
            "click on pill should make pill active");
        form.destroy();
    });
```

3. Add the following code in `/views/template.xml` to register it in the test suite:

```
...
<template id="qunit_suite" name="colorpicker test"
         inherit_id="web.qunit_suite">
    <xpath expr="." position="inside">
        <script type="text/javascript"
                src="/my_library/static/tests/colorpicker_tests.js" />
    </xpath>
</template>
...
```

To run this test case, start your server with the following command in the terminal:

```
./odoo-bin -c server.conf -i my_library,web --test-enable
```

To check that the tests have run successfully, search for the following log:

```
... INFO test odoo.addons.web.tests.test_js.WebSuite: console
log: "Color Picker Tests" passed 2 tests.
```

How it works...

In Odoo, JavaScript test cases are added to the `/static/tests/` directory. In *step 1*, we have added a `colorpicker_tests.js` file for the test case. In that file, we have imported the `formView` and `test_utils` references. `web.FormView` is imported because we have created the `int_color` widget for the form view, so to test the widget, we will need the form view.

`web.test_utils` will provide us with the test utilities we require to build the JavaScript test cases. If you don't know how JavaScript import works, refer to the *Extending CSS and JavaScript for the website* recipe in *Chapter 14*, *CMS Website Development*.

Odoo client-side test cases are built with the QUnit framework, which is the jQuery framework for the JavaScript unit test case. Refer to https://qunitjs.com/ to learn more about this. The beforeEach function is called before running the test cases, and this helps to initialize the test data. The reference of the beforeEach function is provided by the QUnit framework itself.

We have initialized some data in the beforeEach function. Let's see how that data is being used in the test case. The client-side test case runs in an isolated (mock) environment, and it doesn't make a connection to the database, so for these test cases, we need to create test data. Internally, Odoo creates the mock server to mimic the **Remote Procedure Call (RPC)** calls and uses the this.data property as the database. Consequently, in beforeEach, we have initialized our test data in the this.data property. The keys in the this.data property are considered a table, and the values contain information about the fields and the table rows. The fields key is used to define table fields, and the records key is used for the table rows. In our example, we have added a book table with two fields: name(char) and color(integer). Note that here, you can use any Odoo fields, even relational fields; for example, {string: "M2o Field", type: "many2one", relation: 'partner'}. We have also added two book records with the records key.

Next, we have added the test cases with the QUnit.test function. The first argument in the function is string to describe the test case. The second argument is the function to which you need to add code for the test cases. This function is called from the QUnit framework, and it passes the assert utilities as the argument. In our example, we have passed the number of expected test cases in the assert.expect function. We are adding two test cases, so we have passed 2.

We want to add to the test case int_color widget in the editable form view, so we have created the editable form view with testUtils.createView. The createView function accepts different arguments, as follows:

- View is the reference of the view you want to create. You can create any type of view for the test case; you just need to pass the view reference here.
- model is the name of the model for which the given view is created. All of the models are listed in the this.data property. We want to create a view for the book model, so in our example, we have used book as a model.
- data is the record that we are going to use in the view.

- `arch` is the definition of the view you want to create. Because we want to test the `int_color` widget, we have passed the view definition with the widget. Note that you can only use the fields that are defined in the model.
- `res_id` is the record ID whose record is being displayed. This option is only used for form views. In our case, the form view will be displayed with the data of the book 1 record, as we added `1` as `res_id`.

After creating the form view with the `int_color` widget, we added two test cases. The first one is used to check the number of color pills on the UI, and the second test case is used to check that the pill is activated correctly after the click. We have the `strictEqual` function from the asserted utility of the QUnit framework. The `strictEqual` function passes the test case if the first two arguments match. If they do not match, it will fail the test case.

There's more...

There are a few more assert functions available for QUnit test cases, such as `assert.deepEqual`, `assert.ok`, and `assert.notOk`. To learn more about QUnit, refer to its documentation at `https://qunitjs.com/`.

Adding tour test cases

You have now seen Python and JavaScript test cases. Both of these work in an isolated environment, and they don't interact with each other. To test integration between JavaScript and Python code, tour test cases are used.

Getting ready

For this recipe, we will continue using the `my_library` module from the previous recipe. We will add a tour test case to check the flow of the book model. Also, make sure you have installed the `web_tour` module or have added the `web_tour` module dependency to the manifest.

How to do it...

Follow these steps to add a tour test case for `books`:

1. Add a `/static/src/js/my_library_tour.js` file, and then add a tour as follows:

   ```
   odoo.define('my_library.tour', function (require) {
   "use strict";

   var core = require('web.core');
   var tour = require('web_tour.tour');
   var _t = core._t;

   tour.register('library_tour', {
       url: "/web",
       test: true,
       rainbowManMessage: _t("Congrats, you have listed a book."),
       sequence: 5,
       }, [tour.stepUtils.showAppsMenuItem(),

       // Place step 3 here
   ]);
   });
   ```

2. Add steps for the test tour:

   ```
   {
       trigger: '.o_app[data-menu-xmlid="my_library.library_base_menu"]',
       content: _t('Manage books and authors in <b>Library app</b>.'),
       position: 'right'
   }, {
       trigger: '.o_list_button_add',
       content: _t("Let's create new book."),
       position: 'bottom',
   }, {
       trigger: 'input[name="name"]',
   ```

```
            extra_trigger: '.o_form_editable',
            content: _t('Set the book title'),
            position: 'right',
            run: function (actions) {
                actions.text('Test Book');
            },
        }, {
            trigger: '.o_form_button_save',
            content: _t('Save this book record'),
            position: 'bottom',
        }
```

3. Add the my_library_tour.js file in the test assets:

```
<template id="assets_tests" name="Library Assets Tests"
inherit_id="web.assets_tests">
    <xpath expr="." position="inside">
        <script type="text/javascript" src="/my_library/static/tests/my_library_tour.js" />
    </xpath>
</template>
```

4. Add a /tests/test_tour.py file, and run the tour through HttpCase, as follows:

```
from odoo.tests.common import import HttpCase, tagged

class TestBookUI(HttpCase):

    @tagged('post_install', '-at_install')
    def test_01_book_tour(self):
        """Books UI tour test case"""
        self.browser_js("/web",
            "odoo.__DEBUG__.services['web_tour.tour'].run('library_tour')",
            "odoo.__DEBUG__.services['web_tour.tour'].tours.library_tour.ready",
            login="admin")
```

In order to run test cases, start the Odoo server with the following option:

```
./odoo-bin -c server.conf -i my_library --test-enable
```

Now check the server log. Here, you will find the following logs if our test cases ran successfully:

```
...INFO test odoo.addons.my_library.tests.test_tour.TestBookUI:
console log: Tour library_tour succeeded
```

How it works...

In order to create tour test cases, you need to create the UI tour first. If you want to learn more about UI tours, refer to the *Improve onboarding with tours* recipe in *Chapter 15, Web Client Development*.

In *step 1*, we registered a new tour with the name `library_tour`. This tour is exactly like the tour we created in the *Improve onboarding with tours* recipe in *Chapter 15, Web Client Development*. In *step 2*, we added the steps for the tours.

Here we have two main changes compared to the onboarding tour. First, we have added a `test=true` parameter for the tour definition; second, we have added one extra property, `run`. In the `run` function, you have to write the logic to perform the operation that is normally done by the user. For example, in the fourth step of the tour, we ask the user to enter the book title.

To automate this step, we have added a `run` function to set the value in the `title` field. The `run` function passes the action utility as the parameter. This provides some shortcuts to perform basic actions. The most important ones are as follows:

- `actions.click(element)` is used to click on a given element.
- `actions.dblclick(element)` is used to double-click on a given element.
- `actions.tripleclick(element)` is used to triple-click on a given element.
- `actions.text(string)` is used to set the input values.
- `actions.drag_and_drop(to, element)` is used to drag and drop an element.
- `actions.keydown(keyCodes, element)` is used to trigger particular keyboard events on an element.
- `actions.auto()` is the default action. When you don't pass the `run` function in the tour step, `actions.auto()` is performed. This usually clicks on the trigger element of the tour step. The only exception here is an input element. If the trigger element is `input`, the tour will set the default value `Test` in the input. That is why we don't need to add `run` functions to all of the steps.

Alternatively, you can perform whole actions manually if default actions are not enough. In the next tour step, we want to set a value for the color picker. Note that we have used the manual action because default values won't help here. Consequently, we have added the `run` method with the basic jQuery code to click on the third pill of the color picker. Here, you will find the trigger element with the `this.$anchor` property.

By default, registered tours are displayed to the end user to improve the onboarding experience. In order to run them as a test case, you need to run them in Headless Chrome. To do so, you need to use the `HttpCase` Python test case. This provides the `browser_js` method, which opens the URL and executes the command passed as the second parameter. You can run the tour manually, like this:

```
odoo.__DEBUG__.services['web_tour.tour'].run('library_tour')
```

In our example, we have passed the name of the tour as the argument in the `browser_js` method. The next parameter is used to wait for a given object to be ready before performing the first command. The last parameter in the `browser_js()` method is the name of the user. This username will be used to create a new test environment, and all of the test actions will be performed on behalf of this user.

Running client-side test cases from the UI

Odoo provides a way to run client-side test cases from the UI. By running the test case from the UI, you will be able to see each step of the test case in action. This way, you can verify that the UI test case is working exactly as we wanted.

How to do it...

You can run both the `QUnit` test case and the tours test case from the UI. It is not possible to run Python test cases from the UI as it runs on the server side. In order to see the options to run test cases from the UI, you need to enable developer mode.

Running QUnit test cases from the UI

Click on the bug icon to open the drop-down menu, as shown in the following figure. Click on the **Run JS Tests** option:

Figure 18.1 – Option to run test cases

This will open the QUnit suite and it will start running the test cases one by one, as shown in the following screenshot. By default, it will only show failed test cases. To show all the passed test cases, uncheck the **Hide passed tests** checkbox, as shown in the following screenshot:

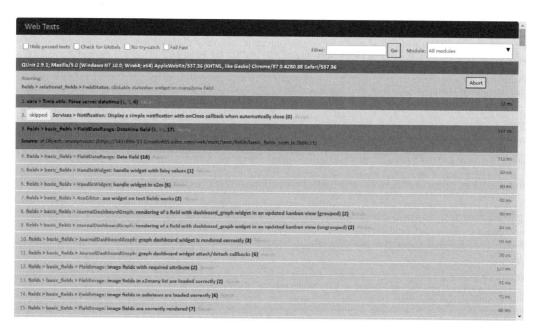

Figure 18.2 – Results of QUnit test cases

Running tours from the UI

Click on the bug icon to open the drop-down menu, as shown in the following screenshot, and then click on **Start Tour**:

Figure 18.3 – Option to run tour test cases

This will open the dialog with a list of registered tours, as you can see in the following screenshot. Click on the play button on the side to run the tour:

Figure 18.4 – List of tour test cases

The test tours only display in a list if you have enabled test assets mode. If you don't find the `library_tour` tour in the list, make sure you have activated test assets mode.

How it works...

The UI for QUnit is provided by the QUnit framework itself. Here, you can filter the test cases for the modules. You can even run a test case for just one module. With the UI, you can see the progress of each test case, and you can drill down to each step of the test case. Internally, Odoo just opens the same URL in Headless Chrome.

Clicking on the **Run tours** option will display the list of available tours. By clicking on the play button on the list, you can run the tour. Note that when the tour runs via the command-line options, it runs in the rolled-back transaction, so changes made through the tour are rolled back after the tour is successful. However, when the tour runs from the UI, it works just as though a user was operating it, meaning changes made from the tour are not rolled back and stay there, so use this option carefully.

Debugging client-side test cases

Developing complex client-side test cases can be a headache. In this recipe, you will learn how you can debug the client-side test cases in Odoo. Instead of running all of the test cases, we will just run the one. Additionally, we will display the UI of the test case.

Getting ready

For this recipe, we will continue using the `my_library` module from the previous recipe.

How to do it...

Follow these steps to run a test case in debug mode:

1. Open the `/static/tests/colorpicker_tests.js` file and update the `QUnit.test` test with `QUnit.only`, like this:

    ```
    ...
    QUnit.only('int_color field test cases', function (assert) {
    ...
    ```

2. Add the `debug` parameter in the `createView` function, as follows:

    ```
    var form = testUtils.createView({
        View: FormView,
        model: 'book',
        data: this.data,
        arch: '<form string="Books">' +
    ```

```
            '<group>' +
                '<field name="name"/>' +
                '<field name="color" widget="int_color"/>' +
            '</group>' +
        '</form>',
    res_id: 1,
    debug: true
});
```

Open the developer mode and open the drop-down menu by clicking on the bug icon on the top menu, and then click on **Run JS Tests**. This will open the QUnit suite:

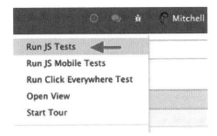

Figure 18.5 – Option to run test cases

This will run only one test case, which is our color picker test case.

How it works...

In *step 1*, we have replaced QUnit.test with QUnit.only. This will run this test case only. During the development of the test case, this can be time saving. Note that using QUnit.only will stop the test case from running via the command-line options. This can only be used for debugging or testing, and it can only work when you open the test case from the UI, so don't forget to replace it with QUnit.test after the development.

In our example of the QUnit test case, we have created the form view to test the int_color widget. If you run the QUnit test cases from the UI, you will learn that you are not able to see the created form views in the UI. From the UI of the QUnit suite, you are only able to see the logs. This makes developing a QUnit test case very difficult. To solve this issue, the debug parameter is used in the createView function. In *step 2*, we have added debug: true in the createView function. This will display the test form view in the browser. Here, you will be able to locate **Document Object Model** (**DOM**) elements via the browser debugger.

> **Warning**
>
> At the end of the test case, we destroy the view through the `destroy()` method. If you have destroyed the view, then you won't be able to see the form view in the UI, so in order to see it in the browser, remove that line during development. This will help you debug the test case.

Running QUnit test cases in debug mode helps you develop test cases very easily and quickly.

Generating videos/screenshots for failed test cases

Odoo uses Headless Chrome. This opens new possibilities. Starting from Odoo 12, you can record videos of the failed test cases, or you can take screenshots of the failed test cases as well.

How to do it...

Recording a video for the test case requires an `ffmpeg` package.

1. To install this, you need to execute the following command in the terminal (note that this command only works on a Debian-based OS):

   ```
   apt-get install ffmpeg
   ```

2. To generate a video or screenshot, you will need to provide a directory location to store the video or screenshots.

3. If you want to generate screencast (video) of a test case, use the `--screencasts` command like this:

   ```
   ./odoo-bin -c server.conf -i my_library --test-enable
   --screencasts=/home/pga/odoo_test/
   ```

4. If you want to generate screenshots of a test case, use the `--screenshosts` command like this:

   ```
   ./odoo-bin -c server.conf -i my_library --test-enable
   --screenshots=/home/pga/odoo_test/
   ```

How it works...

In order to generate screenshots/screencasts for failed test cases, you need to run the server with the path to save the video or image files. When you run the test cases, and if a test case fails, Odoo will save a screenshot/video of the failed test case in the given directory.

To generate a video of a test case, Odoo uses the `ffmpeg` package. If you haven't installed this package on the server, then it will only save a screenshot of a failed test case. After installing the package, you will be able to see the `mp4` file of any failed test case.

> **Note**
> Generating videos for test cases can consume more space on disks, so use this option with caution and only when it is really necessary.

Keep in mind that screenshots and videos are only generated for failed test cases, so if you want to test them, you need to write a test case that fails.

Populating random data for testing

So far, we have seen test cases that have been used to detect errors or bugs in business logic. However, at times we need to test our development with large amounts of data. Generating large amounts of data can be a tedious job. Odoo provides a set of tools that helps you to generate a lot of random data for your model. In this recipe, we will use the `populate` command to generate test data for the `library.book` model.

Getting ready

For this recipe, we will continue using the `my_library` module from the previous recipe. We will add the `_populate_factories` method, which will be used to generate test data.

How to do it...

Follow these steps to generate data for the `library.book` model:

1. Add a `populate` folder in the `my_library` module. Also, add an `__init__.py` file with this content:

    ```
    from . import library_data
    ```

2. Add a `my_library/populate/library_data.py` file and add this code to generate the book's data:

    ```
    from odoo import models
    from odoo.tools import populate

    class BookData(models.Model):
        _inherit = 'library.book'
        _populate_sizes = {'small': 10, 'medium': 100, 'large': 500}
        def _populate_factories(self):
            return [
                ('name', populate.constant('Book no {counter}')),
            ]
    ```

3. Run this command to generate the book's data:

    ```
    ./odoo-bin populate --models=library.book --size=medium -c server.conf -i my_library
    ```

This will generate 100 units of data for the books. After generating the data, the process will be terminated. To see the book's data, run the command without the `populate` parameters.

How it works...

In *step 1*, we added the populate folder in the `my_library` module. This folder contains the code to populate the test data.

In *step 2*, we added code to populate the book data. To generate random data, the _populate_factories method was used. The _populate_factories method returns factories for model fields, which will be used to generate random data. The library.book model has the required name field, so in our example, we have returned the generator for the name field. This generator will be used to generate random data for the books record. We have used the populate.constant generator for the name field; this will generate different names when we iterate during data generation.

Just like populate.constant, Odoo provides several other generators to populate data; here is a list of those generators:

- populate.randomize(list) will return a random element from the given list.
- populate.cartesian(list) is just like randomize(), but it will try to include all the values from the list.
- populate.iterate(list) will iterate over a given list and once all the elements are iterated, it will return based on randomize or random elements.
- populate.constant(str) is used to generate formatted strings. You can also pass the formatter parameter to format values. By default, the formatter is a string-format function.
- populate.compute(function) is used when you want to compute a value based on your function.
- populate.randint(a, b) is used to generate a random number between the a and b parameters.

These generators can be used to generate test data of your choice.

Another important attribute is _populate_sizes. It is used to define the number of records you want to generate based on the --size parameter. Its value always depends on the business object.

In *step 3*, we have generated a data books model. To populate test data, you will need to use the --size and --model parameters. Internally, Odoo uses the _populate method to generate random records. The _populate method itself uses the _populate_factories method to get random data for records. The _populate method will generate data for the models given in the --model parameter and the amount of test data will be based on the _populate_sizes attribute of the model. Based on our example, if we use --size=medium, the data for 100 books will be generated.

> **Note**
> If you run the `populate` command multiple times, the data will be generated multiple times as well. It's important to use this carefully: if you run the command in a production database, it will generate test data in the production database itself. This is something you want to avoid.

There's more...

At times, you would like to generate relational data too. For example, with books, you might also want to create author or rent records. To manage such records, you can use the `_populate_dependencies` attribute:

```
class BookData(models.Model):
    _inherit = 'library.book'
    _populate_sizes = {'small': 10, 'medium': 100, 'large': 500}
    _populate_dependencies = ['res.users', 'res.company']
    ...
```

This will populate the data for dependencies before populating the current model. Once that is done, you can access the populated data via the `populated_models` registry:

```
company_ids = self.env.registry.populated_models['res.company']
```

The line given here will give you the list of companies that is populated before generating test data for the current model.

19
Managing, Deploying, and Testing with Odoo.sh

In 2017, Odoo released Odoo.sh, a new cloud service. Odoo.sh is a platform that makes the process of testing, deploying, and monitoring Odoo instances as easy as possible. In this chapter, we will look at how Odoo.sh works, when you should use it over other deployment options, and its features.

In this chapter, we will cover the following recipes:

- Exploring some basic concepts of Odoo.sh
- Creating an Odoo.sh account
- Adding and installing custom modules
- Managing branches
- Accessing debugging options

- Getting a backup of your instance
- Checking the status of your builds
- All Odoo.sh options

> **Note**
> This chapter is written under the assumption that you have Odoo.sh access. It is a paid service, and you will need a subscription code to access the platform. If you are an Odoo partner, you will get a free Odoo.sh subscription code. Otherwise, you will need to purchase it from `https://www.odoo.sh/pricing`. You can still go through this chapter even if you don't have a subscription code. It contains enough screenshots to help you understand the platform.

Technical requirements

All the code used in this chapter can be downloaded from the GitHub repository, at `https://github.com/PacktPublishing/Odoo-14-Development-Cookbook-Fourth-Edition/tree/master/Chapter20/00_initial_module`.

Exploring some basic concepts of Odoo.sh

In this recipe, we will look at some of the features of the Odoo.sh platform. We will answer some basic questions, such as when you should use it, and why should it be used.

What is Odoo.sh?

Odoo.sh is a cloud service that provides the platform with the ability to host Odoo instances with custom modules. Putting it simply, it is Odoo's **Platform as a Service** (**PaaS**) cloud solution. It is fully integrated with GitHub. Any GitHub repository with valid Odoo modules can be launched on Odoo.sh within minutes. You can examine the ongoing development by testing multiple branches in parallel. Once you have moved your instance to production, you can test some new features with a copy of the production database; this helps to avoid regression. It also takes daily backups. With Odoo.sh, you can deploy Odoo instances efficiently, even if you don't have sound knowledge of DevOps. It automatically sets up an Odoo instance with top-notch configurations. Note that Odoo.sh is the Enterprise edition of Odoo. You cannot use the Odoo Community edition because Odoo.sh will only load the Enterprise edition.

Why was Odoo.sh introduced?

Before Odoo.sh was introduced, there were two ways to host Odoo instances. The first was to use Odoo Online, which is a **Software as a Service (SaaS)** cloud service. The second method was the on-premises option, in which you needed to host an Odoo instance and configure it on your server yourself. Now, both of these options have pros and cons. In the Odoo online option, you don't need to carry out any configuration or deployment, as it is a SaaS service. However, you cannot use custom modules on this platform. On the other hand, with the on-premises option, you can use custom modules, but you need to do everything yourself. You need to purchase the server, you need to configure the database and NGINX, and you need to set up the mail server, daily backups, and security.

For this reason, there was a need for a new option that provided the simplicity of Odoo online and the flexibility of the on-premises option. Odoo.sh lets you use custom modules without complex configuration. It also provides additional features, such as testing branches, staging branches, and automated tests.

> **Note**
> It is not completely true that customization is not possible on Odoo online. With Odoo Studio and other techniques, you can carry out customization. The scope of this customization, however, is very narrow.

When should you use Odoo.sh?

If you don't need customization or you only need a small amount of customization that is possible in Odoo online, you should go for Odoo online. This will save both time and money. If you want a significant amount of customization and you have teamed up with expert DevOps engineers, you can choose the on-premises option. Odoo.sh is suitable for when you have good knowledge of Odoo customization but you do not have any expertise in DevOps. With Odoo.sh, there's no need to carry out complex configurations; you can start using it straight away, along with your customization. It even configures the mailing server.

Odoo.sh is very useful when you are developing a large project with agile methodology. This is because on Odoo.sh, you can test multiple development branches in parallel and deploy the stable development in production in minutes. You can even share the test development with the end customer.

What are the features of Odoo.sh?

Odoo has invested a lot of time in the development of the Odoo.sh platform, and it is packed with features as a result. Let's have a look at the features of Odoo.sh. Note that Odoo adds new features from time to time. In this section, I have mentioned the features that are available at the time of writing this book, but you might find some further features as well:

- **GitHub integration**: This platform is fully integrated with GitHub. You can test every branch, pull, or commit here. For every new commit, a new branch will be pulled automatically. It will also run an automated test for the new commits. You can even create/merge branches from the Odoo.sh UI itself.

- **Web shell**: Odoo.sh provides the web shell in the browser for the current build (or production server). Here, you can see all the modules and logs.

- **Web code editor**: Just like the web shell, Odoo.sh provides the code editor in the browser. Here, you can access all of the source code and also get the Odoo interactive shell for the current build.

- **SSH access**: By registering your public keys, you can connect to any container via SSH.

- **External dependencies**: You can install any Python packages. To do this, you just need to add `requirement.txt` in the root of your GitHub repository. Right now, you can only install Python packages. It is not possible to install system packages (apt packages).

- **Server logs**: You can access the server log for each build from this browser. These logs are in real time and you can also filter the logs from here.

- **Automated tests**: Odoo.sh provides your own runbot, which you can use to perform a series of automated tests for your development. Whenever you add a new commit or a new development branch, Odoo.sh will automatically run all of the test cases and show the status of the tests. You can access the full test log, which will help you find issues if a test case fails.

- **Staging and development branches**: Odoo.sh provides two types of branches: the development branch and the staging branch. In the development branch, you can test ongoing development with demonstration data. The staging branch is used when the development is finished and you want to test the feature before merging it into production. The staging branch does not load the demonstration data; instead, it uses a copy of the production server.

- **Mail server**: Odoo.sh automatically sets up a mail server for the production server. Just like Odoo online, Odoo.sh does not need any extra configuration for email, although it is possible to use your own mail server.

- **Mail catcher**: The staging branch uses a copy of your production database, so it has information about your real customers. Testing on such a database can make it possible to send emails to real customers. To avoid this issue, the email feature is only activated on production branches. Staging and development branches do not send real emails, but instead, they use a mail catcher so that you can test and see emails in the staging and development branch.

- **Share the build**: With Odoo.sh, you can share the development branches with your customer so they can test them before merging the feature into production.

- **Faster deployment**: As Odoo.sh is fully integrated with GitHub, you can merge and deploy the development branches directly from the browser with a simple drag-and-drop procedure.

- **Backup and recovery**: Odoo.sh keeps full backups for the production instance. You can download or restore any of these backups in just a few clicks. Refer to the *Getting a backup of your instance* recipe to learn more about backups. Odoo.sh keeps 14 full backups for up to 3 months: 1 per day for 7 days, 1 per week for 4 weeks, 1 per month for 3 months.

- **Community modules**: You can test install any community module in a few simple clicks. You can also test free modules directly from the app store.

Creating an Odoo.sh account

In this recipe, we will create an Odoo.sh account and an empty repository for the custom add-ons.

Getting ready

For this recipe, you will need a GitHub account on which you can add custom modules. You will also need an Odoo.sh subscription code. If you are an Odoo partner, you will get a free Odoo.sh subscription code. Otherwise, you will need to purchase it from `https://www.odoo.sh/pricing`.

How to do it...

Follow these steps to create an Odoo.sh account:

1. Open `https://www.odoo.sh` and click on **Sign in** in the top menu. This will redirect you to the GitHub page:

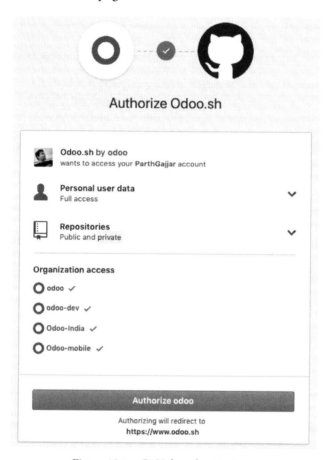

Figure 19.1 – GitHub authentication

2. Give authorization to your repositories, which will redirect you back to Odoo.sh. Fill in the form to deploy the instance:

Creating an Odoo.sh account   599

Figure 19.2 – Create an Odoo.sh instance

3. This will deploy the instance and you will be redirected to the Odoo.sh control panel. Wait for the build status to be successful; then, you can connect to your instance with the **CONNECT** button displayed in the following screenshot:

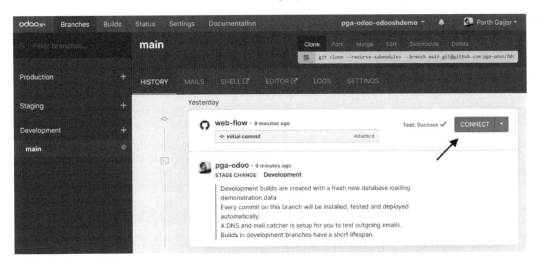

Figure 19.3 – Connect to the development instance

Upon clicking **CONNECT**, you will be automatically logged in to your instance. If you are an admin, by clicking on the arrow button at the side, you can connect as other users as well.

How it works...

The Odoo.sh platform is integrated with GitHub. You need to give full authorization to Odoo.sh, so that it can have access to your repositories. Odoo.sh will also create the webhooks. GitHub webhooks notify the Odoo.sh platform when a new commit or branch has been added to your repository. When you sign in for the first time, Odoo.sh will redirect you to GitHub. GitHub will show a page similar to the screenshot in *step 1*, in which you will need to provide access to all of your private and public repositories. If you are not the owner of the repository, you will see the button to make an access request to the owner for the rights.

After you grant repository access to Odoo.sh, you will be redirected back to Odoo.sh, where you will see the form to deploy the Odoo instance. To create a new instance, you will need to add the following information:

- **GitHub repository**: Here, you will need to set the GitHub repository with your custom modules. The modules in this repository will be available to the Odoo instance. You will see a list of all your existing repositories. You can select one of them or create a new one.

- **Odoo version**: Choose the Odoo version you want to deploy. You can select from the currently supported Odoo LTS versions. Make sure you select the version that is compatible with the modules in the GitHub repository. For our example, we will select version 14.0.

- **Subscription code**: This is the code to activate the instance. You will receive the code via email after purchasing an Odoo.sh plan; if you are an official Odoo partner, you can ask for this code from Odoo.

- **Hosting location**: Here, you need to choose a server location based on your geographic location. The server that is nearest will give the best performance. The latency displayed under the hosting location is based on your location. So if you are creating an instance for your customer and the customer is in another country, you will need to select a server location that is near the customer's location with lower latency.

Once you submit this form, your Odoo instances will be deployed and you will be redirected to the Odoo.sh control panel. Here, you will see your first build. It will take a few minutes, and then you will be able to connect to your Odoo instance. If you check the left panel, you will see that there are no branches in the production and staging sections and that only one branch is in the development section. In the next few recipes, we will see how you can create staging and production branches.

There's more...

Right now, Odoo.sh only works with GitHub. Other version-control systems, such as GitLab and Bitbucket, are not supported right now. If you want to use a system other than GitHub, you can use the intermediate GitHub repository that is linked to your actual repository via the submodule. In the future, Odoo will add support for GitLab and Bitbucket, but this is not the priority at the moment, according to the Odoo officials. The method suggested here is just a workaround if you want to use GitLab or Bitbucket.

Adding and installing custom modules

As we described earlier, in the *Exploring some basic concepts of Odoo.sh* recipe, on the Odoo.sh platform, you can add custom Odoo modules. The platform is integrated with GitHub, so adding a new commit in the registered repository will create a new build in the respective branch. In this recipe, we will add a custom module in our repository and access that module in Odoo.sh.

Getting ready

For our example, we will choose the `my_library` module from *Chapter 18, Automated Test Cases*. You can add any valid Odoo module in this recipe, but we will use the module with test cases here, as the Odoo.sh platform will perform all the test cases automatically. For simplicity, we have added this module in the GitHub repository of this book, at `Chapter20/r0_initial_module/my_library`.

How to do it...

Follow these steps to add your custom modules to Odoo.sh:

1. Get your Git repository on your local machine, add the `my_library` module in it, and then execute the following command to push the module in the GitHub repository:

   ```
   git add .
   git commit -am"Added my_library module"
   git push origin master
   ```

2. Open your project in Odoo.sh. Here, you will find a new build for this commit. It will start running test cases and you will see the following screen:

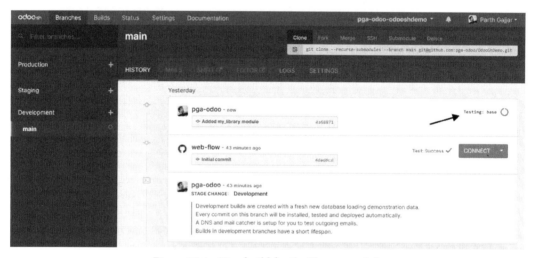

Figure 19.4 – New build for the library module

3. After a new commit is pulled in your Odoo.sh project, you will see the installation progress on the right side. Wait for the installation to be complete, then access your instance by clicking on the green **CONNECT** button. It will open the Odoo instance with the `my_library` module:

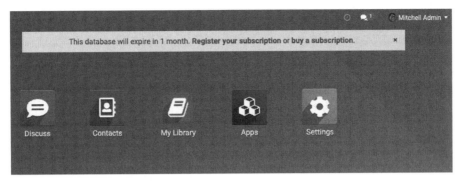

Figure 19.5 – Library module installed

Explore and test the my_library module. Note that this is not a production build, so you can test it however you like.

How it works...

In *step 1*, we uploaded the my_library module on the GitHub repository. Odoo.sh will be notified about these changes instantly, through a webhook. Then, Odoo.sh will start building a new instance. It will install all your custom modules and their dependencies. A new build will automatically perform the test cases for the installed modules.

> **Note**
> By default, Odoo.sh will only install your custom modules and their dependencies. If you want to change this behavior, you can do it from the module installation section of the global settings. We will look at these settings in detail in the next few recipes.

In the **HISTORY** tab, you will be able to see the full history of the branch. Here, you can find some basic information about the build. It will display the commit message, the author information, and the GitHub link of the commit. On the right side, you will get the live progress of the build. Note that the builds in the development section will install the modules with demonstration data. In the next few recipes, you will see the difference between the production, development, and staging branches, in detail.

After a successful build, you will see a button to connect the instance. By default, you will be connected with the admin user. Using **CONNECT** as a drop-down menu, you can log in as a demo and portal user, instead.

There's more...

Odoo.sh will create a new build for every new commit. You can change this behavior from the **SETTINGS** tab of the branch:

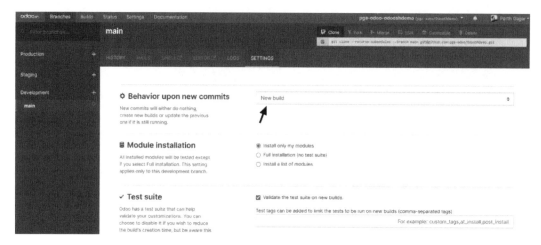

Figure 19.6 – Development branch options

Here, you will find several options. One of them is **Behavior upon new commits**. It has three possible values:

- **New Build**: This option will create a new build for each commit.
- **Do Nothing**: This option will ignore the new commit and do nothing.
- **Update Previous Build**: This will use an existing build for the new commit.

The **Module installation** and **Test suite** options will help you control the test suites. You can disable testing and you can run specific test cases with these options.

Managing branches

In Odoo.sh, you can create multiple development and staging branches along with the production branch. In this recipe, we will create different types of branches and see the differences between them. You will see the full workflow of how you can develop, test, and deploy the new features.

Getting ready

Visit `https://www.odoo.sh/project` and open the project we created in the *Creating an Odoo.sh account* recipe. We will create a development branch for the new feature and then test it in the staging branch. Finally, we will merge the feature in the production branch.

How to do it...

In this recipe, we will create all types of branches in Odoo.sh. At the moment, we don't have any branches in production, so we will start by creating a production branch.

Creating the production branch

Right now, we only have one `main` branch in the **Development** section. The last build of the `main` branch shows a green label that reads `Test: success`, meaning that all of the automated test cases have run successfully. We can move this branch into the **Production** branch, as the test case status shows that everything is fine. In order to move your `main` branch into the **Production** branch, you just need to drag the `main` branch from the **Development** section and drop it in the **Production** section, as shown in the following screenshot:

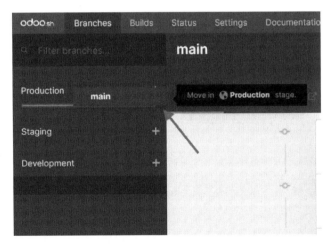

Figure 19.7 – Move the main branch to Production

This will create your **Production** branch. You can access the **Production** branch with the **Connect** button on the right side. Once you open the production instance, you will notice that there are no applications installed in the production database. This is because the production instance requires you or your end customer to install and configure the operation according to the requirements. Note that this is a production instance, so in order to keep the instance running, you need to enter your Enterprise subscription code.

Creating a development branch

You can create development branches directly from the browser. Click on the plus (+) button next to the **Development** section. This will show two types of input. One is the branch to fork, and the other is the name of the development branch. After filling in the input, hit the *Enter* key.

This will create a new branch by forking the given branch, as shown in the following screenshot:

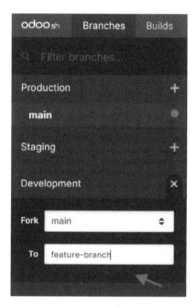

Figure 19.8 – Create a new development branch

> **Note**
> If you don't want to create a development branch from the UI, you can create it directly from GitHub. If you add a new branch in the GitHub repository, Odoo.sh will create a new development branch automatically.

Branches in development are usually new feature branches. As an example, we will add a new field in the `library.book` model. Follow these steps to add a new HTML field in the `books` model:

1. Increase the module version in the `manifest` file:

    ```
    ...
    'version': '14.0.2',
    ...
    ```

2. Add a new field in the `library.book` model:

    ```
    ...
    color = fields.Integer()
    description = fields.Html()

    def make_available(self):
    ...
    ```

3. Add a `description` field in the book's form view:

    ```
    ...
        </group>
        <notebook>
            <page string="Description">
                <field name="description"/>
            </page>
        </notebook>
    </sheet>
    ...
    ```

4. Push the changes in the feature branch by executing the following command in the terminal:

    ```
    git commit -am"Added book description"
    git push origin feature-branch
    ```

This will create a new build on Odoo.sh. After a successful build, you can test this new feature by accessing the instance. You will be able to see a new HTML field in the book's form view. Note that this branch is the development branch, so the new feature is only available to this branch. Your production branch is not changed.

Creating a staging branch

Once you complete the development branch and the test cases are successful, you can move the branch to the **Staging** section. This is the pre-production section. Here, the new feature will be tested with a copy of the production database. This will help us to find any issues that might be generated in the production database. To move from the development branch to the **Staging** branch, just drag and drop the branch into the **Staging** section:

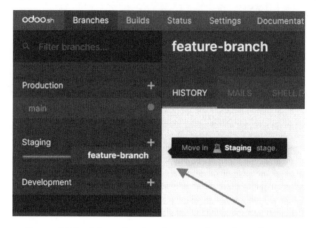

Figure 19.9 – Move the development branch to Staging

Once you move the **Development** branch to the **Staging** section, you can test your new development with production data. Just like any other build, you can access the **Staging** branch with the **CONNECT** button on the right. The only difference is that you will be able to see the data of the production database, in this case. Here, your development module is only upgraded automatically if you have increased the module version from the manifest.

> **Note**
> The staging branch will use a copy of the production database, so the staging instance will have real customers and their emails. For this reason, in the staging branch, real emails are disabled so that you don't send any by accident when testing a new feature in the staging branch.

If you haven't changed the module version, you will need to upgrade the modules manually to see the new features in action.

Merging new features in the production branch

After you test the new development with the production database (in the staging branch), you can deploy the new development into the **Production** branch. Like before, you just need to drag and drop the **Staging** branch into the **Production** branch. This will merge the new feature branch into the main branch. Like the **Staging** branch, your development module is only upgraded automatically if you have increased the module version from `manifest`. After this, the new module is available for the end customer:

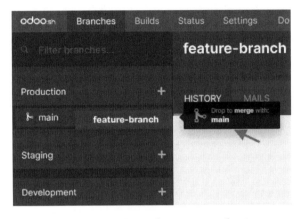

Figure 19.10 – Merge changes to production

Once you drop the staging branch to **Production**, a popup will be displayed with two options:

- **Rebase and Merge**: This will create a pull request and merge it with the rebase so you will have liner history.

- **Merge**: This will create a merge commit, without fast-forwading..

How it works...

In the previous example, we performed a full workflow to deploy a new feature into production. The following list explains the purposes of the different types of branches in Odoo.sh:

- **Production branch**: This is the actual instance that is used by the end customer. There is only one production branch, and the new features are intended to merge with this branch. In this branch, the mailing service is active, so your end customer can send and receive emails. Daily backup is also active for this branch.

- **Development branches**: This type of branch shows all the active development. You can create unlimited development branches, and every new commit in the branch will trigger a new build. The database in this branch is loaded with the demonstration data. After the development is complete, this branch will be moved to the staging branch. The mailing service is not active in these branches.

- **Staging branches**: This is the intermediate stage in the workflow. A stable development will be moved to the staging branch to be tested with a copy of the production branch. This is a very important step in the development life cycle; it might happen that a feature that works fine in the development branch does not work as expected with the production database. The staging branches give you an opportunity to test the feature with the production database before deploying it in production. If you find any issues with the development in this branch, you can move the branch back to development. The number of the staging branches is based on your Odoo.sh plan. By default, you only have one staging branch, but you can purchase more if you want to.

This is the complete workflow of how new features should be merged into production. In the next recipe, you will see some other options that we can use with these branches.

Accessing debugging options

Odoo.sh provides different features for analysis and debugging purposes. In this recipe, we will explore all of these features and options.

How to do it...

We will be using the same Odoo.sh project for this recipe. Each option will be shown in a different section, with a screenshot.

Branch history

You have already seen this feature in previous recipes. The **HISTORY** tab shows the full history of the branch. You can connect to the builds from here:

Figure 19.11 – The HISTORY tab

In the **HISTORY** tab, you can see all past actions performed on a selected branch. It will display logs, merges, new commits, and database restores.

Mail catcher

The staging branch uses a copy of your production database, so it has information about your customers. Testing the staging branch can send emails to real customers. This is why emails are only activated on production branches. The staging and development branches do not send real emails. If you want to test the email system before deploying any feature into production, you can use the mail catcher where you can see the list of all outgoing emails. The mail catcher will be available in the staging and development branches.

The mail catcher will display an email with the source and any attachments, as shown in the following screenshot:

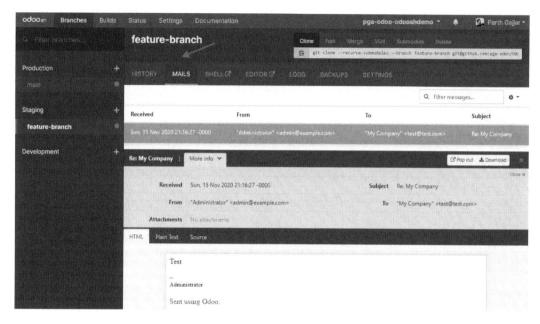

Figure 19.12 – Mail catcher

In the **MAILS** tab, you can see a list of all the captured mail with all attachments. Note that the **MAILS** tab will only be displayed in the staging and development branches.

Web shell

From the **SHELL** tab, you can access the web shell. Here, you can access the source code, the logs, the file store, and so on. It provides all of the shell features with editors such as nano and Vim. You can install the Python package with `pip` and maintain multiple tabs.

Take a look at the following screenshot: you can access the web shell by clicking on **SHELL**:

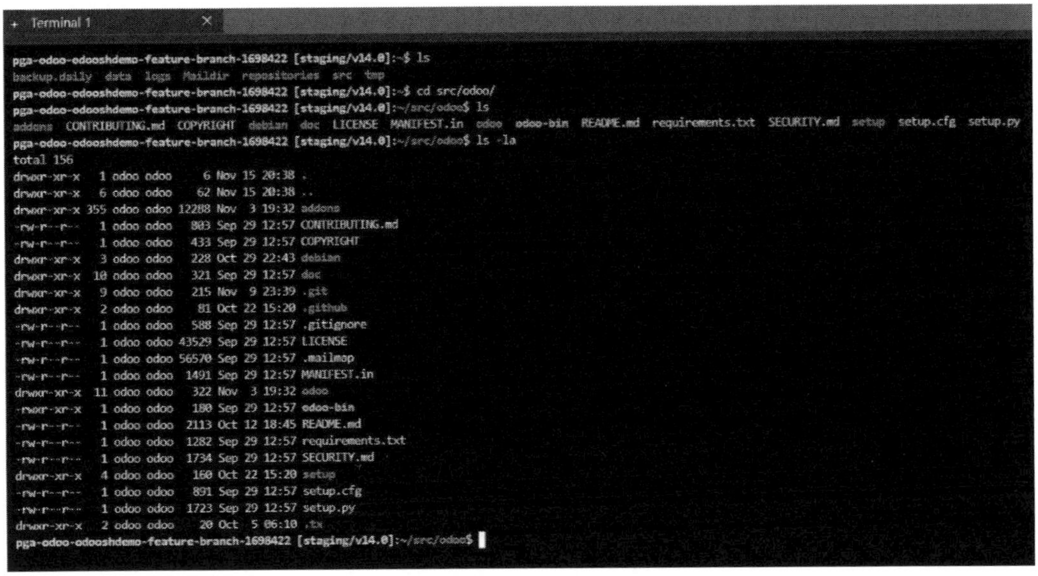

Figure 19.13 – Web shell

With shell access, you can traverse between different directories and perform operations. You can also use the `pip` command to install Python packages.

Here is the directory structure from the root directory:

```
.
├── data
│   ├── addons
│   ├── filestore
│   └── sessions
├── logs
├── Maildir
│   ├── cur
│   ├── new
│   └── tmp
├── repositories
│   └── git_github.com_pga-odoo_odooshdemo.git
├── src
│   ├── enterprise
│   ├── odoo
│   ├── themes
│   └── user
└── tmp
```

These directories can be different based on the type of branch. For example, `Maildir` will only be available in staging and development branches as it uses a mail catcher.

Sometimes you need to restart the server or update the module from the shell. You can use the following command in the shell to restart the server:

```
odoosh-restart
```

To update the module, execute the given command in the shell:

```
odoo-bin -u my_library --stop-after-init
```

The previous command will update the `my_library` module. If you want to update multiple modules, you can pass module names separated by a comma.

Code editor

If you are not comfortable with shell access, Odoo.sh provides a full-featured editor. Here, you can access the Python shell, the Odoo shell, and Terminal. You can also edit the source code from here, as you can see in the given screenshot. After modifying the source code, you can restart the server from the **Odoo** menu at the top:

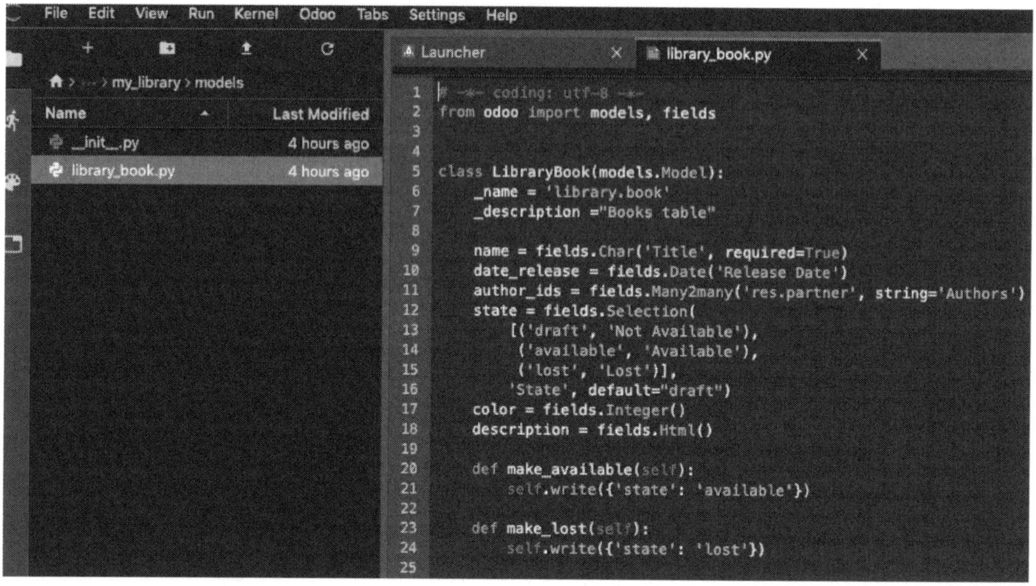

Figure 19.14 – Web code editor

As depicted in the preceding screenshot, you will be able to update files from the editor. Odoo will detect the changes automatically and restart the server. Note that if you make changes in data files, you will need to update the module.

Logs

From the **LOGS** tab, you can access all of the logs for your instance. You can see the live logs without reloading the pages. You can filter the logs from here. This allows you to find issues from the production server. Here is a list of the different log files you can find in the **LOGS** tab:

- `install.log`: This is for the logs that are generated when installing the modules. The logs of all the automated test cases will be located here.
- `pip.log`: You can add Python packages with the `requirement.txt` file. In this log file, you will find the installation log of these Python packages.
- `odoo.log`: This is the normal access log of Odoo. You will find the full access log here. You should look in this log to check production errors.
- `update.log`: When you upload a new module with a different manifest version, your module gets updated automatically. This file contains the logs of these automatic updates.

Take a look at the following screenshot. This shows the live logs for the production branch:

Figure 19.15 – Server log

The preceding screenshot shows that the logs are live; so you will be able to see new logs without reloading. Additionally, you can search for a particular log with the textbox in the top-right corner of the UI.

There's more...

Some commonly used `git` commands are available on top of the module, as shown in the following screenshot. You can run these by using the **Run** button on the left. These commands can't be edited, but if you want to run a modified command, you can copy it from here and then run it from the shell:

Figure 19.16 – Git commands

You can execute these `git` commands in the shell to perform various operations, as depicted in the preceding screenshot.

Getting a backup of your instance

Backups are essential for the production server. Odoo.sh provides a built-in backup facility. In this recipe, we will illustrate how you can download and restore backups from Odoo.sh.

How to do it...

In the production branch, you can access the full information about the backups from the **BACKUPS** tab at the top. This will display a list of backups:

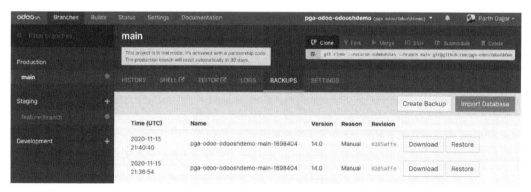

Figure 19.17 – Backups manager

From the buttons at the top, you can carry out backup operations, such as downloading the dump, performing a manual backup, or restoring from a backup. A database backup can take a long time, so it will be done in the background. You will have a notification on the bell icon at the top when it gets completed.

How it works...

Odoo automatically takes a backup of your production instance daily. Odoo also takes an automatic backup whenever you merge a new development branch and update the module. You can also perform a manual backup from the button at the top.

Odoo.sh keeps a total of 14 full backups for the Odoo production instance for up to 3 months—1 per day for 7 days, 1 per week for 4 weeks, and 1 per month for 3 months. From the **BACKUPS** tab, you can access 1 month of backups (all 7 days of the week and 4 weekly backups).

If you are moving to Odoo.sh from the on-premises or online option, you can import your database with the **Import Database** button. If you import your database directly into production, it might cause issues. To avoid this, you should import the database into the staging branch first.

Checking the status of your builds

Whenever you make a new commit, Odoo.sh creates the new commit. It also performs automated test cases. To manage all of this, Odoo.sh has its own version of runbot. In this recipe, we will check the statuses of all the builds.

How to do it...

Click on the **Builds** menu at the top to open the list of builds. Here, you can see a full overview of all of the branches and their commits:

Figure 19.18 – Build status

By clicking on the **Connect** buttons, you can connect to the instances. You can see the status of the build by the background color of the branch.

How it works...

On the runbot screen, you will get extra control over the builds. You can connect to the previous builds from here. Different colors show the status of the build. Green means that everything is fine; yellow indicates a warning, which can be ignored, but it is recommended that you fix it; red means there is a critical issue that you have to fix before merging the development branch into production. Red and yellow branches show the exclamation icon, (!), near the **Connect** button. When you click on this, you will get a popup with the error and warning log. Usually, you need to search the installation log files to find the error or warning logs, but this popup will filter out the other logs and only display the error and warning logs. This means that whenever a build goes red or yellow, you should come here and fix the errors and warnings before merging them into production.

Inactive development branches are destroyed after a few minutes. Normally, a new build will be created when you add a new **Commit** button. If you want to reactivate the build without a new commit, however, you can use the **Rebuild** button on the left side. The builds for the staging branches are also destroyed after a few minutes, apart from the last one, which will remain active.

There's more...

From the **Status** menu in the bar at the top, you can see the overall statistics of your instance. The servers of the platform are continuously monitored. On the **Status** screen, you will see the statistics of the server's availability, which will be computed automatically from the platform's monitoring system. It will show data, including the server uptime. The **Status** page will show the input and output data from the server. The **Status** page will display the following information:

Figure 19.19 – Odoo.sh status

The data displayed in the **Status** tab is collected from the various monitoring tools used by Odoo.sh.

All Odoo.sh options

Odoo.sh provides a few further options under the **Settings** menu. In this recipe, you will see all of the important options used to modify the default behavior of certain things on the platform.

Getting ready

We will be using the same Odoo.sh project that we used in previous recipes. You can access all the Odoo.sh settings from the **Settings** menu in the top bar. If you are not able to see this menu, that means you are accessing a shared project and you don't have admin access.

How to do it...

Open the **Settings** page from the **Settings** menu in the top bar. We'll take a look at the different options in the following sections.

Project Name

You can change the name of the Odoo.sh project from this option. The project name in the input will be used to generate your production URL. Development builds also use this project name as a prefix. In this case, the URL of our feature branch will be something like `https://parthgajjar-odooshdemo-feature-branch-260887.dev.odoo.com`:

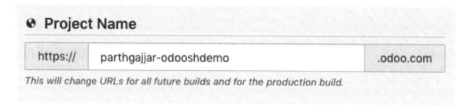

Figure 19.20 – Change the project name

> **Note**
> This option will change the production URL, but you cannot get rid of `*.odoo.com`. If you want to run a production branch on a custom domain, you can add your custom domain in the **Settings** tab of the production branch. You will also need to add a CNAME entry in your DNS manager.

Collaborators

You can share the project by adding collaborators. Here, you can search and add a new collaborator by their GitHub ID. A collaborator can have either **Admin** or **User** access rights. A collaborator with admin access rights will have full access (to the settings as well). A collaborator with user access rights, on the other hand, will have restricted access rights. They will be able to see all builds, but they will not be able to access the backups, logs, shells, or emails of the production or staging branches, though they will have full access to the development branches:

Figure 19.21 – Add collaborators

> **Note**
> You will need to give access to the GitHub repository to these users, too; otherwise, they won't be able to create a new repository from the browser.

Public Access

Using this option, you can share builds with your end customer. This can be used for demonstration or testing purposes. To do so, you need to enable the **Allow public access** checkbox:

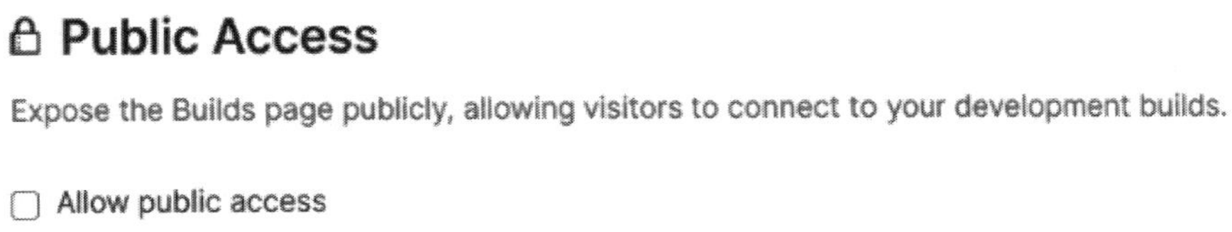

Figure 19.22 – Give public access to builds

Note that the staging branch will have the same password as your production branch. However, in the development branch, you will have the username and password shown in this table:

Username	Password
admin	admin
demo	demo
portal	portal

Table 19.1

Module installation

In the **Settings** tab of the development branch, you will see the **Module installation** option for the development branches. It provides three options, as shown in the following screenshot:

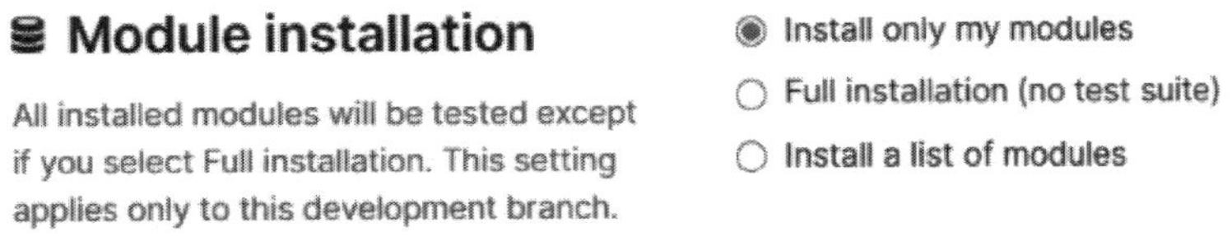

Figure 19.23 – Module installation options

By default, it is set to **Install only my modules**. This option will install all of your custom modules and their dependent modules in the new development branches. Only automated test cases are performed for these modules. The second option is **Full installation**. This option will install all of the modules and perform automated test cases for all of those modules. The final option is **Install a list of modules**. In this option, you will need to pass a list of comma-separated modules, such as `sales`, `purchases`, and `my_library`. This option will install the given modules and their dependencies.

This setting only applies to development builds. Staging builds duplicate the production build, so they will have the same modules that are installed in the production branch and perform test cases for modules that have an updated version manifest.

Submodules

The **Submodules** option is used when you are using private modules as submodules. This setting is only needed for private submodules; public submodules will work fine, without any issues. It is not possible to download private repositories publicly, so you need to give repository access to Odoo.sh. Follow these steps to add access to the private submodules:

1. Copy the SSH URL of your private submodule repository in the input and click on **Add**.
2. Copy the displayed **public key**.
3. Add this **public key** as a deploy key in your private repository settings in GitHub (similar settings are also available on Bitbucket and GitLab):

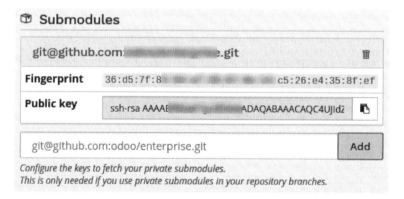

Figure 19.24 – Set the private submodule

You can add multiple submodules too and you can remove submodules from here as well.

Database Workers

You can increase the number of workers for the production build. This is useful when you have more users; usually, a single worker can handle 25 backend users or 5,000 daily website visitors. This formula is not perfect; it can vary based on usage. This option is not free, and increasing the number of workers will increase the price of your Odoo.sh subscription:

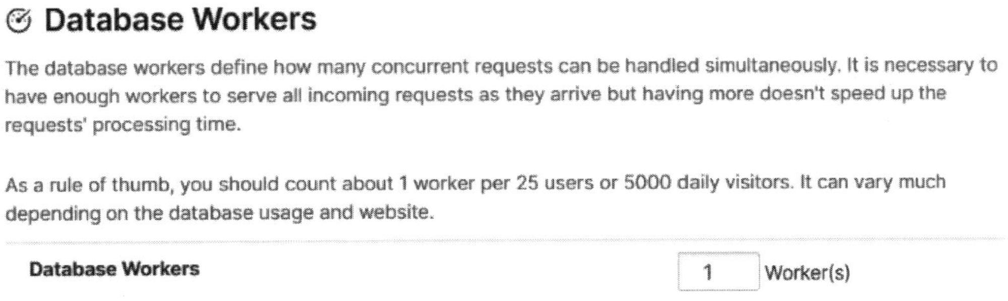

Figure 19.25 – Set Database Workers

These **database workers** are multithreaded, and each one is able to handle 15 concurrent requests. It is necessary to have enough workers to serve all incoming requests as they arrive, but increasing the number of workers does not increase the speed of the requests' processing time. It is only used to handle a large number of concurrent users.

Staging Branches

Staging branches are used to test a new development with the production database. By default, Odoo.sh gives you one staging branch. If you are working on large projects with lots of developers, this might be a bottleneck in the development process, so you can increase the number of **Staging Branches** at an extra cost:

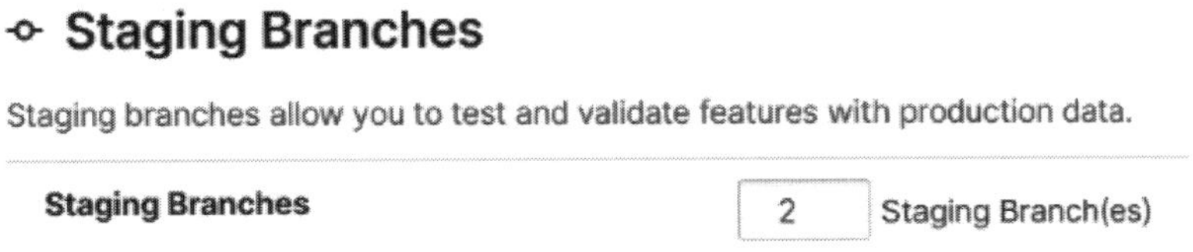

Figure 19.26 – Set staging branches

There's more...

Along with the configuration options, the **Settings** menu will also display some statistics related to the platform.

Database size

This section will display the size of your production database. The Odoo.sh platform charges the database at $1/GB/month. This option helps you keep track of your database. The displayed database size is only for the production database; it does not include the databases of the staging and development branches:

Figure 19.27 – Database size

Odoo source code revisions

This section will display the GitHub revision number of Odoo's project. It will display the revision hash for the Community, Enterprise, and theme projects that are currently being used in the platform. This source code will automatically be updated every week. This option will help you get the exact same versions in your local machine. You can also check this from the web shell, through the `git` command in the repository.

20
Remote Procedure Calls in Odoo

The Odoo server supports **Remote Procedure Calls** (**RPCs**), which means that you can connect Odoo instances from external applications, an example being if you want to show the status of a delivery order in an Android application, which is written in Java. Here, you can fetch the delivery status from Odoo via RPC. With the Odoo RPC API, you can perform any CRUD operations on a database. Odoo RPC is not limited to CRUD operations; you can also invoke public methods of any model. Of course, you will need to have proper access to rights to perform these operations because RPC respects all of the access rights and record rules you have defined in your database. Consequently, it is very safe to use because the RPC respects all access rights and record rules. Odoo RPC is not platform-dependent, so you can use it on any platform, including Odoo.sh, online, or self-hosted platforms. Odoo RPC can be used with any programming language, so you can integrate Odoo with any external application.

Odoo provides two types of RPC API—XML-RPC and JSON-RPC. In this chapter, we will learn how to use these RPCs from an external program. Finally, you will learn how to use Odoo RPC through OCA's `odoorpc` library.

In this chapter, we will cover the following recipes:

- Logging in to/connecting Odoo with XML-RPC
- Searching/reading records through XML-RPC
- Creating/updating/deleting records through XML-RPC
- Calling methods through XML-RPC
- Logging in to/connecting Odoo with JSON-RPC
- Fetching/searching records through JSON-RPC
- Creating/updating/deleting records through JSON-RPC
- Calling methods through JSON-RPC
- The OCA odoorpc library
- Generating API keys

Technical requirements

In this chapter, we will be using the `my_library` module, which we created in *Chapter 19, Managing, Deploying, and Testing with Odoo.sh*. You can find the same initial `my_library` module in the GitHub repository: `https://github.com/PacktPublishing/Odoo-12-Development-Cookbook-Third-Edition/tree/master/Chapter19/r0_initial_module`.

Here, we will not introduce a new language as you may not be familiar with it. We will continue using Python to access the RPC API. You can use another language if you want to, as the same procedure can be applied in any language to access the RPC.

To connect Odoo through the RPC, you will need a running Odoo instance to connect with. Throughout this chapter, we will assume that you have the Odoo server running on `http://localhost:8069`, that you called the `book-db-14` database, and that you have installed the `my_library` module therein. Note that you can connect any valid IP or domain through the RPC.

Logging in to/connecting Odoo with XML-RPC

In this recipe, we will carry out user authentication through RPC to check whether the credentials supplied are valid.

Getting ready

To connect an Odoo instance through RPC, you will need a running Odoo instance to connect with. We will assume that you have the Odoo server running on `http://localhost:8069` and that you have installed the `my_library` module.

How to do it...

Perform the following steps to carry out user authentication through RPC:

1. Add the `odoo_authenticate.py` file. You can place this file anywhere you want because the RPC program will work independently.

2. Add the following code to the file:

   ```python
   from xmlrpc import client

   server_url = 'http://localhost:8069'
   db_name = 'book-db-14'
   username = 'admin'
   password = 'admin'

   common = client.ServerProxy('%s/xmlrpc/2/common' %
       server_url)
   user_id = common.authenticate(db_name, username,
       password, {})

   if user_id:
       print("Success: User id is", user_id)
   else:
       print("Failed: wrong credentials")
   ```

3. Run the following Python script from the Terminal with the following command:

   ```
   python3 odoo_authenticate.py
   ```

This will print a success message with the user ID if you have provided a valid login name and password.

How it works...

In this recipe, we used the Python `xmlrpc` library to access Odoo instances through XML-RPC. This is a standard Python library and you do not have to install anything else in order to use it.

For authentication, Odoo provides XML-RPC on the `/xmlrpc/2/common` endpoint. This endpoint is used for meta methods, which do not require authentication. The `authentication()` method itself is a public method, so it can be called publicly. The `authentication()` method accepts four arguments—database name, username, password, and user agent environment. The user agent environment is a compulsory argument, but if you do not want to pass the user agent parameter, at least pass the empty dictionary.

When you execute the `authenticate()` method with all valid arguments, it will make a call to the Odoo server and perform authentication. It will then return the user ID, provided the given login ID and password are correct. It will return `False` if the user is not present or if the password is incorrect.

You need to use the `authenticate()` method before accessing any data through RPC. This is because accessing data with the wrong credentials will generate an error.

> **Note**
>
> Odoo's online instances (`*.odoo.com`) use OAuth authentication, and so the local password is not set on the instance. To use XML-RPC on these instances, you will need to set the user's password manually from the **Settings | Users | Users** menu of your instance.

Additionally, the methods used to access data require a user ID instead of a username, so the `authenticate()` method is needed in order to get the ID of the user.

There's more...

The `/xmlrpc/2/common` endpoint provides one more method: `version()`. You can call this method without credentials. It will return the version information of the Odoo instance. The following is an example of the `version()` method usage:

```
from xmlrpc import client

server_url = 'http://localhost:8069'
common = client.ServerProxy('%s/xmlrpc/2/common' %
```

```
        server_url)
version_info = common.version()

print(version_info)
```

The preceding program will generate the following output:

```
$ python3 version_info.py
{'server_version': '14.0', 'server_version_info': [14, 0, 0, 'final', 0, ''],
 'server_serie': '14.0', 'protocol_version': 1}
```

Figure 20.1 – Output of the version info program

This program will print version information based on your server.

Searching/reading records through XML-RPC

In this recipe, we will see how you can fetch the data from an Odoo instance through RPC. The user can access most data, except data that is restricted by the security access control and record rules. RPC can be used in many situations, such as collecting data for analysis, manipulating a lot of data at once, or fetching data for display in another software/system. There are endless possibilities, and you can use RPCs whenever necessary.

Getting ready

We will create a Python program to fetch the book data from the `library.book` model. Make sure you have installed the `my_library` module and that the server is running on `http://localhost:8069`.

How to do it...

Perform the following steps to fetch a book's information through RPC:

1. Add the `books_data.py` file. You can place this file anywhere you want because the RPC program will work independently.

2. Add the following code to the file:

    ```
    from xmlrpc import client

    server_url = 'http://localhost:8069'
    db_name = 'book-db-14'
    ```

```python
username = 'admin'
password = 'admin'

common = client.ServerProxy('%s/xmlrpc/2/common' %
    server_url)
user_id = common.authenticate(db_name, username,
    password, {})

models = client.ServerProxy('%s/xmlrpc/2/object' %
    server_url)

if user_id:
    search_domain = ['|', ['name', 'ilike', 'odoo'],
    ['name', 'ilike', 'sql']]
    books_ids = models.execute_kw(db_name, user_id,
        password,
        'library.book', 'search',
        [search_domain],
        {'limit': 5})
    print('Books ids found:', books_ids)

    books_data = models.execute_kw(db_name, user_id,
        password,
        'library.book', 'read',
        [books_ids, ['name', 'date_release']])
    print("Books data:", books_data)
else:
    print('Wrong credentials')
```

3. Run the Python script from the Terminal with the following command:

```
python3 books_data.py
```

The preceding program will fetch the book data and give you the following output:

```
$ python3 books_data.py
Books ids: [1, 3, 4, 7, 8]
Books data: [{'id': 1, 'name': 'Odoo 12 Development Cookbook', 'date_release': '2019-02-13'}, {'id': 3, 'name': 'PostgresSQL basics', 'date_release': '2018-02-15'}, {'id': 4, 'name': 'MySQL basics', 'date_release': '2018-02-15'}, {'id': 7, 'name': 'Odoo basics', 'date_release': '2018-02-15'}, {'id': 8, 'name': 'Odoo 11 Development Cookbook', 'date_release': '2018-02-15'}]
```

Figure 20.2 – Data of books

The output shown in the preceding screenshot is based on data in my database. The data in your Odoo instance may be different data, and so the output will also be different.

How it works...

In order to access the book data, first you have to carry out authentication. At the beginning of the program, we did authentication in the same way as we did in the *Logging in to/connecting Odoo with XML-RPC* recipe earlier. If you provided valid credentials, the `authentication()` method will return the `id` of the user's record. We will use this user ID to fetch the book data.

The `/xmlrpc/2/object` endpoint is used for database operation. In our recipe, we used the `object` endpoint to fetch the book data. In contrast to the `/xmlrpc/2/common` endpoint, this endpoint does not work without credentials. With this endpoint, you can access the public method of any model through the `execute_kw()` method. `execute_kw()` takes the following arguments:

- Database name
- User ID (we get this from the `authenticate()` method)
- Password
- Model name, for example, `res.partner`, or `library.book`
- Method name, for example, `search`, `read`, or `create`
- An array of positional arguments
- A dictionary for keyword arguments (optional)

In our example, we want to fetch the book's information. This can be done through a combination of `search()` and `read()`. Book information is stored in the `library.book` model, so in `execute_kw()`, we use `library.book` as the model name and `search` as the method name. This will call the ORM's `search` method and returns record IDs. The only difference here is that the ORM's `search` method returns a record set, while this search method returns a list of IDs.

In `execute_kw()`, you can pass arguments and keyword arguments for the method provided. The `search()` method accepts a domain as a positional argument, so we passed a domain to filter books. The `search` method has other optional keyword arguments, such as `limit`, `offset`, `count`, and `order`, from which we have used the `limit` parameter to fetch only five records. This will return the list of book IDs whose names contain the `odoo` or `SQL` strings.

However, we need to fetch book data from the database. We will use the `read` method to do this. The `read` method accepts a list of IDs and fields to complete the task. At the end of *step 3*, we used the list of book IDs that we received from the `search` method and then used the book IDs to fetch the `name` and `release_date` of the books. This will return the list of the dictionary with the book's information.

> **Note**
> Note that the arguments and keyword arguments passed in `execute_kw()` are based on the passed method. You can use any public ORM method via `execute_kw()`. You just need to give the method name, the valid arguments, and the keyword arguments. These arguments are going to be passed in the method in the ORM.

There's more...

The data fetched through a combination of the `search()` and `read()` methods is slightly time-consuming because it will make two calls. `search_read` is an alternative method for fetching data. You can search and fetch the data in a single call. Here is the alternative way to fetch a book's data with `search_read()`.

> **Note**
> The `read` and `search_read` methods will return `id` fields even if the `id` field is not requested. Furthermore, for the `many2one` field, you will get an array made up of the `id` and display name. For example, the `create_uid` many2one field will return data like this: `[12, 'Parth Gajjar']`.

It will return the same output as in the previous example:

```
from xmlrpc import client

server_url = 'http://localhost:8069'
db_name = ' book-db-14'
username = 'admin'
password = 'admin'

common = client.ServerProxy('%s/xmlrpc/2/common' % 
    server_url)
user_id = common.authenticate(db_name, username, 
    password, {})
```

```python
models = client.ServerProxy('%s/xmlrpc/2/object' %
    server_url)

if user_id:
    search_domain = ['|', ['name', 'ilike', 'odoo'],
        ['name', 'ilike', 'sql']]
    books_ids = models.execute_kw(db_name, user_id,
        password,
        'library.book', 'search_read',
        [search_domain, ['name', 'date_release']],
        {'limit': 5})
    print('Books data:', books_ids)

else:
    print('Wrong credentials')
```

The `search_read` methods improve performance significantly as you get your result in one RPC call, so use the `search_read` method instead of a combination of the `search` and `read` methods.

Creating/updating/deleting records through XML-RPC

In the previous recipe, we saw how to search and read data through RPC. In this recipe, we will perform the remaining **CRUD** operations through RPC, which are **Create**, **Update** (write), and **Delete** (unlink).

Getting ready

We will create the Python program to `create`, `write`, and `unlink` data on the `library.book` model. Make sure you have installed the `my_library` module and that the server is running on `http://localhost:8069`.

How to do it...

Perform the following steps to create, write, and update a book's information through RPC:

1. Add the `books_operation.py` file. You can place this file anywhere you want because the RPC program will work independently.

2. Add the following code to the `books_operation.py` file:

```python
from xmlrpc import client

server_url = 'http://localhost:8069'
db_name = 'book-db-14'
username = 'admin'
password = 'admin'

common = client.ServerProxy('%s/xmlrpc/2/common' %
    server_url)
user_id = common.authenticate(db_name, username,
    password, {})

models = client.ServerProxy('%s/xmlrpc/2/object' %
    server_url)

if user_id:
    # create new books
    create_data = [
        {'name': 'Book 1', 'release_date':
        '2019-01-26'},
        {'name': 'Book 3', 'release_date':
        '2019-02-12'},
        {'name': 'Book 3', 'release_date':
        '2019-05-08'},
        {'name': 'Book 7', 'release_date':
        '2019-05-14'}
    ]
    books_ids = models.execute_kw(db_name, user_id,
        password,
        'library.book', 'create',
        [create_data])
    print("Books created:", books_ids)

    # Write in existing book record
```

```
        book_to_write = books_ids[1] # We will use ids of
        # recently created books
        write_data = {'name': 'Books 2'}
        written = models.execute_kw(db_name, user_id,
            password,
            'library.book', 'write',
            [book_to_write, write_data])
        print("Books written:", written)

        # Delete the book record
        books_to_delete = books_ids[2:] # We will use ids
        # of recently created books
        deleted = models.execute_kw(db_name, user_id,
            password,
            'library.book', 'unlink',
            [books_to_delete])
        print('Books unlinked:', deleted)

    else:
        print('Wrong credentials')
```

3. Run the Python script from the Terminal with the given command:

```
python3 books_operation.py
```

The preceding program will create four records of the books. Updating the data in the book records and later deleting two records gives you the following output (the IDs created may be different depending on your database):

Figure 20.3 – Book operation output

The `write` and `unlink` methods return `True` if the operation is successful. This means that if you get `True` in response, assume that a record has been updated or deleted successfully.

How it works...

In this recipe, we performed `create`, `write`, and `delete` operations through XML-RPC. This operation also uses the `/xmlrpc/2/object` endpoint and the `execute_kw()` method.

The `create()` method supports the creation of multiple records in a single call. In *step 2*, we first created a dictionary with the book's information. Then we used the book's dictionary to create new records of the books through XML-RPC. The XML-RPC call needs two parameters to create new records—the `create` method name and the book data. This will create the four book records in the `library.book` model. In ORM, when you create the record, it returns a record set of created records, but if you create the record's RPC, this will return a list of IDs.

The `write` method works in a similar way to the `create` method. In the `write` method, you will need to pass a list of record IDs, and the field values, to be written. In our example, we updated the name of the book created in the first section. This will update the name of the second book from Book 3 to Book 2. Here, we passed only one `id` of a book, but you can pass a list of IDs if you want to update multiple records in a single call.

In the third section of the program, we deleted two books that we created in the first section. You can delete records with the `unlink` method and a list of record IDs.

After the program is executed successfully, you will find two book records in the database, as indicated in *Figure 20.3*. In the program, we have created four records, but we have also deleted two of them, so you will only find two new records in the database.

There's more...

When you are performing a CRUD operation through RPC, this may generate an error if you don't have permission to do that operation. With the `check_access_rights` method, you can check whether the user has the proper access rights to perform a certain operation. The `check_access_rights` method returns `True` or `False` values based on the access rights of the user. Here is an example showing whether a user has the rights to create a book record:

```
from xmlrpc import client

server_url = 'http://localhost:8069'
db_name = 'book-db-14'
username = 'admin'
password = 'admin'
```

```python
common = client.ServerProxy('%s/xmlrpc/2/common' %
    server_url)
user_id = common.authenticate(db_name, username,
    password, {})

models = client.ServerProxy('%s/xmlrpc/2/object' %
    server_url)

if user_id:
    has_access = models.execute_kw(db_name, user_id,
        password,
        'library.book', 'check_access_rights',
        ['create'], {'raise_exception': False})
    print('Has create access on book:', has_access )
else:
    print('Wrong credentials')

# Output: Has create access on book: True
```

When you are doing complex operations via RPC, the `check_access_rights` method can be used prior to performing the operation to make sure you have proper access rights.

Calling methods through XML-RPC

With Odoo, the RPC API is not limited to CRUD operations; you can also invoke business methods. In this recipe, we will call the `make_available` method to change the book's state.

Getting ready

We will create the Python program to call `make_available` on the `library.book` model. Make sure that you have installed the `my_library` module and that the server is running on `http://localhost:8069`.

How to do it...

Perform the following steps to create, write, and update a book's information through RPC:

1. Add the `books_method.py` file. You can place this file anywhere you want because the RPC program will work independently.

2. Add the following code to the file:

```python
from xmlrpc import client

server_url = 'http://localhost:8069'
db_name = 'book-db-14'
username = 'admin'
password = 'admin'

common = client.ServerProxy('%s/xmlrpc/2/common' %
    server_url)
user_id = common.authenticate(db_name, username,
    password, {})

models = client.ServerProxy('%s/xmlrpc/2/object' %
    server_url)

if user_id:
    # Create book with state draft
    book_id = models.execute_kw(db_name, user_id,
        password,
        'library.book', 'create',
        [{'name': 'New Book', 'date_release':
        '2019-01-26', 'state': 'draft'}])

    # Call make_available method on new book
    models.execute_kw(db_name, user_id, password,
        'library.book', 'make_available',
        [[book_id]])

    # check book status after method call
    book_data = models.execute_kw(db_name, user_id,
        password,
        'library.book', 'read',
        [[book_id], ['name', 'state']])
    print('Book state after method call:',
```

```
            book_data[0]['state'])
else:
    print('Wrong credentials')
```

3. Run the Python script from the Terminal with the following command:

```
python3 books_method.py
```

The preceding program will create one book using draft and then we will change the book's state by calling the make_available method. After that, we will fetch the book data to check the book's status, which will generate the following output:

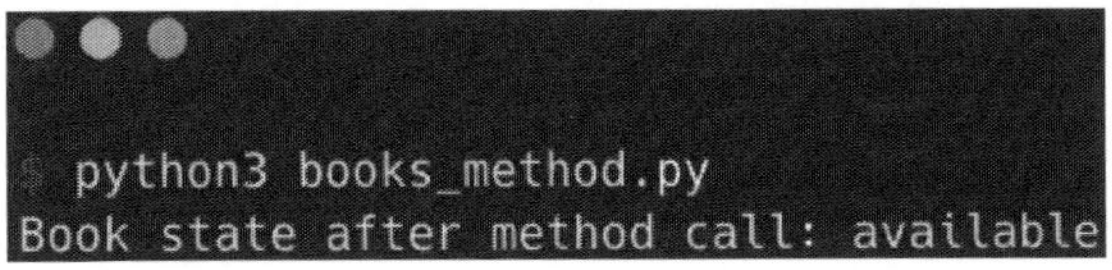

```
python3 books_method.py
Book state after method call: available
```

Figure 20.4 – Changing the state of the book

The program of this recipe will create a new book record and change the state of the book by calling the model method. By the end of the program, we have read the book record and printed the updated state.

How it works...

You can call any modal method from RPC. This helps you to perform business logic without encountering any side effects. For example, you created the sales order from RPC and then called the action_confirm method of the sale.order method. This is equivalent to clicking on the **Confirm** button on a sales order form.

You can call any public method of the model, but you cannot call a private method from RPC. A method name that starts with _ is called a private method, such as _get_share_url() and _get_data().

It is safe to use these methods, as they go through the ORM and follow all security rules. If the method is accessing unauthorized records, it will generate errors.

In our example, we created a book with a state of draft. Then we made one more RPC call to invoke the make_available method, which will change the book's state to available. Finally, we made one more RPC call to check the state of the book. This will show that the book's state has changed to **available**, as indicated in *Figure 20.4*.

Methods that do not return anything internally return `None` by default. Such methods cannot be used from RPC. Consequently, if you want to use your method from RPC, at least add the return `True` statement.

There's more...

If an exception is generated from a method, all of the operations performed in the transaction will be automatically rolled back to the initial state. This is only applicable to a single transaction (a single RPC call). For example, imagine you are making two RPC calls to the server and there is an exception generated in the second call. This will roll back the operation that is carried out in the second RPC call. The operation performed through the first RPC call won't be rolled back. Consequently, you want to perform a complex operation through RPC. It is recommended to perform this in a single RPC call by creating a method in the model.

Logging in to/connecting Odoo with JSON-RPC

Odoo provides one more type of RPC API: JSON-RPC. As its name suggests, JSON-RPC works in the JSON format and uses the `jsonrpc` 2.0 specification. In this recipe, we will see how you can log in with JSON-RPC. The Odoo web client itself uses JSON-RPC to fetch data from the server.

Getting ready

In this recipe, we will perform user authentication through JSON-RPC to check whether the given credentials are valid. Make sure you have installed the `my_library` module and that the server is running on `http://localhost:8069`.

How to do it...

Perform the following steps to perform user authentication through RPC:

1. Add the `jsonrpc_authenticate.py` file. You can place this file anywhere you want because the RPC program will work independently.
2. Add the following code to the file:

    ```python
    import json
    import random
    import requests
    ```

```python
server_url = 'http://localhost:8069'
db_name = 'book-db-14'
username = 'admin'
password = 'admin'

json_endpoint = "%s/jsonrpc" % server_url
headers = {"Content-Type": "application/json"}

def get_json_payload(service, method, *args):
    return json.dumps({
        "jsonrpc": "2.0",
        "method": 'call',
        "params": {
            "service": service,
            "method": method,
            "args": args
        },
        "id": random.randint(0, 100000000),
    })

payload = get_json_payload("common", "login", db_name,
    username, password)
response = requests.post(json_endpoint, data=payload,
    headers=headers)
user_id = response.json()['result']

if user_id:
    print("Success: User id is", user_id)
else:
    print("Failed: wrong credentials")
```

3. Run the Python script from the Terminal with the following command:

   `python3 jsonrpc_authenticate.py`

When you run the preceding program and you have passed a valid login name and password, the program will print a success message with the id of the user, as follows:

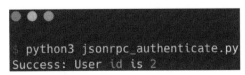

Figure 20.5 – Authenticating via JSON-RPC

The JSON authentication works just like XML-RPC, but it returns a result in the JSON format.

How it works...

JSON-RPC is using the JSON format to communicate with the server using the `/jsonrpc` endpoint. In our example, we used the Python requests package to make POST requests, but if you want to, you can use other packages, such as `urllib`.

JSON-RPC only accepts a payload formatted in the **JSON-RPC 2.0** specification. You may refer to this link to learn more about the JSON-RPC format: https://www.jsonrpc.org/specification. In our example, we created the `get_json_payload()` method. This method will prepare the payload in the valid JSON-RPC 2.0 format. This method accepts the `service` name and the `method` to call and the remaining arguments will be placed in `*args`. We will be using this method in all subsequent recipes. JSON-RPC accepts requests in JSON format, and these requests are only accepted if the request contains a `{"Content-Type": "application/json"}` header. The results of the requests will be in JSON format.

Like XML-RPC, all public methods, including login, come under the common service. For this reason, we passed `common` as a service and `login` as a method to prepare the JSON payload. The login method required some extra arguments, so we passed the database name, username, and password. Then we made the POST request to the JSON endpoint with the payload and headers. If you passed the correct username and password, the method returns the user ID. The response will be in JSON format and you will get the result in the result key.

> **Note**
> Note that the `get_json_payload()` method created in this recipe is used to remove repetitive code from the example. It is not compulsory to use it, so feel free to apply your own adaptations.

There's more...

Like XML-RPC, the version method is also available in JSON-RPC. This version method comes under the common service and is accessible publicly. You can get version information without login information. See the following example showing how to fetch the version info of the Odoo server:

```
import json
import random
```

```python
import requests


server_url = 'http://localhost:8069'
json_endpoint = "%s/jsonrpc" % server_url
headers = {"Content-Type": "application/json"}

def get_json_payload(service, method, *args):
    ... # see full function definition in last section

payload = get_json_payload("common", "version")
response = requests.post(json_endpoint, data=payload,
headers=headers)

print(response.json())
```

This program will display the following output:

```
$ python3 jsonrpc_version_info.py
{'jsonrpc': '2.0', 'id': 583639034, 'result': {'server_version': '14.0',
 'server_version_info': [14, 0, 0, 'final', 0, ''], 'server_serie': '14.0',
 'protocol_version': 1}}
```

Figure 20.6 – Output of the version info program

This program will print version information based on your server.

Fetching/searching records through JSON-RPC

In the previous recipe, we saw how you can do authentication through JSON-RPC. In this recipe, we will see how you can fetch the data from the Odoo instance with JSON-RPC.

Getting ready

In this recipe, we will fetch book information with JSON-RPC. Make sure you have installed the `my_library` module and that the server is running on `http://localhost:8069`.

How to do it...

Perform the following steps to fetch book data from the `library.book` model:

1. Add the `jsonrpc_fetch_data.py` file. You can place this file anywhere you want because the RPC program will work independently.

2. Add the following code to the file:

   ```python
   # place authentication and get_json_payload methods (see
   first jsonrpc recipe)

   if user_id:
       # search for the book's ids
       search_domain = ['|', ['name', 'ilike', 'odoo'],
       ['name', 'ilike', 'sql']]
       payload = get_json_payload("object", "execute_kw",
           db_name, user_id, password,
           'library.book', 'search',
           [search_domain], {'limit': 5})
       res = requests.post(json_endpoint, data=payload,
           headers=headers).json()
       print('Search Result:', res)
       # ids will be in result keys

       # read data for books ids
       payload = get_json_payload("object", "execute_kw",
           db_name, user_id, password,
           'library.book', 'read', [res['result'],
           ['name', 'date_release']])
       res = requests.post(json_endpoint, data=payload,
           headers=headers).json()
       print('Books data:', res)
   else:
       print("Failed: wrong credentials")
   ```

3. Run the Python script from the Terminal with the following command:

   ```
   python3 jsonrpc_fetch_data.py
   ```

The preceding program will give you the following output. The first RPC call will print the book's ID, and the second one will print the information for the book's ID:

```
python3 jsonrpc_fetch_data.py
Search Reasult: {'jsonrpc': '2.0', 'id': 924727329, 'result': [1, 3, 4, 7, 8]}
Books Data: {'jsonrpc': '2.0', 'id': 855811251, 'result': [{'id': 1, 'name': 'Odoo 12 Development
Cookbook', 'date_release': '2019-02-13'}, {'id': 3, 'name': 'PostgresSQL basics', 'date_release':
'2018-02-15'}, {'id': 4, 'name': 'MySQL basics', 'date_release': '2018-02-15'}, {'id': 7, 'name': 'Odoo
basics', 'date_release': '2018-02-15'}, {'id': 8, 'name': 'Odoo 11 Development Cookbook',
'date_release': '2018-02-15'}]}
```

Figure 20.7 – Data of books

The output shown in the preceding screenshot is based on data in my database. The data in your Odoo instance may be different data, and so the output will also be different.

How it works...

In the *Logging in to/connecting Odoo with JSON-RPC* recipe, we saw that you can validate `username` and `password`. If the login details are correct, the RPC call will return `user_id`. You can then use this `user_id` to fetch the model's data. Like XML-RPC, we need to use the `search` and `read` combination to fetch the data from the model. To fetch the data, we use `object` as a service and `execute_kw()` as the method. `execute_kw()` is the same method that we used in XML-RPC for data, so it accepts the same argument, as follows:

- Database name
- User ID (we get this from the `authenticate()` method)
- Password
- Model name, for example, `res.partner`, or `library.book`
- Method name, for example, `search`, `read`, or `create`
- An array of positional arguments (`args`)
- A dictionary for keyword arguments (`optional`) (`kwargs`)

In our example, we called the `search` method first. The `execute_kw()` method usually takes mandatory arguments as positional arguments, and optional arguments as keyword arguments. In the `search` method, `domain` is a mandatory argument, so we passed it in the list and passed the `optional` argument limit as the `keyword` argument (dictionary). You will get a response in JSON format, and in this recipe, the response of the `search()` method RPC will have the book's IDs in the `result` key.

In *step 2*, we made an RPC call with the `read` method. To read the book's information, we passed two positional arguments—the list of book IDs and the list of fields to fetch. This RPC call will return the book information in JSON format and you can access it in the `result` key.

> **Note**
> Instead of `execute_kw()`, you can use `execute` as the method. This does not support keyword arguments, so you need to pass all of the intermediate arguments if you want to pass some optional arguments.

There's more...

Similar to XML-RPC, you can use the `search_read()` method instead of the `search()` and `read()` method combination as it is slightly time-consuming. Take a look at the following code:

```
# place authentication and get_json_payload methods (see first
jsonrpc recipe)

if user_id:
    # search and read for the book's ids
    search_domain = ['|', ['name', 'ilike', 'odoo'],
        ['name', 'ilike', 'sql']]
    payload = get_json_payload("object", "execute_kw",
        db_name, user_id, password,
        'library.book', 'search_read',
        [search_domain, ['name', 'date_release']],
        {'limit': 5})
    res = requests.post(json_endpoint, data=payload,
        headers=headers).json()
    print('Books data:', res)
else:
    print("Failed: wrong credentials")
```

The code snippet is an alternative way to fetching book data with `search_read()`. It will return the same output as in the previous example.

Creating/updating/deleting records through JSON-RPC

In the previous recipe, we looked at how to search and read data through JSON-RPC. In this recipe, we will perform the remaining **CRUD** operations through RPC—**Create**, **Update** (write), and **Delete** (unlink).

Getting ready

We will create a Python program to `create`, `write`, and `unlink` data in the `library.book` model. Make sure you have installed the `my_library` module and that the server is running on `http://localhost:8069`.

How to do it...

Perform the following steps to create, write, and unlink a book's information through RPC:

1. Add the `jsonrpc_operation.py` file. You can place this file anywhere you want because the RPC program will work independently.

2. Add the following code to the file:

```python
# place authentication and get_json_payload method (see
last recipe for more)

if user_id:
    # creates the books records
    create_data = [
        {'name': 'Book 1', 'date_release':
        '2019-01-26'},
        {'name': 'Book 3', 'date_release':
        '2019-02-12'},
        {'name': 'Book 5', 'date_release':
        '2019-05-08'},
        {'name': 'Book 7', 'date_release':
        '2019-05-14'}
    ]
    payload = get_json_payload("object", "execute_kw",
        db_name, user_id, password, 'library.book',
        'create', [create_data])
    res = requests.post(json_endpoint, data=payload,
```

```python
        headers=headers).json()
    print("Books created:", res)
    books_ids = res['result']

    # Write in existing book record
    book_to_write = books_ids[1]
    # We will use ids of recently created books
    write_data = {'name': 'Book 2'}
    payload = get_json_payload("object", "execute_kw",
        db_name, user_id, password, 'library.book',
        'write', [book_to_write, write_data])
    res = requests.post(json_endpoint, data=payload,
        headers=headers).json()
    print("Books written:", res)

    # Delete in existing book record
    book_to_unlink = books_ids[2:]
    # We will use ids of recently created books
    payload = get_json_payload("object", "execute_kw",
        db_name, user_id, password, 'library.book',
        'unlink', [book_to_unlink])
    res = requests.post(json_endpoint, data=payload,
        headers=headers).json()
    print("Books deleted:", res)

else:
    print("Failed: wrong credentials")
```

3. Run the Python script from the Terminal with the following command:

   `python3 jsonrpc_operation.py`

The preceding program will create four books. Writing one book and deleting two books gives you the following output (the IDs created may be different based on your database):

```
$ python3 jsonrpc_operation.py
Books created: {'jsonrpc': '2.0', 'id': 21804281, 'result': [80, 81, 82, 83]}
Books written: {'jsonrpc': '2.0', 'id': 81603666, 'result': True}
Books deleted: {'jsonrpc': '2.0', 'id': 767449164, 'result': True}
```

Figure 20.8 – Book operation output

The `write` and `unlink` methods return `True` if the operation is successful. This means that if you get `True` in response, assume that a record has been updated or deleted successfully.

How it works...

`execute_kw()` is used for the `create`, `update`, and `delete` operations. From Odoo version 12, the `create` method supports the creation of multiple records. So, we prepared the dictionary with information from the four books. Then we made the JSON-RPC call with `library.book` as the model name and `create` as the method name. This will create four book records in the database and return a JSON response with the IDs of these newly created books. In the next RPC calls, we want to use these IDs to make an RPC call for the `update` and `delete` operations, so we assign it to the `books_ids` variable.

> **Note**
> Both JSON-RPC and XML-RPC generate an error when you try to create the record without providing values for the required field, so make sure you have added all the required fields to the `create` values.

In the next RPC call, we used the `write` method to update the existing records. The `write` method accepts two positional arguments; the records to update and the values to write. In our example, we have updated the name of the book by using the ID of the second book from a created book's IDs. This will change the name of the second book from `Book 3` to `Book 2`.

Then we made the last RPC call to delete two book records. To do so, we used the `unlink` method. The `unlink` method accepts only one argument, which is the ID of the records you want to delete. This RPC call will delete the last two books.

There's more...

Like XML-RPC, you can use the `check_access_rights` method in JSON-RPC to check whether you have access rights to perform the operation. This method requires two parameters—the model name and the operation name. In the following example, we check access rights for the `create` operation on the `library.book` model:

```
# place authentication and get_json_payload method (see last
recipe for more)
if user_id:
    payload = get_json_payload("object", "execute_kw",
        db_name, user_id, password,
```

```
        'library.book', 'check_access_rights', ['create'])
    res = requests.post(json_endpoint, data=payload,
        headers=headers).json()
    print("Has create access:", res['result'])

else:
    print("Failed: wrong credentials")
```

This program will generate the following output:

```
$ python3 jsonrpc_access_rights.py
Has create access: True
```

Figure 20.9 – Output for checking access rights

When you are performing complex operations via RPC, the use of the `check_access_rights` method can be used before performing an operation to make sure you have proper access rights.

Calling methods through JSON-RPC

In this recipe, we will learn how to invoke a custom method of the model through JSON-RPC. We will change the status of the book by calling the `make_available()` method.

Getting ready

We will create the Python program to call `make_available` on the `library.book` model. Make sure you have installed the `my_library` module and that the server is running on `http://localhost:8069`.

How to do it...

Perform the following steps to create, write, and update a book's information through RPC:

1. Add the `jsonrpc_method.py` file. You can place this file anywhere you want because the RPC program will work independently.

2. Add the following code to the file:

```
# place authentication and get_json_payload method (see
last recipe for more)
if user_id:
    # Create the book in draft state
    payload = get_json_payload("object", "execute_kw",
        db_name, user_id, password,
        'library.book', 'create', [{'name': 'Book 1',
        'state': 'draft'}])
    res = requests.post(json_endpoint, data=payload,
        headers=headers).json()
    print("Has create access:", res['result'])
    book_id = res['result']

    # Change the book state by calling make_available
    # method
    payload = get_json_payload("object", "execute_kw",
        db_name, user_id, password,
        'library.book', 'make_available', [book_id])
    res = requests.post(json_endpoint, data=payload,
        headers=headers).json()

    # Check the book status after method call
    payload = get_json_payload("object", "execute_kw",
        db_name, user_id, password,
        'library.book', 'read', [book_id,
        ['name', 'state']])
    res = requests.post(json_endpoint, data=payload,
        headers=headers).json()
    print("Book state after the method call:",
        res['result'])
else:
    print("Failed: wrong credentials")
```

3. Run the Python script from the Terminal with the following command:

```
python3 jsonrpc_method.py
```

The preceding command will create one book using `draft` and then we will change the book state by calling the `make_available` method. After that, we will fetch the book data to check the book's status, which will generate the following output:

```
$ python3 jsonrpc_method.py
Book created with id: 86
Book state after the method call: [{'id': 86, 'name': 'Book 1', 'state': 'available'}]
```

Figure 20.10 – Changing the state of the book

The program of this recipe will create a new book record and change the state of the book by calling the model method. By the end of the program, we will have read the book record and printed the updated state.

How it works...

`execute_kw()` is capable of calling any public method of the model. As we saw in the *Calling methods through XML-RPC* recipe, public methods are those whose names that don't start with _ (underscore). Methods that start with _ are private and you cannot invoke them from JSON-RPC.

In our example, we created a book with a state of `draft`. Then we made one more RPC call to invoke the `make_available` method, which will change the book's state to `available`. Finally, we made one more RPC call to check the state of the book. This will show that the book's state has changed to **available**, as seen in *Figure 20.10*.

Methods that do not return anything internally return `None` by default. Such methods cannot be used from RPC. Consequently, if you want to use your method from RPC, at least add the return `True` statement.

The OCA odoorpc library

The **Odoo Community Association (OCA)** provides a Python library called `odoorpc`. This is available at `https://github.com/OCA/odoorpc`. The `odoorpc` library provides a user-friendly syntax from which to access Odoo data through RPC. It provides a similar syntax to the server. In this recipe, we will see how you can use the `odoorpc` library to perform operations through RPC.

Getting ready

The `odoorpc` library is registered on the Python package (`PyPI`) index. In order to use the library, you need to install it with the following command. You can use this in a separate virtual environment if you want:

```
pip install OdooRPC
```

In this recipe, we will perform some basic operations using the `odoorpc` library. We will use the `library.book` model to perform these operations. Make sure you have installed the `my_library` module and that the server is running on `http://localhost:8069`.

How to do it...

Perform the following steps to create, write, and update a book's information through RPC:

1. Add the `odoorpc_library.py` file. You can place this file anywhere you want because the RPC program will work independently.

2. Add the following code to the file:

   ```python
   import odoorpc

   db_name = 'book-db-14'
   user_name = 'admin'
   password = 'admin'

   # Prepare the connection to the server
   odoo = odoorpc.ODOO('localhost', port=8069)
   odoo.login(db_name, user_name, password) # login

   # User information
   user = odoo.env.user
   print(user.name) # name of the user connected
   print(user.company_id.name)
   # the name of user's company
   print(user.email) # the email of user

   BookModel = odoo.env['library.book']
   search_domain = ['|', ['name', 'ilike', 'odoo'],
        ['name', 'ilike', 'sql']]
   books_ids = BookModel.search(search_domain, limit=5)
   for book in BookModel.browse(books_ids):
   ```

```
        print(book.name, book.date_release)

# create the book and update the state
book_id = BookModel.create({'name': 'Test book', 'state':
'draft'})
print("Book state before make_available:", book.state)
book = BookModel.browse(book_id)
book.make_available()
book = BookModel.browse(book_id)
print("Book state before make_available:", book.state)
```

3. Run the Python script from the Terminal with the following command:

   ```
   python3 odoorpc_library.py
   ```

The program will do the authentication, print user information, and perform an operation in the `library.book` model. It will generate the following output:

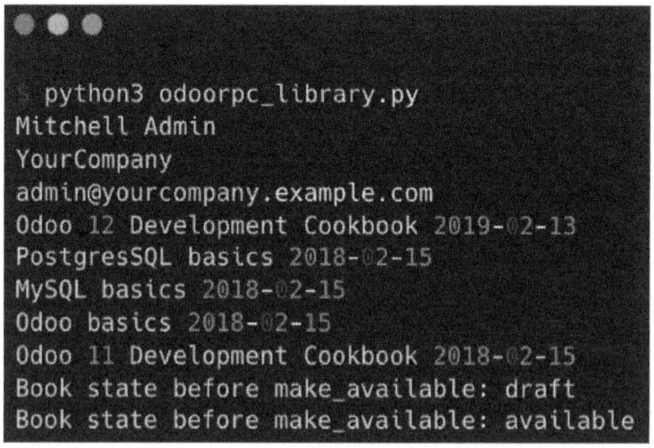

```
 python3 odoorpc_library.py
Mitchell Admin
YourCompany
admin@yourcompany.example.com
Odoo 12 Development Cookbook 2019-02-13
PostgresSQL basics 2018-02-15
MySQL basics 2018-02-15
Odoo basics 2018-02-15
Odoo 11 Development Cookbook 2018-02-15
Book state before make_available: draft
Book state before make_available: available
```

Figure 20.11 – Output of the odoorpc library program

The preceding output is the result of several RPC calls. We have fetched user info, some book info, and we have changed the state of the book.

How it works...

After installing the `odoorpc` library, you can start using it straightaway. To do so, you will need to import the `odoorpc` package and then we will create the object of the ODOO class by passing the server URL and port. This will make the `/version_info` call to the server to check the connection. To log in, you need to use the `login()` method of the object. Here, you need to pass the `database` name, `username`, and `password`.

Upon successful login, you can access the user information at `odoo.env.user`. `odoorpc` provides a user-friendly version of RPC, so you can use this user object exactly like the record set in the server. In our example, we accessed the name, email, and company name from this user object.

If you want to access the model registry, you can use the `odoo.env` object. You can call any model method on the model. Under the hood, the `odoorpc` library uses `jsonrpc`, so you can't invoke any private model method name that starts with an _. In our example, we accessed the `library.book` model from the registry. After that, we called the `search` method with the `domain` and `limit` parameters. This will return the IDs of the books. By passing the book IDs to the `browse()` method, you can generate a record set for the `library.book` model.

By the end of the program, we will have created a new book and changed the book's state by calling the `make_available()` method. If you look closely at the syntax of the program, you will see that it uses the same syntax as the server.

There's more...

Although it provides a user-friendly syntax like the server, you can use the library just like the normal RPC syntax. To do so, you need to use the `odoo.execute` method with the model name, method name, and arguments. Here is an example of reading some book information in the raw RPC syntax:

```
import odoorpc

db_name = 'book-db-14'
user_name = 'admin'
password = 'admin'

# Prepare the connection to the server
odoo = odoorpc.ODOO('localhost', port=8069)
odoo.login(db_name, user_name, password) # login

books_info = odoo.execute('library.book', 'search_read',
    [['name', 'ilike', 'odoo']], ['name', 'date_release'])
print(books_info)
```

See also

There are several other implementations of RPC libraries for Odoo, as follows:

- `https://github.com/akretion/ooor`
- `https://github.com/OCA/odoorpc`
- `https://github.com/odoo/openerp-client-lib`
- `http://pythonhosted.org/OdooRPC`
- `https://github.com/abhishek-jaiswal/php-openerp-lib`

Generating API keys

Odoo v14 has built-in support for the **Two-Factor Authentication** (**2FA**) feature. 2FA is an extra layer of security for user accounts and users need to enter a password and time-based code. If you have enabled 2FA, then you won't be able to use RPC by entering your user ID and password. To fix this, you will need to generate an API key for the user. In this recipe, we will see how you can generate API keys.

How to do it...

Perform the following steps to generate an API key for RPC:

1. Open user preferences and open the **Account Security** tab.
2. Click on the **New API Key** button:

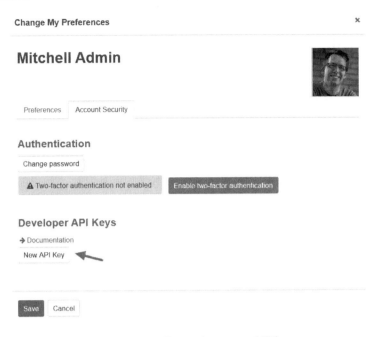

Figure 20.12 – Generating a new API key

3. It will open a popup as in the following screenshot. Enter the API key name and click on the **Generate key** button:

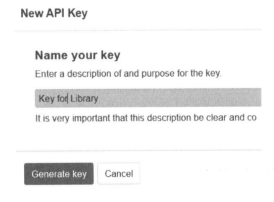

Figure 20.13 – Naming your key

4. This will generate the API key and show it in a new popup. Note down the API key because you will need this again:

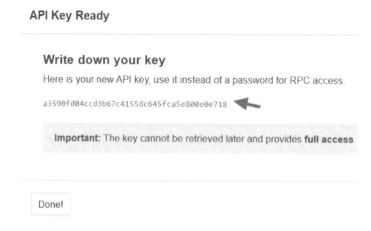

Figure 20.14 – Noting the generated API key

Once the API key is generated, you can start using the API key for RPC in the same way as the normal password.

How it works...

Using API keys is straightforward. However, there are a few things that you need to take care of. The API keys are generated per user and if you want to utilize RPC for multiple users, you would need to generate an API key for each user. Additionally, the API key for a user will have the same access rights as the user would have, so if someone gains access to the key, they can perform all the operations that the user can. So, you need to keep the API key secret.

> **Note**
> When you generate the API key, it is displayed only once. You need to note down the key. If you lose it, there is no way to get it back. In such cases, you would need to delete the API key and generate a new one.

Using the API key is very simple. During RPC calls, you just need to use the API key instead of the user password. You will be able to call RPC even if 2FA is activated.

21
Performance Optimization

With the help of the Odoo framework, you can develop large and complex applications. Good performance is key to the success of any project. In this chapter, we will explore the patterns and tools you need to optimize performance. You will also learn about the debugging techniques used to find the root cause of a performance issue.

In this chapter, we will cover the following recipes:

- The prefetching pattern for recordsets
- The in-memory cache – `ormcache`
- Generating differently sized images
- Accessing grouped data
- Creating or writing multiple records
- Accessing records through database queries
- Profiling Python code

The prefetching pattern for recordsets

When you access data from a recordset, it makes a query in the database. If you have a recordset with multiple records, fetching records on it can make a system slow because of the multiple SQL queries. In this recipe, we will explore how you can use the prefetching pattern to solve this issue. By following the prefetching pattern, you can reduce the number of queries needed, which will improve performance and make your system faster.

How to do it...

Take a look at the following code; it is a normal compute method. In this method, self is a recordset of multiple records. When you iterate directly on the recordset, prefetching works perfectly:

```
# Correct prefetching
def compute_method(self):
    for rec in self:
        print(rec.name)
```

But in some cases, prefetching becomes more complex, such as when fetching data with the browse method. In the following example, we browse records one by one in the for loop. This will not use prefetching efficiently and it will execute more queries than usual:

```
# Incorrect prefetching
def some_action(self):
    record_ids = []
    self.env.cr.execute("some query to fetch record id")
    for rec in self.env.cr.fetchall():
        record = self.env['res.partner'].browse(rec[0])
        print(record.name)
```

By passing a list of IDs to the browse method, you can create a recordset of multiple records. If you perform operations on this recordset, prefetching works perfectly fine:

```
# Correct prefetching
def some_action(self):
    record_ids = []
    self.env.cr.execute("some query to fetch record id")
    record_ids = [ rec[0] for rec in self.env.cr.fetchall() ]
    recordset = self.env['res.partner'].browse(record_ids)
    for record_id in recordset:
        print(record.name)
```

This way, you will not lose the prefetching feature and data will be fetched in a single SQL query.

How it works...

When you are working with multiple recordsets, prefetching helps reduce the number of SQL queries. It does this by fetching all of the data at once. Usually, prefetching works automatically in Odoo, but you lose this feature in certain circumstances, such as when you split records as depicted in the following example:

```
recs = [r for r in recordset r.id not in [1,2,4,10]]
```

The preceding code given will split the recordset into parts, and so you cannot take advantage of prefetching.

Using prefetching correctly can significantly improve the performance of the **Object-Relational Mapping** (**ORM**). Let's explore how prefetching works under the hood. When you iterate on a recordset through a `for` loop and access the value of a field in the first iteration, the prefetching process starts its magic. Instead of fetching data for the current record in the iteration, prefetching will fetch the data for all of the records. The logic behind this is that if you are accessing a field in a `for` loop, you are likely to fetch that data for the next record in the iteration as well. In the first iteration of the `for` loop, prefetching will fetch the data for all of the recordsets and keep it in the cache. In the next iteration of the `for` loop, data will be served from this cache, instead of making a new SQL query. This will reduce the query count from O(n) to O(1).

Let's suppose the recordset has 10 records. When you are in the first loop and access the name field of the record, it will fetch the data for all 10 records. This is not only the case for the `name` field; it will also fetch all the fields for those 10 records. In the subsequent `for` loop iterations, the data will be served from the cache. This will reduce the number of queries from 10 to 1:

```
for record in recordset: # recordset with 10 records
    record.name # Prefetch data of all 10 records in the first loop
    record.email # data of email will be served from the cache.
```

Note that the prefetching will fetch the value of all of the fields (except the *2many fields) even if those fields are not used in the body of the `for` loop. This is because the extra columns only have a minor impact on performance compared to the extra queries for each column.

> **Note**
> Sometimes, prefetched fields could reduce performance. In these cases, you can disable prefetching by passing `False` into the `prefetch_fields` context, as follows: `recordset.with_context(prefetch_fields=False)`.

The prefetch mechanism uses the environment cache to store and retrieve record values. This means that once the records are fetched from the database, all subsequent calls for fields will be served from the environment cache. You can access the environment cache using the `env.cache` attribute. To invalidate the cache, you can use the `invalidate_cache()` method of the environment.

There's more...

If you split recordsets, the ORM will generate a new recordset with a new prefetch context. Performing operations on such recordsets will only prefetch the data for the respective records. If you want to prefetch all the records after `prefetch`, you can do this by passing the prefetch record IDs to the `with_prefetch()` method. In the following example, we split the recordset into two parts. Here, we passed a common prefetch context in both recordsets, so when you fetch the data from one of them, the ORM will fetch the data for the other and put the data in the cache for future use:

```
recordset = ... # assume recordset has 10 records.
recordset1 = recordset[:5].with_prefetch(recordset._ids)
recordset2 = recordset[5:].with_prefetch(recordset._ids)
```

The prefetch context is not limited to splitting recordsets. You can also use the `with_prefetch()` method to have a common prefetch context between multiple recordsets. This means that when you fetch data from one record, it will fetch data for all other recordsets too.

The in-memory cache – ormcache

The Odoo framework provides the `ormcache` decorator to manage the in-memory cache. In this recipe, we will explore how you can manage the cache for your functions.

How to do it...

The classes of this ORM cache are available at /odoo/tools/cache.py. In order to use these in any file, you will need to import them as follows:

```
from odoo import tools
```

After importing the classes, you can use the ORM cache decorators. Odoo provides different types of in-memory cache decorator. We'll take a look at each of these in the following sections.

ormcache

This one is the simplest and most-used cache decorator. You need to pass the parameter name upon which the method's output depends. The following is an example method with the ormcache decorator:

```
@tools.ormcache('mode')
def fetch_mode_data(self, mode):
    # some calculations
    return result
```

When you call this method for the first time, it will be executed, and the result will be returned. ormcache will store this result based on the value of the mode parameter. When you call the method again with the same mode value, the result will be served from the cache without executing the actual method.

Sometimes, your method's result depends on the environment attributes. In these cases, you can declare the method as follows:

```
@tools.ormcache('self.env.uid', 'mode')
def fetch_data(self, mode):
    # some calculations
    return result
```

The method given in this example will store the cache based on the environment user and the value of the mode parameter.

ormcache_context

This cache works similarly to `ormcache`, except that it depends on the parameters plus the value in the context. In this cache's decorator, you need to pass the parameter name and a list of context keys. For example, if your method's output depends on the `lang` and `website_id` keys in the context, you can use `ormcache_context`:

```
@tools.ormcache_context('mode', keys=('website_id','lang'))
def fetch_data(self, mode):
    # some calculations
    return result
```

The cache in the preceding example will depend on the `mode` argument and the values of `context`.

ormcache_multi

Some methods carry out an operation on multiple records or IDs. If you want to add a cache on these kinds of method, you can use the `ormcache_multi` decorator. You need to pass the `multi` parameter, and during the method call, the ORM will generate the cache keys by iterating on this parameter. In this method, you will need to return the result in dictionary format with an element of the `multi` parameter as a key. Take a look at the following example:

```
@tools.ormcache_multi('mode', multi='ids')
def fetch_data(self, mode, ids):
    result = {}
    for i in ids:
        data = ... # some calculation based on ids
        result[i] = data
    return result
```

Suppose we called the preceding method with [1,2,3] as the IDs. The method will return a result in {1:... , 2:..., 3:... } format. The ORM will cache the result based on these keys. If you make another call with [1,2,3,4,5] as the IDs, your method will receive [4, 5] as the ID parameter, so the method will carry out the operations for the 4 and 5 IDs and the rest of the result will be served from the cache.

How it works...

The ORM cache keeps the cache in dictionary format (the cache lookup). The keys of this cache will be generated based on the signature of the decorated method and the values will be the result. Put simply, when you call the method with the x, y parameters and the result of the method is x+y, the cache lookup will be { (x, y) : x+y}. This means that the next time you call this method with the same parameters, the result will be served directly from this cache. This saves computation time and makes the response faster.

The ORM cache is an in-memory cache, so it is stored in RAM and occupies memory. Do not use ormcache to serve large data, such as images or files.

> **Warning**
> Methods using this decorator should never return a recordset. If you do this, they will generate psycopg2.OperationalError because the underlying cursor of the recordset is closed.

You should use the ORM cache on pure functions. A pure function is a method that always returns the same result for the same arguments. The output of these methods only depends on the arguments, and so they return the same result. If this is not the case, you need to manually clear the cache when you perform operations that make the cache's state invalid. To clear the cache, call the clear_caches() method:

```
self.env[model_name].clear_caches()
```

Once you have cleared the cache, the next call to the method will execute the method and store the result in the cache, and all subsequent method calls with the same parameter will be served from the cache.

There's more...

The ORM cache is the **Least Recently Used** (**LRU**) cache, meaning that if a key in the cache is not used frequently, it will be removed. If you don't use the ORM cache properly, it might do more harm than good. For instance, if the argument passed in a method is always different, then each time Odoo will look in the cache first and then call the method to compute. If you want to learn how your cache is performing, you can pass the SIGUSR1 signal to the Odoo process:

```
kill -SIGUSR1 496
```

Here, 496 is the process ID. After executing the command, you will see the status of the ORM cache in the logs:

```
> 2020-11-08 09:22:49,350 496 INFO book-db-14 odoo.tools.cache:
1 entries,       31 hit,     1 miss,      0 err, 96.9% ratio,
for ir.actions.act_window._existing
> 2020-11-08 09:22:49,350 496 INFO book-db-14 odoo.tools.cache:
1 entries,        1 hit,     1 miss,      0 err, 50.0% ratio,
for ir.actions.actions.get_bindings
> 2020-11-08 09:22:49,350 496 INFO book-db-14 odoo.tools.cache:
4 entries,        1 hit,     9 miss,      0 err, 10.0% ratio,
for ir.config_parameter._get_param
```

The percentage in the cache is the hit-to-miss ratio. It's the success ratio of the result being found in the cache. If the cache's hit-to-miss ratio is too low, you should remove the ORM cache from the method.

Generating differently sized images

Large images can be troublesome for any website. They increase the size of web pages and consequently make them slower as a result. This leads to bad SEO rankings and visitor loss. In this recipe, we will explore how you can create images of different sizes; by using the right images, you can reduce the web page size and improve the page loading time.

How to do it...

You will need to inherit `image.mixin` in your model. Here is how you can add `image.mixin` to your model:

```
class LibraryBook(models.Model):
    _name = 'library.book'
    _description = 'Library Book'
    _inherit = ['image.mixin']
```

The mixin will automatically add five new fields to the `books` model to store images of different sizes. See the *How it works...* section to learn about all five fields.

How it works...

The `image.mixin` instance will automatically add five new binary fields to the model. Each field stores image with a different resolution. Here is a list of the fields and their resolutions:

- `image_1920`: 1,920x1,920
- `image_1024`: 1,024x1,024
- `image_512`: 512x1,512
- `image_256`: 256x256
- `image_128`: 128x128

Of all the fields given here, only `image_1920` is editable. The other image fields are read-only and update automatically when you change the `image_1920` field. So, in the backend form view of your model, you need to use the `image_1920` field to allow the user to upload images. But by doing so, we are loading large `image_1920` images in the form view. However, there is a way to improve performance by using `image_1920` images in the form view but displaying smaller images. For instance, we can utilize the `image_1920` field but display an `image_128` field. To do this, you can use the following syntax:

```
<field name="image_1920" widget="image"
    options="{'preview_image': 'image_128'}" />
```

Once you have saved the image to the field, Odoo will automatically resize the image and store it to the respective field. The form view will display the converted `image_128` as we use it as `preview_image`.

> **Note**
> The `image.mixin` model is `AbstractModel`, so its table is not present in the database. You need to inherit it in your model in order to use it.

With this `image.mixin`, you can store an image with a maximum resolution of 1,920x1,920. If you save an image with a resolution higher than 1,920x1,920, Odoo will reduce it to 1,920x1,920. While doing so, Odoo will also preserve the resolution of the image, avoiding any distortion. As an example, if you upload the image with a 2,400x1,600 resolution, the `image_1920` field will have a resolution of 1,920x1,280.

There's more...

With `image.mixin`, you can get images with certain resolutions, but what if you want to use an image with another resolution? To do so, you can use a binary wrapper field image, as in the following example:

```
image_1500 = fields.Image("Image 1500", max_width=1500, max_height=1500)
```

This will create a new `image_1500` field, and storing the image will resize it to 1,500x1,500 resolution. Note that this is not part of `image.mixin`. It just reduces the image to 1,500x1,500, so you need to add this field in the form view; editing it will not make changes to the other image fields in `image.mixin`. If you want to link it with an existing `image.mixin` field, add the `related="image_1920"` attribute in the field definition.

Accessing grouped data

When you want data for statistics, you often need it in a grouped form, such as a monthly sales report, or a report that shows sales per customer. It is time-consuming to search records and group them manually. In this recipe, we will explore how you can use the `read_group()` method to access grouped data.

How to do it...

Perform the following steps:

> **Note**
> The `read_group()` method is widely used for statistics and smart stat buttons.

1. Let's assume that you want to show the number of sales orders on the partner form. This can be done by searching sales orders for a customer and then counting the length:

```
# in res.partner model
so_count = fields.Integer(compute='_compute_so_count',
    string='Sale order count')

def _compute_so_count(self):
    sale_orders = self.env['sale.order'].
search(domain=[('partner_id', 'in', self.ids)])
```

```
        for partner in self:
            partner.so_count = len(sale_orders.
filtered(lambda so: so.partner_id.id == partner.id))
```

The previous example will work, but not optimally. When you display the `so_count` field on the tree view, it will fetch and filter sales orders for all the partners in a list. With this small amount of data, the `read_group()` method won't make much difference, but as the amount of data grows, it could be a problem. To fix this issue, you can use the `read_group` method.

2. The following example will do the same as the preceding one, but it only consumes one SQL query, even for large datasets:

```
# in res.partner model
so_count = fields.Integer(compute='_compute_so_count',
string='Sale order count')

def _compute_so_count(self):
    sale_data = self.env['sale.order'].read_group(
        domain=[('partner_id', 'in', self.ids)],
        fields=['partner_id'], groupby=['partner_id'])
    mapped_data = dict([(m['partner_id'][0], m['partner_
id_count']) for m in sale_data])
    for partner in self:
        partner.so_count = mapped_data[partner.id]
```

The previous code snippet is optimized as it obtains the sales order count directly via SQL's `GROUP BY` feature.

How it works...

The `read_group()` method internally uses the `GROUP BY` feature of SQL. This makes the `read_group` method faster, even if you have large datasets. Internally, the Odoo web client uses this method in the charts and the grouped tree view. You can tweak the behavior of the `read_group` method by using different arguments.

Let's explore the signature of the `read_group` method:

```
def read_group(self, domain, fields, groupby, offset=0,
limit=None, orderby=False, lazy=True):
```

The different parameters available for the `read_group` method are as follows:

- `domain`: This is used to filter records. This will be the search criteria for the `read_group` method.
- `fields`: This is a list of the fields to fetch with the grouping. Note that the fields mentioned here should be in the `groupby` parameter, unless you use some aggregate functions. The `read_group` method supports the SQL aggregate functions. Let's say you want to get the average order amount per customer. In this case, you can use `read_group` as follows:

  ```
  self.env['sale.order'].read_group([], ['partner_id',
  'amount_total:avg'], ['partner_id'])
  ```

  If you want to access the same field twice but with a different aggregate function, the syntax is a little different. You need to pass the field name as `alias:agg(field_name)`. This example will give you the total and average number of orders per customer:

  ```
  self.env['sale.order'].read_group([], ['partner_id',
  'total:sum(amount_total)', 'avg_total:avg(amount_
  total)'], ['partner_id'])
  ```

- `groupby`: This parameter will be a list of fields by which the records are grouped. It lets you group records based on multiple fields. To do this, you will need to pass a list of fields. For example, if you want to group the sales orders by customer and order state, you can pass `['partner_id ', 'state']` in this parameter.
- `offset`: This parameter is used for pagination. If you want to skip a few records, you can use this parameter.
- `limit`: This parameter is used for pagination; it indicates the maximum number of records to fetch.
- `lazy`: This parameter accepts Boolean values. By default, its value is `True`. If this parameter is `True`, the results are grouped only by the first field in the `groupby` parameter. You will get the remaining `groupby` parameters and the domain in the `__context` and `__domain` keys in the result. If the value of this parameter is set to `False`, it will group the data by all fields in the `groupby` parameter.

There's more...

Grouping by date fields can be complicated because it is possible to group records based on days, weeks, quarters, months, or years. You can change the grouping behavior of the date field by passing `groupby_function` after `:` in the `groupby` parameter. If you want to group the monthly total of the sales orders, you can use the `read_group` method:

```
self.env['sale.order'].read_group([], ['total:sum(amount_total)'], ['order_date:month'])
```

Possible options for date grouping are `day`, `week`, `month`, `quarter`, and `year`.

See also

Refer to the documentation if you want to learn more about PostgreSQL aggregate functions: `https://www.postgresql.org/docs/current/functions-aggregate.html`.

Creating or writing multiple records

If you are new to Odoo development, you might execute multiple queries to write or create multiple records. In this recipe, we will look at how to create and write records in batches.

How to do it...

Creating multiple records and writing on multiple records works differently for each, under the hood. Let's see each of these records one by one.

Creating multiple records

Odoo supports creating records in batches. If you are creating a single record, simply pass a dictionary with the field values. To create records in a batch, you just need to pass a list of these dictionaries instead of a single dictionary. The following example creates three book records in a single `create` call:

```
vals = [{
    'name': "Book1",
    'date_release': '2018/12/12',
}, {
    'name': "Book2",
    'date_release': '2018/12/12',
```

```
    }, {
        'name': "Book3",
        'date_release': '2018/12/12',
    }]

self.env['library.book'].create(vals)
```

The code snippet will create the records for three new books.

Writing on multiple records

If you are working on multiple versions of Odoo, you should be conscious of how the `write` method works under the hood. As of version 13, Odoo handles `write` differently. It uses a delayed approach for updates, which means that it does not write data in the database immediately. Odoo writes the data to the database only when necessary or when `flush()` is called.

Here are two examples of the `write` method:

```
# Example 1
data = {...}
for record in recordset:
    record.write(data)

# Example 2
data = {...}
recordset.write(data)
```

If you are using Odoo v13 or above, then there will not be any issues regarding performance. However, if you are using an older version, the second example will be much faster than the first one because the first example will execute a SQL query in each iteration.

How it works...

In order to create multiple records in a batch, you need to pass value dictionaries in the form of a list to create new records. This will automatically manage batch-creating the records. When you create records in a batch, internally doing so will insert a query for each record. This means that creating records in a batch is not done in a single query. This doesn't mean, however, that creating records in batches does not improve performance. The performance gain is achieved through batch-calculating computing fields.

Things work differently for the `write` method. Most things are handled automatically by the framework. For instance, if you write the same data on all records, the database will be updated with only one UPDATE query. The framework will even handle it if you update the same record again and again in the same transaction, as follows:

```
recordset.name= 'Admin'
recordset.email= 'admin@example.com'
recordset.name= 'Administrator'
recordset.email= 'admin-2@example.com'
```

In the previous code snippet, only one query will be executed for `write` with final values of `name=Administrator` and `email=admin-2@example.com`. This does not have a bad impact on performance as the assigned values are in the cache and written in later in a single query.

Things are different if you are using the `flush()` method in between, as shown in the following example:

```
recordset.name= 'Admin'
recordset.email= 'admin@example.com'
recordset.flush()
recordset.name= 'Administrator'
recordset.email= 'admin-2@example.com'
```

The `flush()` method updates the values from the cache to the database. So, in the previous example, two UPDATE queries will be executed; one with data before the flush and a second query with data after the flush.

There's more...

The delayed update is only for Odoo version 13, and if you are using an older version, then writing a single value will execute the UPDATE query immediately. Check the following examples to explore the correct usage of the `write` operation for an older version of Odoo:

```
# incorrect usage
recordset.name= 'Admin'
recordset.email= 'admin@example.com'

# correct usage
recordset.write({'name': 'Admin', 'email'= 'admin@example.com'})
```

Here, in the first example, we have two UPDATE queries, while the second example will only take one UPDATE query.

Accessing records through database queries

The Odoo ORM has limited methods, and sometimes it is difficult to fetch certain data from the ORM. In these cases, you can fetch data in the desired format, and you need to perform an operation on the data to get a certain result. Due to this, it becomes slower. To handle these special cases, you can execute SQL queries in the database. In this recipe, we will explore how you can run SQL queries from Odoo.

How to do it...

You can perform database queries using the `self._cr.execute` method:

1. Add the following code:

    ```
    self.flush()
    self._cr.execute("SELECT id, name, date_release FROM library_book WHERE name ilike %s", ('%odoo%',))
    data = self._cr.fetchall()
    print(data)

    Output:
    [(7, 'Odoo basics', datetime.date(2018, 2, 15)), (8, 'Odoo 11 Development Cookbook', datetime.date(2018, 2, 15)), (1, 'Odoo 12 Development Cookbook', datetime.date(2019, 2, 13))]
    ```

2. The result of the query will be in the form of a list of tuples. The data in the tuples will be in the same sequence as the fields in the query. If you want to fetch data in dictionary format, you can use the `dictfetchall()` method. Take a look at the following example:

    ```
    self.flush()
    self._cr.execute("SELECT id, name, date_release FROM library_book WHERE name ilike %s", ('%odoo%',))
    data = self._cr.dictfetchall()
    print(data)

    Output:
    [{'id': 7, 'name': 'Odoo basics', 'date_release': datetime.date(2018, 2, 15)}, {'id': 8, 'name': 'Odoo
    ```

```
11 Development Cookbook', 'date_release': datetime.
date(2018, 2, 15)}, {'id': 1, 'name': 'Odoo 12
Development Cookbook', 'date_release': datetime.
date(2019, 2, 13)}]
```

If you want to fetch only a single record, you can use the `fetchone()` and `dictfetchone()` methods. These methods work like `fetchall()` and `dictfetchall()`, but they only return a single record, and you need to call the `fetchone()` and `dictfetchone()` methods multiple times if you want to fetch multiple records.

How it works...

There are two ways to access the database cursor from the recordset: one is from the recordset itself, such as `self._cr`, and the other is from the environment, in particular, `self.env.cr`. This cursor is used to execute database queries. In the preceding example, we saw how you can fetch data through raw queries. The table name is the name of the model after replacing . with _, so the `library.book` model becomes `library_book`.

If you have noticed, we have used `self.flush()` before executing a query. The reason behind this is that Odoo uses cache excessively and the database might not have the correct values. `self.flush()` will push all the delayed updates to the database and conduct all the dependent computations as well, and you will get correct values from the database. The `flush()` method also supports a few parameters that help you control what is being flushed in the database. The parameters are as follows:

- The `fname` parameter needs a list of fields that you want to flush to the database.
- The `records` parameter needs a recordset, and it is used if you want to flush certain records only.

If you are executing INSERT or UPDATE queries, you will also need to execute `flush()` after executing the query because the ORM might not be aware of the change you made and it might have cached records.

You need to consider a few things before you execute raw queries. Only use raw queries when you have no other choice. By executing raw queries, you are bypassing the ORM layers. You are therefore also bypassing security rules and the ORM's performance advantages. Sometimes, wrongly built queries can introduce SQL injection vulnerabilities. Consider the following example, in which the queries could allow an attacker to perform SQL injection:

```
# very bad, SQL injection possible
self.env.cr.execute('SELECT id, name FROM library_book WHERE
name ilike + search_keyword + ';')

# good
self.env.cr.execute('SELECT id, name FROM library_book WHERE
name ilike %s ';', (search_keyword,))
```

Don't use the string format function either; it will also allow an attacker to perform SQL injection. Using SQL queries makes your code harder to read and understand for other developers, so avoid using them wherever possible.

> **Information**
> A lot of Odoo developers believe that executing SQL queries makes operations faster as it bypasses the ORM layer. This is not completely true, however; it depends on the case. In most operations, the ORM performs better and faster than RAW queries, because data is served from the recordset cache.

There's more...

Operations done in one transaction are only committed at the end of the transaction. If an error occurs in the ORM, the transaction is rolled back. If you have made an INSERT or UPDATE query and you want to make it permanent, you can use `self._cr.commit()` to commit the changes.

> **Note**
> Note that using `commit()` can be dangerous because it can put records in an inconsistent state. An error in the ORM can cause incomplete rollbacks, so only use `commit()` if you are completely sure of what you're doing.

If you are using the `commit()` method, then there's no need to use `flush()` afterward. The `commit()` method flushes the environment internally.

Profiling Python code

Sometimes, you will be unable to pinpoint the cause of an issue. This is especially true of performance issues. Odoo provides some built-in profiling tools that help you find the real cause of an issue.

How to do it...

Perform the following steps to do this recipe:

1. Odoo's profiler is available at `odoo/tools/profiler.py`. In order to use the profiler in your code, import it into the file:

   ```
   from odoo.tools.profiler import profile
   ```

2. After importing it, you can use the `profile` decorator on the methods. To profile a particular method, you need to add the `profile` decorator to it. Take a look at the following example. We put the `profile` decorator in the `make_available` method:

   ```
   @profile
   def make_available(self):
       if self.state != 'lost':
           self.write({'state': 'available'})
       return True
   ```

3. So, when this method is called, it will print the full statistics in the logs:

   ```
   calls     queries    ms
   library.book ----------------------- /Users/pga/odoo/
   test/my_library/models/library_book.py, 24

   1         0          0.01       @profile
                                   def make_available(self):
   1         3          12.81          if self.state !=
   'lost':
   1         7          20.55              self.
   write({'state': 'available'})
   1         0          0.01           return True

   Total:
   1         10         33.39
   ```

How it works...

After adding the `profile` decorator on your method, when you call that method, Odoo will print the full statistics in the log, as shown in the previous example. It will print the statistics in three columns. The first column will contain the number of calls or how many times a line is executed. (This number will increase when the line is inside a `for` loop or the method is recursive.) The second column represents the number of queries fired with the given line. The last column is the time taken by the given line in milliseconds. Note that the time displayed in this column is relative; it is faster when the profiler is off.

The `profiler` decorator accepts some optional arguments, which help you to get detailed statistics of the method. The following is the signature of the `profile` decorator:

```
def profile(method=None, whitelist=None, blacklist=(None,),
files=None,
 minimum_time=0, minimum_queries=0):
```

The following is a list of parameters supported by the `profile()` method:

- `whitelist`: This parameter will accept a list of model names to display in the log.
- `files`: This parameter will accept a list of filenames to display.
- `blacklist`: This parameter will accept a list of model names that you do not want to display in the log.
- `minimum_time`: This will accept an integer value (in milliseconds). It will hide logs whose total time is less than the given amount.
- `minimum_queries`: This will accept an integer value of the number of queries. It will hide the logs whose total number of queries is less than the given amount.

There's more...

One further type of profiler that is available in Odoo generates a graph for the executed method. This profiler is available in the `misc` package, so you need to import it from there. It will generate a file with statistics data that will generate a graph file. To use this profiler, you need to pass the file path as an argument. When this function is called, it will generate a file at the given location. Take a look at the following example, which generates the `make_available.prof` file on the desktop:

```
from odoo.tools.misc import profile
...
@profile('/Users/parth/Desktop/make_available.profile')
def make_available(self):
    if self.state != 'lost':
```

```
        self.write({'state': 'available'})
        self.env['res.partner'].create({'name': 'test',
'email': 'test@ada.asd'})
    return True
```

When the `make_available` method is called, it will generate a file on the desktop. To convert this data into graph data, you will need to install the `gprof2dot` tool and then execute the following command to generate the graph:

```
gprof2dot -f pstats -o /Users/parth/Desktop/prof.xdot    /Users/parth/Desktop/make_available.profile
```

This command will generate the `prof.xdot` file on the desktop. Then, you can display the graph with `xdot` with the following command:

```
xdot /Users/parth/Desktop/prof.xdot
```

The preceding `xdot` command will generate the graph shown in the following figure:

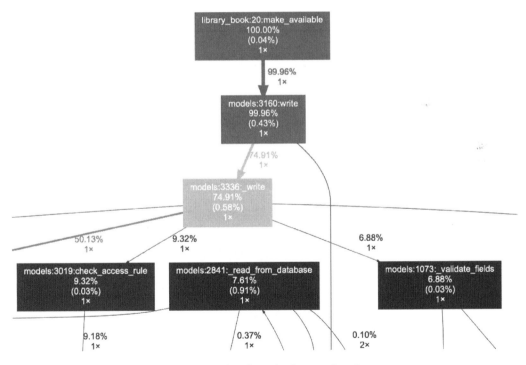

Figure 21.1 – Graph to check execution times

Here, you can zoom in, check the call stack, and look at details of the execution times for the methods.

22
Point of Sale

So far in this book, we have explored two different code bases. The first one is the backend code base, which is used to create views, actions, menus, wizards, and so on. The second one is the backend code base, which is used to create web pages, controllers, snippets, and so on. In this chapter, we will explore a third code base, which is used for the Point of Sale application. You might wonder why the Point of Sale application needs a different code base. This is because it uses a different architecture, in order to work offline as well. In this chapter, we will see how to modify the Point of Sale application.

In this chapter, we will cover the following recipes:

- Adding custom JavaScript/SCSS files
- Adding an action button on the keyboard
- Making RPC calls
- Modifying the Point of Sale screen UI
- Modifying existing business logic
- Modifying customer receipts

> **Note**
> The Point of Sale application is mostly written in JavaScript. This chapter is written assuming that you have a basic knowledge of JavaScript. This chapter also uses the OWL framework, so if you are unaware of these JavaScript terms, check out *Chapter 16, The Odoo Web Library (OWL)*.

Throughout this chapter, we will be using an add-on module called `pos_demo`. This `pos_demo` module will have a dependency on `point_of_sale` as we are going to do customization in the Point of Sale application. To get started with this recipe quickly, we have prepared an initial `pos_demo` module, and you can grab it from the `Chapter21/r0_initial_module/pos_demo` directory in the GitHub repository of this book.

Technical requirements

All the code used in this chapter can be downloaded from the following GitHub repository: `https://github.com/PacktPublishing/Odoo-14-Development-Cookbook-Fourth-Edition/tree/master/Chapter22`.

Adding custom JavaScript/SCSS files

The Point of Sale app uses different asset bundles for managing JavaScript and style sheet files. In this recipe, we will learn how to add **SCSS** and **JavaScript** files to the Point of Sale asset bundle.

Getting ready

In this recipe, we will load an SCSS style sheet and a JavaScript file into the Point of Sale application.

How to do it...

To load assets in the Point of Sale application, follow these steps:

1. Add a new SCSS file at `/pos_demo/static/src/scss/pos_demo.scss` and insert the following code:

   ```
   .pos .pos-content {
       .price-tag {
           background: #00abcd;
           width: 100%;
           right: 0;
           left: 0;
           top: 0;
       }
   }
   ```

2. Add a JavaScript file at `/pos_demo/static/src/js/pos_demo.js` and add the following:

   ```
   console.log('Point of Sale JavaScript loaded');
   ```

3. Register these JavaScript and SCSS files into the `point_of_sale` assets:

   ```xml
   <?xml version="1.0" encoding="utf-8"?>
   <odoo>
       <template id="assets" inherit_id="point_of_sale.assets">
           <xpath expr="." position="inside">
               <script type="text/javascript"
                       src="/pos_demo/static/src/js/pos_demo.js"></script>
               <link rel="stylesheet"
                     href="/pos_demo/static/src/scss/pos_demo.scss"/>
           </xpath>
       </template>
   </odoo>
   ```

Install the `pos_demo` module. To see your changes in action, start the new session from the **Point of Sale | Dashboard** menu.

How it works...

In this recipe, we loaded one JavaScript file and one SCSS file into the Point of Sale application. In *step 1*, we changed the background color and the border radius of the pricing label of the product card. After installing the pos_demo module, you will be able to see changes to the pricing labels:

Figure 22.1 – Updated price label

In *step 2*, we added the JavaScript file. In it, we added the log to the console. In order to see the message, you will need to open your browser's developer tools. In the **Console** tab, you will see the following log. This shows that your JavaScript file is loaded successfully. Right now, we have only added the log to the JavaScript file, but in upcoming recipes, we will add more to it:

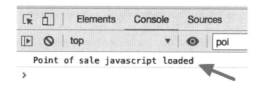

Figure 22.2 – JavaScript loaded (log in the console)

In *step 3*, we added the JavaScript file and the SCSS file into the Point of Sale assets. The external ID of the Point of Sale assets is point_of_sale.assets. Here, only the external ID is different; everything else works like regular assets. If you don't know how assets work in Odoo, refer to the *Static-assets management* recipe in *Chapter 14, CMS Website Development*.

There's more...

Odoo also has an add-on module for Point of Sale solutions for restaurants. Note that this Point of Sale restaurant module is just an extension of the Point of Sale application. If you want to do customization in the restaurant module, you will need to add your JavaScript and SCSS files to the same `point_of_sale.assets` asset bundle.

Adding an action button on the keyboard

As we discussed in the previous recipe, the Point of Sale application is designed in such a way that it works offline. Thanks to this, the code structure of the Point of Sale application is different from the remaining Odoo applications. The code base of the Point of Sale app is largely written with JavaScript and provides different utilities for customization. In this recipe, we will use one such utility and create an action button at the top of the keyboard panel.

Getting ready

In this recipe, we will be using the `pos_demo` module created in the *Adding custom JavaScript/SCSS files* recipe. We will add a button at the top of the keyboard panel. This button will be a shortcut for applying a discount to the order lines.

How to do it...

Follow these steps to add a 5% discount action button to the keyboard panel for the Point of Sale application:

1. Add the following code to the `/static/src/js/pos_demo.js` file, which will define the action button:

```
odoo.define('pos_demo.custom', function (require) {
    "use strict";

    const PosComponent = require('point_of_sale.PosComponent');
    const ProductScreen = require('point_of_sale.ProductScreen');
    const Registries = require('point_of_sale.Registries');

    class PosDiscountButton extends PosComponent {
```

```
        async onClick() {
            const order = this.env.pos.get_order();
            if (order.selected_orderline) {
                order.selected_orderline.set_discount(5);
            }
        }
    }
    PosDiscountButton.template = 'PosDiscountButton';
    ProductScreen.addControlButton({
        component: PosDiscountButton,
        condition: function () {
            return true;
        },
    });
    Registries.Component.add(PosDiscountButton);
    return PosDiscountButton;
});
```

2. Add the QWeb template for the button in the /static/src/xml/pos_demo.xml file:

```
<?xml version="1.0" encoding="UTF-8"?>
<templates id="template" xml:space="preserve">

    <t t-name="PosDiscountButton" owl="1">
        <span class="control-button "
            t-on-click="onClick">
            <i class="fa fa-gift"></i>
            <span>5%</span>
            <span>Discount</span>
        </span>
    </t>

</templates>
```

3. Register the QWeb template in the `manifest` file as follows:

```
'qweb': [
     'static/src/xml/pos_demo.xml'
]
```

4. Update the `pos_demo` module to apply the changes. After that, you will be able to see a **5% Discount** button above the keyboard:

Figure 22.3 – Discount button

After clicking this, the discount will be applied to the selected order line.

How it works...

In Odoo v14, code based on the Odoo Point of Sale application is completely re-written using the OWL framework. You can learn more about the OWL framework in *Chapter 16, The Odoo Web Library (OWL)*.

To create the action button in the Point of Sale application, you will need to extend `PosComponent`. Now, `PosComponent` is defined in the `point_of_sale.PosComponent` namespace, and so to use it in your code, you will need to import it. In *step 1*, we imported screens with `require('point_of_sale.PosComponent')`. Then we created `PosDiscountButton` by extending `PosComponent`. If you want to learn how the `require` mechanism works in Odoo JavaScript, refer to the *Adding CSS and JavaScript for a website* recipe in *Chapter 14, CMS Website Development*. In *step 1*, we have also imported `point_of_sale.ProductScreen` and `point_of_sale.Registries`. Now, `point_of_sale.ProductScreen` is used to add a button to the Point of Sale screen via the `addControlButton` method. Finally, we have added a registered button to `point_of_sale.Registries`, which is the global registry that contains all OWL components.

`PosComponent` has some built-in utilities that give access to useful information such as order details, Point of Sale configuration, and more. You can access it via the `this.env` variable. In our example, we have accessed the current order information via the `this.env.pos.get_order()` method. Then, we used the `set_discount()` method to set a 5% discount.

In *step 2* and *step 3*, we added the OWL template, which will be rendered over the Point of Sale keyboard. If you wish to learn more about this, please refer to *Chapter 16, The Odoo Web Library (OWL)*.

There's more...

The `addControlButton()` method supports one more parameter, which is `condition`. This parameter is used to hide/show the button based on some condition. The value of this parameter is a function that returns a Boolean. Based on the returned value, the Point of Sale system will hide or show the button. Take a look at the following example for more information:

```
ProductScreen.addControlButton({
    component: POSDiscountButton,
    condition: function() {
        return this.env.pos.config.module_pos_discount;
    },
});
```

The `condition` discount button is only displayed if the discount is enabled from the Point of Sale configuration.

Making RPC calls

Though the Point of Sale application works offline, it is still possible to make RPC calls to the server. The RPC call can be used for any operation; you can use it for CRUD operations, or to perform an action on the server. In this recipe, we will make an RPC call to fetch information about a customer's last five orders.

Getting ready

In this recipe, we will be using the `pos_demo` module created in the *Adding an action button on the keyboard* recipe. We will define the action button. When the user clicks on the action button, we will make an RPC call to fetch the order information and display it on the popup.

How to do it...

Follow these steps to display the last five orders for the selected customer:

1. Add the following code to the `/static/src/js/pos_demo.js` file; this will add a new action button to fetch and display the information about the last five orders when a user clicks on the button:

```javascript
class PosLastOrderButton extends PosComponent {
    // Place step 2 here
}
PosLastOrderButton.template = 'PosLastOrderButton';
ProductScreen.addControlButton({
    component: PosLastOrderButton,
    condition: function () {
        return true;
    },
});
Registries.Component.add(PosLastOrderButton);
```

2. Add the `onClick` function to the `PosLastOrders` component to manage button clicks:

```
async onClick() {
    var self = this;
    const order = this.env.pos.get_order();
    if (order.attributes.client) {
        var domain = [['partner_id', '=', order.attributes.client.id]];
        this.rpc({
            model: 'pos.order', method: 'search_read',
            args: [domain, ['name', 'amount_total']],
            kwargs: { limit: 5 },
        }).then(function (orders) {
            if (orders.length > 0) {
                var order_list = _.map(orders, function (o) {
                    return { 'label': _.str.sprintf("%s - TOTAL: %s", o.name, o.amount_total) };
                });
                self.showPopup('SelectionPopup', { title: 'Last 5 orders', list:order_list });
            } else {
                self.showPopup('ErrorPopup', { body: 'No previous orders found' });
            }
        });
    } else {
        self.showPopup('ErrorPopup', { body: 'Please select the customer' });
    }
}
```

3. Add the QWeb template for the button to the `/static/src/xml/pos_demo.xml` file:

```
<t t-name="PosLastOrderButton" owl="1">
    <span class="control-button" t-on-click="onClick">
        <i class="fa fa-shopping-cart"></i>
```

```
                <span></span>
                <span>Last Orders</span>
         </span>
    </t>
```

4. Update the `pos_demo` module to apply the changes. After that, you will be able to see the **Last orders** button above the keyboard panel. When this button is clicked, a popup will be displayed with the order information:

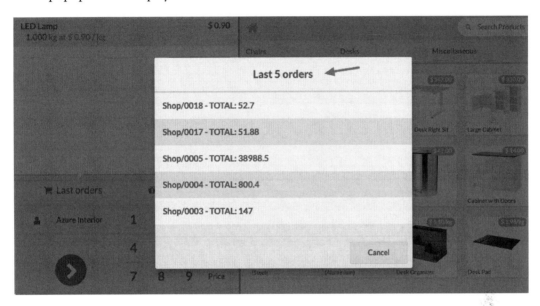

Figure 22.4 – Last five orders of a customer

If no previous orders are found, a warning will be displayed instead of an order list.

How it works...

In *step 1*, we created and registered the action button. If you want to learn more about the action button, refer to the *Adding an action button on the keyboard* recipe of this chapter. Before going into the technical details, let's understand what we wanted to accomplish with this action button. Once clicked, we want to display information for the last five orders for the selected customer. There will be a few cases where the customer is not selected, or customers have no previous orders. In such cases, we want to show a popup with an appropriate message.

The RPC utility is available with the `this.rpc` attribute of the component. In *step 2*, we added the click-handler function. On clicking the action button, the click-handler function will be called. This function will make the RPC call the server to fetch the order information. We used the `rpc()` method to make RPC calls. The following is a list of the parameters you can pass in the `rpc()` method:

- `model`: The name of the model on which you want to perform the operation
- `method`: The name of the method you want to invoke
- `args`: A list of compulsory positional arguments accepted by the method
- `kwargs`: A dictionary of the optional arguments accepted by the method

In this recipe, we used the `search_read` method to fetch data through RPC. We passed the customer domain to filter the orders. We also passed `limit` keyword arguments to fetch only five orders. `rpc.query()` is an asynchronous method and returns a `Promise` object, so to handle the result, you will need to use the `then()` method, or you can use the `await` keyword.

> **Note**
> The RPC call does not work in offline mode. If you have a good internet connection and you do not use offline mode frequently, you can use RPCs. Although the Odoo Point of Sale application works offline, a few operations, such as creating or updating a customer, require an internet connection, as those features use RPC to call internally.

We have displayed the previous order information in the popup. We have used `SelectionPopup`, which is used to display a selectable list; we used it to show the last five orders. We have also used `ErrorPopup` to display a warning message when a customer is not selected or no previous orders were found.

In *step 3*, we added the QWeb template for the action button. The Point of Sale application will render this template to display the action button.

There's more...

There are plenty of other popup utilities. For example, `NumberPopup` is used to take number input from the user. Refer to the files in the `addons/point_of_sale/static/src/xml/Popups` directory to see all these utilities.

Modifying the Point of Sale screen UI

The UI of the Point of Sale application is written with the OWL QWeb template. In this recipe, we will learn how you can modify UI elements in the Point of Sale application.

Getting ready

In this recipe, we will be using the `pos_demo` module created in the *Making RPC calls* recipe. We will modify the UI of the product card and display the profit margin per product.

How to do it...

Follow these steps to display the profit margin on the product card:

1. Add the following code to the `/static/src/js/pos_demo.js` file to fetch the extra field for the product's actual price:

    ```
    const pos_model = require('point_of_sale.models');
    pos_model.load_fields("product.product", ["standard_price"]);
    ```

2. Add the following code to `/static/src/xml/pos_demo.xml` in order to display a profit margin product card:

    ```
    <t t-name="ProductItem" t-inherit="point_of_sale.ProductItem"
        t-inherit-mode="extension" owl="1">
        <xpath expr="//span[hasclass('price-tag')]" position="after">
            <span t-if="props.product.standard_price"
                  class="sale_margin">
                <t t-set="margin"
                   t-value="props.product.get_price(pricelist, 1) - props.product.standard_price"/>
                <t t-esc="env.pos.format_currency(margin)"/>
            </span>
        </xpath>
    </t>
    ```

3. Add the following style sheet to style the margin text:

```
.sale_margin {
    top: 21px;
    line-height: 15px;
    right: 2px;
    background: #CDDC39;
    position: absolute;
    border-radius: 10px;
    padding: 0px 5px;
}
```

Update the `pos_demo` module to apply the changes. After that, you will be able to see the profit margin on the product card:

Figure 22.5 – Profit margins for products

If the product cost is not set on a product, then the product card will not display a profit margin, so make sure you set the product cost.

How it works...

In this recipe, we want to use the `standard_price` field as the purchase cost of the product. This field is not loaded by default in Point of Sale applications. In *step 1*, we added the `standard_price` field for the `product.product` model. After this, the product data will have one more field: `standard_price`.

In *step 2*, we extended the default product card template. You will need to use the `t-inherit` attribute to extend the existing QWeb template. Then, you need to use XPath to select the element on which you want to perform the operation. If you want to learn more about XPaths, refer to the *Changing existing views – view inheritance* recipe of *Chapter 9, Backend Views*.

To fetch the product sale price, we have used the `product` properties sent from the parent OWL component. `get_price()` is a method of the `product` model, and we receive the `product` properties in the `ProductItem` component. Then, we calculated the margin by using the product price and product cost. If you want to learn more about this, please refer to *Chapter 16, The Odoo Web Library (OWL)*

In *step 3*, we added the style sheet to modify the position of the margin element. This will add a background color to the margin element and place it under the price pill.

Modifying existing business logic

In the previous recipes, we saw how to fetch data through an RPC and how to modify the UI of the Point of Sale application. In this recipe, we will see how you can modify or extend the existing business logic.

Getting ready

In this recipe, we will be using the `pos_demo` module created in the *Modifying the Point of Sale screen UI* recipe, which is where we fetched the purchase price of a product and displayed the product margin. Now, in this recipe, we will show a warning to the user if they sell the product below the product margin.

How to do it...

Most of the business logic of the Point of Sale application is written in JavaScript, so we just need to make changes to it to achieve the goal of this recipe. Add the following code to `/static/src/js/pos_demo.js` to show a warning when the user sells a product below the purchase price:

```javascript
const UpdatedProductScreen = ProductScreen =>
    class extends ProductScreen {
        _setValue(val) {
            super._setValue(val);
            const orderline = this.env.pos.get_order().selected_orderline;
            if (orderline && orderline.product.standard_price) {
                var price_unit = orderline.get_unit_price() * (1.0 - (orderline.get_discount() / 100.0));
                if (orderline.product.standard_price > price_unit) {
                    this.showPopup('ErrorPopup', { title: 'Warning', body: 'Product price set below cost of product.' });
                }
            }
        }
    };

Registries.Component.extend(ProductScreen, UpdatedProductScreen);
```

Update the `pos_demo` module to apply the changes. After the update, add the discount on the order line in such a way that the product price becomes less than the purchase price. A popup will appear with the following warning:

Modifying existing business logic   697

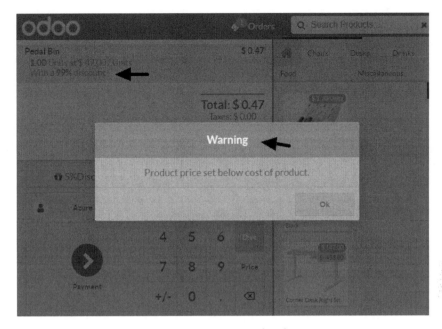

Figure 22.6 – Warning on a big discount

Note that when you set the product price below the actual cost, a warning will be displayed, and it will continue to pop up every time you take an action, such as when you change the quantity for the product order.

How it works...

The Point of Sale component register provides an extend method to make changes to an existing function. Internally, it is monkey patching the actual component definition.

In our example, we have modified the _setValue() method. The _setValue() method of ProductScreen is called whenever the user makes a change to the order line. We wanted to show a warning if the user set the product price below the product cost. So, we defined a new _setValue() method and called the super method; this will make sure that whatever actions the user performs are applied. After the call to the super method, we wrote our logic, which checks whether the product sale price is higher than the actual cost of the product. If not, then we show a warning to the user.

> **Note**
>
> Using `super` can break things if it's not used carefully. If the method is inherited from several files, you must call the `super` method; otherwise, it will skip the logic in the subsequent inheritance. This sometimes leads to a broken internal data state.

We placed our business logic after the default implementation (`super`) is called. If you want to write business logic before the default implementation, you can do so by moving the `super` call to the end of the function.

Modifying customer receipts

When you are customizing a Point of Sale application, a common request you get from customers is to modify customer receipts. In this recipe, you will learn how to modify customer receipts.

Getting ready

In this recipe, we will be using the `pos_demo` module created in the *Modifying existing business logic* recipe. We will add one line to the Point of Sale receipt to show how much money the customer saved in the order.

How to do it...

Follow these steps to modify a customer receipt in the Point of Sale application:

1. Add the following code to the `/static/src/js/pos_demo.js` file. This will add extra data in the receipt environment:

    ```js
    var models = require('point_of_sale.models');
    var _super_order = models.Order.prototype;
    models.Order = models.Order.extend({
        export_for_printing: function () {
            var result = _super_order.export_for_printing.apply(this, arguments);
            var savedAmount = this.saved_amount();
            if (savedAmount > 0) {
                result.saved_amount = this.pos.format_currency(savedAmount);
            }
    ```

```
            return result;
        },
        saved_amount: function() {
            const order = this.pos.get_order();
            return _.reduce(order.orderlines.models,
                function (rem, line) {
                    var diffrence = (line.product.lst_price *
line.quantity) - line.get_base_price();
                    return rem + diffrence;
                }, 0);
        }
    });
```

2. Add the following code in /static/src/xml/pos_demo.xml. This will extend the default receipt template and add our customization:

```
<t t-name="OrderReceipt" t-inherit="point_of_sale.OrderReceipt"
    t-inherit-mode="extension" owl="1">
    <xpath expr="//div[hasclass('before-footer')]" position="before">
        <div style="text-align:center;">
            <div t-if="receipt.saved_amount">
                You saved
                <t t-esc="receipt.saved_amount"/>
                on this order.
            </div>
        </div>
    </xpath>
</t>
```

Update the `pos_demo` module to apply the changes. After that, add a product with the discount and check the receipt; you will see one extra line in the receipt:

Figure 22.7 – Updated receipt

The receipt will not display the **amount saved** screen if it is zero or negative.

How it works...

There is nothing new in this recipe. We just updated the receipt by using the previous recipes. In *step 1*, we overrode the `export_for_printing()` function to send more data to the receipt environment. Whatever you are sending from the `export_for_printing()` method will be available in the QWeb template of the receipt. We compared the product's base price with the product price in the receipt to calculate how much money the customer saved. We sent this data to the receipt environment via the `saved_amount` key.

In *step 2*, we modified the default QWeb template of the receipt. The template name of the actual receipt is `OrderReceipt`, so we used it as a value in the `t-inherit` attribute. In *step 1*, we'd already sent the information needed to modify the receipt. In the QWeb template, we get the saved amount in the `receipt.saved_amount` key, so we just add one more `<div>` element before the footer. This will print the saved amount in the receipt. If you want to learn more about overriding, refer to the *Modifying the Point of Sale screen UI* recipe.

23
Managing Emails in Odoo

Email integration is the most prominent feature of Odoo. You can send and receive emails directly from the Odoo user interface. You can even manage email threads on business documents, such as leads, sales orders, and projects. In this chapter, we will explore a few important ways to deal with emails in Odoo.

Here, we'll cover the following topics:

- Configuring incoming and outgoing email servers
- Managing chatter on documents
- Managing activities on documents
- Sending emails using the Jinja template
- Sending emails using the QWeb template

- Managing the email alias
- Logging user changes in a chatter
- Sending periodic digest email

Technical requirements

All the code used in this chapter can be downloaded from `https://github.com/PacktPublishing/Odoo-14-Development-Cookbook-Fourth-Edition/tree/master/Chapter23`.

Configuring incoming and outgoing email servers

Before you start sending and receiving emails in Odoo, you will need to configure the incoming and outgoing email servers. In this recipe, you will learn how to configure email servers in Odoo.

Getting ready

There is no development needed for this recipe, but you will require email server information, such as the server URL, port, server type, username, and password. We will use this information to configure the email servers.

> **Note**
> If you are using **Odoo Online** or **Odoo.sh**, you do not need to configure the email servers. You can send and receive emails without any complex configurations on those platforms. This recipe is for on-premises Odoo instances.

How to do it...

Configuring incoming and outgoing email servers involves a few steps that are common to the processes for incoming and outgoing servers and a few steps that are unique to each kind of server. So, first we will see the common configuration steps, and then we will configure the incoming and outgoing email servers individually. The following are the steps that are required for both incoming and outgoing email servers:

1. Open the **General Settings** form menu, at **Settings | General Settings**.
2. Go to the **Discuss** section and enable **External Email Servers**. This will display the following options:

Figure 23.1 – Setting an alias domain

3. In the **Alias Domain** field, enter the domain name on which your email server is running. Then save the configuration.

Configuring the incoming email server

Perform the following steps to configure the incoming email server:

1. Open **General Settings** and click on the **Incoming Email Servers** link. This will redirect you to a list view of incoming email servers.

2. Click on the **Create** button, which will open the following form view. Enter the details of your incoming email server (see the *How it works...* section for an explanation of each field):

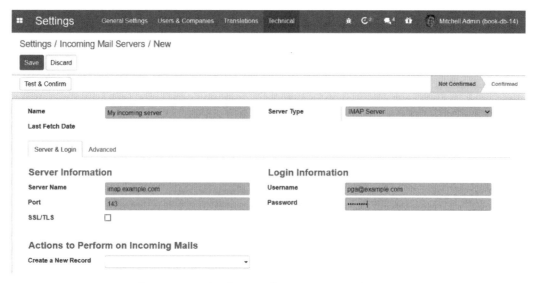

Figure 23.2 – Configuring the incoming email server

3. Click on the **Test & Confirm** button to verify your configuration. It will show an error message if you have wrongly configured the incoming email server.

Configuring the outgoing email server

Follow these steps to configure the outgoing email server:

1. Open **General Settings** and enable the **External Email Servers** option, then click on the **Outgoing Email Servers** link. This will redirect you to the list view of outgoing email servers.

2. Click on **Create**, which will open the following form view. Enter the details of your outgoing email server (see the *How it works...* section for explanations of each field):

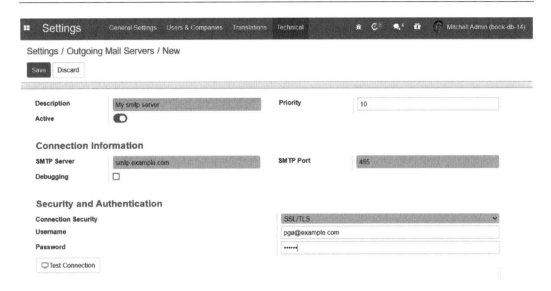

Figure 23.3 – Configuring the outgoing email server

3. Click on **Test Connection** at the bottom of the screen to verify your configuration. It will show an error message if you have wrongly configured the outgoing email server.

The outgoing email server will display the error dialog even if you have configured it properly. Look for the **Connection Test Succeeded! Everything seems properly set up!** message in the error dialog body. It means your outgoing server is configured correctly.

How it works...

The steps given in this recipe are self-explanatory and do not require further explanation. But the outgoing email and incoming email records have several fields, so let's see their purpose.

Here is a list of the fields used to configure the incoming email server:

- **Name**: The name of the server, which helps you identify a specific incoming email server when you have configured multiple incoming email servers.
- **Server Type**: Here you need to choose from three options: **POP**, **IMAP**, and **Local**. The value of this field will be based on your email service provider.
- **Server Name**: The domain of the server on which the service is running.
- **Port**: The number of the port on which the server is running.
- **SSL/TLS**: Check this field if you are using SSL/TLS encryption.

- **Username**: The email address for which you are fetching emails.
- **Password**: The password for the email address provided.
- **Active**: The `Active` field is used to enable or disable the incoming email server.
- **Keep Attachment**: Turn off this option if you do not want to manage attachments from incoming emails.
- **Keep Original**: Turn on this option if you want to keep the original email along with the preceding one.

The following is a list of fields used for configuring the outgoing email server:

- **Description**: The description of the server, which helps you identify a specific incoming email server when you have configured multiple incoming email servers.
- **Priority**: This field is used to define the priority of the outgoing email server. Lower numbers get higher priority, so email servers with a lower priority number will be used most.
- **SMTP Server**: The domain of the server on which the service is running.
- **SMTP Port**: The number of the port on which the server is running.
- **Connection Security**: The type of security used to send the email.
- **Username**: The email account used for sending the emails.
- **Password**: The password for the email account provided.
- **Active**: The `Active` field is used to enable or disable the outgoing email server.

There's more...

By default, incoming emails are fetched every 5 minutes. If you want to change this interval, follow these steps:

1. Activate developer mode.
2. Open **Scheduled Actions** at **Settings | Technical | Automation | Scheduled Actions**.
3. Search for and open the scheduled action named **Mail: Fetchmail**.
4. Change the interval using the field labeled **Execute Every**.

Managing chatter on documents

In this recipe, you will learn how to manage chatter on your documents and add a communication thread to a record.

Getting ready

For this recipe, we will reuse the `my_library` module from *Chapter 8, Advanced Server-Side Development Techniques*. You can grab an initial copy of the module from the `Chapter23/ 00_initial_module` directory of the GitHub repository for this book. In this recipe, we will add chatter to the `library.book.rent` model.

How to do it...

Follow these steps to add chatter on the records of the `library.book.rent` model:

1. Add the `mail` module dependency in the `__manifest__.py` file:

    ```python
    ...
    'depends': ['base', 'mail'],
    ...
    ```

2. Inherit `mail.thread` in the Python definition of the `library.book.rent` model:

    ```python
    class LibraryBookRent(models.Model):
        _name = 'library.book.rent'
        _inherit = ['mail.thread']
        ...
    ```

3. Add chatter widgets on the form view of the `library.book.rent` model:

    ```xml
    ...
    </sheet>
    <div class="oe_chatter">
        <field name="message_follower_ids" widget="mail_followers"/>
        <field name="message_ids" widget="mail_thread"/>
    </div>
    </form>
    ...
    ```

4. Install the `my_library` module to see the changes in action:

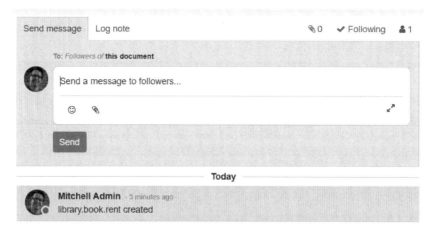

Figure 23.4 – Chatter on the rent form view

As shown in the preceding screenshot, after installing the module, you will be able to see chatter in the form view.

How it works...

In order to enable chatter on any model, you will need to install the `mail` module first. This is because all the code required to enable chatter or mailing capabilities is part of the `mail` module. That's why in *step 1*, we added the `mail` module dependency in the `manifest` file of the `my_library` module. This will automatically install the `mail` module whenever you install the `my_library` module.

The fields and methods required to operate chatter are part of the `mail.thread` model. The `mail.thread` model is an abstract model and is just used for inheritance purposes. In *step 2*, we inherited the `mail.thread` model in the `library.book.rent` model. This will add all the necessary fields and methods required for chatter in the `library.book.rent` model. If you don't know how model inheritance works, refer to the *Using abstract models for reusable model features* recipe in *Chapter 4, Application Models*.

In the *first two steps*, we added all the fields and methods required for chatter. The only remaining thing for chatter is adding a user interface in the form view. In *step 3*, we added a message thread and follower widget. You might be wondering about the `message_follower_ids` and `message_ids` fields. These fields are not added in the `library.book.rent` model definition but they are added from the `mail.thread` model through inheritance.

There's more...

When you post messages in a chatter, emails will be sent to the followers. If you notice in the example of this recipe, the borrower of the book is not the follower of the records, so they will not receive the messages. If you want to send an email notification to the borrower, you will need to add them to the borrower list. You can add the follower manually from the user interface, but if you want to add them automatically, you can use the message_subscribe() method. Take a look at the following code—when we place a book on rent, the given code will automatically add borrowers to the list of followers:

```python
@api.model
def create(self, vals):
    res = super(LibraryBookRent, self).create(vals)
    res.message_subscribe(partner_ids=[res.borrower_id.id])
    return res
```

Similarly, if you want to remove followers from the list, you can use the message_unsubscribe() method.

Managing activities on documents

When using chatter, you can also add activities. These are used to plan your actions on the record. It is kind of a to-do list for each record. In this recipe, you will learn how to enable activities on any model.

Getting ready

For this recipe, we will be using the my_library module from the previous recipe, *Managing chatter on documents*. We will add activities to the library.book.rent model.

How to do it...

Follow these steps to add activities to the library.book.rent model:

1. Inherit mail.activity.mixin in the Python definition of the library.book.rent model:

```python
class LibraryBookRent(models.Model):
    _name = 'library.book.rent'
    _inherit = ['mail.thread', 'mail.activity.mixin']
    ...
```

2. Add the `mail_activity` widget in the chatter of the `library.book.rent` model:

   ```
   ...
   <div class="oe_chatter">
       <field name="message_follower_ids" widget="mail_followers"/>
       <field name="activity_ids" widget="mail_activity"/>
       <field name="message_ids" widget="mail_thread"/>
   </div>
   ...
   ```

3. Update the `my_library` module to apply the changes. This will display chatter activities:

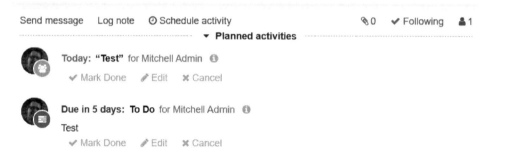

Figure 23.5 – Activity manager on the rent form view

This is how the user will be able to manage different chatter activities. Note that an activity scheduled by one user is visible to all other users too.

How it works...

Activities are part of the `mail` module and you can optionally enable them in chatter. In order to enable activities on records, you need to inherit `mail.activity.mixin`. Similar to the `mail.thread` model, `mail.activity.mixin` is also an abstract model. Inheriting `mail.activity.mixin` will add all the necessary fields and methods in the module. These methods and fields are used to manage activities on records. In *step 1*, we added `mail.activity.mixin` into the `library.book.rent` model. Because of this, the inheritance of `library.book.rent` will get all the methods and fields required to manage activities.

In *step 2*, we added the `mail_activity` widget in the form view. This will display the UI for managing activities. The `activity_ids` field is added in the `library.book.rent` model through inheritance.

Activities can be of different types. By default, you can create activities with types such as `Email`, `Call`, `Meeting`, and `To-Do`. If you want to add your own activity type, you can do it by going to **Settings | Technical | Email | Activity Types** in developer mode.

There's more...

If you want to schedule an activity automatically, you can use the `activity_schedule()` method of the `mail.activity.mixin` model. This will create the activity on a given due date. You can schedule the activity manually with the `activity_schedule()` method, as follows:

```
@api.model
def create(self, vals):
    res = super(LibraryBookRent, self).create(vals)
    if res.return_date:
        res.activity_schedule('mail.mail_activity_data_call',
                              date_deadline=res.return_date)
    return res
```

This example will schedule a call activity for the librarian whenever someone borrows a book. The deadline of the activity will be set as the return date of the book, so the librarian can make a call to the borrower on that date.

Sending emails using the Jinja template

Odoo supports creating dynamic emails through Jinja templates. Jinja is a text-based templating engine used to generate dynamic HTML content. In this recipe, we will create a Jinja email template and then send emails with its help.

Getting ready

For this recipe, we will be using the `my_library` module from the previous recipe, *Managing activities on documents*. We will add the Jinja template to send an email to the borrower to tell them the book is overdue.

How to do it...

Follow these steps to send a reminder email to the borrower:

1. Create a new file called `my_library/data/mail_template.xml` and add the email template:

```xml
<?xml version="1.0" encoding="utf-8"?>
<odoo noupdate="1">
    <record id="book_return_reminder" model="mail.template">
        <field name="name">Book Return Reminder</field>
        <field name="email_from">${object.book_id.create_uid.email}</field>
        <field name="email_to">${object.borrower_id.email}</field>
        <field name="subject">Reminder for book return</field>
        <field name="model_id" ref="my_library.model_library_book_rent"/>
        <field name="body_html">
            <![CDATA[
                <p>Dear ${object.borrower_id.name},</p>
                <p>You had rented the
                    <b>${object.book_id.name}</b> book on ${format_date(object.rent_date)}
                    <br/>
                    The due date of book is <b style="color:red;">${format_date(object.return_date)}.</b>
                </p>
                <br/>

                <p>Best regards,
                <br/> Librarian</p>
            ]]>
        </field>
    </record>
</odoo>
```

2. Register the template file in the `manifest` file:

```
...
'data': [
    'security/groups.xml',
    'security/ir.model.access.csv',
    'views/library_book.xml',
```

```
        'views/library_book_categ.xml',
        'views/library_book_rent.xml',
        'data/mail_template.xml'
    ],
    ...
```

3. Add a `Send reminder` button in the form view of the `library.book.rent` model to send the email:

```
...
<header>
    <button name="book_return" string="Return the Book" states="ongoing" type="object"/>
    <button name="book_return_reminder" string="Send reminder" states="ongoing" type="object"/>
    <field name="state" widget="statusbar"/>
</header>
...
```

4. Add the `book_return_reminder()` method to the `library.book.rent` model:

```
...
def book_return_reminder(self):
    template_id = self.env.ref('my_library.book_return_reminder')
    self.message_post_with_template(template_id.id)
```

Update the `my_library` module to apply the changes. This will add a **Send reminder** button in the form view of the `library.book.rent` model. When they click on the button, followers will get the following message:

Figure 23.6 – Email sent via a Jinja template

The procedure shown in this recipe is useful when you want to send updates to your customers through emails. Because of the Jinja template, you can send emails dynamically based on individual records.

How it works...

In *step 1*, we created an email template using Jinja. Jinja templates help us generate a dynamic email based on record data. The email template is stored in the `mail.template` model. Let's see the list of fields you will need to pass in order to create a Jinja email template:

- `name`: The name of the template that is used to identify a specific template.
- `email_from`: The value of this field will be the email address from which this email is sent.
- `email_to`: The value of this field will be the email address of the recipient.
- `email_cc`: The value of this field will be used for the email address to send a copy of the email.
- `subject`: This field contains the subject of the email.
- `model_id`: This field contains the reference of the model. The email template will be rendered with the data of this model.
- `body_html`: This field will contain the body of the email template. It is a Jinja template so you can use variables, loops, conditions, and so on. If you want to learn more about Jinja templates, go to `http://jinja.pocoo.org/docs/2.10/`. Usually, we wrap the content in the CDATA tag so the content in the body is considered as character data and not as markup.
- `auto_delete`: This is a Boolean field that deletes an email once the email is sent. The default value of this field is `False`.
- `lang`: This field is used to translate the email template into another language.
- `scheduled_date`: This field is used to schedule emails in the future.

> **Information**
>
> You can use `${}` in the `email_form`, `email_to`, `email_cc`, `subject`, `scheduled_date`, and `lang` fields. This helps you to set values dynamically. Take a look at *step 1* in our recipe—we used `${object.borrower_id.email}` to set the `email_to` field dynamically.

If you look closely at the content of the `body_html` field, you will notice we used `${object.borrower_id.name}`. Here, the object is the record set of the `library.book.rent` model. During the rendering, `${object.borrower_id.name}` will be replaced with the borrower's name. Like `object`, some other helper functions and variables are passed in the rendering context. Here is the list of helpers passed to the renderer context:

- `object`: This variable will contain the record set of the model, which is set in the template by the `model_id` field.
- `format_date`: This is a reference to the method used to format date-time objects.
- `format_datetime`: This is a reference to the method used to convert UTC date and time into the date and time for another time zone.
- `format_amount`: This is a reference to the method used to convert `float` into `string` with the currency symbol.
- `format_duration`: This method is used to convert float into time—for instance, to convert 1.5 to 01:30.
- `user`: This will be the record set of the current user.
- `ctx`: This will contain the dictionary of the environment context.

> **Note**
> If you want to see the list of templates, activate developer mode, and open the **Settings | Technical | Email | Templates** menu. The form view of the template also provides a button to preview the rendered template.

In *step 2*, we registered the template file in the `manifest` file.

In *step 3*, we added a button in the form view to invoke the `book_return_reminder()` method, which will send the email to the followers.

In *step 4*, we added the `book_return_reminder()` method, which will be invoked by clicking the button. The `message_post_with_template()` method is used to send the email. The `message_post_with_template()` method is inherited in the model through `mail.thread` inheritance. To send the email, you just need to pass the template ID as the parameter.

There's more...

The `message_post_with_template()` method is used to send emails with the Jinja template. If you just want to send an email with plain text, you can use the `message_post()` method:

```
self.message_post(body="Please return your book on time")
```

The preceding code will add the **Please return your book on time** message in the chatter. All of the followers will be notified with this message. If you just want to log the message, call the method with the `subtype_id` parameter.

Sending emails using the QWeb template

In the previous recipe, we learned how to send emails using the Jinja template. In this recipe, we will see another way to send dynamic emails. We will send emails with the help of the QWeb template.

Getting ready

For this recipe, we will use the `my_library` module from the previous recipe, *Sending emails using the Jinja template*. We will use the QWeb template to send an email to the borrower informing them that their book is overdue.

How to do it...

Follow these steps to send a reminder email to the borrower:

1. Add the QWeb template into the `my_library/data/mail_template.xml` file:

```
<template id="book_return_reminder_qweb">
    <p>Dear <span t-field="object.borrower_id.name"/>,</p>
    <p>You had rented the
        <b>
            <span t-field="object.book_id.name"/>
        </b> book on <span t-field="object.rent_date"/>
        <br/>
        The due date of book is
        <b style="color:red;">
            <span t-field="object.return_date"/>
        </b>
```

```
            </p>
            <br/>

            <p>Best regards,
            <br/>
            Librarian
        </p>
</template>
```

2. Add a `Send reminder (QWeb)` button in the form view of the `library.book.rent` model to send the email:

```
...
<header>
    <button name="book_return" string="Return the Book" states="ongoing" type="object"/>
    <button name="book_return_reminder" string="Send reminder" states="ongoing" type="object"/>
    <button name="book_return_reminder_qweb" string="Send reminder(QWeb)" states="ongoing" type="object"/>
    <field name="state" widget="statusbar"/>
</header>
...
```

3. Add the `book_return_reminder_qweb()` method in the `library.book.rent` model:

```
...
def book_return_reminder_qweb(self):
    self.message_post_with_view('my_library.book_return_reminder_qweb')
```

4. Update the my_library module to apply the changes. This will add a **Send reminder (QWeb)** button in the form view of the library.book.rent model. When the button is clicked, followers will get a message like this:

Figure 23.7 – Email sent via the QWeb template

The procedure shown in this recipe works exactly like the previous recipe, *Sending emails using the Jinja template*. The only difference is the template type, as this recipe uses QWeb templates.

How it works...

In *step 1*, we created a QWeb template with the book_return_reminder_qweb ID. If you look in the template, you'll see we are not using the format_date() data field method anymore. This is because the QWeb rendering engine handles this automatically and displays the date based on the user's language. For the same reason, you are not required to use the format_amount() method to display the currency symbols. The QWeb rendering engine will manage this automatically. If you want to learn more about QWeb templates, refer to the *Creating or modifying templates – QWeb* recipe from *Chapter 14, CMS Website Development*.

In *step 2*, we added a button in the form view to invoke the book_return_reminder_qweb() method, which sends the email to the followers.

In *step 3*, we added the `book_return_reminder_qweb()` method, which will be invoked by a button click. The `message_post_with_view()` method is used to send the email. The `message_post_with_view()` method is inherited in the model through `mail.thread` inheritance. To send the email, you just need to pass the web template's XML ID as the parameter.

Sending emails with the QWeb template works exactly the same as in the previous recipe, but there are some subtle differences between the QWeb email template and the Jinja email template. Here is a quick comparison between both templates:

- There is no simple way to send extra parameters in the email templates. You have to use a record set in the object variable to fetch dynamic data. On the other hand, with QWeb email templates, you can pass extra values in the renderer context through the `values` parameter:

    ```
    self.message_post_with_view(
        'my_library.book_return_reminder_qweb',
        values={'extra_data': 'test'}
    )
    ```

- To manage the date format, time zone, and amount with currency symbols, in the Jinja template you have to use the `format_date`, `format_tz`, and `format_amount` functions, while in QWeb templates, it is managed automatically.

- It is not possible to modify an existing template for other modules in Jinja, whereas in QWeb templates you can modify the email template through inheritance. If you want to learn more about QWeb inheritance, refer to the *Creating or modifying templates – QWeb* recipe in *Chapter 14, CMS Website Development*.

- You can select and use a Jinja template directly from the message composer. In the following screenshot, the drop-down menu in the bottom-right corner is used to select a Jinja template:

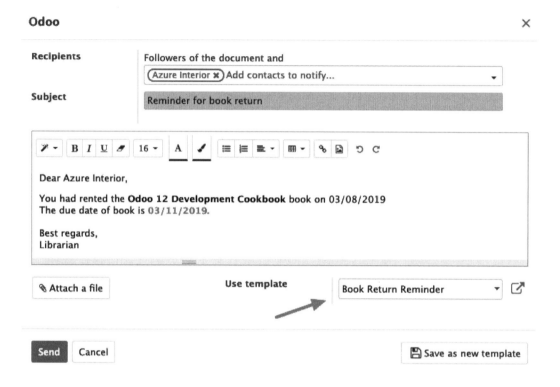

Figure 23.8 – Template selection option

- Using QWeb, selecting a template directly from the message composer is not an option.

There's more...

All methods (`message_post`, `message_post_with_template`, and `message_post_with_view`) respect the user's preference. If the user changes the notification-management option from the user preferences, the user will not receive emails; instead, they will receive notifications in Odoo's UI. This is the same for customers; if a customer opts out of emails, they will not receive any updates through email.

Additionally, the Odoo message thread follows a concept called **subtypes**. Subtypes are used to receive emails only for information you are interested in. You can pass an extra parameter, subtype_id, in message_post_* methods to send emails based on the subtype. Usually, the user will manage their subtypes from the dropdown of the **Follow** button. Let's suppose the user has set their subtypes as follows:

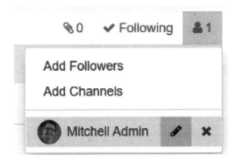

Figure 23.9 – Option to edit subtype

Based on the user's preference, the user will only get emails for Discussions messages.

Managing the email alias

Email aliasing is the feature in Odoo that is used to create a record through incoming emails. The simplest example of an email alias is sales teams. You just need to send an email to sale@yourdomain.com and Odoo will create a new record for crm.lead in the sales team. In this recipe, we will create one email alias to create a book's borrowing record.

Getting ready

For this recipe, we will be using the my_library module from the previous recipe, *Sending emails using the QWeb template*. We will create our email alias with the rent@yourdomain.com email address. If you send an email to this email address with the book's name in the subject, a record is created in the library.book.rent model.

How to do it...

Follow these steps to add an email alias for the `library.book.rent` model:

1. Add the email alias data in the `my_library/data/mail_template.xml` file:

    ```xml
    <record id="mail_alias_rent" model="mail.alias">
        <field name="alias_name">rent</field>
        <field name="alias_model_id" ref="model_library_book_rent"/>
        <field name="alias_user_id" ref="base.user_admin"/>
        <field name="alias_contact">partners</field>
    </record>
    ```

2. Add the following imports in the `my_library/models/library_book_rent.py` file:

    ```python
    import re
    from odoo.tools import email_split, email_escape_char
    ```

3. Override the `message_new()` method in the `library.book.rent` model:

    ```python
    @api.model
    def message_new(self, msg_dict, custom_values=None):
        self = self.with_context(default_user_id=False)
        if custom_values is None:
            custom_values = {}
        regex = re.compile("^\[(.*)\]")
        match = regex.match(msg_dict.get('subject')).group(1)
        book_id = self.env['library.book'].search([
            ('name', '=', match),
            ('state', '=', 'available')], limit=1)
        custom_values['book_id'] = book_id.id
        email_from = email_escape_char(email_split(msg_dict.get('from'))[0])
        custom_values['borrower_id'] = self._search_on_partner(email_from)
        return super(LibraryBookRent, self).message_new(msg_dict, custom_values)
    ```

Update the `my_library` module to apply the changes. Then send an email to `rent@yourdomain.com`. Make sure you have included the book's name in the email subject, for example, *[Odoo 14 Development Cookbook] Request to borrow this book*. This will create the new `library.book.rent` record and it will be displayed as follows:

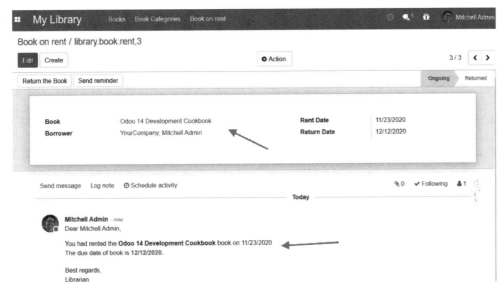

Figure 23.10 – Record generated via email

Whenever you send an email to `rent@yourdomain.com` with the book's name in the email subject, Odoo will generate a new borrowing record. Note that this will work only if the book is available in the library.

How it works...

In *step 1*, we created the `mail.alias` record. This alias will handle the `rent@yourdomain.com` email address. When you send the email to this address, Odoo will create a new record in the `library.book.rent` model. If you want to see the list of active aliases in the system, open **Settings | Technical | Email | Aliases**. Here is a list of the fields available to configure the alias:

- `alias_name`: This field holds the local part of the email address; for example, the rent part in `rent@yourdomain.com` is the local part of the email address.
- `alias_model_id`: The model reference on which the record should be created for the incoming email.

- `alias_user_id`: When incoming emails are received, records are created with the environment of the user in this field.
- `alias_contact`: This field holds the security preferences for the alias. Possible options are `everyone`, `partners`, `followers`, and `employees`.
- `alias_defaults`: When an incoming email is received, its record is created in the model specified on the alias. If you want to set default values in the record, give the values in the form of a dictionary in this field.

In *step 2*, we added the necessary imports. In *step 3*, we overrode the `message_new()` method. This method is invoked automatically when a new email is received on the alias email address. This method will take two parameters:

- `msg_dict`: This parameter will be the dictionary that contains information about the received email. It contains email information such as the sender's email address, the receiver's email address, email subject, and email body.
- `custom_values`: This is a custom value used to create a new record. This is the same value you set on the alias record using the `alias_defaults` field.

In our recipe, we overrode the `message_new()` method and fetched the book's title from the email subject through a regular expression. Then we fetched the email address of the sender with the help of the tools we imported in *step 2*. We used the sender's email address to find the borrower's record. Then we updated `custom_values` with these two values: `books_id` and `borrower_id`. We pass this updated `custom_values` data to the `super()` method, which will create a new `library.book.rent` record with the given `books_id` and `borrower_id` values. This is how the record is created when you send an email to the alias.

Note that this recipe generates an error when you don't send the proper email subject, such as `[book name] remaining subject`. You can update the program according to your business logic to avoid errors.

There's more...

Some business models have a requirement that means you need a separate alias per record. For example, the sales team model has separate aliases for each team, such as sale-in@example.com for Team India and sale-be@example.com for Team Belgium. If you want to manage such aliases in your model, you can use mail.alias. mixin. In order to use it in your model, you will need to inherit the mixin:

```
class Team(models.Model):
    _name = 'crm.team'
    _inherit = ['mail.alias.mixin', 'mail.thread']
```

After inheriting the mixin, you will need to add the alias_name field into the form view so the end users can add aliases by themselves.

Logging user changes in a chatter

The Odoo framework provides a built-in facility to log field changes in a chatter. In this recipe, we will enable logging on some of the fields, so when changes are made in them, Odoo will add the logs in the chatter.

Getting ready

For this recipe, we will be using the my_library module from the previous recipe, *Managing the email alias*. In this recipe, we will log changes from a few fields in the library.book model.

How to do it...

Modify the definitions of the fields, to enable logs for the fields when you change them. This is shown in the following code snippet:

```
class LibraryBookRent(models.Model):
    _name = 'library.book.rent'
    _inherit = ['mail.thread', 'mail.activity.mixin']

    book_id = fields.Many2one('library.book', 'Book',
required=True)
    borrower_id = fields.Many2one('res.partner', 'Borrower',
required=True)
    state = fields.Selection([('ongoing', 'Ongoing'),
('returned', 'Returned')], 'State', default='ongoing',
required=True,  tracking=True)
```

```
    rent_date = fields.Date(default=fields.Date.today,
 tracking=True)
    return_date = fields.Date(tracking=True)
```

Update the `my_library` module to apply the changes. Create a new record in the `library.book.rent` model, make some changes in the fields, and then return the book. If you check the chatter, you will see the following logs:

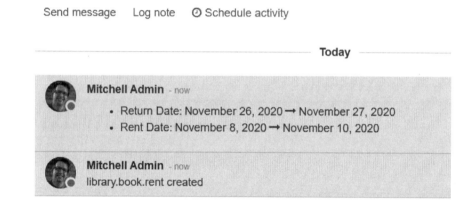

Figure 23.11 – Change log in the chatter

Whenever you make changes to `state`, `rent_date`, or `return_date`, you will see a new log in the chatter. This will help you to see the full history of the record.

How it works...

By adding the `tracking=True` attribute on the field, you can enable logging for that field. When you set the `tracking=True` attribute, Odoo will add a log that changes in the chatter whenever you update the field value. If you enable tracking on multiple records and you want to provide sequence in the tracking values, you can also pass a number in the tracking parameter like this: `tracking=20`. When you pass `tracking=True`, then the default sequence is used, which is `100`.

In our recipe, we added `tracking=True` on the `state`, `rent_date`, and `return_date` fields. This means Odoo will log the changes when you update the values of the `rent_date`, `return_date`, or `state` fields. Take a look at the screenshot in the *How to do it...* section; we have only changed the `rent_date` and `return_date` fields.

Note that the `track_visibility` feature only works if your model inherits the `mail.thread` model because the code-related chatter and logs are part of the `mail.thread` model.

Sending periodic digest emails

The Odoo framework has built-in support for sending out periodic digest emails. With digest emails, you can send an email with information about business KPIs. In this recipe, we will send data about rented books to the librarian (or any other authorized person).

Getting ready

For this recipe, we will be using the `my_library` module from the previous recipe, *Logging user changes in a chatter*.

How to do it...

Follow these steps to generate digest emails for book rent records:

1. Inherit the `digest.digest` model and add fields for the KPIs:

    ```python
    class Digest(models.Model):
        _inherit = 'digest.digest'
        kpi_book_rent = fields.Boolean('Book Rent')
        kpi_book_rent_value = fields.Integer(compute='_compute_kpi_book_rent_value')

        def _compute_kpi_book_rent_value(self):
            for record in self:
                start, end, company = record._get_kpi_compute_parameters()
                record.kpi_book_rent_value = self.env['library.book.rent'].search_count([
                    ('create_date', '>=', start),
                    ('create_date', '<', end)
                ])
    ```

2. Inherit the `digest.digest` model's form view and add the KPI fields:

    ```xml
    <?xml version='1.0' encoding='utf-8'?>
    <odoo>
        <record id="digest_digest_view_form" model="ir.ui.view">
            <field name="name">digest.digest.view.form.inherit.library</field>
    ```

```xml
                <field name="model">digest.digest</field>
                <field name="inherit_id" ref="digest.digest_digest_view_form"/>
                <field name="arch" type="xml">
                    <xpath expr="//group[@name='kpi_general']" position="after">
                        <group name="kpi_library" string="Library">
                            <field name="kpi_book_rent"/>
                        </group>
                    </xpath>
                </field>
            </record>
</odoo>
```

Update the module to apply the changes. Once you update the module, enable developer mode and open **Settings | Technical | Emails | Digest Emails**, as seen in the following screenshot:

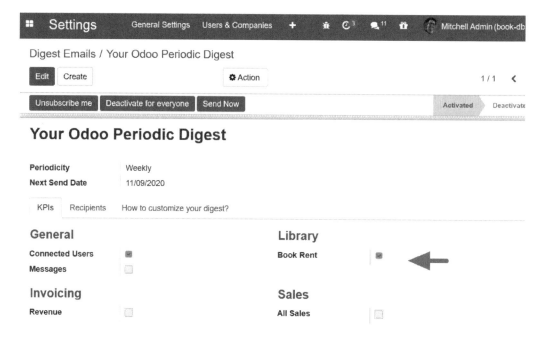

Figure 23.12 – Enabling the digest email for book rent data

Once you enable this and if you have subscribed to digest emails, you will start receiving digest emails.

How it works...

In order to build a customized digest email, you need two fields. The first field will be a **Boolean field**, used to enable and disable the KPI, while the second field will be the **compute field** and will be called to acquire the KPI value. We created both of the fields in *step 1*. If you check the definition of the `compute` field, it uses the `_get_kpi_compute_parameters` method. This method returns three parameters: a start date, an end date, and the company record. You can use these parameters to generate the value for your KPI. We have returned the number of books rented during a particular period of time. If your KPI is multi-website-compatible, then you can use a company parameter.

In *step 2*, we added a field to the digest form view. This field is used to enable/disable digest emails. When you enable it, you will start receiving digest emails:

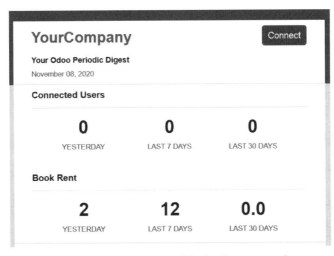

Figure 23.13 – Digest email for book rent records

Enable developer mode, then open **Settings | Technical | Emails | Digest Emails**. Here you can configure the recipients of the digest emails and set the periodicity for the digest emails. You can also enable/disable digest emails from here.

24
Managing the IoT Box

Odoo provides support for the **Internet of Things** (**IoT**). The IoT is a network of devices/sensors that exchange the data over the internet. By connecting such devices with a system, you can use them. For instance, by connecting a printer with Odoo, you can send PDF reports directly to the printer. Odoo uses a piece of hardware called the **IoT Box**, which is used to connect devices such as printers, calipers, payment devices, footswitches, and more. In this chapter, you will learn how to set up and configure the IoT Box. Here, we'll cover the following topics:

- Flashing the IoT Box image for Raspberry Pi
- Connecting the IoT Box with a network
- Adding the IoT Box to Odoo
- Loading drivers and listing connected devices
- Taking input from devices
- Accessing the IoT Box through SSH
- Configuring a point of sale
- Sending PDF reports directly to a printer

Note that the goal of this chapter is to install and configure the IoT Box. Developing hardware drivers is outside the scope of this book. If you want to learn about the IoT Box in more depth, explore the `iot` module in the Enterprise edition.

Technical requirements

The IoT Box is a Raspberry Pi-based device. The recipes in this chapter are based on the Raspberry Pi 3 Model B+, available at `https://www.raspberrypi.org/products/ raspberry-pi-3-model-b-plus/`. The IoT Box is the part of the Enterprise edition, so you will need to use the Enterprise edition to follow the recipes in this chapter.

All the code used in this chapter can be downloaded from the following GitHub repository: `https://github.com/PacktPublishing/Odoo-14-Development-Cookbook-Fourth-Edition/tree/master/Chapter24/05_capture_image/my_library`.

Flashing the IoT Box image for Raspberry Pi

In this recipe, you will learn how to flash a microSD card with an image of the IoT Box. Note that this recipe is only for those who have purchased the blank Raspberry Pi. If you have purchased the official IoT Box from Odoo, you can skip this recipe as it is preloaded with the IoT Box image.

Getting ready

Raspberry Pi 3 Model B+ uses a microSD card, so we have used a microSD card for this recipe. You will need to connect a microSD card to your computer.

How to do it...

Perform the following steps to install an IoT Box image onto your SD card:

1. Insert a microSD card into your computer (use an adapter if your computer doesn't have a dedicated slot).

2. Download the IoT Box image from Odoo's nightly builds. The image is available at `https://nightly.odoo.com/master/iotbox/`.

3. Download and install **balenaEtcher** on your computer. You can download this from `https://www.balena.io/etcher/`.

4. Open **balenaEtcher**, select the **IoT Box** image (we are using version 20.10 of the IoT Box image), and choose to flash your microSD card. You'll see the following screen:

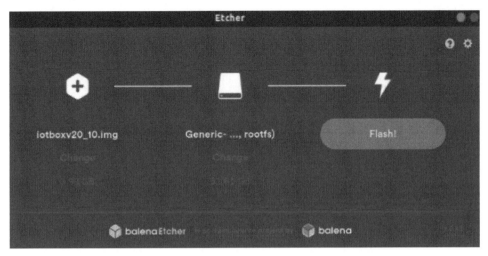

Figure 24.1 – Flashing the SD card with the IoT Box image

5. Click on the **Flash!** button and wait until the process completes.
6. Remove the microSD card and place it in the Raspberry Pi.

After these steps, your microSD card should be loaded with the IoT Box image and ready to be used in the IoT Box.

How it works...

In this recipe, we have installed the IoT Box image on a microSD card. In the second step, we downloaded the IoT Box image from the Odoo nightly builds. On the nightly page, you can find different images for the IoT Box. You need to choose the latest image from the Odoo nightly builds. When writing this book, we used the latest image, which was `iotboxv20_10.zip`. The Odoo IoT Box image is based on the Raspbian Stretch Lite OS and the image is loaded with the libraries and modules required to integrate the IoT Box with the Odoo instance.

In *step 3*, we downloaded the **balenaEtcher** utility tool to flash the microSD card.

> **Note**
> In this recipe, we used **balenaEtcher** to flash the microSD card, but you can use any other tools to flash the microSD card.

In *step 4*, we flashed the microSD card with the IoT Box image. Note that this process can take several minutes. After the completion of the process, the microSD card will be ready to be used.

Perform the following steps if you want to verify whether the image was flashed successfully:

1. Mount the microSD card into Raspberry Pi.
2. Connect it with the power supply and attach the external display through an HDMI cable (in practical usage, an external display is not compulsory; we have used it here just for verification purposes).
3. The OS will boot up and show the following page:

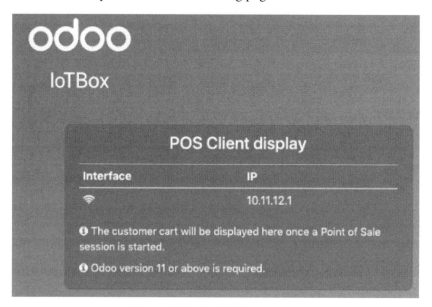

Figure 24.2 – The IoT Box screen

If you are not using a display, you can just connect the IoT Box to a power supply and after some time, you will see the Wi-Fi network of the IoT Box.

There's more...

In previous versions of Odoo, PosBox was used in point-of-sale applications. The IoT Box supports all the features of PosBox, so if you are using the Community edition of Odoo and you want to integrate devices, you can use the same IoT Box image to connect Odoo instances with different devices. See the *Configuring a point of sale* recipe for more information.

Connecting the IoT Box with a network

The IoT Box communicates with an Odoo instance through the network. Connecting the IoT Box is a crucial step and if you make a mistake here, you might encounter errors when connecting the IoT Box with Odoo.

Getting ready

Mount the microSD card with the IoT Box image into the Raspberry Pi and then connect the Raspberry Pi with the power supply.

How to do it...

Raspberry Pi 3 Model B+ supports two types of network connection—Ethernet and Wi-Fi.

Connecting the IoT Box through Ethernet is simple; you just need to connect your IoT Box with the RJ45 Ethernet cable, and the IoT Box is then ready to be used. Connecting the IoT Box through Wi-Fi is complicated as you might not have a display attached to it. Perform the following steps to connect the IoT Box through Wi-Fi:

1. Connect the IoT Box with the power supply (if the Ethernet cable is plugged into the IoT Box, remove it and restart the IoT Box).
2. Open your computer and connect to the Wi-Fi network, named **IoTBox**, as shown in the following screenshot (no password is needed):

Figure 24.3 – IoT Box Wi-Fi network

3. After connecting to the Wi-Fi, you'll see a popup with the IoT Box home page as shown in the following screenshot (if this does not work, open the IP address of the box in the browser):

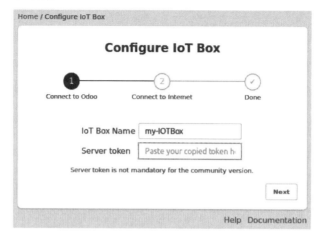

Figure 24.4 – Connecting to the IoT Box

4. Set **IoT Box Name** and keep **Server token** empty, then click on **Next**. This will redirect you to a page where you can see a list of Wi-Fi networks:

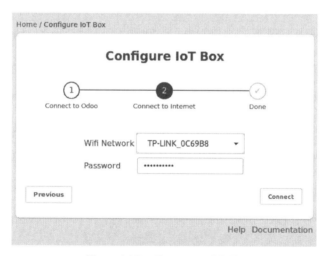

Figure 24.5 – Connect to Wi-Fi

> **Note**
> You can use a server token if you are using the Enterprise edition and you want to connect the IoT Box with Odoo right away. You can get a server token from your Odoo instance; refer to the next recipe to learn more about it.

5. Select the Wi-Fi network that you want to connect to and fill in the **Password** field. After doing this, click on the **Connect** button. If you entered the correct information, you will be redirected to the final page:

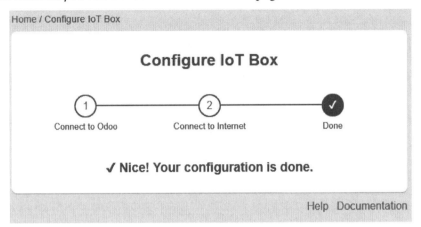

Figure 24.6 – Confirmation page

After performing these steps, your IoT Box is connected to the network and ready to be integrated with the Odoo instance.

How it works...

Connecting the Odoo instance to the IoT Box through Ethernet is simple; just connect your IoT Box with the RJ45 Ethernet cable and the IoT Box is ready to be used. It's different when you want to connect the IoT Box with Wi-Fi; this is difficult because the IoT Box doesn't have a display or GUI. You do not have an interface to enter your Wi-Fi network password. Consequently, the solution to this problem is to disconnect your IoT Box from the Ethernet cable (if it is connected) and restart it. In such cases, the IoT Box will create its own Wi-Fi hotspot, named **IoT Box** or similar, as shown in *step 2*. You need to connect the Wi-Fi with the name **IoT Box**; luckily, it does not require a password. Once you connect to the **IoT Box** Wi-Fi, you'll get a popup, as shown in *step 3*. Here, you can name your IoT Box something like `Assembly-line IoT Box`. Keep the server token empty for now; we will learn more about it in the *Adding the IoT Box to Odoo* recipe. Then click on the **Next** button.

Upon clicking the **Next** button, you will be shown a list of Wi-Fi networks, as shown in *step 4*. Here, you can connect the IoT Box to your Wi-Fi network. Make sure you choose the right network. You need to connect the IoT Box with the same Wi-Fi network as the computer on which the Odoo instance is going to be used. The IoT Box and the Odoo instance communicate within a **local area network** (**LAN**). This means that if both are connected to different networks, they cannot communicate and so IoT will not work.

After choosing the right Wi-Fi network, click on **Connect**. Then the IoT Box will turn off its hotspot and reconnect to your configured Wi-Fi network. That's it—the IoT Box is ready to be used.

Adding the IoT Box to Odoo

Our IoT Box is connected to the local network and ready to be used with Odoo. In this recipe, we will connect the IoT Box with the Odoo instance.

Getting ready

Make sure the IoT Box is on and that you have connected the IoT Box to the same Wi-Fi network as the computer with the Odoo instance.

There are a few things you need to take care of, otherwise the IoT Box will not be added to Odoo:

- If you are testing the IoT Box in a local instance, you will need to use `http://192.168.*.*:8069` (your local IP) instead of `http://localhost:8069`. If you use localhost, the IoT Box will not be added to your Odoo instance.

- You need to connect the IoT Box with the same Wi-Fi/Ethernet network as the computer on which the Odoo instance is being used. Otherwise, the IoT Box will not be added in your Odoo instance.

- If your Odoo instance is running with multiple databases, IoT Box will not auto-connect with the Odoo instance. Use the `--db-filter` option to avoid this issue.

How to do it...

In order to connect the IoT Box with Odoo, first you will need to install the `iot` module on your Odoo instance:

1. To do so, go to the **Apps** menu and search for the **Internet of Things** module. The module will look like as follows. Install the module and we are good to go:

Figure 24.7 – Installing the iot module

2. After installing the `iot` module, you can connect your instance with the IoT Box. Then connect your IoT Box manually with the Odoo instance by clicking on the **IoT** menu.

3. Click on the **Connect** button on the control panel. This will show the following popup. Copy the **Token** value:

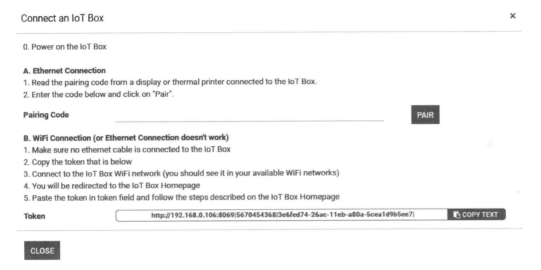

Figure 24.8 – Dialog to connect the IoT Box with Odoo

4. Open the IP of the IoT Box with port `8069`. This will display the home page of the IoT Box. Click on the **configure** button in the **Name** section:

Figure 24.9 – The IoT Box home page

5. Set the **IoT Box Name** setting and paste in the server token. Then click on the **Connect** button. This will start configuring the IoT Box. Wait for the process to complete:

Figure 24.10 – The IoT Box home page

6. Check the **IoT** menu in your Odoo instance. You will find a new IoT Box:

Figure 24.11 – Successfully connected IoT Box

How it works...

Connecting `IoTBox` with Odoo is important. This way, Odoo will know the IP of the IoT Box. The IP will be used by Odoo to communicate with devices connected with that device. This will also make sure, in case of multiple IoT Boxes, that Odoo communicates with the right one. The rest is straightforward.

If you want to add an IoT Box to an Odoo instance during Wi-Fi configuration, that can be done. In the *Connecting the IoT Box with the network* recipe, we kept the **Server token** field empty. You just need to add the server token in this step:

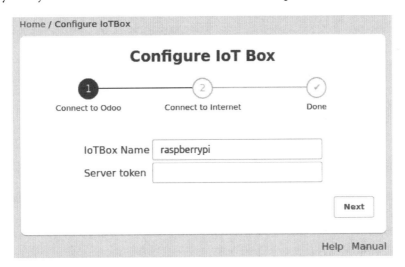

Figure 24.12 – Adding the server token during Wi-Fi configuration

> **Note**
> Avoid using the DHCP network when using the IoT Box. This is because the IoT Box network configuration is added based on the IP address. If you use the DHCP network, then the IP address is assigned dynamically. So, there is a chance that your IoT Box will stop responding due to the new IP address. To avoid this issue, you can map the MAC address of the IoT Box to the fixed IP address.

Connecting an IoT Box with a pairing code

There is one more alternative way to connect an IoT Box, which is through a **pairing code**. The pairing code can be found on the **Point of Sale** (**POS**) display page of the IoT Box. There are two ways to open a POS client display. The first is by connecting the IoT Box with an external display. When you start your IoT Box with a display connected, it will open the POS client display by default. The second way is to open the POS client via the IoT Box IP. The URL for the POS client display is as follows: `<IoTBOX IP>:8069/point_of_sale/display`. Once you open the POS client display, you will be able to see the pairing code as follows:

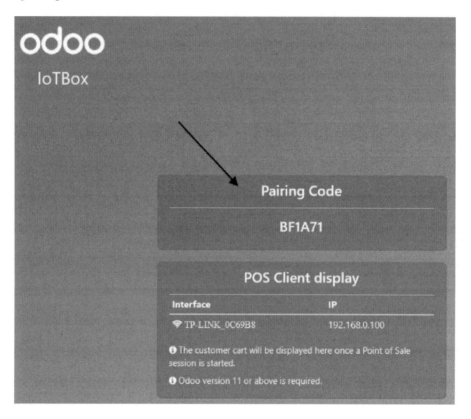

Figure 24.13 – The pairing code for the IoT Box

Then you just need to use the pairing code in the IoT Box connection dialog in your Odoo instance.

> **Note**
> The pairing code will not be displayed if you are not connected to the internet.

In the preceding figure, we have seen how you can get the pairing code for the POS client display. But if you have an Ethernet connection and a printer, you can get the pairing code without a display. You just need to connect the IoT Box with the Ethernet and the printer. Once the IoT Box is booted, it will print a receipt with the pairing code. Then you just need to use the pairing code in the IoT Box connection dialog in your Odoo instance.

There's more...

If you want to connect an existing IoT Box with any other Odoo instance, you will need to clear the configuration. You can clear the IoT Box configuration with the **Clear** button in the Odoo server configuration page of the IoT Box:

Figure 24.14 – Clearing the IoT Box configuration

Loading drivers and listing connected devices

The IoT Box is not just limited to the Enterprise edition. You can use it like PoSBox in the Community edition. The device's integration is part of the Enterprise edition, so the `IoTBox` image does not come with device drivers; you need to load them manually. Usually, if you connect the IoT Box with and Enterprise Odoo instance, the IoT Box loads the device driver interfaces automatically. But sometimes, you might have custom drivers or drivers that are not loaded correctly. In that case, you can manually load the drivers. In this recipe, we will see how you can load drivers and get a list of connected devices.

Getting ready

Make sure the IoT Box is on and that you have connected it to the same Wi-Fi network as the computer with the Odoo instance.

How to do it...

Perform the following steps to load device drivers into the IoT Box:

1. Open the IoT Box home page and click on the **handlers list** button at the bottom:

Figure 24.15 – Handlers list

2. The **handlers list** button will redirect you to the **Handlers list** page, where you will find the **Load handlers** button. Click on the button to load the drivers:

Figure 24.16 – Drivers list

3. Go back to the **IoT Box** home page. Here, you will see a list of the connected devices:

Figure 24.17 – Connected devices

After performing these steps, the IoT Box will be ready with the devices you specified and you can start using the devices in your applications.

How it works...

You can load the drivers from the home page of the IoT Box. You can do this using the **Load handlers** button at the bottom. Note that this will only work if your IoT Box is connected with the Odoo instance using the Enterprise edition. After loading the drivers, you will be able to see a list of devices on the IoT Box home page. You can also see a list of connected devices in the Odoo instance through the **IoT | Devices** menu. In this menu, you will see a list of connected devices for each IoT Box:

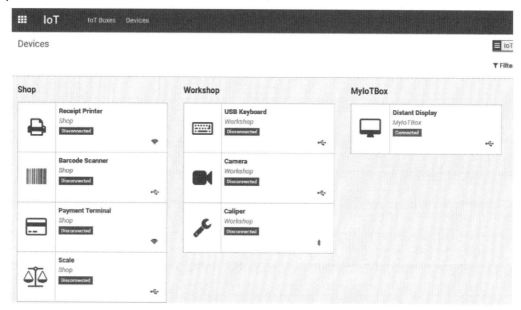

Figure 24.18 – Connected devices list

Right now, the IoT Box supports a few hardware devices, such as cameras, footswitches, printers, and calipers. The list of devices that are recommended by Odoo can be found here: https://www.odoo.com/page/iot-hardware. If your device is not supported, you can pay for driver development.

Taking input from devices

The IoT Box only supports limited devices. Right now, these hardware devices are integrated with the manufacturing application. But if you want, you can integrate supported devices with your module. In this recipe, we will capture a picture from a camera through our IoT Box.

Getting ready

We will be using the `my_library` module from the *Logging user changes in a chatter* recipe of *Chapter 23, Managing Emails in Odoo*. In this recipe, we will add a new field to capture and store images when a borrower returns a book. Make sure the IoT Box is on and that you have connected a supported camera device with it.

How to do it...

Perform the following steps to capture a picture using a camera with the IoT Box:

1. Add a dependency in the manifest file:

    ```
    ...
    'depends': ['base', 'mail', 'quality_iot'],
    ...
    ```

2. Add new fields in the `library.book.rent` model:

    ```
    ...
    device_id = fields.Many2one('iot.device', string='IoT
    Device',
      domain="[('type', '=', 'camera')]")
    ip = fields.Char(related="device_id.iot_id.ip")
    identifier = fields.Char(related='device_id.identifier')
    picture = fields.Binary()
    ...
    ```

3. Add these fields into the form view of the `library.book.rent` model:

    ```
    <group>
        <field name="book_id" domain="[('state', '=', 'available')]"/>
        <field name="borrower_id"/>
        <field name="ip" invisible="1"/>
        <field name="identifier" invisible="1"/>
        <field name="device_id" required="1"/>
        <field name="picture" widget="iot_picture"
               options="{'ip_field': 'ip', 'identifier': 'identifier'}"/>
    </group>
    ```

4. Update the `my_library` module to apply the changes. After the update, you will have a button to capture pictures:

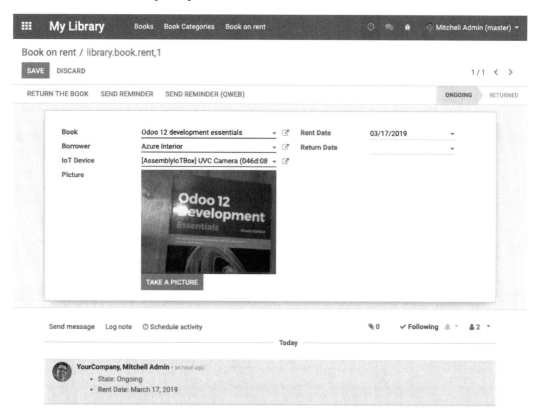

Figure 24.19 – Capturing an image via IoT

Note that the button will not capture the image if the webcam is not connected to the IoT Box or drivers are not loaded in the IoT Box.

How it works...

In *step 1*, we added a dependency to the `quality_iot` module in the manifest file. The `quality_iot` module is part of the Enterprise edition and contains a widget that allows you to request an image from a camera through the IoT Box. This will install the `stock` modules, but for the sake of simplicity, we will use `quality_iot` as a dependency. If you do not want to use this dependency, you can create your own field widget. Refer to the *Creating custom widgets* recipe in *Chapter 15, Web Client Development*, to learn more about widgets.

In *step 2*, we added the fields required to capture an image from the camera. To capture the image, we need two things: the device identifier and the IP address of the IoT Box. We want to give the user the option to select the camera, so we added a `device_id` field. The user will choose a camera to capture the image, and based on the selected camera device, we extracted IP and device identifier information from related fields. Based on these fields, Odoo will know where to capture the image, if you have multiple IoT Boxes. We have also added a binary field, `picture`, to save the image.

In *step 3*, we added fields in the form view. Note that we used the `iot_picture` widget on the `picture` field. We added the `ip` and `identifier` fields as invisible fields because we do not want to show them to the user; rather, we want to use them in the `picture` field options. This widget will add the button in the form view; upon clicking the button, Odoo will make a request to the IoT Box to capture the image. The IoT Box will return image data as the response. This response will be saved in the `picture` binary field.

There's more...

The IoT Box supports Bluetooth calipers. If you want to take measurements in your module, you can use the `iot_measure` widget to fetch them in Odoo. Note that as with `iot_picture`, here you will also need to add the `ip` and `identifier` invisible fields in the form view:

```
<field name="measure" widget="iot_measure"
       options="{'ip_field': 'ip', 'identifier':
'identifier'}"/>
```

This will fill the `measure` field with the data captured from the IoT caliper.

Accessing the IoT Box through SSH

The IoT Box is running on Raspbian OS, and it is possible to access the IoT Box through SSH. In this recipe, we will learn how to access the IoT Box through SSH.

Getting ready

Make sure the IoT Box is on and you have connected the IoT Box to the same Wi-Fi network as the computer with the Odoo instance.

How it works...

In order to connect the IoT Box through SSH, you will need the IP address of the IoT Box. You can see this IP address in its form view. As an example, in this recipe, we will use `192.168.43.6` as the IoT Box IP address, so replace this with your IP address. Perform the following steps to access the IoT Box through SSH:

1. Open the Terminal and execute the following command:

   ```
   $ ssh pi@192.168.43.6
   pi@192.168.43.6's password:
   ```

2. The Terminal will ask you for a password; enter `raspberry` as the password.

3. If you added the right password, you can access the shell. Execute the following command to see the directory:

   ```
   total 24
   -rw-r--r-- 1 root root     6 Oct 26 08:12 iotbox_version
   drwxr-xr-x 5 pi   pi    4096 Oct 23 09:05 odoo
   -rw-r--r-- 1 pi   pi      36 Nov 15 13:10 odoo-db-uuid.conf
   -rw-r--r-- 1 pi   pi       0 Nov 15 13:10 odoo-enterprise-code.conf
   -rw-r--r-- 1 pi   pi      26 Nov 15 13:10 odoo-remote-server.conf
   -rw-r--r-- 1 pi   pi      11 Nov 15 13:10 token
   -rw-r--r-- 1 pi   pi      26 Aug 20 12:03 wifi_network.txt
   ```

As you have SSH access, you can explore the full filesystem of the IoT Box.

How to do it...

We used the Pi user with the password `raspberry` to access the IoT Box through SSH. SSH connection is used when you want to debug a problem in the IoT Box. SSH doesn't need any explanation, but let's see how Odoo works in the IoT Box.

Here is some information that might help you debug the issue:

- The IoT Box is internally running some Odoo modules. The name of these modules usually starts with `hw_` and they are available in the Community edition. You can find all the modules in the `/home/pi/odoo/addon` directory.

- If you want to see the Odoo server log, you can access it from the `/var/log/odoo/odoo-server.log` file.
- Odoo is running through a service named `odoo`; you can use the following command to `start`, `stop`, or `restart` the `service`:

```
sudo service odoo start/restart/stop
```

- Customers mostly turn the IoT Box off by disconnecting the power. This means that the IoT Box OS does not shut down properly in such cases. To avoid corruption of the system, the IoT Box filesystem is read-only.

There's more...

Note that the IoT Box is only connected with the local machine. Consequently, you cannot access the shell directly from a remote location (through the internet). If you want to access the IoT Box remotely, you can paste the `ngrok` authentication token key in the IoT Box's remote debug page, as shown in the following screenshot. This will enable the TCP tunnel from the IoT Box so you can connect the IoT Box through SSH from anywhere. Learn more about `ngrok` at `https://ngrok.com/`:

Figure 24.20 – Debugging with an ngrok token

Once you add your token, you will be able to access the IoT Box from remote locations.

Configuring a point of sale

The IoT Box works with point-of-sale applications. In this recipe, we will learn how to configure the IoT Box for point-of-sale applications.

Getting ready

Make sure the IoT Box is on and you have connected IoT Box to the same Wi-Fi network as the computer with the Odoo instance. Also, install the point-of-sale application if it is not already installed.

How to do it...

Perform the following steps to configure the IoT Box for the point-of-sale application:

1. Open the point-of-sale application, and open **Settings** from the POS session dropdown:

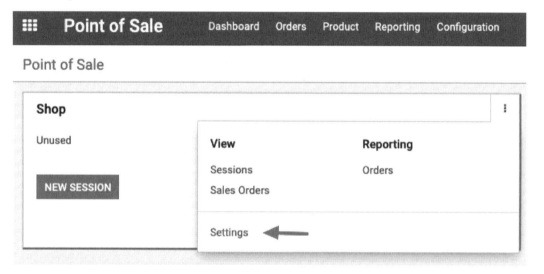

Figure 24.21 – POS session settings

2. Click on the **Settings** button. You will be redirected to the **Settings** page. Search for the **Connected Devices** section and click on the **IoT Box** checkbox. This will enable more options:

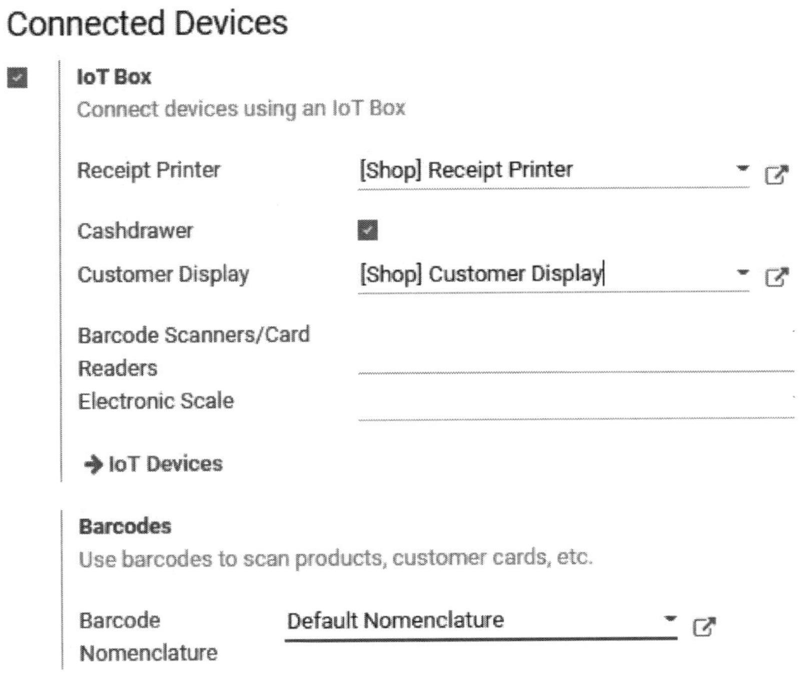

Connected Devices

IoT Box
Connect devices using an IoT Box

Receipt Printer	[Shop] Receipt Printer
Cashdrawer	✓
Customer Display	[Shop] Customer Display
Barcode Scanners/Card Readers	
Electronic Scale	

→ IoT Devices

Barcodes
Use barcodes to scan products, customer cards, etc.

Barcode Nomenclature	Default Nomenclature

Figure 24.22 – Selecting IoT devices

3. Select the devices that you want to use in a point-of-sale session. If you are going to use hardware, such as a barcode scanner, select the relevant devices.

4. Save the changes by clicking the **Save** button in the control panel.

After the configuration, you will be able to use the IoT Box in the point-of-sale application.

How it works...

The IoT Box can be used with point-of-sale applications like the PosBox. In order to use the IoT Box in a point-of-sale application, you have to connect the IoT Box to the Odoo instance. If you don't know how to connect the IoT Box, follow the *Adding the IoT Box to Odoo* recipe. Once you have connected the IoT Box to Odoo, you will be able to select the IoT Box in the point-of-sale application, as shown in *step 2*.

Here, you can select the hardware you want to use in the point-of-sale session. After saving the change, if you open the point-of-sale session, you will be able to use the enabled hardware at the point of sale. If you enabled specific hardware from the settings but the hardware is not connected to the IoT Box, you will see the following warning in the top bar:

Figure 24.23 – IoT Box connection issues

You can click on these warnings to try to connect again.

There's more...

The point-of-sale application is part of the Community edition. If you are using the Community edition, instead of the **IoT Box** selection, you will see the **IoT Box IP Address** field in the point-of-sale settings:

Figure 24.24 – IoT Box settings in the Community edition

If you want to integrate hardware in the Community edition, you will need to use the IP address of the **IoT Box** in the field.

Sending PDF reports directly to a printer

The IoT Box runs the CUPS server by default. CUPS is a printing system that allows a computer to act as a printing server. You can learn more about it at https://www.cups.org/. So, as the IoT Box runs CUPS internally, you can connect network printers with the IoT Box. In this recipe, we will see how you can print PDF reports directly from Odoo.

Getting ready

Make sure the IoT Box is on and you have connected the IoT Box with Odoo.

How to do it...

Follow these steps to print reports directly from Odoo:

1. Open the IoT Box home page via IP.
2. Click on the **Printer Server** button at the bottom:

Figure 24.25 – Options to configure the printer

3. This will open the CUPS configuration home page. Configure your printer here.
4. Once you have configured the printer, you will be able to see the printer in the IoT device list. Activate developer mode and open **Settings| Technical | Actions | Report**.
5. Search for the report that you want to print, open the form view, and select the printer in the **IoT Device** field, as shown in the following screenshot:

Figure 24.26 – Options to select an IoT device

Once this configuration is done, report PDFs will be sent directly to the printer.

How it works...

This recipe is straightforward in terms of configuration, but there are a few things that you should know. The IoT Box uses the CUPS server to print reports. You can access the CUPS home page at `http://<IoT Box IP>:631`.

With CUPS, you can add/remove your printer. On the home page of CUPS, you will be able to see all the documentation that you need to help you connect different types of printers. Once you have configured the printer, you will find your printer in the IoT device list. Then, you can select this IoT device (printer) in the report record. Usually, when you print a report in Odoo, it will download a PDF of the report. But when this configuration is done, instead of downloading the report, Odoo will send the PDF report directly to the selected printer. Note that only reports whose record has the printer set in the IoT device field will be sent to the printer.

Other Books You May Enjoy

If you enjoyed this book, you may be interested in these other books by Packt:

The Art of CRM

Max Fatouretchi

ISBN: 978-1-78953-892-2

- Deliver CRM systems that are on time, on budget, and bring lasting value to organizations
- Build CRM that excels at operations, analytics, and collaboration
- Gather requirements effectively: identify key pain points, objectives, and functional requirements
- Develop customer insight through 360-degree client view and client profiling
- Turn customer requirements into a CRM design spec
- Architect your CRM platform

- Bring machine learning and artificial intelligence into your CRM system
- Ensure compliance with GDPR and other critical regulations
- Choose between on-premise, cloud, and hybrid hosting solutions

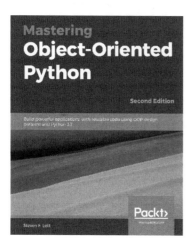

Mastering Object-Oriented Python

Steven F. Lott

ISBN: 978-1-78953-136-7

- Explore a variety of different design patterns for the __init__() method
- Learn to use Flask to build a RESTful web service
- Discover SOLID design patterns and principles
- Use the features of Python 3's abstract base
- Create classes for your own applications
- Design testable code using pytest and fixtures
- Understand how to design context managers that leverage the 'with' statement
- Create a new type of collection using standard library and design techniques
- Develop new number types above and beyond the built-in classes of numbers

Leave a review - let other readers know what you think

Please share your thoughts on this book with others by leaving a review on the site that you bought it from. If you purchased the book from Amazon, please leave us an honest review on this book's Amazon page. This is vital so that other potential readers can see and use your unbiased opinion to make purchasing decisions, we can understand what our customers think about our products, and our authors can see your feedback on the title that they have worked with Packt to create. It will only take a few minutes of your time, but is valuable to other potential customers, our authors, and Packt. Thank you!

Index

Symbols

2 Factor Authentication (2FA) 656
--dev option
  about 210
  working 210, 211
@http.route decorator 426
_populate_dependencies attribute
  using 592
/xmlrpc/2/common endpoint
  version() method, example 628

A

abstract models
  using, for reusable model
      features 147-149
access
  limiting, to fields in models 333, 334
access-control lists (ACLs) 329
activities
  managing, from kanban card 405-407
activity view
  defining 319, 320
add-on module
  about 82, 83
  access security, adding 101-104

changes, applying 75, 76
creating 83, 84
file structure, organizing 89-92
installing 83-85
installing, from GitHub 74, 75
list updating 56, 58
manifest, completing 86-89
menu items, adding 95-99, 100
versioning 202-204
views, adding 95-97, 99, 100
add-ons path
  configuring 60-62
  working 61
Affero General Public License
      version 3 (AGPLv3) 31
API decorators
  using 152-156
API keys
  generating 656, 658
  using 658
  working 658
archive option
  enabling, for records 410, 411
asset bundles, Odoo
  about 430
  features 432

web.assets_backend 431
web.assets_common 431
web.assets_frontend 431
web_editor.summernote 431
web.report_assets_common 431
website.assets_editor 431
website.assets_frontend 431
assets, Odoo
  about 430
  working with 433
automated actions
  about 393
  using, on event conditions 397-399
  using, on time conditions 393-396
automated actions, on record updates
  benefits 400
  drawbacks 400
auto-reload 210

B

Boolean field 729
Bootstrap
  URL 448
branches
  managing 604
  working 609, 610
business logic
  extending, in model 176-178
buttons
  adding, to form view 276

C

calendar views
  attributes 311
  defining 310
  working 311

chatter
  managing, on documents 707
  message_subscribe() method, using 709
  user changes, logging 725, 726
  working 708
chatter activities
  activity_schedule() method, using 711
  managing, on documents 709, 710
  working 710
chatter widgets 300
check_access_rights method 637
class inheritance (extension) 140
client-side code
  debugging 507-509
client-side QUnit test cases
  adding 575-577
  assert functions 579
  working 577-579
client-side QWeb templates
  using 489-491
client-side test cases
  debugging 586-588
  Headless Chrome, setting up for 574, 575
  running, from UI 583
  working 587
code reuse 243
cohort view
  defining 313, 314
command-line interface 215
Community Edition 30
complex modules
  configuration options 66
compute field 729
compute method
  used, for defining onchange methods 250, 251
conditionals 445

construct 442
context
  about 233, 277
  parameters, passing to forms and actions 277-280
  used, for computing default values 243
context node 295
controller 505
converters 423
country information, of visitor
  obtaining 468-470
create() method
  extending 179-182
cross-site request forgery 418
Cross-Site Request Forgery (CSRF) 463
CSS
  adding, for website 435-438
CSV files
  used, for loading data 200, 201
custom assets
  about 432
  bundle, creating 432, 433
Customer Relationship Management (CRM) 30
custom JavaScript/SCSS files
  adding, to Point of Sale asset bundle 682-684
custom language URL code
  modifying, for website 365, 367
custom metatags
  adding 466
custom settings options
  adding 255, 256, 258, 259
custom widgets
  creating 483-488

D

dashboard view
  defining 315-317
data
  fetching, in groups with read_group() method 186, 187
  loading, with CSV files 200, 201
  loading, with XML files 193-197
database queries
  records, accessing through 674, 676
data fields
  adding, to model 112-118
data files 91
data migrations
  running 202-204
data normalization 252
Datetime fields 313
datetime Python module
  reference link 389
deactivated (archived) partner records 278
debugging options
  accessing 610
  branch history 611
  code editor 614
  logs 615
  mail catcher 611, 612
  web shell 612-614
debug mode options 223, 224, 226, 228
default values
  computing, with context 243
delegation inheritance
  used, for copying features to another model 144-147
dependency handling 73

developer mode 54
development branch
   creating 606, 607
devices
   input, obtaining from 746, 748, 749
Document Object Model (DOM) 587
documents
   chatter activities, managing 709, 710
   chatter, managing 707, 708
document-style forms
   defining 298, 299
   working 299, 300
domain
   filters, defining on record lists 281-283
   pitfalls, of searching fields 284
drivers connected devices
   loading 743-745
   working 746
duplicate data structures 144
dynamic attributes 443, 444
dynamic form elements
   modifying, attr attribute used 300, 301
dynamic record stages
   library.rent.stage model,
      creating 373, 374
   managing 370-373
dynamic relations
   adding, reference fields used 138-140
dynamic routes
   managing 448-451
dynamic snippet
   about 452
   offering, to user 455-459

E

email alias
   fields list 723
   mail.alias.mixin, using 725
   managing 721, 723
   working 723, 724
emails
   sending, with Jinja template 711-714
   sending, with QWeb template 716, 717
embedded views
   defining 301, 302
empty recordset
   obtaining, for different model 158-160
Enterprise Edition 30
Enterprise Resource Planning
      (ERP) 30, 431
error message
   reporting, to user 156-158
event conditions
   automated actions, using 397-399
event triggers 386
existing handler
   modifying 424-426
   working 425
external IDs
   using 190, 191, 193
Extra Rights 328

F

failed test cases
   videos/screenshots, generating
      for 588, 589
fields 445
file
   translation strings, exporting to 358-361
file structure
   organizing, of add-on module 89-92
float field
   using, with configurable
      precision 119, 120

Font Awesome
  URL 300
forcecreate flags
  using 198, 199
form view
  attachments, displaying side
    by side 303-305
  attrs attributes 274
  button element 272
  buttons, adding 276
  content, adding 270-276
  field element 273
  form element 272
  group element 272
  groups attributes 274
  header element 272
  notebook tag 273
  oe_edit_only class 275
  oe_inline class 275
  oe_read_only class 275
  OWL field, adding to 529-533
  page tag 273
  stat button, adding to 407-409
  tags 274, 275
  widgets, adding to 270-276

G

gantt view
  defining 317, 318
  item, hovering 318
GeoIP 468
gettext tools
  used, for translations 362, 363
git commands
  using 616
GitHub
  add-on module, installing from 74, 75

Git repositories 31
global record rules 338
GNU gettext documentation
  reference link 364
graph view
  defining 311
  working 312
grouped data
  accessing 668, 671

H

Headless Chrome
  about 574
  setting up, for client-side
    test cases 574, 575
HTTP routes 419, 424

I

IAP account credit
  offers, displaying 563, 565, 566
  working 566
IAP client module
  creating 557, 559-561
  services, checking 562, 563
  working 561, 562
IAP concepts
  about 538
  working 538, 539
IAP credits
  authorizing 551-553, 556
  charging 551-553, 556
  working 554, 556
IAP service
  registering, in Odoo 541-544
  working 544, 545
IAP service flow 539, 540

IAP service module
    creating 545, 546, 548-550
    working 550
image size
    generating 666, 667
incoming email server
    configuring 702, 704, 706
    fields list 705, 706
    working 705
inheritance
    used, for adding features
        to model 140-142
    used, for copying model
        definition 142, 143
init hooks
    implementing 259, 260
inline template 520
input
    obtaining, from website users 460-463
instance directory layout
    generating 65
    standardizing 62-64
interactive kanban card
    creating 380-383
    working 383, 384
IoT Box
    accessing, through SSH 749-751
    adding, to Odoo 738-741
    connecting, with network 735-738
    connecting, with pairing code 742
IoT Box image
    flashing, for Raspberry Pi 732-734
ipdb debugger
    reference link 223

J

JavaScript
    adding, for website 435-438
Jinja template
    fields list 714
    message_post_with_template()
        method, using 716
    reference link 714
    used, for sending emails 711-714
    versus QWeb template 719
    working 714, 715
JSON-RPC
    check_access_rights method 649
    methods, calling through 650-652
    records, creating through 647, 649
    records, deleting through 647, 649
    records, fetching through 643, 645
    records, searching through 643, 645
    records, updating through 647, 649
    search_read() method, using 646
    used, for connecting to Odoo 640-642
    used, for logging into Odoo 640-642
    version() method 642
JSON-RPC 2.0 specification
    reference link 557, 642
JSON-RPC2 transaction API
    reference link 557

K

kanban board
    about 375
    features 378
kanban card
    activities, managing 405-407

Index 767

displaying, in columns 308-310
quick create form, adding to 378-380
kanban stages
  managing 375, 377
  working 377
kanban views
  defining 305-307
  helper functions 308
  progress bar, adding 384, 385
  working 307

L

language
  installing 350-352
language-related settings
  configuring 353, 354
Least-Recently Used (LRU) cache 665
LESS 432
Lesser General Public License
    v3.0 (LGPLv3) 30
Library Books model
  access, limiting to fields 333, 334
  adding, to module 92-94
  computed fields, adding 132-137
  constraint validations, adding 129-132
  data fields, adding to 112-118
  features, adding with
    inheritance 140, 141
  hierarchy, adding 127-129
  monetary field, adding 120-122
  record representation 111
  relational fields, adding 122-126
  representation and order,
    defining 108-111
  security access, adding to 329-332
listing connected devices
  loading 743-745

working 746
list views
  create attribute 287
  defining 285, 286
  delete attribute 287
  editable attribute 287
  edit attribute 287
  sum attribute 287
  working 286
local add-on modules
  installing 67, 71
  installing, from command line 70
  installing, from web interface 68, 69
  upgrading 67, 71, 72
  upgrading, from command line 70
  upgrading, from web interface 68, 69
local area network (LAN) 737
loops 442, 443

M

many-to-many (m2m) relations 122, 126
many-to-one (m2o) relations 122, 125
mapbox
  reference link 320
mapped() method
  properties 173
map view
  defining 320, 321
marketing campaign
  tracking 471-473
menu item
  adding 263-265
  adding, to add-on module 95-97, 99-101
menus, in security groups
  hiding 347, 348
message_new() method, parameters
  custom_values 724

msg_dict 724
method calling
  with modified context 233-235
method execution
  tracing, with Python debugger 218-223
methods
  calling, through JSON-RPC 650-652
  calling, through XML-RPC 637, 639
  calling, with Odoo shell 215-217
  debugging, by producing server
    logs 211-213, 215
mixin 479
model definition
  copying, inheritance used 142, 143
model methods
  defining 152-156
model, renderer, controller (MRC) 504
model, view, controller (MVC) 504
modified context
  used, for calling method 233-235
module
  creating, with scaffold
    command 103, 105
multiple records
  creating 671-673
  writing 671-673
multiple websites
  managing 473-476
my-custom-event 523

N

namespaces
  using 190-193
nested set model
  URL 127
network
  IoT Box, connecting with 735-738
  path, making accessible from 414-418
new view
  creating 495, 496, 498-505, 507
non-global record rules 338
noupdate attribute
  using 198, 199

O

Object Relational Mapping
  (ORM) 94, 235, 661
Odoo
  accessing, as superuser 98, 99
  connecting, with JSON-RPC 640-642
  connecting, with XML-RPC 626, 628
  IAP service, registering 541-544
  IoT Box, adding to 738-741
  logging, with JSON-RPC 640-642
  logging, with XML-RPC 626, 628
  translation files, importing into 364, 365
Odoo Community Association
  (OCA) 74, 652
Odoo developer tools
  activating 54-56
Odoo, devices
  reference link 746
Odoo ecosystem 30
Odoo editions 30
Odoo editions, comparison
  reference link 31
Odoo Enterprise edition
  about 320
  cohort view 314
odoo.execute method 655
Odoo instance
  configuration file, storing
    in 50, 51, 53, 54

Index   769

Odoo mobile app
  JavaScript 513-515
  mobile utilities 515
  URL 515
odoorpc library
  about 654
  reference link 652
  working 654, 655
Odoo server databases
  database backup, restoring 46, 47
  database instance, backing up 46
  database instance, duplicating 44, 45
  database instance, removing 45
  managing 49
  working 48
Odoo.sh account
  creating 597, 598, 600, 601
  working 600
Odoo.sh account, instances
  GitHub repository 600
  hosting location 600
  Odoo version 600
  subscription code 600
Odoo shell
  REPL shell interface, using 218
  used, for calling methods 215-217
Odoo.sh options
  about 619
  collaborator 620, 621
  database size 624
  database workers 623
  module installation 621
  project name 620
  public access 621
  source code revisions 624
  staging branch 623
  submodules 622
Odoo.sh platform

  about 594
  backup 616, 617
  build status, checking 617-619
  concepts, exploring 594
  custom modules, adding 601-604
  custom modules, installing 601-604
  need for 595
  using 595
Odoo.sh platform, features
  about 596
  automated tests 596
  backup and recovery 597
  build, sharing 597
  community modules 597
  development branch 596
  external dependencies 596
  faster deployment 597
  GitHub integration 596
  mail catcher 597
  mail server 597
  server logs 596
  SSH access 596
  staging branch 596
  web code editor 596
  web shell 596
old URLs
  redirecting 476, 477
onchange methods
  calling, on server side 248, 250
  defining 245, 246
  defining, with compute method 250, 251
  field values, computing 247, 248
  working 247
one-to-one (o2m) relations 122, 125
Optimize SEO option 465
ormcache_context decorator 664
ormcache decorator
  about 663

in-memory cache, managing 662, 665
ormcache_multi decorator 664, 665
outgoing email server
  configuring 702, 704-706
  fields list 706
  working 705
OWL component
  creating 518-520
  reactivating 523-526
  user actions, managing 521-523
  working 520, 521
OWL component life cycle
  about 526-528
  working 528
OWL component life cycle, methods
  constructor() 528
  mounted() 528
  patched() 529
  willPatch() 528
  willStart() 528
  willUnmount() 529
OWL field
  adding, to form view 529-533
  working 534, 535
OWL library
  reference link 521

P

pairing code
  IoT Box, connecting with 742
parameters, passed to handlers
  consuming 422, 423
path, making accessible from network
  about 414, 415
  odoo.http.route, using 416
  request object 418
  return values 416, 417

PDF reports
  sending, to printer 755, 756
periodic digest emails
  sending 727, 728
  working 729
pivot view
  defining 311
  working 312
Platform as a Service (PaaS) 594
Point of Sale application
  action button, adding on
    keyboard 685-688
  business logic, modifying 695-697
  customer receipts, modifying 698-700
  RPC calls, making 689-692
  screen UI, modifying 693-695
Point of Sale asset bundle
  custom JavaScript/SCSS files,
    adding 682-684
Point of Sale (POS)
  about 742, 754
  configuring 752, 753
  working 753
Point of Sale restaurant module 685
PostgreSQL aggregate functions
  reference link 671
printer
  PDF reports, sending to 755, 756
production branch
  creating 605
  features, merging 609
profile() method
  parameters 678
progress bar
  adding, in kanban views 384, 385
  working 385
Promise
  reference link 495

Prototype inheritance 142
publish management
  for website-related records 478, 479
publish mixin 480
pudb debugger
  reference link 223
Pull Request (PR)
  about 31
  applying 77, 78
  trying 77, 78
Python code
  about 91
  evaluating 389
  profiling 677-679
  working 678
Python code server action
  creating 392
  limitations 392
  using 390, 391
Python debugger (PDB)
  about 211
  using, to trace method
     execution 218-223
Python test cases
  adding 569, 570
  classes 571
  reference link 570
  working 570

Q

quick create form
  adding, to kanban card 378-380
QUnit test cases
  running, from UI 584
QWeb 437
QWeb attributes
  conditionals 445

dynamic attributes 443, 444
fields 445
inline editing 446, 447
loops 442, 443
subtemplates 446
variables, setting 446
QWeb-based PDF reports
  creating 400-402, 404
  working 403, 404
QWeb template
  about 492
  creating 439-441
  methods, using 720
  modifying 439-441, 447
  used, for sending emails 716, 718
  versus Jinja template 719
  working 718
QWeb template design
  reference link 448

R

random data
  populating for testing 589-591
Raspberry Pi
  IoT Box image, flashing for 732-734
raw SQL queries
  executing 236-239
read_group() method
  about 668, 669
  parameters 670
  used, for fetching data in
     groups 186, 187
  working 187, 188, 669
record access
  limiting, with record rules 335-338
record rules
  about 335

fields 337
used, for limiting record access 335-338
records
  accessing, through database
    queries 674, 676
  archive option, enabling for 410, 411
  creating 160-163
  creating, through JSON-RPC 647, 649
  creating, through XML-RPC
    633, 635, 636
  customizing 182-185
  deleting, from XML files 205, 206
  deleting, through JSON-RPC 647, 649
  deleting, through XML-RPC
    633, 635, 636
  fetching, through JSON-RPC 643, 645
  reading, through XML-RPC 629, 631
  searching 166, 168, 169
  searching, through JSON-RPC 643, 645
  searching, through XML-RPC 629, 631
  updating, through JSON-RPC 647, 649
  updating, through XML-RPC
    633, 635, 636
recordset records
  values, updating 164-166
recordset relations
  traversing 172-174
recordsets
  accessing, as superuser 345, 346
  combining 169
  filtering 171, 172
  pattern, prefetching 660-662
  sorting 174, 175
  working 170
redirect button
  adding, to book's form view 480
redirection options
  301 Moved permanently 477

302 Moved temporarily 477
308 Redirect / Rewrite 477
404 Not Found 477
redirection rule 476
reference fields
  used, for adding dynamic
    relations 138-140
related fields, stored in other models
  exposing 137, 138
relational fields
  adding, to model 122-125
remote procedure call (RPC) 157
renderer 505
RequireJS
  URL 438
ReStructuredText (RST) format
  about 87
  reference link 87
Return on Investment (ROI) 471
route decorator 418
RPC calls
  making, to server 492-494
RPC libraries, for Odoo
  reference links 656

S

scaffold command
  used, for creating module 103-105
SCSS
  about 432
  URL 438
search filter side panel
  adding 291, 292
  items, displaying 293
search views
  defining 287, 288
  filters, grouping with group tag 290

Index   773

responding, to context keys 291
working 289, 290
security access
  adding, to models 329-332
security groups
  additional fields 328
  assigning, to users 324-328
  creating 324-328
  using, to activate features 339-344
self.env.ref() function 192
SEO options
  managing 464, 465
separation of concerns 252
server actions
  creating 386, 387
  working 388, 389
server logs
  about 211
  producing, to debug methods 211-213, 215
server side
  onchange methods, calling 248, 250
sitemaps
  managing, for website 466-468
snippet option
  creating 459
Software as a Service (SaaS) 595
specific view
  custom view, using 270
  ir.actions.act_window.view 269
  opening, with action 268, 269
  opening, with window action 267
SQL view model
  defining 252-254
SSH
  IoT Box, accessing through 749-751
staging branch
  creating 608

stat button
  adding, to form view 407-409
state field
  using 374
static assets
  managing 430
static hierarchies 129
static resources
  serving 427
  working 428
static snippet
  about 452
  offering, to user 452-454
status bar 272
subtypes 721
superuser
  Odoo, accessing as 98, 99
  recordsets, accessing as 345, 346

T

tablet mode 266
tagged Python test cases
  running 571, 572
  working 572, 573
text file editor
  reference link 361
texts
  translating, through web client user interface 355-358
text strings 361
time conditions
  automated actions, using 393-396
tour
  adding, to library 510-512
tour test cases
  adding 579-582
  running, from UI 585, 586

working 582, 583
translation files 352, 353
　importing, into Odoo 364, 365
translation strings
　exporting, to file 358-361
tree element. *See* list views

U

UI
　client-side test cases, running from 583
　QUnit test cases, running from 584
　tour test cases, running from 585, 586
unaccent 291
Urchin Tracking Module (UTM) 471
user
　dynamic snippet, offering to 455-459
　static snippet, offering to 452-454
user actions
　managing, in OWL component 521-523
　modifying 230-232
　sudo() recordset, using 233
　working 232
user changes
　logging, in chatter 725, 726
user guide
　wizard, writing for 239-242
user preferences
　configuring 350-352
user redirecting 244
users
　dynamic snippet, offering to 455-459
　security groups, assigning to 324-328
　static snippet, offering to 452-454

V

videos/screenshots
　generating, for failed test cases 588, 589
view elements, in security groups
　hiding 347, 348
view inheritance
　attribute node 296
　existing views, changing 293-295
　order of evaluation 297
　position attribute 296
　tricks, for tweaking behavior 297
views
　adding, to add-on module 95-97, 99-101
Voice over Internet Protocol (VoIP) 30

W

web-accessible paths
　access, restricting 419-422
web assets 91
web client user interface
　texts, translating through 355-358
website
　CSS, adding for 435-438
　JavaScript, adding for 435-438
　sitemaps, managing for 466-468
website-related records
　publish management 478, 479
website users
　input, obtaining from 460-463
WebSockets 574
werkzeug 451
window action
　adding 263-266
　target attribute 266
　used, for opening specific view 267-269

wizard
  about 149, 243
  writing, for user guide 239,
    240, 241, 242
write() method
  extending 179-182

X

XML files
  functions, invoking from 206-208
  records, deleting from 205, 206
  used, for loading data 193-197
XML-RPC
  check_access_rights method 636
  methods, calling through 637, 639
  records, creating through 633, 635, 636
  records, deleting through 633, 635, 636
  records, reading through 629, 631
  records, searching through 629, 631
  records, updating through 633, 635, 636
  search_read method, using 632, 633
  used, for connecting to Odoo 626, 628
  used, for logging into Odoo 626, 628